# Diagnostic-Prescriptive Reading Instruction

# Diagnostic-Prescriptive Reading Instruction

A Guide for Classroom Teachers

Second Edition

Martha Collins-Cheek
Louisiana State University

Earl H. Cheek Jr.
Louisiana State University

wcb

Wm. C. Brown Publishers
Dubuque, Iowa

To Kristy and Jo-Jo-----

LB
1050
.C575
1984

Library of Congress Catalog Card Number: 83–71875

ISBN 0–697–00086–9

Printed in the United States of America

2  00086  01

# contents

# preface

The first edition of this text evolved from our work as classroom teachers attempting to teach reading to students with many different needs and interests; our experience as reading specialists teaching students with severe reading disabilities; and finally from our experience as teachers in a university observing and interacting with undergraduate and graduate students seeking to improve elementary and middle school reading instruction. With this perspective, we wrote a text for the *current or prospective* classroom teacher wishing to meet the many reading needs in each class using diagnostic-prescriptive teaching strategies. This practical approach has been well received; thus, the second edition reflects the same step-by-step process with updated research and an expansion in selected areas.

The first three chapters of the text deal with the diagnostic-prescriptive reading model, the classroom teacher's role in the diagnostic-prescriptive reading program, and the role of the content teacher in providing diagnostic-prescriptive reading instruction. An understanding of these chapters not only helps teachers in implementing the concept of diagnostic-prescriptive instruction—they also learn their roles and responsibilities in the reading program.

The remaining chapters are divided into five steps that outline the diagnostic-prescriptive model. Step 1 (chapters 4 and 5) is concerned with presenting informal and formal diagnostic procedures for assessing the reading strengths and weaknesses of each student in the teacher's classroom.

Step 2 (chapter 6) is titled "Synthesizing Data" and focuses on assisting the classroom teacher in organizing, analyzing, interpreting, and using the diagnostic information. In step 3 (chapter 7), techniques for organizing the classroom are discussed. Included are suggestions for the use of management systems, individualization, grouping, the arrangement of facilities, and the use of materials.

Ideas for using prescriptive reading instruction in the classroom are given in step 4 (chapters 8–14). Chapters 8–13 present suggestions for prescriptive teaching along with ideas for implementing prescriptive reading instruction in each of the skill areas: pre-reading, word recognition, comprehension, study skills, and personal reading. Students with special needs are included in the prescriptive

reading program; specific suggestions are given in chapter 14 for meeting the needs of students with physical impairments, psychological impairments, educational differences, and language variations.

In the final step, step 5, the need for a diagnostic-prescriptive reading program is summarized, and assistance is given the classroom teacher in fitting all of the parts together for the successful implementation of a program designed to meet the individual reading needs of all students.

Each chapter is preceded with questions to suggest its objectives and vocabulary which should be noted as the chapter is read. All vocabulary is defined in the chapter and in the glossary. The chapters close with a summary, exercises in applying the information in a classroom, and a list of further suggested readings. The appendixes include a list of reading skills, an interest and attitude inventory, sample interpretive reports on students, an observation checklist, guidelines for evaluating reading management systems, and several bibliographies of student and teacher materials. The instructor's manual which is available to professors using this text in their class contains sample multiple choice, matching, and essay questions. Additionally, the manual provides suggestions for using the text, audiovisual materials which may supplement the information, and transparency masters to correspond to the figures and tables in the text.

**New to This Edition**

The second edition of *Diagnostic-Prescriptive Reading Instruction* reflects an update of research in each chapter, within the text and in the suggested readings. Some additions were also made in the content of each chapter. For example, the section on the reading process in chapter 1 presents an overview of many models of reading including a skills perspective as well as a linguistic perspective. In chapter 4 the sequence of presentation of the informal instruments has been reorganized to reflect the order of usage by the classroom teacher. This chapter also includes the addition of a discussion of the Reading Miscue Inventory and a sample of how this procedure is used in conjunction with an Informal Reading Inventory.

The formal testing instruments have been updated in chapter 5. Chapter 9 contains an expansion in the section on listening comprehension to reflect current research in the area. Chapter 11, which presents ideas on comprehension instruction, has been revised extensively to include much of the current research and implications in the area. Included in this revision are: 1) an expansion of the information on factors affecting comprehension; 2) an expanded section on the various taxonomies of comprehension; 3) a presentation of factors to consider in diagnosing comprehension as well as some basic guidelines for teaching comprehension; and 4) a discussion of miscomprehension.

Study skills instruction has been expanded in chapter 12 with the inclusion of information on factors which influence studying. Chapter 13 includes additional information on motivating students to read. Teaching students with special needs is the topic of chapter 14 which has been greatly expanded to provide more specific information on teaching the mainstreamed student and the culturally disadvantaged student.

Martha D. Collins-Cheek
Earl H. Cheek, Jr.

# acknowledgments

The second edition of this text was prepared with input from many colleagues and students. These suggestions have been incorporated to provide a text which is designed to meet the daily needs of the classroom teacher, the reading specialist, and clinician, as well as the future teacher. Because you have been so generous with your assistance, we wish to express our sincere appreciation to our professional friends for these vital contributions. We have attempted to present the current information on diagnostic-prescriptive teaching in a useful manner. However, we recognize the need for constant improvement and refinement and welcome your comments.

Our special thanks go to _____ and _____ who were most helpful in the review of this manuscript and our editor Susan Soley. Of tremendous assistance was our typist Karla Lemoine who typed diligently to make the deadlines! Thanks also must be extended to our friends and students who have supported us through this effort. Your patience and encouragement will always be greatly appreciated!

# Diagnostic-Prescriptive Reading Instruction

# 1

The teachers at Seabreeze School are concerned that the reading instruction being provided in their school is not meeting the individual needs of many students. The reading program was discussed in a meeting of the team chairpersons, and they decided to invite the principal to the next meeting to talk over the current program as well as alternatives for improving it. Between the meetings, the teachers met with other teachers, reviewed their professional literature, and conferred with some outside consultants. The one suggestion that continually surfaced as a concept worthy of further consideration was diagnostic-prescriptive reading instruction. When this concept was discussed in the meeting with the principal, the entire faculty soon realized that each had a different idea about the teaching of reading as well as the components of a diagnostic-prescriptive reading program. They developed a number of questions for further study, as they considered improving their school reading program.

These questions, which arise in the mind of any teacher who is considering implementing a diagnostic-prescriptive reading program, will be addressed in the first chapter of this book. They should be reviewed and discussed before exploring the remainder of the book, which presents the specific steps involved in establishing a diagnostic-prescriptive reading program.

What is the reading process?

What is meant by the concept of diagnostic-prescriptive instruction?

How is a diagnostic-prescriptive reading program different from the typical school reading program?

Why is a diagnostic-prescriptive reading program needed?

How does diagnostic-prescriptive instruction relate to the reading process?

Who is involved in a diagnostic-prescriptive reading program?

# What is diagnostic-prescriptive reading instruction?

As this chapter is read, consideration should be given to these terms:

**Vocabulary to Know**

Diagnosis

Diagnostic-prescriptive instruction

Prescription

Reading process

Scope and sequence

**The Reading Process**

The act of reading requires complex thought processes by means of which a person interprets printed symbols as meaningful sound units and comprehends them as thought units in order to understand the message being presented. Thus, reading is sometimes defined as a process which is used to identify printed symbols and associate meaning with these symbols in order to respond to ideas conveyed by the writer.

The reading process has been researched and defined by many writers. Accordingly, there are various theories and models of reading instruction, including Gray's taxonomic model, the psychometric models of Holmes and Singer, and the psychological models, which include the ideas of the behavioralists, such as Skinner and Gagné, as well as the cognitive theorists, such as Gibson.[1] Additionally, the understanding of the reading process has been greatly enhanced by the research of Smith, who describes reading as information processing; by the linguistic models from researchers such as Bloomfield, Chomsky, Goodman and Ruddell; and by Rosenblatt's transactional model.[2] All of these models have had an impact on definitions of the reading process. Furthermore, Singer has suggested that a series of models is probably necessary to explain and predict reading performance.[3] For a more thorough analysis of the various reading models, sources such as Williams, Dechant and Smith, and Singer and Ruddell are most helpful.[4] Because each of the models defining the reading process reflects some ideas from other models, there is no pure model.

As researchers attempt better to understand the reading process, they give much attention to the newer models proposed by the linguists, psycholinguists, and sociolinguists. Goodman views reading as a psycholinguistic process, an interaction between thought and language. He states that "reading is a complex

process by which a reader reconstructs, to some degree, a message encoded by a writer in graphic language."[5] In this definition, the major goal is meaning. The reader may not perceive and identify every graphic cue, but must recognize errors in decoding as they affect meaning. The student who is reading for meaning corrects errors that interfere with comprehension. Errors that are dialectical and do not interfere with understanding may not be corrected. Goodman suggests that a divergent dialect itself is not an obstacle in learning to read; the problem for the divergent-dialect speaker is the rejection of the dialect by teachers.[6]

Other linguists, such as Frank Smith, develop the concept that in the reading process the reader's past experiences, expectations about meaning, and word recognition strategies operate simultaneously to enable the reader to obtain meaning from the printed page. Furthermore, Smith believes that it is impossible to learn the sound of a word by building up from the sounds of letters.[7] "Reading does not easily lend itself to compartmentalization," Smith states.[8] This statement seems to summarize a major emphasis on the linguist's concept of the reading process.

**Figure 1.1**
A Definition of the
Reading Process

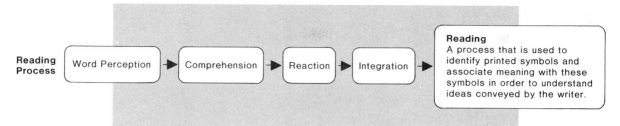

One of the older but most frequently used definitions of reading is that of William S. Gray, which suggests that reading is a four-step process that includes:

1. *Word Perception:* The reader perceives the printed word.
2. *Comprehension:* The reader understands the meaning of the word as used in the context.
3. *Reaction:* The reader reacts to the idea presented by the writer. The reaction is based on the reader's feelings and past experiences.
4. *Integration:* The reader integrates the new ideas gained from reading into his or her personal perspective and applies the ideas to daily activities.[9]

Although Gray's definition of the components of the reading process may be considered simplistic and compartmentalized, nevertheless these components identify the complexity of the reading process. Remember that the reasons for reading are to derive pleasure and knowledge from the printed page. The reading process thus involves much more than the mere recognition of words: it necessitates understanding of the message conveyed by the words. Comprehension is the essential component. This is emphasized in all definitions of reading, including Gray's definition, in which word perception is only a first step followed by three others relating to various levels of understanding (see figure 1.1).

A person who comments that a student reads well but cannot understand what has been read has a very limited perspective of the reading process. The classroom teacher must realize that reading instruction involves the development of both word recognition skills and comprehension skills. The student is not reading unless the words that are recognized are also understood. Thus, these areas cannot be taught as totally separate units, but must be developed simultaneously.

Because understanding is the essential aspect of reading, teachers must also recognize the importance of language understanding and background experiences as aids in comprehension. Writers transmit ideas and feelings, using their backgrounds of experiences and their unique language style. Readers must then, in order to obtain meaning from these written words, relate their individual backgrounds of experiences and understanding of language. The extent to which the reader is able to relate to the words of the writer determines the degree to which understanding will occur.

The reading process involves more than the skills which allow the perception or recognition of words and understanding. It involves language and experiences, combined with the assimilation of the various skills; only when these components work together do we encounter successful or mature readers.

Reading is a simple word but a complex process. Actually, reading is closely interrelated with thinking, language, and experiences; however, just how each of these areas impacts the reading process seems to be unique to the individual. Why does one student learn to read while another does not? Because we cannot provide a definitive answer to this question, teachers must be aware of the many aspects of the process as well as individual needs of each student.

## The Concept of Diagnostic-Prescriptive Instruction

*Diagnosis* is a familiar term that has been used in the field of medicine and related areas for hundreds of years. This word may be defined as the act of determining the nature of a disease or problem through careful examination and study. Using this same definition, educators have adopted during the last half century the idea of diagnosing students in school in order to ascertain their strengths and weaknesses in various academic areas.

*Prescription* is likewise a term that educators have borrowed from other areas. A prescription is a specific direction that is recommended following a careful diagnosis. Thus, this term is used in education when students receive instruction based on their identified educational needs.

These terms have been combined to form a relatively new concept in the teaching of reading—the concept of diagnostic-prescriptive instruction. This concept has been discussed for many years, but only recently have classroom teachers been faced with its implementation in a planned program. *The concept of diagnostic-prescriptive instruction in reading means that the individual strengths and weaknesses of each student are identified through various diagnostic procedures and that appropriate instruction is provided based on the diagnosis.* In order to implement this concept, the faculty must be committed to the idea, and the administration must assume a leadership role in the reading program. In addition, the following components are necessary (see figure 1.2):

1. *A scope and sequence of reading skills.* This hierarchy of skills is an essential component of the diagnostic-prescription program. The reading skills to be taught at each level, from kindergarten through the highest level, must be identified and arranged in the order in which they are to be introduced. While each student may not progress through this hierarchy in precisely the same order, formulation of the scope and sequence of reading skills provides a framework for sequential skill development in the program.
2. *Procedures to facilitate continuous diagnosis of each student.* Diagnostic information from a variety of sources is a second essential component of a diagnostic-prescriptive program. This does not mean that the teacher must spend a great deal of time in testing individual students. Chapters 4 and 5 present procedures for obtaining diagnostic data.

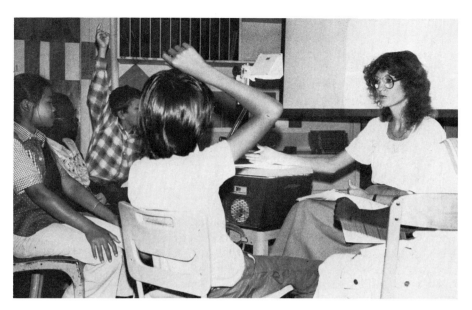

3. *A variety of materials and teaching techniques for prescriptive instruction.*
   In a diagnostic-prescriptive program, the student is diagnosed and instructed
   as an individual, although the instruction may be done in a small group.
   Prescriptive instruction requires careful instruction and a variety of materials in order to develop the language and reading skills identified as important for each student. These materials must be organized for accessibility.
   Chapter 7 provides specific ideas for their organization. Chapters 8–14 give
   prescriptive techniques.

4. *The use of guided or directed reading lesson procedures.* The concept of
   diagnostic-prescriptive instruction is based on meeting the individual students's needs. This idea may be misinterpreted to mean that the student is
   tested on a particular skill, assigned a workbook or some other material to
   develop the skill, and tested again at some later date. This is *not* diagnostic-
   prescriptive instruction. A better label for this type of instruction is the "plug-
   in approach." In an attempt to avoid the "plug-in approach," prescriptive
   instruction should follow a guided or directed reading lesson format. This
   procedure, which is more specifically outlined in chapter 8, requires that the
   teacher be actively involved in teaching, and that the student be provided
   with opportunities to apply the skills as they are taught.

5. *Methods for keeping records on each student.* In a diagnostic-prescriptive
   program, it is essential to use a procedure for keeping records as each student's strengths and weaknesses are identified and prescriptive instruction
   is provided. Detailed information about each of thirty or more students is
   impossible to remember. Therefore, some convenient record such as a check-
   sheet or a skill card must be used. Although these records require teacher
   time, they are essential components of the program.

**Figure 1.2**
Model for Diagnostic-
Prescriptive Reading
Instruction

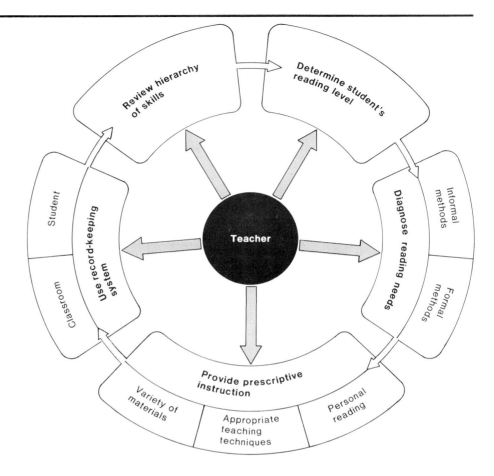

## Comparing Traditional and Diagnostic-Prescriptive Instruction

The preceding description of the elements of a diagnostic-prescriptive program suggests how it differs from more traditional reading instruction. A description of the procedures for teaching reading which might be observed in two elementary classrooms will facilitate comparison of the two kinds of instruction.

Mr. Johnson has thirty-one students in his classroom. He has reviewed their records and has achievement test data on each one. At the beginning of the school year, Mr. Johnson organizes his class into three reading groups, and each group moves through the designated basal reader in a step-by-step procedure. The test at the end of each unit in the basal reader is given before going on to the next unit. Few changes are made in the three groups.

The teacher's manuals for the basal readers are the major teaching tools used by Mr. Johnson. He follows these guidebooks very closely and has never really considered the scope and sequence of reading skills to be developed in his class-

room. To assist in managing his classroom, Mr. Johnson provides seatwork for the students to do during the reading class when they are not in the reading group. This seat work consists of ditto sheets, randomly selected cards from a kit, board work, and workbook pages. In Mr. Johnson's class, the teacher has most of the responsibility to provide for all of the student's activities.

Ms. Perez also has thirty-one students in her class. These students are organized into three basic groups, but work in different skill and interest groups, or individually, as necessary, to achieve predetermined objectives. The three reading groups are quite flexible; their composition changes as needs are diagnosed. Ms. Perez uses various diagnostic procedures, such as informal reading inventories, observation, work sheets, and criterion-referenced tests. Before school opened, Ms. Perez met with other faculty members to determine the scope and sequence of skills being followed in the school. She believed that this was very useful information, since she does not always follow the teacher's manuals for the basal series. In fact, Ms. Perez employs various approaches, such as language experience and individualized reading, together with the basal material to meet the students' needs. She provides direct instruction in reading for every student each day, either in groups or in a one-to-one situation. As Ms. Perez works with one group or student, however, others in the class are involved in activities designed to develop their individual skill needs.

On one particular day, Ms. Perez was working with three students using a language experience approach to express their ideas regarding a recent fire at a neighborhood store. Several other students were involved in free reading and preparing for individual conferences with the teacher. Four boys were at the listening center working on the skills of following oral directions and locating details in the selection. Other students were in the skills center working with activities designed to strengthen their dictionary skills. Two students were working together, using various activities to improve their sight word vocabulary. Five students were involved in miscellaneous tasks including seatwork, manipulative games, and writing, all of which related to their specific, diagnosed needs.

In this classroom, a variety of materials and approaches is used in order to provide prescriptive instruction. Ms. Perez believes that the additional time required to plan for such instruction is well spent. She feels that her students are more involved with their learning, since they know why they are expected to do the various assignments and can become self-directed during the school day.

These classrooms are different. The atmosphere is more positive, and the rate of learning is faster in Ms. Perez's class. Students are taught as individuals whose reading needs have been identified and for whom presecriptive instruction is provided. These ideas are summarized in table 1.1. Further illustration is given in figure 1.3.

**Table 1.1**

Comparison of Reading Instruction in the Diagnostic-Prescriptive Classroom and the Traditional Classroom

| | Diagnostic-prescriptive Classroom | Traditional Classroom |
|---|---|---|
| *Scope and sequence* | Reading skills are identified and a scope and sequence of skills is used to guide instruction. | The basal reader is followed, with the assumption that all skills are developed. |
| *Diagnosis* | Continuous diagnosis is done using students' work as well as informal reading inventories, observation, criterion-referenced tests, and various procedures to determine specific skill strengths and weaknesses. | Student needs are generalized from such information as standardized tests and unit tests in the basals. |
| *Prescription* | A variety of materials and approaches are used to meet the diagnosed needs of the students. Instruction may be provided in groups or to individuals as necessary. Grouping arrangements are flexible according to the students' changing needs. | The basal reader is followed very closely. Skills are taught as directed in the basal program. Instruction is provided in the basal groups, which are often not changed during the school year. |
| *Personal reading* | Time and activities are scheduled to encourage students to use the reading skills as they read for enjoyment and to locate information. | The students read the stories in the basal reader and, if interested, they read library books. |
| *Records* | The teacher keeps class records to guide daily instruction. Individual student records are used in communicating with parents and follow the student from level to level. These record-keeping forms are based on the hierarchy of reading skills. | There is no systematic record-keeping system. |

## The Need for Diagnostic-Prescriptive Instruction

The foregoing comparison clearly indicates the need for diagnostic-prescriptive instruction. But to ascertain this need, it is necessary to look into only one classroom, anywhere, at any level. Upon review, it will be evident that no two students in the classroom are exactly alike in their reading development. The teacher may locate six students who are near the same reading level, but each of these students has different skill needs and interests. The teacher must identify their individual skill needs and interests in order to provide appropriate instruction for each student.

As suggested earlier in this chapter, the reading process is not a simple process but consists of many interrelated components which are integrated by the reader. Thus, readers react to the printed word in different ways based on their abilities and experiences. When teachers understand that the process of reading is not an exact, step-by-step procedure followed in the same way by all students, then differences in learning are better understood. Such understanding helps one to realize that the traditional three-group organizational plan using one set of materials cannot be successful in teaching all students to read. The complex nature of the reading process itself shows the need for the methods of diagnostic-prescriptive reading instruction.

**Figure 1.3**
Noticeable Differences
between the Traditional
Classroom and the
Diagnostic-Prescriptive
Classroom
Courtesy of Julie Reische

Traditional
Classroom

Diagnostic-Prescriptive
Classroom

*What Is Diagnostic-Prescriptive Reading Instruction?*

Once again the medical analogy is useful. A person visits a physician for a checkup or possibly for treatment of a specific problem. The physician uses various methods to obtain more information, which leads to the decision to require certain tests. Using the outcome of the tests and other information, the physician develops a prescription for treating the patient. This prescription may cure the patient's ills, or it may need to be changed or modified. Detailed records are kept so that the physician can recall the specific problems, the date of the diagnosis, the prescription provided, and the results of the prescription. Now compare this diagnostic-prescriptive procedure to the provision of reading instruction in the classroom.

In September, the teacher is faced with a new group of students. Little is known about the students' reading ability. They may all be ten years old and in the fifth grade, but their similarity ends at this point. The teacher, like the physician, must determine the specific needs of each student, using various diagnostic procedures including questioning, observation, and testing. Based on this information, appropriate prescriptive instruction is provided as needed in group or individual situations. Records must be kept so that the teacher will know and be able to share with parents specific information regarding each student's progress in reading.

Another analogy shows the need for diagnostic-prescriptive instruction from a different perspective. Mrs. Jones went to her physician complaining of a backache and dizziness. After a cursory examination, the physician recommended that she rest in bed for a few days and take a prescribed medication. Mrs. Smith visited the same physician the next day complaining of a headache and a sore throat. After a cursory examination, the physician recommended rest for a few days and a prescribed medication. Mrs. Jones and Mrs. Smith were neighbors, and as they compared their superficial diagnoses, similar little blue pills, and continuing problems, they decided to seek other medical advice.

Now consider Susan and Ricardo. Susan is eleven years old, in the fifth grade, and reads at approximately a third-grade level. She has one sister, comes from a middle income home, and has had a wide variety of experiences. Susan's teacher has placed her in the third reading group. Ricardo is ten years old, in the same fifth-grade class and reads at approximately a mid-two level. He has five brothers and two sisters, comes from a lower income home, and has never been outside his immediate neighborhood. Ricardo's teacher placed him in the same third reading group as Susan because this was the lowest group in the class. What are the similarities and differences in these situations?

Adults have alternatives when they are not satisfied.

Students are often captive audiences in classrooms in which their needs are not met.

Adults can verbalize their feelings, while students frequently develop feelings of inadequacy because they are in a frustrating situation.

In all of these cases, prescriptions were provided based on little or no diagnostic data. Thus, no significant improvements occurred, physically or mentally.

Physicians who do not adequately diagnose and prescribe do not improve their patients' health. Teachers who do not properly diagnose and prescribe do not improve their students' learning environment.

Teachers are not physicians, and the analogy is not meant to suggest that teaching children to read is the same as diagnosing a cold. In fact, the teacher is dealing with the human brain, which is a most complex entity, and with the learning process, which is more difficult to define than a temperature of 102° F. Additionally, teachers have no "miracle drugs" to prescribe. These and other factors make it imperative that the classroom teacher use some systematic procedure in providing reading instruction. Teacher and student time is precious. Without utilizing specific diagnostic data, much time is lost teaching reading skills that the students may already know or skills that they may not be ready to learn.

Accountability is a term that educators hear every day. Parents ask if their children are being taught to read. The public asks why so many students are leaving the secondary schools unable to read and write at even a seventh-grade level. Teachers must respond to these questions. A study by Farr, Fay and Negley suggests that students are reading better today than in 1944–45.[10] Other reports from the National Assessment program provide similar information.[11] The classroom teacher must provide this positive information to the public. Additionally, through the use of diagnostic-prescriptive instruction, the teacher can report the specific individual strengths and weaknesses of each student. This type of classroom documentation is essential!

Each student has specific needs. Teachers must discover and respond to these needs if students are to reach their full potential in reading. The diagnostic-prescriptive concept provides the necessary framework for developing each student's reading skill to the maximum level.

## Staff Involvement in the Diagnostic-Prescriptive Reading Program

The school reading program traditionally has required the involvement of all members of the school staff. This does not change when a diagnostic-prescriptive program is implemented. The fact is that more involvement is required as the program is coordinated from level to level and all personnel become part of the reading team.

The specific roles of the classroom and content teachers are outlined in chapters 2 and 3. These persons are obviously extremely important in the diagnostic-prescriptive reading program. However, there are others who are essential to the program's success. These include the principal, the media specialist, the school reading teacher, the guidance counselor, teachers of music, art, and physical education, and teachers in exceptional education. In addition to the faculty, a successful diagnostic-prescriptive reading program must have parent involvement. To understand how all of these people are involved in the program, it is necessary to look at their specific contributions.

The *principal* is the key to a successful diagnostic-prescriptive reading program. The principal must understand the reading process as well as the concept of diagnostic-prescriptive instruction, provide necessary staff time for planning, locate materials for instruction, support the faculty as they face the initial frustrations of change, and help parents and students understand the changes occurring in the reading program. An enthusiastic principal with a positive attitude toward the program will evoke a positive response from teachers, students, and parents. Thus, total faculty involvement becomes much easier.

The school *media specialist* or *librarian* also has an essential role in the diagnostic-prescriptive reading program. Media specialists have at their disposal an extensive collection of reading materials that can be used to motivate most students to read. They should share these materials with the students through book reviews, storytelling, creative dramatics, and displays, in order to make them aware of the wealth of information to be found in books. The media specialist reinforces the development of reading by helping the student to apply the skills in reading for enjoyment or reading to locate information. Because students must continuously apply reading skills as they are developed in the classroom, this reinforcement must be a shared responsibility of the media specialist and the classroom teacher. Periodically during the school year, classroom teachers should provide the media specialist with current information about the reading level of each student; the media specialist must also know the readability level of the materials in the library. Thus informed, this program can give students knowledgeable assistance in selecting books at the appropriate level. The specialist who enjoys books and respects the individual needs of students makes an extremely valuable contribution to the diagnostic-prescriptive reading program.

The role of the school *reading teacher* varies, depending on the job description provided for the position. In some schools this person is a resource teacher who works in the classroom helping teachers to meet their students' reading needs. In this capacity, the reading teacher in a diagnostic-prescriptive program helps the classroom teacher to develop diagnostic skills, such as observation and informal testing, and also provides ideas for prescription development based on the diagnoses. In addition, the reading resource teacher is valuable in assisting the classroom teacher by furnishing necessary staff development, locating materials, and demonstrating diagnostic and prescriptive techniques as well as skills in managing instruction. The involvement of the resource teacher is most important, as this person does the "legwork" and enables the teacher to concentrate on the instructional program.

In other schools this person may have the role of a special reading teacher who works only with the poorer readers. In this capacity the reading teacher must follow the same program and sequence of reading skills which are used by the classroom teacher. The reading teacher works with the classroom teacher in diagnosing the students' problems and providing prescriptive instruction. Reading instruction is given by both the classroom teacher and the reading teacher working as a team to provide maximum learning opportunities for the student. The classroom teacher is responsible for the students' reading instruction; the reading

teacher should furnish supplemental assistance to help designated students develop the necessary reading skills. The essential consideration is that these two persons work together, sharing diagnostic data, prescriptive procedures, and notes on successes and failures.

*Music, art,* and *physical education* teachers are also members of the diagnostic-prescriptive reading program team. These persons must work with the classroom teacher in identifying students with specific reading deficiencies, and assisting with prescriptive instruction in their related areas. For example, the music program can be a great help to the student with poor auditory skills by providing instruction in the identification of various instruments by their sounds. The art teacher can design instruction to help younger students develop their tactile senses and visual perception, or provide follow-up activities related to their classroom reading instruction. The physical education teacher can work with the classroom teacher to design specific exercises or activities which develop in young students necessary motor skills, such as eye-hand coordination and visual tracing. With older students, the physical education teacher can often recommend books, activities, or assignments and elicit a more positive response than the classroom

teacher. Thus, the classroom teacher needs to communicate with the physical education teacher, to identify students with specific needs, such as following directions, listening comprehension, or remembering details, or a poor attitude toward reading. Together, classroom and physical education teachers can embark upon a joint program to provide appropriate prescriptive instruction.

*Teachers in exceptional education* may have some self-contained classes of students at either extreme of the mental ability scale; or they may serve as resource teachers as their students are placed in regular classes ("mainstreamed"). In either case, they are involved in the diagnostic-prescriptive reading program. The role of exceptional education teachers who have self-contained classrooms is outlined in chapter 2, in the discussion of the classroom teacher's role in the diagnostic-prescriptive program. Teachers must realize that in the diagnostic-prescriptive program a continuum of skills is used, and students progress at a rate appropriate for their learning abilities. The educable mentally retarded student learns the skills at a slower rate than the average student; the gifted student learns them at a faster rate. Regardless of the rate, each student must be given many opportunities to use the skills in reading situations.

The teacher in exceptional education whose students are mainstreamed provides assistance in the diagnostic-prescriptive reading program by helping the classroom teacher to diagnose specific skills needs, but assists more significantly in prescription. Students with exceptionalities such as hearing and vision impairments, as well as the educable mentally retarded, need additional teaching assistance in order to develop the necessary reading skills. The exceptional education resource teacher, like the reading teacher, must continuously coordinate with the classroom teacher in reading instruction.

*Guidance counselors* at all levels have major responsibilities in the diagnostic-prescriptive reading program. They do not necessarily deal with direct reading instruction in the classroom, but serve to support the teacher in providing reading instruction. Among the responsibilities of counselors are helping to develop positive attitudes toward school and reading, helping the teacher investigate personal problems which may impede learning, promoting communication among the faculty, and aiding in parent-teacher conferences to communicate students' strengths and weaknesses as identified in the program.

*Parents* are also involved in the diagnostic-prescriptive reading program in order to improve its effectiveness. They may serve as volunteers or aides, or they may participate only in parent-teacher organization meetings or conferences. Regardless of the extent of their involvement, parents must realize that in the diagnostic-prescriptive program instruction is based on the student's individual needs. Parents then view progress in reading in terms of individual achievement rather than just letter grades. Since each student is making progress in areas of diagnosed reading problems, it defeats the purpose of the program to use grades as the only indicator of progress. When parents understand this, they cooperate with the program by participating in conferences which report student progress, and by learning ways to give further assistance in the home. Most parents want to help their children to become good readers. For many years, parents have felt

like outsiders in the schools and have not known how to help. In diagnostic-prescriptive reading programs, parents are provided with definite information about their children's strengths and weaknesses in reading, as well as specific ideas about how to help them. The astute teacher will help parents to use this information and thus expand the school team. When parents are involved in the reading program, students will view reading as important.

As these descriptions suggest, everyone in the school is involved in the diagnostic-prescriptive reading program. Teamwork is essential—faculty members and parents must work together. The entire staff continuously shares their observations and collaborate in designing all areas of the curriculum to enhance the students' learning. A diagnostic-prescriptive reading program is student-centered, using the teachers, parents, materials, and other resources to meet the specific needs of the individual student (see figure 1.4). The leadership of the principal, cooperation of the parents, and collaboration of the faculty are all parts of a complex puzzle which, when put together, will create a program that produces students who can read and who enjoy reading!

**Summary**

The concept of diagnostic-prescriptive instruction is based on the premise that each person is an individual with unique needs. This is true in reading. Because each student has individual strengths and weaknesses in reading, diagnostic-prescriptive instructional procedures are needed. Thus, the classroom teacher must identify these individual differences and provide instruction which will help each student become a better reader.

Five components are identified, in addition to administrative leadership and teacher commitment, as being necessary for the implementation of a diagnostic-prescriptive reading program. They are (1) a scope and sequence of reading skills; (2) procedures to facilitate continuous diagnosis of each student; (3) a variety of materials and teaching techniques for prescriptive instruction; (4) the use of guided or directed reading lesson procedures; and (5) methods for keeping records on each student. Teachers are encouraged to consider these components as they design strategies for daily instruction.

Each faculty member should be involved in the implementation of a diagnostic-prescriptive reading program. Additionally, the administration provides the leadership for the program, and parents must understand the program and be involved in giving necessary assistance at home. The diagnostic-prescriptive reading program requires teamwork in order to develop better readers who are able to function in a complex society.

The topics discussed in this chapter provide a basic understanding of the concept of diagnostic-prescriptive reading instruction. This fundamental information is a useful background for the remaining chapters, which address more specifically the roles of the classroom and content teachers in the diagnostic-prescriptive reading program and the steps involved in putting it into practice.

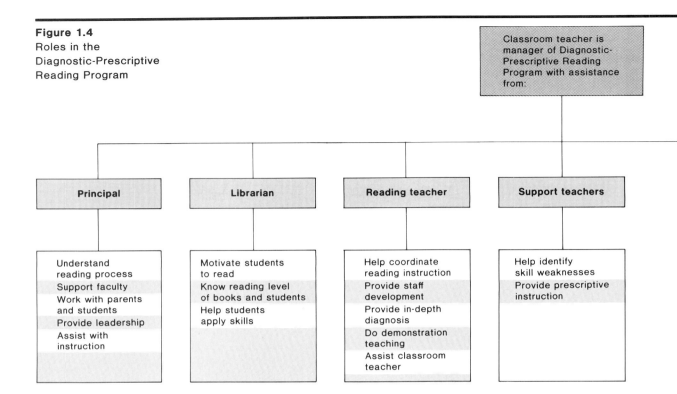

**Figure 1.4**
Roles in the
Diagnostic-Prescriptive
Reading Program

Classroom teacher is manager of Diagnostic-Prescriptive Reading Program with assistance from:

**Principal**

Understand reading process
Support faculty
Work with parents and students
Provide leadership
Assist with instruction

**Librarian**

Motivate students to read
Know reading level of books and students
Help students apply skills

**Reading teacher**

Help coordinate reading instruction
Provide staff development
Provide in-depth diagnosis
Do demonstration teaching
Assist classroom teacher

**Support teachers**

Help identify skill weaknesses
Provide prescriptive instruction

## Applying What You Read

You are selected as a faculty representative to discuss changes needed in the school or district reading program. During the first meeting, some say they have read about a concept known as diagnostic-prescriptive reading instruction; however, no one seems to know very much about it. Outline the information you could share with the committee on the concept of diagnostic-prescriptive reading instruction.

The principal in your school has asked that you lead a discussion on the involvement of the faculty in a diagnostic-prescriptive reading program. Outline your ideas.

The faculty in your school wishes to compare their current reading program with a diagnostic-prescriptive program. Propose the major idea that should be compared.

Compare the reading program in the elementary or middle school which you attended, to the diagnostic-prescriptive reading program described in this chapter.

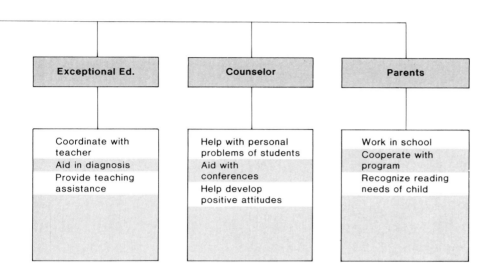

| Exceptional Ed. | Counselor | Parents |
|---|---|---|
| Coordinate with teacher<br>Aid in diagnosis<br>Provide teaching assistance | Help with personal problems of students<br>Aid with conferences<br>Help develop positive attitudes | Work in school<br>Cooperate with program<br>Recognize reading needs of child |

**Notes**

1. William S. Gray, "Reading and Physiology and Psychology of Reading," in *Encyclopedia of Educational Research;* Jack A. Holmes and Harry Singer, *The Substrata-Factor Theory; The Substrata-Factor Differences Underlying Reading in Known Groups;* B. F. Skinner, *Verbal Behavior;* Robert M. Gagné, *The Conditions of Learning;* E. J. Gibson, "The Ontogeny of Reading," *American Psychologist.*
2. Frank Smith, *Understanding Reading: A Psycholinguistic Analysis of Reading and Learning to Read;* Leonard Bloomfield and Clarence L. Barnhart, *Let's Read: A Linguistic Approach;* Noam Chomsky, *Language and Mind;* Kenneth S. Goodman, "Behind the Eye: What Happens in Reading," in *Reading Process and Program;* Robert B. Ruddell, *Reading-Language Intruction; Innovative Practices;* L. M. Rosenblatt, "Towards a Transactional Theory of Reading," *Journal of Reading Behavior.*
3. Harry Singer, "Theoretical Models of Reading," *Journal of Reading Behavior.*
4. Joanna P. Williams, "Learning to Read: A Review of Theories and Models," *Reading Research Quarterly;* Emerald V. Dechant and Henry P. Smith, *Psychology in Teaching Reading;* Harry Singer and Robert Ruddell, eds., *Theoretical Models and Processes of Reading.*

5. Goodman, "Behind the Eye," p. 5.
6. Kenneth S. Goodman with Catherine Buck, "Dialect Barriers to Comprehension Revisited," *The Reading Teacher.*
7. Smith, *Understanding Reading,* p. 126.
8. Frank Smith, *Psycholinguistics and Reading,* p. 8.
9. William S. Gray, *On Their Own in Reading,* pp. 35–37.
10. Roger Farr, Leo Fay and Harold Negley, *Then and Now: Reading Achievement in Indiana* (1944–45 and 1976).
11. Education Commission of the States, *National Assessment of Educational Progress: A Project of the Education Commission of the States.*

## Other Suggested Readings

Artley, A. Sterl. "Psycholinguistics Applied to Reading Instruction." *Reading Horizons* 20 (Winter 1980):106–11.

Bean, Rita M. "Role of the Reading Specialist: A Multifaceted Dilemma." *The Reading Teacher* 32 (January 1979):409–13.

Botel, Morton, and Granowsky, Alvin. "Diagnose the Reading Program Before You Diagnose the Child." *The Reading Teacher* 26 (March 1973):563–65.

Canady, Robert J. "Psycholinguists in a Real-Life Classroom." *The Reading Teacher* 34 (November 1980):156–59.

Cheek, Martha Collins, and Cheek, Earl H. "This Reading Program Ensures Success." *The Executive Educator* 3 (June 1981):30–31.

Cohen, Elizabeth; Intili, JoAnn K.; and Robbins, Susan H. "Teachers and Reading Specialists: Cooperation or Isolation?" *The Reading Teacher* 32 (December 1978):281–87.

Downing, John. "Reading-Skill or Skills?" *The Reading Teacher* 35 (February 1982):534–37.

Elijah, David, and Legenza, Alice. "A Major Revision of the Reading Model for Classroom Teachers." *Reading Horizons* 21 (Winter 1981):108–13.

Gibson, Eleanor, and Levin, Harry. *The Psychology of Reading.* Cambridge, Mass.: MIT Press, 1975.

Goodman, Kenneth S. "Effective Teachers of Reading Know Language and Children." *Elementary English* 51 (September 1974):823–28.

Goodman, Yetta, and Watson, D. "A Reading Program to Live With: Focus on Comprehension." *Language Arts* 54 (November-December 1977):868–79.

Hall, MaryAnne, and Ramig, Christopher J. *Linguistic Foundations for Reading.* Columbus, Ohio: Charles E. Merrill Publishing Company, 1978.

Harris, Larry A., and Smith, Carl B. *Reading Instruction.* 3rd ed. New York: Holt, Rinehart & Winston, 1980. Chapters 1, 2 and 3.

Hollander, Sheila K. "Reading: Process and Product." *The Reading Teacher* 28 (March 1975):550–54.

Horn, Janis L. "The Reading Specialist as an Effective Change Agent." *The Reading Teacher* 35 (January 1982):408–11.

Lexier, Kenneth A. "Common Oversimplifications of the Reading Process." *Journal of Reading* 21 (April 1978):601–05.

Manning, Gary L., and Manning, Maryann. "What Is the Role of the Principal in an Excellent Reading Program." *Reading World* 21 (December 1981):130–33.

Ngandee, Kathleen M. and Strum, Carolyn B. "The Reading Specialists' Role as Perceived by Administrators, Special Education Instructors, Classroom Teachers, and Specialists." *Reading Horizons* 22 (Fall 1981):29–32.

Pearson, P. David. "A Psycholinguistic Model of Reading." *Language Arts* 53 (March 1976):309–14.

Sawyer, Diane J. "The Diagnostic Mystique—A Point of View." *The Reading Teacher* 27 (March 1974):555–61.

Shuy, Roger. "What Should the Language Strand in a Reading Program Contain?" *The Reading Teacher* 35 (April 1982):806–12.

Shuy, Roger W., ed. *Linguistic Theory: What Can It Say About Reading?* Newark, Delaware: International Reading Association, 1977.

Strange, Michael, and Allington, Richard L. "Use the Diagnostic-Prescriptive Model Knowledgeably." *The Reading Teacher* 31 (December 1977):290–92.

Tovey, Duane R. "The Psycholinguistic Guessing Game." *Language Arts* 53 (March 1976):319–22.

Zintz, Miles V. *The Reading Process.* 3rd ed. Dubuque, Iowa: William C. Brown Co. Publishers, 1980.

# 2

The teachers at Seabreeze School were engaged in a lively discussion concerning the implementation of diagnostic-prescriptive instruction in their school reading program. Now that they had a clearer understanding of the reading process and were convinced of the need for a diagnostic-prescriptive program, the next step was to determine more specifically the role of the classroom teacher in such a program. As they talked they listed some of the basic functions that the classroom teacher should assume.

*Be familiar with each student's reading abilities.* Awareness of the student's strengths and weaknesses in reading enables the teacher to provide better instruction, eliminating many of the trial and error procedures necessary without the use of the diagnostic-prescriptive model.

*Use diagnostic-procedures continuously.* Continuous diagnosis enables the teacher to develop an accurate, clear, up-to-date profile for each student.

*Analyze each student's reading abilities.* This should be done at the beginning of the school year and continued as an ongoing process throughout the year.

*Exercise leadership in the classroom.* The teacher must decide which students should be placed in what reading groups at the beginning of the year and continuously adjust group membership. The teacher must also keep parents informed of the program's success as well as their child's progress.

*Provide prescriptive instruction.* The teacher must provide instruction based on diagnostic information and the learning styles of individual students.

The teachers at Seabreeze recognized these ideas as essential to the successful implementation of the diagnostic-prescriptive model. As their discussion continued, they raised the questions shown here, which are to be discussed in this chapter.

Who is the self-contained classroom teacher?

Why is diagnosis of reading difficulties the responsibility of the classroom teacher?

How can diagnosis be related to the daily classroom instructional program in reading?

Why is the identification of reading skills necessary to the classroom diagnostic-prescriptive program?

What reading skills are important for the classroom teacher to include in the diagnostic-prescriptive program?

How does the classroom teacher organize and relate the reading skills to the diagnostic-prescriptive program?

How can the classroom teacher assess achievement of the reading skills?

# What is the classroom teacher's role in the diagnostic-prescriptive reading program?

As this chapter is read, the following terms should be noted:

**Vocabulary to Know**

Assessment
Classroom teacher
Comprehension skills
Continuous diagnosis
Hierarchy of skills
Personal reading

Prereading skills
Reading skills
Scope and sequence
Study skills
Word recognition skills

**The Classroom Teacher and Diagnosis**

This chapter emphasizes the role of the self-contained classroom teacher in the diagnostic-prescriptive reading program. *A self-contained classroom teacher is one who has responsibility for a group of students who remain in the same classroom with that teacher for the entire school day.* In this role, the teacher has the responsibility for teaching all students in this classroom all the subjects they will encounter for an entire school year. This is a great deal of responsibility, since the teacher in a self-contained classroom must be an expert in several areas of instruction.

There are certainly advantages to this setting, especially for younger students. Rapport between student and teacher develops more quickly, and the anxiety created by having several teachers is prevented. The primary disadvantages of a self-contained setting are that one person usually does not teach all subjects with equal enthusiasm, and that possible student-teacher personality differences are unrelieved during the day. The latter problem can and should be resolved by moving the student to another classroom. The former, however, is not as easily resolved.

Despite continuous debate, the fact is that most elementary schools use self-contained instructional units; therefore, the teacher must strive for excellence within this setting. It is the classroom teacher who sets the tone and encourages learning. The teacher in a self-contained classroom should facilitate student participation and provide an atmosphere that enlivens the processes through which learning occurs.

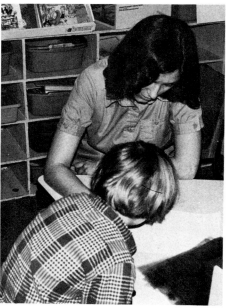

Such teachers must have a wide range of talents and must excel in the teaching of reading, which is especially significant. Since reading forms the foundation for learning in all subjects, adequate instruction must be provided in both the development and the application of reading skills. Learning is further enhanced if the classroom teacher is careful to provide an environment conducive to reading.

Historically, classroom teachers have not been encouraged to diagnose reading problems in the classroom because this was primarily within the purview of the reading clinician or reading specialist. Teachers have relied on the teacher's guide for the materials used and only referred students for special reading diagnosis when they could no longer cope in the classroom. Many felt that reading diagnosis was too time consuming. As a result, often little diagnostic information was obtained about each student in the classroom. This information usually came from standardized group tests, which yielded scores that were questionable at best, especially under the conditions in which they were administered (i.e., school lunchrooms, auditoriums, etc.). However, this diagnostic information was used by teachers to the best possible advantage. If a school or school system had a reading specialist available, then diagnostic information on some of the more severely disabled readers could be obtained; however, teachers realized the inadequacy of this data in determining the specific needs of students in each classroom.

The result of this deficiency of diagnostic data was that students were often grouped incorrectly. Teachers used a basic three-group format and found that within the confines of these three groups, there were students who ran the gamut in reading levels. Diagnosis was based primarily on the aforementioned standardized scores, recommendations from teachers who had taught a student previously, some teacher observations, and teacher intuition. In many instances the missing element was the lack of a systematic approach to diagnosis. Thus, there was no identification of the reading skills to be taught, leaving the teacher unaware of exactly what needed to be diagnosed. This was a rather haphazard approach to teaching reading. Many slower readers were frustrated when they were unable to keep pace with the majority of the class, while the higher level students were not challenged sufficiently in their reading.

As classroom teachers have received more information on reading instruction in recent years, they have realized the need to refine their diagnostic techniques in order to determine the individual reading needs of their students. The difficulties experienced by the self-contained classroom teacher are being alleviated by a trend toward a more systematic diagnostic approach to reading. This has resulted in greater emphasis on diagnostic-prescriptive techniques for instruction.

After realizing that continuous diagnosis was necessary and that assistance from outside sources such as reading specialists was insufficient, classroom teachers correctly concluded that they must assume the responsibility for diagnosing their students' needs in their own classrooms. Certainly with the advent of the emphasis on accountability, and competency testing, the classroom teacher could

no longer accept the trial and error previously associated with diagnostic information.[1] The push for more appropriate instruction based upon the specific needs of each student has become a matter of teacher-student survival. The importance of systematic, accurate diagnosis cannot be overemphasized, since the student's progress in reading depends on the diagnostic information gathered and the prescriptive instruction provided. A thorough diagnostic-prescriptive program ensures each student a greater chance of success.

In order to assist classroom teachers with the transition to such programs, school systems have initiated in-service training designed to acquaint their teachers with techniques for diagnosing strengths and weaknesses in reading. Also, colleges have instituted preservice and graduate programs to further the concept of diagnostic-prescriptive instruction. Although this concept is relatively new, classroom teachers have recognized its benefits for their students and have proceeded vigorously.

As a point of clarification, the systematic diagnostic approach referred to in the preceding pages does not suggest using a clinical testing approach in the classroom, but simply the use of appropriate diagnostic procedures as necessary to learn about individual needs in reading. Systematic diagnosis would be developed around informal testing procedures designed specifically for the classroom teacher, which are discussed extensively in chapter 4. It is recommended that the classroom teacher's diagnosis be built upon this design. Formal diagnostic procedures may be necessary to supplement the informal techniques. These are discussed in chapter 5.

Diagnosis precedes the development of an instructional program for each student, and is continuous throughout the year. A major responsibility of the classroom teacher is to use diagnostic-prescriptive information to greatest advantage by continuously updating previous diagnoses and adjusting prescriptive instructional procedures. As students and their experiences change during the year, so should their reading instruction.

## Reading Diagnosis and the Classroom Instructional Program

Diagnosis is the foundation for planning the daily as well as long-range instructional program for classroom reading instruction. Thus, reading diagnosis cannot be separated from prescriptive teaching, even on a daily basis. The two are so closely intertwined that even though formal diagnosis may not occur every day, less formalized diagnostic information is obtained from prescriptive teaching through observation, student work, and so forth.

Continuous diagnosis is vital to the development of each student's instructional program, since it allows day-to-day adjustments that keep individual instruction tailored to current progress and problems. If diagnosis occurs at infrequent intervals, the quality of reading instruction declines, and the students' progress suffers needlessly. Infrequent diagnosis often leads to radical changes in instruction that disrupt the continuity of the learning process. Continuous diagnosis enables the teacher to recognize reading difficulties before they become severe enough to cause anxiety for both student and teacher. Gradual and subtle changes may then be prescribed that keep instruction focused on specific needs.

Classroom teachers sometimes feel that they do not have the necessary time to diagnose students, often because the idea of diagnosis suggests formal tests. This is not the case. Once systematic diagnosis is begun, using many diagnostic procedures, teachers realize that time is actually saved because classroom instruction becomes more efficient. Without diagnosis, instructional programs do not function efficiently because teachers can only guess the specific strengths and weaknesses of the student. Good diagnostic information enables the classroom teacher to plan each student's instructional program in a logical, sequential manner that makes maximum use of both student and teacher time.

Observation is one of the classroom teacher's primary diagnostic tools. This may be either formal or informal. Since both of these are discussed at some length in chapter 4, suffice it to say that teachers can make very effective use of observation in planning the daily instructional program of each student. Information concerning students' progress can and should be gathered all during the school day, especially during the periods of prescriptive reading instruction. Clues to a student's successes and failures in reading are easily observed during these periods. For example, during a follow-up activity designed to reinforce the skill of sequencing ideas, the teacher observed that two students were unable to correctly sequence four ideas after reading a paragraph. To help them understand the concept of sequencing, the teacher adjusted their instruction, working with them on two- and three-step sequencing before asking them to complete the original assignment.

Diagnosis, of course, is only one of the cornerstones of diagnostic-prescriptive instruction, but its importance cannot be overemphasized. Used correctly, diagnosis assumes a vital role in day-to-day instruction. It should be viewed positively as a tool that assists the teacher in providing the most effective reading instruction for each student.

## Reading Skill Development and the Classroom Teacher

Reading skill development forms the basis of a sound reading program. Deficiencies in basic reading skills affect not only the students' ability to read but also their self-image and performance in all academic learning. The development of a sound foundation in reading skills not only makes for improved learning and a more positive attitude, but greatly enhances the probability that students will read as a leisure-time activity.

Instruction in reading skills has been the classroom teacher's major role in teaching students to read for quite a few years. However, there has been a debate as to the overall importance of developing these skills. Proponents of skill development believe that students cannot become proficient readers without the development of at least the basic reading skills;[2] but there are those who believe that an overemphasis on reading skills has occurred and perhaps even slowed the development of reading for some students.[3] In an effort to improve the quality of reading instruction and to provide students with better opportunities for learning experiences, there has been a forceful "back to basics" movement. The primary reason for this movement is criticism from the public in response to the

number of students who are having difficulty in the basic academic areas.[4] A major thrust of this "back to basics" movement has been heavy emphasis on skill development through competency testing.[5] Classroom teachers have perhaps overreacted in their haste to improve instruction and, as a result, placed too heavy an emphasis upon isolated reading skill development. In some school systems reading skill development is so separated from actual reading experiences that the students never realize why they are learning the skills. For example, during a visit to a primary classroom the observer was greeted by a little boy who immediately wanted to relate his reading activities. The conversation went something like this:

*Boy:* Hey, you know what I'm doing in reading?
*Observer:* No, tell me about what you are doing.
*Boy:* I'm working on inferences.
*Observer:* What are you doing with inferences?
*Boy:* I don't know but they are back here in my folder.

Too much skill development and too few provisions for application lead students to equate reading with a mass of apparently unrelated, isolated skills. The result is students who know the skills but cannot apply them and thus do not read.

On the other hand, reading instruction with little or no emphasis on the formal teaching of skills is also open to question. Again, the concern is whether or not students can actually become good readers if little attention is given to skill development. Most people can cite at least one example of a student who never was formally taught to read and yet developed good reading habits. Such situations do indeed exist; however, even these students must receive some instruction in order to continue to develop their reading proficiency.

A basic premise of diagnostic-prescriptive instruction is that the development of reading skills is necessary. Therefore, skill development will be advocated, but with the caution that too much emphasis on isolated skills is just as harmful as too little emphasis. There must be a balance—instruction in reading skills must be a part of the total school program for teaching students to read. Some portion of the time for reading instruction should be dedicated to teaching the skills, so that the basic foundation of reading can be developed, just as some of the time should be devoted to reading for enjoyment in order to apply the skills.

If skill development is to be encouraged, then a knowledge of the skills on the part of the classroom teacher is essential. In addition, it is essential for the classroom teacher to know the order in which the skills are taught at all levels. Each school reading program should have skills listed so that classroom teachers are aware of their position in the hierarchy of skill development. Teachers should remember that a hierarchy of skills should be used to guide instruction, and that the various areas are developed simultaneously.

Because skill development is such a significant part of diagnostic-prescriptive instruction, some of the more important categories of skills necessary for successful reading instruction are reviewed here. They will be discussed in detail in chapters 9–13, and a detailed listing of the skills is in appendix A.

The first category of skills to be reviewed is *prereading* skills. These are considered to be the basic skills necessary for developing a foundation that will enable a student to master higher-level reading skills and to learn to read. The majority of these skills apply directly to all areas of learning. Having developed these skills, the student is able to build on to this basic foundation and begin the formal act of reading. They are often referred to as readiness skills, a term used to describe those skills that a student must learn in order to get ready to read. The major areas of prereading skills include oral language development, visual perception, auditory perception, listening comprehension, and visual-motor development.

As experience demonstrates, students who develop these prereading skills have greater success in beginning reading. This initial success affects later reading at all levels. Unfortunately, some youngsters are lost at this early stage, even before actual reading instruction begins. Often students who have difficulty in learning these skills come from a lower socioeconomic background where reading is not highly regarded and where lack of experience prevents their advancement in school. A large number of the students performing poorly at this stage come from culturally different backgrounds where parents must be more concerned with getting food on the table and other basic survival needs than with encouraging their children to develop the preliminary skills necessary for reading. Therefore, without question, this prereading or readiness category is a major responsibility for the classroom teacher. The student's emotional development, as well as success in learning to read, depends on this positive beginning.

**Prereading Skills**

## Word Recognition Skills

A second category of skills necessary for reading is *word recognition* or decoding skills. These encompass a wide range of sub-skills which provide students with different techniques for identifying a word. The skills in this category are those involved in learning sight words, phonetic and structural analysis of words, and the use of context to identify an unknown word. This is a critical series of skills, since learning how to decode words is such a basic step in learning to read.

Classroom teachers must be cautioned not to overemphasize this category of skills to the exclusion of other areas. If this occurs, students will become proficient at calling words, sounding out letters, and analyzing word parts, but they may have absolutely no idea of what these words mean! Another word of caution to the teacher regarding word recognition skills: there are *many* word recognition skills that students must master in order to read proficiently. Teachers cannot exclude any of these skills from their teaching; thus, it is not a question of whether to teach sight words or phonics, but a fact that both skill areas must be developed through the diagnostic-prescriptive process.

## Comprehension Skills

A third category of reading skills includes those known as *comprehension skills;* these are essential in the reading process. Comprehension skills are those through which the reader understands, organizes thought processes, and employs critical thinking skills. They enable the student to use the word recognition skills learned to gain an understanding of a selection. Words learned by sight or through word analysis become more than just symbols; through comprehension the reader acquires meaning from the printed page and the reading process comes to a successful conclusion.

Comprehension skills are organized into three basic areas: (1) *literal,* (2) *interpretive,* and (3) *critical.* These areas are defined in more detail in chapters 4 and 11. Classroom teachers need to provide instruction for these three levels of comprehension and maintain a balance in the types of questions used in developing comprehension. Guszak analyzed, through observation in grades two, four and six, the types of questions teachers ask, the responses of pupils to teachers' questions, and the questioning strategies teachers use in reading assignments.[6] Teachers' questions were grouped in the following six categories: recognition, recall, translation, conjecture, explanation, and evaluation. At grade two, the categories of recall and recognition (literal comprehension) constituted 78.8 percent of all questions asked; at grade four, 64.7 percent; and at grade six, 57.8 percent. Such findings clearly suggest that a balance is not being kept in developing comprehension skills at the various levels.

## Study Skills

The fourth category of reading techniques is *study skills.* These are considered to be higher-level skills which require the application of many other reading skills. They are skills that a large number of students fail to grasp, and without which they have difficulty in content reading. Study skills are initially introduced in the primary grades as students learn to use the dictionary and parts of their books such as the table of contents. These skills are expanded at each level. Classroom teachers must assume the responsibility for initially teaching the study skills and helping students to apply them in the content areas.

Deficiencies in study skills create a frustrating atmosphere for students, since assignments in the upper elementary, middle, and high schools require the use of many of these skills. Study techniques are essential to understanding the concepts and technical, specialized vocabulary of the various content areas, as well as in using charts, tables, and graphs, and adjusting rate according to material and purpose. Further discussion of study skills is provided in chapter 12.

The fifth category of reading skills with which the classroom teacher must be concerned is *personal reading skills*. These are unlike the others in that they are not cognitive skills but rather are in the affective domain of learning. This area deals with the students' attitudes toward reading and their use of reading as a leisure-time activity. Good personal reading skills must be developed if the students are to use the skills taught in the other four categories. However, without sufficient development of the prereading, word recognition, comprehension, and study skills, students do not usually develop the cognitive reading skills as well as positive attitudes towards reading. This is not an easy task, but it is essential in a diagnostic-prescriptive reading program.

Identification of the reading skills is an essential part of the diagnostic-prescriptive framework, since skill development is an essential phase of reading instruction.

**Personal Reading Skills**

After this brief discussion of the five categories of reading skills, it is necessary to think about organizing these skills and about their relationship to diagnostic-prescriptive instruction. Classroom teachers must recognize that skills are sequential, that is, some skills are learned earlier than others. Skills, therefore, follow a hierarchy of development from a lower to a higher level. The lower-level skills form a foundation to which higher-level, more complex skills are added, enabling the student to read more difficult material. Diagnostic-prescriptive reading instruction is developed around this concept of a hierarchy of reading skills.

**Organizing the Reading Skills for Diagnostic-Prescriptive Instruction**

Examples of this sequential skill development are found in the basal reading series used in many schools. These basals use a scope and sequence of skills that indicates the level at which a specific skill should be introduced. Most of these hierarchies of skills assume a fairly normal developmental process on the part of the student. In other words, a student entering school in the first grade would be introduced to a specific skill at a particular time during the year. The introduction of skills at specific times based on normal development is good for those students moving along at a normal pace. For readers having difficulty progressing at a normal pace, however, the effectiveness of such a system becomes questionable. Often, the classroom teacher is not prepared to adjust instruction to the student's own rate of development, and as a result the student does not learn a specific skill at the proper time.

In order to eliminate this possibility, the classroom teacher must be familiar with the hierarchy of skills and make adjustments to meet the needs of each student. In a diagnostic-prescriptive program, the classroom teacher is familiar with the scope and seqeuence of skills, and follows it according to the students' needs rather than page by page from the teacher's manual. New skills are introduced as each student learns the prerequisite skills. Through diagnosis and prescription, the teacher has a much more accurate idea of each student's level of development and can prevent frustrating experiences by continually prescribing instruction at the appropriate level.

The first task in organizing reading skills, then, is to determine a scope and sequence of skills. This means deciding which skills are introduced at a particular level. Not all schools follow a scope and sequence; some prefer to assume that the basal series used in their reading program is structured to fulfill their needs. As explained earlier, however, this results in the teaching of material rather than students. Since basal reading series are used in most schools,[7] it is advantageous to analyze the scope and sequence of these series. Several other scope and sequence lists should also be examined in an effort to determine which, if any, best meets the school's needs; These lists may be used as models to develop a hierarchy of reading skills for a particular school or school system.

Criteria for the analysis and comparison of scope and sequence lists are necessary if the end product is to be useful to the classroom teacher. One simple yet valuable criterion is the teacher's perception of which reading skills are important to include. After analyzing several hierarchies, teachers might discover that none of them identifies the same skills that are taught in their classrooms.

By combining various skills identified in several scope and sequence lists, teachers can develop a list suited to the needs of their students. A related criterion is the completeness of the list. Are all categories of reading skills included? Is there comprehensive listing of the various specific sub-skills?

The most important criterion for the analysis of scope and sequence lists is that there be a logical hierarchy of skills. The various basal programs and other scope and sequence lists indicate to a certain extent that some skills should be introduced before others. There are, of course, differences among them, especially concerning the middle- and upper-level skills, but these are minor differences of philosophical opinion. The most important fact to remember is that some skills must logically precede others. For example, auditory discrimination skills must be taught before students can be expected to develop the phonetic skill of determining the initial sound in *dog*. Additionally, students must have some proficiency in word recognition prior to decoding words on the printed page.

In reviewing a hierarchy of reading skills, the classroom teacher should note the levels at which specific skills are introduced. In a few cases, they may discover that the logic of the sequence of skills is not sound. For example, some prereading skills may be introduced at a higher level than expected. Such a delay in introducing a necessary skill causes students to miss a link in the learning chain and may eventually result in reading problems.

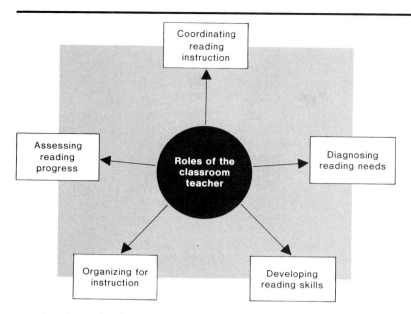

Another criterion to be used in evaluating a hierarchy of reading skills is the way the skills are reviewed and reinforced. Having introduced a skill, the scope and sequence list should provide for review and reinforcement of it at the various levels. Additionally, the list should be designed so that skills in different categories (word recognition, comprehension, study skills, personal reading) are developed simultaneously. Students should continue to learn word recognition and comprehension skills even as they apply them through the use of study skills and personal reading. Thus, the continuum followed to develop the reading skills in a diagnostic-prescriptive program should be spiral rather than vertical.

Another responsibility of the classroom teacher in the diagnostic-prescriptive program is to continuously assess the reading skill development of all students. This is the diagnostic aspect of the program; it is discussed in chapters 4 and 5.

**Assessment and the Classroom Teacher**

Most basal series provide assessment procedures for evaluating the progress which a student makes in skill development. Usually these procedures are in the form of mastery tests at the end of a particular segment in the basal. These assessment items may not be satisfactory to teachers working with the diagnostic-prescriptive concept, and must always be expanded through the use of other diagnostic procedures.

Because the assessment of reading skills is such an integral phase of diagnostic-prescriptive instruction, it is recommended that chapters 4 and 5 be carefully examined to assure a thorough understanding of how the various diagnostic procedures may be used to complement one another, and to provide maximum information. If continuous diagnosis is to take place, teachers must be familiar with various means of assessing a student's progress in skill development.

## Coordination and the Classroom Teacher

A diagnostic-prescriptive reading program requires the involvement and coordination of an entire school faculty. Classroom teachers cannot go in separate directions in implementing the program, but must work together. This cooperation is essential as students progress from grade to grade. Thus, classroom teachers should work together to design a scope and sequence of reading skills which can be used throughout the school to facilitate continuous progress for each student.

Individual school personnel working with staff from the central office could develop a scope and sequence of reading to be used in the entire school system. This would provide more coordination of the reading program and be of great assistance as students move from school to school within the system. Regardless of whether this hierarchy of skills is developed for the individual school or for the school system, the classroom teachers are responsible for sharing such information with all teachers. Without the use of a school-wide scope and sequence, reading instruction becomes isolated in each classroom. Teaching time is lost in trying to determine the level of each student at the beginning of the year, and students often receive double instruction in skills they know while other skills are never introduced. Therefore, it is imperative that classroom teachers work together in using a scope and sequence reading skills and report information about students' progress to parents and other teachers.

Coordination with resource teachers is also necessary. Classroom teachers should realize that the responsibility for teaching reading to each student in the classroom is theirs; resource teachers are responsible for supplementing or reinforcing the reading instruction given in the classroom. This means that the classroom teacher must identify the reading skills being developed with each student, then share this information with the resource teacher. Otherwise, the student may receive two or more entirely different types of instruction. A diagnostic-prescriptive reading program directs instruction to the identified needs of the students. Thus, classroom teachers should provide resource teachers with information on the student. Likewise, resource teachers can share their information with classroom teachers.

Coordination and cooperation are key components in diagnostic-prescriptive reading instruction. As leaders of the instructional team, classroom teachers must see that everyone in the school is working together for the benefit of the students (see figure 2.1).

## Summary

The classroom teacher has become the diagnostician for the classroom as reading programs strive to strengthen the reading capabilities of all students. In order to provide diagnostic-prescriptive instruction in all classrooms, teachers must recognize the reading needs of the students and serve as facilitators for prescriptive instruction. The classroom teacher's role also involves the relationship of diagnosis to daily classroom instruction, and the identification as well as the organization of reading skills.

In relating diagnosis to daily classroom instruction, it is suggested that not only long-range diagnosis, but also short-range or day-to-day diagnosis be used. Continuous diagnosis is essential to achieve the most effective instructional program.

Identification of the reading skills is an essential part of the diagnostic-prescriptive procedure. Knowledge of the reading skills and their location in a hierarchy is necessary to encourage the type of skill development needed.

Methods of organizing reading skills, such as analyzing, developing, and using a scope and sequence, were also discussed in this chapter. A scope and sequence which ensures efficient reading instruction is a necessary part of the diagnostic-prescriptive framework.

The latter part of this chapter discussed the classroom teachers' responsibility for the assessment and coordination of reading skill development. Assessing reading skills is crucial to diagnostic-prescriptive instruction; without teacher coordination, instruction to meet individual needs cannot be provided.

**Applying What You Read**

As a self-contained elementary classroom teacher, identify the scope and sequence of reading skills followed in your classroom. Then identify the scope and sequence used in your school. How could the skills hierarchy be used to facilitate a diagnostic-prescriptive program in the school?

The teachers in your school felt that it is their responsibility to teach the necessary reading skills, but that the diagnosis of reading strengths and weaknesses is the responsibility of the reading specialist. How would you respond to this?

The five categories of skills identified as necessary for the development of a good reader are prereading skills, word recognition skills, comprehension skills, study skills, and personal reading skills. Do you feel that all of these categories are necessary? Why or why not? Which categories are developed in your school reading program?

Continuous diagnosis is a very important part of a diagnostic-prescriptive program. What is continuous diagnosis? Why is it so important? How could a diagnostic-prescriptive program function without it? Is continuous diagnosis done in your classroom or school? How?

**Notes**

1. Jeanne C. Chall, "Minimum Competency in Reading," *Kappan;* Ron Raybin; "Minimum Essentials and Accountability," *Kappan;* Shirley Boes Neill, "A Summary of Issues in the Minimum Competency Movement," *Kappan.*
2. Theodore Clymer, "What is 'Reading'?: Some Current Concepts," *Innovation and Change in Reading Instruction;* Albert J. Harris and Edward R. Sipay, *How to Increase Reading Ability.*
3. Kenneth S. Goodman, "Reading: A Psycholinguistic Guessing Game," *Theoretical Models and Processes of Reading;* Robert B. Ruddell, *Reading-Language Instruction.*

4. James L. Jarrett, "I'm for Basics, But Let Me Define Them," *Kappan.*
5. "The Minimum Competency Testing Movement," *Kappan.*
6. Frank J. Guszak, "Teacher Questioning and Reading." *The Reading Teacher.*
7. New England Educational Assessment Project, *Reading Instruction in New England's Public Schools.*

**Other Suggested Readings**

Blair, Timothy R., and Rupley, William H. "Diagnosis of Teacher's Reading Instruction As Well As The Pupil's Reading Program." *Reading Horizons* 21 (Fall 1980):34–38.

Cushenberry, Donald C. "The New Role for Teachers for Improving Reading Skills (How to Survive With Less Title I Reading Money)." *Reading Horizons* 22 (Spring 1982):180–83.

Farr, Roger, and Brown, Virginia L. "Evaluation and Decision-Making." *The Reading Teacher* 24 (January 1971):341–46.

Gray, Mary Jane. "Does the Teacher's Attitude Toward Reading Affect the Attitude Toward Reading Held by Students?" *Reading Horizons* 21 (Summer 1981): 239–43.

Lass, Bonnie. "What Research Says About the Quality Reading Teacher." *Educational Technology* 21 (June 1981):28–31.

Leibert, Robert E., editor. *Diagnostic Viewpoints in Reading.* Newark, Delaware: International Reading Association, 1971.

Orlow, Maria, "Low Tolerance for Frustration: Target Group for Reading Disabilities." *The Reading Teacher* 27 (April 1974):669–74.

Robinson, Richard D., and Pettit, Neila T. "The Role of the Reading Teacher: Where Do You Fit In?" *The Reading Teacher* 31 (May 1978):923–27.

Sawyer, Diane J. "The Diagnostic Mystique—A Point of View." *The Reading Teacher* 27 (March 1974):555–61.

Wilson, Robert M. *Diagnostic and Remedial Reading for Classroom and Clinic.* 4th ed. Columbus, Ohio: Charles E. Merrill, 1981:Chapter 4.

Zintz, Miles V. *Connective Reading.* 4th ed. Dubuque, Iowa: William C. Brown Company Publishers. 1981.

# 3

At Seabreeze School there are teachers who have self-contained classrooms, and teachers who have departmentalized classrooms and teach only specific content areas. Thus, in planning a diagnostic-prescriptive reading program, an area of special interest and concern to teachers, administrators, and reading specialists is the relation of reading instruction to the content areas. Over the years, content teachers often have been educated to teach only a specific content area. They have received little if any preparation for understanding reading problems or individual reading needs as related to the teaching of content material. Suddenly, at the upper elementary and middle school levels, these teachers are being asked to deal with reading problems in the schools. Content teachers sometimes feel that major responsibility for teaching reading belongs to primary school teachers, and that their responsibility is to teach a specific subject matter at the upper levels. Thus, many content teachers ask why they are expected to teach reading when they are supposed to teach a content area. This is a difficult question, but it must be dealt with if the content teacher is to realize why teaching reading is so vital to the content area.

This chapter will address this question as well as several others which were raised by the content teachers at Seabreeze School.

Why does a content teacher have to teach reading?

Why do students have difficulty reading content material?

How is reading in the content areas different from reading basal materials?

What reading skills relate to the various content areas?

Who is involved in implementing a program which integrates reading into the content areas?

How can the content teacher assist the student in reading content materials?

# What is the content teacher's role in the diagnostic-prescriptive reading program?

As this chapter is read, the following terms should be noted.

Vocabulary to Know

Basal reader

Comprehension

Concepts

Individualized instruction

Readability

Readiness

Reading skills

Reference skills

Specialized vocabulary

SQ3R

Structural analysis

Study skills

Syllabication

Technical vocabulary

Vocabulary development

Word recognition

The statement that every teacher is a teacher of reading often creates an immediate negative response from the content teacher. It may evoke insistence that he or she is a history teacher, not a reading teacher, or it may call forth a panicked response of "What am I to do?" Both reactions are understandable; and to deal with either it is necessary to comprehend why the content teacher is also a teacher of reading.

**Every Teacher Is a Teacher of Reading**

**Readiness for Reading**   Readiness for reading is an important variable. Content teachers need to review information on child growth and development, then spend some time in a primary classroom to fully appreciate the concept of readiness for reading. First-grade teachers face a new group of squirming students each September. A few of these students can already read, some will be ready to read in a few weeks or months, and others will require a year or more of readiness work before they are ready to read. The mental age of students in a typical first-grade class on the first day of school may range from three to eight years of age, and their individual needs must be met. At the end of the first grade, the range has probably increased, with the second-grade teacher finding a range of mental ages from about four to ten. Some students still may not be ready to begin formal reading instruction at the end of the first, second, or third grades. However, social and emotional factors often do not permit the students to be held in the first grade

for several years! Some students, therefore, reach the middle grades unable to read as well as many feel they should; they enter school without the necessary readiness (prereading) skills and never catch up. Content teachers must realize how far students have advanced during the primary grades and help them continue to progress from where they are.

**Individualized Instruction is Essential for Learning in the Classroom.** Teachers at both the elementary and middle school levels must realize that students need instruction in skill development at the appropriate reading level if they are to make continuous progress. This is not to say that each student receives one-to-one instruction, but it is essential that small-group and one-to-one instruction be used as necessary. This topic is dealt with in more detail in Chapter 7. It is sufficient to say at this point that if the individual learning needs of students are not met each year, students slowly fall farther and farther behind until they become so frustrated that no learning occurs. Teachers often find students who cannot perform in the classroom and who do not care about learning. This is characteristic of students who have been frustrated to the point of rebelling or withdrawing from the situation. Content teachers must attempt to motivate these students to learn again—quite a challenge!

**Content Reading is Different from Reading a Basal** Changing from the basal readers used in the elementary grades to the content materials in the upper elementary and middle school levels can be difficult for many students. This transition begins in about the third or fourth grade and presents problems to both good and poor readers. These difficulties arise from the different format, the application of the reading skills, the vocabulary load, and the many concepts presented. For example, many basal readers have a stated main idea, *whereas most content materials have an implied main idea.* Perhaps this seems to be a minor point, and for some students it creates no problem. However, for many students, especially the poor reader, it is a significant obstacle. To personalize this difficulty, consider for a moment that you have been working with a selection in which the main idea has been clearly stated. The teacher asks you what the paragraph or selection was about, and you read a specific sentence. Then you are promoted to the fourth grade, introduced to social studies or science materials, and suddenly expected to infer the major premise of the material you are reading. You are asked what the selection is about and begin to look for a sentence to read; it's not there so you read something anyway, only to be told that you are wrong. This is quite confusing, especially for a poor reader!

Another difficulty in reading content materials relates to the *transfer of reading skills from basal readers to content materials.* Unless teachers show students how to apply the skills learned from the basal program, it is very difficult for many students to transfer the skills. Because of the more consistent language patterns used in basal readers, students not only experience problems in transferring skills, but also become confused when facing the *literary style commonly*

*used in content materials.* Students who are already exhibiting reading difficulties become more confused by this turn of events and develop deeper feelings of inadequacy and frustration.

Content materials also require the use of *higher-level* reading skills. In many basal programs more emphasis is placed on the literal comprehension skills, which primarily require recall of information, than on the interpretive and critical reading skills.[1] However, in content material, the student must use the higher-level comprehension skills in order to understand what is being read. Comprehension and study skills at the inferential, interpretive, and application levels are emphasized in content materials. Unless great care is taken in teaching them, the stress on these higher-level skills creates frustration and leads to a decrease in students' performance as well as a corresponding decline in their self-concept.

Coping with *compact presentation* is another difficulty encountered by students changing from basal to content materials. Students have difficulty understanding content selection because many new concepts and facts are presented in a very brief span of time as compared to the basal format, which presents just a few concepts or ideas at a time. In addition, encountering a *mass of unrelated facts* in content reading poses further problems for students. Although the trend in content reading is toward emphasizing how to learn rather than simply learning many facts, students are often faced with a barrage of unrelated facts from all content areas, whereas in basal readers, they encountered a relatively limited

number of facts to be synthesized. This places severe stress on poor readers, who have difficulty learning even the limited number of facts presented in the basal reader. In order for the student to function and progress at a satisfactory level, the content teacher must emphasize the learning process rather than the importance of learning facts. Unfortunately, content teachers may not be aware that such problems exist and blame the students for their poor performance rather than considering the material or the teaching style used.

Another major problem encountered when changing from the basal readers to content materials is that of understanding the *many new words introduced*. The vocabulary load suddenly becomes much greater as many more new words are introduced over a shorter span of time. This is especially true in the beginning sections of content materials, when new vocabulary seems to fill every page. Again, in the basal, the student is accustomed to having relatively few new words introduced at one time and devoting large amounts of the class period to learning them. Although content teachers sometimes introduce new vocabulary in class, they often require students to become familiar with these words on their own. Content teaching implies much more independence in the student; but content teachers should realize that students must be taught how to learn on their own. It cannot be assumed that they will select the appropriate vocabulary necessary for learning; more guidance from content teachers is needed when new vocabulary is being introduced.

Closely related to understanding new words is the problem of *introducing technical and specialized vocabulary in each of the content areas*. Many of these words are familiar to the students, but the appropriate or precise meaning may not be clear and must be introduced if students are to comprehend the material. Without question, such new vocabulary is on a level of difficulty much higher than that encountered in basal readers. While all teachers help students to develop their vocabulary, it is the responsibility of each content teacher to develop and clarify the specialized and technical vocabulary appropriate to the particular content.

*Specialized vocabulary* is vocabulary which changes in meaning from one content area to another. For example, the word *mass* means a collection of data in mathematics, the weight of some material in science, or a religious ceremony in literature or social studies. As a result of these variations of definitions, students must be taught the special meaning of this word in relation to the appropriate content area to which it pertains. *Technical vocabulary* is vocabulary that is essential to the understanding of a specific content area. Since it relates to only one field, it is usually critical to the understanding of concepts in that content area. An example of a technical vocabulary word is *genes*. In order for students to comprehend the concept of genetics, they must first understand the meaning of this technical word. Another example of a technical word in social studies is *serf*. If students are to understand a lesson on the Middle Ages, they must know the meaning of this word and its significance in terms of social stratification during that period. The student's comprehension of content materials is dependent upon learning the meaning of technical words such as these.

*Comprehending the numerous concepts* presented is another difficulty in reading content materials. So many new concepts are introduced in such a short span of time that students often experience frustration. Content teachers must understand the need to adjust instruction so that those with reading problems have the opportunity to learn the concepts being introduced. Unless they grasp the introductory concepts in content areas, students become totally lost as the year progresses, because many concepts within the content areas build on one another. The poor reader needs more time and adjusted instruction in order to gain some knowledge of the basic concepts being introduced. This often frustrates the content teacher. Without these basic concepts, however, such students have little chance for success in the content areas and are sometimes regarded as non-learners. At this point, frustration mounts and the self-image becomes more negative, increasing the likelihood that these students will become non-functioning members of society.

*Reading in a variety of sources* causes difficulty in dealing with content materials when students have worked previously with only one text at a time. At the upper levels in the content areas, students are encouraged to supplement their textbook material with information from outside sources, and are expected to use many sources in their quest for information relating to specific topics. They switch from one type of material to another and may be unfamiliar with the use and format of these other resources. In addition, since different types of materials have various levels of reading difficulty, there are some materials that poor readers are unable to use simply because of the readability factor. These difficulties need to be taken into consideration by the content teacher so that poor readers will not be expected to work with some types of sources as efficiently as good readers. For example, reference materials are generally written on a high readability level. This problem cannot be totally alleviated in order to cope with the poor reader's inability to function on a higher level. However, the content teacher can attempt to assign other materials appropriate to the reading level of the students involved. Acquiring some knowledge in a content area is preferable to gaining none.

The *readability level of the content material* itself often causes the poor and average reader great difficulty. Teachers use basal readers written on a variety of readability levels. In the content areas, however, usually only one book is available for each grade level, and these texts are frequently two or more grade levels higher in readability than they purport to be.[2] Thus, the content teacher must locate various texts and library books on different readability levels.

Understanding the relationships among the content area subjects may be difficult for students changing from basal readers. The concept that all content learning is similar should be stressed. For example, although each content area has its own technical and specialized vocabulary, the methods for learning this vocabulary are the same. In a similar fashion, inferential comprehension is inherent in all content areas; the same method of inference used in learning one can also be used in learning another. All content teachers must work together to stress the similarity of learning methods for all content areas. The benefit to the students will offset any inconvenience experienced by the teachers.

In content materials *different organizational patterns* are found; this is in contrast to basal reading materials. Four organizational patterns have been identified: enumeration, relationships, problem-solving, and persuasive.[3] These different organizational patterns not only cause difficulty for students as they attempt to apply their reading skill knowledge from a basal reader to a content text, but also create problems in terms of understanding the format used in presenting the information. For example, the teacher may assign a specific paragraph or selection for the class to read, and ask that the students identify the sentence or sentences in which the cause-effect relationship is stated. Because a great many of the cause-effect relationships found in basal reading materials are stated, and are situational in nature, they are not as difficult for students to locate. Unfortunately for the student, the relationship pattern found in content materials is

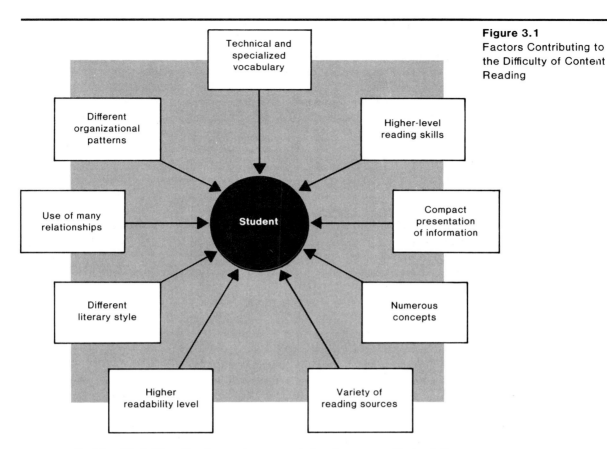

**Figure 3.1**
Factors Contributing to the Difficulty of Content Reading

not so easily identified. Usually, the student must infer the cause-effect relationship from the information given, or first identify the effect or result, (which is frequently easier to find,) and then determine the cause. Because of the impact of organizational patterns on reading content materials, it is essential that teachers assist students in identifying these patterns so that they may better understand the structure of the information to be read.

Teachers and students should realize that the reading skills taught in the basal reader form the foundation for acquiring information in content reading; they should also understand that the application and transfer of these skills are not automatic. Because of the factors of difficulty in content reading (see figure 3.1), it is essential that content teachers help students to read content materials. The belief that reading instruction begins and ends with the elementary schools and that content teachers have no obligation to concern themselves with reading problems in their classrooms does not reflect the actual situation. The reading problem in our middle schools has sorely taxed the content teachers. They are perplexed and may even resent primary-level teachers for not having relieved

them of this difficult task. Although content teachers are asked to teach a specific subject, they must also become involved in diagnostic-prescriptive reading instruction in their classrooms. The fact is that no matter how well a student reads, *it is essential that specific reading skills be developed as appropriate for each content area.* This is the major role of the content teacher. Thus, the pre-and inservice education programs must assist the content teacher in meeting this need. Fortunately, the trend toward integrating reading instruction into the content area is expanding. There is an increasing effort on the part of school systems to assist their content teachers in implementing a program based on diagnostic-prescriptive reading instruction in the content areas.

The integration of reading with the content areas will greatly assist all students in reading content materials. Content teachers are already teaching these skills in their classrooms, but they are, in many instances, unaware of this. Content teachers should learn which skills are needed to read the content materials, use a diagnostic-prescriptive approach to teaching, then adjust their instruction to meet the individual needs of each student. Thus, the poor readers will have a reasonable chance for success, while the better readers will be challenged in their learning experiences.

## Reading Skills for the Content Areas

The discussion of reading in the content area has involved the use of the term *reading skills.* These skills comprise the acquisition of the expertise required to grasp specific concepts essential to the reading process, whether in the primary grades or in the content areas. Although in many instances the use of the term *reading skills* in the content area carries the connotation of converting the content teacher into a reading teacher, content teachers should consider the development of reading skills as another way of enhancing the learning capabilities of their students. Content teachers are unique, in that their material is especially suited to the use of reading skills as an essential part of diagnostic-prescriptive instruction. Thus, these teachers should become more aware of the need for some skill development on the part of the students in the content areas, recognizing that reading skills are an integral part of the total program.

Obviously, reading skills are essential in order for students to learn content material, and they are taught every day by every content teacher. However, content teachers may not know that they are already developing these skills. Therefore, it is the responsibility of reading specialists to assist content teachers in becoming consciously aware of the reading skills which are involved in all content areas. This will help them to determine the strengths and weaknesses of each student and to provide a program which will develop the skills most appropriate to the content. All students have weaknesses in some of the various reading skills. Accordingly, it becomes imperative that the content teacher be able to diagnose strengths and deficiencies in the skill areas so that content instruction can be tailored to individual needs. A logical question, then, is, "What are the reading skills which relate to various content areas?"

In an effort to assist the content teacher, the reading skills for four primary content areas are identified in table 3.1. This outline of skills is divided into four major parts for each of the content areas represented. The skill areas are *word recognition, vocabulary development, comprehension,* and *study skills.* Each of these areas contains specific reading skills essential to the students' satisfactory performance in the several content areas.

One group of skills with which content teachers are concerned is that of *word recognition.* Although many skills fit into this category, it is recommended that the content teacher deal with only two of the major skill areas: structural analysis and syllabication. Included in structural analysis are plural forms, verb tense, prefixes and suffixes, and compound words. These subdivisions stress the analysis of word structure for purposes of pronunciation as well as comprehension.

A second word recognition skill of interest to content teachers is syllabication. This is one of the skills needed for decoding new vocabulary. Since students in the content areas are introduced to an extensive technical and specialized vocabulary, this is an indispensable skill in analyzing the parts of the word. Syllabication is essential as one proceeds to decode words by dividing them into parts.

The area of *comprehension* comprises those skills necessary to the proper understanding of what is being read. These skills are generally considered to comprise three basic types: literal, interpretive, and critical. At the literal level, the reader is concerned with what the author said. Questions or statements at this level require the reader to locate and verify explicitly stated details. An example of a statement at this level is: *Name several things mentioned by the author as causes of pollution.*

**Table 3.1**

Selected Learning Skills for Content Areas

| | Literature | Mathematics | Science | Social Studies |
|---|---|---|---|---|
| *Word recognition* | | | | |
| Structural analysis | √ | √ | √ | √ |
| Syllabication | √ | √ | √ | √ |
| *Vocabulary development* | | | | |
| Word meanings | √ | √ | √ | √ |
| Affixes | √ | √ | √ | √ |
| Context clues | √ | √ | √ | √ |
| Abbreviations | √ | √ | √ | √ |
| *Comprehension* | | | | |
| Reading for purpose | √ | √ | √ | √ |
| Recall of important points | √ | √ | √ | √ |
| Paraphrasing | √ | √ | √ | √ |
| Propaganda techniques | √ | | | √ |
| Critical analysis | √ | √ | √ | √ |
| Inferences | √ | √ | √ | √ |
| Making judgments | √ | | √ | √ |
| Relationship in formulas and equations | | √ | √ | |
| Restating verbal problems | | √ | √ | |
| Identifying speaker | √ | | | |
| Emotional reactions | √ | | | |
| Following directions | √ | √ | √ | √ |
| Understanding details | √ | √ | √ | √ |
| Sequence of ideas | √ | | √ | √ |
| Symbol interpretation | √ | √ | √ | √ |

At the interpretive level, the reader is concerned with interpreting what the author has said. Questions or statements at this level require the reader to locate and verify explicitly stated details, then make a generalization showing their relationship. An example of a question at this level is: *On the basis of several things mentioned by the author as causing pollution, what is the common cause?*

At the critical level, the focus is on analyzing and extending the author's meaning as it extends beyond the printed page. Questions or statements at this level require the reader to locate and verify explicitly stated details, make a generalization about them, then extend their meaning beyond the printed page in order to use them in an intellectual or practial way. An example of a statement at this level is: *Read this article along with other available sources, including*

| | Literature | Mathematics | Science | Social Studies |
|---|---|---|---|---|
| Relationships | √ | | √ | √ |
| Figurative speech | √ | | | |
| Identification of setting | √ | | | |
| Understanding main idea | √ | √ | √ | √ |
| Drawing conclusions | √ | √ | √ | √ |
| Predicting outcomes | √ | √ | √ | √ |
| Summarizing and organizing | √ | | √ | √ |
| Fact and opinion | √ | | √ | √ |
| Problem-solving | √ | √ | √ | √ |
| Cause-effect relationships | √ | | √ | √ |
| Generalizations | √ | | √ | √ |
| Understanding mood | √ | | | |
| Comparing and contrasting | √ | √ | √ | √ |
| Author's purpose | √ | | | √ |
| *Study skills*<br>Using reference books | √ | | √ | √ |
| Locating information | √ | √ | √ | √ |
| Using parts of a book | √ | √ | √ | √ |
| Outlining | √ | | | √ |
| Reading graphs, tables, charts | √ | √ | √ | √ |
| Skimming and scanning | √ | √ | √ | √ |
| Reading rate according to purpose | √ | √ | √ | √ |
| Study techniques | √ | √ | √ | √ |

*chapter 4 in your textbook, and the pamphlet "What is Pollution?" to determine the effect that the author's suggestion would have on ecological balance.*

The area of *vocabulary development* is especially important for content teachers, since deficiencies in these skills usually adversely affect the student's comprehension. Skill in dealing with word meanings, with prefixes and suffixes, enhances a student's interest and performance in reading. The use of context clues is another vocabulary skill that is especially important, since their proper use enables the student to grasp the meaning of a content selection without necessarily being able to decode and pronounce all the words in that selection. Other skills necessary to vocabulary development are knowledge of abbreviations and of the meaning and appropriate use of synonyms, antonyms, and homonyms.

The fourth group of reading skills, which is essential to the content teacher, is *study skills*. In this category, reference skills are especially important; without proficiency in using the dictionary and locating information, gaining understanding from the textbook or other sources is difficult.

Another study skill of great importance to the content areas is known as SQ3R. This is a study procedure that is especially beneficial when used as a teacher-guided activity in the introduction of a new chapter or a new textbook. It can be used in groups or for the class as a whole. SQ3R comprises the following five steps.

*Step 1: S = Survey.* The reader surveys the material, giving careful attention to the title, introductory pages, heading, organization of the material, and summary. Following this survey, the reader should try to recall as much information as possible before going on to the next step.

*Step 2: Q = Question.* As the reader reviews what is remembered from the survey, specific questions should be formulated to be answered as the material is read. These questions assist the reader in establishing purposes for reading.

*Step 3: R = Read.* With specific questions in mind, as a purpose given by the teacher, the student reads the material to locate answers. It is possible that answers to all of the questions will not be found, and in that case other resources must be sought. In addition, the student should be encouraged to use these unanswered questions to stimulate class discussion.

*Step 4: R = Recite.* After reading the material, the student should recite the answers to the questions formulated prior to reading. This assists in remembering and leads the reader to summarize the ideas presented. Recitation will help the reader to become more critical in analyzing the information and possibly question the logic of some of the author's ideas. This recitation is a personal matter; it is not a recitation to the class.

*Step 5: R = Review.* At this point, the reader reviews the ideas presented in the entire selection and may outline them mentally or on paper. The reader should attempt to fill in the specific details from what was read. If the student cannot review the material in this manner, then assistance is needed in developing the higher-level comprehension skills of interpretive and critical reading.[4]

There are variations of SQ3R for various content areas: the PQSRT technique is recommended by George Spache for studying science materials, and Leo Fay has proposed the SQRQCQ technique for use in reading mathematics. Both procedures are outlined in the following pages.

*Science: PQRST*

*Step 1: P = Preview.* Rapidly skim the total selection.

*Step 2: Q = Question.* Raise questions to guide the careful reading that will follow.

*Step 3: R = Read.* Read the selection, keeping the questions in mind.

*Step 4: S = Summarize.* Organize and summarize the information gained from reading.

*Step 5: T = Test.* Check your summary against the selection to determine if the summary was accurate.[5]

*Mathematics: SQRQCQ*

*Step 1: S = Survey.* Read the problem rapidly to determine its nature.

*Step 2: Q = Question.* Decide what is being asked, what the problem is.

*Step 3: R = Read.* Read for details and interrelationships.

*Step 4: Q = Question.* Decide what processes should be used.

*Step 5: C = Compute.* Carry out the computation.

*Step 6: Q = Question.* Ask if the answer seems correct, check the computation against the problem facts and the basic arithmetic facts.[6]

Other general skills necessary for proper use of a textbook include outlining, using parts of the book, adjusting reading rate according to the purpose given for reading a particular selection, and the correct use of skimming, scanning, and previewing. There are other useful reading skills used in specific content areas. For example, in social studies, skills such as reading maps and interpreting graphs, tables, and charts are necessary for thorough understanding.

After identifying the specific reading skills inherent in each of the content areas, the content teacher's next step is to diagnose the student's strengths and weaknesses in each skill area. Procedures are outlined in chapters 4 and 5.

When the diagnostic information has been collected, a prescriptive program of instruction is made for the student. Specific activities which can be used in prescription development are outlined in chapters 10 and 13.

## Involvement in Implementing the Program

In implementing any new idea in a school program, it must be recognized that the more the faculty and administration are involved, the better the new idea will be received. A key ingredient in any successful program is the administration. The leader of the program for integrating reading skills into the content areas should be the principal of the school. If the principal sees no relevance in dealing with this problem, then neither will the teachers. Perhaps even worse, they may see no problem at all. Therefore, the principal must feel a commitment to encourage teachers to integrate reading into the content areas. The principal's influence can either make or break such an effort on the part of the teachers. Fortunately many school administrators possess the vision to understand the problems which students experience in changing from primary grade material to content area material.

After the principal has assumed the leadership role, the faculty must be willing to make a concerted effort to improve their instructional program so that the problems students encounter in reading content materials can be dealt with in the most effective manner. When the teachers have decided to effect these changes

in their program, then cooperating with each other becomes of utmost importance. The enthusiasm and spirit of cooperation with which the content teachers approach the implementation of an instructional program will determine to a great extent the success or failure of such a program. The commitment of the faculty to effecting a change becomes an integral part of the total program which involves not only teachers, but administrators and students as well.

The principal's commitment to the concept of integrating reading into the content areas, and the teachers' determination to implement the program successfully are vital in the development of a sound program. However, teachers may find that the administration does not seem to care about these problems, or that other teachers do not share their concern, or both. The content teacher must then implement these changes in the classroom as well as possible and share successful ideas with the administration and faculty. Such teachers may find themselves in isolated positions for a while; however, the reward will come as students begin to demonstrate their enjoyment of content. In addition, these students will let other teachers know what is going on in their classroom—so the lonely teachers will begin to hear questions from curious teachers. *Slowly* change will occur.

Content teachers should also recognize that they must work with one another in diagnosing and prescribing for their students. Discussions with other teachers regarding their observations of certain students, and of areas that have been identified as problem spots, will add to the diagnostic information needed to provide the best instruction for the students. Content teachers are not reading specialists, but they are teachers who must be concerned with the learning needs of students and make every effort to provide the appropriate instruction for each student.

## Summary

In considering the content teacher's role in diagnostic-prescriptive reading instruction, the major premise of this chapter is that teachers in the content areas must, of necessity, integrate the reading skills with their subject matter in order for students to learn the content material. This is being dramatically illustrated by the number of students who are having difficulty reading the content materials and by the large number of teachers who are frustrated because they are not prepared to deal with students who cannot read the textbook. Therefore, the very survival of the content teacher demands the use of techniques other than the traditional methods of instruction. Integrating reading instruction into the content areas will assist in solving these problems.

As described in this chapter, there are numerous concerns that must be dealt with in using diagnostic-prescriptive reading instruction in the content areas. They include the need for strong administrative support of the program as well as a cooperative faculty dedicated to meeting the needs of the individual student.

Problems encountered by students in the content areas are discussed. Some of the specific difficulties involved in changing from basal readers to content materials are (1) the transfer of learning skills from basal readers to content materials; (2) dealing with higher-level reading skills; (3) coping with the compact presentation of content materials; (4) understanding the amount of new words

introduced, including technical and specialized vocabulary; (5) comprehending the numerous concepts presented; (6) reading in a variety of sources; (7) encountering a mass of unrelated facts; (8) understanding the relationships among the content area subjects; and (9) identifying different organizational patterns found in content materials.

Reading skills for each of four content areas (social studies, science, mathematics, and literature) were identified. These skills were divided into four major categories encompassing word recognition, vocabulary development, comprehension, and study skills.

A more concentrated effort in integrating reading skills into the content areas is necessary. Content teachers should use the knowledge gained from diagnosis and follow a prescriptive program designed for individual students. This will enable them to provide the best possible instruction for all of their students.

**Applying What You Read**

Select several basal readers and compare them with content textbooks used at the same grade level.

Determine essential vocabulary that should be introduced when teaching a concept of your choice. Develop activities that can be used to teach the vocabulary.

In your present or future role as a content teacher, reading specialist, or administrator, how would you initiate a program which integrates reading skills with the content areas?

Identify the reading skills that relate most directly to the content area you teach. Outline ideas for developing these skills in your classroom.

**Notes**

1. Frank Guszak, "Teacher Questioning and Reading." *The Reading Teacher.*
2. Barbara K. Clarke, "A Study of the Relationship Between Eighth Grade Students' "A Study of the Relationship Between Tenth Grade Students' Reading Ability and Their Comprehension of Certain Assigned Textbooks."
3. Earl H. Cheek and Martha Collins Cheek, "Organizational Patterns: Untapped Sources for Better Reading," *Reading World.* 278–83.
4. Francis P. Robinson, *Effective Study,* p. 27.
5. George Spache, *Toward Better Reading,* p. 94.
6. Leo Fay, "Reading Study Skills: Math and Science," in *Reading and Inquiry,* p. 93.

**Other Suggested Readings**

Cheek, Earl H., Jr., and Cheek, Martha Collins. *Reading Instruction Through Content Teaching.* Columbus, Ohio: Charles E. Merrill Publishing Company, 1983.
Eeds, Maryann. "What To Do When They Don't Understand What They Read—Research Based Strategies for Teaching Reading Comprehension." *The Reading Teacher* 34 (February 1981):565–75.

Harp, M. William. "Read the Assignment and Answer the Questions." *Language Arts* 54 (February 1977):168–71.

Herber, Harold L. *Teaching Reading in Content Areas.* 2nd ed. Englewood Cliffs, New Jersey: Prentice-Hall, 1978.

Johns, Jerry L., and McNamara, Lawrence P. "The SQ3R Study Technique: A Forgotten Research Target." *Journal of Reading* 23 (May 1980):705–08.

Lipton, Jack P., and Liss, Jody A. "Attitudes of Content Area Teachers Towards Teaching Reading." *Reading Improvement* 15 (Winter 1978):294–300.

Moore, Mary A. "C2R: Concentrate, Read, Remember." *Journal of Reading* 24 (January 1981):337–39.

Paradis, Edward E., and Arth, Alfred A. "Reading: Vanguard of Junior High/Middle School Curriculum." *Language Arts* 52 (March 1976):329–34.

Readence, John E.; Bean, Thomas W.; and Baldwin, R. Scott. *Content Area Reading: An Integrated Approach.* Dubuque, Iowa: Kendall-Hunt Publishing Company, 1981.

Rieck, Billie Jo. "How Content Teachers Telegraph Messages Against Reading." *Journal of Reading* 20 (May 1977):646–48.

Robinson, H. Alan. *Teaching Reading and Study Strategies: The Content Areas.* 2nd ed. Boston: Allyn and Bacon, 1978.

Smith, Ellen R., and Standal, Timothy C. "Learning Styles and Study Techniques." *Journal of Reading* 24 (April 1981):599–602.

Vacca, Richard T. *Content Area Reading.* Boston: Little, Brown and Company, 1981.

Vaughan, Joseph L., Jr. "A Scale to Measure Attitudes Toward Teaching Reading in Content Classrooms." *Journal of Reading* 20 (April 1977):605–09.

# Diagnosis

S tep 1 revolves around the use of informal and formal diagnostic instruments in implementing diagnostic-prescriptive reading instruction. The teachers at Seabreeze School have investigated various diagnostic procedures that may be used by the self-contained and departmentalized classroom teachers. Their findings are summarized in chapters 4 and 5.

**4**

Informal diagnostic procedures are the primary tools used by the classroom teachers at Seabreeze School to assess student strengths and weaknesses in reading. Simplicity, accuracy, and speed are factors that they consider to be important. The classroom teachers needs quick, inexpensive, and accurate methods of determining the reading strengths and weaknesses of students. With so few reading specialists in many school districts, the role of the reading specialist has changed from that of a remedial teacher to one of working with teachers in implementing ideas in the classroom. Reading specialists have minimal time to devote to testing students. In addition, the information they gain by observation during test administration is diagnostic data needed by the classroom teacher in diagnosis. Thus, classroom teachers are responsible for the diagnosis of their students, while reading specialists provide assistance by further diagnosing those students identified by the teacher as severely disabled readers. Therefore, the classroom teacher at Seabreeze School, like other classroom teachers with classes of twenty-five to thirty-five students, must do most of the diagnosis and prescription development for students in the classroom. Because of the teacher-pupil ratio and other factors, it is imperative that simple diagnostic tools be at the disposal of classroom teachers so that relevant data can be expeditiously gathered.

Because classroom teachers are realizing that the responsibility for appropriate diagnosis and prescription is theirs, they are giving more attention to the area of classroom diagnosis. Some of the common questions regarding informal diagnosis asked by the teachers at Seabreeze School are discussed in this chapter.

Why are informal measures so important?

What are the various informal diagnostic procedures?

What is an informal reading inventory, and how is it used?

How can informal procedures be used to greater advantage in the classroom?

What does a teacher look for when using observation as a technique for informal diagnosis?

What are the best diagnostic procedures content teachers can use?

What are some informal procedures for diagnosing comprehension problems?

Which measures can best be used to assess the development of word recognition skills?

# What informal diagnostic procedures can the classroom teacher use?

As this chapter is read, the following terms should be noted.

**Vocabulary to Know**

Attitude scales
Cloze procedure
Comprehension
Criterion-referenced tests
Critical reading
Frustration level
Graded basal series
Graded word lists
Group Reading Inventory
Hesitations
Independent level
Informal diagnosis
Informal Reading Inventory

Insertions
Instructional level
Interest surveys
Interpretive comprehension
Literal comprehension
Mispronunciations
Objective-based tests
Observation
Omissions
Readability
Repetitions
Substitutions
Word recognition inventories

**An Overview**

Informal diagnostic procedures are nonstandardized techniques used by teachers to determine their students' strengths and weaknesses in reading. The skill areas to be measured are (1) *prereading skills,* which include oral language and auditory and visual perception skills; (2) *decoding* or *word recognition skills,* more specifically knowledge of sight words, phonics, contextual and structural analysis skills, and dictionary skills; (3) *context processing* or *comprehension skills,* including literal, interpretive, and critical reading skills; (4) *study skills,* such as reference skills and using parts of a book; and (5) *personal reading,* which involves the application of the skills and the enjoyment of reading. An extensive listing of the specific skills in each of these areas appears in appendix A. Teachers should also consider students' interests and their attitudes toward reading as informal diagnostic data is obtained. Because success in reading depends on students' interest and attitude as well as ability to use the various skills, diagnosis of all areas is essential.

**Figure 4.1**
Informal Diagnostic
Procedures

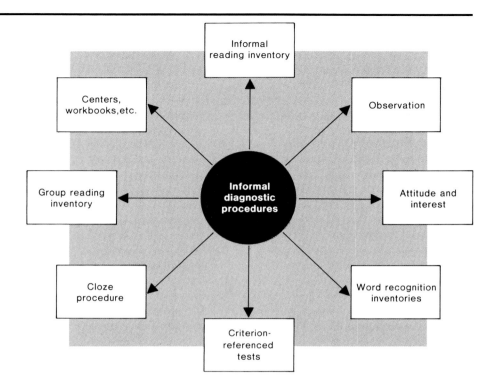

These areas can be diagnosed using many different informal procedures. The more common techniques are discussed in this chapter (see figure 4.1). They include informal reading inventories, observations, criterion-referenced or objective-based tests, interest and attitude inventories, cloze procedure, group reading inventories, and word recognition inventories. These informal instruments may be developed by the individual classroom teacher, the school district, or by commercial sources. Examples that teachers can use or adapt are provided in this text.

Informal diagnostic procedures provide essential information for

Determining the students' strengths and weaknesses in reading.
Grouping students for reading instruction and further skill development.
Selecting materials and teaching techniques appropriate to the students' level, needs, and interests.
Tracing the students' growth in reading over a period of time.
Providing specific information to parents during conferences.

Before beginning the discussion of the various informal techniques, one should consider a preliminary step which provides the teacher with an initial insight into the reading level together with an indication of some of the students' strengths and weaknesses. This screening inventory, sometimes called a Simplified Reading

Inventory, saves considerable time in locating a starting point for the other informal procedures. The procedure requires that each student read a short selection to the teacher. At the elementary level, basal readers can be used. Content teachers can use other books. Publishing companies usually specify an approximate level for their books, but a readability formula should be used to determine or verify the readability level of the material. For information regarding the different readability formulas, see chapter 7.

Following the oral reading, the teacher asks five to ten questions about the material. The questions should be of different types, including *literal,* requiring recall of information stated in the passage, *interpretive,* requiring understanding of the meaning not directly stated in the passage, and *critical,* requiring use of the literal and interpretive meanings to evaluate the information. More than one oral reading error per twenty words, or difficulty in responding to about thirty percent of the comprehension questions, indicates that the material is too difficult. An oral reading error includes the mispronunciation of a word or the pronunciation of a word by the teacher.

This procedure "tries the material on for size" and makes possible a quick assessment of whether or not the material is too difficult or too easy for the student. Although this is a rather crude diagnostic device, it prevents the assignment of reading material which is too difficult or too easy. In addition, it gives the classroom teacher an idea of some of the impediments to a student's reading, such as difficulty in identifying basic sight words, or failure to note the context when word recognition errors are made. Of course, this preliminary step should be immediately followed by more refined diagnostic techniques. However, it assists in assigning materials to students at the very beginning of the school year and in determining what other diagnostic procedures should be employed. One humane note: students should not be required to read a lengthy passage before the entire class. It is not necessary to let everyone know that reading is difficult for a student!

The remainder of this chapter discusses specific informal diagnostic procedures that the classroom teacher can develop and use. Remember, *every procedure is not to be used with every student.* Teachers should select techniques which appear necessary and appropriate. Informal diagnostic procedures can provide a wealth of information; as teachers become more experienced in using them, they become more observant and more sophisticated in the interpretation of their observations.

## Attitude and Interest Inventories

In attempting to ascertain the reasons for students' reading problems, frequently the most important variable in the reading process is overlooked: the student. While making elaborate interpretations of diagnostic information and explaining students' failures to learn to read well, teachers often overlook the students' feelings about the reading process, about themselves, and their interests. The students know better than anyone how they feel about reading and why they either like or dislike to read. Thus, they need the opportunity to express freely their

feelings toward reading and their interests in reading. Consequently teachers must be familiar with various procedures to assess students' interests and attitudes. Obviously, the observation techniques outlined in another section would be quite helpful. However, other techniques compatible with observation may be used with individuals or groups. This section will review these various procedures. A sample interest and attitude form is found in appendix E.

Attitude

The students' attitudes toward reading are a key variable in whether or not they read well. The student who reads poorly naturally does not like to read. Yet students often feel that they cannot freely express their attitudes toward reading. Instead, they attempt to convince teachers that they like reading, if only they could read, while at the same time disliking themselves for being unable to read well. In this way a personal conflict begins which may develop into emotional problems. The reading problem is then compounded. By encouraging students to express their feelings teachers can overcome some of the guilt feelings which students develop about disliking reading. Students must be allowed opportunity to evaluate their reading ability and to express themselves in a way that will assist the teacher in improving reading skills and facilitating cooperation in the process. Attitude inventories enable the teacher to obtain a better idea of the students' overall behavior and may reveal some clues as to students' feelings about the

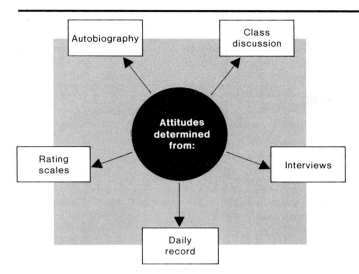

**Figure 4.2**
Informal Sources for
Determining Attitudes
toward Reading

world, their peers, their environment, and, most important, themselves. The teacher will also acquire some insight into the mental processes and attitudes of the student. Remember, *a poor self-image is one of the most crippling problems for poor readers.*

Attitude inventories can be divided into two basic categories: retrospective and introspective. The retrospective inventory allows students to examine the reasons for their successes or failures in reading. It may be a simple analysis of why they pronounced a word as they did or a more complex investigation of why they have difficulty with reading. Although this give-and-take analysis is made a part of each day's classroom activities, both students and teacher gain much insight into the learning processes of other students. Disabled readers learn new techniques for improving their reading by listening to good readers report their reasons for certain responses; and there are also opportunities for good readers to learn from the disabled reader.

The introspective inventory requires students to think about the processes they use in reading, as they read. They tell what went on in their minds while they were reading. This is actually an analysis or critical review of their reading processes. For example, do they concentrate on what they are reading, do they read too fast or too slow, or do they use context clues to aid in their comprehension? These are important ideas of which students need to be aware. Their awareness will assist them in improving both their reading skills as well as their attitudes toward reading.

Although theoretically these two categories can be defined, practically speaking it is difficult to completely separate the various inventories into neat categories. The main concern is that the classroom teacher use varying techniques to ascertain students' attitudes toward reading. Most inventories assess both the retrospective and the introspective areas. The following pages provide some ideas that may be used to determine student attitudes in reading (see figure 4.2).

**Autobiography.**

One of the more common procedures to learn more about a student is to use a reading autobiography, which may be formulated orally or in writing, depending upon the student's skills. Those disabled readers who are unable to write will usually prefer to employ the oral autobiography or to record their message on a tape recorder. Many disabled readers feel frustration, bitterness, and discouragement about their inability to read well; the autobiography gives them the personal attention they desire and need in order to express their feelings about their difficulties in reading. As a written exercise, the reading autobiography may be composed in various formats. Teachers may choose a checklist form of autobiography, which can be easily written and evaluated. This format, however, does not allow students to express their feelings frankly, since it places contraints on their responses. Hence, it may be more meaningful to provide students with leading questions and ask them to write about their feelings toward reading. Here are some leading questions that may be used:

How do you feel when you have to read?
What do you think when your teacher says it's time for reading?
What is your least favorite subject in school? Why?
When did you read your first book? How did you feel?
What do you like most (or least) about reading?

The teacher should provide a few stimulating questions which are not to be answered directly, but are to serve as guidelines for the students in recounting a developmental history of their reading experiences. This type of autobiography furnishes a great deal more in-depth information about individual students, their attitudes toward other students in the class, their feelings about themselves in relationship to their peers, their sentiments about reading, and perhaps even their reactions toward the classroom teacher. This also allows the teacher to study various forms of spelling and grammar used, vocabulary development, sentence structure, and organizational pattern, while it enables the student to show the teacher how well he or she has developed in the use of written expression.

The reading autobiography allows students to gain insight into their reading difficulties and put them into perspective. It is hoped that students will then evaluate their positions, set some goals for themselves, and make the additional efforts needed to improve their reading ability.

**Class discussions.**

Class discussions are useful times during which students can interact with each other and with their teacher. This interaction provides poor readers with an opportunity to verbalize their feelings in a given area. In addition, these discussions allow students to learn how others deal with the printed word, how they decode a word, how they use clues to determine the appropriate meaning of an unfamiliar word, or how they locate the answer to a specific question. These periods of interaction among students also allow the teacher to determine how the students' thought processes work. This can provide insight into ways of adjusting instruction better to meet student needs.

To initiate class discussions, the teacher may use student responses to questions asked about their reading material. This often leads to very stimulating discussions concerning how students located or could have located the answers. It also helps students to realize that people learn in different ways.

Through class discussions the teacher should help students verbalize their problems in reading and determine ways to solve the problems. Class discussions can help all students learn to work together to aid one another, and assist some students in realizing that they are not alone with their reading problems.

*Interviews.* The one-to-one relationship in an interview encourages free expression of the frustrations and difficulties a student is encountering in the reading process. Although this procedure is not frequently used, it can be quite informative to the teacher and refreshing to the student. The disabled reader often feels frustrated and even hostile toward the teacher as well as others in the class. Teachers should realize that a short period of time given exclusively to such a student may help overcome this hostility and prevent further damage to the student's self-image. Perhaps the reason so many students are being labeled as behaviorally disordered, emotionally disturbed, or any of many appellations applied to students today, is that teachers and other adults do not spend five minutes with the young people who obviously want and desperately need individual attention and an opportunity to express their feelings toward school and the areas of study.

*Daily Record.* Teachers need to note how students use their time during the day. It is helpful to document just what various students do with their spare time by using a checklist or narrative notes. The teacher may select certain students to observe during the day and mark the checklist at specified times. Using this procedure throughout a school year will document changes in students' attitudes toward reading.

To facilitate use of this procedure, the teacher may ask students to keep their own daily record of the books they read or the activities they were involved with during their spare time. Students who enjoy reading will read in their leisure time. With respect to students who are not using their time in reading-related activities, this record will assist the teacher in showing them how they are spending their time.

*Rating Scales.* More formal procedures such as rating scales are sometimes used in ascertaining students' feelings toward reading. Many such scales have been developed, most of them for use with secondary students. Sample attitude scales appear in appendix F. Teachers may wish to adapt these scales for use with elementary students by simplifying the words or reading them orally. Questions from other scales may be adapted to elementary use by allowing answers in the shape of a face. For example:

When my mother brings me a book, I feel

Teachers must realize that reading problems cannot be thoroughly diagnosed or properly treated unless they give careful attention to students' attitudes toward reading. Various techniques must be used to discover students' real feelings towards themselves and reading. With this information, the teacher can then attempt to build more positive attitudes about reading. Reading skills are improved more easily and reading itself becomes more enjoyable when students can openly express their feelings.

## Interests

In determining ways to improve students' attitudes toward reading, the teacher must first consider their interests. Many times teachers are of the opinion that a strong emphasis on the development of word-recognition skills, sight words, and comprehension skills will suffice in the diagnostic-prescriptive process without due regard to the concept of interest. Although it may be possible to improve students' reading abilities without meeting their interests, it is much easier to motivate them to read when their interests are considered.

One of the more significant developments in recent years has been the increase in the use of high-interest/low-vocabulary materials. Teachers have discovered that an interested student is easier to teach than one who is not. Fortunately, publishers have also discovered this fact, and there has been a much-needed increase in the development of high-interest material. A reliance on the traditional basal reading systems often tends to further discourage the already frustrated poor reader and fails to motivate the gifted reader.[1] However, current readers reflect a change in content to represent the reading interests of students.

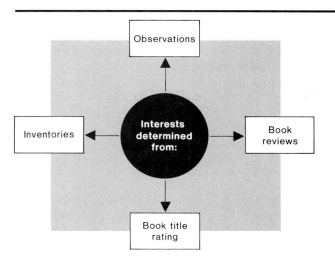

**Figure 4.3**
Informal Sources for
Determining Interests in
Reading

High-interest materials often evoke greater effort from the student using them, and students demonstrate a higher reading ability when the material interests them. Low achieving students comprehend materials that they consider highly interesting better than they comprehend low-interest material. These students also tend to transcend their frustrational reading levels when reading materials which are highly interesting to them.[2] Teachers find teaching to be a much more enjoyable experience when students are interested in the content of the materials and successful in the reading experience.

Teachers must realize that a seventh-grade student reading on a second-grade level cannot be given second-grade materials to read. The student becomes frustrated, embarrassed, and resentful, and is likely to become a discipline problem. Although materials which are written at the students' reading level and meet their interest will not cure all the discipline and attitude problems which a teacher will encounter, they can certainly play a great role in making the day a little brighter for both teacher and student.

There are various ways of determining the interests of students; some are perhaps more effective than others. The following ideas give some insights into discovering the types of subjects which interest your students and how these relate to the reading process (see figure 4.3).

*Observation.*

A very simple way to determine interests is by observing students. Watch them choose books; try to decide if they choose the books they want or the ones they think the teacher wants them to choose. If the latter is true, then the teacher needs to reorient students so that they select books for their own enjoyment. A second trait to observe is how closely students concentrate on their reading. If they show a propensity to being easily distracted, then it is likely that the interest in the book is low. Observe also the students' reactions when a story is read to the class. Note those who are extremely interested in the story and those who

show no interest at all. Select a number of different titles to read to the class in an attempt to meet the interests of the various students in the classroom. Oral reading by the teacher can be a powerful tool for motivation; do not destroy it by choosing books of low interest to the students!

**Reviews.** Having the students write brief reviews of their reading provides the teacher an opportunity to see what kinds of materials they enjoy. This activity should in no way be construed as a "book report," which almost always bores the students. The reviews should be only long enough to yield an understanding of the student's interest. One idea that works well with young readers is to have them "sell" a book to a friend after reading it. In order to "sell" the book, the student must tell enough of the story to interest the friend in reading it. The teacher can learn much about a student's interest by keeping a record of the books being "sold."

A related method of determining student interest is to note the books or stories that students choose to read. A useful activity in this case would be to have students bring to class stories that interested them and share them with the class. Through this kind of activity students reveal much about their interests; this gives the teacher an opportunity to gear assignments toward those particular interests.

Another means of eliciting student response concerning books is the establishment of a graffiti board. Cover a bulletin board with heavy paper and encourage students to write book titles and their reactions to help others decide on reading them. This is a helpful way for teachers to determine students' interest by observing their response to the various books.

**Book Title Rating.** Another effective method of determining interests is to have students rate titles of books according to their interest. The classroom teacher could select a series of titles and list them on the chalkboard or on duplicated sheets. Students would then evaluate them according to their likes or dislikes. It is important to determine the kinds of titles in which each student appears to be most interested.

**Inventories.** One of the more common ways to determine student interest is the interest inventory. Interest inventories have been used for many years and are regarded as an effective tool for determining the areas in which students exhibit specific interests. The information gained provides the teacher with insight into the student's likes, dislikes, and attitudes, and even some insight into the student's values, peer interaction, and self-concept.

A word of caution should be added regarding the interpretation of these instruments. The results of an inventory should be reviewed periodically, since interests change quickly as students get older. They develop more diverse interests, have more experiences, encounter changes in the peer group, and are influenced by various teachers and adults. Thus, information from interest inventories must be updated continuously. Another factor to be considered is that students may answer contrary to their beliefs in an effort to create a favorable impression. As classroom teachers, the authors have found that students frequently respond positively to the question, "Do you like to read?" The teacher must realize that this

is often an effort not to offend the teacher as well as to create a favorable impression; sometimes it is even an effort to hide guilt feelings. The students feel that the teacher will surely feel hurt and dislike them if they respond negatively, since students believe that all teachers like to read.

An interest inventory is easy to develop and use, since the only criterion to be followed is to develop questions designed to explore the interests of the student. The teacher determines the types of questions to be asked, put them into a questionnaire format (which may be as brief or detailed as the teacher wishes), then administers the inventory individually or in groups. After administering the inventory, the teacher should interpret the results and use the information gained to structure the students' activities around their interests, which may improve their attitudes toward reading. Teachers may wish to use inventories that are already developed; sources for examples that may be used with elementary students are listed in appendix C.

In order to help a student overcome reading problems or to prevent the development of problems, the teacher must be aware of and use materials appropriate to the students' interest. Teachers sometimes generalize and think that all second graders are interested in animal stories. This is not true. Just as all adults have individual interests, all students have individual interests. Know your students and try to use their interests as your guide in instruction.

One of the most informative diagnostic procedures is the informal reading inventory. An IRI is a compilation of reading selections from various grade levels with comprehension questions to accompany each selection. The selections used can be passages from a graded basal reading series, passages from miscellaneous materials, or passages written by the teacher. An IRI is administered individually, enabling the classroom teacher to determine the student's specific word recognition and comprehension difficulties while observing both oral and silent reading habits. This instrument is especially useful in determining the strengths and weaknesses in sight vocabulary, word attack, and comprehension skills (see figure 4.4).

**The Informal Reading Inventory (IRI)**

The IRI should be used during the beginning weeks of school to diagnose more carefully those students having difficulty in the screening inventory, and to place new students. In addition, it should be used frequently with all students to determine their needs in reading and to ascertain reading levels as students are moved from one material to another. Although teachers may believe there is not enough time continuously to assess individual students, they must realize that if individual needs are to be met it is essential to have the data from an IRI. As they are used, the time needed for administration will decrease, and the information gained will increase. Soon the teacher will wonder how reading instruction was provided without the information from the IRI.

**Figure 4.4**
Basic Steps in Using an
Informal Reading
Inventory

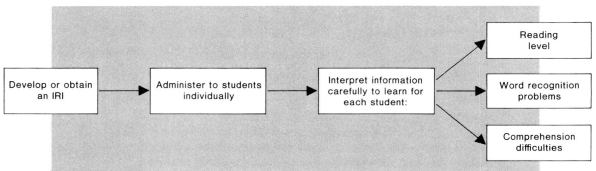

Many school districts and individual schools have developed their own IRI's, and most publishing companies provide them to accompany their basal series. Other sources for obtaining IRI's are educational publishers of professional materials. Some of the IRI's available in published form are listed in appendix B.

Since many commercially developed informal reading inventories are available, teachers must be aware of their advantages and disadvantages. Jongsma and Jongsma found variety among these instruments in the content, style, and length of the passages, with readability estimates used as the primary means of passage validity and scaling. Differences in directions to the examiner were noted, as well as discrepancies on what constituted an error in oral reading. Factual recall questions were the dominant type of comprehension assessments. Additionally, they found no data on any of the eleven tests evaluated to validate the correspondence between reading levels established through informal reading inventory testing and classroom performance.[3]

These commercial instruments, however, offer the teacher complete word lists, passages, and questions which are already developed and ready to use. Most of the inventories provide multiple passages at each level to assess oral and silent reading.

Because some teachers may desire to construct their inventory, or may be called upon to assist in developing one for their school or district, the following section describes the construction of an IRI.

## Construction of an IRI

An IRI consists of a series of graded passages of approximately 100 to 200 words. Passages at the lower levels, such as preprimer, may have fewer than 100 words, while passages at the upper levels, such as senior high, may have more than 200 words. As was stated earlier, these passages may be selected from graded basal reading series which are unfamiliar to the student, from children's books whose readability level has been determined by the publisher or by the teacher, or from any other graded materials the teacher wishes to use. The passages may also be written by the teacher.

Some words of caution concerning the construction of an IRI are pertinent at this time. The first concern relates to a common problem of teachers: lack of time. Constructing an inventory is a time-consuming task which is better attempted as a group project than an individual one. In addition, the development of an IRI requires knowledge of the reading process as well as test construction. Thus, if an individual teacher who feels competent in reading is working alone on an IRI, there should be consultative assistance from someone with expertise in test construction.

Another concern is the readability levels of the selections used. Readability levels of a graded basal series or other graded materials are sometimes not carefully checked. Thus, the actual readability level of the material may not be what it purports to be. This particular consideration becomes more relevant when the information is used to determine accurately the independent and instructional reading levels of a student. Passages used in an IRI, whether they are written by the teacher or taken from other materials, should be checked, using a readability formula like those outlined in chapter 7. Decisions concerning these areas of caution need to be made before proceeding with the following specific tasks in the construction of an IRI.

**Task 1** (Optional) *Select a list of words that can be used to assess the student's sight vocabulary level.* This first step assists in determining an approximate level at which to begin to administer the graded reading selections. A teacher may use word lists which are already developed and leveled, such as the *Dolch Basic Sight Word List* or the *Slosson Oral Reading Test.* In addition, the teacher may prepare a word list using words from the basal reader or a graded word list such as the *Cheek Master Word List.*[4]

To develop a word list from a basal or another more extensive list of words, select at random about twenty words from each level of the basal (preprimer through the highest available level), or from each grade indicated on the word list. These words should be typed by level on a sheet for teacher use and placed individually on index cards for student use. Remember, such a list only measures sight vocabulary. It does *not* measure the most important area of reading—comprehension. For more information on word lists, see the section "Word Recognition Inventories" in this chapter. A sample graded word list appears in table 4.1.

**Task 2** *Obtain two passages of approximately 100 to 200 words for each readability level (preprimer through senior high school).* One of the passages will be used to assess oral reading skills, and the second selection will be used to measure silent reading proficiency. Although some teachers may use the same passage for both silent and oral reading assessment, they should realize that the information obtained will not be as definitive if one passage is used twice. For optimal results, plan to obtain two passages for each of the readability levels. If the passages are taken from a graded basal series, be sure to check their readability level.

**Table 4.1**
Sample Graded Word List (Teacher Page)

| Readability Level 1.0–2.0 | Readability Level 2.1–3.0 | Readability Level 3.1–4.0 | Readability Level 4.1–5.0 |
|---|---|---|---|
| as | both | automobile | aside |
| better | buy | brick | bound |
| can | climb | cloud | castle |
| different | deer | decide | correct |
| far | empty | electric | dictionary |
| game | finally | fifth | experience |
| hat | garden | grain | further |
| ice | having | indeed | honest |
| laugh | iron | lying | imagination |
| me | leaves | measure | liquid |
| next | matter | narrow | medicine |
| over | nest | path | native |
| play | person | power | paragraph |
| red | quickly | root | professor |
| side | roof | shed | route |
| sun | shape | sorry | slope |
| three | slow | stuck | sum |
| us | test | tight | tough |
| who | upon | usual | whenever |
| you | written | weight | youth |

Words selected from *Cheek Master Word List* (Waco, Texas: Education Achievement Corporation, 1974).

It is essential to select passages which will interest students, regardless of age. Remember that you may have a seven-year-old who reads at an eighth-grade level or a fourteen-year-old who reads at a second-grade level. Obviously, if a student's interest in the content of the material is high, a more accurate and complete diagnosis is likely. High interest content has a greater effect on increasing comprehension instructional level than on increasing word recognition instructional level. High interest materials have a greater effect for boys than for girls, as well as on average and below average readers when compared to above average readers.[5] Therefore, examine the material being used for the IRI to be sure that the passages are as interesting as possible; you will obtain better results from the inventory.

If a teacher chooses to write the passages, several additional points are to be considered. Writing selections which communicate well with the reader is sometimes difficult. The writer must consider not only the interest and readability level of the passage, but also the concepts presented. An additional concern is syntax, the way the material is written. To check the communicability of the material, the writer may ask selected students to read the passage as a "field test," then ask them to tell what they remember about the passage. This helps to identify sentences which may be unclear. Care in selecting or writing the passages used for the IRI is the key to the development of a reliable instrument.

**Table 4.2**

Sample Questioning Patterns for Assessing Selected Comprehension Skills

| | Literal Questions |
|---|---|
| Details | What color is the house? |
| Cause-effect situations | Why was the store owner angry? |
| Sequence | What happened first in the story? |
| Main idea | What was this story about? |
| Character traits and actions | How did Bob act when he saw his bicycle? |
| | **Interpretive Questions** |
| Predict outcomes | How do you think the story ended? |
| Figurative language | What does "laughed his head off" mean in this story? |
| Mood and emotional reaction | How did Mary feel when she saw Kristy? |
| Author's purpose and point of view | How did the author feel about pollution? |
| Abstract words | What ideas in the paragraph help demonstrate the concept of democracy as it is known in the United States? |
| | **Critical Reading Questions** |
| Fallacies in reasoning | What words or ideas in the story seem to stereotype Wendy? |
| Facts and opinions | What is the writer's opinion of the use of nuclear energy? What facts are given to substantiate this opinion? |
| Relevant and irrelevant information | What information would be necessary to make plane reservations for a trip to California? |

**Task 3** *Develop comprehension questions for each of the passages.* After the series of graded passages has been chosen or written and the readability level of each passage determined, the next step is to develop a series of comprehension questions for each passage. It is strongly suggested that a minimum of five and a maximum of ten questions be used. Although using ten questions requires more teacher time, the greater number ensures a more precise evaluation of the students' comprehension.

Questions should measure the three levels of understanding: literal, interpretive, and critical. There should be questions relating to each of the various reading skills, such as understanding details, the main idea, sequence of events, cause-effect relationships, comparisons and contrasts, mood, author's opinion, inference. Be sure to include questions at all of the three levels mentioned above. Note also that some skills may be measured at both the literal and interpretive levels, depending upon the information contained in the material and the wording of the questions. Samples of various types of questions are provided in table 4.2.

In developing questions for the IRI, there are certain guidelines to keep in mind. To expedite the process, it is best to read the passages and prepare as many questions as possible, then classify each question in the light of the skill being measured. Following this classification, select the best questions to sample adequately the students' performance at each of the three levels of comprehension, as well as their proficiency in as many specific skills as possible. The questions can then be tested with selected students to determine their quality. Poor questions should be replaced with others from the list.

More specific information on questioning techniques useful in developing an IRI appears in publications by Valmont, Johnson and Kress, and Livingston.[6]

**Task 4** *Develop response sheets for use while administering the inventory.* The teacher needs response sheets on which to record the student errors made during the administration of the IRI. These sheets may have various formats, ranging from a one-page sheet with blanks for recording errors to copies of each page of the inventory, on which the teacher marks oral reading errors and other responses. Combining the latter with the single-page response sheet as a summary is preferable.

The single-page response sheet should provide spaces to record information such as:

Student's name
Name of person administering the inventory
Date of administration
Levels of the IRI passages used during oral reading
Responses to the comprehension questions following oral reading—the simplest procedure to use is a plus and minus for right and wrong responses
Words asked during silent reading
Responses to the comprehension questions following silent reading
A summary of oral and silent reading word errors
A summary of comprehension question responses
Special notes and comments
The instructional and independent level of the student

Figure 4.5 shows a sample one-page response sheet.

Response sheets of the second kind should show copies of the passages which the student is reading, together with the comprehension questions directly following the passage. As the student reads the teacher makes appropriate marks and comments on the sheet. This information may then be transferred to the one-page response sheet if both are being used. In the next section specific instructions for marking the passages as the students read are provided.

**Figure 4.5**
Summary Record Sheet

Student Name: _____     Date: _____
Administrator: _____     Levels Used: __;__;__;__;__;__:

## Words Missed (Oral Reading)

| Level____ | Level____ | Level____ | Level____ | Level____ | Level____ |
|---|---|---|---|---|---|
| S-U | S-U | S-U | S-U | S-U | S-U |

## Comprehension Check (Oral Reading)

| Level____ | Level____ | Level____ | Level____ | Level____ | Level____ |
|---|---|---|---|---|---|
| 1.____ | 1.____ | 1.____ | 1.____ | 1.____ | 1.____ |
| 2.____ | 2.____ | 2.____ | 2.____ | 2.____ | 2.____ |
| 3.____ | 3.____ | 3.____ | 3.____ | 3.____ | 3.____ |
| 4.____ | 4.____ | 4.____ | 4.____ | 4.____ | 4.____ |
| 5.____ | 5.____ | 5.____ | 5.____ | 5.____ | 5.____ |
| 6.____ | 6.____ | 6.____ | 6.____ | 6.____ | 6.____ |
| 7.____ | 7.____ | 7.____ | 7.____ | 7.____ | 7.____ |
| 8.____ | 8.____ | 8.____ | 8.____ | 8.____ | 8.____ |
| 9.____ | 9.____ | 9.____ | 9.____ | 9.____ | 9.____ |
| 10.____ | 10.____ | 10.____ | 10.____ | 10.____ | 10.____ |
| S-U | S-U | S-U | S-U | S-U | S-U |

Observation Notes on Oral Reading: _____

_____

_____

_____

_____

## Words Asked (Silent Reading)

| Level____ | Level____ | Level____ | Level____ | Level____ | Level____ |
|---|---|---|---|---|---|
| S-U | S-U | S-U | S-U | S-U | S-U |

**Figure 4.5**—*Continued*

**Comprehension Check** (Silent Reading)

| Level_____ | Level_____ | Level_____ | Level_____ | Level_____ | Level_____ |
|---|---|---|---|---|---|
| 1._____ | 1._____ | 1._____ | 1._____ | 1._____ | 1._____ |
| 2._____ | 2._____ | 2._____ | 2._____ | 2._____ | 2._____ |
| 3._____ | 3._____ | 3._____ | 3._____ | 3._____ | 3._____ |
| 4._____ | 4._____ | 4._____ | 4._____ | 4._____ | 4._____ |
| 5._____ | 5._____ | 5._____ | 5._____ | 5._____ | 5._____ |
| 6._____ | 6._____ | 6._____ | 6._____ | 6._____ | 6._____ |
| 7._____ | 7._____ | 7._____ | 7._____ | 7._____ | 7._____ |
| 8._____ | 8._____ | 8._____ | 8._____ | 8._____ | 8._____ |
| 9._____ | 9._____ | 9._____ | 9._____ | 9._____ | 9._____ |
| 10._____ | 10._____ | 10._____ | 10._____ | 10._____ | 10._____ |
| S-U | S-U | S-U | S-U | S-U | S-U |

Observation Notes on Silent Reading: _____

_____

_____

_____

_____

_____

Independent Level: _____

Instructional Level: _____

Frustration Level: _____

**Task 5** *Type the passages which the student will read.* If the passages are written by the teacher or taken from materials which may be inconvenient to use, each should be typed on a separate sheet or a large index card. The paper should be of good quality and the cards large enough for the student to manage easily. A point to remember is that the type and spacing should be appropriate to the student; for example, a primary type and double-spaced line should be used for the younger student.

One set of the lower-level passages should be typed for use with older students who are reading at a primary level, even though the passage is available in a book, since these students may feel insulted and embarrassed by the juvenile appearance of the book. In addition, these students may read information from cards when they cannot read the same information from a book. Books have become such a symbol of failure that they cannot read from them! Keep these ideas in mind as you work with older students.

Following these five steps very closely will greatly assist the teacher in constructing an IRI. But what happens after construction? The two most important events are left: administration and interpretation. These must occur almost simultaneously; therefore, they are discussed together in the next section.

One of the practical aspects of the IRI, if designed properly, is that it can be easily and quickly administered by the classroom teacher. For this purpose the teacher requires the appropriate passages for the student, a response sheet for recording and summarizing information, and the teacher copies, which contain the comprehension questions and on which the teacher can mark errors. The teacher is now ready to administer an IRI to determine the individual's independent, instructional, and frustration levels in reading.

Specific criteria for each of these levels have been debated for several years, but the question of which criteria are most accurate remains unresolved. The most commonly used criteria are those provided by Emmett Betts in 1957. Further research regarding the criteria has been done by William Powell. Studies by Pikulski, Hays, and Ekwall present evidence that supports retaining the traditional Betts criteria.[7] Thus, teachers must be aware of this discrepancy and be consistent in the use of a selected criteria. The specific criteria given by both Powell and Betts for each of these levels are found in table 4.3. The levels are defined below.

*Independent level:* The level on which students read for recreational purposes. The material is easy enough to read quickly, with maximum comprehension of the information.

*Instructional level:* The level on which instruction in reading is provided. The student can read the material, but has some difficulty with the recognition of words and comprehension to the extent specified in the criteria.

*Frustration level:* At this level, the student has extreme difficulty in pronouncing words and comprehending the material. This is the level at which the student should *not* be reading for instructional purposes, and certainly not for leisure.

Researchers and practitioners generally agree on the following steps in the administration of an IRI.

1. Rapport is established with the student. This is done through a discussion of what the teacher will ask the student to do and is enhanced by developing readiness for reading each of the selections.
2. The teacher uses a word list to ascertain the student's word recognition level. If the *Dolch Basic Sight Word List* is used, specific criteria have been established to assist in determining the grade placement.[8]

| *Dolch Words Known* | *Equivalent Reader Levels* |
|---|---|
| 0–75 | Preprimer |
| 76–120 | Primer |
| 121–170 | First reader |
| 171–210 | Second reader or above |
| Above 210 | Third reader or above |

**Table 4.3**

Criteria Used in Scoring Informal Reading Inventories

**Powell Differentiated Criteria**

| Book Level (1-2) | Word Pronunciation | Comprehension |
|---|---|---|
| Independent | 94% or more | 81% or more |
| Instructional | 87% or more | 55%–80% |
| Frustration | 86% or less | 54% or less |
| Book Level (3-5) | Word Pronunciation | Comprehension |
| Independent | 96% or more | 86% or more |
| Instructional | 92% or more | 60%–85% |
| Frustration | 91% or less | 59% or less |
| Book level (6+) | Word Pronunciation | Comprehension |
| Independent | 97% or more | 91% or more |
| Instructional | 94% or more | 65%–90% |
| Frustration | 93% or less | 64% or less |

**Betts Criteria**

| Level | Word Pronunciation | Comprehension |
|---|---|---|
| Independent | 99% or more | 90% or more |
| Instructional | 95% or more | 75% or more |
| Frustration | 90% or less | 50% or less |

Source: William R. Powell, "Measuring Reading Performance," ERIC, November 1978, ED 155 589; Emmett A. Betts, *Foundations of Reading Instruction* (New York: American Book Company, 1957), p. 449. Copyright © 1957, American Book Company.

If the teacher has developed a graded word list from other lists, the grade placement can be determined by using the general criterion that the student should miss no more than one of every five words. This would be the student's instructional level on the word list portion of the IRI. With this information, data from the screening inventory, or teacher knowledge of the student, the teacher can proceed with the IRI reading selections.

3. The teacher chooses a selection approximately two grade levels below the student's estimated instructional level. Readiness for reading the selection is developed by introducing the selection and giving the student a purpose for reading the material.

4. The student reads the paragraph orally. The teacher marks the oral reading errors on the response sheet as the student reads. The following marking procedure is suggested.

*words pronounced by the teacher* =  P  over the word

*mispronounciation* =  mp  over the word with the word written above as mispronounced

*substitution* =  ———  through the word with new word written above

*omission* =  ◯  circle the words or punctuation omitted

*hesitation* =   /   between words on which hesitation of more than 5
     seconds occurs.

*repetition* =   ⌇⌇⌇⌇⌇   over the word

*insertion* =   ∧   with word written in

A sample marked paragraph appears in figure 4.6. If a one-page response sheet is used, then the teacher records only the words pronounced for the student, repetitions, omissions, substitutions, insertions, and those words mispronounced.

5. The teacher asks the comprehension questions following the oral reading, and indicates correct and incorrect responses on the sheet.

6. The teacher counts and may later record on the summary response sheet the words pronounced for the student, the mispronunciations, substitutions, omissions, insertions, and repetitions. Using the criteria for word recognition as outlined in table 4.3, the teacher determines whether the passage is on the student's independent, instructional, or frustration level.

7. The second passage is used for silent reading. The teacher introduces the passage and gives the student a purpose for reading it.

8. The student reads the passages silently, and the teacher records the words the student asks while reading.

9. The teacher asks the comprehension questions following the silent reading and indicates on the response sheet the correct and incorrect answers.

10. The teacher counts and records on the summary sheet the words asked by the student, and the satisfactory or unsatisfactory responses are indicated.

Once again using the criteria for comprehension in table 4.3, the teacher determines whether the student's comprehension of the material indicates the independent, instructional, or frustration level. If the errors on either the word recognition portion of the oral reading or the comprehension section of the silent reading indicate the frustration level, an easier passage should be selected. If the passage is at the student's instructional level the teacher moves to the next higher level and attempts to ascertain the student's frustration level. Few errors in both areas, as outlined in the criteria, indicates the student's independent reading level. The teacher then moves to more difficult passages in an effort to determine the student's instructional and frustration levels. Several levels may be skipped if the material seems extremely easy for the student.

## Interpretation of an IRI

Through experience in administering IRI's and observing students' reading habits, the classroom teacher can gain much diagnostic information about each student. The following discussion introduces the significant factors to note in administering the IRI, together with and some suggestions for interpretation. As the classroom teacher becomes more familiar with the IRI, the observations and possible interpretations will greatly increase.

**Figure 4.6**
Sample Marked
Selection

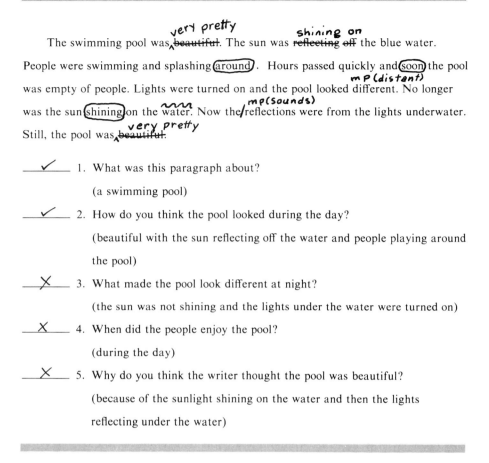

The swimming pool was ~~beautiful~~ *very pretty*. The sun was ~~reflecting off~~ *shining on* the blue water. People were swimming and splashing (around). Hours passed quickly and (soon) the pool was empty of people. Lights were turned on and the pool looked different. *m p (distant)* No longer was the sun (shining) on the water. Now the / reflections *m p (sounds)* were from the lights underwater. Still, the pool was ~~beautiful~~ *very pretty*.

✓ 1. What was this paragraph about?

(a swimming pool)

✓ 2. How do you think the pool looked during the day?

(beautiful with the sun reflecting off the water and people playing around the pool)

✗ 3. What made the pool look different at night?

(the sun was not shining and the lights under the water were turned on)

✗ 4. When did the people enjoy the pool?

(during the day)

✗ 5. Why do you think the writer thought the pool was beautiful?

(because of the sunlight shining on the water and then the lights reflecting under the water)

*General Observations.*

When interpreting the errors made in oral reading, the teacher should consider these points:

Dialectical or regional pronunciations should not be counted as errors. This type of mispronunciation does not affect comprehension, although the teacher may wish to note the pronunciation.

Young students often hesitate while reading orally. The teacher may wish to mark these hesitations, but not count them as errors. Fluency in reading comes with practice, which the young reader has not had.

Repetitions should be noted, but the teacher may elect not to count them as errors. This is a habit that can be corrected. Repetitions slow the rate of reading but usually do not indicate a lack of comprehension.

Substitutions, omissions, and insertions should be noted and counted as errors; however, teachers must also indicate whether these changes hinder comprehension. Errors which could fit the context of the sentence and do not affect comprehension are less severe than those which have no relationship to the sentence. For example:

1. The ~~cat ran~~ car got around under the ~~house~~ home.

2. The ~~cat ran~~ kitten went under the ~~house~~ porch.

While both sentences have many errors, those in the first sentence are more serious because of their effect on comprehension.

*Word Recognition.* Errors noted in the recognition of words on the word list and in the oral reading section of the IRI, reveal significant information about the student's word recognition skills. Some responses to note, and possible interpretations of these observations, follow.

Does the student attempt to pronounce words which he or she is not sure of, or ask that they be pronounced? Failure to attempt to pronounce a word indicates that the student has poor word attack skills and does not know how to break words into parts to determine their correct pronunciation.

Does the student frequently hesitate prior to pronouncing a word? This indicates that the student is analyzing the word because of uncertainty. Word analysis is an essential skill for proper decoding of words; however, if this is a frequent occurrence, the student may become a very slow reader and may have poor comprehension. Easier materials and assistance in developing a basic sight vocabulary should be provided to help overcome the problem.

Does the student often repeat a word several times before going on to the next? Students use this as a way to gain time when they do not know the next word. Note how the next word following the repetition is pronounced. Usually the student who uses this technique is unsure and needs to be encouraged to move on more quickly. Games that allow the student to pronounce each word in a sentence only once may be used to help overcome the problem.

Does the student mispronounce the words? This may indicate one of several different problems; specific types of mispronunciations are described below.

The student may call the word another word that differs by only one letter or sound. This is an indication that the student is not looking at the entire word and is not using context clues as a word recognition technique. Note whether the errors seem to be with the initial, medial, or final sounds, then assist the students in looking at the entire word as they read (this will slow the rate initially).

The student may express the word a synonym for the actual word, such as *kitten* for *cat*. This indicates that the student is using context clues quite extensively rather than noting the sounds in the word. Although this is a problem that should not be overlooked, it will not handicap the student's comprehension skills as severely as some of the other word recognition errors.

Does the student more frequently miss basic sight words for which most phonic generalizations do not apply, or miss words which can be easily analyzed? Many students have great difficulty in recognizing the basic sight words and confuse them with one another. If this error is noted, one way of assisting the student is by using activities which require recognition of words in context. If, on the other hand, the student consistently misses words which can be analyzed by using either phonetic analysis, structural analysis, or a combination, then the teacher should note the type of skill the student is not using and provide additional instruction in that area.

Does the student make consistent insertions or omissions? Students who make these errors and do not correct themselves, are not observing attentively the context of the information. Because of their errors, these students usually have difficulty in comprehending the material. If omissions are the problem, the teacher must determine whether the student knows the word and is just skipping it, or if the word is skipped because it is not known. These are two entirely different problems. The student who continuously inserts words may do so in an effort to keep words flowing when a specific word is not known. Students who consistently either insert or omit words should be carefully screened to determine whether a vision problem is contributing to the errors.

*Comprehension.*    Often the student who has difficulty with word recognition skills will also have difficulty with comprehension. However, some students have little difficulty in recognizing the words, but are unable to process the information for comprehension. Thus, when interpreting the data reflecting comprehension, the teacher must determine whether comprehension errors occur because the student does not recognize the words or because the material is not understood. Lack of understanding may be the result of poor language development, or background experiences, or difficulty in processing the information. Note the following as the student's comprehension is checked.

Does the student not understand the material because of word recognition errors? If this is the problem, the student should be able to respond to questions about materials in which no word recognition errors occurred. If easier materials seem to improve comprehension significantly, the student may be diagnosed as having word recognition difficulties which contribute to the comprehension problems. Correcting the word recognition problem should improve the comprehension skills. If the student

makes few errors in word recognition, but continues to have difficulty comprehending the material, then further diagnosis is needed to determine the cause(s) of the comprehension errors.

Does the student respond better to questions measuring literal, interpretive, or critical reading skills? If the teacher has appropriately labeled each question according to the area and specific skill being measured, a rapid review of the errors will indicate the comprehension problem area(s). With this information, the teacher can provide instruction to strengthen the deficient skill areas.

Errors on an IRI can be evaluated quantitatively, according to the number of recorded word recognition and comprehension errors, as well as qualitatively by categorizing the errors and their relationship to comprehension. This detailed analysis of oral reading errors or miscues was initially presented by Goodman and Burke in the *Reading Miscue Inventory* (RMI).[9] The RMI is an outgrowth of a series of studies conducted since 1964 by Yetta Goodman and Kenneth Goodman. These studies focused on the reading process from a psycholinguistic viewpoint (see chapter 1), and analyzed oral reading errors in order to better understand how the reader derives meaning from language.

**Analysis of Miscues on IRI**

Four basic assumptions provide the foundation for the development of the RMI:

1. All readers bring an oral language system to the reading process.
2. All readers bring the sum total of their past experiences to the reading process.
3. Reading materials represent the language patterns of past experiences of the author.
4. Reading is an active language process, which involves constant interaction between the reader and the text.[10]

The *Reading Miscue Inventory* is administered following five basic steps. First, the student reads an unfamiliar selection to the teacher for a period of fifteen to twenty minutes. This is recorded on tape. The teacher is not allowed to provide any assistance to the student during this period of time. While the student is reading, the teacher records errors or miscues on a specially prepared worksheet. After reading the selection, the student is asked to retell as much of it as possible. The teacher may ask probing questions during this time in order to gain more information.

The second step involves the marking of the miscues. The tape is replayed, and the teacher checks the worksheet for accuracy, and calculates a score. The types of miscues marked are substitutions, omissions, insertions, reversals, and repetitions.

In the third step, copies of the *RMI* Coding Sheet and the *RMI* questions are used. On the Coding Sheet, each miscue is listed and the appropriate inventory questions are asked about each miscue. This process enables the examiner to determine the comprehension relationships and the grammar meaning relationships. This information is then transferred to the *RMI* Reader Profile.

The fourth step is the preparation of the Reader Profile for each student. Patterns of strengths and weaknesses are indicated in graph form. Used continuously, the graphs indicate patterns of a student's progress in reading.

The fifth step involves the planning of a reading program for the students. Teachers may plan programs for individuals or groups.[11]

The *Reading Miscue Inventory* differs from other oral reading tests in that each error is carefully evaluated to determine its impact on comprehension, and the acceptability of the error. In miscue analysis the teacher determines the depth of the error. Goodman suggests that "The ability to use the information gained from miscue analysis in working with learners is . . . dependent on the teacher's moving to a view of reading and reading instruction consistent with views of reading as a meaning-getting, language process."[12]

This instrument is very helpful to the teacher in careful analysis of oral reading errors and their impact on the student's understanding. It is essential, however, that the teacher study the materials carefully and practice extensively with the instrument, as this analysis of errors is extremely detailed. Yetta Goodman has suggested that "To simply count miscues is to short circuit a complex process."[13] When properly used, the miscue analysis procedure in the *RMI* certainly assists the teacher in the evaluation of a student's errors.

Classroom teachers may find the *RMI* to be too complex an instrument to use with all students. However, it provides excellent diagnostic data for students experiencing difficulty in reading. For further information on this instrument, the following sources should be reviewed, in addition to those previously cited as references.

> P. David Allen and Dorothy Watson, eds., *Findings of Research in Miscue Analysis: Classroom Implications* (Urbana, Illinois: Clearinghouse on Reading and Communication Skills, 1976).
>
> Kenneth S. Goodman, "Analysis of Oral Reading Miscues: Applied Psycholinguistics," *Reading Research Quarterly* 5 (Fall 1969):9–30.

Classroom teachers may, however, use categorization schemes such as those in the *RMI* to analyze patterns of reading behavior when interpreting any commercial or teacher-made IRI. Using the passage at the student's instructional reading level and the categories generally noted on the IRI, i.e. substitutions, insertions, mispronunciation, and omissions, the teacher can determine the impact of the errors on meaning and make qualitative judgements regarding the severity of the errors. Some questions which should be considered are

*Mispronunciation*
—Was there an attempt to use some type of word recognition skill in pronouncing the word?
—What type of mispronunciation was made—a sight word or other word with an irregular pattern, a proper noun, a multisyllabic word, or a complex word which is infrequently used?

—Did the student have any portion of the word correct, if so what: initial, medial, or final?

—Was the word correctly pronounced in another part of the selection when more context clues were available?

*Substitution*

—Was the substitution correct syntactically?

—Was the substitution correct semantically, thus not severely affecting the meaning?

—Did the substituted word look similar to the word in the text, i.e. horse for house?

—Could the word fit logically into the context of the selection?

—Was the substituted word a real or nonsense word?

—Is the text word a part of the student's vocabulary, as compared to the word which was substituted?

*Omissions*

—Was the omitted word needed in the text for a complete thought to be expressed?

—Did the student note that a word was omitted as the remainder of the selection was read?

—Did the omission affect the meaning of the text?

—Were the same types of words omitted throughout the selection, i.e. nouns, verbs, sight words, words with affixes, etc.?

—Did the omissions occur as isolated incidents in various selections?

*Insertions*

—Did the insertion affect the meaning of the text?

—Was the insertion made to make an earlier mispronunciation or omission make sense?

—Did the insertion serve to embellish the narrative by adding descriptive or clarifying words?

—Do insertions occur frequently to keep the reading of the selection moving smoothly, or as isolated incidents?

*Meaning*

—Did the student understand the meaning of the passage although miscues were made?

—Were the errors related to dialect differences and have no impact on understanding? (Note: Errors which reflect dialect differences are not counted as miscues.)

—Did the student answer the comprehension questions using the words which were considered miscues, or were the miscues corrected mentally and the correct answer given to the questions?

As miscues are analyzed, these questions should be considered to help the teacher determine the qualitative aspect of the errors.

**Figure 4.7**
Sample Marked
Selection

United States
The ~~U.S.~~ government (has) asked car makers to build smaller and more ~~efficient~~, new eficent

cars. This is an ~~effort~~ to get people to buy (those) cars that use less ~~gas~~. The ~~price~~ of fuel fuel cost

we use in our homes has ~~risen~~ sharply. ~~Thus,~~ people try to use less energy in their risen This

~~home.~~ They take very good care of ~~their heating~~ systems so (that) they use less fuel. Also, new house the heater

laws have been passed that give people tax ~~breaks~~ when they build ~~homes~~ that use less bonus houses

fuel. These homes have good ~~heating~~ systems. They also have ~~insulation~~ that keep(s) heater insides

more heat in(side) the home. People are ~~now~~ using less energy. not

_____ ✓ 1. Who has asked car makers to build more efficient cars?

_____ ✗ 2. What does efficient mean?

_____ ✓ 3. Why do people use less fuel in their homes?

_____ ✗ 4. What is used in houses to keep the heat inside?

_____ ✓ 5. What can people do to use less fuel?

_____ ✓ 6. Why do you think fuel has increased in cost?

**Table 4.4**
Summary of Word Recognition Miscues

| Substitutions | Mispronunciations | Omissions | Insertions | Pronounced |
|---|---|---|---|---|
| United States (U.S.) | eficent (efficient) | has | new | effort |
| fuel (gas) | risen (risen) | those | very | |
| cost (price) | | that | new | |
| This (Thus) | | keep(s) | | |
| house (home) | | in(side) | | |
| the (their) | | | | |
| heater (heating) | | | | |
| bonus (breaks) | | | | |
| houses (homes) | | | | |
| heater (heating) | | | | |
| insides (insulation) | | | | |
| not (now) | | | | |

Figure 4.7 presents a passage from an IRI which has been marked. The errors are summarized in Table 4.4 and the miscues classified in Table 4.5. Teachers may use this simplifed procedure to analyze the impact of the miscues on the student's understanding of a passage. Those miscues which create difficulty in understanding the information are considered to be definitely more serious than miscues which do not affect comprehension.

**Table 4.5**
Classification for Miscues

| Student Miscue | Text | Graphic Similarity | | | Syntax Error | Semantics Error | Meaning Change |
|---|---|---|---|---|---|---|---|
| | | Initial | Medial | Final | | | |
| United States | U.S. | yes | no | no | no | no | No |
| fuel | gas | no | no | no | no | no | No |
| cost | price | no | no | no | no | no | No |
| This | Thus | yes | no | yes | yes | yes | Yes |
| house | home | yes | no | yes | no | no | No |
| the | their | yes | no | no | no | no | No |
| heater | heating | yes | yes | no | yes | yes | No |
| bonus | breaks | yes | no | yes | no | yes | No |
| houses | homes | yes | no | yes | no | no | No |
| heater | heating | yes | yes | no | yes | no | No |
| insides | insulation | yes | no | no | yes | yes | Yes |
| not | now | yes | yes | no | yes | yes | Yes |
| eficent | efficient | yes | no | yes | — — | — — | Yes |
| risen | risen | yes | no | yes | — — | — — | Yes |
| — — | has | — — | — — | — — | — — | — — | No |
| — — | those | — — | — — | — — | — — | — — | No |
| — — | that | — — | — — | — — | — — | — — | No |
| keep | keeps | yes | yes | no | yes | no | No |
| in | inside | yes | no | no | no | no | No |
| new | — — | — — | — — | — — | no | no | No |
| very | — — | — — | — — | — — | no | no | No |
| new | — — | — — | — — | — — | no | no | No |
| — — | effort | — — | — — | — — | — — | — — | Yes |

Thus, by using an IRI to evaluate not only the number but also the severity of the miscue, the teacher obtains more diagnostic data about the student, data which greatly assists in planning prescriptive instruction.

The versatility of the IRI also facilitates determination of a listening comprehension or capacity level score. To determine the listening capacity level, the teacher reads a series of selections to the student, moving from easier to more difficult material. These selections are taken from teacher-made IRI, graded materials, basal series, or published informals. After each selection is read, the teacher asks a series of comprehension questions accompanying the selection. Satisfactory performance corresponds to the same criteria that determine the instructional level for the IRI (see table 4.3). When the student falls below the instructional level, the assessment is discontinued. If further assessment of listening comprehension is desired, several standardized instruments are available. Examples are listed in appendix B.

Informal reading inventories are valuable diagnostic instruments which furnish much insight into the strengths and weaknesses in reading of each student. Remember, however, to follow procedures carefully and exercise caution in interpreting the data.

**Listening Comprehension**

**Observation**

One of the more important methods of diagnostic evaluation is teacher observation. It can be used alone, but is more often employed in conjunction with other diagnostic instruments. Because students work and play together in the classroom during a prolonged period of time, the classroom teacher has the best opportunity to observe students' traits and attitudes, interaction that takes place among them, and changes in individual behavior. From such observation the astute teacher derives the first indication that a problem is developing. Teachers have many opportunities during the school day to observe the reading patterns of their students; and it is particularly important to observe students reading silently as well as orally. Students may change their reading styles and act differently, depending upon the type of reading they are doing. It is also essential to observe students working in reading groups as well as individually.

In the cases of many students, the observations of reading problems are fairly simple, although the underlying problems are quite complex. Characteristics such as overaggressiveness in play, hyperactivity, propensity to distraction are easily observable; and awareness of these characteristics often helps the teacher to develop the atmosphere necessary for improving the performance of these problem readers.

There are some words of caution in dealing with observation. Remember that observation is only one of many tools needed for diagnosing students' reading problems; overreliance on observation could adversely affect the prescription developed for a student. Remember, too, that since students are always changing and growing, an up-to-date observation should be used rather than one that was made six months earlier. The teacher should continuously note the reading behavior of each student. Another critical fact to remember is that the teacher can observe only a limited amount of a particular student's activities, and should not generalize extensively on the basis of the behavior patterns noted. Teachers should realize that their own attitudes and values may affect their evaluation of a student; they must be careful to note only facts and reserve opinions until discussing the conclusions reached following many observations. Finally, although it may often seem necessary to act immediately upon observation of certain behavior, the classroom teacher will generally gain more useful information through structured observation over a long period of time, and should plan to use this method.

Structured observation may take either of two forms: (1) a *checklist* (the most commonly used form) or (2) *anecdotal records*. Anecdotal records are detailed notes concerning individual students, with dates recorded for each observation. These records often reveal consistent patterns of behavior, which may be significant in working with a student. The anecdotal record may be most helpful in observing a student with a severe reading disability, in order to gain more insight into the student's reading behaviors. Such records are not recommended for large numbers of students, since recording the observations takes a great deal of time from the teacher's primary function: teaching. Checklists, which are less time-consuming and more flexible, are best for large groups. A checklist is a versatile instrument, in that it can be one page or several pages in length; however, a checklist does not lend itself to the in-depth observation of a student over a long period of time; for the latter purpose, an anecdotal record is more advisable.

Checklist record forms should follow consistent criteria to guide classroom observation: (1) items should deal with specific behavior which can be observed, (2) space for additional observations and comments should be provided, and (3) items should be limited so that using the checklist is not an overwhelming task. The teacher should be familiar with the types of observations to be measured by the checklist used. Some of the standard items that such a list might be expected to include are the following:

Rate of reading assignments.
Understanding of material read.
Skill in oral reading.
Classroom participation in discussion.
Desire to read assigned or other material.
Types of material read during leisure time.
Skill in responding to various types of questions.
Ability to recognize new words.
Variety of vocabulary used.

Observation may take place during the regular reading time or at any time when the student is reading. The teacher can informally observe designated students for a few minutes during the class time over a period of days to note selected items. Specific steps in using an observation checklist as an informal diagnostic tool are as follows:

1. Select or design a checklist which meets the needs of your classroom situation.
2. Make copies of the checklist in order to have one for each student who will be observed.
3. Become very familiar with the checklist so that you will know what to look for during the observation time.
4. Arrange for short periods of time to observe the student in a reading situation.
5. Select one or two specific areas on the checklist, then observe the student to note strengths and weaknesses in these areas.
6. Note any problems the student seems to have in the areas being observed at this particular time.
7. Select other areas to be observed at different times.

Observation checklists are available from various sources, or they may be developed by the classroom teacher. Sources for checklists that may be adapted for classroom use are listed in appendix C. In addition to these sources, most basal reading programs provide checklists for noting student strengths and weaknesses. A sample checklist appears in appendix G. Classroom teachers may wish to review several checklists and then design one which more satisfactorily meets their own special needs.

Observation using the anecdotal record requires the teacher to note carefully the behavior and reactions of the student during a specified time. The most difficult problem for an observer using the anecdotal record is to keep fact separate from opinion. Only the actual facts or events are to be recorded; no interpretations or opinions are added until all observations for the student are complete (see figure 4.8).

Perhaps the most difficult phase of the observation process is interpreting the results. It is one thing to record a student's actions and statements during the day, but quite another to identify the underlying reasons for the behavior observed. An example of behavior which may be very difficult to interpret would be an emotional reaction recorded during the observation period. Use a cautious approach to determining the reasons for such an emotional upheaval. Before drawing any conclusions or making decisions based on observation, note the frequency with which the problem seemed to appear and the consistency of the problem from day to day. Remember that observation checklists involve less subjective evaluation than anecdotal records; thus, it may be helpful to use one to support or reject the findings of the other. Observation should be viewed as a beneficial part of all areas of diagnosis; however, teachers must be very aware of their students and cautious in interpreting the information gained from observing them.

**Figure 4.8**
Sample Anecdotal
Record

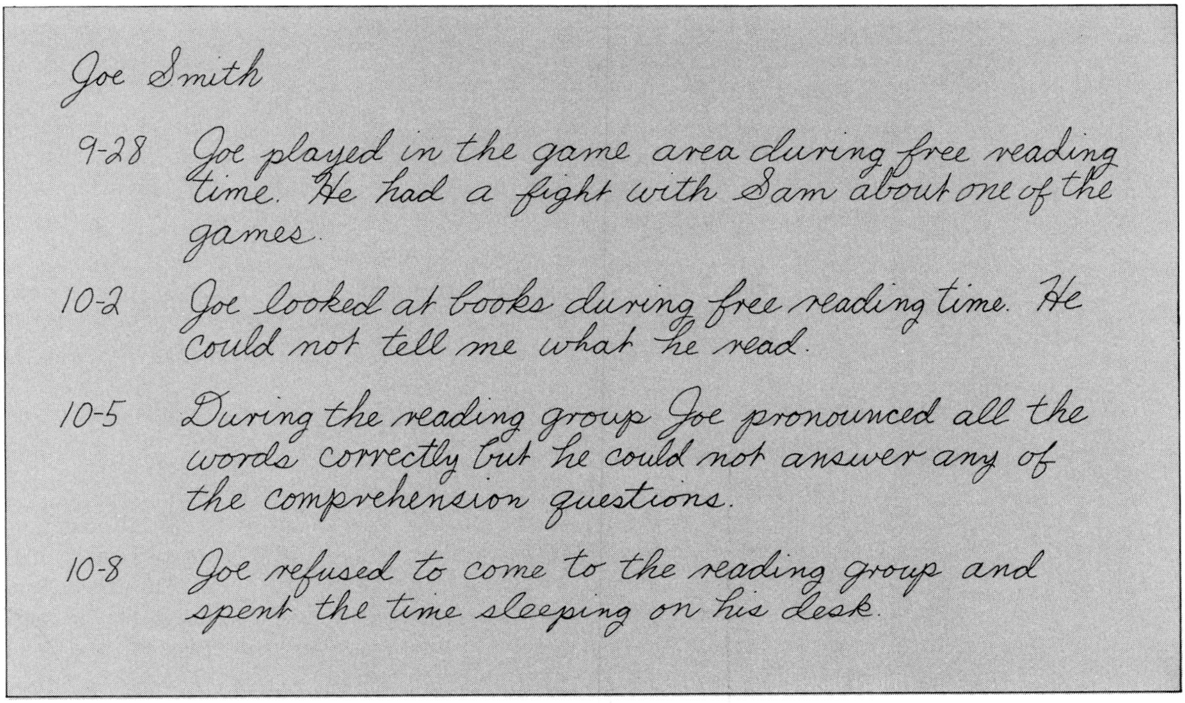

Joe Smith

9-28    Joe played in the game area during free reading time. He had a fight with Sam about one of the games.

10-2    Joe looked at books during free reading time. He could not tell me what he read.

10-5    During the reading group Joe pronounced all the words correctly but he could not answer any of the comprehension questions.

10-8    Joe refused to come to the reading group and spent the time sleeping on his desk.

**Word Recognition Inventories**

Word recognition inventories assist the classroom teacher in learning more about a student's word recognition skills. As outlined in the discussion of the Informal Reading Inventory, the teacher may use a word list as a part of the IRI or use only the oral reading selection to aid in diagnosing word recognition difficulties. In addition to these procedures, the teacher may use a word list to measure knowledge of a specific group of words, or use informal activities which require the student to recognize or analyze words. The following pages provide some ideas concerning informal procedures to use in analyzing word recognition difficulties.

**Word Lists.**

Teachers should develop word recognition inventories based on their needs. Specific directions for developing inventories using word lists were provided at the beginning of this chapter. This section will present information on the various word lists that teachers may wish to review.

One of the more widely used word lists is the *Dolch Basic Sight Word List*, which was developed in 1941 from three lists that were in wide use at that time. The words on the Dolch List were drawn from a variety of sources composed of

the following: 510 words from a list published by the Child Study Committee of the International Kindergarten Union, the first 500 words from the Gates List, and the entire 453 words of the Wheeler and Howell List.[14] The Dolch List consists of 220 basic sight words comprising those words occurring most frequently in basal readers on the first, second, and third grade levels. There is some doubt about the present-day relevancy of the list; however, it is still widely used by classroom teachers and reading specialists.

The relevancy of the Dolch List has been studied by Johnson and by Hillerich.[15] Johnson's study suggested that the Dolch List has become outdated compared to the Kucera-Francis word list. Hillerich, however, in reviewing some fourteen different studies, arrived at the following conclusions:

1. The recentness of a list is no assurance of its importance.
2. The language base of the word count may be more important than the date it was compiled.
3. The structure words in our language tend to remain constant, although the language is continually changing.
4. The Dolch List, unlike some other word lists, does not seem particularly outmoded.

The Dolch List, outlined by grade level, is provided in table 4.6.

A more recent inventory is the Kucera-Francis Corpus, which also contains 220 service words.[16] This list was compiled from a word bank of over one million words from many sources. From this bank of words a list of 220 of the most frequently occurring words was derived. Some authorities believe that because of its recentness this inventory is more appropriate for use today than the Dolch List. The Kucera-Francis Corpus differs in content from the Dolch List in that eighty-two, or 37 percent, of the words on the Kucera-Francis Corpus are not on the Dolch List.[17] The Kucera-Francis Corpus appears in table 4.7.

Other valuable word lists which have recently been developed are: *Basic Elementary Reading Vocabularies,* by Albert Harris and Milton Jacobson; *A Revised Core Vocabulary: A Basic Vocabulary for Grades 1–8, An Advanced Vocabulary for Grades 9–13,* by Standford Taylor, Helen Frackenpohl, and Catherine White; *Word Frequency Book,* by John B. Carroll, Peter Davies, and Barry Richman; and "Sight Words for Beginning Readers" by Wayne Otto and Robert Chester.[18] These lists were developed more recently than the Dolch List and are used in current research. The *Cheek Master Word List,* mentioned earlier in this chapter, is compiled from four previously mentioned word lists.[19] It consists of 1,720 words and was developed for readability levels 1.0 to 5.0. This word list appears in appendix H.

Formal word recognition inventories are available to assist teachers who do not wish to develop their own lists. One of the more commonly used lists is the *Slosson Oral Reading Test* (SORT), which is discussed in chapter 5.[20] Another formal instrument which has an oral reading section designed as a word recognition inventory is the *Wide Range Achievement Test* (WRAT); this can be used for ages five through adult and can provide a grade equivalent score.[21]

**Table 4.6**

Dolch Basic Sight Words

| Preprimer | Primer | First Grade | Second Grade | Third Grade |
|-----------|--------|-------------|--------------|-------------|
| a | all | after | always | about |
| and | am | again | around | better |
| away | are | an | because | bring |
| big | at | any | been | carry |
| blue | ate | as | before | clean |
| can | be | ask | best | cut |
| come | black | by | both | done |
| down | brown | could | buy | draw |
| find | but | every | call | drink |
| for | came | fly | cold | eight |
| funny | cat | from | does | fall |
| go | did | give | don't | far |
| help | do | going | fast | full |
| here | four | has | first | got |
| I | get | had | five | grow |
| in | good | her | found | hold |
| is | have | him | gave | hot |
| it | he | his | goes | hurt |
| jump | into | how | green | if |
| little | like | just | its | keep |
| look | must | know | made | kind |
| make | new | let | many | laugh |
| me | no | live | off | light |
| my | now | may | or | long |
| not | on | of | pull | much |
| one | our | old | read | myself |
| play | out | once | right | never |
| red | please | open | sing | only |
| run | pretty | over | sit | own |
| said | ran | put | sleep | pick |
| see | ride | round | tell | seven |
| the | saw | some | their | shall |
| three | say | stop | these | show |
| to | she | take | those | six |
| two | so | thank | upon | small |
| up | soon | them | us | start |
| we | that | then | use | ten |
| where | there | think | very | today |
| yellow | they | walk | wash | together |
| you | this | were | which | try |
|  | too | when | why | warm |
|  | under |  | wish |  |
|  | want |  | work |  |
|  | was |  | would |  |
|  | well |  | write |  |
|  | went |  | your |  |
|  | what |  |  |  |
|  | white |  |  |  |
|  | who |  |  |  |
|  | will |  |  |  |
|  | with |  |  |  |
|  | yes |  |  |  |

Source: E.W.Dolch, *Dolch Basic Sight Word Test* (Champaign, Illinois: Garrard Publishing Company, 1942). Reproduced by permission of Garrard Publishing Company, Champaign, Illinois.

**Table 4.7**
Kucera-Francis Corpus

| | | | | |
|---|---|---|---|---|
| the | more | where | come | fact |
| of | no | much | since | though |
| and | if | your | against | water |
| to | out | may | go | less |
| a | so | well | came | public |
| in | said | down | right | put |
| that | what | should | used | thing |
| is | up | because | take | almost |
| was | its | each | three | hand |
| he | about | just | states | enough |
| for | into | those | himself | far |
| it | than | people | few | took |
| with | them | Mr. | house | head |
| as | can | how | use | yet |
| his | only | too | during | government |
| on | other | little | without | system |
| be | new | state | again | better |
| at | some | good | place | set |
| by | could | very | American | told |
| I | time | make | around | nothing |
| this | these | would | however | night |
| had | two | still | home | end |
| not | may | own | small | why |
| are | then | see | found | called |
| but | do | men | Mrs. | didn't |
| from | first | work | thought | eyes |
| or | any | long | went | find |
| have | my | get | say | going |
| an | now | here | part | look |
| they | such | between | once | asked |
| which | like | both | general | later |
| one | our | life | high | knew |
| you | over | being | upon | |
| were | man | under | school | |
| her | me | never | every | |
| all | even | day | don't | |
| she | most | same | does | |
| there | made | another | got | |
| would | after | know | united | |
| their | also | while | left | |
| we | did | last | number | |
| him | many | might | course | |
| been | before | us | war | |
| has | must | great | until | |
| when | through | old | always | |
| who | back | year | away | |
| will | years | off | something | |

Source: From Henry Kucera and W. Nelson Francis, *Computational Analysis of Present-Day American English* (Providence, Rhode Island: Brown University Press, 1967). Reproduced by permission of Brown University Press, Providence, Rhode Island.

Much diagnostic information concerning the development of word recognition skills can be obtained through other informal techniques used continuously in the classroom. Activities such as workbook pages, games, and writing assignments provide additional insight into word recognition difficulties. For example, if students experience difficulty or show total lack of skill in activities requiring them to use context clues or structural analysis skills, the teacher can provide appropriate instruction to meet their needs.

Informal assessments of word recognition difficulties should be an integral part of any ongoing diagnostic-prescriptive program, especially at the elementary school level. As teachers note errors through observation and occasional informal appraisal, they can do much to alleviate many word recognition difficulties before they become major reading problems.

Word lists assist the classroom teacher in the identification of sight word deficiencies. In addition, they give the teacher some insight into techniques which students use to decode words. Teachers should keep notes as to whether students have difficulty with initial, medial, or final sounds or whether they have no skill in analyzing words; such information is essential for prescriptive instruction. Teachers should, however, keep in mind that these word recognition inventories assess only one area of reading; they do not measure comprehension, and the scores cannot be used to obtain a definite reading level for the student.

Criterion-referenced and objective-based tests are recent developments in testing. These tests are designed to measure what a learner knows or can do relative to a specific objective. The criterion-referenced test is based on objectives that contain the specific conditions, outcomes, and criteria which are expected for satisfactory completion of the task. The objective-based test is also based on specific objectives, but no predetermined criteria for achievement are provided. This lack of specific criteria is the technical difference between criterion-referenced and objective-based tests.

These tests, in contrast to norm-referenced or standardized tests, do not compare one student's performance with that of another. Each student is evaluated on his or her ability to perform the specific skill being measured, rather than in comparison to established norms on a group of related test items. Thus, the criterion-referenced or objective-based test is becoming more popular as a diagnostic tool used by local and state testing programs. These tests provide a more realistic view of achievement in reading, since students are tested on specific objectives directly related to specific reading skills.

In order to evaluate the use of criterion-referenced reading instruments more easily, examine the contrast between them and norm-referenced instruments, as outlined by Otto.

1. Standardized tests have a low degree of overlap with the objectives of instruction at any given time and place. The overlap for criterion-referenced measures is absolute, for the objectives are the referents.

**Table 4.8**
Contrast of Norm-referenced and Criterion-referenced Tests

| Point of Comparison | Norm-referenced | Criterion-referenced |
| --- | --- | --- |
| Purpose | Determines a student's grade level achievement. | Determines extent to which student objectives are being achieved. |
| Testing Procedure | Each student takes a complete test. | Items may be randomly assigned as purposes dictate. |
| Achievement Standard | Comparison with other students of same age. | Performance of individual in regard to the objective. |
| Reporting of Results | Grade-level achievement norms for individuals or groups. | Percentage score on number of items correct for specific objective. |
| Implications for Teaching | Teaching for the test constrains classroom activity and invalidates the test. | Teaching for the objectives is desirable and expected if the objectives have been carefully formulated. |

2. Norm-referenced tests are not very useful as aids in planning instruction because of the low overlap just mentioned. Criterion-referenced measures can be used directly to assess the strengths and weaknesses of individuals with regard to instructional objectives.

3. Again because of their nonspecificity, norm-referenced tests often require skills or aptitudes that may be influenced only to a limited extent by experiences in the classroom. This cannot be so for criterion-referenced measures because the referent for each test is also the referent for instruction.

4. Standardized tests do not indicate the extent to which individuals or groups of students have mastered the spectrum of instructional objectives. Again, there is no such problem with criterion-referenced measures because they focus on the spectrum of instructional objectives in a given situation.[22]

Table 4.8 provides a further contrast of the two types of tests.

The primary advantage of criterion-referenced tests is that they get directly at the performance of individuals with regard to specified instructional objectives; thus they facilitate the management of a diagnostic-prescriptive system of instruction.

There are, however, some limitations inherent in criterion-referenced tests. Otto describes such problems as the following:

1. Objectives involving hard-to-measure qualities, such as appreciation or attitudes, may be slighted.

2. Objectives involving the retention and transfer of what is learned may become secondary to the one-time demonstration of mastery of stated objectives.

3. Specifying the universe of tasks (determining critical instructional objectives) to be dealt with is of extreme importance. Good tests will do nothing to overcome the problem of bad objectives. But note that the problem here is no different for norm-referenced testing.

4. Determining proficiency standards can be troublesome. Perfect or near-perfect performance should be required if (a) the criterion objectives call for mastery; (b) the skill is important for future learning; (c) items are objective type and guessing is likely. Less demanding performance may be adequate if any of the three conditions do not prevail.[23]

Instead of attempting to choose between either norm-referenced or criterion-referenced instruments, teachers should use them to complement each other, choosing the most appropriate instrument for their particular purpose and testing situation. Teachers interested in knowing how students are performing in relation to national standards should use a standardized or norm-referenced test. Teachers who need diagnostic information about a student's performance on a specific skill should use a criterion-referenced or objective-based test.

Criterion-referenced tests are being used more frequently as schools develop management systems to aid in implementing diagnostic-prescriptive reading programs. In addition, statewide testing programs are using objective-based tests to determine student performance on specific minimum objectives or standards. As a result, these tests are becoming more readily available for teacher use. Many of the current basal reading programs contain criterion-referenced tests to aid in classroom diagnosis. These tests are based on the scope and sequence of skills for the series and are used as part of a management system for the basal series.

In addition, specially designed management systems containing criterion-referenced tests can be purchased to use with various materials. Such systems include

*High Intensity,* by Random House, Inc.
*Fountain Valley Teacher Support System in Reading,* by Zweig Associates, Inc.
*Individualized Criterion-Referenced Testing,* by Educational Development Corporation
*Prescriptive Reading Inventory,* by CTB-McGraw-Hill
*Wisconsin Design for Reading Skill Development,* by NCS Interpretive Scoring System

Teachers should exercise caution in using criterion-referenced tests from a management system for reading. Here are two suggestions for the proper use of such tests. First, follow the scope and sequence of skills outlined for the school, since many management systems are not outlined according to a horizontal and vertical hierarchy of skills. Second, do not fall into the trap of the "test-teach-test" syndrome, which encourages the development of reading skills in isolation. A further discussion of this topic is provided in chapter 7 in the section on management systems.

Teachers who do not have these criterion-referenced tests developed for them, or are not satisfied with the tests that are provided, can prepare their own tests to measure specific objectives. The specific steps to follow in doing so are listed below.

1. Identify the objective that will become the basis for the test item.
2. Specify the objective so that you define exactly what is to be measured.

   Example A: *To understand what is read.* This objective is incorrectly stated. It is not specific; it gives no idea of the outcome or what is to be done to achieve the objective.

   Example B: *After reading a paragraph, the student will identify the main idea of the paragraph.* This objective is more specific and could be used to develop an objective-based test item.

   Example C: *Given three reading selections, each containing a stated main idea and followed by four choices of response, the student will underline the choice that states the main idea for each selection. The student must correctly answer two of the three.* This is the type of objective often used in criterion-referenced test items. It is very specific, leaving little room for doubt as to what is expected. The problem is that the objective is so cumbersome that teachers often find it not very practical for classroom use. Thus, the objective in Example B is more commonly used.

3. Develop the test items to measure the objective as specified. If the teacher uses objectives as specific as the one in Example C, then the item is already designed. However, if a more general objective is used, as in Example B, then the teacher must determine the format, the number of selections to use, the procedure to be used in administration, and criteria for the performance expected for each student. Teachers may use selections from readers and library books or selected items from workbooks to aid in developing test items. An assessment to measure a specific objective usually consists of from three to eight items that measure the specific skill as outlined in the objective. Some assessments are designed for use with individuals, but most can be administered to small groups.

Criterion-referenced tests are essential components of a diagnostic-prescriptive reading program. They are easy to administer and are excellent for determining the specific skill needs of students in the classroom.

## Cloze Procedure

An important and versatile informal procedure for use by elementary and secondary classroom teachers in determining students' reading levels and in discovering the possible causes of reading problems is the cloze procedure. It was developed by Wilson Taylor in 1953 primarily as a tool for measuring readability;[24] however, further research indicates that the cloze procedure can also be used as an alternative to the Informal Reading Inventory for determining students' reading levels.[25]

A cloze test can be developed without special training in test construction. To develop and administer a cloze test, gather reading selections from textbooks, basal readers, or any other material that is appropriate and unfamiliar to the students, and follow the steps listed below.

1. Select a passage of approximately 250–300 words on a level at which the student is or should be reading.
2. Check the readability level of the passage using a readability formula as outlined in chapter 7.
3. Retype the passage. Beginning with the second sentence, delete every fifth word. Replace each deleted word with a line, making sure that each line is of the same length. Do not delete words from the first or last sentences. There should be approximately fifty blank spaces in the selection.
4. Make copies of the test for students to complete.
5. Direct the students to fill in each blank with the words they think best complete the sentences.
6. Score the papers by counting as correct only those responses that exactly match the original selection. Using a percentage score of correct responses, determine the student's reading level:

58%–100% correct = Independent level
44%– 57% correct = Instructional level
 0%– 43% correct = Frustration level[26]

Teachers will find this technique quite useful in learning more about their students. The passages used at the various readability levels may be stapled together in booklet form for students to work through as an assignment. The objective of the cloze procedure is to provide an estimate of the level of the material the student can satisfactorily read, but it can also be used to gain more diagnostic information through alternative interpretation. It can serve as a method of evaluating students' comprehension. For example, if the student fills in the blanks with totally irrelevant words, it is very likely that the material is not understood. This is a valuable clue for the teacher to use in evaluating the student's ability to comprehend certain material. More diagnostic information can be gathered by examining the types of words substituted in the blanks and whether or not the student uses other words in the sentence to assist in figuring out the omitted words. Those students unable to use these context clues have not fully developed their reading skills. In addition, to determine the extent of the student's vocabulary, students may be asked to list as many words as they can think of which could complete each blank. Students with limited vocabularies will encounter difficulty in completing the assignment, indicating to the teacher their need for further vocabulary study to understand the material.

The cloze procedure is a good diagnostic technique for use in content materials from the elementary grades through high school, since it can be administered to groups of students, thereby minimizing the loss of teaching time in diagnosis, and maximizing the amount of information gained from an instrument. A sample cloze test is provided in Figure 4.9.

**Figure 4.9**
Sample Cloze
Selection.

River Deposits

Much of a stream's load is deposited before the river reaches the sea. The amount of sediment _____ a stream can carry _____ on its speed. When _____ stream is slowed down, _____ can no longer carry _____ of its load. The _____ is dropped at the _____ , at the mouth, or _____ the bed of the _____ .

Few youthful streams carry _____ full load of sediment. _____ , youthful streams seldom deposit _____ sediment. Mature streams, however, _____ their limit of fragments. _____ slight slowing of their _____ causes mature streams to _____ some of their load. _____ wear down the land _____ 0.3 in 9000 _____ . But only one fourth _____ this sediment reaches the _____ . The rest is deposited _____ the drainage basin.

Floodplains _____ built next to channels _____ mature rivers. When water _____ out of a flooded _____ channel, sediment is dropped _____ the flooded land. These _____ form mounds or natural _____ parallel to the channel. _____ levee is made of _____ coarsest material. Beyond the _____ , fine muds are spread _____ over the alluvial plains. _____ plains usually are swamp _____ covered with excellent soil. _____ of the cultivated land _____ Egypt is sediment deposited _____ the yearly flood of _____ Nile River. The Mississippi _____ is also very fertile _____ new soil is brought _____ the alluvial plain each _____ by the spring floods _____ the river.

Deltas are _____ where rivers flow into _____ , standing water. At this _____ the river's speed is _____ reduced. Sediment carried by _____ river spreads out at _____ mouth as the river _____ into quiet water. The _____ material settles out first. _____ material are carried farther, _____ eventually most of the _____ settles onto the delta. _____ wave action is strong, _____ , the waves and currents _____ prevent the formation of _____ delta. Then sediment from the river's load becomes a part of the shore deposits.

Reprinted with permission of Charles E. Merrill Publishing Company and Margaret S. Bishop, Phyllis G. Lewis, and Berry Sutherland.

A Group Reading Inventory (GRI) is a procedure used by content teachers to diagnose the specific reading skills necessary to learn the concepts in a content area lesson. The teacher must first *identify the concepts* or content to be taught during a particular period of time. Using these concepts, the teacher must then *identify the reading skills* which must be used to learn the content. The GRI can be developed when these two aspects, concepts and reading skills are identified as in the example below.

| Concept Generalizations | Reading Skills |
|---|---|
| To determine the location of Pearl Harbor. | Using the atlas |
| To understand the meaning of the quote "I shall return." | Interpretation |
| To understand the significance of the Battle of the Coral Sea. | Cause-effect relationships<br>Main idea |
| To understand the term "unconditional surrender." | Word meanings<br>Prefixes |
| To realize the impact of the use of the atomic bomb on Hiroshima and Nagasaki. | Drawing conclusions<br>Anticipating outcomes<br>Evaluation |

For each of the identified reading skills, three to five questions should be developed, using the content materials at an appropriate readability level for the students. The student uses the materials to answer the questions. Sample questions developed from the previous example appear in the following outline.

*Sample Questions for Group Reading Inventory*

I. Vocabulary Development
   A. Word Meaning: Directions—Turn to page 30. Write a brief definition of the term "unconditional surrender."
   B. Prefixes: Directions—Turn to page 30. Now that you have defined the term "unconditional surrender," what does the prefix *un* mean?

II. Comprehension
   A. Author's purpose: Directions—Turn to page 25. What does MacArthur mean by the quote, "I shall return"?
   B. Cause-effect relationships: Directions—Turn to page 28. What is the significance of the Battle of the Coral Sea?
   C. Evaluation: Directions—Turn to page 31. How important was the decision to use the atomic bomb on Hiroshima and Nagasaki?
   D. Anticipating outcomes: Directions—Turn to page 32. How has this decision to use the atomic bomb in World War II affected present-day relationships between countries?

III. Reference Skills
   Using the atlas: Directions—Turn to the map on page 35. Locate the Pearl Harbor naval base.

Thus, the student is asked to read specified materials and to provide written responses to the questions prior to beginning the unit. With information gathered about each student's knowledge of necessary reading skills, the teacher can determine which alternative teaching procedures would be most effective to help each student develop better skills and learn the content material more easily.

One of the advantages of the GRI is that it can be administered several times during the year, since different material is used each time. Because it is important to ascertain the students' progress at various times throughout the year, and because it is a group test, it has obvious advantages over other informal and standardized instruments, especially for the content teacher. Using this instrument, the teacher can assess the progress students have made in learning reading skills. An important point to remember is that not all students are progressing at the same learning rate; therefore, it is necessary to use materials at various levels to assess the skills. Usually the textbook may be used with those reading at or above level, a textbook from a little lower level with those who are two or three years below grade level, and an elementary textbook for those much below level. Unless this differentiation is made, the teacher will be unable to determine whether the student does not know the skill or just cannot read the material.

## Miscellaneous Sources

Classroom teachers sometimes overlook many sources from which they can informally obtain much diagnostic information without ever testing a student. These sources include the daily work of the student, such as workbook pages, learning center activities, and instructional games. Additionally, the teacher should use information from parent conferences and discussions with the students' other teachers to assist in a diagnostic-prescriptive reading program. These miscellaneous sources of data exist in every classroom and should be used in order to provide continuous diagnosis in reading.

*Daily classroom activities* should be used to assess progress in specific skill development, and to note strengths and weaknesses as well as feelings toward the tasks. Observant classroom teachers make notes regarding individual student errors during the basal reading time. Errors such as difficulty with specific word recognition skills or responding to literal comprehension questions must be noted so that appropriate instruction can be provided. Workbook pages should serve as a source to reinforce observations made in the reading group or to alert the teacher to look for particular difficulties. The *workbook exercises* can serve as excellent criterion-referenced tests for the teacher who has identified the specific tasks to be taught in the reading class. Thus, in a diagnostic-prescriptive reading program, workbook pages are not used for busywork, but are an integral part of the diagnostic procedures.

Likewise, *learning centers* should be used as an informal diagnostic resource. As students participate in the prescribed activities of the learning centers, teachers should notice, through observation and student feedback, the areas of strengths and weaknesses. For example, a learning center devoted to the study of contractions allows the teacher to determine which students have no understanding of

contractions, which can understand simple contractions, and which have mastered the more complex contractions. Furthermore, the teacher can use the learning center activities to reinforce instruction and assess the development of skills.

*Instructional games,* whether purchased or teacher-made, can provide the same types of diagnostic information as the learning centers. Teachers may group students to work as teams with specific games and ask them to report the difficulties encountered in the activity. Using these diagnostic procedures will assist the classroom teacher in several ways:

1. Less teaching time is spent in administering paper-pencil tests.
2. More diagnostic data is continuously being used to assist in providing appropriate instruction.
3. Students are not continuously facing testing situations and developing a careless attitude toward tests.
4. Evaluation is an integral part of the instructional program, a fact which enhances the concept of diagnostic teaching.

In addition to these sources of data, remember that the students' *parents* can provide excellent information which aids in diagnosis. Brief conversations with parents will give answers to questions such as:

Does the student spend any time reading at home?
Do the parents read at home or do they read to the student?
What is the family's attitude toward reading?
How does the mother or father feel about the student's performance in school?
What kind of family life does the student have?
Are there reading materials in the home?

Parents are a valuable source of information. They can assist by answering these general types of questions; for students with severe reading difficulties, parents can provide information as to possible physical or emotional difficulties that may have contributed to the reading problem. In a diagnostic-prescriptive reading program, everyone and everything is used to assist in supplying the appropriate instruction to the individual student.

Classroom teachers must rely to a great extent on informal testing procedures in order to provide appropriate instruction. As mentioned previously, experience is one of the best teachers in interpreting the various informal assessments. However, there are some special suggestions which may help the teacher who is just beginning to use informal diagnostic procedures in the classroom.

**Tips on Informal Testing**

*Make these testing situations as informal as possible.* Much diagnosis can be made by using observation techniques and analysis of classroom work.
*Check the readability levels of all materials used in informal testing.* Unless the teacher knows the readability level of the materials, the level on which the student succeeds or fails cannot be determined.

*Various instruments should be used in informally diagnosing reading difficulties.* No one instrument can provide all the needed data.

*Limit the testing time according to an individual student's interest and attention span.*

*Verify data from one instrument by using your opinion, or another form or procedure for testing a given area.* Do not draw conclusions based on limited information from one observation or test.

*Ask for assistance from fellow teachers.* Consult with others as you review the diagnostic information on students. It is quite likely that another person can assist you in obtaining more information from the informal tests.

## Summary

Several informal diagnostic procedures were presented in this chapter. Because of the growing importance of the classroom teacher's role in diagnostic-prescriptive instruction, all of these instruments are designed for use by the classroom teacher. By using these informal procedures to the fullest, teachers will gain specific information about each student in the class.

Attitude and interest surveys are essential in the informal diagnostic process in order to obtain information which assists in encouraging students to read. This data also gives teachers greater insight into the affective aspects of reading instruction. Such information as poor self-images, lack of interest in reading materials, and hostility toward peers may be revealed from these procedures.

Perhaps the most useful informal diagnostic measure is the Informal Reading Inventory (IRI). This instrument was discussed in great detail, with specific directions for construction, administering, scoring, and interpreting included. Suggestions and guidelines were also given for interpreting miscues and their impact on comprehension. Directions for obtaining a listening comprehension score from the IRI were also included.

Another valuable diagnostic procedure is observation. Many important bits of information can be obtained by using the two observational techniques: anecdotal records and a checklist. In using observation for diagnostic purposes, the teacher should be cautious in interpreting the data, since primarily subjective data are produced.

Also discussed were word recognition inventories. These are procedures used to assist in diagnosing word recognition difficulties and to measure the students' knowledge of a specific group of words. The primary method of obtaining this diagnostic information is through the use of word lists. Several word lists were presented, with directions for their appropriate use.

Criterion-referenced and objective-based tests were identified as another informal diagnostic procedure. These tests are designed to measure what a learner knows or can do relative to a specific objective. Such tests are becoming more popular because, unlike standardized tests, they do not measure one student's performance against another's; rather, the students are evaluated with respect to their ability to perform the specific skill being measured.

Two other instruments discussed are designed primarily for use with content area materials. These are the cloze procedure and the Group Reading Inventory (GRI). The cloze procedure is designed as a group test which indicates reading strengths at the independent, instructional, and frustration levels. The GRI is designed to measure the specific reading skills necessary to learn the concepts in a content area lesson. Some miscellaneous sources for obtaining additional diagnostic information were described. These include workbook pages, learning center activities, instructional games, parent conferences, and discussions with the students' other teachers.

Each of the informal diagnostic procedures discussed contributes to a better understanding of the students' capabilities. Used properly, the information obtained facilitates more adequate assessment of the students' strengths and weaknesses, and increases the effectiveness of the diagnostic-prescriptive process.

**Applying What You Read**

Using passages from a basal reading series, follow the steps outlined in this chapter and begin to develop your own informal reading inventory.

Administer an informal reading inventory to five students and identify their areas of strengths and weaknesses.

Using a checklist, observe several students and record your observations. Determine what other informal assessment instruments may be needed to more specifically diagnose their reading problems.

Develop your own interest inventory. Administer this inventory to several of your poor readers. Compare the results with the results from materials already used with these students.

Determine six specific objectives to be attained in your reading program over a specific period of time.

Develop criterion-referenced tests that measure the students' mastery of these objectives.

Make a list of sources of diagnostic data that are currently available in your classroom. How are you using this information?

Use one of the informal reading inventories previously administered and analyze the miscues as described in this chapter.

**Notes**

1. Florence T. Pieronek, "Do Basal Readers Reflect the Interests of Intermediate Students?" *The Reading Teacher.*
2. Loretta Frances Belloni and Eugene A. Jongsma, "The Effects of Interest on Reading Comprehension of Low-Achieving Students," *Journal of Reading.*
3. Kathleen S. Jongsma and Eugene A. Jongsma (Reviewers), "Test Review: Commercial Informal Reading Inventories," *The Reading Teacher.*
4. Earl H. Cheek, *Cheek Master Word List,* pp. 5–18.
5. Susan M. Walker, Ronald G. Noland, and Charles M. Greenshields, "The Effect of High and Low Interest Content on Instructional Levels in Informal Reading Inventories," *Reading Improvement.*
6. William J. Valmont, "Creating Questions for Informal Reading Inventories," *The Reading Teacher;* Marjorie Seddon Johnson and Roy a Kress, *Informal Reading*

*Inventories;* Howard F. Livingston, "Measuring and Teaching Meaning with an Informal Reading Inventory," *Elementary English.*

7. Eldon E. Ekwall, "Informal Reading Inventories: The Instructional Level," *The Reading Teacher.* Eldon Ekwall, "Should Repetitions Be Counted As Errors?" *The Reading Teacher.* Warren S. Hays, "Criteria for the Instructional Level of Reading," 1975, Microfiche ED 117 665. John Pikulski, "A Critical Review: Informal Reading Inventories," *The Reading Teacher.*

8. Maude McBroom, Julia Sparrow, and Catherine Eckstein, *Scale for Determining a Child's Reader Level.*

9. Yetta M. Goodman and Carolyn L. Burke, *Reading Miscue Inventory.*

10. Goodman and Burke, *Reading Miscue Inventory,* pp. 5.

11. Goodman and Burke, *Reading Miscue Inventory,* pp. 6–7.

12. Kenneth S. Goodman, "Miscues: Windows on the Reading Process," in *Miscue Analysis,* edited by Kenneth Goodman, p. 8.

13. Yetta M. Goodman, "Reading Diagnosis—Qualitative or Quantitative?" *The Reading Teacher.*

14. Child Study Committee on the International Kindergarten Union, *A Study of the Vocabulary of Children Before Entering First Grade;* Arthur I. Gates, *A Reading Vocabulary for the Primary Grades;* H. E. Wheeler and Emma A. Howell, "A First Grade Vocabulary Study," *Elementary School Journal.*

15. Dale D. Johnson, "The Dolch List Re-Examined," *The Reading Teacher;* Robert L. Hillerich, "Word Lists: Getting It All Together," *The Reading Teacher.*

16. Henry Kucera and W. Nelson Francis, *Computational Analysis for Present-Day American English.*

17. Johnson, "The Dolch List," pp. 450–51.

18. Albert J. Harris and Milton D. Jacobson, *Basic Elementary Reading Vocabularies;* Stanford, E. Taylor, Helen Frackenpohl, and Catherine White, *A Revised Core Vocabulary: A Basic Vocabulary for Grades 1–8, An Advanced Vocabulary for Grades 9–13;* John B. Carroll, Peter Davies, and Barry Richman, *Word Frequency Book;* Wayne Otto and Robert Chester, "Sight Words for Beginning Readers," *The Journal of Educational Research.*

19. Cheek, *Cheek Master Word List.*

20. Richard L. Slosson, *Slosson Oral Reading Test.*

21. J. F. Jastak; S. W. Bijou, and S. R. Jastak, *Wide Range Achievement Test.*

22. Wayne Otto, "Evaluating Instruments for Assessing Needs and Growth in Reading," *Assessment Problems in Reading,* pp. 17–18.

23. Otto, "Evaluating Instruments," p. 18.

24. Wilson L. Taylor, "Cloze Procedure: A New Tool for Measuring Readability," *Journalism Quarterly.*

25. Eugene R. Jongsma, "The Cloze Procedure: A Survey of the Research."

26. John Bormuth, "The Cloze Readability Procedure," *Elementary English.*

**Other Suggested Readings**

Alexander, J. Estill, and Filler, Ronald Claude. *Attitudes and Reading.* Newark, Delaware: International Reading Association, 1976.

Blanton, William E.; Farr, Roger; and Tuinman, Jaap. eds. *Measuring Reading Performance.* Newark, Delaware: International Reading Association, 1974.

Brecht, Richard D. "Testing Format and Instructional Level with the Reading Inventory." *The Reading Teacher* 31 (October 1977):57–60.

Cheek, Martha Collins, and Cheek, Earl H. "Diagnosis—A Part of Content Area Reading." *Reading Horizons* 19 (Summer 1979):308–13.

Cunningham, James W., and Cunningham, Patricia M. "Validating a Limited—Cloze Procedure." *Journal of Reading Behavior* 10 (Summer 1978):211–13.

Cunningham, James W., and Tierney, Robert J. "Evaluating Cloze as a Measure of Learning from Reading." *Journal of Reading Behavior* 11 (Fall 1979):287–92.

Duzat, Sam V. "Informal Diagnosis: The Nucleus." *Classroom Practice in Reading.* Edited by Richard A. Earle. Newark, Delaware: International Reading Association, 1977.

Ekwall, Eldon E. *Teacher's Handbook on Diagnosis and Remediation in Reading.* Boston: Allyn and Bacon, 1977.

Englert, Carol Sue, and Semmel, Melvyn I. "The Relationship of Oral Reading Substitution Miscues to Comprehension." *The Reading Teacher* 35 (December 1981):273–80.

Estes, Thomas H., and Vaughan Joseph I. "Reading Interest and Comprehension: Implications." *The Reading Teacher* 27 (November 1973):149–53.

Harris, Larry A. and Niles, Jerome A. "An Analysis of Published Informal Reading Inventories." *Reading Horizons* 22 (Spring 1982):159–74.

Heathington, Betty S., and Alexander, J. Estill. "A Child-based Observation Checklist to Assess Attitudes Toward Reading." *The Reading Teacher* 31 (April 1978): 769–71.

Johns, Jerry L. "Initiating Assessment of Student Needs in Content Areas." *Reading Horizons* 18 (Winter 1978):134–36.

Johns, Jerry.; Garton, Sharon; Schoenfelder, Paula; and Skriba, Patricia. *Assessing Reading Behavior: Informal Reading Inventories.* Newark, Delaware: International Reading Association, 1977.

Kaminsky, Sally. "Taking a Closer Look at the Cloze Procedure." *Reading World* 19 (October 1979):12–18.

Kender, Joseph, and Rubenstein, Herbert. "Recall Versus Reinspection in IRI Comprehension Tests." *The Reading Teacher* 30 (April 1977):776–79.

Moray, Geraldine. "What Does Research Say about the Reading Interests of Children in the Intermediate Grades?" *The Reading Teacher* 31 (April 1978):763–68.

Peterson, Joe; Greenlaw, M. Jean; and Tierney, Robert J. "Assessing Instructional Placement with the IRI; The Effectiveness of Comprehension Questions." *Journal of Educational Research* 71 (May/June 1978):247–50.

Pikulski, John P., and Pikulski, Edna C. "Cloze, Maze, and Teacher Judgment." *The Reading Teacher* 30 (April 1977):766–70.

Rakes, Thomas A. "A Group Instructional Inventory." *Journal of Reading* 18 (May 1975):595–98.

Redelheim, Paul S. "A Multidimensional Test of Reading Attitude for Children." *The Reading Teacher* 30 (November 1976):181–86.

Schell, Leo M. and Hanna, Gerald S. "Can Informal Reading Inventories Reveal Strengths and Weaknesses in Comprehension Subskills?" *The Reading Teacher* 35 (December):263–67.

Siegel, Florence. "Adapted Miscue Analysis. "*Reading World* 19 (October 1979):36–43.

Smith, Edwin H.; Guice, Billy M.; and Cheek, Martha C. "Informal Reading Inventories for the Content Areas: Science and Mathematics." *Elementary English* 46 (May 1972):659–66.

Tortelli, James P. "Simplified Psycholinguistic Diagnosis." *The Reading Teacher* 29 (April 1976):637–39.

# 5

The teachers at Seabreeze School defined formal diagnostic procedures as those instruments which are administered using specific guidelines and which provide norms to compare a student's scores with those of other students of the same age or grade level. Like other classroom and content area teachers at the elementary and middle school levels, the teachers at Seabreeze are most familiar with the formal testing procedures associated with administering group achievement tests. Although these are formal testing procedures, unfortunately they usually do not qualify as diagnostic reading tests. This chapter is designed to familiarize the teacher with other formal diagnostic procedures that may be used in conjunction with the informal diagnostic procedures presented in Chapter 4.

At Seabreeze School, the teachers want to use formal diagnostic procedures to explore further students' reading problems in order to provide more appropriate prescriptive instruction. They realize that some formal diagnostic instruments are administered to groups of students, while others must be administered individually. Most of these tests are relatively simple to administer. The teacher needs only to review the materials and administer the instrument several times under the supervision of a trained person prior to using it in the classroom.

This chapter reviews a variety of formal diagnostic procedures, including oral reading tests, diagnostic reading tests, auditory discrimination tests, intelligence tests, and survey reading tests, as well as auditory and visual screening measures which the teachers at Seabreeze examined. Specific questions addressed in the chapter include:

What are formal diagnostic procedures?

Why are formal procedures important in reading diagnosis?

What types of formal diagnostic procedures are available to evaluate reading difficulties?

What are some differences between individually-administered and group-administered formal diagnostic procedures?

How does the teacher select appropriate tests for use with given students?

What are the various individually-administered formal diagnostic instruments? How do they compare?

What are the various group-administered formal diagnostic instruments? How do they compare?

How are the different tests administered?

# What formal diagnostic procedures can the classroom teacher use?

These terms should be noted as this chapter is read.

Formal diagnostic procedures
Group achievement tests
Group administered formal tests
Group diagnostic tests
Group intelligence tests
Group survey tests
Individual auditory and visual
  screening tests
Individual auditory discrimination
  tests
Individual diagnostic reading tests
Individual intelligence tests
Individual oral reading tests
Individually-administered formal
  tests

**An Overview**

Formal diagnostic procedures are the standardized techniques used by teachers and reading specialists to learn more about students' strengths and weaknesses in reading. They are often used to supplement informal procedures. These instruments are important because they are designed to measure specific areas in reading which informal instruments do not measure, or for which only superficial information is provided. Because many of them are so specialized, it may be necessary to administer a battery of several instruments in order to develop the total picture of a poor reader's strengths and weaknesses. However, the classroom teacher usually administers only selected tests to gain more information on a specific problem area identified by informal diagnostic procedures. Thus, large amounts of teacher time are not always necessary for formal diagnostic procedures; they are administered only as the teacher needs more information.

Formal like informal diagnostic procedures, have both advantages and disadvantages. For the teacher, the chief disadvantages may be the time needed for the individually-administered instruments and the acquisition of a sufficient number of copies of a test for use as necessary. To deal with these problems, teachers should (1) use group tests whenever possible and request the assistance of the reading teacher if numerous individual tests are needed, and (2) select initially only one or two formal tests which seem to meet best the general needs of students, then build a test file in the school over several years.

The advantages of formal diagnostic procedures definitely outnumber the disadvantages. Although the time factor for individual testing may be viewed as a disadvantage, the one-to-one testing situation is an advantage in itself, because it allows the teacher to learn more about the student. Additionally, formal diagnostic procedures provide the teacher with a more complete profile of each student, as well as with some comparison of each student with others of a similar age. Although diagnosis is not based on this comparative data, it is sometimes necessary to have this data to communicate better with parents.

The tests presented in this chapter are classified as group or individual tests, with further breakdowns according to types. The tests classified as individual formal diagnostic procedures must be administered to only one student at a time. These often are time consuming and require increased proficiency and experience on the part of the examiner. However, they yield much valuable information and assist in determining more accurately students' strengths and weaknesses.

Group-administered formal tests are just that, tests administered to an entire group. They are useful because they can be used to test large or small groups of students. These tests usually do not yield as much information on the individual student, and the teacher does not obtain helpful information learned in an individual testing situation.

Because of the various factors involved in implementing diagnostic-prescriptive instruction, a concern of the classroom teacher is when to use these formal tools. Practically speaking, using group tests is probably a more realistic objective than using individual tests. As already stated, group tests are relatively easy to administer, since the time involved is minimal and an entire class can be tested at one time. The teacher's schedule can be adjusted to accommodate this type of testing; however, disadvantages such as the lack of specific information and scoring and interpreting test results sometimes dissuade teachers from using these tests as fully as possible.

Individual formal instruments are time consuming, since students must be tested on a one-to-one basis. Many of these instruments require large amounts of time not only for administration, but also for scoring and interpretation. They are best used as supplements to informal measures and formal group measures. However, they play an important role in an in-depth diagnosis of a small number of students in a teacher's classroom.

Because of the constraints associated with individual formal instruments, testing time is more wisely spent using group tests in conjunction with the informal procedures already discussed in chapter 4. Nevertheless, in the case of a severely disabled reader, the teacher may wish to use one or two well-chosen individually-administered instruments. The teacher needs a workable knowledge of these instruments in order better to understand reports from the reading specialist or to request further testing from other outside sources. *Regardless of the pros and cons of using formal diagnostic procedures, teachers must be familiar with them in order to provide better prescriptive reading instruction in their*

*classes.* To assist the teacher in selecting appropriate formal diagnostic procedures, the tests discussed in this chapter are summarized in table 5.1 (group tests)
and table 5.2 (individual tests). Using these tables as references, teachers can
select those testing instruments which best meet their needs at a given time. A
further resource that assists in selecting tests is provided by Mavrogenes, Hanson, and Winkley.[1]

The first section of this chapter deals with those instruments generally referred
to as group-administered tests. There are many types of group tests used for varying purposes; what they have in common is that they all can be administered in
a group situation. The various types include survey reading tests, diagnostic reading tests, achievement tests, and intelligence tests. Each type has a specific purpose, different from the others. The use of each is dependent upon the testing
conditions and information desired. All four types are discussed in this section.

**Group Test
Procedures**

Survey reading tests are widely used to ascertain reading levels. The primary reason for their popularity is the ease in which they are administered by classroom teachers. Moreover, the manuals for these instruments are usually quite clear and concise in describing the appropriate manner for administering, scoring, and interpreting the data. Other reasons for their popularity include the time factor, norms, and test construction. Survey reading tests can be administered and scored in a relatively short period of time, especially as compared to individually administered tests. They are standardized, using national norms, and some, such as the *Gates-MacGinitie Reading Tests,* provide local norms. In most instances these instruments are carefully constructed by persons with expertise in test construction and in the area of reading.

Survey reading tests have disadvantages as well. One disadvantage which is actually a characteristic of a survey test, is the information obtained lacks depth. For example, only two or, at the most, three scores are obtained from these instruments. The scores are in the general areas of vocabulary, comprehension, and (often) rate of reading. They are reported in either grade equivalents, stanines, percentiles, or perhaps all three. Although this is the purpose of a survey instrument, it is also considered a limitation. Even though scores in only these general areas are obtained, one suggestion for turning this disadvantage into an advantage is to analyze each item in the instrument so that more detailed diagnostic information about a student can be obtained.

Another disadvantage of survey reading tests is that the scores obtained are almost always inflated and represent the students' frustration levels; teachers should note that the scores do not indicate the students' instructional or independent levels. However, these scores may represent the most accurate information available, and can be helpful if used as a starting point for diagnosis in conjunction with an informal reading inventory.

The advantages and disadvantages of survey reading tests are presented for review in the belief that teachers must determine whether or not such instruments would be beneficial in their classrooms. One important consideration is that their primary purpose is to serve as a *screening device*. The most appropriate way to use this instrument is to administer it to the entire class, determine grade equivalent scores for each student, make an item analysis to obtain more diagnostic information, set up initial groups using the results of this instrument and any other available information, then begin to administer other diagnostic tests, such as the Informal Reading Inventory, to students about whom more in-depth information is desired. Used in this manner, the survey reading test can provide helpful information.

**Gates-MacGinitie Reading Tests, Second Edition**
Arthur I. Gates and Walter H. MacGinitie
Houghton Mifflin Company, Boston, Massachusetts, 1978 (Grades Readiness-12)

**Table 5.1**

Formal Group Tests

| Test | Appropriate Levels | Subtest Scores |
|---|---|---|
| **Survey Tests** | | |
| *Gates— MacGinitie Reading Tests* | Grades Readiness-12 | Vocabulary, Comprehension, Total |
| *Iowa Silent Reading Test* | Grades 6-12, College | Vocabulary, Comprehension, Directed Reading, Reading Efficiency |
| **Diagnostic Reading Tests** | | |
| *Doren Diagnostic Reading Test of Word Recognition Skills* | Grades 3-4 and Disabled Readers | Twelve subtests of word recognition skills |
| *Stanford Diagnostic Reading Test* | Grades 1.6-13 | Varies with form—Auditory Vocabulary, Phonetic Analysis, Structural Analysis, Comprehension |
| **Achievement Tests** | | |
| *California Achievement Test* | Grades K-12 | Reading, Spelling, Language, Mathematics, Reference Skills |
| *Comprehensive Test of Basic Skills* | Grades 0.1-13.6 | Reading, Language, Arithmetic, Study Skills |
| *Metropolitan Achievement Test* | Grades K-12.9 | Reading Comprehension, Language, Mathematics, Science, Social Studies |
| *Stanford Achievement Test* | Grades 1.5-9 | Reading Comprehension, Language, Mathematics, Science, Social Science, Auditory Skills |
| **Intelligence Tests** | | |
| *California Short-Form Test of Mental Maturity* | Grades K-Adult | I.Q., Mental Age |
| *Otis-Lennon Mental Ability Test* | Grades K.5-12 | I.Q., Mental Age |
| *Short Form of Academic Aptitude* | Grades 1.5-12 | Language and Nonlanguage Capabilities, I.Q. |

The *Gates-MacGinitie Reading Tests* are among the better-known group survey reading test batteries. This instrument was developed in 1965 by Arthur Gates and Walter MacGinitie; however, it was primarily a revision of the *Gates Primary Reading Tests,* the *Gates Advanced Primary Reading Tests,* and the *Gates Reading Survey.* The most recent revision occurred in 1978, with the publication of the second edition. Approximately five years were devoted to its development, and there are some obvious changes that strengthen the overall battery.

The battery continues to use the booklet format, which facilitates test administration and hand-scoring. One of the main advantages of this instrument is that a classroom teacher can administer the instrument one day, hand-score the booklets, and have the grade equivalents, stanines, or percentiles available for use the next day.

Another useful feature of the second edition is that the test materials are almost totally new and relate to current experiential patterns of students. This edition was also field-tested with students of various socio-economic and racial backgrounds in order to develop items that decrease cultural bias in the instrument. As a result, new national norms were developed.

One of the major revisions of the second edition concerns the first-grade test. In an effort to strengthen this level, a wide range of reading skills, from pre-reading to beyond first grade, were used. Other levels have also been strengthened by the addition of more interesting comprehension passages which correspond more closely in difficulty and suitability of the material to the specified grade level.

One criticism of the first edition was its cumbersome scoring key. The second edition uses newly designed scoring keys, or self-scoreable answer sheets, which enable the teacher to score the booklets much faster. Another interesting service provided by the publisher is the machine-scored profile sheet, which not only reports the testing data, but also includes a brief diagnostic evaluation of the student. For those school systems which send in their tests for scoring, this is an added advantage.

There are seven levels of the *Gates-MacGinitie Reading Tests* available for use by school systems, all of which have at least two test forms at each level. Each level provides three scores: vocabulary, comprehension, and a total reading score. The levels are divided as follows:

Basic R, Grade 1
Level A, Grade 1
Level B, Grade 2
Level C, Grade 3
Level D, Grades 4, 5, and 6
Level E, Grades 7, 8, and 9
Level F, Grades 10, 11, and 12[2]

This test has been widely used as a screening device in reading, and has proven to be a valuable instrument for use with groups of students.

## Iowa Silent Reading Test (ISRT)
Roger Farr, Coordinating Editor
The Psychological Corporation, New York, New York, 1973 (Grades 6–12, College)

This test battery was originally published in 1927 and included grades 4–8 in the elementary section, and grades 9–14 in the advanced section. The latest revision, published in 1973, has three levels: Level 1, Grades 6–9; Level 2, Grades 9-Community College, and Level 3, above-average readers in the eleventh and twelfth grades. Since the focus of this book is on elementary and middle school students, Level 1 is the primary level of interest, Levels 2 and 3 are mentioned only for informational purposes.

Several areas are tested on the ISRT: vocabulary, reading comprehension, directed reading, and reading efficiency. The principal difference in the 1973 ISRT and its predecessors is the way in which reading skills are assessed. These skills are evaluated through the use of various types of reading material rather than only the basic textbook. Testing for literal information has been minimized, and more stress has been placed on applying skills and knowledge.

For example, in the vocabulary section of Level 1, Grades 6–9, word knowledge is measured with words which are carefully selected as to level of difficulty and frequency of use. Another feature in the Comprehension section of Level 1 is the use of high-interest materials emphasizing various reading styles and content. Inferential comprehension is tested in conjunction with literal meaning. In the Directed Reading section of Level 1, also referred to as work-study skills, proficiency in the use of the dictionary is tested, using imaginary words that follow phonemic principles. Library skills and knowledge of other sources of information are also tested. The skills of skimming and scanning are assessed, using materials from encyclopedias. The final area measured in Level 1 is Reading Efficiency, also referred to as rate with comprehension. This test is designed to indicate a student's speed and accuracy, using a modified cloze item procedure.

An interesting addition to this revised version is a separate "Guide for Interpretation and Use." It is designed to inform the instructor of the rationale for the ISRT and to assist in the interpretation of the test data.[3] The ISRT is another screening instrument for teachers at the middle school levels and above. Remember, however, that these instruments should be evaluated by the teacher in relation to the objectives of their school reading program.

## Diagnostic Reading Tests

Group diagnostic reading tests are used quite extensively in school systems throughout the country. They have a valuable role in assisting teachers in gathering rapidly diagnostic information about their students. Their popularity is further enhanced because they are easy to administer.

Other factors that contribute to their success are such features as the manual, the time factor, and the norms. The manuals which accompany these instruments are easily understood and facilitate the successful administration, scoring, and interpretation of the tests. For example, the manual that accompanies the *Stanford Diagnostic Reading Test* is extremely thorough and quite detailed. The time required for administering these instruments is relatively brief compared to that required for individually-administered instruments. A classroom teacher's time is so valuable that rapidity is imperative in reviewing diagnostic instruments. Of equal importance are the norm factors. These instruments are standardized, using national norms, and therefore they allow school systems to compare their school population with others, if they wish.

The primary advantage of the group diagnostic reading test is that a great deal of information is obtained during a relatively brief expenditure of time. In contrast to group survey reading tests, which yield only vocabulary, comprehension, and rate-of-reading scores, group diagnostic reading tests furnish much more in-depth information. They provide several subtest scores which aid in ascertaining areas of strengths and weaknesses. For example, the *Stanford Diagnostic Reading Test* yields scores in several areas, including structural analysis, auditory discrimination, auditory vocabulary, and literal and inferential comprehension. The basic difference between the two types of instruments, other than subtest information, is the time and expense involved. Usually, group survey reading tests require less time than group diagnostic reading tests, and are less expensive.

This type of instrument also has disadvantages. The primary disadvantage of group diagnostic tests is the lack of teacher-student interaction during the testing situation. Teachers obtain much diagnostic data when they observe individual students while diagnostic tests are administered. This individual observation and interaction of course, is not possible when tests are group administered. Other disadvantages of the various tests are explored in the discussions in the following pages. Teachers should note, however, that the primary objective of the group diagnostic reading test is to provide as much in-depth information in as short a period of time as possible.

**Doren Diagnostic Reading Test of Word Recognition Skills**
Margaret Doren
American Guidance Service, Inc., Circle Pines, Minnesota, 1973 (Grades 3–4 and Disabled Readers)

This test was first published in 1956 by Margaret Doren and was revised in 1973. It is designed to provide in-depth measurement of word recognition skills. There are twelve subtests measuring several skill areas:

Skill 1—Letter Recognition
Skill 2—Beginning Sounds
Skill 3—Whole Word Recognition
Skill 4—Words within Words
Skill 5—Speech Consonants
Skill 6—Ending Sounds
Skill 7—Blending
Skill 8—Rhyming
Skill 9—Vowels
Skill 10—Discriminate Guessing
Skill 11—Spelling
Skill 12—Sight Words

The primary purpose of the *Doren* test is to assist in diagnosing strengths and weaknesses in the various word recognition areas. In contrast to most group diagnostic instruments, this test does not yield scores in terms of grade equivalents, stanines, or percentiles. Instead, scores are determined by the use of the Individual Score Sheet and the Individual Skill Profile. Scores that fall below a specified level into the shaded area on the Individual Skill Profile are indicators of weakness in those skill areas.

Another unusual feature of the *Doren* test is that there is no specified time for completing the test; students are given as much time as necessary. It is suggested, however, that if a few slower students delay the majority, they should be allowed to finish later.[4]

This instrument exhibits strengths in the following areas:

Teacher testing time: because the instrument is a group test, the time required to administer it is minimal.

Administration: the instrument can be easily administered by classroom teachers.

Interpretation: the manual provides a relatively comprehensive interpretive section.

The limitations of the *Doren* are restricted primarily to two areas:

A low interest level, which would hinder its use with older disabled readers.

The absence of a comprehension section. Although this is a test of word recognition ability, the addition of a comprehension section would enhance its usefulness.

After a careful examination of the *Doren* test, the teacher should find that it evaluates thoroughly each student's word recognition skills and is an adequate group diagnostic tool for classroom use.

### Stanford Diagnostic Reading Test (SDRT)
Bjorn Karlsen, Richard Madden, and Eric F. Gardner
The Psychological Corporation, New York, New York, 1976 (Grades 1.6–13)

The *SDRT* is one of the more widely used group diagnostic reading tests. This instrument was first published in 1966. In 1974, Level III for grades 10–12 was added. The latest revision was published in 1976, and the original levels were replaced by four new levels. These are Red Level (Grades 1.6–3.5), Green Level (Grades 2.6–5.5), Brown Level (Grades 4.6–9.5), and Blue Level (Grades 9–13). Each level has two forms (A and B), thus facilitating its use in a pre- and post-test situation, if desired. The areas measured on each level are:

*Red Level:* Auditory vocabulary, auditory discrimination, phonetic analysis, word reading (word recognition), and comprehension.

*Green Level:* Auditory vocabulary, auditory discrimination, phonetic analysis, structural analysis, and literal and inferential comprehension.

*Brown Level:* Auditory vocabulary, literal and inferential comprehension, phonetic analysis, structural analysis, and reading rate.

*Blue Level:* Literal and inferential comprehension, word meaning, word parts, phonetic analysis, structural analysis, scanning and skimming, and fast reading.

The primary purpose of the *SDRT* is to assist in diagnosing strengths and weaknesses. Scores are reported in stanines, percentiles, and grade equivalents. By using the student profile sheet, the teacher is able to discern immediately the areas in which each student exhibits strengths or weaknesses in reading.[5]

One of the definite strengths of the revised edition of the *SDRT* is the excellent manual which has been developed. The manual for the 1966 edition was adequate, but the manual for the 1976 edition is outstanding. For example, the Red Level manual has ninety-five pages with detailed information for administering the test, scoring, interpreting the results, and using the student profile. The section on interpreting the data is one of its best features.

Another outstanding strength of the *SDRT* concerns the distribution of the items in the curve. There is a greater concentration of scores in the lower end of the distribution, which increases its reliability. This instrument is directed toward poor readers so as to make possible a closer examination of their reading abilities. With this objective in mind, some items were designed to improve the poor readers' chances of answering them, thereby creating a concentration of scores at the lower end of the distribution.

Other strengths of the *SDRT* include such factors as teacher time, administration and interpretation, silent reading as well as auditory subtests, and ideas for prescription development. Since the *SDRT* is a group instrument, it does not require a great deal of the teacher's time. It can be administered in a total of about two hours, and generates much useful information in this relatively brief period. Like other group diagnostic tests, the *SDRT* does not require the classroom teacher to be a testing specialist in order to administer and interpret it. The directions in the manual are quite clear and specific as to proper administration, and the interpretive section of the manual, as already mentioned, is excellent.

The *SDRT* contains a good mixture of listening and silent reading subtests, allowing students to demonstrate their capabilities either through auditory or visual modes. A final strength of this test involves the development of prescriptions: the information provided greatly facilitates the preparation of instructional strategies.

Some limitations of the *SDRT* are that it is not designed for severly disabled readers, and it does not measure students in beginning first grade. However, the majority of the students in a classroom can be adequately diagnosed by this instrument.

This test is obviously well suited for use by the classroom teacher and is an excellent group diagnostic tool for obtaining initial diagnostic information.

## Achievement Tests

Achievement tests are designed to measure the depth of a student's knowledge of various broad areas of the curriculum, the extent to which specific information has been acquired, or the extent to which certain skills have been mastered. These tests are intended to determine whether specific instruction regarding the broad areas of the curriculum has been effective.

Achievement tests are rigidly standardized, using norms developed from a large sampling of the appropriate school-age population. They are group administered instruments which survey several curriculum areas taught in the schools. The information elicited is similar to that obtained from survey reading tests, in that it is not in-depth diagnostic information. By their very nature, achievement tests are not designed to be diagnostic instruments. They provide information that is general rather than specific. Scores are reported in grade equivalents, stanines, or percentiles.

The majority of achievement tests measure basically the same curriculum areas: language, mathematics, reading, science, and social studies. School systems are anxious to determine how effective their instruction is and to test as many areas of instruction as possible; it appears that achievement tests are the least expensive manner of obtaining this broad range of information. Thus, they account for a large percentage of the standardized instruments used in the school systems.

Five of the more widely used achievement tests and their subtest areas are outlined below.

**California Achievement Test**
CTB/McGraw Hill, Monterey, California, 1977, 1978
(Grades K–12)

Measures reading, spelling, language, mathematics, and reference skills.

**Comprehensive Test of Basic Skills**
CTB/McGraw Hill, Monterey, California, 1973, 1974, 1977 (Readiness), 1981
Grades 0.1–12.9)

Measures reading, language, mathematics, reference skills, science and social studies. Readiness measures letter names, letter forms, listening, sounds, visual discrimination, and sound matching.

**Metropolitan Achievement Test**
The Psychological Corporation, New York, New York, 1977, 1978
(Grades K–12.9)

Measures reading comprehension, mathematics, and language.

**SRA Achievement Series**
Science Research Associates, Chicago, Illinois, 1978
(Grades K–12)

Measures reading, mathematics, language arts, reference materials, social studies, and science.

**Stanford Achievement Test**
The Psychological Corporation, New York, New York, 1973
(Grades 1.5–9)

Measures reading comprehension, language skills, mathematics skills, science, social science, and auditory skills.

All types of instruments have strengths and limitations, and achievement tests are no exception. Some of these are listed below.

*Strengths*

School systems receive information covering a wide range of curriculum areas.
Classroom teachers can easily administer these tests.
Strict norming procedures are followed.
The data can assist in evaluating students' progress over a period of time.
Some tests provide criterion-referenced test data on specific reading skills.

*Limitations*

Lack of depth in information necessitates an item analysis to ascertain any diagnostic data.
Scores received are on the students' frustration level.
Improper administration procedures, such as massing large groups of students together in the cafeteria or auditorium, may occur; these circumstances often result in fallacious data.
Requires the use of silent reading skills, thus reflecting, in many instances, a reading problem rather than knowledge of the material being tested.
Occasionally, test results are not promptly returned to classroom teachers.
Local norms may not be available.

With proper use under appropriate conditions, and with recognition of their strengths and limitations, achievement tests can fulfill a useful role as broad group survey instruments providing valuable assistance to school districts in evaluating their total curriculum. If the criterion-referenced test data is available and requested by the school district, achievement tests can provide some individual diagnostic data on students' strengths and weaknesses in specific skills.

Intelligence tests are designed as predictive instruments. Their purpose is to predict the level of proficiency that might be anticipated from a student's performance of a specific activity. These instruments measure not only past learning, but also learning that is unexpected or unplanned. Intelligence tests are often referred to as aptitude tests, since they are concerned with measuring a student's potential for acquiring additional information resulting in a higher level of performance, assuming that additional educational opportunities are provided.

Intelligence tests, like achievement tests, adhere to strict standardization procedures, using a large number of students from various regions of the country to develop national norms, and thus enhancing the usability of the instruments. These tests are designed for administration either on an individual or group basis. Only group intelligence tests are discussed here, since individually-administered instruments are described in another section of this chapter. These group-administered instruments reflect an effort to obtain a rather general evaluation of a student's aptitude, furnishing information in such areas as verbal concepts, mathematical capabilities and following directions. Scores are provided in terms of stanines, percentiles, and standard scores, with the batteries providing an I.Q. and indicating mental age.

Since school systems are interested in the information provided by intelligence tests, several publishing companies provide these instruments, in conjunction with achievement tests. Two examples of tests that are so grouped are the *California Achievement Test* and the *California Short-Form Test of Mental Maturity* as well as the *Stanford Achievement Test* and the *Otis-Lennon Mental Ability Test*.

Three of the more widely used intelligence tests with a listing of the areas measured are given below.

**California Short-Form Test of Mental Maturity**
CTB/McGraw Hill, Monterey, California, 1963
(Grades K–Adult)

Measures logical reasoning, numerical reasoning, verbal concepts, and memory.

**Otis-Lennon Mental Ability Test**
The Psychological Corporation, New York, New York, 1979
(Grades K.5–12)

Measures the ability to classify through the use of pictures and geometrical designs, following directions, and using quantitative reasoning, verbal concepts, and analogies.

**Short Form Test of Academic Aptitude**
CTB/McGraw Hill, Monterey, California, 1970
(Grades 1.5–12)

Measures vocabulary, analogies, sequences, and memory. An unique feature of this instrument is the use of the Reference Scale Score, which examines students' mental growth and evaluates their language and nonlanguage capabilities. This is used in lieu of an I.Q.; however, I.Q. scores are available if school systems request them.

Group intelligence tests probably generate more debate concerning their usefulness than any other type of instrument. Certainly there are strengths and limitations inherent in these instruments; some of these are listed below.

*Strengths*

School systems receive information evaluating their students' aptitude for achievement.
Classroom teachers can administer these instruments.
Strict norming procedures are followed.

*Limitations*

Many items in these tests are culturally biased.
The tests lack a performance factor.
When reading is required, the score obtained reflects a lack of reading ability rather than aptitude.
As with achievement tests, improper administration procedures, such as massing large groups of students together in the cafeteria or auditorium, may occur, and these conditions often cause fallacious data to be obtained.
A poor score may adversely affect the teacher's attitude toward a student.

Despite attempts by many educators to de-emphasize group intelligence tests, many school systems regard this information as an integral component of the evaluation process. Under optimum testing conditions, these scores may be helpful in evaluating a student's performance. Unfortunately, such optimum conditions rarely exist. More often, the information gained from group intelligence tests is not a fair evaluation of a student's ability. Thus, information gained from group intelligence tests should be carefully evaluated from the standpoint of a student's cultural and socio-economic background, experiential history, reading proficiency, and other variables that can affect the results of the testing.

## Individual Test Procedures

Different types of individually-administered instruments are discussed in the following section of this chapter. These tests are categorized as oral reading tests, diagnostic reading tests, auditory discrimination tests, auditory and visual screening tests, and intelligence tests.

Each category is treated in detail, and the various instruments are listed and described. An attempt is made to discuss instruments most useful to the classroom teacher. Tests were chosen according to what the authors believe to be the frequency of their use, though conceding that some outstanding instruments may be omitted.

## Oral Reading Tests

In the nineteenth century, oral reading was the most important aspect of this reading. Proper enunciation and pronunciation of words were the mark of an educated person. Students were taught to read through emphasis on oral activities; school stressed such activities as round-robin oral reading and choral reading. It was assumed that a person with good oral skills likewise possessed good

**Table 5.2**
Formal Individual Tests

| Test | Appropriate Levels | Subtest Scores |
|---|---|---|
| **Oral Reading** | | |
| *Gilmore Oral Reading Test* | Grades 1–8 | Accuracy, Comprehension, Rate |
| *Gray Oral Reading Test* | Grades 1–16 and adults | Total |
| *Slosson Oral Reading Test* | Grades 1–8 and High School | Reading Level |
| **Diagnostic Reading** | | |
| *Botel Reading Inventory* | Grades 1–12, Reading Levels 1–4 | Word Recognition, Word Comprehension, Phonics, Potential Level |
| *Diagnostic Reading Scales* | Grades 1–6 | Independent, Instruction, Frustration Levels, Eight Phonic Tests |
| *Durrell Analysis of Reading Difficulty* | Grades 1–6 | Oral Reading, Silent Reading, Listening, Flash Words, Word Analysis, Spelling, Handwriting, Visual Memory, Hearing Sounds |
| *Gates-McKillop-Horowitz Reading Diagnostic Tests* | Grades 1–6 | Oral Reading, Words—Flash, Words—Untimed, Phrases—Flash, Knowledge of Word Parts, Visual Form of Sounds, Auditory Blending, Four Supplementary Tests |
| Sipay Word Analysis Test | Grades 2–12 | Sixteen Tests of Word Analysis Skills |
| *Woodcock Reading Mastery Tests* | Grades K–12 | Letter Identification, Word Identification, Word Attack, Word Comprehension, Passage Comprehension, Total |
| **Auditory Discrimination** | | |
| *Wepman Auditory Discrimination* | Ages 5–8 | Satisfactory/Unsatisfactory |
| **Auditory and Visual Screening** | | |
| *Audiometer* | All ages | Auditory Acuity |
| *Telebinocular* | All ages | Visual Acuity |
| *Ortho-Rater* | All ages | Visual Acuity |
| **Intelligence** | | |
| *Peabody Picture VocabularyTest* | Ages 2.6 to 18 | I.Q., Mental Age |
| *Slosson Inteligence Test* | Ages 4 and above | I.Q., Mental Age |

silent reading skills; this assumed correlation between oral and silent reading went virtually unchallenged for many years. Recently, however, there has been growing concern about the emphasis on oral reading; this has resulted in less stress on oral exercises and more emphasis on silent reading.

In the early 1900's the ideas of Parker and Huey began to influence reading instruction.[6] Huey suggested that reading in daily life was done silently, while students were taught oral reading at school. Parker considered oral reading, like speech, to be a means of expression, while silent reading was a matter of attending to the printed material. These comments prompted research into the areas of oral versus silent reading. The results suggested the superiority of silent over oral reading, and led to changes in testing procedures. Some felt so strongly about the importance of silent reading that they urged that oral reading not be taught.[7] The debate has continued; most teachers now realize that both oral and silent reading must be taught, and that oral reading is an excellent means of diagnosing a student's word recognition difficulties.

In administering oral reading tests, the teacher asks the student to read aloud, then marks the errors made, carefully noting such difficulties as mispronunciations, omissions, repetitions, substitutions, unknown words, and sometimes hesitations. Comprehension questions are asked in order to measure the student's understanding of material when reading orally. With this information the teacher can assist in correcting many reading difficulties. Each oral reading test has its own marking and scoring procedures which the instructor should review. The marking system is usually similar to that presented in the discussion of Informal Reading Inventories in chapter 4.

The three oral reading tests to be discussed in this section are the *Gilmore Oral Reading Test, Gray Oral Reading Test,* and *Slosson Oral Reading Test.*

### Gilmore Oral Reading Test
John V. Gilmore and Eunice C. Gilmore
The Psychological Corporation, New York, New York, 1968
(Grades 1–8)

The *Gilmore Oral Reading Test* (see figure 5.1) consists of ten paragraphs in each of the two forms, Forms C and D. These paragraphs progress from first-grade level to eighth-grade level, with one paragraph per level. Five comprehension questions follow each paragraph. The manual suggests that approximately fifteen to twenty minutes per student are necessary for administration.

In administering the test the teacher must record the errors made in reading the paragraph, the time required for reading each paragraph, and the responses to the comprehension questions. This information is recorded on an individual record blank used for each student. Eight types of oral reading errors are noted: substitutions, mispronunciations, words pronounced by the examiner, disregard of punctuation, insertions, hesitations, repetitions, and omissions.

FORM C-6

Mary and Dick's father supervises the repair department of a large garage. He is also a trained mechanic specializing in the electrical system of the car. Father, who enjoys his job, has frequently taken Mary and Dick to the garage on Saturday mornings. During these visits he has taught them much about the construction of automobiles. Thus he is preparing his son and daughter for the time when they will possess drivers' licenses. Father wisely insists that familiarity with the basic mechanism of an automobile is absolutely essential for a person who wishes to develop into an intelligent driver. Dick hopes that he, too, will be able to work on automobiles after he has completed high school.

TIME_____Seconds

1. Where does Father work?
2. In what part of the automobile is Father a specialist?
3. When did the children learn about the construction of an automobile?
4. Why does Father insist upon familiarity with a car's mechanism?
____ 5. What does Dick want to do in the future?

| ERROR RECORD | Number |
|---|---|
| Substitutions | |
| Mispronunciations | |
| Words pronounced by examiner | |
| Disregard of punctuation | |
| Insertions | |
| Hesitations | |
| Repetitions | |
| Omissions | |
| Total Errors | |

Using the explicit directions provided in the manual, the teacher can administer and score this test with little difficulty. The test, which is timed, provides an accuracy score, a comprehension score, and a rate score. The raw scores measuring accuracy and comprehension can be converted to stanines, grade equivalents, and a general rating. The rate score has only a general rating.[8]

Readability studies indicate that the accuracy scores are satisfactory; however, the comprehension and rate scores fall below accepted standards. Additionally, the comprehension score is based primarily on short-term recall and is not the kind of comprehension measured by most silent reading tests. The content seems most suitable for the nondisadvantaged student.[9]

This oral reading test, like the *Gray Oral Reading Test,* is considered to be among the better measures of oral reading accuracy. For further reviews of this test, see Oscar K. Buros, *Reading Tests and Reviews.*

## Gray Oral Reading Test

William S. Gray, edited by Helen M. Robinson
The Psychological Corporation, New York, New York, 1967
(Grades 1–16 and Adults)

The *Gray Oral Reading Test* is a major revision of the *Standardized Oral Reading Paragraphs* first published by William S. Gray in 1915. The principal purposes of this test are to assess oral reading and to assist in diagnosing reading problems. This revised test has four equivalent forms with thirteen passages in each form, ranging in levels of difficulty from first grade to college.

Errors on the *Gray Oral Reading Test* are specified in eight areas: aid, gross mispronunciation, partial mispronunciation, omission, insertion, substitution, repetition, and inverting word order (see figure 5.2). The test is timed, and a score is obtained for each passage, based on the time required for reading and the number of errors made. Following the reading of a passage, four literal comprehension questions are asked. No norms are provided for the comprehension questions.[10]

> Harris states that
> The content of the passages is varied, and in general the style of writing is appropriate. Difficulty ascends regularly and in fairly even steps. The length of the passages is quite similar, except at first-grade level. The four forms seem quite equivalent in content as well as in form, although small differences in difficulty are reported.[11]

Specific procedures for administering and scoring this test are provided in the manual, which is quite adequate. For further information on this test, one should read the reviews provided in Buros, *Reading Tests and Reviews.*

**Figure 5.2**

Summary Sheet for
*Gray Oral Reading Test*
From the Examiner's
Record Booklet of the
*Gray Oral Reading Test,*
*Form A*, copyright © 1963,
The Bobbs-Merrill Co., Inc.
Reprinted with permission.

EXAMINER'S RECORD BOOKLET

for the

GRAY ORAL READING TEST

FORM A

Name_____ Grade_____ Age_____

School_____ Teacher_____ Sex_____

City_____ State_____

Examiner_____ Date_____

## SUMMARY

| Passage Number | No. of Errors | Time (in Seconds) | Passage Scores | Comprehension |
|---|---|---|---|---|
| 1. | | | | |
| 2. | | | | |
| 3. | | | | |
| 4. | | | | |
| 5. | | | | |
| 6. | | | | |
| 7. | | | | |
| 8. | | | | |
| 9. | | | | |
| 10. | | | | |
| 11. | | | | |
| 12. | | | | |
| 13. | | | | |
| Total Passage Scores | | | | |
| Grade Equivalent | | | | |

## TYPES OF ERRORS

| | | |
|---|---|---|
| 1. | Aid | |
| 2. | Gross Mispronunciation | |
| 3. | Partial Mispronunciation | |
| 4. | Omission | |
| 5. | Insertion | |
| 6. | Substitution | |
| 7. | Repetition | |
| 8. | Inversion | |

### OBSERVATIONS
*(Check statement and circle each part)*

_____ Word-by-word reading
_____ Poor phrasing
_____ Lack of expression
_____ Monotonous tone
_____ Pitch too high or low; voice too loud,
            too soft, or strained
_____ Poor enunciation
_____ Disregard of punctuation
_____ Overuse of phonics
_____ Little or no method of word analysis
_____ Unawareness of errors
_____ Head movement
_____ Finger pointing
_____ Loss of place

COMMENTS:_____

_____

_____

_____

THE **BOBBS-MERRILL** COMPANY, INC.
A SUBSIDIARY OF HOWARD W. SAMS & CO., INC.
Publishers · INDIANAPOLIS · NEW YORK

Copyright © 1963, The Bobbs-Merrill Co., Inc. Indianapolis 6, Indiana

**Slosson Oral Reading Test (SORT)**
Richard L. Slosson
Slosson Educational Publications, Inc., East Aurora, New York, 1981
(Grades 1–8 and high school)

The *Slosson Oral Reading Test* "is based on the ability to pronounce words at different levels of difficulty. The words have been taken from standardized school readers and the Reading Level obtained from testing median or standardized school achievement."[12] Advertisements and accompanying materials which come in the kit of materials containing the SORT and the *Slosson Intelligence Test* (SIT), discussed in another section of this Chapter, indicate that a second edition of the tests were published in 1981. However, careful review of the *SORT* indicates no changes in the words with the test sheet still bearing a 1963 copyright date.

This oral reading test consists of ten lists of twenty words each and measures only word pronunciation in isolation. It makes no attempt to ascertain comprehension of oral reading. The test is not timed, except that hesitation on a word for more than five seconds counts as an error. The test should take from three to five minutes to administer. The student's raw score, or total number of words correct, can be converted to a Reading Level using the tables provided.

In a review of the *SORT,* Spache suggests the following:

1. The *SORT* is primarily a measure of sight word vocabulary.
2. The lack of a pronunciation key leaves the decision of correctness to the teacher. The author considers dialectical pronunciations as errors.
3. The meaningfulness of a score from a word-calling test such as *SORT* is questionable in determining a student's reading ability above the primary grades.
4. The test was compared only with the *Gray Oral Reading Test,* which also has no measure of comprehension. Thus, the test was not validated with any test that measures comprehension in determining reading ability.
5. No information regarding the population involved in the standardization of this test has been provided.
6. The reliability seems to be inflated.[13]

If the teacher selects the *SORT* as a diagnostic tool, it should be viewed as a test of word recognition techniques rather than an oral reading test. Thus, the teacher should note the mispronunciations made by the student, as well as the types of word analysis skills employed in attempting an unknown word.

**Diagnostic Reading Tests**

Standardized diagnostic reading tests are designed to provide in-depth analysis of reading difficulties. The individual diagnostic reading tests discussed in this section provide the most thorough diagnosis of reading problems. These tests are used with students who exhibit more severe reading difficulties on informal or group tests or for whom the teacher desires more detailed information.

The individual standardized diagnostic tests are time consuming to use with a large number of students; however, the teacher can use these instruments with selected students, as needed. These tests have various subtests, which assist the teacher in identifying precisely individual reading problems.

In this section, six individual diagnostic reading tests are discussed. There are many more such tests; however, these were selected because they seem to be those most commonly used. For a complete listing of the individual diagnostic reading tests, see Buros, *Reading Tests and Reviews.*[14]

The following tests are presented in this section:

*Botel Reading Inventory*
*Diagnostic Reading Scales*
*Durrell Analysis of Reading Difficulty*
*Gates-McKillop-Horowitz Reading Diagnostic Tests*
*Sipay Word Analysis Test (SWAT)*
*Woodcock Reading Mastery Tests (WRMT)*

**Botel Reading Inventory**
Morton Botel
Follett Publishing Company, Chicago, Illinois, 1978
(Grades 1–12; Reading Levels 1–4)

The *Botel Reading Inventory* is considered by some to be a diagnostic reading test and by others to be an informal reading inventory. This distinction is made because of the lack of information as to the reliability or validity of the instrument. The authors recognize this limitation; however, the instrument is categorized in this book as a diagnostic reading test because of its various subtests, which provide more specific data on word identification than does the typical informal inventory. Parts of the instrument are administered individually and other parts in a group situation.

The inventory consists of two batteries, A and B, each having the following subtests: Word Recognition Test, Word Opposites Test (Reading), Word Opposites Test (Listening), and Phonemic Inventory Test. In the 1978 revision, the Phonemic Inventory Test, Battery A and Battery B, are packaged together. The administration manual is an essential component for the proper use of this instrument.

The Word Recognition Test contains twenty words at each reading level, pre-primer through fourth grade. The student reads the lists, beginning with one on which 100 percent accuracy should be attained, and continuing until accuracy falls below 70 percent on two successive levels.

The Word Opposites Test (Reading) is administered to learn more about the student's word comprehension. Words at levels from first grade through senior high school are used with ten multiple choice items at each level. This test is also

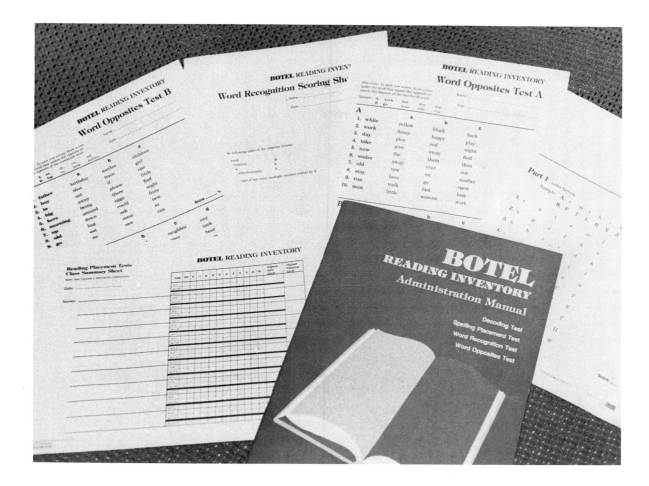

used with a separate response sheet for the Word Opposites Test (Listening), which is to measure reading potential.

The Phonemic Inventory Test assesses knowledge of initial consonant sounds, consonant blends, consonant digraphs, rhyming words, long and short vowel sounds, double vowels, vowels plus *r,* syllabication, and accent. For students at the fourth-grade level or above, a test of nonsense words is given. If the student is successful in pronouncing these words, the other phonics tests are not given.[15]

Teachers may use this test in conjunction with other measures to gain more information about students' word recognition skills. However, the instructor must recognize that little data are provided as to the reliability and validity of the instrument, a condition which leaves it open to much debate and criticism.

### Diagnostic Reading Scales
George D. Spache
CTB/McGraw Hill, Inc., Monterey, California, 1981
(Grades 1–6 and disabled readers in grades 7–12)

The *Diagnostic Reading Scales* consist of a series of tests designed to analyze oral and silent reading skills as well as auditory comprehension. The testing materials include an examiner's manual, an examiner's record book, and a student's reading book. The examiner's record book is expendable. This test was revised in 1981. The purpose of this revision was

> . . . to update, expand, and facilitate use of the test. The major thrust of the revision centered around reassigning grade levels to the reading selections. The new level assignments were based on analyses of revised readability formulas and results from the national study for the revision of the *DRS*.[16]

Additionally, the word analysis and phonics tests were revised and expanded with nonsense words used instead of isolated letters and their sounds. The manual for the examiner was revised and a cassette provided to aid in training in the use of the *DRS*.

The test book contains three word-recognition lists, two sets of eleven graded reading passages, and twelve supplementary word-analysis and phonics tests. The word recognition lists form the first part of the test battery. These lists have three basic purposes:

To function as a pretest, indicating the entry level for testing in the reading selections
To reveal the student's methods of decoding words in isolation
To evaluate the student's sight-word vocabulary

Using the level from the word recognition list, the teacher selects a passage to be read orally. The passages range in difficulty from a grade placement of 1.4 to 2.5, and there are two passages at each level. The student's oral reading performance is evaluated according to word recognition and comprehension errors. The specific number of errors allowed is indicated for each paragraph. As the student reads, the teacher marks the following errors: omissions, additions, substitutions or mispronunciations, repetitions (two or more words), and reversals.

Hesitations and self-corrections are not counted as errors. Words are not pronounced for the student. When the student fails, either in word recognition or comprehension, the oral reading should stop. Spache considers the Instructional Level a measure of oral reading and comprehension and is usually one level below the point of failure in the oral reading selections.

Once the Instructional Level is determined, the student's Independent Level is ascertained by means of silent reading. Spache contends that "the majority of children can read silently with adequate comprehension at levels above the Instruction Level.[17] Thus, the student reads silently until more than the allowed number of comprehension questions are missed. The Independent Level is the final level at which the student shows the minimal level of comprehension.

The reading passages are also used to determine the student's Potential Level, or the level at which the student can listen and respond satisfactorily to questions. The Potential Level is determined by reading the next passage above the Independent Level to the student and then asking questions. The Potential Level is the last level at which the student gives the appropriate number of correct responses.

Following the use of the reading passages, the twelve supplementary word analysis and phonics tests are administered. The content of the tests are

1. Initial Consonants
2. Final Consonants
3. Consonant Digraphs
4. Consonant Blends
5. Initial Consonant Substitution
6. Initial Consonant Sounds Recognized Auditorily
7. Auditory Discriminations
8. Short and Long Vowel Sounds
9. Vowels with r
10. Vowel Diphthongs and Digraphs
11. Common Syllables or Phonograms
12. Blending[18]

The revised edition of the *Diagnostic Reading Scales* has been subjected to little critical review as to its quality. Questions regarding the reliability and validity of the test were addressed by Spache in the *Technical Bulletin,*[19] with other comments in *Diagnosing and Correcting Reading Disabilities.*[20]

The main caution concerning this instrument is that it uses the terms Instructional and Independent Levels in a way which is different from their customary use in the Informal Reading Inventory. The authors remind teachers to be cognizant of the difference in terminology, and to avoid using the terms to mean the same as in other instruments. Perhaps it would be easier to note the levels as Oral Reading Level and Silent Reading Level in order to avoid confusion.

This test is useful for the classroom teacher or the reading clinician at the elementary and middle school levels. The detailed information provided can be used with data from other instruments to obtain an in-depth profile of the reader.

### Durrell Analysis of Reading Difficulty, 3rd edition
Donald D. Durrell and Jane H. Catterson
The Psychological Corporation, New York, New York, 1980
(Grades K–6)

The *Durrell Analysis of Reading Difficulty* is a series of tests and situations in which the various aspects of a student's reading may be observed. It consists of a manual of directions, a booklet of reading paragraphs, a tachistoscope, various cards for use with the tachistoscope, and an individual record blank. Approximately thirty to ninety minutes of testing time are necessary to administer this test, which is composed of the following subtests.

Eight Oral Reading paragraphs with comprehension questions are provided. The student is to read at least three selections. The teacher should find the "basal paragraph" or paragraph in which one or less errors are made. The "upper level" is found when seven or more errors are made in a single paragraph, or the student takes more than two minutes to read the paragraph. During the oral reading, the teacher is to mark omissions, mispronunciations, repetitions, words pronounced for the student, insertions, punctuation marks ignored, and hesitations. Each paragraph is timed. Following the oral reading of each paragraph, comprehension questions are asked. The checklist of errors is marked at the completion of this section. Three kinds of data are collected on these passages: oral reading errors, comprehension, and time for reading. Scoring includes the time element as the most important factor.

The Silent Reading subtest uses the second set of eight paragraphs. The student is timed as the designated paragraph is read silently. When the paragraph has been completed, the student is asked to tell everything remembered about the story. Following this unaided recall, the teacher asks questions to assist the student in remembering more about the story. The grade norms are based on time and memory scores.

The third subtest is Listening Comprehension which consists of six paragraphs. The teacher begins reading the paragraph appropriate for the student's grade or chronological age. After listening to the material read, the student responds to comprehension questions. The listening comprehension level is determined when no more than one question in eight is missed.

The tachistoscope is used on the Word Recognition and Word Analysis subtests. Lists of words are printed on strips of cardboard. A word is flashed for the student to recognize and if the word is missed, it is shown again with time provided for word analysis. The teacher must note carefully the responses during the flash and the analysis. The test is stopped when seven successive errors are made in each area. All or part of these tests may be administered as necessary to learn more about the performance of the student.

A Listening Vocabulary subtest is provided to furnish a second index of reading capacity, using the same words which appeared in the Word Recognition and Word Analysis subtests. The scores obtained on the Listening Vocabulary subtest are compared to the scores on the Word Recognition and Word Analysis subtests.

Sounds in Isolation is a subtest designed to require students to produce the sounds of isolated letters, letter groups, and word parts. Included in the word parts are affixes.

Other subtests include Spelling, Phonic Spelling of Words, Visual Memory of Words (primary and intermediate) and Identifying Sounds in Words. An additional subtest also included to aid in diagnosing the kindergarten age student is the Prereading Phonics Abilities subtests which measures knowledge of letter names, ability to write letters, knowledge of letter sounds, and skill in matching written and spoken words.[21]

This test provides numerous checklists to assist in deriving maximum information from each subtest. These checklists, used in conjunction with the Profile Chart on the front of the test booklet, will provide much diagnostic data on the student. The main criticism of the earlier edition of this test as well as this edition is its lack of information on reliability and validity. Regardless of this criticism, the test has proven over the years to be an excellent source of diagnostic information on poor readers. Teachers should, however, be aware of the lack of technical information on this test, and consult such reviews as Schell and Jennings[22] before deciding to use the entire instrument.

## Gates-McKillop-Horowitz Reading Diagnostic Tests, 2nd edition
Arthur I. Gates, Anne S. McKillop, and Elizabeth Cliff Horowitz, Teachers College Press, New York, New York, 1981
(Grades 1–6)

The *Gates-McKillop-Horowitz Reading Diagnostic Tests* consist of a detailed manual of directions, the test materials, and the pupil record booklet. The teacher uses one copy of the pupil record booklet for each student, since individual responses are recorded in the booklet. As with all tests, the teacher needs to be very familiar with the manual prior to using the instrument. Since the purpose of this instrument is to obtain as much diagnostic information as possible on the student, the manual suggests the following:

Data from other tests should be used for information and correlated with this instrument.
There is no specific order for the administration of these subtests.
Not all subtests must be given to the students.
After following the specified procedures in administering the tests, the teacher may gain more diagnostic data by allowing the student to work independently on the items not completed on a specific subtest. Care should be taken to keep this record separate from the original recording so that errors in scoring will not result.

The test is composed of eight basic parts, two of these being further divided into more specific subtests. These are briefly described in the order of their presentation in the manual.

The Oral Reading subtest has seven paragraphs, which increase in difficulty. These readings are designed to assess the student's use of context and meaning clues, as well as word-form clues, in word recognition. Both phonetically regular and irregular words appear in the paragraphs. Also included in this subtest are four individual sentences, primarily containing phonetically regular words, which are intended to measure the student's use of meaning or word-form clues. During the oral reading, the teacher is to mark the following types of errors: hesitations, additions, omissions, repetitions, mispronunciations, and self corrections. The student reads until eleven or more errors are made on each of two consecutive paragraphs. The total number of errors is expressed as a raw score, which can then be converted into a grade norm.

The next two subtests are Words: Flash and Words: Untimed, which are designed to determine the student's ability to decode isolated words. The Flash subtest measures instant recognition of words while the Untimed subtest allows for the application of word analysis skills. The test information can be converted to a grade score.

The six subtests in Knowledge of Word Parts: Word Attack, which proceeds from the largest units, nonsense words, to the smallest units, individual letters. The nonsense words are used to determine skill in syllabication, employing two or more frequently used syllables. The next parts of this subtest measure the decoding skills of recognizing and blending common word parts and reading words. One-syllable words containing consonant combinations are used in recognizing and blending common word parts, while one-syllable words without consonant combinations are used in the reading words test. The student's performance on these two parts determines whether or not the remainder of the test should be given. Knowledge of isolated sounds is assessed on the letter sounds section by asking the student to give the sound corresponding to each of the individual printed letters or letter combinations. The student's ability to recognize and name upper- and lower-case letters is measured in the portions naming capital letters and lower-case letters.

Vowel knowledge is assessed on the Recognizing the Visual Form of Sounds subtest. The student is required to associate a graphic symbol with the vowel sound heard in words pronounced by the test administrator.

Auditory Blending and Auditory Discrimination are two subtests in which no visual component is involved. Auditory Blending measures whether a student can orally combine given sounds to make a word. The ability to hear the difference between similar-sounding phonemes which are presented orally is assessed on the Auditory Discrimination subtest.

Subtests are also included to evaluate spelling of isolated words (both phonetically regular and irregular words) in informal writing. The Informal Writing Sample subtest assesses the student's facility in written verbal expression as well as handwriting.[23]

The *Gates-McKillop-Horowitz Reading Diagnostic Tests* are measures of the oral reading, writing, and spelling skills of students in grades 1–6. Evaluation of word analysis skills is stressed, with no attention given to silent reading or comprehension. The Manual of Directions refers the examiner to the *Gates-MacGinitie Reading Tests* for information on comprehension and vocabulary.

This test is very comprehensive in its identification of word analysis difficulties; however, the teacher must be quite familiar with the instrument in order to use it appropriately. Additionally, the test must be carefully interpreted by a person who is trained in reading test interpretation. The teacher may wish to use some of these subtests with select individuals in the classroom, but the time element would prohibit its wide usage as a classroom diagnostic tool.

**Sipay Word Analysis Tests (SWAT)**
Edward R. Sipay
Educators Publishing Service, Inc., Cambridge, Massachusetts, 1974
(Grades 2–12)

The *Sipay Word Analysis Tests* consist of sixteen subtests designed to measure word analysis skills. There is also an initial test, the Survey Test, which is administered to help decide which of the subtests need to be administered. The test components include a general test manual, a mini-manual for each subtest, test cards, answer sheets, and an individual report form.

Because of the number of subtests of the *SWAT,* they are not discussed, but merely listed below.

Test 1—Letter Names
Test 2—Symbol-Sound Association: Single Letters
Test 3—Substitution: Single Letters
Test 4—Consonant-Vowel-Consonant Trigrams
Test 5—Initial Consonant Blends and Digraphs
Test 6—Final Consonant Blends and Digraphs
Test 7—Vowel Combinations
Test 8—Open Syllable Generalization
Test 9—Final Silent E Generalization
Test 10—Vowel Versatility
Test 11—Vowels Plus R
Test 12—Silent Consonants
Test 13—Vowel Sounds of Y
Test 14—Visual Analysis
Test 15—Visual Blending
Test 16—Contractions

Much emphasis is placed on summarizing and interpreting the findings of each subtest; the mini-manual provides necessary information as well as suggestions for follow-up testing. In addition, an individual report form can be used in summarizing and reporting the findings for each student.

The *SWAT* provides two types of scores. Specific strengths and weaknesses scores are used following the criteria of

68–100% correct: can or probably can perform the task
51–67% correct: may be able to perform the task
0–50% correct: cannot or probably cannot perform the task

Performance objective scores are also given, using a criterion of at least 95% accuracy.[24]

This test is extremely specific in identifying strengths and weaknesses in word analysis skills. The results should provide accurate information for the teacher to use in prescriptive teaching of these skills. Sipay seems to have given careful thought to providing a test which measures these skills as they are actually used in reading, and attempts to test the skills in an activity-oriented setting.

### Woodcock Reading Mastery Tests (WRMT)

Richard W. Woodcock

American Guidance Service, Inc., Circle Pines, Minnesota, 1973

(Grades Kindergarten–12)

The *Woodcock Reading Mastery Tests* are available in two alternative forms, each consisting of five subtests. These subtests include Letter Identification, Word Identification, Word Attack, Word Comprehension, and Passage Comprehension. Scores can be obtained for each subtest, and for a total reading score results when all are combined. The materials needed for this test include a manual, response forms, and an easel notebook containing all the test materials. The raw scores on these tests can be converted to grade scores, age scores, percentile ranks and standard scores. In addition, a Mastery Scale is provided, "which predicts the individual's relative success with reading tasks at different levels of difficulty."[25] Two other features regarding norms include separate norms for boys and girls, and procedures for adjusting the norms according to the socioeconomic status for a given community.

The Letter Identification test has forty-five items; these measure the student's skill in recognizing upper- and lower-case letters in four styles of type, Roman, sans serif, cursive, and a speciality typeface.

The Word Identification includes 150 words ranging in difficulty from beginning first-grade words to those for advanced twelfth-grade students. The student pronounces each word until five or more consecutive words are missed. Suggested starting points are given for each level.

The Word Attack test provides fifty items to determine the student's ability to identify nonsense words, using phonic and structural analysis skills. The nonsense words proceed from simple to complex, and the test stops when five or more consecutive errors are made.

The seventy items on the Word Comprehension test use an analogy format to test the student's knowledge of word meanings. Like the other subtests, this one is halted when five or more consecutive errors are made.

The modified cloze procedure is used with eighty-five items in the Passage Comprehension test. The student reads silently a sentence or short passage which has a word missing. The student is then asked to give the word that goes in the blank space. Acceptable words are provided for the teacher. The passages range in difficulty from first grade to college level.[26]

The *Woodcock Reading Mastery Tests* provide data which could be used as a guide to further testing; however, they do not furnish enough information for prescriptive teaching, unless very careful analysis of the errors on each subtest is made. The data plotted on the Mastery Profile will guide the teacher in the use of more specific measures, possibly criterion-referenced tests, to gain additional knowledge about the student's strengths and weaknesses in reading.

Auditory discrimination may be defined as the ability to distinguish likenesses and differences in sounds. It is only one aspect of an area known as auditory perception. The correlation of auditory discrimination skill development with reading proficiency has long been disputed in the field of reading education. Writers such as Robeck and Wilson, Durrell and Murphy, contend that auditory discrimination skills are extremely important and are directly related to reading.[27] Others, like Smith, and Deutsch and Feldman, have found no evidence that auditory discrimination training has any positive impact on reading achievement.[28] In addition to this debate over the importance of auditory discrimination skills, there is also concern regarding the procedures used to assess them. Dykstra maintains that the various auditory discrimination tests are not equivalent in prescriptive ability or in their relationship to reading. He found the most effective test for predicting reading achievement to be one which requires the student to select a picture of an object with the same initial sound as a spoken word.[29] Oakland concluded that phonemic auditory discrimination tests correlated better with reading achievement than nonphonemics tests.[30]

Although questions regarding auditory discrimination continue to surface, such tests remain in testing programs. They may be given as separate instruments or as a part of another test, such as the *Stanford Diagnostic Reading Test* or the *Gates-McKillop-Horowitz Reading Diagnostic Tests*. The most commonly used separate auditory discrimination test is the *Wepman Auditory Discrimination Test*.

### Wepman Auditory Discrimination Test
Joseph M. Wepman
Language Research Associates, Chicago, Illinois, 1973
(Ages 5–8)

The revised *Wepman Auditory Discrimination Test* consists of forty pairs of words on each of the two forms. The teacher pronounces each pair, and the student states whether the words are the same or different. The teacher has the student face in another direction, so that the possibility of lip reading does not enter into the score.

Before administering this test, the teacher should be sure that the student understands the meaning of the terms same and different. Some examples are provided for practice. Teachers must be careful to pronounce the words correctly and not to overemphasize likenesses and differences in the pairs.

The score is based on the number of correct responses. Norms are provided for ages five to eight, but the test may also be used with older students.

Physical factors such as poor auditory and visual acuity account for many difficulties diagnosed in reading. The teacher who suspects a reading problem should first try to determine whether the problem is in part caused by a physical handicap which can be corrected. Because instructors may not have necessary equipment properly to diagnose these acuity problems, careful observation is very

valuable until a more thorough diagnosis can be made. The following lists present signs of vision and hearing problems.

*Indicators of Visual Acuity Problems*

Headache in forehead or temples
Rubbing eyes frequently
Tilting head
Holding book too close to face
Losing place in reading
Blinking excessively
Frequent errors in copying
Tense during visual work
Squinting or covering one eye
Nausea or dizziness
Reddened eyes
Poor sitting position
Excessive head movement in reading
Avoiding close visual work
Frequent styes or encrusted eyelids
Blurring of print while reading
Excessive tearing
Fatigued and distraught while reading

*Indicators of Auditory Acuity Problems*

Monotonous voice pitch
Cupping hand behind ear
Turning ear toward speaker
Misunderstands directions frequently
Requests speaker to repeat statements
Generally inattentive
Poor pronunciation abnormal to age
Turning record player/radio to unusually loud volume
Difficulty in auditory discrimination tasks
Hears ringing or buzzing sounds in ear
Has blank expression
Strained posture in listening
Excessive amounts of wax in ears

*Visual Acuity*

There is disagreement about the exact degree to which vision contributes to reading achievement. There seems, however, to be a correlation. In a survey of sixty-nine students referred to the university reading clinic, the authors noted that twenty-three, exactly one-third, were referred for further visual examinations. The teacher should be familiar with terms used to describe various types of visual problems, some of which are listed below.

*Amblyopia:* commonly called "lazy eye." This is lowered acuity in one eye, possibly because of suppression.

*Aniseikonia:* the image of an object is formed in a different size or shape in each eye.

*Astigmatism:* a blurring vision due to an uneven curvature of the front of the eye. Not usually related to reading problems.

*Convergence:* the degree to which the eyes turn in to focus on the same object.

*Fixation:* skill in holding fusion on a given object.

*Fusion:* the ability of both eyes to align so that the object is centered. Without proper fusion, double vision results.

*Hyperopia:* farsightedness, or the ability to see objects at a distance but not close.

*Myopia:* nearsightedness, or the ability to see objects close but not at a distance.

*Strabismus:* lack of binocular coordination due to a muscular imbalance of one or both eyes.

In assessing visual acuity, schools have previously used the *Snellen Chart* or the *E Chart*. These charts measured only distance vision. In addition, vision is tested in only one eye at a time; this is unnatural. These tests are not recommended for use in determining whether a student has a vision problem contributing to a reading difficulty. Other instruments are presented in the following pages. This list is not exhaustive, but it provides information concerning the various types of visual screening instruments available. Additional information on visual screening can be found in *Screening Vision in Schools.*[31]

**Keystone Visual Survey Tests**
Keystone View Company, Davenport, Iowa

The *Keystone Telebinocular* (figure 5.3) is a viewer used with a series of slides to measure the following areas: Simultaneous Perception, Vertical Imbalance, Lateral Posture at Far Point, Fusion at Far Point, Usable Vision of Both Eyes at Far Point, Stereopsis, Color Blindness, Lateral Posture at Near Point, Fusion at Near Point, Visual Acuity of Both Eyes at Near Point, Visual Acuity of Right Eye at Near Point, and Visual Acuity of Left Eye at Near Point. These tests can be used to screen for possible nearsightedness, farsightedness, astigmatism, muscular imbalance, lack of fusion at the near and far points, binocular efficiency, stereopsis level or depth perception, and color blindness.

Teachers need no specialized training to administer this test, but care should be taken in recording and interpreting the record form. This screening instrument, like all others, tends to over-refer for further analysis. However, it is a very thorough screening device in reading diagnosis.

**Figure 5.3**
Keystone Telebinocular
Reproduced by permission
of Keystone View
Company, 2212 East 12th
St., Davenport, IA 52803.

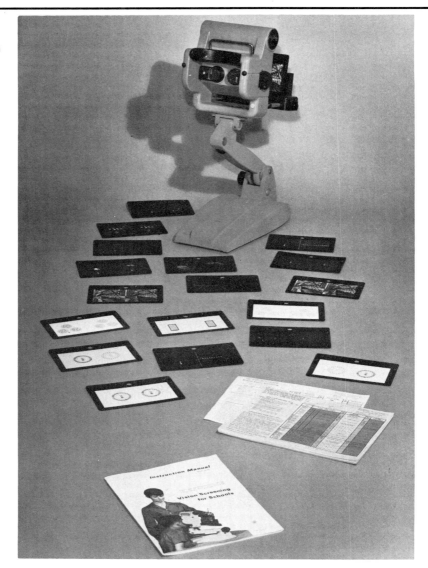

### Ortho-Rater
Bausch and Lomb Optical Company, Rochester, New York

The *Ortho-Rater* (figure 5.4) is a vision screening device originally designed for adult and industrial use. The subtests were restandardized by Helen M. Robinson for use in schools and clinics. This instrument, like the *Keystone Visual Screening Tests,* tends to over-refer students, especially young children.

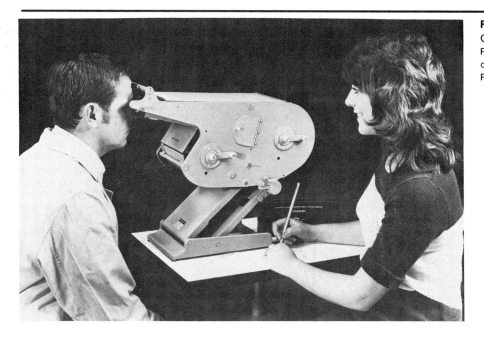

**Figure 5.4**
Ortho-Rater
Reproduced by permission
of Bausch and Lomb, Inc.,
Rochester, New York.

The tests included with this instrument are Acuity Far (right right), Acuity Far (left eye), Far Sightedness (right eye), Far Sightedness (left eye), Phoria Far, Phoria Near, Depth Perception, and Color Blindness.

*Auditory Acuity*

Auditory or hearing acuity is the ability to hear pitches of sounds at varying levels of loudness. The different degrees of loudness are measured in decibels, while the pitch or frequency of sounds is discussed in cycles per second or hertz.

Auditory acuity is measured by an instrument known as an audiometer (figure 5.5). There are many different types of audiometers; however, they all function in basically the same way.

The teacher places earphones on the student and faces the student away from the instrument. Setting the audiometer at the correct decibels according to the manual, the instructor begins testing at various frequencies. The student is directed to signal when a sound is heard. The tones are cut off by an interrupter switch to allow the teacher to change the frequencies and decibels, if necessary. The teacher records the responses on an audiogram. When testing is complete, the marks are joined by a line to provide a profile of the student's hearing in each ear. The frequencies to be tested range from about 125 to 8000 cycles per second. Students with a hearing loss between 500 and 2500 cycles per second in one or both ears should be referred for a closer examination. These students may experience difficulty in school because the female teacher's voice tends to be at a higher frequency. Additionally, some consonant sounds are at a higher frequencies.

**Figure 5.5**
Teacher Using
Audiometer

Teachers should note that some slight hearing losses may be transitory, because of ear infections and other temporary conditions. The instructor may therefore wish to recheck the student in several weeks prior to referring for further testing. More specific information on the administration and interpretation using various audiometers is contained in the manuals that accompany the instruments. Several companies which provide the more frequently used audiometers are listed below. It should be noted that, although some companies provide tests which can be administered in a group situation, they are not as reliable as individually-administered tests.

*Auditory Instrument Division*
Zenith Radio Corporation
6501 W. Grand Avenue
Chicago, Illinois 60635

*Beltone Electronics Corporation*
Hearing Test Instruments Division
4201 W. Victoria Street
Chicago, Illinois 60646

*Maico Hearing Instruments*
7375 Bush Lake Road
Minneapolis, Minnesota 55435

Many other companies such as Grayton Electric, Audiometer Sales Corporation, Royal Industries, Precision Acoustics Corporation, and Sonotone Corporation provide audiometers that are adapted for school use.

The use of intelligence tests as aids in reading diagnosis or predictors of reading success can be either supported or discredited by research. However, the general conclusion is that group intelligence tests are more a measure of reading ability than intelligence. Individual intelligence tests seem to be better indicators of potential. Verbal mental ability tests, such as the verbal section of the *Wechsler Intelligence Scale for Children (WISC),* correlate more highly with reading comprehension. Studies like that of Bond and Dykstra suggested that at the first-grade level, correlation between mental ability and reading comprehension is generally in the .40's and .50's.[32] Allen indicated that this correlation rose into the .70's by the fourth grade.[33] Thorndike found that the .70 correlation tended to remain into the freshman year of college.[34] Spache and Spache conclude that an I.Q. score may be a fairly good predictor of reading ability for students with an extremely high I.Q. or for those are who mentally retarded.[35] Sewell found that the I.Q. correlated moderately with achievement for both black and white first graders, but was a more reliable predictor for whites than for blacks.[36]

Teachers should not conclude that an I.Q. test must be administered in order to diagnose a reading problem. Intelligence tests usually provide little information beyond that gained by observation or by the administration of an individual reading test. The intelligence tests with subtests which seem to be most helpful in reading diagnosis are the *Wechsler Intelligence Scale for Children,* the *Wechsler Adult Intelligence Scale,* and the *Stanford-Binet Intelligence Scale.* These tests must be administered by a specially certified person and take a great deal of time; thus, many teachers are unable to use them for diagnostic purposes. If these tests are administered, the teacher should request information on each of the subtest scores. This information can assist in determining strengths and weaknesses in learning, and in providing better prescriptive instruction. Sources such as *How to Use WISC Scores in Reading Diagnosis* by Searls are most helpful in making maximum use of the information.[37]

Should the teacher believe that an intelligence measure may provide more necessary information, and if individual I.Q. test data are not available, there are two individual intelligence measures which can be administered by the teacher: the *Peabody Picture Vocabulary Test* and the *Slosson Intelligence Test.*

**Peabody Picture Vocabulary Test (PPVT)**
Lloyd M. Dunn
American Guidance Service, Inc., Circle Pines, Minnesota, 1965 and 1981
(Ages 2.6 and 18)

The *PPVT* is designed to provide an estimate of a student's verbal intelligence by assessing hearing vocabulary. This is done using 150 sets of four pictures: the student selects the named picture for each set. The kit includes a spiral-bound book containing the pictured plates, a manual, and individual test record booklets. There are two forms, Forms A and B, which are included in one kit. The test requires about ten to fifteen minutes for administration. An I.Q., a percentile score, and a mental age indication can be obtained from the raw score.

Validity, reliability, and relationship with reading success are the points often questioned relative to the 1965 edition of the *PPVT*. Spache has suggested that the reliability of the estimate is improved if both forms are administered.[38] He states that the influence of socioeconomic or linguistic handicaps on the score is not significant. Ekwall's research, however, indicated that the *PPVT* is a highly unreliable measure of intelligence for individual students.[39] Pikulski reported that the *PPVT* and *Slosson Intelligence Test* correlated equally well with the *WISC* for students with reading disabilities.[40] Thus, the teacher should recognize that the studies regarding this instrument provide varying information dependent upon the population, and that this test is strictly a measure of intelligence based on the student's vocabulary knowledge. Wilson suggests that "it is valuable to refer to the M.A. score on the *PPVT* as the child's auding age and to the I.Q. as the auding quotient."[41] Because vocabulary and language knowledge are so important to success in reading, this test is better used as a predictor of reading success than of intelligence.

**Slosson Intelligence Test (SIT)**
Richard L. Slosson
Publishers Test Service, Monterey, California, 1963 and 1981
(Ages infant to adult)

The *SIT* is a verbal measure of intelligence that was developed to emulate the *Stanford-Binet*. Many items were adapted from the *Stanford-Binet* (Form L-M), with this test being used as the criterion validity for the *SIT*. The test follows a question-answer format. The manual suggests that the test can be administered in ten to twenty minutes; however, the experience of the authors is that about fifteen to thirty minutes are necessary.

This test was developed as a short screening instrument for teachers and others without extensive training in test administration. Armstrong and Mooney found that the results were equally valid when the test was given by a teacher or a test administrator.[42]

The *SIT,* like all other verbal measures of intelligence, penalizes the student with limited experiences in language. Thus, the classroom teacher must use these measures cautiously.

Few changes have been made in the second edition of the *SIT*. However, this edition contains sections on validity, independent sampling, other research findings, as well as an extended bibliography. Moreover, an item analysis can be purchased as a supplement to aid in screening for strengths and weaknesses in various areas.

**Summary**

This chapter has presented an overview of various formal diagnostic procedures available for use by the classroom teacher. Some of the instruments discussed require special training; others do not. However, classroom teachers willing to devote a minimum amount of time to the study of the tests can administer and interpret the instruments mentioned.

Two broad categories of diagnostic procedures were discussed, with several types of instruments in each category. The major categories were group and individual testing procedures.

There were four types of group-administered tests presented:

Survey reading tests
Diagnostic reading tests
Achievement tests
Intelligence tests

Under individually-administered procedures, five types of tests were presented:

Oral reading tests
Diagnostic reading tests
Auditory discrimination tests
Auditory and visual screening tests
Intelligence tests

These instruments, with their individual strengths and limitations, were presented to assist teachers in becoming more knowledgeable of tests that may help in diagnosing student needs in reading.

**Applying What You Read**

Under what circumstances would an individually-administered diagnostic instrument be preferable to a group-administered diagnostic instrument?

What type of instrument would be better suited for screening a fourth-grade class for specific word recognition and comprehension skills? Why?

Your school is selecting some formal diagnostic tools to use in the reading program. What individual tests would you recommend? Why? What group tests would you recommend? Why?

Are there any instances in which you as a classroom teacher might want to use the results from group I.Q. tests? Why or why not?

A second-grade student in your classroom has a reading problem and exhibits difficulties with sight words, auditory and visual perception, as well as word analysis skills. What type of formal diagnostic instrument could you use with this student? What specific tests would you recommend? Why?

Identify a battery (2 or 3 tests) of formal tests which you would like to have available in your classroom. Tell why you selected each.

**Notes**

1. Nancy A. Mavrogenes, Earl F. Hanson, and Carol K. Winkley, "A Guide to Tests of Factors that Inhibit Learning to Read," *The Reading Teacher.*
2. Walter H. MacGinitie et al., *Gates-MacGinitie Reading Tests Teacher's Manuals.*
3. Roger Farr, ed., *Iowa Silent Reading Test, Manual of Direction.*
4. Margaret Doren, *Doren Diagnostic Reading Test of Word Recognition Skills Manual,* 2nd ed., pp. 12–28.

5. Bjorn Karlsen, Richard Madden, and Eric F. Gardner, *Stanford Diagnostic Reading Test: Manual for Administering and Interpreting.*

6. Francis W. Parker, *Talks on Pedagogies;* Edmund B. Huey, *The Psychology and Pedagogy of Reading.*

7. Nila Banton Smith, *American Reading Instruction,* 3rd ed., pp. 158–64.

8. John V. Gilmore and Eunice C. Gilmore, *Gilmore Oral Reading Test: Manual of Directions.*

9. Albert J. Harris, "Review of Gilmore Oral Reading Test," in *Reading Tests and Reviews,* ed. Oscar K. Buros, pp. 127–28.

10. Helen M. Robinson, ed., *Manual: Gray Oral Reading Test.*

11. Albert J. Harris, "Review of Gray Oral Reading Test," in *Reading Tests and Reviews,* ed. Oscar K. Buros, p. 368.

12. Richard L. Slosson, *Slosson Oral Reading Test,* p. 1.

13. George D. Spache, *Diagnosing and Correcting Reading Disabilities,* pp. 218–220.

14. Oscar K. Buros, ed., *Reading Tests and Reviews II,* p. 255.

15. Morton Botel, *Botel Reading Inventory,* revised.

16. George D. Spache, *Diagnostic Reading Scales,* Examiner's Manual, p. 10.

17. George D. Spache, *Diagnostic Reading Scales,* revised, p. 18.

18. George D. Spache, *Diagnostic Reading Scales,* Examiner's Manual, pp. 9–16.

19. George D. Spache, *Diagnostic Reading Scales: Technical Bulletin.*

20. Spache, *Diagnosing and Correcting Reading Disabilities,* pp. 203–214.

21. Donald D. Durrell and Jane H. Catterson, *Durrell Analysis of Reading Difficulty: Manual of Directions.*

22. Leo M. Schell and Robert E. Jennings, "Test Review: Durrell Analysis of Reading Difficulty (3rd Edition)," *The Reading Teacher.*

23. Arthur I. Gates, Anne S. McKillop, and Elizabeth Cliff Horowitz, *Gates-McKillop-Horowitz Reading Diagnostic Tests,* 2nd ed., Manual of Directions.

24. Edward R. Sipay, *Sipay Word Analysis Tests.*

25. Richard W. Woodcock, *Woodcock Reading Mastery Tests: Manual,* p. 1.

26. Woodcock, *Woodcock Reading Mastery Tests: Manual,* pp. 1–5.

27. Mildred C. Robeck and John A. R. Wilson, *Psychology of Reading: Foundations of Instruction;* Donald D. Durrell and Helen A. Murphy, "The Auditory Discrimination Factor in Reading Readiness and Reading Disability." *Education.*

28. Frank Smith, *Psycholinguistics and Reading;* Cynthia P. Deutsch and Shirley C. Feldman, "A Study of the Effectiveness of Training for Retarded Readers in the Auditory Skills Underlying Reading." Title VII, Project No. 1127 Grant.

29. Robert Dykstra, "Auditory Discrimination Abilities and Beginning Reading Achievement," *Reading Research Quarterly.*

30. Thomas D. Oakland, "Auditory Discrimination and Socioeconomic Status as Correlates of Reading Ability," *Journal of Learning Disabilities.*

31. Fred W. Jobe, *Screening Vision in Schools.*

32. Guy L. Bond and Robert Dykstra, "The Cooperative Research Program in First Grade Reading Instruction," *Reading Research Quarterly.*

33. M. Allen, "Relationship Between Kuhlmann-Anderson Intelligence Tests and Academic Achievement in Grade IV," *Journal of Educational Psychology.*

34. Robert L. Thorndike, *The Concepts of Over and Underachievement.*

35. George D. Spache and Evelyn B. Spache, *Reading in the Elementary School,* 4th ed.

36. Trevor E. Sewell, "Intelligence and Learning Tasks as Predictors of Scholastic Achievement in Black and White First-Grade Children," *Journal of Psychology.*
37. Evelyn F. Searls, *How to Use WISC Scores in Reading Diagnosis.*
38. Spache, *Diagnosing and Correcting Reading Disabilities,* p. 88.
39. Eldon E. Ekwall, *Diagnosis and Remediation of the Disabled Reader,* p. 177.
40. John Pikulski, "The Validity of Three Brief Measures of Intelligence for Disabled Readers," *Journal of Educational Research.*
41. Robert M. Wilson, *Diagnostic and Remedial Reading for Classroom and Clinic,* 3rd ed.
42. Robert J. Armstrong and Robert F. Mooney, "The Slosson Intelligence Test: Implications for Reading Specialists," *The Reading Teacher.*

**Other Suggested Readings**

Bond, Guy L.; Tinker, Miles A. and Wasson, Barbara B. *Reading Difficulties: Their Diagnosis and Correction,* 4th edition. (Englewood Cliffs, New Jersey: Prentice-Hall, Inc., 1979). Chapter 7.

Drahozal, Edward C., and Hanna, Gerald S. "Reading Comprehension Subscores: Pretty Bottles for Ordinary Wine." *Journal of Reading* 21 (February 1978): 416–20.

Dechant, Emerald. *Diagnosis and Remediation of Reading Disabilities.* Englewood Cliffs, New Jersey: Prentice-Hall, Inc., 1981. Chapter 3.

Fry, Edward. "Test Review: Metropolitan Achievement Tests." *The Reading Teacher* 34 (November 1980):196–201.

Geissal, Mary Ann, and Knafle, June D. "A Linguistic View of Auditory Discrimination Tests and Exercises." *The Reading Teacher* 31 (November 1977):134–41.

Gunning, Thomas G. "Wrong Level Test: Wrong Information." *The Reading Teacher* 35 (May 1982):902–05.

Harris, Albert J., and Sipay, Edward R. *How to Increase Reading Ability.* 7th ed. New York: David McKay Company, 1980.

Hayward, Priscilla. "Evaluating Diagnostic Reading Tests." *The Reading Teacher* 21 (March 1968):523–28.

Jenkins, Joseph R., and Pany, Darlene. "Curriculum Biases in Reading Achievement Tests." *Journal of Reading Behavior* 10 (Winter 1978):345–57.

Klein, Alice E. "Redundancy in the Comprehensive Tests of Basic Skills." *Educational and Psychological Measurement* 40 (Winter 1980):1105–10.

Pikulski, John J. "Assessing Information about Intelligence and Reading." *The Reading Teacher* 29 (November 1975):157–63.

Robinson, H. Alan, and Hanson, Earl. "Reliability of Measures of Reading Achievement." *The Reading Teacher* 21 (January 1968):307–13.

Schubert, Delwyn G. and Walton, Howard N. "Visual Screening—A New Breakthrough." *The Reading Teacher* 34 (November 1980):175–77.

Smith, William Earl, and Beck, Michael D. "Determining Instructional Reading Level with the 1978 Metropolitan Achievement Tests." *The Reading Teacher* 34 (December 1980):313–19.

Spache, George D. *Investigating the Issues of Reading Disabilities.* Boston: Allyn and Bacon, 1976.

# 2

# Synthesizing Data

S tep 2 is a key link in using the diagnostic information for prescriptive teaching. The teachers at Seabreeze School realize that much time can be wasted in diagnosis if the data are not properly organized, interpreted, and summarized. Thus, chapter 6 provides suggestions for teachers to use in order to obtain maximum information from data on each student.

**6**

The teacher at Seabreeze School realize that synthesizing data from the diagnostic information gathered on each student is an essential step in the development of a diagnostic-prescriptive reading program. Since students are continuously diagnosed during the school year, large amounts of data are collected. However, the information gained is little more than a series of test scores, observational information, and miscellaneous data gathered about each student. In order for information to have any significance to the teacher, student, parents, or others involved in the program, the teachers must synthesize the data. To accomplish this, the Seabreeze teachers identified a series of tasks to be carried out. These include organizing, analyzing, and interpreting the data, providing recommendations for instruction, and summarizing the findings (see figure 6.1).

The completion of these four tasks is essential if the diagnostic information obtained is to have a meaningful impact on the teaching process. Synthesizing the data to form a meaningful whole enables the teacher to prescribe more adequately the most effective techniques and materials to use with each student. It allows other school personnel to understand better the reasons for the use of specific procedures in dealing with the reading development of individual students.

During the period when the diagnostic information is obtained, the teacher gains valuable insights into the student's personality, attitude, value system, peer relationships, and, perhaps to some extent, cultural and environmental factors that can and do affect a student's performance in reading. These affective aspects of diagnosis are extremely important in the synthesizing process, and are as relevant as the cognitive information obtained through informal and formal testing procedures. Both cognitive and affective determiners go hand-in-hand in developing the most effective prescription for teaching a student to read. As the faculty at Seabreeze discussed these areas, they asked these questions:

What do the various terms used on the test instruments, such as raw score, stanine, and grade equivalent, mean to the teacher?

What procedures should be used in synthesizing data?

How are data organized for teacher use?

What are the interrelationships between analysis and interpretation of diagnostic information?

Why are these interrelationships so vital to the diagnostic-prescriptive process?

How are diagnostic data analyzed and interpreted?

How does the teacher effectively summarize diagnostic information to enhance the instructional process?

How can the diagnostic information be organized for daily classroom use in providing prescriptive instruction?

# After diagnosis, what is done with the information, and how is it summarized for use?

As you read this chapter, be aware of the following terms.

Analysis
Correlation
Data
Grade equivalent
Grade level
Grade placement
Interpretation
Mean
Median

Normal curve
Percentile
Range
Raw score
Reliability
Standard score
Stanine
Summarizing
Validity

**Vocabulary to Know**

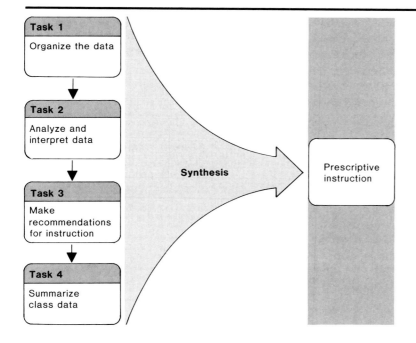

**Figure 6.1**
Four Basic Tasks in Synthesizing Diagnostic Data for Prescriptive Instruction

**Measurement Terms Defined**

As teachers review diagnostic information and begin to analyze and interpret the data, they should be familiar with the terminology used in the test materials. The authors have defined fifteen terms which seem to be most frequently used in diagnostic data.

*Correlation:* The degree of relationship between two variables expressed by the coefficient of correlation, which extends along a scale from 1.00 through .00 to − 1.00; 1.00 denotes a perfect positive relationship; a coefficient of .00 denotes no relationship, and a coefficient of − 1.00 denotes a perfect negative relationship.

*Grade equivalent:* A derived score converted from the raw score on a standardized text, usually expressed in terms of a grade level divided into tenths. The grade equivalents in sixth grade, for example, range from 6.0 to 6.9 with 6.9 indicating six years, nine months or the end of the sixth grade.

*Grade level:* The actual grade in which the student is enrolled.

*Grade placement:* The level at which the student is placed for instruction. The student in the fourth grade with a low second-grade reading level may have a grade placement of 2.3 at the fourth-grade level. This term may also be used on some tests as a synonym for grade equivalent.

*Mean:* The average of a set of numbers derived by taking the sum of the set of measurements and dividing it by the number of measurements in the set.

*Median:* The central number in a set. There are equal numbers of scores which fall above and below the median number in a set.

*Normal curve:* Same as the bell curve, which has more scores at the mean or median and a decreasing number in equal proportions at the left and right of the center. (See figure 6.2).

*Percentile:* The percentage score that rates the student relative to the percentage of others in a group who are below the score. A student at the 47th percentile has done better on the test than 47 percent of the other people taking the test. Percentile scores may be reported in *quartiles* and *deciles,* in which case a 50th percentile is in the second quartile and the fifth decile. Percentiles, quartiles, and deciles cannot be averaged, added together, subtracted, or treated arithmetically in any manner.

*Range:* The distance between the largest and smallest numbers in a set, calculated by subtracting the smallest score from the largest score. For example, the score on a test may be 10, 8, 15, 22, 36, and 20; the range, calculated by subtracting 8 from 36, would be 28.

*Raw Score:* An untreated test score usually obtained by counting the number of items correct. The raw score is used to determine the other scores, such as grade equivalent and percentile.

*Reliability:* A term that refers to the consistency with which the test agrees with itself or produces similar scores when readministered over a period of time by the same individual.

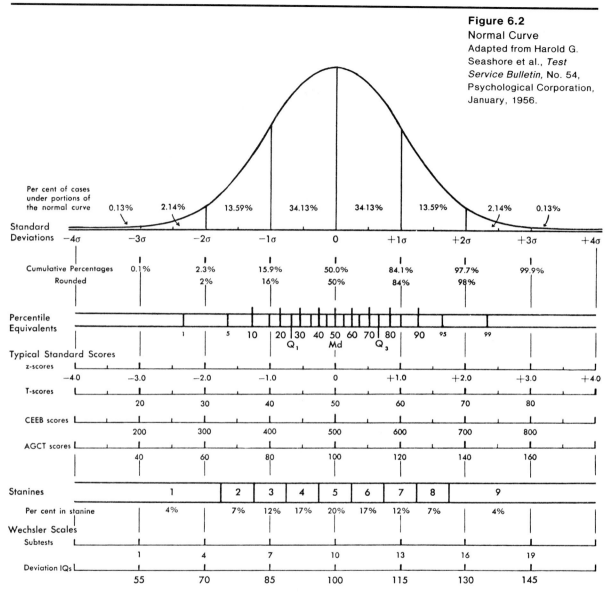

**Figure 6.2**
Normal Curve
Adapted from Harold G. Seashore et al., *Test Service Bulletin*, No. 54, Psychological Corporation, January, 1956.

Per cent of cases under portions of the normal curve

| 0.13% | 2.14% | 13.59% | 34.13% | 34.13% | 13.59% | 2.14% | 0.13% |

Standard Deviations
−4σ  −3σ  −2σ  −1σ  0  +1σ  +2σ  +3σ  +4σ

Cumulative Percentages  0.1%  2.3%  15.9%  50.0%  84.1%  97.7%  99.9%
Rounded  2%  16%  50%  84%  98%

Percentile Equivalents
1  5  10  20 30 40 50 60 70 80  90  95  99
Q₁  Md  Q₃

Typical Standard Scores
z-scores
−4.0  −3.0  −2.0  −1.0  0  +1.0  +2.0  +3.0  +4.0

T-scores
20  30  40  50  60  70  80

CEEB scores
200  300  400  500  600  700  800

AGCT scores
40  60  80  100  120  140  160

Stanines
1  2  3  4  5  6  7  8  9

Per cent in stanine
4%  7%  12%  17%  20%  17%  12%  7%  4%

Wechsler Scales
Subtests
1  4  7  10  13  16  19

Deviation IQs
55  70  85  100  115  130  145

NOTE: *This chart cannot be used to equate scores on one test to scores on another test. For example, both 600 on the CEEB and 120 on the AGCT are one standard deviation above their respective means, but they do not represent "equal" standings because the scores were obtained from different groups.*

*After Diagnosis, What Is Done with the Information, and How Is It Summarized for Use?*

*Standard deviation:* A term used to describe the deviations of scores from the mean, which varies with the range in a set of scores. Thus, the greater the range in scores, the larger the standard deviation can be.

*Standard score:* A raw score expressed in some form of standard deviation units. They can be dealt with arithmetically and are easier to interpret than raw scores. Various types of standard scores include z-scores, T-scores, CEEB scores, and stanines.

*Stanines:* A 9-point scale which is another form of a standard score with a mean of 5 and a standard deviation of about 2. The 9 stanines fit along the base of the normal curve with Stanines 1, 2, and 3 considered below average, Stanines 4, 5, and 6 average, and Stanines, 7, 8, and 9 above average.

*Validity:* The extent to which a test measures what it is designed to measure. A test may be reliable but not valid, in that it does not measure what it purports to measure.

To provide further assistance in visualizing these various terms in relation to the normal curve, the teacher should carefully study figure 6.2. In selecting as well as interpreting tests, teachers should note the types of data provided as well as the reliability and validity of the instruments.

## Organizing the Data

After the diagnostic information has been obtained, the first task is to organize it in a format which will enhance its usefulness. It is important that this information be recorded in a logical sequence so that the teacher may refer to it as needed. Accessibility of data is an important aspect of diagnostic-prescriptive instruction and ensures a more adequate learning environment for the student. Organization enhances instruction and is an indispensable aspect of synthesizing data. Data can be organized in various ways; and as they become more accustomed to diagnostic-prescriptive instruction; teachers will develop and refine their ideas for organizing diagnostic information. It is essential that the data be organized initially in some usable format.

It may be helpful to use a folder for each student so that the information can be readily available for the teacher's use. The folder may contain tests, observations, and other pertinent data useful for prescriptive instruction. Remember that the information should be strictly objective and factual. Personal opinions concerning the student's behavior or home life have no place in a student's diagnostic-prescriptive folder, which is open for review by many people.

As data are collected, the teacher may wish to consider a four-step organizational plan used by the authors. The categories or steps in this plan are concerned with basic information about the student, his or her background, identifying diagnostic information, interpretation of the data, and listing recommendations for prescriptive instruction. They are outlined in figure 6.3.

The first step is concerned with recording *basic information,* such as the student's name, chronological age, and the dates during which diagnostic information was obtained. Another important factor is whether or not the student is

**Figure 6.3**
Organization of Data

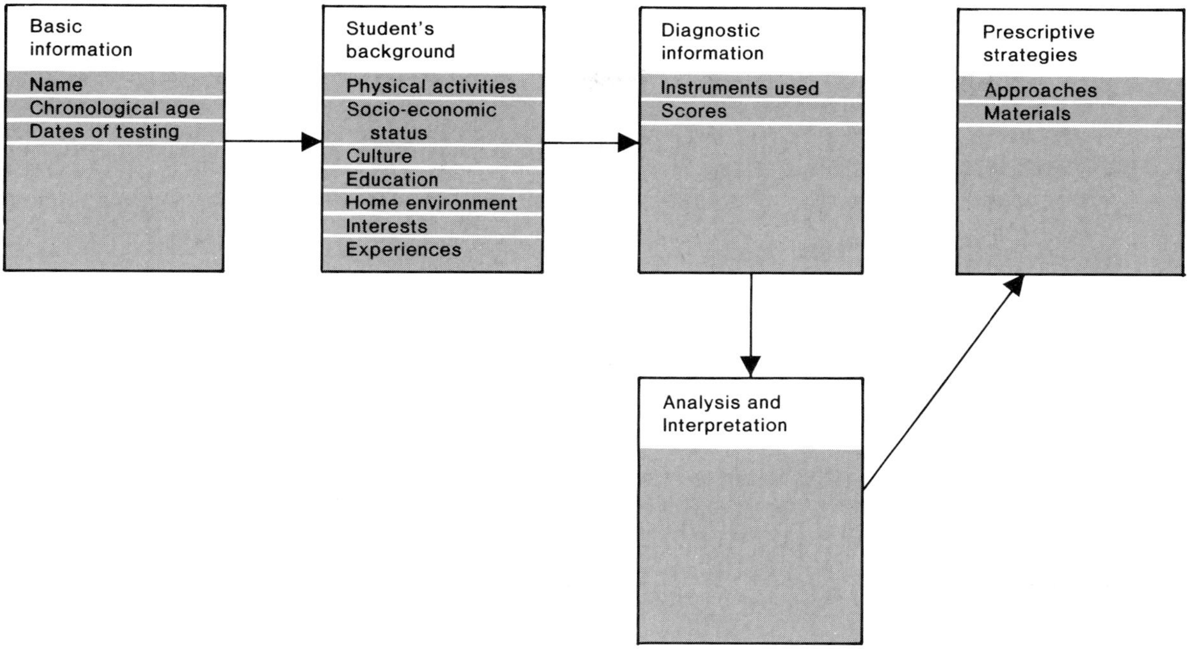

| Basic information | | Student's background | | Diagnostic information | | Prescriptive strategies |
|---|---|---|---|---|---|---|
| Name | | Physical activities | | Instruments used | | Approaches |
| Chronological age | | Socio-economic status | | Scores | | Materials |
| Dates of testing | | Culture | | | | |
| | | Education | | | | |
| | | Home environment | | | | |
| | | Interests | | | | |
| | | Experiences | | | | |

| Analysis and Interpretation |
|---|
| |

in the correct grade level; some students may have been retained in previous grades. Although this step may appear somewhat simplistic, it is imperative that it be reported correctly, as many test norms use this information. The teacher may record this basic information on the front of the student folder or on a separate sheet of paper inside the folder. For students with severe reading problems, for whom more formal case reports are developed, the instructor would use this as introductory information.

In the second step, the *student's background* is explored. This is valuable because of the many factors that affect a student's reading ability. Such variables as physical condition, cultural and socioeconomic background, educational factors, the home environment, interests, and experiential background are all very useful in developing the appropriate instructional program for a student. This is an area which perhaps influences the student's educational progress more than any other. The authors have seen many students with adequate reading skills and ability, who theoretically should have been able to read, but could not because of any number of other factors that adversely affected them. Foremost among these are unstable homes, poor experiential backgrounds, cultural differences, and language differences. Unfortunately, there are so many factors which adversely affect a student's ability to read that the teacher experiences great difficulty in dealing effectively with them. Learning to read is not always contingent

upon the improvement of oral language abilities, learning phonetic and structural analysis skills, and improving comprehension; many outside forces heavily influence reading progress. For this reason, it is imperative that as much background information as possible be available to the teacher. This not only allows teachers to be better informed about their students, but further enhances the prospect for success in improving the student's reading capabilities. To organize this data, the teacher may find it useful to list significant information about the student as obtained from parent conferences or from the student. Possible leading questions that might be asked are listed below.

*Parent*

> Were there any difficulties with the pregnancy, or with the birth process or development of the child?
> How many children are in the family?
> How does this child get along with others in the family? Father? Mother?
> Have you noticed that your child has difficulty with reading?
> When did you first notice the difficulty?
> What kind of activities does the family enjoy together?
> How much reading does each of the family members engage in during the week?
> What is the longest trip that your child has taken?
> Do you take your child with you when you go shopping, visiting, or on trips?
> How does your child feel about school? Reading?

*Student*

> Do you like to read? What types of material?
> Do you have your own books at home? What is your favorite?
> Do your parents read to you? When?
> What is your favorite activity after school?
> What do you like to do best with your father? Mother? Brothers? Sisters?
> Have you been to the zoo? Grocery store? On trips to other states?

In addition, the teacher may wish to use parent information sheets and interest inventories such as that in appendix E to gather more information regarding the student's background. This information should be listed on the inside of the student's folder or on a separate sheet kept in the folder. The teacher must remember that the purpose of this information is to assist in better diagnosing the student's reading problem and providing appropriate prescriptive instruction.

The third step in organizing data deals with the *identification of the diagnostic information*. The teacher should list on a summary page the instruments used with their scores. Other informal diagnostic information such as observation checklists, interest and attitude surveys, criterion-referenced tests, and notes on daily work, should also be listed with the necessary information. The teacher should arrange or formulate the information so that data are readily accessible and easy to use. This step is essential to the task of *analysis and interpretation* of the data, discussed in the following section.

The fourth step in organizing the data is concerned with *listing prescriptive or instructional strategies* for the student. After the data have been interpreted in terms of the student's strengths and weaknesses, and the background information analyzed, the teacher is ready to recommend the instructional strategies to be used in teaching.

This can be accomplished by using either a list format or a narrative format for enumerating materials and approaches for teaching. A list format saves time and presents the information in such a manner that the teacher need only turn to the prescriptive section in the folder to locate the procedures recommended for instruction. The instructor should list the appropriate approach or method of teaching for each student, and the materials to be used. Once this is done, the teacher may easily refer to each student's folder to determine the skills to be developed or the appropriate methods or procedures to be used in the instructional process. It is essential to remember that prescriptions can and do change. This is a characteristic of the diagnostic-prescriptive instructional process and, in fact, one of its underlying principles. Chapters 8–14 deal specifically with prescriptive instruction for the students.

Organization of data is a necessary step in the process of synthesizing and using diagnostic information. Successful completion of this organization enhances the instructional process, allowing teachers to make better use of the facilities and materials available to them.

The second task in the synthesis of the diagnostic information involves the analysis and interpretation of the data. Analysis is essential to the overall process of diagnostic-prescriptive instruction, and involves the objective evaluation of the data. For example, a student might receive a third stanine score on the phonetic analysis subtest of the *Stanford Diagnostic Reading Test,* Red Level. An analysis of this data would indicate a below-average score in this area. On further analysis of this subtest score, the teacher realizes that the student experienced great difficulty with vowels, but little difficulty with consonants. Thus, the objective analysis involves evaluating the types of errors made by the student, without interpreting the consequences of these errors.

Analysis of the scores taken from test data enables the teacher to look at the individual phases of the total picture, so that essential questions about particular problems can be raised and answered. Looking at a total score is not likely to reveal the information needed for prescribing an appropriate instructional program. For example, two students may score at a low, third-year level on an informal reading inventory; however, a closer analysis of the data may indicate that one student showed strengths in word recognition skills, while the other was stronger in comprehension.

**Analyzing and Interpreting the Data**

**Figure 6.4**
Brief Analysis of Data

```
            Name: Joe Hunter                                Grade: 3
       Interests: Racing cars, motorcycles, and machine guns
                  Likes to make things with tools
                  Likes to watch television

  Sucher-Allred Reading Placement Inventory
     Satisfactory comprehension; poor sequencing skills
     Poor phrasing—ignores punctuation
     Omits word endings
     Weak in medial sounds
        Independent level:   Primer
        Instructional level: 2²
        Frustration level:   3¹

  Stanford Diagnostic Reading Test—Red Level
     Difficulty in auditory discrimination
     Poor vocabulary
     Unsure when tested using a cloze format
        Auditory Discrimination:
           Stanine 4—Grade equivalent 1.9
        Phonetic Analysis:
           Stanine 6—Grade equivalent 3.2
        Auditory Vocabulary:
           Stanine 5—Grade equivalent 2.6
        Word Reading:
           Stanine 5—Grade equivalent 2.8
        Reading Comprehension:
           Stanine 5—Grade equivalent 3. 1
        Total Comprehension:
           Stanine 5—Grade equivalent 2.6
```

By analyzing the individual test scores, a teacher can gain a better understanding of the student's strengths and weaknesses. Does the student exhibit strengths in sight vocabulary, literal comprehension, and word recognition skills? Does the student experience difficulty in the area of inferential comprehension? Does the student show an interest in certain reading materials but not in others? These are types of questions that can be answered in diagnosing reading difficulties. Without looking at all the individual components, it is difficult for the instructor to arrive at an adequate understanding of the student's capabilities. Thus, analysis of the test data is of major importance in determining why a particular student does or does not experience difficulty in reading.

For many students, analysis can be made rather briefly; or it can be an in-depth interpretation of a student's strengths and weaknesses. Since the teacher's time is so valuable, an in-depth evaluation of each student is not possible. For most students, brief, but thorough examination of the data should suffice for the

development of an appropriate prescription. In fact, the teacher may wish to summarize briefly the data on a half-page or so for each student, to be referred to as needed. Figure 6.4 gives an example of one way to briefly analyze the data for an individual student.

Interpretation is a necessary adjunct to analysis of the data. In this procedure the data are further evaluated, while the strengths and weaknesses of each student are interpreted, with an exploration of the underlying causes for poor test results. Adequate interpretation is essential to prescription. Without it, strengthening a poor reader's skills become almost impossible.

In interpreting test data, certain patterns from the various tests are normally observable. These give valuable clues to the development of a complete diagnosis, to serve as a basis for appropriate instruction. There are many difficulties that may enter into the interpretation of a student's reading problems. Students may exhibit not only strengths and weaknesses in the reading skills, but behavior patterns and attitudinal tendencies which influence ability. Other areas of concern when interpreting test data are experiential factors, socioeconomic factors, home environmental factors, and physical conditions. All of these can adversely affect the student's reading ability and must be considered in interpreting diagnostic data.

Some of the more prevalent reading difficulties that affect reading ability are classified by Bond, Tinker, and Wasson.[1]

*Classification of Reading Difficulties*

A. Faulty word identification and recognition
   1. Failure to use context and other meaning clues
   2. Ineffective visual analysis of words
   3. Limited knowledge of visual, structural, and phonetic elements
   4. Lack of ability in auditory blending or visual synthesis
   5. Overanalytical
      a. Analyzing known words
      b. Breaking words into too many parts
      c. Using a letter-by-letter or spelling attack
   6. Insufficient sight vocabulary
   7. Excessive locational errors
      a. Initial errors
      b. Middle errors
      c. Ending errors

B. Inappropriate directional habits
   1. Orientational confusions with words
   2. Transpositions among words
   3. Faulty eye movements

C. Deficiencies in basic comprehension abilities
1. Limited meaning vocabulary
2. Inability to read by thought units
3. Insufficient sentence sense
4. Lack of paragraph organization sense
5. Failure to appreciate author's organization

D. Limitation in special comprehension abilities
1. Inability to isolate and retain factual information
2. Poor reading to organize
3. Ineffective reading to evaluate
4. Insufficient ability in reading to interpret
5. Limited proficiency in reading to appreciate

E. Deficiencies in basic study skills
1. Inability to use aids in locating materials to be read
2. Lack of efficiency in using basic reference material
3. Inadequacies in using maps, graphs, tables, and other visual materials
4. Limitations in techniques of organizing material read

F. Deficient in ability to adapt to reading needs of content fields
1. Inappropriate application of comprehension abilities
2. Limited knowledge of specialized vocabulary
3. Insufficient concept development
4. Poor knowledge of symbols and abbreviations
5. Insufficient ability in using pictorial and tabular material
6. Difficulties with organization
7. Inability to adjust rate to suit purposes and difficulty of material

G. Deficiencies in rate of comprehension
1. Inability to adjust rate
2. Insufficient sight vocabulary
3. Insufficient vocabulary knowledge and comprehension
4. Ineffectiveness in word recognition
5. Overanalytical reading
6. Insufficient use of context clues
7. Lack of phrasing
8. Using "crutches"
9. Unnecessary vocalization
10. Inappropriate purposes

H. Poor oral reading
1. Inappropriate eye-voice span
2. Lack of phrasing ability
3. Unfortunate rate and timing
4. Emotionally tense oral reader

When interpreting diagnostic information from various sources, the data must be interrelated. For example, a student who is observed experiencing difficulty in recognizing words while working with the basal group, who scores at a $2^1$ instructional level on the informal reading inventory because of many errors with medial vowel sounds and basic sight words, and who makes numerous mistakes with vowel sounds on the Phonetic Analysis subtest of the *Stanford Diagnostic Reading Test,* obviously has a problem with vowel sounds. By interrelating the diagnostic information, the teacher can interpret the data, and may conclude that the student needs to work on vowel sounds and basic sight word recognition. Further analysis would indicate the specific vowel sounds causing the most difficulty.

Because accurate interpretation is so vital to the development of an appropriate instructional strategy, the following section is devoted to the analysis and interpretation of the reading capabilities of a student at Seabreeze School. More thorough interpretation of other students is presented in appendix I. All the students are in a normal classroom setting, and their teachers have summarized the information according to the four steps outlined in the section on organizing the data. For one student, only two tests were administered; a more extensive diagnosis was made for the other students. Classroom teachers would not write such detailed analyses and interpretations of most students in their classrooms; however, the teacher may write such reports for some students who have more severe reading difficulties. Teachers must have adequate knowledge of this process in order to use the diagnostic-prescriptive procedure to fullest advantage.

In the classrooms from which these students were selected, the teachers first administered a group diagnostic instrument, the *Stanford Diagnostic Reading (SDRT).* This test provided information regarding strengths and weaknesses in several specific areas. It also identified students experiencing extreme difficulties in reading, as well as average and above average readers. For some students, the teacher may wish to obtain further diagnostic data from an informal reading inventory and other informal techniques. Other students need more in-depth diagnosis, using a battery of tests. Student 1 has taken only the *SDRT* and the *Sucher-Allred Reading Placement Inventory.* Students presented in Appendix I were administered a battery of tests.

### Student 1

George is seven years old and an only child. He is preparing to enter the second grade at Seabreeze School. George is a cooperative and responsible student who enjoys school. Two of his favorite subjects are art and music. He also enjoys outdoor activities, such as swimming and bicycle riding.

On the *Stanford Diagnostic Reading Test,* Red Level, George scored consistently at the fourth stanine, which is considered to be in the low average range. There are five subtests on this level of the *SDRT.* His scores were as follows:

Auditory Vocabulary: Stanine 4
Grade equivalent 1.8

Auditory Discrimination: Stanine 4
Grade equivalent 1.8

Phonetic Analysis: Stanine 4
Grade equivalent 1.7

Word Reading: Stanine 4
Grade equivalent 1.6

Reading Comprehension: Stanine 4
Grade equivalent 1.4

The subtest can be further analyzed to indicte more specific difficulties.

*Subtest 1: Auditory Vocabulary*—measures the ability to understand the spoken word. On this subtest, George responded correctly to twenty-one out of thirty-six items. Many of the items answered incorrectly dealt with vowels, indicating possible difficulty in recognizing vowel sounds in written words after hearing them.

*Subtest 2: Auditory Discrimination*—measures the ability to hear likenesses and differences in the beginning and ending of words. George responded correctly to thirty-one of forty items. Six errors involved the discrimination of long and short vowels after hearing them pronounced in various words.

*Subtest 3: Phonetic Analysis*—measures the ability to identify the letter or combination of letters representing the initial or final sounds of words that begin or end with some of the more common sounds. George responded correctly to twenty-eight of forty items. As in Subtests 1 and 2, the majority of errors involved recognizing long and short vowels. He also experienced difficulty with the *nk* blend and the *br* consonant cluster, and tended to confuse *p* and *q.*

*Subtests 4: Word Reading*—essentially a test of word recognition. In this subtest, George had to identify words which describe a specific illustration. He correctly responded to twenty-two of forty-two items. This subtest, as well

as the other three, indicates some weakness in George's basic sight vocabulary.

*Subtest 5: Reading Comprehension*—assesses the ability to read and understand sentences and short paragraphs.

## Part A

This section assesses the ability to read different types of sentences and identify the picture which best illustrates the meaning of the sentence. No specific pattern evolved, but a limited sight vocabulary again caused problems. George could not read many of the words well enough to understand the sentences and choose the correct picture; this may indicate not only difficulty with sight words, but also with an understanding of word meaning.

## Part B

This section measures the ability to read and understand short paragraphs in a modified cloze format. Only five items were answered correctly. Analysis of the errors in this subtest indicates that George is able to pick out key words in a sentence to match with a particular picture, but without the aid of a picture his comprehension decreases rapidly.

On the *Sucher-Allred Reading Placement Inventory* George scored as follows:

*Word Recognition Test*
Primer—eleven of fifteen words correct; three others attempted.
First Reader—eight of fifteen words correct; two others attempted.

*Oral Reading Test*
Primer—frustration level.
No independent or instructional level obtained.

On the *Word Recognition Test,* George missed basic sight words and began to exhibit difficulty in analyzing words toward the end of the test, e.g., *gone* for *sing.* There was also some indication of difficulty with beginning consonant sounds, e.g., substituting *run* for *fun.*

On the *Oral Reading Test* at the Primer level, the teacher pronounced four words for George. In addition, he had one substitution error, *the* for *got,* and two repetition errors at the beginning of sentences. There were also some basic sight vocabulary errors at this level. In spite of these word recognition errors, his comprehension was high with no errors at this level.

## Interpretation

Needs to develop understanding and use of vowel sounds.
Basic sight vocabulary needs attention.
Strength in comprehension with poor word analysis skills contributing to errors in comprehension.
Needs language development to extend vocabulary.

To gain further experience in analyzing and interpreting a student's reading difficulties, other students with poorly developed reading skills are evaluated in appendix I. Detailed evaluations of these students, using several diagnostic instruments, are presented. Evaluations of this type should be reserved for the more severely disabled readers. Even though the information gained is worthwhile, the teacher's time is too valuable to conduct evaluations of this type for all students. Some tips that will assist the teacher in writing reports such as this and those presented in appendix I are given below.

*Follow an organized procedure for presenting the information.* The teacher may wish to use the steps outlined in this chapter or some other plan that provides the necessary information. It is much easier to organize information when a basic outline or planned procedure is followed.

*Give specific data first, including the name of the test, date administered, and scores.* This basic information is essential for future reference and communicating with others. Be sure to check the information carefully as it is transferred from the primary source.

*Provide a brief analysis and interpretation of the data, using only the information obtained from the diagnostic assessments.* Teachers must carefully study the test scores, the correct and incorrect answers of the items, as well as the actions of the student, and interrelate this information to properly diagnose strengths and weaknesses in reading.

*Prepare a summarized list of the information, giving both the reading strengths and weaknesses of the students.* Diagnostic information is more usable when it is succinctly presented. Thus, significant findings from the analysis and interpretation discussion should be listed for easy reference.

*List specific recommendations for instruction to help improve the student's reading.* Using the diagnostic data, the teacher must give specific suggestions for providing prescriptive instruction. These suggestions should be listed in order to aid the teacher in giving appropriate instructions.

*Communicate the ideas so that other teachers as well as parents will understand the information.* This is a professional report which should be beneficial not only to the classroom teacher but also to others who are interested in the student's reading progress. Keep the information objective and present it in a positive manner. Reports such as these may stay in the student's folder for many years.

## Recommendations for Using Data

After organizing, analyzing and interpreting the diagnostic information, the teacher is ready for the third task, which is to use the data for recommending specific instructional strategies. Since these recommendations or prescriptions are based on the strengths and weaknesses revealed in the diagnostic data, it is essential that the teacher use them to the greatest advantage. In order for diagnostic-prescriptive instruction to be successful, appropriate recommendations must be based upon adequate diagnosis.

Because recommendations and prescription development are such essential elements in the diagnostic-prescriptive reading program, specific information and techniques are presented in more detail beginning in chapter 8. It should be noted at this time, however, that when specific suggestions are provided for prescriptive teaching, they should be summarized and listed in a usable manner. The teacher usually does not read a lengthy narrative set of recommendations which give only general suggestions. Specifics presented in a succinct and organized manner greatly assist the teacher in providing appropriate instruction.

**Summarizing Findings for Classroom Use**

The primary purpose of this chapter is to further develop the teacher's capabilities of organizing, analyzing, and interpreting diagnostic information. However, the diagnostic information gathered, analyzed, and interpreted for each student in the classroom is almost totally ineffective without some techniques for summarizing it for classroom use. Information that is not summarized will not be used. Thus, the teacher's fourth task is to summarize the data so that they are readily accessible for daily use in classroom instruction. To be used effectively for developing prescriptions, diagnostic information must be available in a format that is clear and easy to use, allowing the teacher to determine immediately the strengths and weaknesses of each student, along with relevant information such as interests and instructional level.

Diagnostic information should be used for developing reading skills groups and interest groups as well as for individualizing instruction. Because these groups are very flexible, the teacher should have the data available to shift students to appropriate activities during the school day. The authors have used different formats for organizing the information; classroom charts seem to be the easiest to use.

A chart with the scope and sequence of skills listed across the top and students' names down the side is one way to summarize the students' strengths and weaknesses in skill development (see figure 6.5). The information can be determined from the various informal and formal tests and observations, this constitutes an integral part of managing diagnostic-prescriptive instruction for a classroom of students.

The teacher will also need a chart which lists the scores and other data from the tests. This chart has the students' names down the side and the instruments listed across the top (see table 6.1). This provides the necessary summary information regarding general strengths and weaknesses.

Some diagnostic-prescriptive reading systems provide other means of summarizing classroom data. School systems or individual schools may computerize the information and furnish a classroom summary sheet to each teacher. This type of summary saves teacher time, but necessitates continuous updating.

**Figure 6.5**
Skills Chart

| | Word Analysis | | | | | | | Comprehension | | | | |
|---|---|---|---|---|---|---|---|---|---|---|---|---|
| | Short vowel sounds | Long vowel sounds | Variant vowel sounds | Variant consonant sounds | Basic sight words | Compound words | Contextual Analysis | Details | Main idea | Sequence | Conclusions | Cause/Effect |
| Sally | | | | | ✓ | ✓ | | | | ✓ | | ✓ |
| John | | | ✓ | ✓ | ✓ | | | | | | ✓ | ✓ |
| Pam | ✓ | | ✓ | | ✓ | ✓ | ✓ | | ✓ | ✓ | ✓ | ✓ |
| Fred | | | | | | | | | | | | |
| Jane | | | | | | ✓ | | | | ✓ | | ✓ |
| Jack | | | | | ✓ | | ✓ | ✓ | ✓ | ✓ | | ✓ |

✓ = skill deficiency

**Table 6.1**
Summary of Classroom Diagnostic Data

| | ***Stanford Diagnostic Reading Test*, Green Level** | | | | | | ***Sucher-Allred*** | | |
|---|---|---|---|---|---|---|---|---|---|
| | Aud. Voc. | Aud. Disc. | Phonetic Analysis | Struct. Analysis | Comprehension Lit. | Comprehension Inf. | Word List Inst. Level | Oral Reading Inst. | Oral Reading Indep. |
| | | | *Stanines* | | | | | | |
| Lucy | 6 | 6 | 7 | 6 | 6 | 5 | H4 | H4 | M3 |
| Juan | 5 | 5 | 5 | 5 | 5 | 4 | M3 | M3 | L2 |
| Bettye | 6 | 6 | 6 | 6 | 6 | 6 | M4 | M4 | M3 |
| Sam | 2 | 3 | 3 | 2 | 2 | 1 | M1 | M1 | P |
| Delores | 5 | 4 | 5 | 4 | 5 | 4 | H2 | H2 | H1 |
| Frank | 5 | 6 | 5 | 5 | 5 | 5 | M3 | M3 | M2 |

Study Skills

| Fact/Opinion | Predicting outcomes | Follow directions | Abbreviations | Mood/emotional reactions | Relevant/Irrelevant information | Dictionary | Title page | Table of Contents | Maps, etc. | Specialized vocabulary | Card catalog | Outline |
|---|---|---|---|---|---|---|---|---|---|---|---|---|
| ✓ | ✓ | | | ✓ | | ✓ | | ✓ | ✓ | ✓ | ✓ | ✓ |
| ✓ | ✓ | | | | | | | | | ✓ | ✓ | ✓ |
| ✓ | | ✓ | | | ✓ | ✓ | ✓ | ✓ | ✓ | ✓ | ✓ | ✓ |
| ✓ | | | | ✓ | ✓ | | | | ✓ | | | ✓ |
| ✓ | | ✓ | | | | | | | | ✓ | ✓ | |
| ✓ | ✓ | | | | | | | ✓ | | ✓ | ✓ | ✓ |

| Durrell Analysis of Reading | | | | | | Wepman | Slosson I.Q. |
|---|---|---|---|---|---|---|---|
| Oral Read. | Silent Read. | List. Comp. | Word Analysis | Vis. Mem. | Sounds | | |
| | | | | | | | |
| | | | | | | | |
| | | | | | | | |
| | | | | | | | |
| L 1 | L 1 | H3 | M1 | L 1 | L 1 | 20/30 | Low Average |

Still another way of summarizing classroom data is through the use of individual cards for each student. The cards are available commercially and can be coded around the edges with holes indicating strengths and weaknesses in various skills. The teacher develops skill groups by inserting a long knitting needle into a designed hole on the cards for the entire classroom. Those cards that do not fall off the needle have been coded to indicate a weakness in the given skill; thus, those students comprise a skill group for a designated period of time. This is a useful way of grouping students. The weaknesses of this technique include the frequency with which the cards must be updated, the cost of the cards, and the interpretation of the code for placing the holes. These are, however, minor difficulties which have been overcome by many teachers who use this procedure quite satisfactorily in the classroom.

## Reading Expectancy

As teachers review the summarized data for their classrooms, there is usually some discussion as to how various students are progressing, based on their grade level, age, test scores, teacher observation, and any number of other factors. Teachers and administrators attempt to evaluate students' reading potential through the use of reading expectancy formulas. Before discussing the various formulas used, the authors wish to caution teachers to use the results of these formulas only as indicators of reading potential. Most of the formulas are based on the use of an intelligence quotient, which may definitely distort the results. The results of these reading expectancy formulas should be used only as a guide. They provide a rough estimate which should not be used as the basis for making definite decisions about a student.

There are several reading expectancy formulas that are generally discussed:

Harris Formula for Reading Expectancy
Bond and Tinker Reading Expectancy Formula
Horn Reading Expectancy Formula
Monroe's Formula for Reading Grade Expectancy
Durrell Listening Capacity Measure

Each of these formulas varies in its procedures. The second Harris Formula for Reading Expectancy is a refinement of Monroe's formula and is similar to the Horn formula.[2] The formula is

$$\frac{2MA + CA}{3} = \text{Reading Expectancy Age}$$

The original Harris formula[3] is

$$\text{Reading Expectancy} = MA - 5.0$$

The Bond and Tinker Reading Expectancy Formula[4] is probably the most widely used formula:

$$\text{Reading Expectancy} = \text{Years in School} \times \frac{IQ}{100} + 1.0$$

Alice Horn has proposed a set of formulas in which the mental age becomes more important as the student becomes older.[5] These formulas follow.

At age 6.0 to 8.5

$$\text{Reading Expectancy} = \frac{MA + CA}{2} - 5.0$$

At ages 8.6 to 9.9

$$\text{Reading Expectancy} = \frac{3MA + 2CA}{5} - 5.0$$

At ages 10.0 to 12.0

$$\text{Reading Expectancy} = \frac{2MA + CA}{3} - 5.0$$

At ages above 12.0

$$\text{Reading Expectancy} = \frac{3MA + CA}{4} - 5.0$$

Monroe's formula was one of the earliest predictors of reading expectancy.[6] This procedure is quite complex and is seldom used at this time.

The use of a listening comprehension measure as a predictor of reading potential has been suggested by many writers, such as Durrell and Sullivan, Strang, and Ransom.[7] This is probably the best indicator of reading potential, as it is not directly affected by the use of I.Q. scores in a formula. Information regarding listening comprehension measures is presented in chapters 4 and 5.

A study in which the original Harris formula, the second Harris formula, the Bond and Tinker formula, and the formulas of Horn were compared with actual observed reading scores of a population of fourth and fifth grade students, found the following results:

The Harris I formula is the best predictor of actual reading grade of the four reading expectancy formulas under examination.

The Harris I formula is the best predictor of actual reading grade within the middle I.Q. range (90–109, 110–129).

The Bond formula is the poorest formula predictor of reading grade within the middle I.Q. range (90–109, 110–129).

No formula serves as an adequate predictor of reading grade within the low I.Q. range (70–89).

While all four formulas serve as adequate predictor within the high I.Q. range (130–149), none of the four is a significantly better predictor of reading.[8]

Knowing this, teachers should be selective and exercise great caution in the use of reading expectancy procedures.

**Summary**

Synthesizing diagnostic information is an important aspect of the diagnostic-prescriptive process. In order for diagnostic information to be used effectively, it must be as clear and well organized as possible. This can be achieved more readily by using specific guidelines for synthesizing data. The data must be organized, analyzed, and interpreted before recommendations for instruction can be developed. From this information teachers should organize a usable summary format.

Perhaps the key to the successful implementation of diagnostic-prescriptive instruction is the analysis and interpretation of the diagnostic information, since this leads directly to the recommendations for prescriptive instruction. It is primarily the responsibility of the classroom teacher to detect the strengths and weaknesses of each student. By achieving this objective, the instructor is able to implement effectively a prescriptive program for the student.

**Applying What You Read**

In your classroom, you have administered a group reading test and an individual test to the five lowest students. How would you summarize this data for your daily use?

As a middle school teacher, you have two students for whom you need to write in-depth reports regarding their performance. Outline the information that should be included in the report.

How would you as an elementary or middle school teacher summarize and use diagnostic information in your classroom?

**Notes**

1. Guy L. Bond, Miles A. Tinker, and Barbara B. Wasson, *Reading Difficulties: Their Diagnosis and Correction,* 4th ed., 1979, pp. 155–157. Reprinted by permission of Prentice-Hall, Inc. Englewood Cliffs, N.J.
2. Albert J. Harris and Edward R. Sipay, *How to Increase Reading Ability,* 6th ed.
3. Albert J. Harris, *How to Increase Reading Ability,* 4th ed.
4. Bond and Tinker, *Reading Difficulties.*
5. T. L. Torgenson and G. S. Adams, *Measurement and Evaluation for the Elementary School Teacher,* pp. 84–85.
6. Marion Monroe, *Children Who Cannot Read.*
7. Donald D. Durrell and H. B. Sullivan, *Durrell-Sullivan Reading Capacity and Achievement Manual for Primary and Intermediate Tests;* Ruth Strang, *Diagnostic Teaching of Reading;* Grayce A. Ransom, *Preparing to Teach Reading.*
8. Kathleen Dore-Boyce, Marilyn S. Misner, and Lorraine D. McGuire, "Comparing Reading Expectancy Formulas," *The Reading Teacher.*

**Other Suggested Readings**

Dechant, Emerald. *Diagnosis and Remediation of Reading Disabilities.* Englewood Cliffs, New Jersey: Prentice-Hall, 1981. Chapters 1 and 13.
Hansen, Cheryl L., and Eaton, Marie D. "Reading." In Norris G. Harding, Thomas C. Lovitt, Marie D. Eaton, and Cheryl L. Hansen (Eds.) *The Fourth R: Research in the Classroom.* Columbus, Ohio: Charles E. Merrill Publishing Company, 1978, pp. 41–92.

Johnson, Marjorie S., and Kress, Roy A. "Task Analysis for Criterion-Referenced Tests." *The Reading Teacher* 24 (January 1971):355–59.

Ladd, Eleanor M. "More Than Scores From Tests." *The Reading Teacher* 24 (January 1971):305–11.

McGinnis, Dorothy J., and Smith, Dorothy E. *Analyzing and Treating Reading Problems*. New York: Macmillan Publishing Co., Inc., 1982. Chapters 12 and 18.

McGinnis, George H. "Measuring Underachievement in Reading." *The Reading Teacher* 25 (May 1972):750–53.

Massad, Carolyn Emrick. "Interpreting and Using Test Norms." *The Reading Teacher* 26 (December 1972):286–92.

Prescott, George A. "Criterion-Referenced Test Interpretation in Reading." *The Reading Teacher* 24 (January 1971):347–54.

Rodenborn, Leo Y. "Determining, Using Expectancy Formulas." *The Reading Teacher* 28 (December 1974):286–91.

Strang, Ruth. *Diagnostic Teaching of Reading*. 2nd ed., chapter 14. New York: McGraw-Hill Book Company, 1969.

# Organizing the Classroom for Instruction

D iagnostic information is best used for prescriptive instruction in reading when the classroom is properly organized and managed. The teachers at Seabreeze School recognize that Step 3 is crucial to the success of their program. Therefore, they carefully considered the ways in which their classes are organized and arranged in order to meet the diagnosed needs of the students. The ideas in Chapter 7 are provided to assist in this area.

# 7

Classroom teachers at the elementary and middle school levels continuously ask how they can use all of this diagnostic-prescriptive information to provide appropriate instruction for thirty students in one classroom without additional assistance. Teachers at Seabreeze School asked for smaller classes, aides, or volunteers—anything to lower the adult-pupil ratio. This assistance may be helpful, but research does not really support their request.[1] Lower adult-pupil ratios do not directly result in increased student achievement. The teacher who has thirty students, is well organized, and can manage the classroom produces students with higher performance levels than the teacher who has an unorganized classroom with fifteen students. There are many factors in the classroom that affect a student's ability to learn: one of the most important deals with classroom organization and management. While this area is extremely important to successful teaching, often it is not dealt with in pre- and in-service training programs. Teachers then find themselves assigned to the classroom, not knowing how to deal effectively with their time, resources, facilities, and students. Therefore, this chapter is provided to share some ideas on ways to organize and manage elementary and middle school classrooms. The major limitation of this description is that ideas about classroom organization and management lend themselves more to demonstration than to presentation by means of the printed word. Nevertheless, the following questions will be addressed in this chapter.

What are the various procedures for grouping?

How does a teacher determine who goes into which group?

How is the furniture arranged in the classroom to facilitate diagnostic-prescriptive instruction?

How is diagnostic-prescriptive information organized to aid the teacher in instruction?

What are learning centers?

What does the teacher do with the other groups while working with one group?

How are materials selected and used in a diagnostic-prescriptive reading program?

In selecting materials, how does the teacher determine if the reading level is appropriate to the students?

# How does the teacher organize the classroom to facilitate diagnostic-prescriptive instruction?

To aid in understanding this chapter, careful attention should be given to the following terms.

**Vocabulary to Know**

| | |
|---|---|
| Achievement groups | Interest groups |
| Assessments | Learning centers |
| Cross-age tutoring | Management |
| Facilities | Management systems |
| Grouping procedures | Use of material |
| Heterogeneous | Peer tutoring |
| Homogeneous | Organization |
| Individualization | Skills groups |
| | Teacher effectiveness |

**Overview**

Each classroom teacher develops organizational procedures which help in managing reading instruction. There is no magic list which will work for everyone. However, as teachers think about classroom organization and plan for the implementation of diagnostic-prescriptive reading instruction, the following ideas may be helpful.

1. No single classroom pattern or structure is better than another; the local situation, the strengths of individual teachers, and the abilities of the students involved will help to dictate the best system for a particular school.
2. Many criteria should be considered in deciding upon a particular organizational plan: results of informal or formal tests, students' interests, and specific goals of instruction are but a few.
3. Organizational patterns should be flexible; they should be altered as better ways are discovered.
4. There is no absolute criterion which specifies the proper size for groups within a class. Corrective or remedial work usually requires small groups on the other hand, where children can assume considerable responsibility for independent work, the number involved may be greater.

5. Children learn from each other; opportunities to share within a group are basic to good instruction.
6. Organization is a technique or a system, not a "method of instruction." Organization can only facilitate, or hinder, effective instruction.[2]

Teacher effectiveness studies[3], although not totally conclusive as to what makes an effective teacher of reading, have certainly consistently indicated that teacher organization relates to the nature of the on-task behavior of students. Furthermore, the studies have concluded that reading achievement depends on reading instruction and that teachers improve behaviors through direct instruction and reinforcement.

We have stressed that students are different in many respects: chronological age, maturity, interests, experiential background, and environmental background. It is for these very reasons that the classroom teacher's responsibility is so awesome. In order to achieve optimum results from each student and from the learning environment, the teacher must consider all the factors which affect a student's ability to benefit from the instruction received. Without good classroom organization and concern for the needs of each individual student, effective instruction will not likely take place.

Better organized teachers know their students, establish clear and reasonable expectations, have rules and procedures which are consistent with student needs and are consistently followed; they also communicate this information to the students. As a part of the classroom organization students not only receive instruction, but also are involved in explanations, feedback, monitoring, and continuous reinforcement. To help these ideas become more practical in the elementary or middle school classroom, let us for a moment imagine that the first day of school is near, and each teacher is preparing to teach a group of thirty or more students. Imagine the confusion as one attempts to prepare for the opening of school. There are many things to be done to organize reading instruction for the coming year. Books, supplies, desks, tables, etc., must be organized; but most important of all, the organizational techniques for instruction must be decided upon with preparation to implement these plans when the students arrive.

The teacher must decide which management procedures will be used in the classroom. How many groups will there be? How will the groups be organized? What procedures will be used with the groups? These are the initial questions to be answered before confronting the eager faces on the first day of school.

## Management Procedures

Each teacher has his or her own system of managing a classroom; some systems are quite effective, while others create additional work. The management of a classroom is perhaps one of the more difficult tasks confronting the teacher. It is a task which requires an innovative and creative mind as well as skills in organizing and planning for instruction.

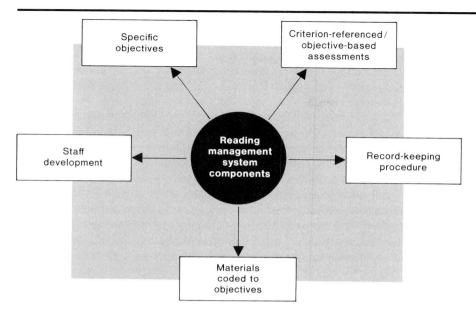

**Figure 7.1**
Components of a
Reading Management
System

This section presents some techniques for managing a classroom. Included are ideas for using management systems in organizing for instruction, suggestions for individualizing instruction to meet student needs, and various techniques for grouping students.

When the idea of a management system is initially mentioned to teachers, many respond that they already have their own systems for managing their classroom. This is as it should be; however, many teachers use a very traditional approach in classroom management. A "routine" is established and followed so that the teacher can supervise student activities at all times. In many instances this system of management means that the students receive instruction from the teacher in their own reading group, but they are required to do busy work at their desks while the teacher works with another group. Unfortunately, this results in repetitive assignments and overuse of workbooks, ditto sheets, and copying from the chalkboard. Many students are alienated by the boredom or frustration which these activities may cause. Rather than helping the teacher to manage the classroom, this system actually adversely affects instruction. Although this may be the teacher's system for managing reading instruction, it is not in the true sense a reading management system and does not result in effective instruction.

A reading management system provides diagnostic information based on the objectives of the reading program and furnishes suggestions which can be used to develop prescriptions for group or individual instruction. Thus, a management system can be used in a very individualized reading program or in group work. The reading management system has several specific components (see figure 7.1):

*Management
Systems*

Specific objectives arranged according to the school's scope and sequence or hierarchy of reading skills.

Criterion-referenced or objective-based pre- and post-assessments to determine knowledge of the skills.

Student and classroom profiles to keep records of the skills learned.

References for activities or materials useful in developing the skills.

Educational materials and staff development sessions to assist the teachers in using effectively the management system.

Teachers must realize that a management system is not a reading program. *A management system is a set of materials used to help the teacher organize and manage the reading program in the classroom.* Thus, in order to use a management system, the teacher must have a scope and sequence or hierarchy of reading skills which are taught as a continuum from level to level. The management system may be used to manage skills taught through the basal reader or, by arranging the objectives from the management system in an appropriate hierarchy, many different approaches and materials may be used for instruction.

There are many commercially developed reading management systems on the market today. Most basal reading series include some type of management system as well as several computerized systems. In addition, some school districts and states have chosen to develop their own management systems. Each must be studied very carefully before deciding to purchase, adopt, adapt, or develop a management system. Some guidelines which may be used are found in Appendix J.

Teachers may be familiar with a management system and understand its various components, yet still feel hesitant to use it as a device for organizing a classroom. This is because few people talk about the "hows" of using a management system. How do you start? How does it relate to the basal program? How do students work? How do you keep the records? How do you test and teach continuously? Answers to these questions are needed before a teacher can use a management system. The following pages outline a step-by-step procedure for using a management system either with a basal reader or with an eclectic approach to teaching reading.

*Step 1: Review the materials and become familiar with all components of the management system.* Teachers must work with the materials in order to develop a workable knowledge of their strengths and weaknesses. However, initially teachers should know what the materials in the system can offer. Review the objectives provided in the system, as well as the assessments. Determine how these materials are similar to or different from what has been used in the past. Keep in mind that the management system materials are not what is used for teaching, but should be regarded as materials to help determine students' strengths and weaknesses in reading.

*Step 2: Determine which skills will be taught in a given lesson.* If using a basal reader, the teacher will note the skills introduced in the lesson; if using a variety of materials, select several appropriate reading skills from the scope and sequence listing. Always select only a few skills so that testing is kept to a minimum at any one time.

*Step 3: Select the objectives from the management system which correspond to the identified skills.* Be sure that appropriate objectives are selected so as to correspond with the skills taught in the lesson. The lesson is enhanced through the use of the objectives and assessments in a management system.

*Step 4: Select or develop pre-assignments to measure the objective.* The teacher should be able to select one assessment for each objective from the management system materials. These may be ready for student use or may need to be duplicated if they are paper-pencil tests. Keep in mind that the teachers in the school or district may determine other ways of assessing certain skills in order better to measure the skill, to avoid the boredom of format, and to utilize ongoing classroom activities more advantagously as means of diagnosis.

*Step 5: Administer the assessments to the students.* Because various groups of students in the classroom will be working on different reading skills, these assessments are usually administered in small groups. Some assessments which do not lend themselves to paper-pencil type testing or group administration may have to be administered individually. Teachers may begin to question how they can devote time to individual testing and often request an aide. An aide is very helpful but often not available.

Some alternatives may be to

Ask for parent or community volunteers,

Schedule one portion of a day each week or every two weeks for individual testing, and provide some library time or total class work to be done while the teacher administers the tests, or

Use students from upper grade levels to assist in the test administration.

Teachers should try to incorporate these assessments into their daily teaching activities in order to avoid continuous isolated skill testing. Thus, students may be involved in a specified learning center activity or game which will serve as the assessment for a given objective.

*Step 6: Score the assessments and record the information on the student and/or class profile.* For students who pass the pre-assessment, instruction on this objective is not necessary. Another skill may be selected for this student as a test objective for instructional purposes. For those students who do not pass the pre-assessment, the teacher must provide appropriate instruction to teach the skill. Regardless, the record sheet is to be marked to indicate a pass or fail on the assessment test which was administered.

*Step 7: Provide instruction on appropriate skills for those students who did not pass the assessments.* If a basal reader approach is being used, then the skills are taught to the students who need the instruction during the skill development portion of the lesson. Students who already know the skill SHOULD NOT be given the instruction again just because the teacher does not have anything else to do with them or because it will change the group. If this is done, then the teacher is not providing diagnostic-prescriptive instruction. If a more individualized approach is used, then skill development may be provided individually or to a small group of students who need to learn this particular skill.

In providing instruction to develop the necessary skills, the teacher may use a reference key to skills developed in various materials. Many commercial companies will key their materials to identified objectives, or teachers may work as a team to identify the specific location in various materials which assist in teaching a skill. This organization of skills and materials greatly assists the teacher in providing more variety in prescriptive instruction.

*Step 8: Post-test to determine if the skill has been learned.* Following instruction in the skill, the teacher must use her judgment in deciding which students have learned the skill and which ones need more instruction. For those who seem to possess the skill, a post-test is administered. If the student passes the post-test, the record sheet is appropriately marked.

*Step 9: Reteach the skill as necessary.* For the student who does not pass the post-assessment or who is not ready to take the post-assessment, the teacher must provide additional instruction. This may be individual or small group instruction.

*Step 10: Provide ample opportunity for the student to use the skill in independent reading.* Reading skills are of little value unless the student uses them in reading. Thus, the teacher must be sure that students are taught how to use the skill and that they should use the skills when reading independently or with content materials. In using a management system, it is very easy for the skills to become isolated; this is not practical and care should be taken to insure that it does not happen! The only way to assure this is to provide the student with ample opportunities to read materials. Figure 7.2 provides a schematic illustration of the steps to be followed in implementing a management system.

Management systems have strengths as well as weaknesses which should be considered as they are used. Some of the strengths are:

1. Because of diagnostic testing data, the student may be instructed on his level, thus avoiding instruction which is either too difficult or too easy.
2. The diagnostic teaching information concerning each student assists the teacher in grouping within the classroom and possibly across grade levels. This provides skill instruction as needed by the individual student.
3. The record keeping procedures provide a way for the teacher to keep track of the individual skill needs of the student. This is useful in communicating information concerning student progress to the parent and to the student.
4. Student and teacher time is not wasted working on skills which the student already possesses.

There are always two sides to every issue; and management systems are certainly not without their share of critics. Therefore, it is only fair to present some of the weaknesses of management systems.

1. Because management systems lend themselves to a routine of test-teach-test, they may be used in such a way as to restrict the innovative teacher's creativity and lead to a boring classroom environment. This may be avoided when the system is properly used. Furthermore, changes in management systems have placed greater emphasis on active teacher participation and group instruction. This could lead to a more efficient approach, allowing students the time to create and foster their natural interest in reading.[4]
2. When skills are taught in isolation without considering their application and the independent reading, students' interests are not met. Thus, skills are learned but the student is unable to apply the skills and is not interested in reading.
3. Criterion-referenced tests are relatively new in education, and some critics question the validity of such tests when used with the management system.
4. One concern mentioned earlier is the debate over the concept of mastery of the skills at a given point. Critics question whether or not the learning of a skill begins and ends in a neat, measurable span of time.

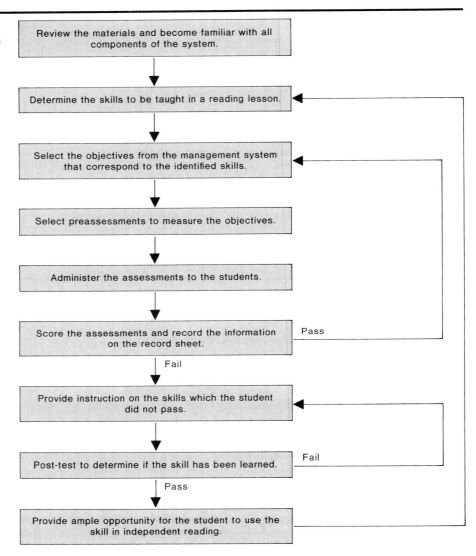

**Figure 7.2**
Steps in Implementing a Management System in the Classroom

Review the materials and become familiar with all components of the system.

Determine the skills to be taught in a reading lesson.

Select the objectives from the management system that correspond to the identified skills.

Select preassessments to measure the objectives.

Administer the assessments to the students.

Score the assessments and record the information on the record sheet.

Pass

Fail

Provide instruction on the skills which the student did not pass.

Post-test to determine if the skill has been learned.

Fail

Pass

Provide ample opportunity for the student to use the skill in independent reading.

5. Because cognitive skills are more easily measured, most management systems stress these almost to the exclusion of the affective and psychomotor skills, which also influence or determine reading performance. Therefore, the classroom teacher must attempt to keep a balance in the reading program.

Other advantages and disadvantages of the management systems have been cited by Duffy, Johnson, Johnson and Pearson, and Klein.[5] These are concerns which must be seriously considered when initiating the use of a management system.

This discussion of management systems points out the advantages as well as the disadvantages of using such a system. One point that is not debatable, however, is that if diagnostic-prescriptive instruction is to be provided, the teacher must use some organized procedure to assist in managing the learning environment. In order to promote good participation and progress, there is an obvious need to motivate the student. Therefore, the wise classroom teacher should use an organizational system designed (1) to ensure proper assessment of students' needs, and (2) to prescribe appropriate instructional activities. Since motivation and interest play such a major role in successful instruction, it is imperative that the classroom teacher avoid assigning dull, repetitive tasks, then rationalizing this comfortable routine as an example of the advantageous use of a management system. Rather, the teacher should maintain flexibility, vary tasks, stress creative aspects of learning, and employ within the management system the types of activities which improve the learning environment. Remember that the use of a management system does not preclude the assignment of creative and interesting tasks.

Individualized instruction is a topic which has been discussed at some length in the past few years. At one point during this discussion, many educators believed that individualized instruction was limited to one-to-one instruction. Each student had to be working on a different assignment in order for instruction to be considered individualized. However, the term individualization is now interpreted to mean that every student must be working on tasks which are geared to his or her instructional level; it is not necessary that each student work on a particular task separately from all the others. It is essential, however, that each student work on an assignment designed to meet his or her individual needs. Thus, it is entirely possible and indeed probable that a student will be receiving individualized instruction within a grouping format, since there may be other students in the classroom who need instruction on the same skill at the same level. In individualizing instruction, whether it is done separately for each student or within a group, it is necessary to obtain some diagnostic information so that a logical placement of the student in the instructional setting may be made. Information received from the assessments in the management system, or from other informal assessments, is used at this time.

**Individualization**

Of the various ways of providing individualized instruction, working with groups is probably foremost. Grouping is discussed in some detail later in this chapter; at this point, it is necessary to note that in individualized instruction students are grouped because diagnostic information indicates that all in the group need the same type of instruction on the same skill, not because it's easier for the teacher to work with a group!

Another technique used in individualizing instruction is to allow periods of independent reading. Again, students do not have to do this alone and apart from the class. It is an activity that encourages students to make some independent

decisions about what they would like to read. Student participating in independent reading activities should be allowed some flexibility and be given an opportunity to express themselves in activities which grow out of independent reading. Perhaps the student would enjoy writing a poem or short story, or working with a group of other students in role-playing activities, presenting a play, making a pretend movie with real cameras (or, if not too expensive, a real movie), or developing a series of short stories for publication on the school press (ditto machine). These types of activities promote growth and the ability to make decisions; they also augment the learning environment. In addition, they add interest to the school environment, often developing an eagerness to learn. This technique used in individualizing instruction is not to be confused with the individualized reading approach, which uses library books as the main source of instruction. This approach is discussed in greater detail in chapter 8.

An interesting technique for individualizing instruction, which has been used by content teachers, is the use of contracts in assigning tasks for instruction and as an organizational procedure. Teachers involved with reading instruction have used this technique with some success, especially in middle school remedial reading classes. The theory behind the use of contracts is that the teacher and the student will arrive together at a logical starting point for instuction. They will agree upon a goal to be reached and specific objectives to be accomplished. A period of time for completion of the task, as well as the specific tasks, will be agreed upon, with both parties more or less bound to abide by their part of the contract. Sometimes the student and teacher will actually sign the contract in order to instill a more formal sense of responsibility. Another unused facet of this agreement is that students may contract for the grade they wish to receive for their work. Of course the grade received, if grades are given, will depend upon the quality of the work. Teachers should note, however, that if this technique is used, the student must continue to have some direct instruction. Students do not improve their reading by being assigned materials; effective teachers first provide instruction, then contract with students for reinforcement activities.

This arrangement can be used to a certain extent with poor readers, but there are limitations to consider. Such elements as the student's ability to work independently for the period of time specified in the contract, the reading skills required by the student, and the availability of appropriate materials and activities must be weighed before the teacher decides to use a contract with a student. The poor reader will need a short-term contract in order to feel a sense of accomplishment before becoming frustrated. In addition, the contract usually works better with older students than with younger ones. However, used in moderation, this technique is a good motivating device for the more gifted student and sometimes also for the slower student. A sample contract is provided in figure 7.3.

Paraprofessionals and volunteers can greatly assist the instructor in implementing an individualized program. The trained paraprofessional can work with individuals or small groups carrying out the plans made by the teacher. This allows the teacher extra time to work with individual students and to serve as a manager of instruction. However, in effectively using aides in the classroom,

**Figure 7.3**
Sample Contract

Name: *Wendy Crowden*                                    Grade: *5th*

Starting Date: *Feb. 1, 19--*                            Ending Date: *Feb 5, 19--*

**Objectives:**

1. To decode words containing vowel sounds represented by the letters *oi, oy, ou,* and *ow.*
2. To recognize fact from opinion in reading selections.
3. To follow directions independently in completing this contract.

**Assignments:**

*Objective #1:*

– Work with the teacher in Group 3 to review the vowel sounds.
– Select 2 of the following tasks. Complete and give them to the teacher. – *The New Phonics We Use,* Book D, pp. 56-57, 47-50.
  – *Phonics Workbook,* Book B, pp. 147-149, 151-154.
  – *Reading Booster Code Book,* pp. 71-76.
  – *Learning Center A.*

*Objective #2:*

– Work with the teacher in Group 1 to discuss distinguishing fact and opinion.
– Select 1 of the following tasks. Complete and give it to the teacher.
  – *Basic Reading Skills,* pp. 106-109.
  – *Study Skills for Information Retrieval,* Book 1, p. 75; Book 2 p. 75; Book 3, p. 72.
– Complete the activities in Learning Center C.

*Objective #3:*

– Check your work to be sure that you followed directions!

*Wendy Crowden*                          *Mrs. Bailey*
_____                          _____
Student                                  Teacher

**Figure 7.4**
Individualized
Instruction

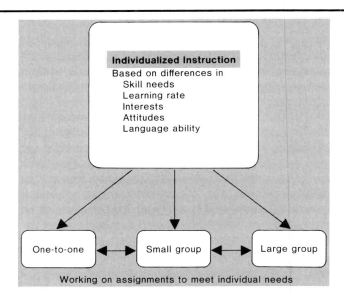

Individualized Instruction

Based on differences in
Skill needs
Learning rate
Interests
Attitudes
Language ability

One-to-one    Small group    Large group

Working on assignments to meet individual needs

teachers must be very well organized. Hiatt found that teachers with aides spent twenty-nine minutes per day in disciplining students while those without aides spent approximately forty minutes. Eleven minutes may seem significant until a final statistic is noted—only six of the eleven minutes were used for instruction![6] Organized teachers who individualize instruction tend to provide more instruction, with or without aides.

Teachers must realize that some one-to-one instruction is essential. When a student fails to progress in a small group situation or has difficulty with some particular skill, individual attention is needed. Yet instruction on a one-to-one basis is neither needed nor desirable with every student on a continuous basis. Students need the social interaction developed by working in large and small groups. (See figure 7.4) Musgrave provides many ideas for teachers to consider in individualizing instruction in elementary or middle school classrooms.[7] Further ideas about individualizing instruction in reading are available in articles by Wallen, Slater, Reeves, and Eisenhardt.[8] Although individualized instruction on a one-to-one basis has declined during the last few years, teachers should recognize the value of this management technique and note that authorities predict a revival of emphasis in this area during the late 1980s.[9]

## Grouping

In elementary schools the use of grouping is probably more widespread than any other type of instructional management procedure. Grouping allows the classroom teacher considerable flexibility in implementing the instructional program, permitting the teacher to devote more time to individuals than would ordinarily be possible in a whole-class type of format. Grouping also facilitates better adaptation of materials and resources to individual needs.

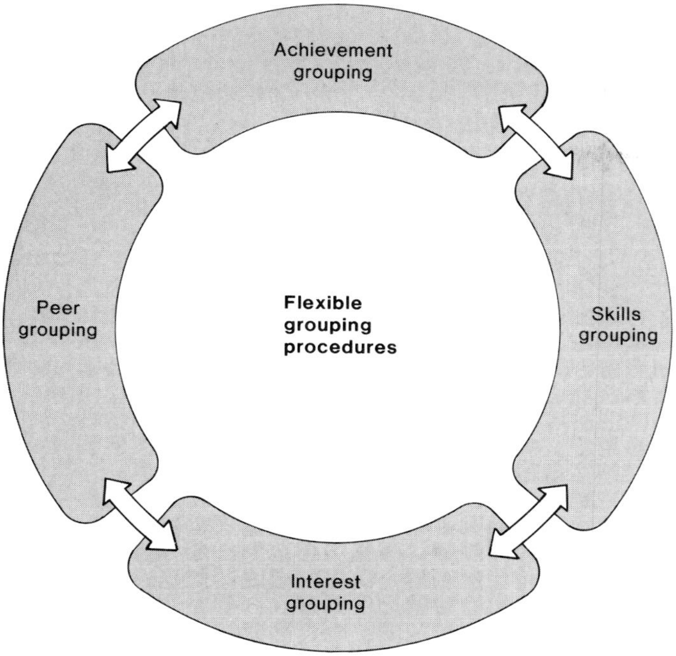

**Figure 7.5**
Intraclass Grouping
Formats

Various types of grouping procedures are used in schools and classrooms. Procedures differ from classroom to classroom, and especially from the elementary to the middle school levels. The two main types of grouping often debated are *homogeneous* and *heterogeneous*. Homogeneous grouping is used more at the upper levels when students are ability-grouped or assigned to tracks. At the elementary level more heterogeneous grouping patterns are usually found. One of the greatest problems is the idea that homogeneous grouping alleviates the need for smaller groups within the individual classroom. Whether a classroom is homogeneously or heterogeneously grouped according to the school management design, further grouping within the classroom is essential. It is unlikely that there will be thirty students in a classroom whose performance is exactly the same and who need exactly the same instruction.

The population of a classroom may be grouped in two ways—intraclass and interclass. In an intraclass format, students can be grouped in various ways for instructional purposes. These are basically achievement groups, skills groups, interest groups, and cross-age or peer groups (see figure 7.5). Each of these techniques for grouping will be examined more carefully.

*Intraclass Formats.*

*Achievement Grouping*    Probably the most widely used grouping technique is that of achievement grouping. In this format, based upon their demonstrated achievement, students are divided into several groups. Those performing at the highest level are grouped together, and those performing at the lowest level are

grouped together, with one or more groups organized between the highest and the lowest level. It is rather common practice for the classroom teacher to use this method in forming three reading groups. However, the authors suggest that the instructor have a minimum of three groups initially and, as soon as management procedures permit, that these be extended to perhaps as many as five groups, in order better to meet the reading levels of the students in a class. Teachers should remember that in a typical fifth-grade classroom which is heterogeneously grouped, reading levels may range from low first to ninth level. Therefore, it is essential that more than three groups be used in an effort to accommodate this wide variation.

Since achievement grouping is, as a general rule, the most widely used grouping procedure, one should exercise caution in designating student placement. Try to avoid, through continuous evaluation of the student, a situation in which the student is labeled a poor reader and not given an opportunity to improve his or her position in the classroom. Teachers must be flexible in their grouping techniques, encouraging students to move from one group to another as their needs dictate. Research indicates that students frequently are not moved into other achievement groups during the school year.[10] Once placed in a certain reading group, they usually remain with it for the year. This is unfortunate, since students' learning rate changes during the school year, and all within a group do not progress together.

In addition, the teacher should be cautious as to what instruments are used to place students in achievement groups. Many times achievement tests do not accurately reflect the students' knowledge or skill. Thus, using these tests as a basis for grouping is very hazardous. If used for grouping purposes, achievement test results should be considered in conjunction with teacher observations and other individualized measures. No one instrument alone can serve as the tool for grouping students. However, test scores should be used as an aid in grouping. Instructional grouping based only on teacher judgement tends to create greater socioeconomic segregation than grouping based on test scores alone.[11]

Teachers also seem to praise lower ability groups more than the higher achievement groups, although the students read on a lower level and answer more questions incorrectly.[12] Moreover, in teaching achievement groups, instructors tend to treat the group as a teaching unit, rather than considering individual student needs. Low level groups generally receive highly structured instruction in decoding and basic comprehension skills, while the top level group enjoys more flexibility in procedures and assignments as well as instruction in the more sophisticated comprehension skills.[13] Thus, teachers should consider other grouping patterns in addition to achievement groups in managing reading instruction.

*Skills Grouping*     A second grouping format involves the use of reading skills for the purpose of student placement. Skills grouping is used to place students in specific groups for instruction in a given skill. It is entirely possible that this placement will be different from the achievement grouping placement. For example, a student may be in the high reading group but have difficulty with a

reading skill that others in the group seem to have mastered. Such a student would work in a skill group which may be composed of students from several other achievement groups who also have difficulty with this skill. The primary method of implementing this type of management procedure is to group the students on the basis of their strengths and weaknesses in a specific reading skill area.

When one or more students exhibit difficulty in using a specific skill, the teacher must, through skill grouping or one-to-one instruction, provide the appropriate instruction for them. This type of grouping is usually for a short period of time, since the primary purpose is to strengthen a skill deficiency. When the skill is learned, the student leaves this skill group and moves to another, as needed.

*Interest Grouping*     Another type of grouping that has been used rather successfully is interest grouping. This allows students who have similar interests to work together in order to explore their interests in greater depth. A positive aspect of this type of grouping is that students from all achievement levels are intermingled, which provides for considerable interaction without regard to reading level. Used interchangeably with achievement and skill grouping, this type of instructional grouping format should prove to be highly successful, since it motivates students to learn and work together. One of the weaknesses of achievement grouping is the lack of opportunity for students from different levels to interact and discuss subjects of importance to them. Interest grouping provides this opportunity, thus overcoming one of the reasons students become disenchanted with learning to read. In addition, interest grouping helps to make reading enjoyable and interesting, rather than a frustrating chore. Therefore, interest

grouping helps motivate students who never seem to become enthusiastic over any of the reading material assigned to them. The use of interest grouping will also allow students from deprived backgrounds to learn by interacting with young people from more diversified experiential backgrounds. Learning about other students' experiences helps to improve the oral language development of the poorer readers and in turn improves their reading. Interest grouping is a very useful procedure which teachers should use continuously in their classes, inasmuch as internal social processes in groups contribute to subsequent differential opportunities for students[14]; social development and reading groups are related!

*Peer Grouping*    A fourth type of grouping which has proven very helpful in elementary and middle school classrooms, is the concept of student or peer tutoring. This type of grouping may also be referred to as cross-age tutoring, an instructional format, in which an older student usually works with a younger student in an effort to improve the reading skills of the latter. It has been found, however, that in many cases the older students also improve their reading skills, especially if they are poor readers.[15] Therefore, an added advantage of this program is that students who would not ordinarily read books they consider childish, will read them so that they can be better able to help "their" student. Thus, in peer tutoring everyone seems to benefit, the student, the tutor, and the teacher!

In some cases, students in the same classroom may tutor one another. This procedure is used when a student is having difficulty with a concept or skill which another member of the class seems to understand. Teachers sometimes find that other students can be of greater assistance in teaching a concept to a confused student than can the instructor. Additionally, the tutor usually progresses as much, if not more than the person he/she is tutoring.[16]

In experiences with peer tutoring, the authors have found this to be a very effective way to motivate the poor reader. This procedure has a very positive effect on learning to read; students exhibit increased interest in learning to read and have a more positive attitude toward themselves. Furthermore, students doing the tutoring develop a more positive self-image and show greater interest in their school work.

One way the authors have used the peer tutoring concept is with fifteen-year-old nonreaders tutoring kindergarten and first graders in an adjoining school. The older students had a dual incentive for reading "easy" materials: they had to learn to read them in order to provide the story hour for these classes. One of the most amusing yet most beautiful occasions was the day these older boys had to learn to read "The Three Bears" because of a request from a little kindergarten girl. They could not let her down, and they could not read the story with only a two-day notice, so they decided to put on a play about the story and only learn to read certain parts! We drew straws for the Goldilocks part, put on wigs and costumes, and created a smash hit with these younger students. The boys were so pleased with themselves that they began to take requests for stories! Needless to say they had a very proud teacher!

The various procedures for intraclass grouping discussed in the preceding pages should be of assistance as teachers organize their classroom learning environment. The teacher serves as manager of the instructional program, and must use a variety of intraclass grouping procedures in order to provide the most appropriate instruction for each student. A student may be involved in all four types of groups during one day. The authors have used all these procedures and found them to be quite successful. Needless to say, no instructional plan yet devised can compensate for poorly organized classroom settings and ineffective teaching; therefore, it is essential that good diagnostic-prescriptive procedures be implemented by means of good management and organizational techniques.

*Interclass Formats.* Interclass or cross-class grouping is the second major grouping procedure. With this type of grouping, students from several classes are integrated in common reading classrooms according to their achievement levels. In other words, parallel scheduling among classes is used to facilitate reading instruction. The purpose of interclass grouping is to permit the teachers involved to develop homogeneous units. Several groups are formed, as determined by the reading levels of the students involved, then each teacher works with a specific group. This type of grouping may be limited to one grade level or may cross several grade levels. For example, all the students in the fifth grade would be divided into groups according to their reading levels. Then each fifth-grade teacher would work with a particular group during the time designated for reading. Crossing grade levels would involve dividing students from several grade levels into groups according to their

reading levels, regardless of age or maturity. Teachers would then work with students from mixed grade levels. Since this grouping procedure may create a poor self-concept for older students reading on a lower-level, great caution must be exercised in using it.

An assumption often made concerning this type of grouping is that it reduces the range of abilities in each classroom. In reality, however, it does not reduce the range of abilities significantly, since the selection criteria used are often relatively weak. This type of grouping has been found to be useful in short-term periods, but its effectiveness is greatly reduced over longer periods of time. When this procedure is used, instructors must realize that it does not preclude the need for grouping within the classroom. As was pointed out in the discussion on homogeneous grouping: no matter how a classroom of students is grouped, further small groupings are needed.

Another significant problem with interclass grouping is that the teacher assigned to a particular student may know little about that student because the instructor has contact for only about an hour per day. This creates some difficulties in correlating appropriate activities for the student. Also, reading becomes separated from the other learning activities. This reduces the effectiveness of instruction, since when it is taught in separate groups, reading is not integrated into the broad spectrum of learning.

**Figure 7.6**
Pros and Cons of
Interclass Grouping

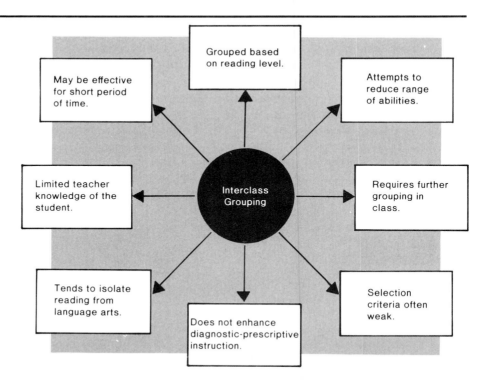

*Chapter 7*

Although interclass grouping is used in many schools caution must be exercised in dealing with the problems which have been identified. Students can readily be "lost" in the shuffle from teacher to teacher. More important, it is extremely difficult for the teacher to diagnose reading problems and provide effective prescriptive instruction when teacher-student contact time is so limited.

The use of diagnostic information is an integral part of the classroom teacher's responsibilities, as this information is essential in determining how best to organize the groups within the classroom. The data which the teacher receives from classroom-oriented diagnostic instruments should be carefully evaluated and used to assign each student to a group that will enhance prospects for improving his or her reading level. One note of caution which is necessary to mention again at this point: the original diagnosis will undergo changes during the year, which means that the student's grouping assignments change. Therefore, *it is imperative that classroom teachers use continuous diagnosis in order to make the necessary adjustments in the students' grouping assignments.* This procedure is stressed, because some teachers may make an initial grouping assignment, allow a routine to set in, and forget to re-evaluate the student's group placement.

**Organizing Groups**

One of the more critical aspects of grouping is the manner in which these groups are organized. Since the type of groups generally used has been discussed in some detail, let us now examine ways to develop these groups in the classroom. Because the majority of classroom teachers have a three-group instructional format, the sample design will use three groups.

Table 7.1 presents a basic design for implementing an instructional program in reading in the elementary and middle school grades. This design uses three groups and a Directed Reading Lesson format (see chapter 8), the design can be easily expanded and adapted for use with more than three groups so long as the basic organization is kept intact. The three groups are achievement groups, with other grouping patterns to be used as needed within the design. The time variable may be adjusted by the instructor to reflect hours actually spent in reading and language arts. This plan may be used for several days if the time for reading is short.

In order effectively to manage groups and use a design such as the one presented in Table 7.1, the teacher should be aware of some lessons learned by the authors.

1. *Time the activities* for each group so that one group does not finish its assignment while the other groups have much longer to work. Try to keep the time for various assignments for the groups about the same.
2. *Provide alternatives* for the students when they finish their assignments. Because it is impossible to have all students finish their work at exactly the same time, it is necessary for the teacher to provide activities when the assigned work is completed. For example, a reading center provides an opportunity for the student to enjoy independent reading activities, or an activities center can give additional assistance in developing reading skills. Students

need to be aware of their alternatives as they finish assignments so that they will not need to disturb the teacher's work with another group, or others in the class.

3. *Appoint a leader* for each group. If students have questions as they work they can direct them to the leader; in this way they will not disturb the other groups or the teacher. If neither the leader nor the group can answer the questions, then the leader may ask the teacher. This procedure also helps control the student who constantly seeks attention by asking questions of the teacher.

4. *Provide interesting activities* which develop language skills. Teachers must realize that paper-pencil tasks become very boring to students; thus, manipulative activities should be provided. In addition, games and learning centers can be used to furnish other activities when students finish their assignments. In far too many classrooms, students are expected to spend their time doing ditto sheets and copying from the board. This is often a waste of student time and paper!

5. Use some time for *total class activities*. At the beginning of each school day or each class, take a few minutes for a total class activity. This may include listening to a record or story, singing a song, or playing a game. Social skills, as well as language skills, are greatly helped by such activities.

   During this time, the teacher may give group assignments, making certain that students understand what they are to do as well as what they can do when they finish assignments. Depending on the students' age level and attention span, the teacher will need to bring the class together as a total group every ten to thirty minutes for a brief break. Otherwise, students become confused as they move from area to area and tend to lose interest in their work.

6. *Provide activities which are appropriate* to the student's level and needs. Do not provide the same listening activity or skills activities for several groups. In table 7.1, the headings are the same for each group, but the activities for each group must be designed to meet individual levels and needs. Although it takes much time to develop centers, games, and activities, this is necessary for each group!

In an effort to demonstrate the usefulness of grouping procedures in the content area, a format for implementing these procedures in a content-classroom was also developed. More effective instruction can take place in the content areas if attention is given to individual students through some grouping procedures. The role of the content teacher, as stated in chapter 3, has changed from that of a conveyor of information to one of facilitating instruction and attending more to the individual needs of students. Necessity has dictated this change because of the increased problems that students have had in coping with content material. Therefore, it is hoped that an instructional design for content-area teaching will help content teachers to incorporate reading instruction in their classes at the elementary and middle school levels.

**Table 7.1**

Organizational Format for Reading Instruction in an Elementary Classroom

| Time* | Group 1 | Group 2 | Group 3 |
|---|---|---|---|
| 9:00-9:20 | *Review skills from last lesson.* May work in learning centers and various skills groups. May be in skills or interest groups with Groups 2 or 3. | *Language development.* May work on language activities such as writing, listening, etc. | *Introduce new skills.* (Teacher) Students from Groups 1 and 2 may be included. |
| 9:20-9:40 | *Language development.* Use listening center, writing area, or discussion activities. Some may work with group 2. | *Introduce new skills.* (Teacher) Students from Group 1 may be involved. | *Skill work.* Students from Groups 1 and 2 may be involved. |
| 9:40-10:00 | *Introduce new skills.* (Teacher) Use chalkboard, activities, etc. | *Skill work.* Students from Group 1 may be involved. | *Language development.* May need to work in skills centers or with Groups 1 or 2, or on other related language activities. |
| 10:00-10:20 | *Skill work.* Use workbooks, charts, etc. | *Introduce story.* (Teacher) | *Review skills from last lesson.* |
| 10:20-10:40 | *Additional reading activities.* Skill groups for those who need more work, independent reading and activity for others. Good time for interest groups. | *Review skills from last lesson.* May also work on skills with Group 1 or in interest group. | *Introduce story.* (Teacher) |
| 10:40-11:00 | *Introduce story.* (Teacher) Build background for reading, using pictures, charts, etc. | *Silent reading.* | *Review skills.* |
| 11:00-11:20 | *Silent reading (at desks).* | *Oral reading/comprehension check.* (Teacher) | *Silent reading.* Need to read story at least two times. |
| 11:20-11:40 | *Oral reading/comprehension check.*† (Teacher) Read orally only for specific purpose and discuss what was read silently. | *Follow up.* | *Oral reading/comprehension check.*† (Teacher) |
| 11:40-12:00 | *Follow up.* | *Review skills.* May also include students from groups 1 and 3. | *Follow up.* |

*Times given are for illustration and must be adjusted to the teacher's schedule. Group 3 is considered the low group in this class; thus, the teacher begins with this group.
†The teacher may work with two groups, using group leaders and activities that allow him or her to move from group to group.

Figure 7.7 presents the basic design for implementing reading instruction in the content areas. Three groups are used, and various activities presented to provide the classroom teacher with a choice of activities in classroom instruction. This format can be easily expanded for use with more than three groups. Since some activities require more time than others, the content specialist should determine the average amount of time that the activities will require in order to establish a framework for presenting them. This design follows the Directed Reading Activity format (chapter 8) and the SQ3R procedure for reading the material (chapter 3).

Content teachers may benefit from the organizational suggestions previously discussed. By adjusting instruction to the reading levels and interest of the students, content teachers will find that students gain more information about the content area and show more interest in the classroom. Thus, organizing and managing the classroom becomes an easier task.

## Arranging the Facilities

As teachers use various ideas in organizing and managing their classrooms, they will need to consider how the classroom facilities may be arranged to assist the program. The types of facilities needed will depend upon the particular management ideas of each teacher. However, certain limitations are always involved in considering physical arrangements. Regardless of the teachers' ideas or needs, time, space, finances, and the goals of the individual school must be considered.

Given the limitations imposed, it is the obligation of each teacher to derive maximum advantage from the facilities available. For example, thirty desks in a room do not obligate the teacher to forego all grouping and individualization ideas in developing teaching plans. The desks must be arranged to provide instruction which meets the needs of the individual students! In an effort to assist the classroom teacher in arranging the facilities properly, two diagrams indicating possible arrangements which stress grouping and individualization procedures, are shown in figures 7.8 and 7.9. They are not to be considered as the only appropriate arrangements of facilities, but rather as two of many ways to arrange the classroom for optimum instruction.

These two diagrams represent classrooms which may be in the traditional school or in the newer, open concept school (modular structure). Regardless of wall arrangement, such a classroom setup provides for flexible groupings and freedom of movement in the room. Ideally, the teacher needs some individual student desks, as well as tables for group work. Ample storage space is needed, since the teacher must be able to store the materials, activities, games, and centers when not in use. As indicated in the diagrams, reading and activity areas must be provided, especially in the elementary grades. If the classroom is not carpeted, it is possible to obtain carpet squares from carpet stores to cover those small areas. Using a little carpet and adding a few big cushions and a rocking chair will encourage students to visit the reading corner in their leisure time.

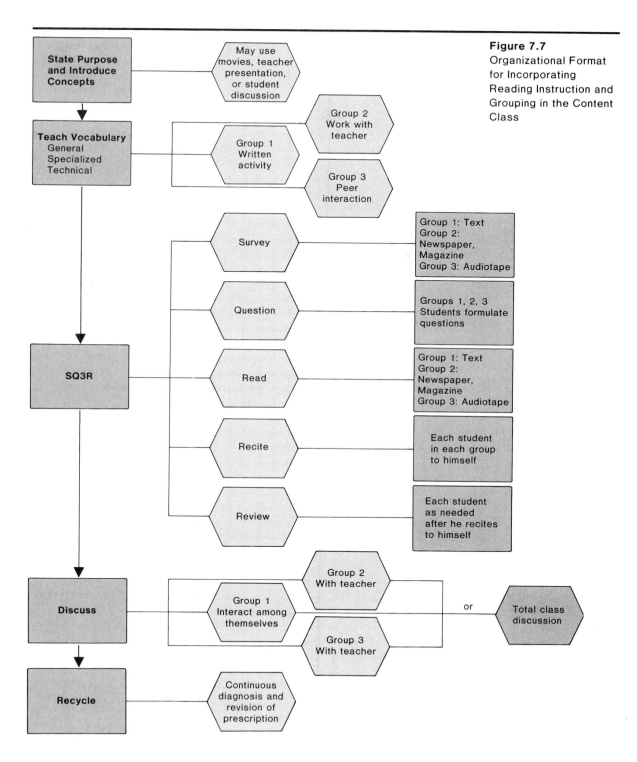

**Figure 7.7**
Organizational Format
for Incorporating
Reading Instruction and
Grouping in the Content
Class

State Purpose
and Introduce
Concepts

May use
movies, teacher
presentation,
or student
discussion

Teach Vocabulary
General
Specialized
Technical

Group 1
Written
activity

Group 2
Work with
teacher

Group 3
Peer
interaction

Survey

Group 1: Text
Group 2:
Newspaper,
Magazine
Group 3: Audiotape

Question

Groups 1, 2, 3
Students formulate
questions

SQ3R

Read

Group 1: Text
Group 2:
Newspaper,
Magazine
Group 3: Audiotape

Recite

Each student
in each group
to himself

Review

Each student
as needed
after he recites
to himself

Discuss

Group 2
With teacher

Group 1
Interact among
themselves

Group 3
With teacher

or

Total class
discussion

Recycle

Continuous
diagnosis and
revision of
prescription

*How Does Classroom Organization Facilitate Diagnostic-Prescriptive Instruction?*

**Figure 7.8**
Room Arrangement

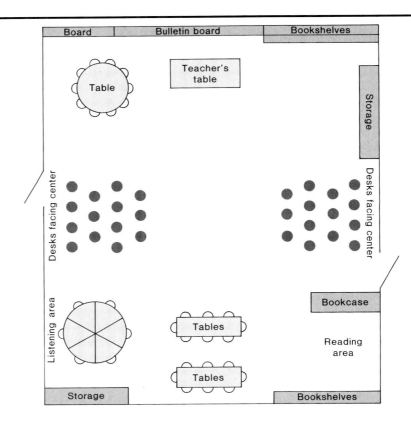

In addition to the availability of desks, tables, chairs, book cases, and storage areas, the teacher must be concerned with the attractiveness of the facilities. A clean, attractive room is very useful in motivating students to learn. Facilities alone do not create a learning environment; their arrangement, usefulness, cleanliness and attractiveness are the key factors. Thus, the teacher should provide attractive bulletin boards, which may contain activities for the students to use in developing various reading skills as well as areas to display the students' work. These displays need to be changed periodically. Teachers may also ask students to be responsible for developing bulletin boards during the year and displaying their work. This encourages the students to feel that they are an important part of the classroom. Attractive bulletin boards and displays add much to the classroom, and sometimes a little paint can brighten old desks and tables to help create a better feeling about the room. Students need to feel at home in the classroom in order to benefit most from instruction.

Here is an example of how changes in the classroom facilities affect learning. A first-year teacher was placed in an inner-city school with fifth and sixth graders who had been "going through" an average of three teachers a year. He was told

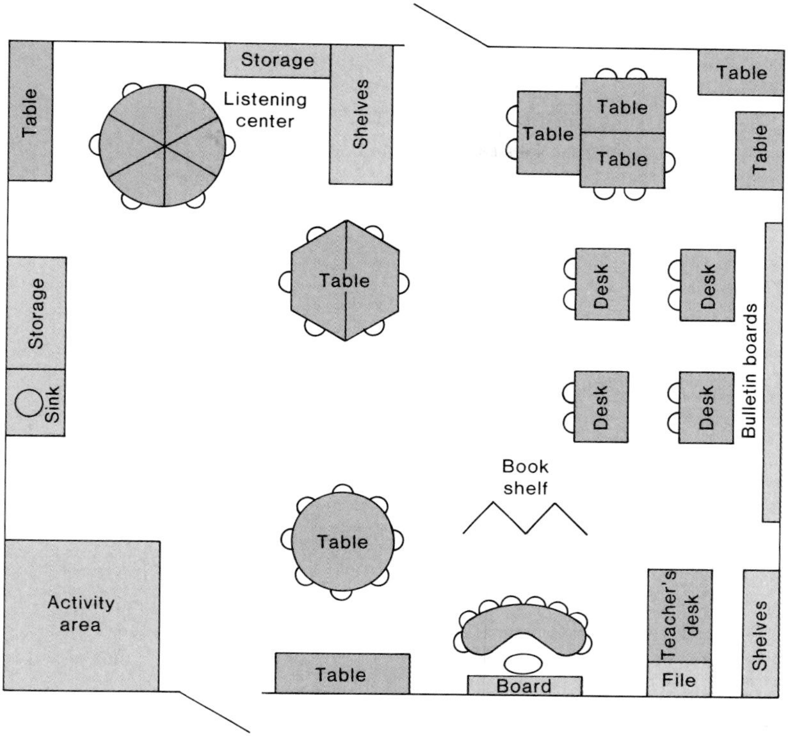

**Figure 7.9**
Room Arrangement

to teach them to read. He tried. The students had no respect for the school, the room, the materials, or the teacher, and the teacher felt very uncomfortable in the room. One day after school as he sat in tears, the idea occurred to him that something had to be done with the room. He presented the idea to the classes the next day, and they were all quite excited—after all, it meant putting away the books for a few days! With the principal's agreement, the classes obtained paint, old carpet, curtains, and tables, and made their classroom into what they wanted. The teacher made some cushions for the reading corner, and the boys turned the old closet space into individual study carrels. Needless to say, these students were proud of their room. This pride was definitely reflected in the changes in their attitude and achievement. The teacher even asked to come back the next year!

Facilities do make a difference. The teacher can arrange the classroom so that it is comfortable, and provide students with the opportunity to adjust the facilities for their individual needs. A warm, comfortable room makes coming to school an enjoyable experience for both the teacher and the students.

**Use of Materials**

The students are assessed, the groups determined, and the facilities comfortably arranged. Now it is time to begin to work with the students. The first question that teachers must ask is "What materials do we have?" This is an essential question, because teachers need a variety of materials in order to provide appropriate prescriptive instruction. However, variety does not mean just a large number of materials, but rather materials which meet the various needs in the classroom.

**Figure 7.10**
Tips to Consider before Selecting Materials

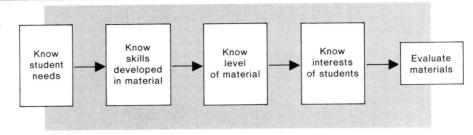

**Selecting Materials**

Student needs as revealed by diagnostic testing is the teacher's first consideration in selecting materials. A second consideration in selecting appropriate materials is to learn what skills they include as well as their level. Suppose that a teacher has a class of third graders who are mostly reading below grade level and have much difficulty in recognizing words. If all the materials are written at about a third-grade level and emphasize comprehension skills, then there is not much variety of materials. In this case, the teacher would require additional materials to meet the students' needs. Another necessary consideration before beginning to review materials carefully for possible selection is to know the students' interests. As discussed in the previous section, considering the students' interests results in improved learning for the student and easier instruction for the teacher. When these basic ideas have been considered, instructors can more thoroughly evaluate the reading materials available. One evaluation form which may be used is provided in figure 7.11. Other evaluation procedures are available from Kaufman, Burns and Roe, Harris and Smith, Cunningham, and Dixon.[17]

**Figure 7.11**
Guidelines for Use in Evaluating Instructional Materials.
Developed by the Florida Right to Read Effort, Florida Department of Education, Tallahassee, Florida, 1975. Reproduced by permission of the Florida Department of Education, Tallahassee, Florida.

Title of material or series: _____
_____

Author(s): _____
Publisher:_____ Copyright date:_____
Address: _____
Price for one unit or part of unit (specify): _____,

Price for teacher's guide or edition: _____
Grade levels: _____

**Figure 7.11**
(continued)

Check
Yes     No

A. Content
   1. meets needs and interest of intended student population ___ ___
   2. contains balanced representation of different socio-economic and ethnic groups ___ ___
   3. provides review and reinforcement of skill ___ ___
   4. is up-to-date and relevant to the times ___ ___
   5. is relevant to assessed needs of district/school/classroom ___ ___
   6. has a clear, concise style ___ ___

B. Scope
   1. is compatible with other materials and techniques being used ___ ___
   2. coordinates well with other subject areas ___ ___
   3. complements objectives of district programs ___ ___
   4. facilitates continuous progress ___ ___
   5. strengthens systematic development of reading skills ___ ___
   6. is adaptable for varying types of teaching ___ ___

C. Readability
   1. is evident in vocabulary load for appropriate level ___ ___
   2. is strengthened by concepts ___ ___
   3. is aided by language structure and length of sentences ___ ___
   4. The approximate readability level is _____

D. Format (For printed material only)
   1. includes appropriate type size and spacing ___ ___
   2. shows adequate margins ___ ___
   3. has quality binding ___ ___
   4. provides for individual replacement of consumable parts ___ ___
   5. has quality illustrations ___ ___

F. Teacher's Guide
   1. provides sufficient direction ___ ___
   2. provides adequate lesson plans ___ ___
   3. provides suggestions for further skill development ___ ___
   4. indexes specific skills ___ ___
   5. defines terms ___ ___

G. Supplementary Materials
   1. are available to implement program ___ ___
   2. are valuable addition to program ___ ___

H. Evaluation
   1. provides individual or group informal inventory ___ ___
   2. provides diagnostic tests ___ ___
   3. provides mastery tests ___ ___
   4. suggests prescriptive/reteaching activity ___ ___

General Rating: Check appropriate line and indicate a reason for your rating.

1. ____ Recommend without reservation
2. ____ Recommend with reservation
3. ____ Accepted as best of limited choice
4. ____ Unsuited for this school at this time
5. ____ Not recommended

_____
Evaluator

Developed by the Florida Right to Read Effort, Florida Department of Education, Tallahassee, Florida, 1975. Reproduced by permission of the Florida Department of Education, Tallahassee, Florida.

In evaluating reading materials, the reviewer must keep in mind the readability level. Publishing companies often provide a readability level for their materials; however, these levels usually reflect an average for the entire set of materials or a level determined in some unknown manner. Thus, teachers can check the readability levels of materials and recognize the limitations of readability formulas. Before discussing the various readability formulas, their general limitations should be reviewed.

Readability formulas furnish only an estimate of the level of a given selection. Because the formulas are based on the word difficulty and sentence length, or number of syllables and sentence length, the complexity of the concepts in the selection is not considered. There is no formula at this time which measures concepts; thus, the teacher must judge whether the level provided by the formula is appropriate for the given student population. Teachers must also recognize that different formulas provide slightly different levels for a material because the formulas are calculated differently. Therefore, no material has an exact level according to the readability formulas. This lack of exactness is further noted as teachers check various passages within a textbook. It is generally observed that each portion of each story in a basal reader has a different readability level. Thus, the level is usually reported by averaging or stating the range of levels.

In using readability formulas to review content materials, the teacher should note that they do not accurately measure mathematics materials which have an abundance of equations. Moreover, the specialized vocabulary that is so essential in all content areas tends to raise the readability levels of the material. It is suggested, therefore, that the instructor be aware of the more difficult terms and teach them prior to asking the students to read the material. It is impossible to eliminate specialized vocabulary in the content areas merely to lower the readability level of the material; rather, it is the responsibility of the teacher to prepare the students by teaching the difficult words and concepts. Further considerations regarding readability are provided by Maxwell, Tibbets, Hittleman, Nelson, and Lange.[18]

After reviewing all of these limitations, teachers often wonder why readability formulas are used. They are used primarily to provide an estimate of the readability level of a selection. This level can be used in conjunction with the teacher's judgment to determine if a material is suitable for a student or group of students.

There are many readability formulas that teachers may use. Some of the more common formulas are the Fry Readability Graph, the Flesch Reading Ease Test, Aukerman's readability formula, the SMOG formula, Dale-Chall readability formula, and the Spache readability formula.[19] The Spache formula is designed to be used with lower elementary level materials, while the Dale-Chall, SMOG, Aukerman and Flesch are for upper elementary, secondary and adult level materials. The Fry formula can be used with materials at all levels. Because this formula is so flexible and easy for the teacher to use, it is provided in figure 7.12.

**Figure 7.12**
The Fry Readability
Graph

# GRAPH FOR ESTIMATING READABILITY — EXTENDED

by Edward Fry, Rutgers University Reading Center, New Brunswick, N.J. 08904

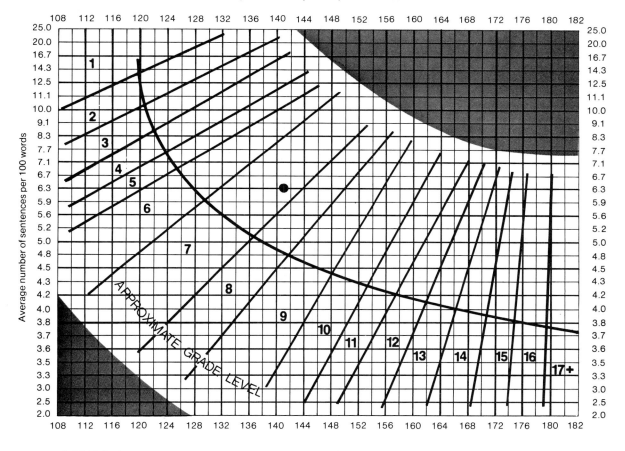

DIRECTIONS: Randomly select 3 one hundred word passages from a book or an article. Plot average number of syllables and average number of sentences per 100 words on graph to determine the grade level of the material. Choose more passages per book if great variability is observed and conclude that the book has uneven readability. Few books will fall in gray area but when they do grade level scores are invalid.

Count proper nouns, numerals and initializations as words. Count a syllable for each symbol. For example, "1945" is 1 word and 4 syllables and "IRA" is 1 word and 3 syllables.

| EXAMPLE: | SYLLABLES | SENTENCES |
|---|---|---|
| 1st Hundred Words | 124 | 6.6 |
| 2nd Hundred Words | 141 | 5.5 |
| 3rd Hundred Words | 158 | 6.8 |
| AVERAGE | 141 | 6.3 |

READABILITY 7th GRADE (see dot plotted on graph)

For further information and validity data see the Journal of Reading December, 1977.

Careful attention must be given to selecting reading materials. There is such an abundance of resources on the market that teachers must evaluate the material very thoroughly before purchase. Some of the materials are excellent and well worth the money, while others are only gimmicks. In addition, teachers should realize that if the material does not meet the needs of the students, then it is of no value in the classroom. This means that teachers must periodically evaluate the materials available in their classroom in relation to student needs, and exchange materials with one another as necessary. Funds are usually not available to purchase new reading materials each year; thus, maximum usage must be made of existing materials. To assist teachers and administrators in their evaluation of reading materials, the Educational Products Information Exchange Institute (EPIE) has produced product reports which analyze basic and supplementary reading materials. These reports are available from EPIE Institute, 463 West Street, New York, New York 10014. The reviews can assist in the thorough evaluation of reading materials, but cannot replace the teacher's analysis, which considers individual student needs.

In discussing reading materials, administrators need to recognize that more than one set of basal readers is helpful in teaching reading. Although materials alone do not enable students to read (and it is well known that some teachers do not need even a set of basals to teach), the fact remains that reading materials help the teacher by providing more abundant resources from which to develop prescriptions. Therefore, the assumption made in this section is that in implementing a diagnostic-prescriptive reading program, the teacher will have basal readers as well as a variety of other materials. However, teachers must be aware of the varying readability levels within basal materials. Eberwein, in a study of three series of basal readers, found that the average readability range was 2.1 grade levels for preprimers to 7.6 levels for fourth, fifth, and sixth grade textbooks. The books did not become progressively more difficult from beginning to end.[20]

## Organizing and Arranging Materials

The arrangement of materials can facilitate instruction and motivate students. Thus, the wise teacher displays different materials during the year rather than putting everything out in August or September. The change in materials is in itself a motivating factor for students. Students feel that they have something new to work with, when in fact it has just been pulled from storage. When teachers use a material for a month or six weeks, give it to another teacher or put it away for a few weeks; variety is provided.

Book shelves or racks are excellent means of displaying library books, basals, and other texts. The materials in the classroom library are changed periodically, but the basal readers remain in the classroom throughout the year. To supplement these materials, the teacher may obtain old basal texts from the school system's surplus material warehouse. These books may be left intact, or taken apart to make mini-stories. The mini-stories can be put in construction paper covers and will form an interesting section for the classroom library. Another way to supplement this resource area is through the use of language-experience story books. As the language-experience approach is used with various students,

their story collections can be illustrated, bound, and placed in the room for others to read. Racks for displaying these materials sometimes may be obtained from department or grocery stores as they remodel or discard material. Students, especially at the upper levels, seem to read more materials when they are attractively displayed on racks.

Kits arranged in various parts of the room or on a table in the far corner of the room allow students an opportunity to move around to obtain materials. Only a few kits displayed at one time avoids the confusion and boredom of doing the same type of work.

For the language-experience approach, a section of the room could contain materials such as a large chart (for primary grades), paper, pictures, and possibly a tape recorder to allow students the opportunity to dictate a story for transcription when no one is available to write.

Materials such as tapes, recorders, and headphones may be placed in a central location for use at the listening center. In addition, paper, pencils, and crayons should be readily available for use in follow-up activities.

In organizing and arranging materials for classroom use, it is best to go over them with a small group, so that students will know where the materials are and how they are organized. This will alleviate some of the problems of giving various assignments, working in small groups, and putting the materials back. Students can be of great assistance in keeping materials in order if they are taught how to use them and if they enjoy the classroom atmosphere.

Although teachers use commercial materials for 94% of their reading instruction,[21] they still need to make games, tapes, or skills kits to better meet students' needs and accommodate their teaching style. Many instructors tend to avoid teacher-made material and rely on the commercial materials for some good reasons. In a study by Shannon

**Developing Materials**

Administrators believed that commercial materials are based on research.
Classroom teachers felt that they were meeting administrative expectations when they used commercial materials.
Administrators, reading teachers, and classroom teachers believed that teachers might not be involved in teaching reading and that teachers truly believe the materials can teach students to read.[22]

Furthermore, teachers frequently believe that the time and money invested in developing materials may not be worth the return. This idea is supported in part by Snyder.[23] However, there are times when teachers must develop their own materials in order to provide appropriate instruction or reinforcement activities. Some ideas for developing materials are given to assist the teacher in providing prescriptive instruction.

To develop listening comprehension skills, the classroom teacher needs a variety of tapes available for independent student activities. Though some teachers may have commercially prepared tapes available, they are usually limited in number and must be supplemented to address the wide range of levels and skills.

Thus, over the years, the teacher accumulates a variety of listening comprehension activities. These can be easily developed, using a short story from the library or one of the stories provided in the various issues of *Instructor*. On the tape, the teacher first provides a purpose for listening, then reads the story, and finally indicates follow-up activities, using questions about the story. By properly labeling these tapes as to emphasize the listening comprehension skills as well as their levels, the instructor will soon have a listening library in the classroom.

Workbooks can be best used when they are set up as skill kits in the classroom. Only three copies of each workbook are needed when used as outlined below.

1. Collect all available workbooks; have at least two copies of each, three if possible.
2. Take two of the workbooks apart, leaving the third intact for reference.
3. Label each page as to its level and the skill developed.
4. If possible, laminate each page or put it in a plastic sheet on which the students can mark; this will also protect the pages as students handle them.
5. Develop a file by placing the pages in folders arranged according to skills. This file may be a metal file cabinet or a box covered with contact paper.
6. The teacher then selects pages on the appropriate levels, as needed for individual or group skill-development sessions.

Games and activities developed by teachers are valuable sources of independent work to develop and reinforce skills. These materials may be made from scraps of paper, juice cans, egg cartons, fruit baskets, or bits of material around the house. Teachers can always think of ways to recycle materials to create usable learning activities. Some activity books which instructors find very useful are listed in appendix D. Figure 7.13 provides a summary of the advantages and disadvantages of teacher-made and commercially developed materials; these are to be considered as teachers develop materials for prescriptive instruction.

**Learning Centers**

From the English infant and primary schools, American schools have adopted the concept of learning centers to provide specialized instruction to individuals or small groups at the elementary and middle school levels. These learning centers contain various materials and activities designed especially for students in a specific group or class. The learning center is basically an open area in which the students are motivated to participate because of the high interest level of the materials. Learning centers may be designed for separate areas such as mathematics, language arts, and science, or for topics such as listening and writing skills.

**Pros and cons of hand-produced and commercially produced materials**

| Hand-Produced | | Commercial | |
| --- | --- | --- | --- |
| Pros | Cons | Pros | Cons |
| 1) Can be designed to meet specific needs and interests of target group. | 1) Durability of the constructed material is sometimes questionable. | 1) Material can be geared to specific needs of children. | 1) May use a too difficult vocabulary or a different approach to skill development. |
| 2) Use an appropriate vocabulary and level of difficulty. | 2) Constant remaking or mending may be required. | 2) Material is durable, legible, and colorful. Looks professional and may be long-lasting. | 2) May be limited in usefulness. |
| 3) Children can be actively involved in game production. | 3) Construction *must* reflect high standards of neatness and legibility. | 3) A wide variety already available on the marketplace. | 3) Require much time to locate, evaluate, purchase. |
| 4) Kits and activity game files can be expanded as needed. | 4) Directions must be carefully thought out. | 4) If teacher time is a factor, may be less expensive than "home made." | 4) Lost items are expensive to replace. |
| 5) Favorite "old" games can be easily adapted. | 5) Construction sometimes requires more time than is warranted. | | 5) Frequently considered too expensive. |
| 6) Materials are sometimes more economical. | 6) Easily available commercial materials are sometimes more economical. | | |

Geraldine V. Snyder, "Learner Verification of Reading Games." *The Reading Teacher* 34 (March 1981):689. Reprinted with permission of Geraldine V. Snyder and the International Reading Association.

**Figure 7.13**
Pros and Cons of Hand-Produced and commercially Produced Materials.

The use of learning centers requires teacher ingenuity and creativity, inasmuch as a variety of activities must be provided in order to develop the area. Manipulative activities as well as materials are needed to make maximum use of the center. It is suggested that teachers begin with one center, then expand to three or four as they become confident in their use and are able to develop the centers. Before beginning to use materials in the learning centers, it is suggested that the teacher do further reading about the concept. The following books may be useful:

Barbara Ingram, Nancy R. Jones, and Marlene LeButt, *The Workshop Approach to Classroom Interest Centers* (West Nyack, N.Y.: Parker Publishing Company, 1975).

Kim Marshall, *Opening Your Class with Learning Stations* (Palo Alto, California: LEARNING Handbook, 1975).

Susan S. Petreshene, *Complete Guide to Learning Centers* (Palo Alto, California: Pendragon House, Inc., 1978), and *Complete Guide to Learning Centers,* Supplement, 1978.

Ann B. Piechowiak and Myra B. Cook, *Complete Guide to the Elementary Learning Center* (New York: Parker Publishing Company, Inc., 1976).

John Thomas. *Learning Centers* (Boston: Holbrook Press, Inc., 1975).

In developing learning centers, teachers may wish to consider the following criteria

have a clear purpose for the center.
state directions in understandable manner.
develop an interesting and motivational center.
provide for immediate feedback.
make the activities durable and useful.
be sure the activities in the center reinforce previous instruction.

Learning centers can assist in classroom organization and management by providing alternative activities which reinforce previous instruction; they also give students an opportunity to work on the activities independently while the teacher instructs other groups. Caution must be exercised to insure that busy work is not glorified and called a learning center. Good learning centers can be excellent reinforcement aids for instruction.

**Resource File**

One last but very important idea which schools are encouraged to consider in order to use available materials to best advantage is that of the resource file. The resource file is developed by the faculty to provide an index of the skills presented in the different materials currently available in the school. The development of this resource file is quite time consuming but most helpful when teachers write prescriptions for students and administrators try to determine the kinds of new materials needed for reading. Such a file may be arranged by skill or by material title. It is easily managed when written on index cards filed alphabetically. For

each material given, specific information is needed, including the exact title of the material, the readability level, the skill developed and the specific page on which the skill is taught. This file may be kept in the office or in the library and updated as new materials are purchased.

Teachers frequently want many materials, but sometimes they do not use them effectively. Materials do not teach students to read—the teacher must do that—but they can greatly assist when effectively used to meet the individual student's needs.

Since teachers use a variety of materials in teaching reading, it is essential that they coordinate the materials used to avoid giving duplicate assignments or assignments in materials with conflicting philosophies. More information is provided in chapter 8 regarding various approaches for teaching reading; at that time a discussion on correlating the various approaches is presented. Accordingly, this topic will not be dealt with in detail here. We will only state that the teacher must know the materials and the students in order to provide the most appropriate prescriptive instruction.

**Summary**

The topics dealt with in this chapter were the optimum use of classroom organization and management procedures, as these can facilitate diagnostic-prescriptive instruction.

The proper use of classroom management techniques improves not only the learning environment, but the quality of teaching as well. Good individualization and grouping procedures are vital to the educational growth of students. Various methods of grouping were discussed, with some emphasis on organizing the classroom in order that these grouping procedures may be implemented. Models of grouping formats for both elementary and content area classrooms were included.

Since the arrangement of classroom facilities is so critical, models were presented which suggest some alternatives to the traditional classroom arrangement.

After the organizational and management procedures were outlined, the next step involved actual implementation of the learning process through the selection and use of materials which are either commercially published or teacher-made. When all of the steps that have been discussed—classroom organization and management, individualization and grouping, arrangement of facilities, and the use of materials—are integrated into a total picture, the process of helping students learn to read through prescriptive instruction can begin.

## Applying What You Read

You are teaching a fourth-grade class. Draw a schematic arranging the furniture as you would like to have it. Outline the types of groups that you may have.

As a new teacher in a middle school, how would you organize your classroom for instruction? What would you do to manage this class?

Develop a grouping procedure for teaching reading to twenty-eight second graders whose achievement levels range from a nonreader to two students reading on a fourth-grade level.

Begin to develop a resource file for three materials you commonly use in your classroom. Identify the title of the material, the readability level, the specific skills developed, and the page numbers on which these skills are presented.

As a content teacher, develop a grouping procedure that can be used in your classroom to develop certain concepts. Identify the concepts and the exact procedures which can be used.

## Notes

1. Richard D. Arnold, "Class Size and Reading Development," in *New Horizons in Reading,* ed. John E. Merritt; Richard L. Harris, "Research Evidence Regarding the Impact of Class Size on Pupil Academic Achievement"; Howard K. Holland and Armand J. Galfo, *An Analysis of Research Concerning Class Size:* Robert L. Thorndike, *Reading Comprehension in Fifteen Countries.* Nello Vignocchi, "What Research Says About the Effect of Class Size on Academic Achievement," *Illinois School Research and Development.*
2. Paul C. Burns and Betty D. Roe, *Teaching Reading in Today's Elementary Schools,* p. 388–89.
3. Carolyn M. Evertson and Linda M. Anderson, "Beginning School," *Educational Horizons.* Gerald G. Duffy, *Teacher Effectiveness Research: Implications for the*

*Reading Profession.* John T. Guthrie, "Effective Teaching Practices," *The Reading Teacher.* William H. Rupley and Timothy R. Blair, "Teacher Effectiveness Research in Reading Instruction: Early Efforts to Present Focus," *Reading Psychology.*

4. Susan B. Neuman. "Creative Reading and the Skills Management Systems," *Reading Improvement.*

5. Gerald Duffy, "Maintaining a Balance in Objective-Based Reading Instruction," *The Reading Teacher;* Dale D. Johnson, "Skills Management Systems: Some Issues," *Language Arts;* Dale D. Johnson and P. David Pearson, "Skills Management Systems: A Critique," *The Reading Teacher;* Marvin L. Klein, "The Reading Program and Classroom Management: Panacea or Perversion?" *Elementary English.*

6. Diana Buell Hiatt, "Time Allocation in the Classroom: Is Instruction Being Shortchanged?," *Phi Delta Kappan.*

7. G. R. Musgrave, *Individualized Instruction.*

8. Carl J. Wallen, "Independent Activities: A Necessity, Not a Frill," *The Reading Teacher;* Mallie Slater, "Individualized Language Arts in the Middle Grades," *The Reading Teacher;* Harriet Ramsey Reeves, "Individual Conferences—Diagnostic Tools," *The Reading Teacher;* Catheryn T. Eisenhardt, "Individualization of Instruction," *Elementary English.*

9. Dayton Rothrock, "The Rise and Decline of Individualized Instruction," *Educational Leadership.*

10. Linda L. Brown and Rita J. Sherbenou, "A Comparison of Teacher Perceptions of Student Reading Ability, Reading Performance, & Classroom Behavior," *The Reading Teacher.* Chris Moacdieh, "Grouping for Reading in the Primary Grades: Evidence on the Revisionist Argument," Paper presented at the Annual Meeting of the American Educational Research Association, Los Angeles, California, April 13–17, 1981. John J. Pikulski and Irwin S. Kiroch, "Organization for Instruction," In Robert C. Calfee and Priscilla A. Drum (Eds.) *Teaching Reading in Compensatory Classes.*

11. Emil J. Haller and Sharon A. Davis, "Does Socioeconomic Status Bias the Assignment of Elementary School Students to Reading Groups?" *American Educational Research Journal.*

12. Jeanne Martin and Carolyn M. Evertson, *Teachers' Interactions with Reading Groups of Differing Ability Levels.*

13. Linda Grant and James Rothenberg, *Charting Educational Futures: Interaction Patterns in First and Second Grade Reading Groups.* Paula R. Stern and Richard J. Shavelson, "The Relationship Between Teachers' Grouping Decisions and Instructional Behavior: An Ethnographic Study of Reading Instruction."

14. Linda Grant and James Rothenberg, *Charting Educational Futures.*

15. Jack Cassidy, "Cross-age Tutoring and the Sacrosanct Reading Period," *Reading Horizons;* Hal Dreyer, "Rx for Pupil Tutoring Programs," *The Reading Teacher;* Joan L. Fogarty and Margaret C. Wang, "An Investigation of the Cross-Age Peer Tutoring Process: Some Implications for Instructional Design and Motivation," *The Elementary School Journal.*

16. Peter A. Cohen, James A. Kulik, and Chen-Lin C. Kulik, "Educational Outcomes of Tutoring: A Meta-analysis of Findings," *American Educational Research Journal.* Ralph J. Melaragno, *Tutoring with Students.*

17. Maurice Kaufman, *Perceptual and Language Readiness Programs: Critical Reviews;* Paul C. Burns and Betty D. Roe, *Teaching Reading in Today's Elementary Schools;* Larry A. Harris and Carl B. Smith, *Reading Instruction,* 3rd ed.; Patricia M. Cunningham, "A Teacher's Guide to Materials Shopping," *The Reading Teacher;* Carol N. Dixon, "Selection and Use of Instructional Materials," In Robert C. Calfee and Priscilla A. Drum (Eds.) *Teaching Reading in Compensatory Classes.*

18. Martha Maxwell, "Readability: Have We Gone Too Far?" *Journal of Reading;* Sylvia-Lee Tibbetts, "How Much Should We Expect Readability Formulas to Do?" *Elementary English;* Daniel R. Hittleman, "Seeking a Psycholinguistic Definition of Readability," *The Readability Teacher;* Joan Nelson, "Readability: Some Cautions to the Content Area Teacher," *Journal of Reading;* Bob Lange, "Readability Formulas Second Looks, Second Thoughts," *The Reading Teacher.*

19. Edward Fry, "Fry's Readability Graph: Clarifications, Validity, and Extension to Level 17," *Journal of Reading;* Rudolph F. Flesch, "A New Readability Yardstick," *Journal of Applied Psychology;* Robert C. Aukerman, *Reading in the Secondary School Classroom;* Harry G. McLaughlin, "SMOG Grading—A New Readability Formula," *Journal of Reading;* Edgar Dale and Jeanne Chall, "A Formula for Predicting Readability," *Educational Research Bulletin;* George D. Spache, *Good Reading for Poor Readers.*

20. Lowell D. Eberwein, "The Variability of Readability of Basal Reader Textbooks and How Much Teachers Know About It," *Reading World.*

21. Educational Products Information Exchange, *Report of a National Study of the Quality of Instructional Materials Most Used by Teachers and Learners.*

22. Patrick Shannon, "Some Subjective Reasons for Teachers' Reliance on Commercial Reading Materials," *The Reading Teacher.*

23. Geraldine V. Snyder, "Learner Verification of Reading Games," *The Reading Teacher.*

## Other Suggested Readings

Bowles, Allen, ed. *Crossroads . . . A Handbook for Effective Classroom Management.* Oklahoma City, Oklahoma: Oklahoma State Department of Education, 1981.

Burns, Paul C., and Roe, Betty D. *Teaching Reading in Today's Elementary Schools.* Chicago: Rand McNally Publishing Company, 1980, 2nd edition. Chapter 10.

Carlson, Ronald. "Reading Level Difficulty." *Creative Computing* (April 1980):60–61.

Clements, Richard O., et al. *The Accuracy of Students' Perceptions of Themselves and Their Classroom,* Report 5082. Washington, D.C.: National Institute of Education, April 1980. ED 192 453.

*Criteria for Evaluating Instructional Materials,* Reading Effectiveness Program. Indianapolis, Indiana: Indiana State Department of Public Instruction, 1977.

Debelak, Marianne, et al. *Creating Innovative Classroom Materials for Teaching Young Children.* New York: Harcourt Brace Jovanovich, Inc., 1981.

Denham, Carolyn and Liberman, Ann, eds. *Time to Learn: A Review of the Beginning Teacher Evaluation Study.* Washington, D.C.: National Institute of Education, May 1980. ED 192 454.

Doyle, Walter. *Classroom Management.* West Lafayette, Indiana: Kappa Delta Pi, 1980.

Duval, Eileen V.; Johnson, Roger E.; and Litcher, John. "Learning Stations and the Reading Class." *Classroom Practice in Reading,* Edited by Richard A. Earle. Newark, Delaware: International Reading Association, 1977.

Emmer, Edmund T.; Evertson, Carolyn M.; and Anderson, Linda M. "Effective Classroom Management at the Beginning of the School Year." *Elementary School Journal* 80 (May 1980):218–28.

Duke, Daniel L., ed. *Helping Teachers Manage Classrooms.* Alexandria, Virginia: Association for Supervision and Curriculum Development, 1982.

Evertson, Carolyn M. *Teacher Behavior, Student Achievement and Student Attitudes: Descriptions of Selected Classrooms, Correlates of Effective Teaching.* Washington, D.C.: National Institute of Education, 1979. ED 204 330.

Farr, Roger, and Roser, Nancy. *Teaching a Child to Read.* New York: Harcourt Brace Jovanovich, 1979, Chapter 9.

Fox, Anne C. and Franke, Mary. "Learning Centers: The Newest Thing in Busy Work?" *Reading World* 18 (March 1979):221–26.

Franke. Jill Catherine. "Learning Centers for Reading in Junior High School." *Journal of Reading* 19 (December 1975):243–46.

Fry, Edward B. *Elementary Reading Instruction.* New York: McGraw-Hill Book Company, 1977. Chapter 12.

Goodman, Donald and Schwab, Sandra. "Computerized Testing for Readability." *Creative Computing* (April 1980):46–51.

Gotowala, Martin C: "Continuous Progress: A Management System." *Classroom Practice in Reading.* Edited by Richard A. Earle, Newark, Delaware: International Reading Association, 1977.

Guthrie, John. "Research Views: Managing Problem Students." *The Reading Teacher* 35 (December 1981):380–82.

Guthrie, John T. "Social Interaction of Reading Groups." *The Reading Teacher* 34 (November 1980):252–53.

Harris, Larry A., and Smith, Carl. *Reading Instruction,* 3rd ed. New York: Holt, Rinehart and Winston, 1980.

Hooper, Beverly. "Reading Expectancy Formulae-Strengths and Limitations To Be Considered." *Reading Horizons* 18 (Winter 1978):128–33.

Howell, Helen. "Peer-Tutoring: Learning Boon or Exploitation of the Tutor?" *Reading Horizons* 19 (Spring 1979):237–39.

Jernigan, Mary L. "Centers Approach in Reading Instruction." *Elementary English* 51 (September 1974):858–60.

Judd, Dorothy H. "Avoid Readability Formula Drudgery: Use your School's Microcomputer." *The Reading Teacher* 35 (October 1981):7–8.

King, R. Tommy. "Learning From A Pal." *The Reading Teacher* 35 (March 1982):682–85.

Kulik, Chen-Lin C. and Kulik, James A. "Research Synthesis on Ability Grouping." *Educational Leadership* 39 (May 1982):619–21.

Lapp, Diane, and Flood, James. *Teaching Reading to Every Child.* New York: Macmilan Publishing Co., 1978. Chapter 15.

Lewis, Tamar with Ruth Long. *Effective Instruction.* Alexandria, Virginia: The Association for Supervision and Curriculum Development, 1981.

McCormick, Sandra, and Collins, Betty M. "A Potpourri of Game-Making Ideas for the Reading Teacher." *The Reading Teacher* 34 (March 1981):692–96.

Madsen, Charles and Madson, Clifford. "A Positive Approach to Classroom Management." *Early Years* 10 (April 1980):44–45.

Martin, Jeanne; Veldman, Donald J.; and Anderson, Linda M. "Within-Class Relationships Between Student Achievement and Teacher Behaviors." *American Educational Research Journal* 17 (Winter 1980):479–90.

Maxwell, Martha. "Readability: Have We Gone Too Far?" *Journal of Reading* 21 (March 1978):525–30.

Mikkelsen, Vincent P. and Joyner, Wilton. "Organizational Climate of Elementary Schools and Reading Achievement of Sixth Grade Pupils." *Reading Improvement* 19 (Spring 1982):67–73.

Morrow, Lesley Mandel. *Organizing for Reading Instruction* (York, Pennsylvania: Strine Publishing Company, 1982).

O'Bruba, William and Campbell, Donald A. "Classroom Management: A Model." *Early Years* 10 (November 1979):55–56.

Odom, Sterling C. "Individualizing a Reading Program." *The Reading Teacher* 24 (February 1971):403–10.

Pikulski, John J., and Jones, Margaret B. "Writing Directions Children Can Read." *The Reading Teacher* 30 (March 1977):598–602.

Ransom, Grayce A. *Preparing to Teach Reading.* Boston: Little, Brown and Company, 1978. Chapter 5.

Simpson, Carl. "Classroom Structure and the Organization of Ability." *Sociology of Education* 54 (April 1981):120–32.

Smith, Lawrence L. "Cross-Age Tutoring—Using the 4 T's," *Reading Horizons* 21 (Fall 1980):44–49.

Standal, Timothy C. "Readability Formulas: What's Out, What's In?" *The Reading Teacher* 31 (March 1978):642–46.

Steinberg, Z. D. and Cazden, C. B. "Children as Teachers of Peers and Ourselves." *Theory into Practice* 18 (1979):258–66.

Vacca, Richard T., and Vacca, Joanne L. "Consider a Stations Approach to Middle School Reading." *The Reading Teacher* 28 (October 1974):18–21.

Veatch, Jeannette. *Reading in the Elementary School,* 2nd ed. New York: John Wiley & Sons, 1978. Chapters 5, 6, and 7.

Weinstein, Carol S., and Weinstein, Neil D. "Noise and Reading Performance in an Open Space School." *The Journal of Educational Research* 72 (March/April 1979):210–13.

Wright, Jane P. "Management Systems and Open Classrooms." *Classroom Practice in Reading.* Edited by Richard A. Earle. Newark, Delaware: International Reading Association, 1977.

# Prescriptive Instruction

At Seabreeze School, the teachers are evaluating their instructional program in reading to determine the extent to which they are providing prescriptive instruction in their classrooms. These teachers realize that quality instruction is the key component in the school reading program. Thus, using the diagnostic data from their reading tests and daily evaluations, as well as the ideas on organizing and managing reading instruction, the teachers are now directing their attention to implementing more prescriptive teaching in their classrooms. Chapters 8–14 are designed to help the teacher provide better prescriptive reading instruction for every student. In these chapters, the terms prescriptive teaching and prescriptive instruction are used interchangeably. A bibliography of references that provide specific activities to aid in prescriptive instruction in the various skill areas appears in appendix D.

**8**

Teachers are the instructional leaders in the classroom. As instructional leaders, the classroom teachers at Seabreeze School realize that they have the tremendous responsibility not only of identifying the reading strengths and weaknesses of each student, but also of providing appropriate instruction to meet each student's needs. Instruction that is based on the diagnosed needs of each student is referred to as prescriptive instruction.

   This chapter provides an overview of prescriptive reading instruction as related to actual classroom practice. Some basic principles underlying prescriptive instruction, together with various approaches for teaching reading, and ideas on developing prescriptions for individuals and groups are discussed. More specifically, the following questions are addressed.

What is prescriptive teaching or instruction?

What are some basic guides for the teacher to follow in providing prescriptive instruction?

How does prescriptive instruction differ in self-contained and departmentalized classrooms?

What does the teacher need to consider before beginning prescriptive reading instruction?

What are the various reading approaches used in prescriptive instruction?

How do the diagnostic data relate to prescriptive instruction?

How does the teacher develop prescriptions? When does a teacher plan for prescriptive reading instruction?

# How can prescriptive teaching be implemented in the classroom?

The following vocabulary terms should be noted as this chapter is read.

**Vocabulary to Know**

Analytic method
Approaches
Augmented alphabet approach
Contextual processing approach
Decoding approach
Directed Learning Activity
Directed Reading Activity
Eclectic approach
Individualized reading approach
Initial Teaching Alphabet

Language experience approach
Linguistic approach
Look-say method
Multi-sensory approach
Neurological impress method
Prescriptive instruction
Programmed approach
Skills approaches
Synthetic method
VAKT
Words in Color

**Prescriptive Teaching**

In thinking further about the concept of diagnostic-prescriptive reading instruction, it is necessary to review and extend the discussion of prescriptive teaching in chapter 1. Prescriptive teaching is reading instruction provided to meet the diagnosed reading needs of each student. This is not to imply that it must be one-to-one instruction. The definition does mean, however, that individual student needs are met through either individual, small group, or large group instruction.

In chapter 1 an analogy with the medical profession was used: the doctor orders a specific medication based on the diagnosed needs of the patient. Teachers need to remember that in providing reading instruction, they too must use diagnostic data to direct the instructional program for each student. One teacher summarized the idea of prescriptive teaching by defining it as *"teaching what you know the student needs rather than what the publishing companies tell you to teach."* This is one way of thinking about prescriptive teaching. As long as teachers follow some type of scope and sequence of skills or reading continuum, whether from the school or publishing company, they will have continuity in skill development from level to level. Basic principles or guides for prescriptive instruction that give the teacher direction in implementing prescriptive teaching in the classroom are discussed in the following pages.

**Prescriptive teaching can be implemented in many ways; there is no one best way.** Each teacher using the concepts of prescriptive reading instruction must determine the best way to put them into effect in the classroom. Just as each student is unique, so also is each teacher's style of teaching, classroom arrangement, and confidence in providing reading instruction. Teachers use ideas provided in this text, from other teachers, and other sources, adapting them to their classrooms. The element which must always exist in prescriptive instruction is that it be based on the students' diagnosed needs.

**Varied approaches and techniques must be used in prescribing for a specific reading problem.** Many approaches for teaching reading have been identified; and research dealing with the different approaches is voluminous. However, as was found in the First Grade Studies, there is no one best approach for teaching reading.[1] Likewise, there is no one technique that is always successful in dealing with diagnosed reading problems. Each student is unique in his or her learning style, reading habits, background experiences, and self-expectations. Thus, a guide which tells a teacher what to do with each student cannot be provided; only suggestions can be made. The teacher must, through careful thought and in some cases trial and error, determine what works best with different students.

**Prescriptive instruction should follow a specified hierarchy of reading skills.** In order for prescriptive reading instruction to provide for continuity in skill development, the teacher should follow a defined scope and sequence of reading skills. Without a continuum of skills, whether from a publishing company or developed within the school system, teachers lack structure for guiding skill development and gaps or inconsistencies develop in the reading skills presented to the students. The hierarchy of skills serves as a guide to the teacher; it is not to be followed rigidly. For example, a student with extremely poor auditory discrimination skills is not expected to overcome this deficiency completely before moving on to other skills. Rather, the student must be helped to capitalize on his or her strengths in visual discrimination, then allowed to progress in other reading skill areas.

Classroom teachers should also note that using a scope and sequence of reading skills means that skills from various areas are developed concurrently. For example, as word recognition skills are taught, so are some comprehension and study skills, as well as the personal reading skills that require the application of the other reading skills. Thus, skills in all basic areas in reading are developed simultaneously.

**Prescriptive instruction must be based on continuous diagnosis.** The diagnosis made by the classroom teacher serves as a guide in identifying students' reading needs. In order for teaching to be truly prescriptive, teachers re-evaluate and diagnose their students continuously. This is not to imply that formal tests are frequently administered. The ongoing diagnosis may be done through observation of the students' performance of assigned tasks, other informal procedures,

and possibly some formal diagnostic tests, if necessary. Regardless of how the information is obtained, the classroom teacher must continuously assess changes in reading performance in order to provide instruction based on the needs of the student.

**Instruction should be flexible in prescriptive teaching.** In following diagnostic-prescriptive procedures for reading instruction, teachers need to be aware that the diagnostic information provides indications of strengths and weaknesses in reading, and that the prescriptive instruction is based upon these indications. Thus, the teacher may begin instruction in an identified area of need only to become aware that the actual need is a lower-level skill or that the student has already developed the skill being taught. The teacher must be flexible enough to make changes in the prescriptive instruction being provided. This may mean moving the student to another group for instruction or offering some individual instruction for a period of time. Flexibility is an essential element of good pre-scriptive instruction.

**Prescriptive teaching requires that all school personnel work together as a team.** As discussed in chapter 1, the entire school staff must work together not only in the continuous diagnosis of students, but also in providing prescriptive instruction. The librarian may assist in developing personal reading skills by en-couraging students to read books at their independent reading level. He or she may also aid in the teaching of study skills by assisting the teacher in developing the specific library and reference skills as necessary. Content teachers can iden-tify the reading skills necessary for learning the content materials and help de-velop these skills in students who do not have them. Reading or language arts teachers should share with the content teachers all diagnostic data available in order to facilitate prescriptive reading instruction in all classes.

The principal and guidance counselor can facilitate prescriptive reading in-struction by locating materials and teaching ideas to assist in meeting special student needs. Additionally, they can provide much positive reinforcement to stu-dents as they improve in reading.

In order for prescriptive reading instruction to have the greatest impact, all of the school faculty must recognize that reading is a tool used in all school work, that each student develops skills according to diagnosed needs, and that each faculty member is responsible for helping students to improve. When a principal and school faculty understand their roles in the school reading program and work together for the benefit of the student, then a prescriptive reading program can function at its best.

**Prescriptive teaching must aid students in applying their knowledge of reading skills to the reading of content as well as other printed materials.** In prescriptive teaching, specific reading skills are identified as areas of need for a student, and instruction is provided to develop the skills. This is the first step in prescriptive instruction. The essential second step is that the student must also be taught how

to use these skills in reading materials for enjoyment and to gain information. Students do not automatically transfer reading skills developed in isolation to their reading tasks. Thus, the development of reading skills does not improve reading performance unless the student can apply the skills as necessary. Teachers must assist in this transfer by showing the student how skills can be used in a given situation. For example, the student who has been taught the skill of sequencing ideas or events should be shown how to use this skill in recalling ideas from a story, in remembering the steps in a science experiment, or determining the chronological order of events in a social studies lesson.

In developing reading skills as well as in teaching their application, the teacher provides direct instruction and uses materials to reinforce and review. Reading skills are not developed by "plugging" students into materials, but rather by explanation from the teacher, with reinforcement as needed, using various activities or materials. When the student has been taught the skills and demonstrated his or her understanding through successfully completing assigned tasks, careful instruction is necessary to help the student apply them in daily life.

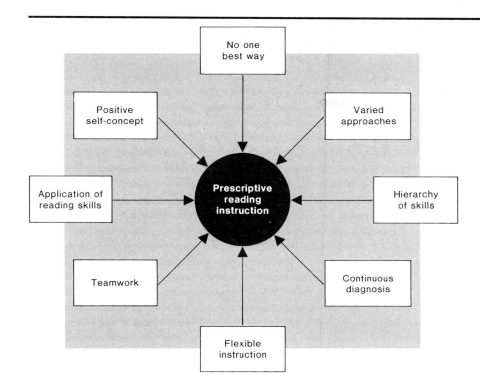

**Figure 8.1**
Basic Principles of
Prescriptive Reading
Instruction

**Prescriptive reading programs must be designed to foster a positive self-image and enjoyment of reading as well as the development of reading skills.** Reading instruction which meets identified needs and is on the appropriate level for the student not only enhances skill development in reading but also helps students to have a more positive attitude toward themselves due to their success in learning. Knowledge of skills and a good self-concept provide an excellent foundation for the enjoyment of reading. Thus, teachers should remember that the end product of the school reading program is a student who can read, and who enjoys reading as a leisure-time activity as well as for informational purposes.

These basic guides provide only general directions for implementing prescriptive instruction. Teachers must interpret and apply them according to their individual teaching styles and classroom needs.

Prescriptive reading instruction is a concept in which most teachers at the elementary and middle school levels believe. However, this concept is not used in some classrooms because of a failure to understand its implementation. The classroom teacher in a self-contained situation can implement prescriptive reading instruction in a somewhat different way than the teacher in a departmental situation. Likewise, the reading specialist working with small groups of students

**Prescriptive Instruction in the Classroom**

who have severe reading problems provides prescriptive instruction through means that differ from those used in the classroom.

To provide prescriptive reading instruction, the teacher needs diagnostic data which have been summarized for each student and organized into a usable format. This information indicates the student's interests, strengths and weaknesses in reading, and instructional reading level. The teacher can use the student's interests and strengths to help improve areas of weakness. For example, the student who has difficulty in remembering details and has an interest in dogs could be given a short selection about dogs. The teacher would ask the student to remember certain facts in the selection and follow up the silent reading with questions requiring the recall of details. When the student has experienced success with these materials, the teacher may use more varied materials to further develop the skill.

The teacher relates the diagnostic data to the reading skills continuum to determine starting points for instruction. Skill development is provided in word recognition, comprehension, and study skills, with continuous opportunities for their application. Several skill deficiencies in each of the areas should be identified for every student. The teacher may then group the students according to needs and determine appropriate ways of providing the necessary instruction. More specific information on prescriptive instruction in the areas of prereading, word recognition, comprehension, study, and personal reading skills appears in chapters 9–13.

The content teacher in a departmental situation implements prescriptive reading instruction by providing instruction in the reading skills which the students do not have, but must use, to learn the content materials. The diagnostic data which the language arts teacher has regarding each student's reading needs can be supplemented by the content teacher through the use of procedures such as a Group Reading Inventory (see chapter 4). The teacher can then develop a class profile of reading skill needs and determine which skills must be developed as the content material is taught.

## Directed Reading Activity

To facilitate prescriptive instruction in all classrooms, both self-contained and departmentalized, the teacher needs to follow a plan. The most commonly used design in reading instruction is the Directed or Guided Reading Activity (DRA). This procedure has been followed for many years by elementary teachers using the basal reader. However, any classroom teacher can use this procedure with or without the basal reader.

The five basic steps of the DRA are described below and should be followed in all reading lessons.

> *Readiness:* Establish readiness for reading material by introducing the topic and the skills needed to read the material. Teach vocabulary words as well as concepts necessary to understand the material to be read.
> *Skill Development:* Using the diagnostic data, provide students with instruction to develop the skills necessary to understand the material to be read. This may be done individually or in small groups.

*Review:* The vocabulary, concepts, and the skills necessary to be successful should be reviewed. At this time, the teacher gives the student a purpose for reading the material and asks for silent reading.

*Guided Reading:* With a purpose for reading clearly stated, the student begins to read the designated material (basal reader, newspaper, library book, experience story, etc.) silently. Following silent reading, ask comprehension questions that relate to the purpose given for reading and to the diagnosed comprehension skill needs of the individual students. For example, the student who has difficulty with the comprehension skill of distinguishing fact and opinion would be asked questions relating to this skill as a review of information taught during the Skill Development portion of the lesson. Following the comprehension check of silent reading, the student may be asked to read portions of the story orally to locate specific information or for some other definite purpose.

*Follow-Up:* Do additional follow-up after the guided reading to develop skill deficiencies, to extend knowledge on a given topic, and to allow students to apply the information learned from reading to some activity. This follow-up session will vary from lesson to lesson and from student to student. It may be used to motivate some students to read; for others it is a time for further skill development. The follow-up session is a valuable time for providing additional prescriptive instruction.

The departmental teacher can use an adapted DRA to provide prescriptive reading instruction in the content areas. The authors refer to this plan as the Directed Learning Activity (DLA). This technique is for students using material written at their instructional reading level. The procedure is designed for use with small groups or a whole class. The following steps present ideas on providing prescriptive reading instruction in the content areas. Step 4 of this plan incorporates the Directed Learning Activity.

**Step 1: Determine the concepts to be stressed in the content material and relate the reading skills needed to understand these concepts.** In order to meet individual student needs and various learning styles, the content teacher must teach concepts rather than just a textbook. Thus, for a given topic, the content specialist identifies the specific concepts to be taught. This way of looking at content material is used for several reasons.

1. With the wealth of knowledge, facts, and materials available today, it is impossible for one textbook to provide all the information students need. Thus, the teacher identifies key concepts and assists students in learning how to use materials to increase their knowledge.
2. No one textbook meets the reading level of every student in a classroom. Therefore the content teacher uses a variety of materials in order to provide students with printed information they can read. If the content specialist is using concepts rather than one textbook, then many materials can be used.

**Directed Learning Activity**

**Figure 8.2**
Steps in the Directed
Reading Activity

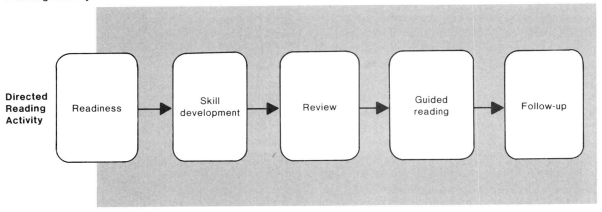

**Directed Reading Activity**

Readiness → Skill development → Review → Guided reading → Follow-up

**Step 2: Identify the reading skills that are necessary for understanding the content materials.**    After the concepts have been identified, the content specialist selects the reading skills that are essential to understanding them. Usually there are four to six reading skills that students use if they are to understand the concepts. Content teachers may use lists of skills such as those in chapter 3 or a more comprehensive list, as in appendix A, to identify the many reading skills that relate to their content area. This may be a rather lengthy list, as different skills are necessary in order to teach various concepts. At a later time, the content specialist will select appropriate skills from this list which will help the student to understand the material.

An example of a concept and related reading skills is shown below:

Social Studies Concept:  Freedom of speech is an essential component of a democracy.

Related Reading Skills:  Vocabulary Development
Generalizations
Cause-Effect
Contrast-Comparisons
Relationships

Once teachers have identified this information, their instructional program will begin to take shape.

**Step 3: Assess student strengths and weaknesses in the reading skills.**    There are several procedures that may be used to diagnose strengths and weaknesses. One procedure, the Group Reading Inventory, is presented in chapter 4.

**Figure 8.3**
Diagnostic Chart for
Content Teachers

| Student name | Concept | | | | | Concept | | | | | Concept | | | | | Concept | | | | | Concept | | | |
|---|---|---|---|---|---|---|---|---|---|---|---|---|---|---|---|---|---|---|---|---|---|---|---|---|
| | Skill | Skill | Skill | Skill | Skill | | | | | | | | | | | | | | | | | | | |
| Ginger | X | | | X | | | | | | | | | | | | | | | | | | | | |
| Lance | X | X | X | X | X | | | | | | | | | | | | | | | | | | | |
| Kristy | | | X | | | | | | | | | | | | | | | | | | | | | |
| Wendy | | X | X | | X | | | | | | | | | | | | | | | | | | | |
| Joe | X | | | | | | | | | | | | | | | | | | | | | | | |
| Harry | | | | X | | | | | | | | | | | | | | | | | | | | |
| Carmen | | | | | | | | | | | | | | | | | | | | | | | | |

X denotes need for additional instruction in the skill.

With the identified concepts and reading skills as well as the diagnostic data on the students, the content specialist may use a file folder or sheet of paper to develop a class chart like the one in figure 8.3. This will assist in organizing the information and aid in prescriptive teaching.

**Step 4: Outline teaching strategies for the development of the concepts and skills.** At this point, the teacher puts together materials which meet the students' diagnosed needs, in order to teach the concepts necessary for learning the content. Using the DLA format as a guide, this is not difficult. The DLA follows this procedure:

*Introduce the concepts and vocabulary.* The content teacher introduces the concept to be studied. This may be done directly, using questions or a movie, or in a more indirect manner based on previous classes. Regardless of the procedure used, the concepts to be studied for a unit or designated period of time need to be carefully introduced. Because the entire class is probably studying the same concepts, this would be a total class

activity. In introducing the concepts and material to be studied, the content specialist also teaches the vocabulary necessary for reading the materials. This includes the general vocabulary as well as the specialized and technical words. Teachers should realize that although a student may be able to pronounce a word, its special meaning as related to the content area may cause difficulty. The responsibility for teaching vocabulary rests with each content teacher. With various reading abilities in the classroom and various materials in use, it may be necessary to teach vocabulary development skills to small groups. Some of the groups can use written activities, while others work with the content teacher or discuss the terminology with one another. Examples of written vocabulary activities follow:

**Science**

*Vocabulary Development:* Give the antonyms for these words.

exhale _____ ventricle _____

**Social Studies**

*Vocabulary Development:* Fill in the missing word:
1. A body of advisors of a head of state is a _____.
2. Refusal to trade with another country is an _____.
3. The title of the highest ranking official of the United States residing in another country is _____.

*Teach/Review Reading Skills.* This phase of the instructional process depends not only upon the identification of those reading skills that are relevant to the student's understanding of the content material, but also includes demonstrating the application of these reading skills appropriately. Although content teachers are not reading specialists, they assist students in adapting previously learned skills to content materials, as well as learning how to apply new skills to these materials.

*Outline the purposes for study.* Students are much more willing to accept some of the requirements made in content areas if they are given specific purposes for study. Teachers usually receive negative responses when they give students a chapter to read with no specific reason for studying it. In addition, students need to know how studying this material relates to their present or future lives. Having a purpose helps students relate to the material and motivates them to study it.

*Read and study the material.* The students have been introduced to the concept, taught the vocabulary, and given a purpose for reading by this time. Now we are ready to ask them to read the material. At this point the

content specialist may help the student use the SQ3R or other appropriate study techniques as outlined in chapter 3. The teacher must remember that students are to read only the material directly related to the concepts introduced. This may or may not be an entire section of the text or other sources. The teacher should also remember to use various materials that are appropriate to the students' levels. This may mean that other instructional tools, such as films, tapes, newspapers, magazines, records, etc., will also be used. Thus, all students will not finish at the same time. This will allow the content specialist to begin the next step at different times to allow for more small group work.

*Discuss the information learned.* As the students complete their reading assignments, the content specialist begins discussions relating to the concepts being studied. These may be stimulated by written questions or they may be group rap sessions. As these discussions are developed, the content teacher must keep in mind the specific reading skills which need to be developed with the various students. This information is obtained from the diagnostic instruments discussed in chapters 4 and 5 and recorded in some format such as the chart in figure 8.3. Sample written activities which may be used to promote discussion and develop appropriate learning skills are outlined below.

### Social Studies

*Details:* Read the following passage and answer these questions. (A short passage on "The Gettysburg Address")
   *Who* wrote "The Gettysburg Address?"
   *What* is the meaning of this passage?
   *Where* was it delivered?
   *When* was this passage delivered?

### Mathematics

*Following Directions:* Give the students a direction carefully and slowly. Then have them write the direction in their own words, going through it step-by-step.

*Follow-up activities.* After small group and total class discussions of the concepts, some follow-up activities should be used to reinforce the subject. These activities may be in the form of other outside readings, reports, special skill development, or art activities. The content specialist can provide additional assistance in developing the reading skills at this time.

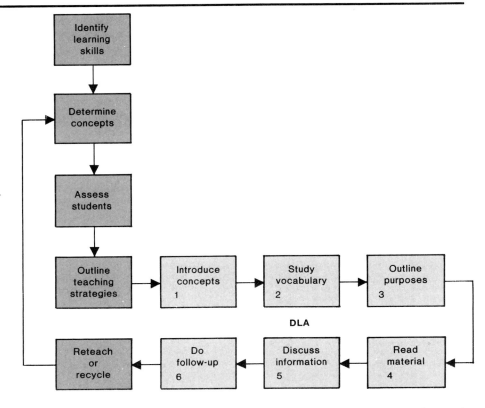

**Figure 8.4**
Procedures for Prescriptive Reading Instruction in the Content Area Classroom.
Earl H. Cheek and Martha Collins Cheek, *Reading Instruction Through Content Teaching* (Columbus, Ohio: Charles E. Merrill Publishing Company, 1983). Reprinted with permission.

**Step 5: Recycle Steps 1, 2, 3, and 4 continuously.** It is essential that diagnosis be a continuous part of prescriptive teaching. If students are to learn content material, content teachers must assume the responsibility of teaching. Teaching students at the appropriate level does not end in the primary grades. If content teachers want students to learn the content presented, they must take students as they are and develop the reading skills they need.

## Approaches for Prescriptive Reading Instruction

In order to provide prescriptive reading instruction, the diagnosed skill needs and the learning styles of the students are to be considered. Thus, teachers should be familiar with many approaches that may be used in prescriptive teaching.

Many approaches have been presented by different writers; for some the term "methods" is synonymous with "approaches." Burns and Roe identify the major approaches as basal reader approach, language experience approach, individualized reading approach, linguistic approaches, intensive phonics approaches, changed alphabet approaches, systems approaches, and eclectic approaches.[2] Fry discusses various methods of teaching reading, including the basal reader, reading systems, individualized reading, programmed instruction, different alphabetic approaches, audiovisual reading materials, language experience approach,

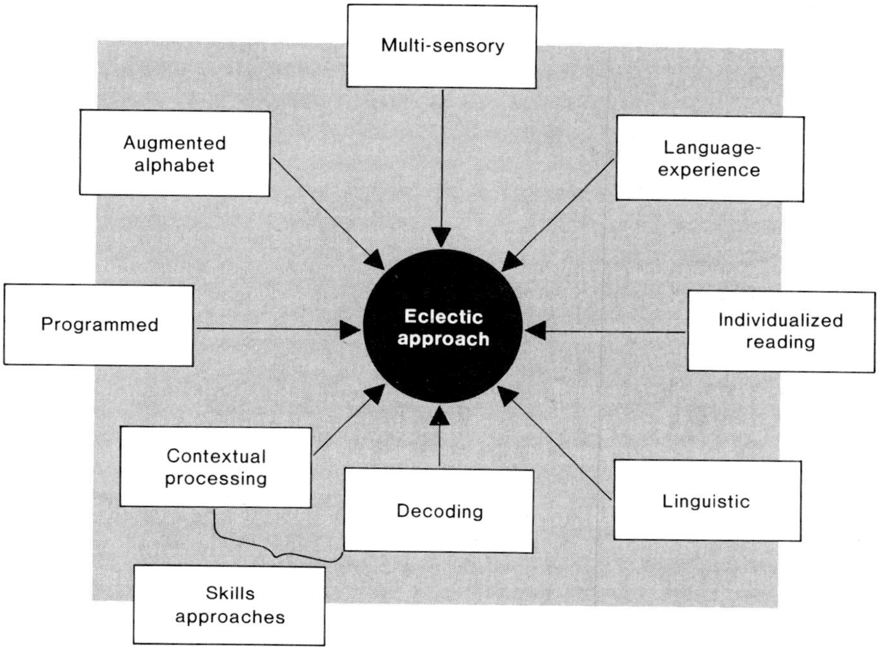

**Figure 8.5**
Approaches for
Teaching Reading

Figure 8.5 Approaches for Teaching Reading

and kinesthetic approach.[3] Other authors, including Ransom, Johnson, and Moe, identify slightly different listings of approaches for teaching reading.[4] Because there is such a diversity in the terminology used in this area, the authors have summarized and defined the approaches to reflect changes in reading instruction in today's schools.

**Multi-Sensory Approach**

The multi-sensory approach involves the senses of touch and muscle movement along with the senses of vision and hearing. Most students learn to read using the basic receptive senses of the eyes and ears. Some learn better through the visual mode than the auditory mode, or vice versa, but these are considered the primary senses necessary for reading. However, some students must have other stimulation in order to learn words in reading. For these individuals, the multi-sensory approach is used. If the classroom teacher recognizes that this approach is necessary, there are several methods which may be used:

Kinesthetic (VAKT)
VAK
Neurological impress

The kinesthetic method was developed by Grace Fernald as a way of teaching nonreaders.[5] This method, also known as the Fernald method or the Visual Auditory Kinesthetic Tactile (VAKT), follows four basic stages in teaching words

*How Can Prescriptive Teaching Be Implemented in the Classroom?*

**Figure 8.6**
Stages in Using the
Fernald Method (VAKT)

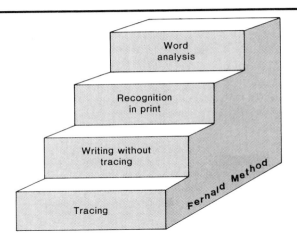

to the nonreader (figure 8.6). The teacher begins with words the student wants to learn, then proceeds to build a story with the words when the student is ready. Words are taught using the following stages.

> *Stage 1: Tracing.* The word is written for the student. The student traces the word and says each part of the word as it is traced. This is repeated until the student can trace the word from memory. The student then writes the word, saying each part as it is written.
>
> *Stage 2: Writing Without Tracing.* When the student seems familiar with the words, he or she looks at the word and writes it from memory without tracing.
>
> *Stage 3: Recognition in Print.* The student looks at a word, is told the word, pronounces it, and writes it from memory.
>
> *Stage 4: Word Analysis.* The student is taught to look for familiar parts of a word and to try to identify new words from the known parts.

This method is designed for use with the student who is experiencing great difficulty in reading.

A similar method is the VAK or visual-auditory-kinesthetic. This method, also developed by Fernald, is a modified VAKT procedure in which Stage 1 has been modified. The major change is that the student pronounces the entire word rather than the word parts as he or she writes. Like the VAKT, this should be used with students who experience difficulty in learning through other approaches.

Neurological impress is another method designed to assist the student with reading problems. In this method, the teacher reads a selection and points to the words, while the student reads along, pronouncing as many words as possible. This method has been adapted for group instruction through the use of earphones and tape recorded stories used while the student looks at the words in the story.[6]

As suggested by Harris and Sipay, this method seems to have more promise as a supplementary procedure, since "the teacher can neither control nor observe where the child's eyes are focused, [and] the child may or may not be looking at the right word, on the right line, as he hears the spoken word."[7]

Thus, examining the methods included within the multi-sensory approach, the classroom teacher should note that they are used primarily with students having difficulty in reading. However, this approach may be used on occasion to assist any student in remembering troublesome sounds, syllables, or words.

The language-experience approach is defined by Hall as "a method in which instruction is built upon the use of reading materials created by writing down children's spoken language."[8] Allen has provided another definition which presents the students' concept of the language-experience approach.

Language-Experience Approach

> What I can think about, I can talk about.
> What I can say, I can write—or someone can write for me.
> What I can write, I can read.
> I can read what I can write and what other people can write for me to read.[9]

These definitions reflect the importance of using the students' language as the basis for the development of reading materials. This approach integrates all the areas in order to strengthen the communication skills of reading, speaking, writing, and listening skills for each student.

The basic idea of developing story or experience charts has been used in schools since the early 1900s. However, through the work of Allen, Stauffer, and Hall this approach has become better understood and accepted for teaching reading to students of any age, preschool through adult.[10] The rationale for the use of this approach is that by using the student's own oral language as dictated, reading can be a successful experience.

In using the language-experience approach in the classroom, the teacher can follow these steps.

> Use the approach with an individual student, a small group, or a large group, depending on the purpose of the lesson.
> Discuss some experience that is common to the group or that seems important to the individual student, using a stimulus such as a field trip, an object, or a picture.
> Prepare the student(s) for telling a story by having them summarize ideas from the discussion or give a title to the ideas discussed.
> Allow each student to contribute to the story by sharing ideas about the experience.
> Write each sentence on the board or a chart.
> Read each idea after it is written, sweeping your hand under each line to emphasize left-to-right progression.
> Read the story together (teacher and students) when it is complete.
> Discuss the story, pointing out capital letters, names, ideas, etc.

**Table 8.1**
Language Experience Approach

| Advantages | Limitations |
|---|---|
| The students' language is the basis for the reading material. | The approach is unstructured; thus, there is no sequential development of skills. |
| Several learning modalities are used—auditory in dictating the story, visual in seeing the words, and kinesthetic in copying or writing the story. | The teacher must assume major responsibility in using this approach as there are no prepared materials and haphazard teaching can result. However, teachers may use the materials, *Language Experiences in Reading*, published by Encyclopedia Britannica, for some direction. |
| Students are motivated to read because the information is interesting to them. | |
| Self-concept is enhanced as the student realizes that others think his ideas are important. | The lack of repetition of vocabulary and vocabulary control may be troublesome for some students. |
| Older students with poor reading skills are interested in the content of the material. | Like any other approach, the overuse of this format in teaching may become boring to the student. |
| Concepts such as left-to-right orientation, capitalization and punctuation, word boundaries, etc. can be easily taught. | The development of the charts is time consuming for the teacher. |
| Oral language skills, which are especially beneficial to the student from an educationally deficient environment, are developed. | |

Copies of the story are made either by the students or duplicated by the teacher.

On the following days, the story is reread and skill development is accomplished by means of the vocabulary and ideas in the story. This last step is extremely important in the development of reading skills, yet it is often overlooked when using the language-experience approach.

This skill development may deal with word parts, letter sounds, capitalization and punctuation, word endings or any other skills needed by the student. Word cards with new vocabulary words may be developed to aid in other reading and writing experiences.

The language-experience approach, like other approaches, has advantages and limitations which must be recognized. These are summarized in table 8.1.

**Individualized Reading Approach**

The individualized reading approach is based on Olson's philosophy about child development, which promotes the ideas of seeking, self-selection, and pacing.[11] This concept was used by Veatch in describing her own views about reading[12] and has become known as the individualized reading approach. In implementing this approach in the classroom the teacher should follow these steps.

Know the reading levels and interests of the students with whom this approach will be used. These can be determined using procedures discussed in chapter 4.

Obtain library books or other materials of interest for the students to read. A large number of books that represent a variety of topics and reading levels is needed. The teacher must select the books very carefully, keeping in mind that different literary forms should be represented.

The readability levels of the books should be determined either by using a readability formula, or library source such as *Children's Catalog.*[13] The books should be organized according to levels so as to aid students in locating material that they can read.

The student selects a book that he or she wants to read. The student is not limited to the books at his or her readability level, as the teacher must realize that interest in a book goes a long way in motivating the student to read. However, the student should be allowed to read several pages to determine whether the book is too difficult and whether it is interesting, before selecting the book to read.

When the book is selected, the student should realize that he or she is expected to read the entire book and then sign up for a conference with the teacher to discuss the story. However, if help is needed while reading, the teacher must be flexible enough to give assistance. During the silent reading, the student may list words which he or she does not recognize or understand.

After completing the story, the student notifies the teacher that he or she is ready for a conference. During the conference, which may last from five to twenty minutes, the teacher asks questions about the story, listens to the student read a short passage in order to diagnose word recognition difficulties, provides some individual skill development instruction, and summarizes the results of the discussion. The conference requires that the teacher be very familiar with the stories read in the classroom and also the reading continuum used in the school.

The individualized reading approach can be used with an entire class of students or an individual student. This approach is not necessarily designed to supplement the basal readers, although it may be used with some students while others use the basal reader, or to add variety to reading instruction. To assist the reader in visualizing this approach in the classroom, a description of the author's use of it is provided. This approach was used because there were no other materials in an overcrowded elementary school. The parents insisted that the students have books, and most of the students hated reading!

On the first day of school I was met by thirty-seven second graders who were not ready for school to begin. With no basal readers, kits, or any instructional material, I had decided to use the language-experience approach with a few students and an individualized reading approach with most of the class.

My first task was to determine the reading levels of the students, which I soon discovered ranged from preprimer to the sixth-grade level. With this information I went to the library to check out books for the students who were reading from low second-grade to sixth-grade level. There I met my first obstacle—the librarian, who allowed me to keep books for only two weeks. As a first-year teacher, I

continued to smile, took my books to the room, checked the readability levels, put a piece of colored tape on each to denote the level, and arranged them on the shelf.

The students were directed to select books from those at their level. They were allowed to read those below their level during extra time and those above their level with permission.

To assure continuity of skill development, I used the scope and sequence chart for the basal series being used in most of the classes in the school. A large chart containing the students' names and the skills was made, laminated and taped on my desk. Using observations and other informal procedures I determined skill strengths and weaknesses and used the chart as my guide for skill grouping and conference discussions.

As the students read their books, they kept a word bank of unknown words. When they finished a book, they placed a name card in a box on my desk to notify me of their need for a conference. They proceeded to another book until they were called for a conference.

During the conference, we discussed words that were difficult, and I asked comprehension questions based on the comprehension needs of the student. Following the conference, I placed a note in my notebook that summarized our discussions. The student was given a gummed label with the title of the book just completed to put on his or her individual reading record poster, which decorated the wall.

Each day the students worked in small groups to develop skills which needed to be strengthened. Many games and activity sheets were used to reinforce this group work.

Every two weeks, five members of the class and I loaded our little red wagon, returned the books to the library, and checked out a new group of books. This procedure continued the entire school year. The results—a group of students who enjoyed reading.

In retrospect, the question arises as to how the teacher could manage this hectic schedule over a long period of time. The response is that when students are excited about reading and are improving in the use of their reading skills, the teacher is rewarded, and energy seems to come from unknown sources.

The advantages and limitations of the individualized reading approach seem apparent from these descriptions. They are summarized in table 8.2.

## Skills Approaches

With the emphasis on skill development in reading, some teachers have begun to use what the authors refer to as the skills approaches. This means that they are teaching reading through the teaching of individual skills. In the use of these approaches, the teacher must keep a balance in the development of decoding and comprehension skills and must provide opportunities for the student to apply the skills in reading materials.

**Table 8.2**
Individualized Reading Approach

| Advantages | Limitations |
|---|---|
| Flexibility and freedom in grouping and adjusting instruction. | Time consuming for the teacher, in that much planning, diagnosis, record-keeping, and knowledge of the reading process is essential. |
| The teacher has regular interaction with the student on an individual basis. | Schools may not have enough library books to loan for an extended period of time. |
| Students read materials that meet their interests. | Teachers must be knowledgeable of children's literature in order to have effective conferences. |
| Students read in a manner that resembles real-life reading situations. | Vocabulary is not controlled. |
| Students build a more positive self-concept, as success in reading comes with working at the appropriate level. | Poor readers have difficulty attending to a book on their own. |
|  | Easy books for students with a limited vocabulary are difficult to locate. |

*Decoding*

The decoding approaches include the phonics method and the whole-word or look-say method. Thus, decoding is defined in a narrow sense to mean the recognition of words either by sound or by sight. For many years, philosophical discussions and reading research debated the use of these approaches in an effort to determine which should be used in teaching reading. Logic and common sense along with research have shown the need for students to be taught phonetic analysis of words and to learn some words by sight recognition, as all words cannot be phonetically analyzed.

The current issue regarding the use of these methods is whether to use analytic (inductive) instruction or synthetic (deductive) instruction in the decoding skills. Analytic instruction teaches through the comparison of words that the student already knows by sight. Synthetic instruction is more intensive. It requires learning individual letter sounds and combining these sounds into words.

The use of these approaches was studied in the First Grade Studies and by Chall.[14] The findings indicated that the use of synthetic phonics instruction in beginning reading resulted in greater success in word recognition. In a follow-up study by Dykstra, these students did not demonstrate superiority in reading comprehension in the second grade.[15] Thus, the best approach for use in beginning reading seems to be a matter of student needs and teacher preference.

**Figure 8.7**
Example of Analytic Method of Decoding

bat    boy    ball

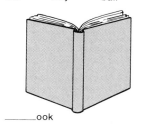

———ook

In implementing the analytic method, the teacher would present an entire word and teach each new word through visual memory. Using visual discrimination skills and visual memory, students remember the words and add them to their sight vocabulary. The teacher selects words that have a similar sound (for example *boy*, *bat*, *ball*) and teaches the initial sound of *b*. Then, when students see the word *book*, they associate the first letter with the same sound as the beginning of *boy*, *bat*, *ball* (see figure 8.7).

Teaching decoding in this manner keeps the sounds in the context of words, assisting the students in learning words as well as sounds simultaneously. Persons who oppose this method feel that without first knowing the individual sounds many students have difficulty recognizing them in words and applying them to other words.

The synthetic method teaches the isolated sounds of the letters, then shows the student how to form these sounds into words. For example, rather than teaching the word *bat* and comparing the initial sound to that of *book,* the synthetic method teaches the sound of *b* as 'bah', *a* as 'aa', and *t* as 'tuh'. The student is then taught to blend these sounds to form the word *bat.*

This method has advantages as well as limitations. The major advantage is that some slower readers who have difficulty recognizing sounds within words seem able to learn the isolated sounds more easily. The limitations of this method include the fact that the English language does not follow a one-to-one pattern in sound-symbol relationships. This creates problems in trying to sound each letter as it is initially taught in the synthetic method. Linguists offer much criticism of this method, as the teaching of isolated letter sounds distorts the sounds and presents them either as representing only one sound or with various sounds depending on the context—the problem is they are not taught in context![16]

The approaches used in decoding have been and continue to be areas of discussion in reading. The teacher must recognize the strengths and weaknesses of each method, know the needs of each student, and use the method which best meets the individual situation. This is prescriptive instruction!

<table>
<tr><td>Contextual<br>Processing</td><td>While debate persists as to the appropriate decoding approach to use with students, achievement test scores continue to indicate more difficulty in comprehension or contextual processing than in decoding. In some school districts, the reaction is to shift the teaching emphasis to develop these skills. Thus another approach seems to be developing in the schools. This approach, like decoding, isolates and attempts to develop a skill area.</td></tr>
</table>

In this procedure the teacher must first know that the students have adequate word recognition skills that permit them to understand the printed word. If this area is deemed satisfactory, the teacher then identifies the contextual processing skills that are deficient and provides instruction to strengthen them. Instruction may be given through the use of many different materials, such as workbooks and kits, or it may be done through oral discussion following the reading of a designated material.

The development of comprehension skills should be an integral part of all reading instruction. It is considered a separate approach only when isolated and used as a total teaching strategy. The major advantage of using this method is that through teaching which emphasizes comprehension, skill deficiencies in this area can be overcome. The major limitations of this approach are (1) a student may not be ready for extensive work in comprehension, since poor word recognition skills may in fact be causing the comprehension difficulty, and (2) if the

teacher isolates the individual comprehension skills when teaching, the student may be unable to apply them in reading situations. More ideas regarding comprehension development are provided in chapter 11.

In discussing the linguistic approach to reading instruction, classroom teachers should recognize that there is no one linguistic approach, and in fact many linguists contend that there is no such thing as a linguistic approach to reading instruction. However, the research of the linguists has produced various ideas about the teaching of reading. Some of the original ideas that were called the linguistic approach resulted from the work of Bloomfield and Barnhart, who proposed that word recognition be taught according to sound patterns.[17] Fries, another linguist, suggested that reading should be taught according to spelling patterns.[18] Both agreed that only regular spelling patterns should be taught initially. These researchers provided progressions for teaching the spelling patterns that were used in developing commercial reading materials such as *Merrill Linguistic Readers* (Columbus, Ohio: Charles E. Merrill, 1975) and *Miami Linguistic Readers* (Indianapolis: D. C. Heath, 1970). The linguistic approach proposed by Fries and Bloomfield and Barnhart seems to be similar to the analytic method discussed previously, with the added dimension of teaching the spelling patterns by means of whole words and transferring this pattern to other words. Emans discusses this idea in greater detail.[19]

Linguists such as Smith, Goodman, and Meredith extended the linguistic approach from word recognition to include the language used and meaning expressed in the reading material. They suggest that "Reading methodology must reflect an understanding of language, of learning, of children, and of children learning language."[20] This philosophy has been incorporated into the new reading materials used in many classrooms and results in the use of methods which consider the students' experiences and language patterns and so help motivate them to read. This has been noted through the increased use of the language-experience approach and changes in basal reader materials that capitalize on the language of all students.

Classroom teachers should be aware of the tremendous impact of linguistics on reading instruction. To gain further information consult the additional references provided in the suggested readings.

The programmed approach develops reading proficiency through the systematic presentation of material and immediate feedback on responses. The approach may use material such as *Programmed Instruction* by Sullivan and Buchanan (Webster, McGraw-Hill), or technological devices such as machines. Some examples of the latter include *Borg-Warner System 80,* the *Hoffman Audiovisual Instructional System,* and computer instructional programs.

Regardless of the medium used in the programmed approach, the basic steps are the same. The material is developed around a set of objectives which specify the expected terminal behavior. The lessons are presented in a step-by-step manner, with each lesson leading toward the accomplishment of a specific objective.

For each response, the learner is given immediate feedback. In some materials the student is directed to another page or lesson to improve an area of weaknesses noted from an incorrect response. This is known as the branching technique. Materials which do not cross reference lessons follow a linear technique.

The strengths in using the programmed approach are:

The materials are motivational to the students, especially the technological devices.

The students develop at their own pace, since the materials are used individually.

The students receive immediate feedback and reinforcement.

The lessons are carefully sequenced for skill development.

The teacher is free to work with students on specific needs rather than spending time in drill work.

The approach is not without limitations. The major weakness is that it lends itself more to the development of word recognition skills than the higher level skills of comprehension. This can result in an unbalanced reading program. A second consideration is that, if overused, this approach becomes very monotonous. This is also true when the novelty of the machine wears off.

Another difficulty with this method is that there must always be only one correct answer. Creative students are not stimulated by this approach. On the other hand, slower students also have difficulty with this procedure, as it is based upon the premise that they can read, which is often not the case. Another limitation is that the materials become very impersonal, as teacher-student interaction is minimal. The teacher loses many opportunities to gain diagnostic information from students when they function so much on their own. An additional limitation of the machine technique is the cost factor. The devices are extremely costly and should be purchased only when the school is equipped with all other reading materials.

## Augmented Alphabet Approach

The augmented alphabet approach incorporates materials which employ some special coding procedure to change the traditional alphabet in order to develop one-to-one sound-symbol correspondences. This change may be in the form of a new set of symbols, as in the *Initial Teaching Alphabet,* or a color coding system, as in *Words in Color*. These materials attempt to simplify the decoding aspect of the reading process by using a specific coded symbol to represent each sound in our language.

The *Initial Teaching Alphabet* (i/t/a) is a forty-four-letter alphabet devised in England by Sir James Pitman and introduced in the United States in 1963 by John Downing. Each of the forty-four symbols (letters) represents one sound. The i/t/a alphabet uses twenty-four of the symbols from the traditional alphabet and adds twenty new symbols. The same symbols represent both upper and lower case letters; capital letters are printed or written larger then the lower case (see figure 8.8).

**Figure 8.8**
The Initial Teaching
Alphabet
Reproduced by permission
of the Initial Teaching
Alphabet Foundation, Inc.

THE INITIAL TEACHING ALPHABET

The method used in teaching with i/t/a is basically the same as with the basal reader. The difference is that the symbols are not the same. With the i/t/a symbols, less time is required in teaching the students to read words than with the traditional letters. Furthermore, writing is emphasized to a greater extent in the i/t/a materials, as students can spell more words using the forty-four symbols. Proponents of this approach recommend it only for beginning reading and recommend the transition to traditional orthography (the twenty-six-letter alphabet) in the primary grades. Strengths often noted concerning the use of this material include:

> In beginning reading the elimination of many failures due to the lack of confusing sound-symbol correspondence

An increase in creative writing because the i/t/a sound-symbol correspondences aid spelling

The limitations of this material are difficult to document. Conclusions of the research studies are hard to compare due to differences in populations, and designs. However, the major limitation involves the change from i/t/a to traditional orthography (t.o.). This change often results in the student's learning to read twice. Proponents of the method dispute this limitation.

Another limitation concerns writing: when students transfer to t.o., their spelling is sometimes adversely affected, as they tend to continue to spell with i/t/a. A third limitation relates to the availability of materials written in i/t/a. While there are some materials available for students to read on their own, there are many more materials written in t.o. Proponents suggest that materials written by the students can supplement the materials used in school. For more research information concerning this method the reader should note the summaries by Aukerman.[21]

Other methods using a varied alphabet include *UNIFON,* which is a forty-letter alphabet; the Laubach Method, which uses phonemic spelling with the twenty-six letters of the alphabet; and *Fonetic English* which has a twenty-nine-letter alphabet. These materials have many of the strengths and weaknesses of the i/t/a materials.

Another method in the augmented alphabet approach uses colors to distinguish the various sound-symbol correspondences. *Words in Color* was developed in 1957 by Caleb Gattegno, using the twenty-six letters of the alphabet and forty-seven shades of colors to represent the forty-seven phonemes in the English language. The materials consist of twenty-one charts of letter sounds, work sheets, and stories using the color coded system. The students are taught to respond to the color symbol and to blend the sounds into words.

This method uses a very novel technique that helps students overcome problems related to the irregularities of the English language. Students who have previously had difficulty in reading often find *Words in Color* to be motivating. More important than the color coding system, however, is the fact that the various sound-symbol correspondences are grouped so the student can see the similarity of sounds regardless of spelling.

Even though this is an interesting method, there are some limitations to its use. The most obvious is that it cannot be used as designed with color-blind students, although it may be adapted for such use. In addition, many of the color shades are quite similar and therefore difficult to distinguish when put together. Another weakness, as with i/t/a, is the limited amount of material available for practice reading. Students may become motivated to read only to realize that there are few materials they can read until they become more proficient in the decoding skills. One major limitation of these materials is their emphasis on word recognition and slight emphasis on comprehension. If this method is used, the classroom teacher must supplement it with a different approach in order to develop comprehension.

Another method that should be mentioned in the discussion of the augmented alphabet approach is the rebus method. Here pictures are substituted for words and combined with other words or symbols to produce sentences. This method is used with beginning readers as an aid to learning words and sentence structure. The use of rebus is becoming more common as the international language symbols are more extensively used.

The augmented alphabet approach uses various methods and materials designed to help the student decode words in a language with many irregularities in its sound-symbol relationships. For some students who have difficulties in this area, the augmented alphabet approach provides an alternative to use in prescriptive teaching.

## Eclectic Approach

Teachers have long recognized that there is no one best way of teaching reading. If there were, this section of the book would be much shorter and there would be far fewer reading materials on the market. The need for a variety of approaches must be stressed in discussing prescriptive instruction, since a major component of prescriptive teaching is the use of the appropriate approach with each student. Thus, the eclectic approach, which combines the desirable aspects of other approaches to meet student needs, becomes the approach most frequently used in the prescriptive reading program.

In discussing the eclectic approach, the authors are including the basal materials as a structured type of eclectic approach rather than a separate approach. This is because the new basal reader materials have changed significantly in the last decade and use various approaches for developing the skills. For example, the story content more closely reflects the children's literature used in the individualized reading approach. The controlled vocabulary and the limited story characters have disappeared. The linguistic philosophies have had a definite impact on the basal materials. Incorporated into most teachers' guides which accompany the basal materials are suggestions for using the language experience approach, ideas for furthering reading through the individualized reading approach, techniques for using the multi-sensory approach to teach letters and words, and specific activities for word recognition and comprehension skill development. The basal reader is no longer designed to function as a self-contained unit but rather as a structured way to guide teachers in the use of various approaches to teach reading. Unfortunately, the basal is often misused and these ideas are not incorporated into the lessons; instead the student may be limited to the reader and a workbook. When used in this manner, the basal is not considered to be a part of the eclectic approach.

As teachers use the eclectic approach, they not only match the method to the student, but they must also be cautious about using conflicting approaches with the same student. For example, a linguistic approach may confuse the student who is learning to decode words phonetically. Likewise, the augmented alphabet approach would require careful introduction and explanation before moving a student into its materials.

To teach reading effectively, the teacher must be familiar with and use a variety of approaches. Thus, the strength of the eclectic approach is that the students' needs can be met. The limitations are that careful planning and coordination on the part of the teacher are essential, and an assortment of materials is necessary. The teacher who believes in diagnostic-prescriptive teaching will overcome these two limitations by taking time to plan and to locate materials, either from other places or by making them. The First-Grade Studies and the follow-up research leave no room for doubt that teachers must use the eclectic approach in order to meet the reading needs of all students.[22]

## Developing Prescriptions

This chapter has addressed basic ideas concerning prescriptive instruction, procedures to use in providing instruction, and the different approaches which should be used in prescriptive teaching. The next specific task confronting the teacher is that of developing prescriptions for instruction. Teachers should remember that in prescriptive instruction, each student has an assignment based on diagnosed needs. This prescription may be written for the student each day or only outlined in the teacher's plans, but it must be designed with the individual in mind.

As teachers develop prescriptions, these ideas need to be kept in mind:

The prescription should guarantee success. Tasks that are performed while working with the teacher should be at the student's instructional reading level, while tasks to be performed alone should be at the independent reading level.

In prescriptive instruction, the teacher should provide direct instruction before asking the student to work alone or with a group. Individual work is done to reinforce the ideas taught by the teacher.

The student is directed to tasks requiring the application of skills which have been taught in isolation.

Prescriptive instruction allow the students opportunities for decision-making. This includes the selection of a learning task from several choices, and the opportunity to express their feelings toward the tasks.

Teachers continuously analyze the students' performances in order to gain the diagnostic information needed to re-evaluate the prescriptive teaching assignments.

Directions given on all tasks need to be specific and clearly stated.

In developing prescriptions, the teacher outlines the plans for the entire class prior to writing prescription cards for students. To organize the instructions for a class, the teacher must have an outline of all the tasks that will be going on at the same time. This planning procedure assists the teacher in grouping students, arranging students in the different centers, and planning for other variables, such as changes in the noise levels in the room. In addition, the teacher needs this "master plan" for instruction as a daily record of what the students have been doing in order to plan for future instruction. The overall plan will probably be

outlined in the teacher's lesson plan booklet and used as a record for directing students in the various tasks. This planning is done daily, with evaluative notes added as observations are made.

From this point the teacher determines how the prescription will be relayed to the student. There are many ways, which range from an individual prescription sheet for each student to oral directions from the teacher. Regardless of the procedure used, the information is based on the teachers' "master plan" for instruction.

Although the teacher can use many techniques for informing the students of their assignments, some teachers feel that prescriptive instruction cannot be provided because of a lack of time to write individual assignment sheets each day. This is a misconception about prescriptive instruction. First, the use of individual sheets or folders is only one way of giving prescriptions in reading; it is not an essential. Second, if individual folders are used, the teacher only has to write new prescriptions for everyone at the same time on the first day of use. Thereafter, the teacher will give new assignments as he or she moves around the classroom, and only a few students need completely new assignments each day. Thus, if the teacher wishes to use this procedure, it is manageable.

**Figure 8.9**

Sample Individual
Prescription

Name: _____

| Date | Skill Needs | Assignment | Remarks |
|------|-------------|------------|---------|
| 11/13 | —Prefix meanings<br>—Sequencing<br>—Use of index | 1. Work with teacher in yellow group.<br><br>2. Work with Jim on Prefix Game #6.<br><br>3. Listen to tape #4 and follow the directions. Take paper and pencil.<br><br>4. Use index in social studies book to complete worksheet. | Only 1 and 2 done. I like the game.<br><br><br><br><br>3 and 4 done now 11/14. |
| 11/15 | —Sequencing<br>—Use of index<br>—Personal reading | 1. Work with Green group in Study Skills center.<br><br>2. Work with teacher — bring work done with yellow group and tape #4.<br><br>3. Select a book to read for fun. | I can put things in order now.<br><br><br><br>Didn't get. |

The main advantage in using the individual assignment sheet and folder is to aid in keeping information on the student in a central location. This is very helpful in parent conferences. However, in addition to the feeling that this is too time consuming for the teacher, there are other concerns. When individual student assignments are written for the student, teachers begin to ignore total class plans and to give only the individual assignments, which soon become mere paper-pencil tasks. The teacher is removed from an instructional role to one of managing papers. Furthermore, skills may be taught in isolation, and students are not provided opportunities to apply them. Soon prescriptive instruction falls into the test-teach-test pattern for reading skill development, and reading instruction becomes very boring. When the teacher is aware of these possible problems and makes an effort to avoid them, individual student sheets can be a most effective way of organizing prescriptive instruction.

When using individual assignment sheets in folders to relay student tasks, the teacher may want to use a format like the one in figure 8.9. Assignments are dated, student choice provided in the selection of some tasks, and student feedback on the work encouraged.

Another way of providing prescriptive information to students is to use assignment cards. The teacher may have a wall chart containing a pocket for each student, then place assignment cards in the pockets to direct the students to their tasks. For students who are unable to read, the teacher may use colored cards to direct them to areas in the room that have their tasks outlined. For other students, the teacher may wish to write specific directions on the cards. Using this procedure, cards may be saved and used again when necessary to save time.

One other idea that may be used in organizing prescriptions is shown in figure 8.10. The various groups or individual students are assigned numbers at the beginning of a specified period of time. The areas in the room are color coded, with necessary assignments placed in each area. Using the chart illustrated in figure 8.10, the teacher assigns students to tasks that are in the various areas, by matching the group number and task color. Be sure that one color represents working with the teacher. The use of this procedure depends on the teacher's plan, since the chart provides the student directions and no individual assignment sheets or cards are given out. The students work primarily in groups; however, special instructions may be given to a student for an individual assignment. At the end of a specified block of time, the color wheel is moved, and the students likewise move to another task.

There are many procedures which the teacher may use in providing prescriptive instruction in the classroom. The organizational plan is up to the instructor. The essential element is that the instruction provided must meet the diagnosed needs of the student. Teachers use the summary charts containing the diagnostic data, the continuum of reading skills, and their observations of the students to give appropriate learning experiences.

**Figure 8.10**
Assignment Wheel for
Prescriptive Instruction

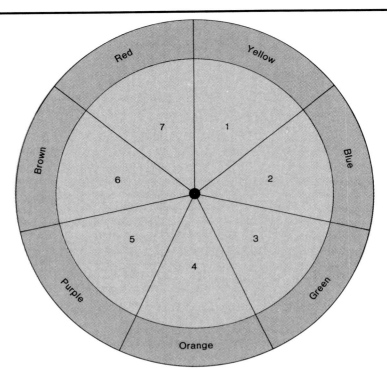

**Summary**

This chapter has provided the classroom teacher with an introduction to prescriptive reading instruction. It includes some basic principles for prescriptive instruction to serve as guides for the teacher. The underlying philosophy is that there is no one best way to implement prescriptive teaching in the classroom; the teacher must adjust these ideas to individual situations.

To present additional instructional ideas, eight approaches to reading instruction were discussed. These included the multi-sensory, language experience, individualized reading, skills, linguistic, augmented alphabet, programmed and eclectic approaches. Advantages and limitations were listed for each approach to assist the teacher in determining the best techniques to use with each student.

Because the teachers in a self-contained classroom and a departmental situation must approach prescriptive reading instruction with a slightly different emphasis, directed teaching procedures were outlined for each. The Directed Reading Activity format was provided for self-contained classroom teachers, while an adaptation of this procedure, the Directed Learning Activity, was furnished for content teachers seeking to integrate prescriptive reading instruction into the content areas. Moreover, some specific techniques were given in order to assist teachers in using prescriptions in reading.

Ways of prescribing for specific difficulties in prereading, word recognition, comprehension, study skills, and personal reading will be presented in chapters 9–14.

You are a new teacher in a school that is beginning a diagnostic-prescriptive reading program. The diagnostic data have been summarized, and you are now ready to organize yourself to provide prescriptive instruction. What would you do?

The principal in your school has asked that every teacher use a variety of approaches in providing prescriptive instruction. To make sure that an effort is made in this direction, each teacher is asked to describe the three most common approaches used in his or her classroom. What three approaches would you identify and why?

A friend of yours teaches sixth-grade social studies. The students need much help in reading, so the school is moving toward the use of diagnostic-prescriptive reading instruction throughout the school. Your friend doesn't understand how prescriptive reading instruction can fit into the social studies class. How could you explain?

1. Guy L. Bond and Robert Dykstra, *Final Report, Project No. X-001.*
2. Paul C. Burns and Betty D. Roe, *Teaching Reading in Today's Elementary Schools,* pp. xii–xiii.
3. Edward B. Fry, *Elementary Reading Instruction,* pp. 134–227.
4. Grayce A. Ransom, *Preparing to Teach Reading,* pp. 72–87; Dale Johnson, "Reading: Current Approaches, Part One," in *Reading: Foundations and Instructional Strategies,* ed. Pose Lamb and Richard Arnold, pp. 194–237; Alden J. Moe, "Reading: Current Approaches, Part Two," in *Reading: Foundations and Instructional Strategies,* ed. Pose Lamb and Richard Arnold, pp. 238–71.
5. Grace M. Fernald, *Remedial Technique in Basic School Subjects.*
6. William C. Jordan, "Prime-o-tec: The New Reading Method," *Academic Therapy Quarterly,* pp. 248–50.
7. Albert J. Harris and Edward R. Sipay, *How to Increase Reading Ability,* 6th ed., p. 403.
8. Mary Anne Hall, *The Language Experience Approach for Teaching Reading,* 2nd ed., pp. 1–2.
9. Roach Van Allen, "The Language-Experience Approach," in *Perspectives on Elementary Reading,* ed. Robert Karlin, p. 158.
10. Roach Van Allen, *Language Experiences in Communication;* Russell G. Stauffer, *The Language-Experience Approach to the Teaching of Reading;* Mary Anne Hall, *Teaching Reading as a Language Experience.*
11. Willard C. Olson, *Child Development.*
12. Jeanette Veatch, *Individualizing Your Reading Program.*
13. Rachel Fidell and Estelle A. Fiddell, eds. *Children's Catalog,* 13th edition.
14. Bond and Dykstra, *Final Report, Project No. X–001;* Jeanne Chall, *Learning to Read: The Great Debate.*
15. Robert Dykstra, "Summary of the Second Phase of the Cooperative Research Program in Primary Reading Instruction," *Reading Research Quarterly.*
16. Charles C. Fries, *Linguistics and Reading.*
17. Leonard Bloomfield and Clarence L. Barnhart, *Let's Read: A Linguistic Approach* (Detroit: Wayne State University Press, 1961).

18. Fries, *Linguistics and Reading.*
19. Robert Emans, "Linguistics and Phonics," *The Reading Teacher.*
20. E. Brooks Smith, Kenneth Goodman, and Robert Meredith, *Language and Thinking in the Elementary School,* p. 271.
21. Robert C. Aukerman, *Approaches to Beginning Reading,* pp. 330–44.
22. This research can be found in the following issues of *The Reading Teacher:* May 1966, October 1966, May 1967, October 1967, January 1969 and March 1969.

**Other Suggested Readings**

*Basic Reading Plus.* Greenwich, Connecticut: Macmillan Professional Magazines, 1976.

Brown, Don A. *Reading Diagnosis and Remediation.* Englewood Cliffs, New Jersey: Prentice-Hall, Inc., 1982. Chapter 10.

Charnock, James. "An Alternative to the DRA." *The Reading Teacher* 31 (December 1977):269–71.

Cheek, Earl H. and Cheek, Martha Collins. *Reading Instruction Through Content Teaching.* Columbus, Ohio: Charles E. Merrill Publishing Company, 1983.

Cunningham, Patricia Marr; Arthur, Sharon V.; and Cunningham, James W. *Classroom Reading Instruction, K–5: Alternative Approaches.* Lexington, Massachusetts: D. C. Heath and Company, 1977.

Downing, John. "Results of Teaching Reading in I.T.A. to Children with Cognitive Deficits." *Reading World* 18 (March 1979):290–99.

Eberwein, Lowell D. "The Variability of Readability of Basal Reader Textbooks and How Much Teachers Know About It." *Reading World* 18 (March 1979):259–72.

Ekwall, Eldon E. and Shanker, James L. *Diagnosis and Remediation of the Disabled Reader.* 2nd edition. Boston: Allyn and Bacon, Inc., 1983.

Fulwiler, Gwen, and Groff, Patrick. "The Effectiveness of Intensive Phonics." *Reading Horizons* 21 (Fall 1980):50–54.

Gentry, Larry A. "A Clinical Method in Classroom Success-Kinesthetic Teaching." *The Reading Teacher* 28 (December 1974):288–300.

Gilliland, Hap. *A Practical Guide to Remedial Reading.* Columbus, Ohio: Charles E. Merrill Publishing Company, 1978.

Glock, Marvin D. "Is there a Pygmalion in the Classroom?" *The Reading Teacher* 25 (February 1972):405–8.

Gold, Patricia Cohen. "Two Strategies for Reinforcing Sight Vocabulary of Language Experience Stories." *The Reading Teacher* 35 (November 1981):141–43.

Gonzales, Phillip C. "What's Wrong with the Basal Reader Approach to Language Development?" *The Reading Teacher* 33 (March 1980):668–73.

Heilman, Arthur, and Holmes, Elizabeth Ann. *Smuggling Language into the Teaching of Reading.* Columbus, Ohio: Charles E. Merrill Publishing Company, 1972.

Jackson, Ruth. "Building Reading Skills and Self-Concepts." *The Reading Teacher* 25 (May 1972):754–58.

Johnson, Joseph C. "Management of an Individualized Reading Instruction and Learning Program." *Elementary English* 50 (September 1973):875–80.

Miller, Wilma. "Organizing a First Grade Classroom for Individualized Reading Instruction." *The Reading Teacher* 24 (May 1971):748–60.

Myers, Collin A. "Reviewing the Literature on Fernald's Technique of Remedial Reading." *The Reading Teacher* 31 (March 1978):614–19.

Quick, Donald M. "Toward Positive Self-Concept." *The Reading Teacher* 26 (February 1973):468–71.

Schwartz, Judy S. "A Language Experience Approach to Beginning Reading." *Elementary English* 52 (March 1975):320–23.

Sebasta, Sam Leaton. "Commentary: Miss Smith and the Traditional Method." *The Reading Teacher* 33 (February 1980):516–18.

Shannon, Patrick. "Some Subjective Reasons for Teachers' Reliance on Commercial Reading Materials." *The Reading Teacher* 35 (May 1982):884–89.

Spiegel, Dixie Lee. "Six Alternatives to the Directed Reading Activity." *The Reading Teacher* 34 (May 1981):914–20.

Stauffer, Russell G., and Harrell, Max M. "Individualized Reading-Thinking Activities." *The Reading Teacher* 28 (May 1975):765–69.

Wilson, Robert M. *Diagnostic and Remedial Reading for Classroom and Clinic,* 4th ed. Columbus, Ohio: Charles E. Merrill Publishing Company, 1981. Chapter 7.

Witman, Carolyn Cattron, and Riley, James D. "Colored Chalk and Messy Fingers: A Kinesthetic-Tactile Approach to Reading." *The Reading Teacher* 31 (March 1978):620–23.

**9**

Teachers at Seabreeze School recognize that the development of prereading skills is essential to a sound foundation for beginning reading instruction. These are skills that children must develop during the early years in order to become proficient readers. Without the progressive development of these skills, students may become inefficient or disabled readers.

The importance of each of these prereading skills is discussed in detail in this chapter. A list of these skills is provided together with ideas to aid the classroom teacher in providing appropriate prescriptive instruction for each student. Other important aspects of this chapter include research as to the importance of the various prereading skills and suggestions for relating the specific diagnostic techniques discussed in previous chapters to the prereading skills. In discussion groups, the Seabreeze School faculty asked the following questions, which are addressed in this chapter.

Why are prereading skills important?
_____

What are the prereading skills?
_____

What does research tell us about this area?
_____

How can the teacher diagnose prereading skills?
_____

What needs in prereading may be discovered through diagnosis?
_____

What are some ideas that may be used in providing prescriptive instruction in prereading skills?

# How are prereading skills developed through prescriptive teaching?

As you read this chapter, note these terms.

**Vocabulary to Know**

Auditory comprehension
Auditory discrimination
Auditory memory
Oral language
Prereading skills
Readiness

Visual comprehension
Visual discrimination
Visual memory
Visual-motor
Word boundaries

**The Importance of Prereading Skills**

Prereading skills are those skills developed prior to the beginning of formal reading instruction. They form a basis for teaching beginning reading skills, and as the student becomes more involved in the reading process, they remain the foundation for the acquisition of the higher level reading skills.

The importance of prereading is implicit in the preceding definition. In order to learn to read, students must develop a foundation in the various areas that comprise the prereading skills. Success in reading depends upon the development of a sound foundation. Without a solid basis for reading development, students experience difficulty in analyzing and comprehending the written word. Even with only a few building blocks missing, many students will not reach their potential in reading, because the missing blocks contain essential skills necessary to learn other reading skills. It is necessary for students to develop prereading skills so that progress in reading may continue to be orderly and sequential.

In considering the importance of prereading skills, it is necessary to examine the various factors that affect reading. It is simple enough to state that a solid foundation in prereading skills is vital to the reading process; however, it is also important to note that not all students are afforded the same opportunities, nor do they all develop at the same rate. These factors have their impact on students prior to school entrance and often continue to cripple them throughout the school years. The three major factors are intelligence, environment, and maturation (see figure 9.1). Each of these factors is discussed in greater detail to give the teacher more insight into the complexity of prereading.

**Figure 9.1**
Factors Influencing
Development in
Reading

Intelligence

**Environment**
Social/cultural awareness
Background of experiences
Oral language
Interests in reading

**Maturation**
Physical
Emotional

Child's
development
in reading

The term intelligence carries the connotation of capability, the ability to under- **Intelligence**
stand. This capability to learn is, of course, indispensable to the acquisition of
the skills necessary for learning to read. High levels of intelligence, as measured
by intelligence tests, usually reflect high verbal ability, varied experiences, a stable homelife, and perhaps fairly well-developed manipulative abilities. Some students obtain intelligence scores which reflect poor ability, when in fact they simply
have not had the opportunity to develop. Thus, teachers must view intelligence
scores as relative to the other factors which affect reading development.

Environment in the home and at school is extremely important in learning to **Environment**
read. Students from environmental conditions which are conducive to learning
to read are more likely to experience success than students from less favorable
environments. Some specific aspects which contribute to the environmental factor include social/cultural awareness, experiential background, oral language
development, and interest in reading.

Students from homes in which reading is not important often enter school
with little expertise in the prereading skill areas. These students may have never
seen a book, newspaper, magazine, or any type of printed material. They have
not been read to nor have they seen others read in the home. Moreover, experiences outside their culture are usually nonexistent, a condition which limits their
understanding of many of the materials and ideas confronting them in school.
These conditions contribute to the students' lack of interest in learning to read,
which means that the teacher must not only develop the prerequisite skills, but
must also motivate the student to learn.

Students who come from such educationally deficient environments are often
lacking in the area of oral language. Oral language is vitally important in the
reading process, in as much as language must first be spoken before it is understood on the printed page. Much more is said about oral language development
in a later section of this chapter. It is sufficient to say here that poor oral language
skills have a tremendous impact on reading; thus, the prime objective of many
preschool programs is to develop oral language skills.

The factor of environment can be summarized by saying that students from
homes with a good educational environment will probably be more successful
readers than those from educationally deprived environments.

The two types of maturation that most directly affect reading development are **Maturation**
physical and emotional maturation. Physical maturation is stimulated by proper
diet and medical attention, while emotional maturation results from a stable home
life which provides love and understanding.

Physical maturation relates to reading in that the student who is immature
physically may have health problems or suffer from malnutrition. This, of course,
affects learning, in general; there is concern on the part of some educators about
a direct link between poor reading achievement and improper nutrition. However, evidence supporting or rejecting this hypothesis is inconclusive.[1]

In addition, physical immaturity affects bone and muscle development, which control the use of the hands and eyes. Physical immaturity often is first noticed because of the student's size or short attention span. This, too, deters learning.

Just as important as physical maturation is emotional maturation. Some students are prepared to attend school well in advance of the required date; others experience considerable anguish and consternation at the thought of substituting the school for home. It is imperative that teachers attend to these students' psychological needs so that school becomes synonymous not only with learning, but also with goodwill and success. Emotionally immature students may fare badly in the school environment, even though they have all the necessary attributes to be successful readers.

Emotionally immature students cannot work on their own and usually have difficulty getting along with their peers. This results in frustration for the student and teacher. Due to the student's short attention span, the teacher must pace instruction to provide much successful learning in small units. At the same time the teacher must work with the parents in developing emotional maturity.

These factors should be recognized as basic elements affecting the acquisition of prereading skills. Teachers must accept the fact that children enter school with differences in their prereading skill knowledge because of differences in their intelligence, environment, and maturation. Hence, the teacher must start with student needs and develop the necessary skills.

**Prereading Skills**

The prereading skills are divided into six basic areas: oral language; visual-motor; visual discrimination/visual memory; visual comprehension; auditory discrimination/auditory memory; and auditory comprehension (see figure 9.2). The specific skills within the areas are listed later in this chapter, and again in appendix A. This section provides a discussion on each of the basic areas and gives some insight into the importance of each area according to research findings.

Oral Language Skill

There is little doubt that oral language development plays a major role in reading instruction. Developing oral language is important because students must first learn oral expression before recognizing that reading represents their spoken language in print. Poor oral language skills affect both word recognition and comprehension skill development. Studies by Loban and Strickland indicate that reading can be influenced either adversely or positively by the language of the reader.[2] Students with good oral language skills tend to have advantages in reading over those with poor oral language skills because of the content of the materials and the language patterns used.

Another essential consideration in developing oral language is the culture from which the student comes. Britton explains that students from a particular culture and dialect group will learn not only to speak the language of that group, but will also think and organize their ideas in accordance with the viewpoints held by their closest contacts.[3] A serious error teachers sometimes make is attempting to change a student's language. It is necessary that the teacher develop an understanding of students' backgrounds and cultures in order to encourage them to extend their learning and expand their language.[4]

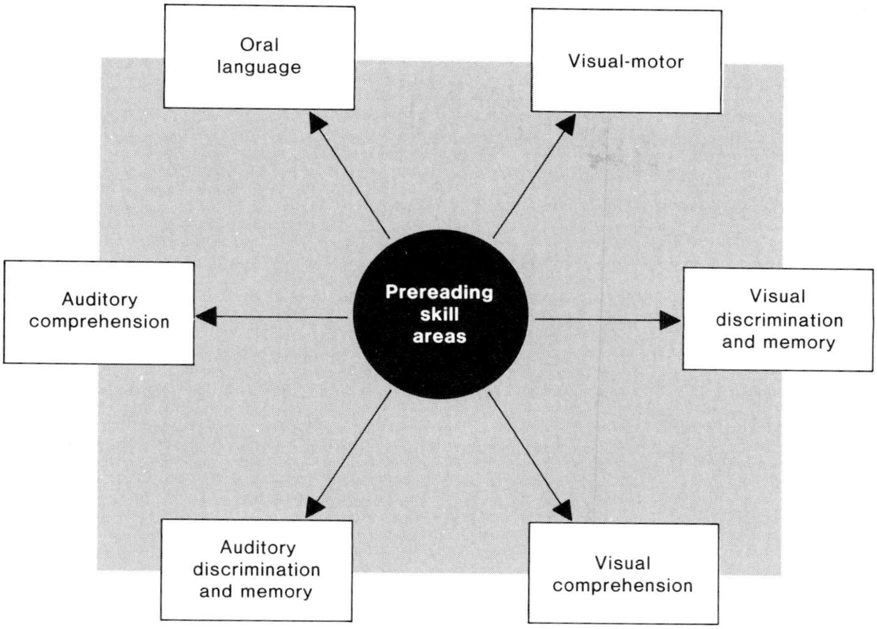

**Figure 9.2**
Prereading Skill Areas

Another essential component of language is syntactic ability. Chomsky examined the relationship between students' knowledge of complex syntactic structures and the amount of reading done by them as well as the amount of material read aloud to them. She found that students who were read to and who read more on their own had a much better knowledge of complex structures than students hearing and reading fewer books.[5]

It is essential that teachers provide an atmosphere which is conducive to the development of oral language skills. An environment of acceptance and respect will encourage students to share their experiences with the teacher and with other students. As students share their various experiences, the teacher will have an opportunity to learn more about their modes of learning, language development, and the socio/cultural factors which affect their learning in a positive or negative manner.

Goodman and Burke propose the following principles for the development of reading programs in the classroom:

1. Language communication involves the transmission of meaning from a language producer to a language receiver.
2. Reading is a receptive but very active language process.
3. What is read is language. Reading materials must always involve the interaction of the three language systems: graphophonic, syntactic, and semantic.
4. People can understand what they read when the material is expressed in language with which they are familiar.

5. People can best understand what they read when the material is related to their own background and experience.
6. People can best understand what they read when the material is interesting.[6]

The development of oral language skills is an integral part of the reading process; because of the special relationship between oral language and the written word, it is essential that teachers take cognizance of the numerous factors that influence the development of these skills.

## Visual-Motor Skills

Teachers should remember that students entering kindergarten have begun to develop their visual-motor skills to a certain extent, but still lack the confidence which will come as they mature. These students need special types of activities that will improve their skills in the visual-motor areas, including such capabilities as eye-hand coordination, directionality, and drawing specific designs using circles and lines.

There is considerable debate about the efficacy of teaching some of the visual-motor skills to young students. Many educators firmly believe that well-developed visual-motor skills are essential to successful reading; others question this point of view. Unfortunately, the research on visual-motor, or as it is frequently called, visual-perceptual training, is inconclusive as to its effectiveness.

For example, studies conducted by Hammill, Goodman, and Wiederholt, and by Robinson found that the visual-perceptual programs used in schools had not clearly demonstrated their effectiveness in enhancing beginning reading instruction. The Robinson study further indicated that although some programs appear to improve perceptual performance in the area trained, the long-term effect is uncertain.[7] Ollila suggests connecting motor skill training as closely as possible to other prereading activities in order to insure the development of prereading skills.[8]

Robinson, Strickland, and Cullinan state that although research is inconclusive regarding the relationship of perceptual training and reading, perceptual training activities may have other benefits, such as developing confidence and self-esteem, which are essential parts of the prereading program.[9]

Even though there is much debate over visual-motor training, there is no debate on at least one visual-motor skill—directionality—which is an essential skill to develop in beginning reading. This skill involves the mastery of left-to-right progression and top-to-bottom orientation. Without appropriate instruction in these skills, some students could develop poor habits in reading words and sentences on the printed page. Studies that found these skills to be essential in the reading process were done by Marshbanks and Levin, Timko, and McKiernan and Avakian.[10]

Until this controversy is resolved, visual-motor training will no doubt continue. Whether or not this training is essential or even useful to reading instruction is perhaps a moot point, since it is already widely used. If, in fact, it actually assists in developing the student's self-concept, then certainly it is a worthwhile addition to the prereading curricula.

As with visual-motor skills, visual discrimination and visual memory skills require students to develop expertise through practice, and these aptitudes are greatly influenced by maturation. Such tasks as matching shapes, recognizing likenesses and differences in objects, designs, numerals, letters, and words, and classifying objects and pictures are among the sub-skills that are stressed. Without proper development of these skills, students will have difficulty distinguishing between letters and words in reading. The inability to properly distinguish between letters would certainly make reading a most frustrating task.

There is no debate concerning the need for visual discrimination and visual memory skills. Because reading is a visual process, the ability to discriminate visually is essential for successful reading. Although the importance of teaching visual discrimination is unquestioned, there is some controversy concerning the need to use nonverbal forms or designs for developing gross discrimination and then moving in a sequential manner to fine discrimination of letters and words.

Among the studies investigating the use of commercially prepared materials for teaching visual discrimination skills are Barrett, Harris, Liebert and Sherk, Olson and Johnson, and Paradis.[11] These studies indicated that exercises using nonverbal stimuli completed by children on workbook pages contribute very little, if anything, to successful reading. Likewise, Durkin and Ollila suggest that the most appropriate instructional procedures for teaching visual discrimination skills involve the use of letters and words, rather than pictures, shapes and numerals.[12] Although much of the research in the area of visual discrimination indicates that instructional time is wasted using shapes, pictures, numerals, etc.,

**Visual Discrimination / Visual Memory Skills**

one study by Stanchfield found positive results. Investigating visual discrimination as one part of a total, sequential program for improving reading readiness skills in kindergarten, Stanchfield found that students taught in this structured program achieved significantly more reading readiness skills than those in the regular kindergarten curricula.[13]

Even with this debate over the use of pictures and shapes prior to using letters and words, there is no doubt that training in visual discrimination and visual memory skills is essential to a sound reading program. This has long been recognized as a basic process of reading. Form discrimination activities which focus on distinguishing features of letters seem to be important learning components related to reading.[14] Students who develop proficiency in the visual discrimination and memory skills are better able to recognize and remember words in reading.

**Visual Comprehension Skills**

After visual discrimination and visual memory skills have been developed, the task of comprehending visually becomes more important. Visual comprehension skills involve interpretive tasks necessary for understanding the visual stimuli presented. Such tasks as identifying details in pictures, identifying missing parts in pictures and symbols, identifying the sequence of pictures, and identifying the common characteristics of objects, are stressed.

Visual comprehension skills are essential in assisting beginning readers in dealing with concrete situations, closure, and sequencing. Mastery of these skills enables students to deal first with pictures, picture stories, and objects on a basic, concrete level and build a foundation for developing abstract interpretive abilities.

Brooks and Bruce found that good readers have the ability to use abstractions and to retain what they have learned; however, poor readers tend to approach a reading situation as though it were a matter of manipulating concrete entities.[15] Saunders notes that difficulties in identifying details in pictures may result from being unable to make contact with the reading task and to maintain perspective, and from experiencing uncertainty, thereby indicating a lack of self-confidence.[16] Whipple and Kodman also found that inadequate development in visual sequencing of symbols was characteristic of poor readers, while normal readers performed significantly better on the task.[17] Wohlwill notes that beginning readers require more repetition in learning tasks related to visual closure.[18] Gollin's earlier study found this to be a characteristic in prereading activities.[19]

From the results of these studies, it is obvious that mastery of visual comprehension skills enhances the student's likelihood of becoming a successful reader. The studies clearly indicate the necessity of integrating these skills into the prereading curricula.

## Auditory Discrimination / Auditory Memory Skills

Like visual skills, auditory discrimination and auditory memory skills are essential to good reading, especially in the development of phonics and other word recognition skills. These skills deal with such tasks as discriminating among various environmental sounds as well as different sounds of letters and words, recognizing sounds in words, and identifying beginning, medial, and ending sounds in words. Of special interest are the tasks of discriminating among different sounds of letters and words and identifying beginning, medial, and ending sounds in words. These are the most essential beginning skills in word recognition.

A primary auditory discrimination skill involves the capability of hearing likenesses and differences in letter sounds. Ollila believes that this is a more important factor than adequate hearing in determining a student's reading readiness;[20] however, other research studies indicate that poor auditory acuity for high-frequency sounds such as /f/, /v/, /d/, /p/, /t/, /g/, /k/, /sh/, and /th/may seriously impair reading achievement.[21] In conjunction with the acuity factor, Smith and Dechant note a greater incidence of high-frequency loss for boys than girls.[22]

There is no doubt that auditory acuity, auditory memory, and auditory discrimination are necessary for progress in word recognition.[23] Walter and Kosowski indicate that unless poor readers are highly motivated, they may pay less attention to reading because auditory discrimination requires so much effort on their part.[24] Many poor readers often exhibit weaknesses in auditory discrimination; thus, it is necessary to design a program for these students using approaches that are not always auditory in nature. For example, a phonics-based approach would not be effective with students who have poor auditory perception skills. Therefore, it becomes necessary for the teacher to be creative in developing these skills for young readers.

**Auditory Comprehension Skills**

Just as visual comprehension is related to interpreting printed symbols, auditory or listening comprehension uses the tools of auditory discrimination and memory to interpret spoken symbols. Such tasks as following directions, associating objects or pictures with an oral description, identifying the main idea, indentifying a sequence of events, and interpreting descriptive language are stressed. The development of these skills enhances the reception of the auditory stimuli presented to the student and increases the quality of information gained from spoken symbols or words.

For understanding information obtained by listening, students should have some command over key components of the language, namely phonology (sound structure), syntax (sentence structure), semantics (word meaning and the relationships among meanings), and text structure (conventions about how events and assertions within a text are typically structured). Various researchers have found that the lack of facility in any one of these components leads to either reduced comprehension or increased processing time. Thus, a good listener orchestrates all of these components simultaneously.[25]

In a literature summary related to teaching listening comprehension, Pearson and Fielding concluded

1. Listening training in the same skills typically taught in reading comprehension curricula tends to improve listening comprehension.
2. Listening comprehension is enhanced by various kinds of active verbal responses on the part of students during and after listening.
3. Listening to literature tends to improve listening comprehension.
4. Certain types of instruction primarily directed toward other areas of language arts may also improve listening comprehension.
5. Direct teaching of listening strategies seems to help students become more conscious of their listening habits.[26]

For many years, auditory comprehension has been identified as an indicator of potential reading ability. In a review of studies which compared reading and listening comprehension at various levels, Sticht, et al. found that in the elementary grades (one–six), almost all of the comparisons favor the listening comprehension mode. However, in grades seven through twelve, the proportion of studies showing an advantage to reading comprehension increases.[27] Although this summary would suggest that in the elementary grades students can rely on their already well developed listening comprehension abilities to assist their less well developed reading abilities, Schell cautions against using a listening comprehension level to determine the reading potential of students in grades 1–3. In a review of research, he found that students were overreferred for help in reading when listening comprehension was used as an indicator of potential.[28] Regardless, often students are able to attend more critically to material read to them than to material they read silently. It is not uncommon for students to be able to comprehend these passages on a higher readability level than their silent reading level. This interesting correlation between listening and reading has resulted in the investigation of this phenomena over a period of several years.

Numerous studies have examined the relationship between listening and reading. Ross found that good listeners rated higher than poor listeners on intelligence, reading, socio-economic status, and achievement, but not on an auditory acuity test.[29] This study indicates that auding requires a finer degree of discrimination than acuity.

Deutsch found that children from lower socio-economic backgrounds were at a distinct disadvantage in learning to read because their language patterns interfered with the comprehension of both oral and written materials.[30] In a related study, Clark and Richards found a significant deficiency in auditory discrimination in economically disadvantaged preschool students.[31]

Many found that for students in the lower grades, students who are poor readers, and for boys in general, listening is the most viable means for achievement.[32] Swalm confirmed his earlier findings in a second study indicating that for students whose reading abilities were below average, listening was significantly more effective than reading. It also indicated that the relationship between a student's reading ability and the readability level of the material was extremely important, and that this factor should determine whether for most effective instruction the teacher should use listening or reading.[33]

Hollingsworth's review of the literature concluded that listening does have a positive effect on reading achievement.[34] In addition, Dechant noted that listening ability is an indicator of the student's potential ceiling in reading ability.[35]

Spache states that, as in the case of using intelligence test results to predict potential for improvement in reading, measures of listening comprehension give tentative clues, not highly accurate estimates.[36]

Although there are those who question the validity of the correlation between listening comprehension and reading potential, research tends to support this contention. Few specialists would totally disregard this concept, even though the research data are not absolutely conclusive. It appears from the data that listening ability provides some indication of a student's potential reading ability.

Auditory or listening comprehension skills must be developed prior to beginning reading instruction in order to assist in the development of reading comprehension skills. However, the development of listening comprehension skills is the responsibility of teachers at every level, as these skills are expanded through adulthood.

Obviously, all of the individual prereading skills are useful to the reading process; thus, the teacher's goal must be to integrate all of the skills into a whole in order to enhance students' reading capabilities. No single skill or set of skills will assure that a student will be a successful reader; however, all of the prereading skills interacting as one will enable students to achieve some degree of success as readers.

## Prescriptive Teaching of Prereading Skills

The last section of this chapter deals with the concept of using prescriptive techniques for teaching the various prereading skills. Part of this section presents several methods of evaluating students' strengths and weaknesses in the prereading skill areas. This is presented in a chart format to enhance its usefulness. The final portion of this section presents the specific prereading skills and some reinforcement techniques for prescriptive teaching.

Assessing students' strengths and weaknesses in the skill areas is vital to the implementation of a successful reading program. In the table presented on ways of evaluating each skill area, several diagnostic procedures are noted. The authors are aware that other diagnostic procedures and instruments of value are not mentioned. This is done primarily in an effort to maintain the theme underlying this book, which is to present practical suggestions that can be used by the classroom teacher. It should also be noted that relatively few formal diagnostic instruments measure performance on the prereading level, and much of the diagnostic information gained at this level is informal in nature, using observations or criterion-referenced instruments.

The procedures presented in table 9.1 are intended to give a means of evaluating students' strengths and weaknesses in the various prereading skill areas. After their needs are evaluated, prescriptive techniques are used to provide appropriate instruction for each student.

As already stated, the final portion of this section is concerned with various skill areas and techniques for implementing prescriptions in each area. The skills and ideas for the prescriptive techniques are presented in table 9.2.

**Table 9.1**
Diagnostic Procedures for Evaluating Prereading Skill Areas

| Skill Areas | Procedures |
|---|---|
| **Oral Language** | Observation checklist<br>*Peabody Picture Vocabulary Test* |
| **Visual-Motor** | Criterion-referenced test<br>*Durrell Analysis of Reading Difficulty* (Handwriting)<br>Observation checklist |
| **Visual Discrimination/<br>Visual Memory** | Criterion-referenced test<br>*Durrell Analysis of Reading Difficulty* (Visual Memory of Word Forms)<br>Observation checklist |
| **Visual Comprehension** | Criterion-referenced test<br>Observation checklist |
| **Auditory Discrimination/<br>Auditory Memory** | Criterion-referenced test<br>*Diagnostic Reading Scales* (Auditory Discrimination)<br>*Durrell Analysis of Reading Difficulty* (Learning to Hear Sounds in Words)<br>*Wepman Auditory Discrimination Test* |
| **Auditory Comprehension** | Criterion-referenced test<br>*Diagnostic Reading Scales* (Listening Comprehension)<br>*Durrell Analysis of Reading Difficulty* (Listening Comprehension)<br>*Durrell Listening-Reading Series*<br>Informal Reading Inventory (Listening Comprehension)<br>*Sequential Tests of Educational Progress* (Listening Comprehension) |

**Table 9.2**
Prereading Skills

| Skill | Prescriptive Techniques |
|---|---|
| Oral Language | |
| *Recognize word boundaries.* | Ask students to clap number of words in a sentence as they talk.<br>Ask students to say a specified number of words. |
| *Use adequate vocabulary.* | Give students a topic and develop word walls (charts covering the walls) containing as many words as they can think of about the topic. Add to this each day.<br>Following a field trip or a film, ask students to use appropriate words to tell about their experience. |
| *Understand basic concepts.* | Use various objects and ask students to point to them according to a specified color, shape, size, etc.<br>Ask students to tell where objects are located when hearing such prepositions as over, under, in, out, etc. |
| *Tell about a picture or object.* | Label objects, pictures or art work in the room and have students dictate a sentence or phrase about their work.<br>Ask students to dictate stories about pictures from newspapers or magazines. |
| *Express ideas in complete sentences.* | Allow students time to tell about a hobby using complete sentences.<br>Ask students to give simple directions using complete sentences. |
| *Relate story in sequence.* | After going on a field trip, allow students to tell about the trip using time sequence.<br>Read a story and ask students to retell the story in the proper order. |
| *Participate in discussions.* | Give a topic and let students work in small groups to discuss their favorite foods, T. V. programs, pets, etc.<br>Give a topic and ask each student to contribute at least one idea. |

| Skill | Prescriptive Techniques |
|---|---|
| **Visual-Motor Skills** | |
| *Coordinate eye-hand movements.* | Give students a set of pick-up sticks and allow them to play the game. |
| | Practice lacing and tying shoes with an old pair of baby shoes. |
| *Execute directionality in coordinated eye-hand movements.* | Have students string colored beads directionally from left to right in a given pattern. |
| | Practice tracing letters on paper using left to right movement. |
| *Draw specified designs, such as circles and lines.* | Give students a tray of sand and ask them to draw circles or lines in the sand. |
| | Draw pictures of various objects using only circles and / or lines. |
| *Reproduce designated designs, numerals, letters, or words.* | Copy letters or shapes using clay to form the design. |
| | Reproduce designs using blocks. |
| *Reproduce own name in manuscript.* | Give students cards containing their names and ask them to trace their names on a textured surface. |
| | Ask students to copy letters in their names in sequence using the chalkboard. |
| **Visual Discrimination / Visual Memory Skills** | |
| *Match shapes, objects, and pictures.* | Give objects and ask students to match them according to shape or size. |
| | Ask students to match pictures that are alike in design. |
| *Recognize likenesses and differences in objects and designs.* | Give students several designs, some of which are alike, and ask them to show you the designs that are different. |
| | Hold an object and direct students to select other objects like it. |
| *Recognize likenesses and differences in numerals, letters, and words.* | Ask students to select from a set of numerals those which are alike. |
| | Give students a letter and ask them to select one from the alphabet chart that is like their letter and one that is different. |

**Table 9.2**
Prereading Skills (continued)

| Skill | Prescriptive Techniques |
|---|---|
| *Match upper- and lowercase letters.* | Give students uppercase letters on the flannel board and ask them to match the lowercase letters.<br>Give students an alphabet board containing lowercase letters and a set of cards containing the uppercase letters. The students are to match the letters. |
| *Identify from memory objects, pictures, or designs briefly presented.* | Show animal pictures taken from magazine cutouts or picture cards. After removing the picture, present several pictures, including the original, and ask students to select the original.<br>Present familiar objects, remove one, and ask students to identify the missing one. |
| *Classify objects or pictures.* | Present three each of several types of fruits and have students classify the fruits according to type.<br>Present pictures of animals, foods, and means of transportation. Have students classify them according to areas. |
| *Recognize own name in manuscript.* | Give each student several cards containing names of students in the room. One card should have the student's own name, to be selected by recognition.<br>Prepare a list of words the student does not know. Include in this list the student's name, which should be selected. |
| *Recognize designated designs, numerals, letters, or words.* | Put a circle or some other design on the board and have students identify the design.<br>Have students recognize warning signs such as STOP, EXIT, POISON by the shape of the sign or words. |
| *Match colors.* | Give students several blocks of different colors, then ask them to match these blocks with colors on pieces of tagboard.<br>Have students match the colors of their shirts and pants with objects of the same color in the classroom. |

| Skill | Prescriptive Techniques |
|---|---|
| *Follow picture, design, letter, or word in sequence.* | Give students a series of colored beads arranged in a definite order. Ask them to replicate this sequence with another set of beads.<br><br>Give students a series of designs that progress from simple to complex. Place one design out of sequence and ask students to put it in sequence. |

**Visual Comprehension Skills**

| Skill | Prescriptive Techniques |
|---|---|
| *Identify details in pictures.* | Show a picture of an event and ask students to name the things they see.<br><br>Have students draw a picture of their house or neighborhood in as much detail as possible. Then ask them to share their picture with the class and describe the details. |
| *Identify missing parts in picture/symbol.* | Show a picture of an object or animal with a detail missing. Ask students to identify what is missing in the picture.<br><br>Show one picture that is intact and then the same basic picture with several details missing. Ask students to identify the missing parts. |
| *Identify sequence of pictures/story from pictures.* | Show a picture of an animal that has been cut into three parts and ask students to arrange the picture in the correct sequence.<br><br>Give students a series of photographs of an event and ask them to arrange the photographs in the correct sequence. |
| *Identify common characteristics of objects.* | Show students a table, a chair, and a desk, then ask them to describe what these objects have in common.<br><br>Give students several different types of one object such as a desk, then ask the students to tell what these objects have in common. |

**Table 9.2**
Prereading Skills (continued)

| Skill | Prescriptive Techniques |
|---|---|
| **Auditory Discrimination / Auditory Memory Skills** | |
| *Discriminate among various environmental sounds.* | Play a tape of an automobile horn, a fog horn, and a boat horn, then ask students to identify the sounds they heard. |
| | Take three paper bags, put rocks in one, sand in another, and coins in the last one; allow students to shake the bags and listen to the sounds, then ask them to identify what they hear. |
| *Discriminate among different sounds of letters and words.* | Give students a series of two letters (*b, v*), then ask the students to clap or raise their hand when the two sounds are the same. |
| | Say several pairs of words, some with the same sounds and some different. Ask students to clap when the words sound the same and stand when they are different. |
| *Identify simple everyday sounds.* | Crumple paper, crack a nut, etc., then ask students to identify the sound. |
| | Hit a board first with a hammer, then a rock, and finally a pencil, then ask students to discriminate between the sounds by replicating the task themselves. |
| *Recognize rhyming words.* | Give students two words that rhyme (cat, bat) and ask them if the ends of words sound alike or different. |
| *Follow simple one- and two-step directions.* | Give students a command ("close the door"). Have them perform the task. |
| | Play a game with students in which directions are given; "Everybody stand up and shake your foot." |
| *Identify sounds in words.* | Give students a specific sound. Then say several words containing the specific sound. Ask students to clap when the sound is heard in each word. |
| | Give students two words with the same beginning sound. Ask them to give the sound with which both words begin. |

| Skill | Prescriptive Techniques |
|---|---|
| *Reproduce simple sounds, letters, and words.* | Play a tape of a tiger growling, then ask students to reproduce the sound.<br>Say two words using different ending sounds (can, pop), then ask students to repeat the ending sounds. |
| *Identify beginning sounds in words.* | Show pictures of several animals. Say two words and ask students to select the picture that begins with the same sound as the two given words.<br>Tell a story about the beach, using descriptive words such as sifting sand, fat fish, etc. Ask students to name the pairs of words that begin with the same sound. |
| *Identify ending sounds in words.* | Show a picture of an object. Ask students to name as many objects as possible that end with the same sound.<br>Play a tape of several words with various endings. Ask each student to find a picture of objects, people, etc., that have the same ending sounds. |
| *Identify medial sounds in words.* | Say several simple words with medial sounds such as fat and big. Ask each student to say at least one word with the same medial sounds as the examples.<br>Give students two words with the same medial sound (*sit, trip*). Ask each student to tell the part of the word that sounds the same. |
| *Use rhyming words to complete sentences.* | Read a sentence that has the last word deleted. Ask students to say the missing word that rhymes with another word in the sentence ("The ham was better than jam.").<br>Give the students a word. Ask them to make up a sentence in which the last word rhymes with another word in the sentence. For example: "The big cat ate a *rat*." |
| *Identify syllables in words.* | Say several polysyllabic words and ask students to hit a drum each time they hear a syllable.<br>Give some monosyllabic words and some polysyllabic words. Ask students to stand when they hear a word with more than one syllable. |

**Table 9.2**
Prereading Skills (continued)

| Skill | Prescriptive Techniques |
|---|---|
| **Auditory (Listening) Comprehension Skills** | |
| *Follow directions.* | Give a one-sentence direction ("I want you to go to the office and bring me a pencil."). Ask students to complete the task. |
| | Have a student give a one-sentence direction to another student, then ask the first student to see that the task is completed. After the second student attempts the task, ask the first student to complete the same task. |
| *Associate object or picture with oral description.* | Describe an object and ask students to tell what it is and to find a picture of the object. |
| | Have a student describe an object, then ask the students to attempt to determine what the object is from the student's description. After the task is completed, have each student draw a picture of the object. |
| *Identify main idea.* | Read a short story. Ask students to listen carefully, then ask them to tell what the story is about. |
| | Read a short story and ask students to find a picture in their books or in a magazine that depicts the main idea. |
| *Identify main character.* | Read a short story to the students, telling them to listen carefully. Ask them to give the name of the main character. |
| | After reading a short story, ask students to draw a picture of how they think the main character looks. |
| *Identify details in sentence and story.* | Place several pictures on a table, then read a sentence ("Dad says we can go to the ballgame."). After reading the sentence, ask students a question about the sentence ("Where did Dad say we could go?"). Finally, ask students to find the picture on the table that answers the question. |
| | Play a recorded short story. Tell students to listen carefully to the details of the story. Then ask several detail questions about it. |

| Skill | Prescriptive Techniques |
|---|---|
| *Identify sequence of events.* | Have a student tell a story. Ask the other students to illustrate in order the main events they heard in the story.<br><br>Tell a story using pictures depicting the sequence of events. Then place the pictures on a table in random order and ask students to put them in the correct sequence. |
| *Identify relationships such as cause-effect and comparisons.* | Describe a situation that occurred on the school bus (several students got into a scuffle). Ask students what the effect was on the class.<br><br>After determining the effect of an incident in a situation, allow students to make suggestions that would prevent a recurrence of such an incident. |
| *Interpret descriptive language.* | Read a short sentence using descriptive language ("She was green with envy."). Ask students the meaning of the sentence.<br><br>After reading a short sentence using descriptive language, ask students to illustrate their impression of the sentence. |
| *Recognize emotions of characters and story.* | Read a short story that is emotionally descriptive. Ask students to illustrate their impression of how the characters felt in the story.<br><br>After hearing a story that is emotionally descriptive, ask students to describe the feelings of the characters in the story by role-playing the characters' feelings. |
| *Draw conclusions.* | Read a story and ask students to tell why the story ended as it did.<br><br>After hearing a story, ask students to illustrate the conclusion. |
| *Anticipate outcomes.* | Read part of a story and ask students to relate how they think the story should end.<br><br>After hearing part of a story, ask students to illustrate their ideas as to how the story should end, and then to present their ideas to the class. |

The preceding tables, depicting informal and formal diagnostic procedures along with prescriptive techniques for each of the prereading skills, represent an effort to present ideas for the classroom teachers' perusal and use. The implementation of these ideas in conjunction with additional activities developed by the teacher will enhance the effectiveness of diagnosis and prescription in the area of prereading.

## Summary

Prereading skills form the foundation for developing all other reading skills. The research and discussions presented in this chapter reiterate this idea in many different ways. The research summaries regarding the five basic areas of prereading skills, oral language, visual-motor, visual discrimination/visual memory, visual comprehension, auditory discrimination/auditory memory, and auditory comprehension, emphasize the need for all of these areas to be developed in an interrelated manner.

The acquisition of the prereading skills is to a great extent influenced by the students' intelligence, environmental background and maturation. Additional information was presented regarding these areas.

The diagnostic information from the previous chapters was related directly to the prereading skills through a chart indicating the skill area and specific diagnostic techniques that are appropriate. The concept of prescriptive teaching of the prereading skills was presented through the identification of specific skills and ideas to aid in the prescriptive teaching of these skills.

## Applying What You Read

You are asked to talk with a school faculty about developing prereading skills. Which three categories of prereading do you feel are most important and why?

Design a program for diagnosing prereading skills. Select the best techniques for diagnosis in your situation.

You have been hired as a kindergarten teacher in an inner-city school. How would you begin to determine the needs of your students? Select five specific prereading skills that you suspect to be their weakest areas and outline techniques for prescriptive instruction.

The teachers in the first and second grades have some students who are having difficulty with auditory discrimination skills. Select three specific skills and outline a prescriptive program for these students.

## Notes

1. Eleanor Chernick, "Effects of the Feingold Diet on Reading Achievement and Classroom Behavior," *The Reading Teacher.* Doris Pertz and Lillian R. Putnam, "An Examination of the Relationship Between Nutrition and Learning," *The Reading Teacher.*
2. Walter Loban, *The Language of Elementary School Children;* Dorothy Strickland, "Black is Beautiful vs. White is Right," *Elementary English.*
3. J. Britton, *Language and Learning.*

4. Kenneth Goodman, "Let's Dump the Up-tight Model in English," *Elementary School Journal.*

5. Carol Chomsky, *The Acquisition of Syntax in Children from 5 to 10.*

6. Yetta Goodman and Carolyn Burke, "Reading: Language and Psycholinguistic Bases," in *Reading: Foundations and Instructional Strategies,* ed. Pose Lamb and Richard Arnold, pp. 92–120.

7. Donald Hammill, Libby Goodman, and J. Lee Wiederholt, "Visual-Motor Processes: Can We Train Them?" *The Reading Teacher;* Helen M. Robinson, "Perceptual Training: Does It Result in Reading Improvement?" in *Some Persistent Questions on Beginning Reading,* ed. Robert C. Aukerman, pp. 135–50.

8. Lloyd Ollila, "Reading: Preparing the Child," in *Reading: Foundations and Instructional Strategies,* ed. Pose Lamb and Richard Arnold, p. 302.

9. Violet B. Robinson, Dorothy S. Strickland, and Bernice Cullinan, "The Child: Ready or Not?" in *The Kindergarten Child and Reading,* ed. Lloyd Ollila, p. 15.

10. Gabrielle Marshbanks and Harry Levin, "Cues by Which Children Recognize Words," *Journal of Educational Psychology;* H. G. Timko, "Letter Position in Trigram Discrimination by Beginning Readers," *Perceptual and Motor Skills;* Jack McKiernan and Margo Avakian, "Directional Awareness Training: Remediation of Receptive Letter Reversals," *Academic Therapy.*

11. Thomas C. Barrett, "The Relationship Between the Measures of Pre-reading Visual Discrimination and First-Grade Achievement: A Review of the Literature," *Reading Research Quarterly;* Albert J. Harris, "Practical Applications of Reading Research," *The Reading Teacher;* Robert E. Liebert and John K. Sherk, "Three Frostig Visual Perception Sub-tests and Specific Reading Tasks for Kindergarten, First, and Second Grade Children," *The Reading Teacher;* Arthur V. Olson and Clifford I. Johnson, "Structure and Predictive Validity of the Frostig Developmental Test of Visual Perception in Grades One and Three," *Journal of Special Education;* Edward Paradis, "The Appropriateness of Visual Discrimination Exercise in Reading Readiness Materials," *Journal of Educational Research.*

12. Dolores Durkin, *Teaching Them to Read,* 3rd ed., pp. 181–82; Lloyd Ollila, "Reading: Preparing the Child," in *Reading: Foundations and Instructional Strategies.*

13. Jo M. Stanchfield, "Development of Prereading Skills in an Experimental Kindergarten Program," in *Some Persistent Questions on Beginning Reading,* ed. Robert C. Aukerman, pp. 20–30.

14. Anne D. Pick, "Some Basic Perceptual Processes in Reading," in *The Young Child,* ed. Willard W. Hartup.

15. Harold F. Brooks and Paul Bruce, "The Characteristics of Good and Poor Readers as Disclosed by the Wechsler Intelligence Scale for Children," *Journal of Educational Psychology.*

16. David R. Saunders, "A Factor Analysis of the Picture Completion Items of the WAIS," *Journal of Clinical Psychology.*

17. Clifford L. Whipple and Frank Kodman, Jr., "A Study of Discrimination and Perceptual Learning with Retarded Readers," *Journal of Educational Psychology.*

18. J. F. Wohlwill, "From Perception to Inference: A Dimension of Cognitive Development," in *Thought in the Young Child,* ed. W. Kessen and C. Kuklman.

19. E. S. Gollin, "Developmental Studies of Visual Recognition of Incomplete Objects," *Perceptual and Motor Skills.*

20. Ollila, "Reading: Preparing the Child," in *Reading: Foundations and Instructional Strategies,* p. 278.
21. Mildred F. Berry and Jon Eisenson, *Speech Disorders: Principles and Practices of Therapy,* p. 448.
22. Henry P. Smith and Emerald V. Dechant, *Psychology in Teaching Reading.*
23. Joseph M. Wepman, "Auditory Discrimination, Speech and Reading," *Elementary School Journal;* Jean R. Harber, "Auditory Closure and Reading," *Reading Horizons;* Cecelia Pollack, Joseph Nahem, and Stanley Krippner, "Developing Auditory Perception Skills in Kindergarten Children," *Academic Therapy.*
24. R. H. Walter and Irene Kosowski, "Symbolic Learning and Reading Retardation," *Journal of Consulting Psychology.*
25. P. David Pearson and Linda Fielding, "Research Update: Listening Comprehension," *Language Arts,* 617–18.
26. P. David Pearson and Linda Fielding, "Research Update: Listening Comprehension," 619–621.
27. Tom G. Sticht; L. J. Beck; R. N. Hanke; G. M. Kleiman; and J. H. James, *Auding and Reading: A Developmental Model.*
28. Leo M. Schell, "The Validity of the Potential Level Via Listening Comprehension: A Cautionary Note," *Reading Psychology.*
29. Ramon Ross, "A Look at Listeners," *Elementary School Journal.*
30. Martin Deutsch et al., *Communication of Information in the Elementary School Classroom.*
31. Ann D. Clark and Charlotte J. Richards, "Auditory Discrimination Among Economically Disadvantaged and Nondisadvantaged Preschool Children," *Exceptional Children.*
32. Wesley A. Many, "Is There Any Difference: Reading vs. Listening?" *The Reading Teacher.*
33. James E. Swalm, "Is Listening Really More Effective for Learning in the Early Grades?" *Elementary English.*
34. Paul M. Hollingsworth, "Can Training in Listening Improve Reading?" *The Reading Teacher.*
35. Emerald V. Dechant and Henry P. Smith, *Psychology in Teaching Reading,* 2nd ed. p. 142.
36. George D. Spache, *Investigating the Issues of Reading Disabilities,* p. 155.

**Other Suggested Readings**

Adams, Marilyn J.; Anderson, Richard C.; and Durkin, Dolores. "Beginning Reading: Theory and Practice." *Language Arts* 55 (January 1978):19–25.

Blaney, Robert L. "Effective Teaching in Early Childhood Education." *The Elementary School Journal* 80 (January 1980):128–32.

Cannella, Clyde G. "Beginning Reading: The Influence of Cognitive Development." *Reading Improvement* 19 (Spring 1982):31–38.

Charlesworth, Rosalind. *Understanding Child Development* (Albany, New York: Delmar Publishers, Inc., 1983).

Dixon, Carol N. "Language Experience Stories as a Diagnostic Tool." *Language Arts* 54 (May 1977):501–505.

Foulke, Patricia N. "How Early Should Language Development and Pre-Reading Experiences Be Started?" *Elementary English* 51 (February 1974):310–15.

Kaufman, Maurice. *Perceptual and Language Readiness Programs: Critical Reviews.* Newark, Delaware: International Reading Association, 1973.

Kavale, Kenneth, and Schreiner, Robert. "Psycholinguistic Implications for Beginning Reading Instruction." *Language Arts* 55 (January 1978):34–40.

King, Ethel. "Prereading Programs: Direct Versus Incidental Teaching." *The Reading Teacher* 31 (February 1978):504–10.

Lowell, Robert E. "Reading Readiness Factors as Predictors of Success in First Grade Reading." *Journal of Learning Disabilities* 4 (December 1971):563–67.

McDonell, Gloria M. and Osburn, E. Bess. "New Thoughts About Reading Readiness." *Language Arts* 55 (January 1978):26–29.

McGee, Lea; Charlesworth, Rosalind; Cheek, Martha Collins; and Cheek, Earl H. "Metalinguistic Knowledge: Another Look at Beginning Reading." *Childhood Education* (January/February 1983).

McGee, Lea, and Tompkins, Gail. "The Video-Tape Answer to Independent Reading Comprehension Activities." *The Reading Teacher* 34 (January 1981):427–33.

Martenson, W. Paul. "Selected Pre-Reading Tasks, Socio-Economic Status and Sex." *The Reading Teacher* 22 (October 1968):45–49.

Meyers, Elizabeth S.; Ball, Helen H.; and Crutchfield, Marjorie. *The Kindergarten Teacher's Handbook*. Los Angeles, California: Gramercy Press, 1973.

Nevius, John R. "Teaching for Logical Thinking is a Prereading Activity." *The Reading Teacher* 30 (March 1977):641–43.

Ollila, Lloyd O., ed. *Beginning Reading Instruction in Different Countries*. Newark, Delaware: International Reading Association, 1981.

Ollila, Lloyd O., ed. *Handbook For Administrators and Teachers: Reading in the Kindergarten*. Newark, Delaware: International Reading Association, 1980.

Pasamanick, Judith. *Talk About: An Early Childhood Language Development Resource*, Book 1 and 2. Little Neck, New York: Center for Media Development, 1976.

Pickert, Sarah M., and Chase, Martha L. "Story Retelling: An Informal Technique for Evaluating Children's Language." *The Reading Teacher* 31 (February 1978):528–31.

Pikulski, John. "Readiness for Reading: A Practical Approach." *Language Arts* 55 (February 1978):192–97.

Sampson, Michael R. and Briggs, L. D. "What Does Research Say About Beginning Reading?" *Reading Horizons* 21 (Winter 1981):114–18.

Sanacore, Joseph. "A Checklist for the Evaluation of Reading Readiness." *Elementary English* 50 (September 1973):858–60.

Sawyer, Diane J. "Readiness Factors for Reading: A Different View." *The Reading Teacher* 28 (April 1975):620–24.

Stanchfield, Jo M. "Development of Pre-reading Skills in an Experimental Kindergarten Program." *The Reading Teacher* 24 (May 1971):699–707.

Stewig, John Warren. "Alphabet Books: A Neglected Genre." *Language Arts* 55 (January 1978):6–11.

Teale, William H. *Early Reading: An Annotated Bibliography*. Newark, Delaware: International Reading Association, 1980.

Todd, Eleanor, and Cheek, Martha Collins. *Paths to Reading: A Resource Guide for Prereading Experiences*. New York: Random House, Inc., 1977.

Waterhouse, Lynn H.; Fischer, Karen M.; and Ryan, Ellen Bouchard. *Language Awareness and Reading*. Newark, Delaware: International Reading Association, 1980.

Weintraub, Sam, and Cowan, Robert J. *Vision/Visual Perception: An Annotated Bibliography*. Newark, Delaware: International Reading Association, 1982.

# 10

Word analysis, decoding, word identification, word processing, word recognition—these terms name the category of skills used to determine how a set of printed symbols is pronounced to form a word to which a meaning can be associated. These skill areas include the use of sight word knowledge, phonics, contextual analysis, and structural analysis.

Of all areas in reading taught at Seabreeze School, word recognition receives the most attention in the classroom and is the most controversial in the public domain. Teachers and parents too often associate good reading with good word recognition skills. Thus, classroom emphasis is sometimes diverted toward the development of the word recognition skills, with little time remaining for the other reading skills, such as comprehension and study skills. The result may be that students become good word callers, but have little understanding of what they read.

The public controversy regarding word recognition centers on whether students should be taught to read through the use of phonics or the look-say or sight approach. Teachers must help the public understand that learning to recognize words is not a matter of learning one set of skills *or* another, but involves learning to use *all* of the word recognition skills, as appropriate.

Because of the importance of this area and the controversies apparently resulting from a lack of understanding of the word recognition skills, the teachers at Seabreeze asked the following questions, which will be addressed in this chapter.

What are the word recognition skills?

What does research say about the development of the word recognition skills?

How does the teacher assist students in learning to use the various word recognition skills?

What are some basic principles for teaching these skills?

Which diagnostic instruments are most appropriate for use in this area?

What prescriptive strategies can be used in developing these skills?

# How are word recognition skills developed through prescriptive teaching?

**Vocabulary to Know**

These terms are important to note as this chapter is read.

Accent
Affix
Analytic phonics
Compound words
Consonants
Context Clue
Contextual analysis
Contractions
Inflectional ending
Phoneme-grapheme correspondences
Phonics

Picture clue
Prefix
Sight words
Structural analysis
Suffix
Syllables
Synthetic phonics
Variant patterns
Vowels
Word recognition skills

**Word Recognition Skills**

Students enter school with a speaking and listening vocabulary as extensive as their background experiences, and exceeding their reading vocabulary. In order to develop a reading vocabulary, students must be taught to recognize printed words. Thus, teachers in the primary grades help students to acquire the skills necessary to recognize words, while teachers at higher levels must continue to extend and reinforce these skills.

In developing word recognition skills, teachers assist students in learning a variety of word recognition techniques so that they are prepared to decode unknown words. Students must develop a *sight word knowledge* consisting of the words they see most frequently in their reading. Readers of all ages continuously expand their sight word knowledge as words are added to their reading vocabulary. However, initially students begin with a limited sight vocabulary consisting of words that cannot be decoded by any other procedure except memory. Another procedure that students are taught to use in recognizing words is *phonics*. Phonics knowledge involves learning to associate specific phonemes, or sounds, with the appropriate graphemes, or symbols. Phonics skills can be used as one procedure for recognizing unknown words but they cannot be used alone.

**Figure 10.1**
Word Recognition Skill
Areas

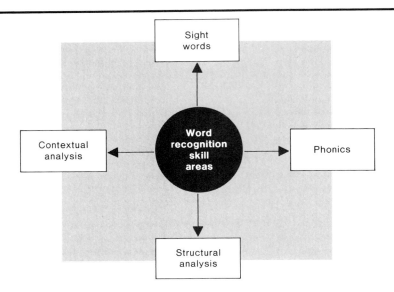

*Structural analysis* skills is taught as another procedure for decoding unknown words. This procedure helps the students to look at word parts, such as syllables, suffixes, contractions, and compound words, to determine the correct pronunciation. *Contextual analysis* skills use the meaning of the phrase, sentence, or passage in conjunction with the other word recognition skills to decode the unknown word. Using all of these skills, students are able to recognize the many words they see in reading material.

Learning to recognize the many words in the English language is complicated by many factors. One major factor relates to the language itself. Because our language is composed of so many other languages and dialects, it is often difficult for students to understand the irregularities encountered. This factor becomes more complex for the student in a program that uses primarily a synthetic phonics method. Thus, caution should be exercised when instruction is provided to help the students decode the variety of words in the English language.

As outlined in figure 9.1 in chapter 9, there are other factors that affect reading development. These factors—intelligence, environment, and maturation—also are to be considered as the teacher provides instruction in the word recognition skills. Intelligence, or the mental age of the student, has an impact on readiness for beginning to learn the various word recognition skills. Parents and teachers realize that the chronological age of six does not automatically indicate that the student is ready for instruction in the word recognition skills in reading.

This readiness for learning the word recognition skills is also affected by environmental factors. As discussed in the previous chapter, many prereading skills are developed before formal reading instruction is begun. These should be started in the home, but when students do not develop some skills in auditory

and visual discrimination prior to school entrance, they must receive this instruction in school. Many students who enter school with these deficiencies seem to have difficulty in overcoming them and learning the various word recognition skills. This difficulty stems from a home environment that has not stimulated language or provided experiences which motivate learning and interest in reading.

Maturation is another factor affecting the development of word recognition skills. In addition to the impact of physical and emotional maturation on the learning of word recognition skills, maturation in terms of speech or language development also plays an influential role in this process. Students who are unable to pronounce a sound, or who do not auditorially distinguish a certain sound in the language, often have immature speech patterns. This immaturity in speech may make learning phonics difficult; thus, the teacher teaches other word recognition skills while developing the speech skills.

Another element to be considered in providing prescriptive instruction in this area is the learning style of the student. Most students learn equally well through the visual or auditory modes. For this reason, students are taught to use a variety of word recognition skills in unlocking words. However, some students have perception or discrimination problems which create problems using either the visual or auditory mode in learning. These are not acuity difficulties, but perception problems that are not easily corrected. Teachers must note these difficulties and adjust instruction accordingly. Students with strength in the visual mode and weakness in the auditory mode will experience more success in learning words by sight or a look-say method. Conversely, students with strength in the auditory mode and weakness in the visual mode will learn to sound out words using phonics. To assist these students in learning words, teachers may wish to use the VAKT method discussed in chapter 8.

Developing the word recognition skills is a complex process which is often complicated by the factors of maturation, learning styles, environment, and intelligence. Teachers who consider these factors to be important in learning to recognize words have begun prescriptive teaching. The following sections present a more in-depth discussion of each word recognition skill area, with a summary of research findings that affect prescriptive teaching.

## Sight Word Knowledge

In defining sight word knowledge as a procedure for recognizing words, it is necessary to note that this procedure or group of skills is sometimes considered a method for teaching beginning reading. The look-say method is based on the premise that the student is taught to recognize words by sight rather than through some analytic process, such as phonics or structural analysis. However, as a procedure for word recognition, it is defined as the development of the reading skills necessary to remember words which occur most frequently in reading and are not easily analyzed through other procedures.

Teachers usually associate sight word knowledge with the Dolch Basic Sight Word List, the Fry New Instant Word List, or the word lists which accompany the basal series. These lists are composed of high-frequency words which should

be recognized quickly in order not to slow the reading rate and interfere with comprehension. Sight words are taught as whole units. Sometimes they may be analyzed in parts after they are known to help students recognize other words with similar components. This is known as analytic phonics, and will be further discussed in the next section.

Teachers find that students sometimes have difficulty remembering the more abstract words included on many sight word lists. In a study regarding the learning of words with a high concrete visual imagery level as compared to words with low imagery level (abstract words), Hargis and Gickling found that high-imagery words were easier to learn than low-imagery words and were remembered longer. Studies by Jorm and Kolker and Terwilliger had similar results, indicating that both good and poor readers' memory of words is enhanced by word imagery.[1] Classroom teachers experience more difficulty in teaching these low-imagery words, such as *was* and *the*, than they do the high-imagery words, such as *cat, mother*, and other nouns that can be visualized.

Teachers also realize that words with similar shapes and sounds seem more difficult for the students to remember. McNeil and Keislar found that students had greater difficulty identifying test words that were similar in letter configuration.[2] Thus, teachers should provide much variety and repetition in helping students learn low-imagery words that are similar in sound and shape. The most common groups include words such as *who, what, where, was, when, were, the, this, them, then, that, there, these, those.*

To assist in learning these essential but difficult words, teachers use many different strategies. King and Muehl found that the appropriate methods for teaching sight words varied with the similarity of the words.[3] Cues such as pictures were helpful in remembering similar words. The use of auditory or visual cues provided faster learning of the similar words, but had little impact on learning words which were not similar.

Goodman and Dallmann, Rouch, Chang, and Deboer, Wood and Brown, and Allington and McGill-Franzen suggest that sight words should be taught in the context of other words.[4] This idea is refuted by Singer, Samuels, and Spiroff, who concluded that "efficiency in learning to associate responses to graphic stimuli is significantly greater when the word is presented in isolation than when presented in sentence context or in association with a picture, or both."[5]

However, as teachers, the authors have found that students tend to remember the more abstract words better when they are in the context of a sentence. This technique of learning sight words combines sight word recognition with contextual analysis and places the word in the context of normal reading. This seems to be a more realistic way of learning sight words.

Further research regarding sight word learning has investigated the correlation of the interest of the words with the speed of learning. Harris concluded that kindergarten children from low socio-economic backgrounds learned high-interest words and words not of high interest equally well. Braun found significant differences favoring interest-loading of words for both boys and girls.[6]

In developing knowledge of sight words, teachers may consider the results of a study by Lahey and Drabman.[7] Using token reinforcement consisting of verbal feedback and tokens that could be exchanged for pennies, they found that the no-token subjects took about twice as long to learn the words as did the token group. This technique may be adapted to help students learn the more difficult sight words. In a study of the use of games to reinforce sight vocabulary, Dickerson found that games serve as better reinforcements than worksheets, and that those games involving the most movement were more effective than the more passive games.[8]

Teachers realize that most words become a part of the students' sight vocabulary as they become more experienced readers. Initially, sight word learning may involve primarily the Dolch Basic Sight Words or some similar list; however, other words are continually added. Although there has been some debate during the last fifteen years as to whether the Dolch Basic Sight Word List will be useful as a valid core list[9], Johns, Edmond, and Mavrogenes have found that this list still accounts for more than fifty-five percent of the words used in materials written for students in grades 3–9.[10]

| | Phoneme | Graphemic Options | Phoneme | Graphemic Options |
|---|---|---|---|---|
| *Readability* | /ā/ | a-e, ay (age, clay) | /h/ | h (heart) |
| *Level 1.0–2.0* | /a/ | a (basket) | /hw/ | hw (whistle) |
| | /ä/ | o,a (pond, start) | /k/ | c, k, ck (cabin, dark, sick) |
| | /aů/ | ou, ow (about, town) | /l/ | l, ll (along, will) |
| | /e/ | e (dress) | /m/ | m (man) |
| | /ē/ | y, ee, e (city, green, she) | /n/ | n (nest) |
| | /ī/ | i-e, i, y, igh (sigh, idea, fly, high) | /ng/ | ng (ring) |
| | /i/ | i, e (begin, return) | /p/ | p (pencil) |
| | /ō/ | o, o-e, ow (ago, hole, yellow) | /r/ | r (rain) |
| | /ò/ | o, a (along, want) | /s/ | s, ss (sail, less) |
| | /ů/ | oo (wood) | /sh/ | sh (shoe) |
| | /ü/ | oo (school) | /t/ | t (ten) |
| | /ə/ | e, o, u, a, i, ou, o-e (hello, does, | /th/ | th (throat) |
| | | cup, above, girl, your) | /th/ | th (that) |
| | /b/ | b (bed) | /v/ | v (vacation) |
| | /ch/ | ch (chair) | /w/ | w (wall) |
| | /d/ | d (deer) | /y/ | y (year) |
| | /f/ | f (first) | /z/ | s (as) |
| | /g/ | g (good) | | |
| *Readability* | /ā/ | a, ai (able, tail) | /ks/ | x (box) |
| *Level 2.1–3.0* | /e/ | ea, e-e, ai, a (bread, else, fair, any) | /kw/ | qu (quarter) |
| | /ē/ | ea (clean) | /əl/ | le (circle) |
| | /i/ | ea, i-e (fear, give) | /n/ | nn (penny) |
| | /ō/ | oa (road) | /ng/ | n (donkey) |
| | /ů/ | u (push) | /ən/ | en, n (dozen, chosen) |
| | /ü/ | ew (grew) | /p/ | pp (upper) |
| | /d/ | ld (could) | /r/ | wr (write) |
| | /f/ | ff (coffee) | /s/ | c (face) |
| | /j/ | g (giant) | /t/ | tt (little) |
| *Readability* | /a/ | a-e (rare) | /d/ | dd (add) |
| *Level 3.1–4.0* | /ē/ | i, ey (radio, key) | /j/ | j (jungle) |
| | /ī/ | ie (pie) | /əl/ | al (final) |
| | /i/ | a-e (village) | /n/ | kn (knife) |
| | /ō/ | ou (court) | /ən/ | on (person) |
| | /ò/ | aw (draw) | /r/ | rr (sorry) |
| | /ü/ | ou (soup) | /s/ | st (cost) |
| | /ə/ | u-e, i-e, e-e, a-e, ea (judge, office, | /sh/ | ti (nation) |
| | | were, are, earn) | /z/ | z (prize) |
| | /ch/ | t, tch (picture, match) | | |
| *Readability* | /ā/ | eigh (weight) | /yə/ | u (regular) |
| *Level 4.1–5.0* | /ē/ | ea-e, ie, ay (leave, chief, Friday) | /f/ | ph, gh (elephant, laugh) |
| | /i/ | y (symbol) | /m/ | mm (summer) |
| | /ò/ | au (author) | /w/ | u (language) |
| | /òi/ | oy, oi (joy, soil) | /z/ | es (does) |
| | /ü/ | o-e (move) | /zh/ | s (usual) |
| | /yü/ | u (unit) | | |

Earl H. Cheek, *Cheek Master Word List,* Waco, Texas: Education Achievement Corporation, 1974.
Reproduced with permission of Education Achievement Corporation, Waco, Texas.

Though research seems inconclusive as to exactly how sight words should be taught, teachers need to consider these findings in relation to individual student needs and develop instructional procedures accordingly. Regardless of how words are taught, students need good visual discrimination skills in order to see likenesses and differences in the sight words. Moreover, it is helpful if the student knows the names of the letters, so that specific letter differences in words can be discussed.

Much practice is necessary to remember sight words. During instruction, teachers initially pronounce the sight word as the student looks at it, then use the word in a sentence, either spoken or written, to assist the student in understanding the meaning. Following this, the student makes a sentence with the word to demonstrate understanding. The word may be compared with other known words to aid memory. Many follow-up games and activities are needed to reinforce the initial teaching activity. Specific ideas are provided in table 10.4.

## Phonics

Phonics is the association of phonemes, or sounds, with graphemes, or symbols. Since the publication of *Why Johnny Can't Read* and *Learning to Read: The Great Debate,* both teachers and the public have renewed their interest in phonics instruction.[11] Prior to this, instruction in the word recognition skills had turned from phonics to the look-say, or sight method. The basic issue in the debate over the teaching of word recognition was not whether to teach phonics, but rather whether beginning reading should be taught through the use of synthetic or analytic phonics. As discussed in chapter 8, analytic phonics begins by teaching an entire word and then teaching the sounds within the word. Synthetic phonics is taught by presenting the isolated sounds in the word and blending them to form the entire word.

The findings of Chall's research indicated that a mode-emphasis method using intensive synthetic phonics produced better results than the teaching of analytic phonics. Similar findings were reported by Bond and Dykstra in the First Grade Studies.[12] However, further follow-up research by Dykstra showed that by the second grade the students taught through a synthetic method were not superior in reading comprehension.[13]

Regardless of the method used for teaching phonics, the teacher must be cognizant of the research regarding what should be taught. Although basal materials and phonics work texts present some organization of phonics skills, there is no one "best" sequence or hierarchy. Analyzing a word list of commonly used words, Cheek proposed a graduated system for teaching phoneme-grapheme correspondences in beginning reading.[14] This information is summarized in table 10.1. In considering the development of phonics skills, Boyd found that the most rapid growth in phonics skills was at the second and third grades, while development at the higher grades was slower.[15]

It is essential for teachers to note that students at the upper levels not only learn phonics at a slower rate, they also seem to lose some phonics skills which were previously learned. This is most vividly pointed out by Plattor and Woestehoff.[16] They found that skills such as letter sounds and rhyming word knowledge seemed to decrease as the students advanced from grades three to six. Yet

reading performance remained good. This finding has significant implications for diagnostic-prescriptive reading programs and state testing programs. Students at the upper levels may reveal deficiencies in the phonics skills because they have already internalized them into their reading practices and have no use for the isolated skills. This does not always indicate a need for prescriptive instruction.

In teaching phonics, rules or generalizations are presented in order to assist the student. Clymer identified some 45 generalizations which were presented in reading materials. He found only 18 of them to be useful according to the specified criteria. Further research concerning these generalizations by Emans and Bailey had similar conclusions.[17] Spache identified 121 different phonics rules in the literature and found only 10 to meet the criteria at least 75 percent of the time. They are:

> Vowels—When *y* is the final letter in a word, it usually has a vowel sound. When there is one *e* in a word that ends in a consonant, the *e* usually has a short sound.
>
> Vowel digraphs—In these double-vowel combinations, the first vowel is usually long and the second silent: *oa, ay, ai, ee.*
>
> Vowel with *r*—The *r* gives the preceding vowel a sound that is neither long nor short. (True also for vowel with *l* or *w.*)
>
> Consonants—When *c* and *h* are next to each other, they form only one sound. *Ch* is usually pronounced as in *kitchen, catch,* and *chair,* not as *sh.* When the letter *c* is followed by *o* or *a,* the sound of *k* is likely to be heard. When *c* is followed by *e* or *i,* the sound of *s* is likely to be heard. When two of the same consonants are side by side, only one is heard.[18]

The usefulness of teaching specific rules has been further researched by Hillerich, Harris et al., and Glass and Burton. Hillerich found that students taught vowel rules showed no superiority in word recognition and were, in fact, inferior in reading comprehension when compared with students who had been taught first to discriminate short and long vowel sounds. Harris et al. suggest a negative correlation between the time devoted to instruction in phonics and the performance in comprehension. In addition, the second- and fifth-grade students in Glass and Burton's study made practically no use of phonics rules in decoding unfamiliar words; yet the teaching of these rules continues to be a major portion of the reading instruction in many schools.[19]

As reading educators have analyzed the findings of research in phonics, they have realized the importance of the work of the linguists. Although many of the phonics generalizations seem to be relatively useless in decoding the English language, Hanna and Moore found English to be 86.9 percent phonetic.[20] Linguists approach the teaching of decoding through the association of letter patterns with sound patterns. Individual sounds are not analyzed as in traditional phonics. Additionally, linguists are concerned with the language process involved in decoding words, rather than just the sounds and pronunciation of words. Decoding, as defined by the linguist, includes meaning.

Research by linguists regarding the teaching of phoneme-grapheme correspondences is extensive. Bloomfield and Barnhart suggested that the beginning reader should be given material designed for teaching the orthographic-phonic regularities of English and that irregular relationships should be introduced later.[21] Contrary to this belief, Levin and Watson and Williams have suggested that multiple phoneme-grapheme correspondences should be introduced early in reading instruction in order to develop a more useful problem-solving approach to reading.[22]

Research in the areas of phonics and linguistics is quite extensive. As linguists and reading specialists work together, the vast amount of knowledge regarding the teaching of sound-symbol relationships is being translated into classroom practice. With renewed emphasis on phonics instruction, textbook publishers and researchers have incorporated the ideas of linguists into materials to help the beginning reader develop more successful word recognition skills.

Classroom teachers are finding changes in the terminology used in many textbooks, as well as modifications in the presentation of phonics. Even though the research findings for phonics instruction are inconclusive on some points, they consistently indicate that some prereading skills are prerequisites for such instruction. Many of the skills discussed in chapter 9 are useful in learning to use sound-symbol correspondences effectively in reading. The prereading skills which relate to the development of phonics include oral language skills; these allow the student to recognize a word as a meaningful unit when it has been decoded, and develop visual and auditory discrimination and memory skills, which aid in distinguishing and remembering the various sounds and symbols.

## Structural Analysis

Structural analysis skills rely on the use of word elements or parts to aid in recognizing unknown words. Skills such as syllabication, prefixes, suffixes, contractions, and compound words are included in this area. Structural analysis differs from phonic analysis in that larger units are dealt with in examining critically the structure of the word.

As in other areas of word recognition, research is inconclusive. The skill area which has received the most attention is syllabication. In the studies done by Clymer, Emans, and Bailey, eight generalizations were identified that related to syllabication. Six of these met the criteria of 75 percent usefulness:

In most two-syllable words, the first syllable is accented.
If *a, in, re, ex, de,* or *be* is the first syllable in a word, it is usually unaccented.
In most two-syllable words that end in a consonant followed by *y,* the first syllable is accented.
If the last syllable of a word ends in *le,* the consonant preceding the *le* usually begins the last syllable.
When the first vowel element in a word is followed by *th, ch,* or *sh,* these symbols are not broken when the word is divided into syllables and may go with either the first or second syllable.
When the last syllable is the sound *r,* it is unaccented.[23]

Syllabication seems to be a skill that is better used after the student can pronounce the word, rather than as an aid in pronunciation.[24] Courtney reinforces this belief as he notes that syllabication principles are of decreasing value above the elementary grades, because of the increase in exceptions.[25] Canney and Schreiner found that intensive instruction in syllabication did not improve the word attack or reading comprehension skills of second graders, although the students could verbalize and apply the syllabication principles being taught.[26]

Additional questions are raised regarding the use of syllabication as a word recognition device, after reviewing a study by Marzano et al.[27] Comparing gains in syllabication and comprehension in middle school students, the authors found little correlation.

Harris and Sipay believe that syllabication knowledge can provide students with some guidelines for dividing polysyllabic words into units which can be analyzed phonetically.[28] Gleitman and Rozin advocate the use of the syllable as a unit for initial acquisition in reading, although this idea is not supported by psycholinguists such as Goodman.[29]

In considering syllabication, one must also address the use of accents. Winkley studied the various accent generalizations and identified seven general conclusions which apply to multisyllabic words.[30] Harris and Sipay identify only two accent generalizations as important for teaching:

Usually accent the first syllable in a two-syllable word.
Affixes are usually not accented.

They further suggest that the good reader primarily uses trial and error in determining the appropriate syllable to accent.[31]

In research regarding other structural analysis skills, Spache questions the teaching of isolated prefixes, suffixes, and roots, in that these units vary within the context of the word, and students seem to use these analysis skills infrequently.[32] Thus, it is suggested that they be taught primarily as visual units or letter clusters.

Schell and McFeely have reviewed the various areas of structural analysis and caution teachers that these skills must be taught in a realistic reading situation rather than as isolated or independent rules.[33] These skills assist students in decoding some unfamiliar words, but may be useful only to the extent that they are taught through application in context.

Contextual analysis is defined by Spache as the ability "to determine word recognition and word meaning by the position or function of a word in a familiar sentence pattern."[34] This is the one area of word recognition skills about which there is no debate. Emans identifies four uses of context clues in word recognition:

**Contextual Analysis**

1. To help children remember words that they may have forgotten.
2. To use with other word recognition skills such as phonics and structural analysis to check the accuracy of words.
3. To assist in the rapid recognition of words by anticipating from other words.
4. To aid in the correct pronunciation of words with multiple meanings and pronunciations.[35]

While other word recognition skills seem to become less useful as the reader matures, the contextual analysis skills become more valuable. Spache concludes that adult readers use letter sounds or word structure very little and rely on contextual analysis as their main tool for understanding strange words.[36] Goodman found that while first-grade students used context to some extent to recognize words, third-graders greatly increased their use of this skill.[37]

Most research regarding context clues relates to the classification of the various types of clues. The most generally accepted classification is that of Ames, who has identified fourteen types of clues:

1. Language experience or familiar expression
2. Modifying phrases or clauses
3. Definition or description
4. Words connected in a series
5. Comparison or contrast clues
6. Synonym clues
7. Tone, setting, and mood clues
8. Referral clues
9. Association clues
10. Main idea and supporting detail pattern

11. Question-answer pattern in paragraph
12. Preposition clues
13. Nonrestrictive clauses or appositive phrases
14. Cause-effect pattern of sentence or paragraph[38]

Using Ames's classification scheme, Rankin and Overholzer attempted to rank the clues from easiest to most difficult. Their findings suggest the order of difficulty as numbered above, is 4, 2, 1, 14, 9, 8, 6, 3, 12, 11, 5, 10, 13, with 4 being the easiest and 13 the most difficult.[39]

Teaching context clues seems complex, but these skills must be taught if students are expected to use them. Emans and Fisher have suggested some simple ways of beginning to develop use of context clues: (1) giving no clue except the context, (2) giving the beginning letter, (3) giving the length of the word, (4) providing the beginning and ending letters, (5) giving a four-word choice, and (6) giving all the consonants in the word.[40] In developing the more complex context clues in Ames's list, the teacher must be more selective in the types of exercises provided.

Juel investigated the extent to which good, average, and poor readers in second and third grade identify words of varying difficulty by a text driven (decoding or sight recognition) or a concept driven (context clues) method. She found that good readers are predominately text-driven, while poor readers are concept-driven, and average readers fluctuate.[41]

In reviewing the research in these various areas of word recognition, it is evident that students must be provided with a background in using all the different word recognition strategies. The importance of each of these areas is summarized by Frenzel in table 10.2.

**Table 10.2**
Four Word Recognition Approaches: Their Dependences, Uses, and Limitations

|  | Dependent Upon | Uses in Word Recognition | Limitations |
|---|---|---|---|
| **Sight words** | Visual memory of words and shapes. Configuration skills. Using high-utility words. Discrimination skills. Associating words and images. | Needed to build initial vocabulary. Foundation for other attack skills. Provides cues in concert with other strategies. Bank of sight words is individual thing. | Impossible to learn thousands of words by sight. Similar configurations are confusing. Detached from meaning. Visual memory inefficient in learning large numbers of words. Pronouncing isolated words is not true reading. Some may not learn well from visual approach. |

**Table 10.2 (continued)**

Four Word Recognition Approches: Their Dependences, Uses, and Limitations

| | Dependent Upon | Uses in Word Recognition | Limitations |
|---|---|---|---|
| **Phonics** | Knowledge of sight words. Ability to associate certain sounds with certain symbols. Synthesizing skills. Analyzing skills. Following a sequential development of decoding skills. Ability to use visual and auditory discrimination skills. Good speaking and listening vocabularies. | Used systematically to attack words, with general commonalities. Used in blending, patterning, and substituting skills. Used to manipulate sounds to obtain acceptable results. Used best in conjunction with other attack options. Operates in reading, spelling, and writing. Applied best to familiar words. | Generalizations may have low utility value. English is inconsistent; irregularities cause problems. Sounding letters in isolation is unrealistic and confusing. Laborious letter-by-letter sounding is slow; child can become overly analytical. Some may not learn well from auditory approach. Piecemeal identification tends to lose bigger meaning. |
| **Structural analysis** | Knowledge of sight words. Synthesizing skills. Analyzing skills. Visual cues to word parts. Good speaking and listening vocabularies. Knowledge of semantic effects of word parts. Following a structure-meaning sequence. | Used along with context, phonics, and sight words. Used in getting meaning via word parts. Aids in building words from known words. Operates in reading, spelling, and writing. Uses structure to determine root, inflection, or derivative. Applied best to familiar bases. | Generalizations may be erroneous or inapplicable. May get meaning without pronunciation. Not all words can be analyzed structurally. Cannot memorize lists of affixes. Some may not transfer structural analysis skills. Overanalysis tends to make each syllable a word. Cannot look for little words in big words. |
| **Context clues** | Speaking and listening vocabularies. Awareness and use of syntactical and semantical signals. Prediction and anticipation skills. Intuitive knowledge of language and its patterns. Comprehension skills. Visual skills. | Used along with phonics and structural analysis skills. Identifies words in a realistic and meaningful setting. Some words must be in context to obtain proper pronunciation and meaning. Might be first consideration in attacking an unfamiliar word. Forces thinking while reading; aids understanding. | Unknown words must be familiar. Guessing may produce incorrect words. Material may not have sufficient or strong context clues. Reliance on one type of signal may produce problems. |

Norman J. Frenzel, "Children Need a Multipronged Attack in Word Recognition," *The Reading Teacher* 31 (March 1978): 627–31. Reprinted with permission of Norman J. Frenzel and the International Reading Association.

## Prescriptive Teaching of Word Recognition Skills

Because word recognition skills are so necessary in the development of comprehension, personal reading, and study skills, teachers must provide appropriate prescriptive instruction to develop the specific areas of need. To assist in the diagnostic-prescriptive process, table 10.3 reviews the diagnostic procedures which are appropriate for evaluating specific strengths and weaknesses in the various word recognition skill areas.

The informal diagnostic procedures of the Informal Reading Inventory, observation checklist, and criterion-referenced tests are proper tools to be used in all areas of word recognition skill diagnosis. In addition to these informal procedures and the formal diagnostic tools listed in table 10.3, the teacher may wish to add other instruments to the list. However, the procedures included are only those discussed in chapters 4 and 5.

In using the Informal Reading Inventories, *Gilmore Oral Reading Test, Gray Oral Reading Test,* and *Reading Miscue Inventory* to diagnose the word recognition skills, teachers should note that there are no specific scores in the various word recognition areas; teachers must use their knowledge of the skills and observe the types of errors made in oral reading.

**Table 10.3**
Diagnostic Techniques for Evaluating Word Recognition Skill Areas

| Skill Areas | Procedures |
| --- | --- |
| **Sight Vocabulary** | *Botel Reading Inventory* (word recognition test) |
| | Criterion-referenced test |
| | *Diagnostic Reading Scales* (word recognition lists) |
| | *Doren Diagnostic Reading Test of Word Recognition* (whole word recognition and sight words) |
| | *Durrell Analysis of Reading Difficulty* (word recognition) |
| | *Gates-McKillop-Horowitz Reading Diagnostic Tests* (words-flashed, untimed) |
| | *Gilmore Oral Reading Test* |
| | *Gray Oral Reading Test* |
| | Informal Reading Inventory |
| | Observation checklist |
| | *Reading Miscue Inventory* |
| | *Slosson Oral Reading Test* |
| | *Stanford Diagnostic Reading Test,* Red Level (word recognition) |
| | *Woodcock Reading Mastery Tests* (word identification) |
| | Word Recognition Inventory |

**Table 10.3 (continued)**
Diagnostic Techniques for Evaluating Word Recognition Skill Areas

| Skill Areas | Procedures |
|---|---|
| **Phoneme-Grapheme Correspondence** (Phonics) | *Botel Reading Inventory* (phonemic inventory test)<br>Criterion-referenced test<br>*Diagnostic Reading Scales*<br>*Doren Diagnostic Reading Test of Word Recognition Skills* (skill 1–2, 4–10)<br>*Durrell Analysis of Reading Difficulty* (word analysis, sounds of letters, hearing sounds in words, phonic spelling of words)<br>*Gates-McKillop-Horowitz Reading Diagnostic Tests* (oral reading test, knowledge of word parts) |
|  | *Gilmore Oral Reading Test*<br>*Gray Oral Reading Test*<br>Informal Reading Inventory<br>Observation checklist<br>*Reading Miscue Inventory*<br>*Sipay Word Analysis Tests* (Tests 1–15)<br>*Stanford Diagnostic Reading Test* (phonetic analysis)<br>*Woodcock Reading Mastery Tests* (word attack test) |
| **Structural Analysis** | *Botel Reading Inventory* (phonemic inventory test—syllabication)<br>Criterion-referenced test<br>*Gates-McKillop-Horowitz Reading Diagnostic Tests* (oral reading test, syllabication test)<br>*Gilmore Oral Reading Test*<br>*Gray Oral Reading Test*<br>Informal Reading Inventory<br>Observation checklist<br>*Reading Miscue Inventory*<br>*Sipay Word Analysis Tests* (test 16—contractions)<br>*Stanford Diagnostic Reading Test*, Green, Brown, Blue Levels (structural analysis) |
| **Contextual Analysis** | Cloze procedure test<br>Criterion-referenced test<br>*Gilmore Oral Reading Test*<br>*Gray Oral Reading Test*<br>Informal Reading Inventory<br>Observation checklist<br>*Reading Miscue Inventory* |

Using the diagnostic data, the teacher should then provide prescriptive instruction in the areas of need. In diagnostic-prescriptive instruction, it is imperative that the teacher spend some time explaining the skill prior to assigning activities that use the skill. This is especially essential in developing word recognition skills, since students tend to learn the skills in isolation, but may be unable to use them in reading materials because they do not understand how to transfer skill knowledge from the worksheet to a written selection. This problem can be dealt with by using carefully planned instructional procedures:

*Discuss the skill with students, explaining how it is used in determining an unknown word.* For example, in teaching contractions, explain that shortened word forms are used in reading just as in speaking. Use a conversation with the students to note the contractions.

*Show students how to use the skill in decoding words.* Using the contractions from the conversation, the teacher could write the abbreviated form of the word and the two complete words to show how to recognize the contraction.

*Provide opportunities for students to develop the skill.* Games, worksheets, and various group activities are ways to provide practice in developing the skill.

*Arrange occasions for students to use the skill in the context of a reading selection.* The teacher may need to remind students of the appropriate skill to use in the situation; however, the skill is not mastered until students have it at their command for application when needed.

**Figure 10.2**
Steps in Teaching
Word Recognition Skills

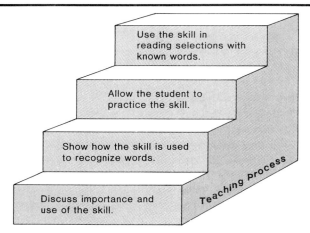

Singer identified ten principles of teaching word recognition skills:

1. Proceed from the familiar to the unfamiliar.
2. Help the student become independent in using word recognition skills.
3. Teach a variety of ways to recognize words.
4. Provide instruction in analyzing new words and much repetition to learn the skill.
5. Use interesting ways to practice learning new words.
6. Use variety in the drill exercises.
7. Let the students know as they make progress.
8. Maximize the probability of success in each lesson.
9. Coordinate instruction among teachers when working with the same student.
10. Follow a sequence of skills in developing word recognition skills.[42]

Table 10.4 gives specific suggestions for developing the different word recognition skills. These ideas are to aid the teacher in providing prescriptive instruction for specific word recognition skill needs. Other ideas are described in the many activity books listed in appendix D.

**Table 10.4**
Word Recognition Skills

| Skill | Prescriptive Techniques |
|---|---|
| **Sight Vocabulary** | |
| *Identify familiar words* | Label familiar objects in the room such as chair, table, etc., then ask students to recognize the familiar word in a sentence. |
| | Give students cards containing familiar words and let them hold up the cards when an object or action is shown by another student. |
| *Identify basic sight words in context* | Use a tape recorder or machine such as a Language Master with cards containing the sight words and ask the student to record the words. The pronunciation can be checked with another tape or the instruction channel of the Language Master. |
| | Give students a flannel board with cards containing the sight words. Let a student put a card on the board and another student pronounce the word and use it in a sentence. |

**Table 10.4**
Word Recognition Skills (continued)

| Skill | Prescriptive Techniques |
| --- | --- |
| **Phoneme-Grapheme Correspondences** | |
| *Reproduce from memory upper- and lowercase letter symbols* | Select one student to be the "letter caller." Ask this student to call the letter and the others to write the designated letter on their individual slates (made from cardboard sprayed with black enamel) or paper. <br><br> Write the upper- or lowercase letter form on the board and ask students to write the form not given by the teacher. |
| *Associate concept of consonants with appropriate letters.* | Tape *A-B-C* letter strips to the floor and ask a student to toss a bean bag on a consonant. <br><br> Place each letter of the alphabet in upper- and lowercase form on individual squares of paper. Ask students to place all of the consonants in a jar. |
| *Associate concept of vowels with appropriate letters* | Ask designated students to hold up individual letter cards. When the letter card contains a vowel the group stands up. <br><br> Play a card game similar to "Old Maid," using cards containing vowels. One card should contain a consonant. The student left with this card is the "Vowel Villain." |
| *Associate sounds and symbols for initial, medial, and final consonant sounds* | Pronounce a word and ask students to write the letter or another word containing the designated sound in a given position. <br><br> Use unfamiliar or nonsense words and ask students to pronounce a part of the word or the entire word. This may be done as a game with points given for each correct response. |
| *Recognize sounds and symbols of variant consonant patterns* | Give students small cards containing the variant consonant patterns. Have them group patterns that represent the same sounds and label the patterns with the sound. <br><br> Pronounce a word containing a designated sound represented by a variant consonant pattern such as si*gn* /n/. Ask the students to name other words containing this variant pattern or other variant patterns representing the /n/ such as *kn*ow. |

| Skill | Prescriptive Techniques |
|---|---|
| *Associate sounds and symbols for initial, medial, and final long and short vowel patterns* | Use words containing a certain vowel sound. Ask students to identify the vowel and vowel sound prior to pronouncing the word. Then give an unfamiliar or nonsense word containing the same sound and ask students to pronounce the word.<br><br>Give students three word cards and a clue, such as "The word I am thinking of has a long *a* sound." Then ask a student to select the word or words that fit the clue. That student may then give a clue to the next student. |
| *Recognize sounds and symbols of variant vowel patterns* | Play a game whereby a vowel sound is given and students identify words containing the vowel sound spelled in different ways.<br><br>Ask students to hold cards representing the various vowel sounds. Give other students word cards containing words with variant vowel patterns. The student matches the word with the appropriate vowel card. |
| *Blend sounds to form words* | Begin with words with two sounds. Give two students big cards containing the appropriate letters. Ask the others to pronounce the letter sounds. As the two students move closer together, the letters are blended more closely until the word is formed.<br><br>Pronounce the sounds that must be blended to form a word and write them on the board as they are pronounced. The student must blend these sounds to form the word. For example, /c/ – /a/ – /t/ to form *cat*. |
| *Substitute initial, medial, and final sounds to form new words.* | Give students a word such as *sit* and ask them to substitute designated letters in certain positions to form new words. This can be done by using letter cards and changing the letter as directed.<br><br>Use a word wheel or tachistoscope idea and change parts of the word by turning the wheel or sliding the tachistoscope card. As the new word is pronounced points may be given. |

**Table 10.4**
Word Recognition Skills (continued)

| Skill | Prescriptive Techniques |
| --- | --- |
| **Structural Analysis** | |
| *Recognize compound words* | Select sets of words, some that form compound words and some that do not. Give the words to the students written as compound words, showing them how to look at the two known words to determine the unknown word. When the words are pronounced, ask students to identify the real compound words.<br><br>Give students sections of the newspaper and marking pens. Ask them to circle each compound word that they find. The student with the most compound words wins the "Compound Detective Award of the Day." |
| *Recognize contractions and original word forms* | Read the students a story containing contractions. Each time they hear a contraction they may stand or hold up a word card containing the two words forming the contraction.<br><br>Use a game board in which each square contains a contraction. When the student "lands" on the square, the two words which form the contraction must be given. |
| *Analyze affixes* | Give students selections containing words with prefixes or suffixes. Ask them to identify the affix that has been added. Then write several of the sentences, using the words without the affix. Discuss how the meaning is changed.<br><br>Use sentences containing words whose meaning can be changed by adding prefixes or suffixes. After the student reads the sentence, ask that the meaning be changed by adding a suffix or prefix. |
| *Recognize inflectional endings* | Give students sentences in which the inflectional endings are omitted. Ask them to add the endings and tell why they are needed.<br><br>Distribute magazines or newspapers and ask students to cut out or mark words with inflectional endings. |
| *Divide unknown words into syllables* | Write several unknown words on the board from a textbook or other reading material. Ask the students to identify the number of vowel sounds in each word. Then ask them to use |

| Skill | Prescriptive Techniques |
|-------|------------------------|
| | the list of syllabication generalizations to divide the word into syllables. Divide the group into teams and let them select words for one another. |
| | Use the same format as above with a game board containing unfamiliar words in each square. The students must divide the word into syllables and pronounce it when they stop on the square. The words can be changed by using rubber cement to attach them to the board. |
| *Accent appropriate syllables in words* | After dividing an unknown word into syllables, ask students to use the accent rules to give the correct pronunciation. |
| | Identify unknown words from the newspaper. Divide them into syllables and accent the correct syllable. Keep score to see who learns the most new words. |

## Contextual Analysis

| | |
|-------|------------------------|
| *Use picture clues to determine unknown words* | Select several sentences that contain an unknown word. Place a picture above the sentences to illustrate the unknown word. Direct the students in using the picture to determine the word. |
| | Give each student a sentence or paragraph with an unknown word and three pictures, of which one depicts the word. Using the context and phonics along with the picture clues, the student should select the correct picture and pronounce the word. |
| *Use context clues to determine unknown words* | Use a modified cloze procedure in which a portion of a word is omitted and must be determined from the context and the given portion of the word. The student getting the word correct must make up a sentence for another student. |
| | Give students a sentence with a word left out and an appropriate number of spaces for the correct word to fit. They must use the context to determine the word. |

The diagnostic procedures and prescriptive teaching ideas included in the preceding tables should assist the classroom teacher in providing instruction in word recognition skills to meet each student's needs. Teachers must always remember that students need to know a variety of word recognition techniques in order to analyze unfamiliar words in reading. Thus, there is no one best way of analyzing words; there is only a best way for analyzing an individual word in a specific situation.

## Summary

This chapter has presented many ideas on teaching word recognition skills. There are four major word recognition skill areas: sight word knowledge, phoneme-grapheme correspondences, structural analysis, and contextual analysis. Within each of these areas, there are specific skills that must be developed in order to recognize words.

Much research has been conducted to determine which word recognition skill is most important in reading and which techniques are the most valuable in teaching the skills. This chapter presented many of the research findings and the conclusive evidence that there is no word recognition skill which can function alone. Students must know the many skills and select the appropriate one to use in a particular situation. Likewise, a variety of techniques must be used to help students learn the word recognition skills.

The tables included in this chapter present a summary of the diagnostic procedures that were most appropriate for the categories of word recognition skills and suggestions for reinforcing these specific skills. As with all skill areas in reading, the teacher must diagnose areas of need prior to providing prescriptive instruction in the word recognition skills. Some general procedures for prescriptive word recognition instruction were also given.

## Applying What You Read

You are teaching in the upper elementary grades. Through diagnostic test data, you find a group of students in your class who have very limited structural analysis skills. What would you do? Design a program for them.

There are several parents in your school who believe that phonics instruction is the answer to all reading problems. How would you explain the importance of the various word recognition skills to them?

Three students in your second-grade class have very poor phonics skills. They also have difficulty with the auditory discrimination skills in prereading. What would you do about teaching the phonics skills to these students? What about the other word recognition skills?

As a first-grade teacher, you have five students who are having difficulty with their sight vocabulary. They can learn the nouns and the more concrete words, but abstract words such as *the, and, what* give them great difficulty. What ideas could be used in developing a prescriptive program for these students?

Contextual analysis requires the use of the meaning of other words in the passage. As a sixth-grade teacher, you have some students who have poor comprehension skills and do not use context clues at all when they read. How could you help them learn to use context clues? How do you think this will affect their comprehension skill development?

**Notes**

1. Charles H. Hargis and Edward F. Gickling, "The Function of Imagery in Word Recognition Development," *The Reading Teacher;* Anthony F. Jorm, "Effect of Word Imagery on Reading Performance as a Function of Reading Ability," *Journal of Educational Psychology;* Brenda Kolker and Paul N. Terwilliger, "Sight Vocabulary Learning of First and Second Graders," *Reading World.*
2. J. D. McNeil and E. R. Keislar, "Value of the Oral Response in Beginning Reading: An Experimental Study Using Programmed Instruction," *British Journal of Educational Psychology.*
3. Ethel M. King and Siegmar Muehl, "Different Sensory Cues as Aids in Beginning Reading," *The Reading Teacher.*
4. Kenneth S. Goodman, "A Linguistic Study of Cues and Miscues in Reading," *Elementary English;* Martha Dallmann, Roger L. Rouch, Lynette Chang, and John J. DeBoer, *The Teaching of Reading,* 4th ed; Martha Wood and Mavis Brown, "Beginning Readers' Recognition of Taught Words in Various Contextual Settings," In Michael L. Kamil and Alden J. Moe (Eds.) *Reading Research: Studies and Applications,* pp. 55–61; Richard L. Allington and Anne McGill-Franzen, "Word Identification Errors in Isolation and In Context: Apples vs. Oranges," *The Reading Teacher.*
5. Harry Singer, S. Jay Samuels, and Jean Spiroff, "The Effect of Pictures and Contextual Conditions on Learning Responses to Printed Words," *Reading Research Quarterly.*
6. Larry A. Harris, "Interest and the Initial Acquisition of Words," *The Reading Teacher;* Carl Braun, "Interest-loading and Modality Effects on Textual Response Acquisition," *Reading Research Quarterly.*
7. Benjamin Lahey and Ronald Drabman, "Facilitation of the Acquisition and Retention of Sight-Word Vocabulary Through Token Reinforcement," *Journal of Applied Behavior Analysis.*
8. Dolores Pawley Dickerson, "A Study of Use of Games to Reinforce Sight Vocabulary," *The Reading Teacher.*
9. John N. Mangieri and Michael S. Kahn, "Is the Dolch List of 220 Basic Sight Words Irrelevant?" *The Reading Teacher;* Dale D. Johnson, Richard J. Smith, and Kenneth L. Jensen, "Primary Children's Recognition of High-Frequency Words," *The Elementary School Journal.*
10. Jerry L. Johns, Rose M. Edmond, and Nancy A. Mavrogenes, "The Dolch Basic Sight Vocabulary: A Replication and Validation Study," *The Elementary School Journal.*
11. Rudolf Flesch, *Why Johnny Can't Read and What You Can Do About It;* Jeanne Chall, *Learning to Read: The Great Debate.*
12. Guy L. Bond and Robert Dykstra, "The Cooperative Research Program in First Grade Reading Instruction," *Reading Research Quarterly.*
13. Robert Dykstra, "Summary of the Second Phase of the Cooperative Research Program in Primary Reading Instruction," *Reading Research Quarterly.*

14. Earl H. Cheek, "The Development of a Hierarchy for Teaching Phoneme-Grapheme Correspondences in Beginning Reading," Ph.D. dissertation.
15. R. D. Boyd, "Growth of Phonic Skills in Reading," in *Clinical Studies in Reading III*, ed. Helen M. Robinson.
16. Emma E. Plattor and Ellsworth S. Woestehoff, "Specific Reading Disabilities of Disadvantaged Children," in *Reading Difficulties: Diagnosis, Correction and Remediation*, ed. William Durr.
17. Theodore Clymer, "The Utility of Phonic Generalizations in the Primary Grades," *The Reading Teacher;* Robert Emans, "The Usefulness of Phonic Generalizations above the Primary Grades," *The Reading Teacher;* Mildred H. Bailey, "The Utility of Phonic Generalizations in Grades One Through Six," *The Reading Teacher.*
18. George D. Spache, *Diagnosing and Correcting Reading Disabilities*, p. 219.
19. Robert L. Hillerich, "The Truth About Vowels," in *Insights into Why and How to Read*, Robert Williams, ed., pp. 63–68; Robert L. Hillerich, "Vowel Generalizations and First Grade Reading Achievement," *Elementary School Journal;* Albert J. Harris, Blanche Serwer, and Laurence Gold, "Comparing Approaches in First Grade Teaching with Disadvantaged Children Extended into Second Grade," *The Reading Teacher;* Gerald G. Glass and Elizabeth H. Burton, "How Do They Decode? Verbalizations and Observed Behaviors of Successful Decoders," *The Reading Teacher.*
20. Paul R. Hanna and James T. Moore, "Spelling—From Spoken Word to Written Symbol," *Elementary School Journal.*
21. Leonard Bloomfield and Clarence Barnhart, *Let's Read: A Linguistic Approach.*
22. Harry Levin and J. Watson, "The Learning of Variable Grapheme-to-Phoneme Correspondences: Variations in the Initial Consonant Position," *A Basic Research Program on Reading;* Joanna P. Williams, "Successive vs. Concurrent Presentation of Multiple Grapheme-Phoneme Correspondences," *Journal of Educational Psychology.*
23. Clymer, "The Utility of Phonic Generalizations in the Primary Grade"; Emans, "The Usefulness of Phonic Generalizations above the Primary Grades; Bailey, "The Utility of Phonic Generalizations in Grades One Through Six.
24. Ruth F. Waugh and K. W. Howell, "Teaching Modern Syllabication," *The Reading Teacher;* Ronald Wardhaugh, "Syl-lab-i-ca-tion," *Elementary English;* L. V. Ruck, "Some Questions About the Teaching of Syllabication Rules," *The Reading Teacher.*
25. Brother Leonard Courtney, "Methods and Materials for Teaching Word Perception in Grades 10–14," in *Sequential Development of Reading Abilities*, ed. Helen M. Robinson.
26. George Canney and Robert Schreiner, "A Study of the Effectiveness of Selected Syllabication Rules and Phonogram Patterns for Word Attack," *Reading Research Quarterly.*
27. Robert J. Marzano, Norma Case, Anne DeBooy, and Kathy Prochoruk, "Are Syllabication and Reading Ability Related?" *Journal of Reading.*
28. Harris and Sipay, *How to Increase Reading Ability*, 6th ed., p. 377.
29. Lila R. Gleitman and Paul Rozin, "Teaching Reading by Use of Syllabary," *Reading Research Quarterly;* Kenneth S. Goodman, "The 13th Easy Way to Make Learning to Read Difficult: A Reaction to Gleitman and Rozin," *Reading Research Quarterly.*

30. Carol Winkley, "Which Accent Generalizations are Worth Teaching?" *The Reading Teacher.*
31. Harris and Sipay, *How to Increase Reading Ability,* p. 379.
32. Spache, *Diagnosing and Correcting Reading Disabilities,* p. 223.
33. Leo M. Schell, "Teaching Structural Analysis," *The Reading Teacher;* Donald C. McFeely, "Syllabication Usefulness in a Basal and Social Studies Vocabulary," *The Reading Teacher.*
34. Spache, *Diagnosing and Correcting Reading Disabilities,* p. 402.
35. Robert Emans, "Use of Context Clues," in *Reading and Realism,* pp. 76–82.
36. Spache, *Diagnosing and Correcting Reading Disabilities,* p. 404.
37. Kenneth S. Goodman, "A Linguistic Study of Cues and Miscues in Reading," *Elementary English.*
38. W. S. Ames, "The Development of a Classification Schema of Contextual Aids," *Reading Research Quarterly.*
39. Earl F. Rankin and Betsy M. Overholzer, "Reaction of Intermediate Grade Children to Contextual Clues," *Journal of Reading Behavior.*
40. Robert Emans and Gladys Mary Fisher, "Teaching the Use of Context Clues," *Elementary English.*
41. Connie Juel, "Comparison of Word Identification Strategies with Varying Context, Word Type, and Reader Skill," *Reading Research Quarterly.*
42. Harry Singer, "Teaching Word Recognition Skills," in *Teaching Word Recognition Skills,* ed. Mildred A. Dawson, pp. 2–14.

**Other Suggested Readings**

Cunningham, Patricia M. "Decoding Polysyllabic Words: An Alternate Strategy." *Journal of Reading* 21 (April 1978):608–14.

Cunningham, Patricia M., Cunningham, James W., and Rystrom, Richard C. "A New Syllabication Strategy and Reading Achievement." *Reading World* 20 (March 1981):208–14.

Dean, Loraine. "Increase Vocabulary with the Word Elements, Mono through Deca." *Elementary English* 47 (January 1970):49–55.

Durrell, Donald D., and Murphy, Helen A. "A Prereading Phonics Inventory." *The Reading Teacher* 31 (January 1978):385–90.

Ehri, Linnea C., Barron, Roderick W., and Feldman, Jeffery M. *The Recognition of Words.* Newark, Delaware: International Reading Association, 1978.

Glazer, Susan M. "Learning to Read Can Become 'Fun and Games'." *Classroom Practice in Reading.* Edited by Richard A. Earle. Newark, Delaware: International Reading Association, 1977.

Goodman, Kenneth S., ed. *Miscue Analysis: Applications to Reading Instruction.* (Urbana, Ill.: NCTE, 1973).

Goodman, Yetta M. "Using Children's Reading Miscues for New Teaching Strategies." *The Reading Teacher* 23 (February 1970):455–59.

Groff, Patrick. "Fifteen Flows of Phonics." *Elementary English* 50 (January 1973):35–40.

Haddock, Maryann. "Teaching Blending in Beginning Reading Instruction *Is* Important." *The Reading Teacher* 31 (March 1978):654–58.

Hall, MaryAnne, and Ramig, Christopher J. *Linguistic Foundations for Reading.* Columbus, Ohio: Charles E. Merrill Publishing Company, 1978.

Johns, Jerry L. "Dolch List of Common Nouns—A Comparison." *The Reading Teacher* 28 (March 1975):538–40.

Lamb, Pose. "How Important is Instruction in Phonics?" *The Reading Teacher* 29 (October 1975):15–19.

McCabe, Don. "220 Sight Words Are Too Many for Students with Memories like Mine." *The Reading Teacher* 31 (April 1978):791–93.

McNeil, John D. "False Prerequisites in the Teaching of Reading." *Journal of Reading Behavior* 6 (December 1974):421–27.

Mangieri, John N., and Kahn, Michael S. "Is the Dolch List of 220 Basic Sight Words Irrelevant?" *The Reading Teacher* 30 (March 1977):649–51.

Maring, Gerald H. "Matching Remediation to Miscues." *The Reading Teacher* 31 (May 1978):887–91.

May, Frank B., and Eliot, Susan B. "A Basic List of 96 Irregular Words for Linguistic Programs." *The Reading Teacher* 31 (April 1978):794–96.

Pikulski, John J. "Using the Cloze Technique." *Language Arts* 53 (March 1976):317–18.

Quandt, Ivan. "Investing in Word Banks—A Practice for Any Approach." *The Reading Teacher* 27 (November 1973):171–73.

Samuels, S. Jay. "Automatic Decoding and Reading Comprehension." *Language Arts* 53 (March 1976):323–25.

Seymour, Dorothy Z. "Word Division for Decoding." *The Reading Teacher* 27 (December 1973):275–83.

Shepherd, James F. "What Every Student Should Know About English Word Formation." *Insights into Why and How to Read.* Edited by Robert T. Williams. Newark, Delaware: International Reading Association, 1976.

Spiegel, Dixie Lee. "Meaning-Seeking Strategies for the Beginning Reader." *The Reading Teacher* 31 (April 1978):772–76.

Waugh, R. P., and Howell, K. W. "Teaching Modern Syllabication." *The Reading Teacher* 29 (October 1975):20–25.

Zeitz, Pearl. "Reading—the Name of the Game." *The Reading Teacher* 28 (March 1975):545–49.

Zuck, L. V. "Some Questions About the Teaching of Syllabication Rules." *The Reading Teacher* 27 (March 1974):583–88.

# 11

The teachers at Seabreeze School realize that comprehension is an indispensable aspect of reading instruction, and is essential to a student's success in reading. They are also aware of the current research interest in reading comprehension. Although their school has a skills hierarchy and they have taught comprehension skills in an orderly progression from beginning reading through high school, these teachers are beginning to wonder what the research implications are for their instructional practices.

Therefore, this chapter presents the current research implications for comprehension instruction. It also seeks to aid classroom teachers in using their knowledge of the comprehension skills as well as the research to provide the best prescriptive instruction to improve students' comprehension. Because most materials and testing programs in reading continue to identify individual comprehension skills, a comprehensive list of these skills is provided, together with ideas to assist the classroom instructor in reinforcing the skills as necessary to meet individual student's needs. Also included are suggestions for using appropriate diagnostic techniques discussed in previous chapters. Some questions addressed in this chapter are:

What factors influence the development of comprehension?

How do the various taxonomies of learning theory relate to comprehension?

What does research tell us about this area?

What are the comprehension skills?

How can comprehension skills be diagnosed by the teacher?

What are some ideas that may be used in providing prescriptive instruction in comprehension?

# How is comprehension developed through prescriptive teaching?

**Vocabulary to Know**

As this chapter is read, the following terms should be noted.

Acronyms
Cause-and-effect relationships
Cognitive development
Comparisons
Comprehension
Contrasts
Critical skills
Discourse analysis
Figurative language

Interactive model
Interpretive skills
Literal skills
Miscomprehension
Organization patterns
Relevant and irrelevant information
Schema theory
Signal words
Synthesis
Taxonomy

**Factors That Influence the Development of Comprehension**

The importance of comprehension in learning to read is seldom questioned. True reading is comprehending or understanding the printed word. Reading does not stop after a word has been analyzed and pronounced correctly; the next step is the understanding of the meaning of that word. Thus as one word is learned and understood, another word must be learned and then another, forming connected discourse allowing a single thought or several thoughts to be transmitted to the reader. This, in turn, facilitates written communication between the writer and the reader. Because the primary purpose of reading is the communication of an idea or ideas to the reader, it is essential for students to develop the skills which will enable them to receive information from the printed page.

Unfortunately, there are some who place so much emphasis on the development of word recognition skills, especially phonetic analysis, that decoding the word has become paramount in the reading process. As a result, a student is often able to pronounce many words in isolation; however, when a word is placed in context, many of these same students will not only have difficulty pronouncing the word, but will also not know its meaning.

The concept of comprehension is somewhat more difficult to understand because of the teacher's inability to observe the ongoing neurological processes.

Comprehension is rather vague; teachers know that it occurs. But it is also necessary to understand how, and in some cases, why not. In contrast to word recognition, which is more easily monitored, the secrets of comprehension are more mysterious and difficult to unlock. Why do some students exhibit more strength in comprehension than others? This is a question which has troubled teachers for quite some time. Obviously, there are many answers to this question, and yet, even with answers, a few students still do not comprehend well in spite of the teacher's best efforts. When examining this complex question, a closer look at students exhibiting weaknesses in comprehension is warranted. There are probably one or more factors interacting to create this difficulty. These factors have been studied by various writers and are summarized on the following pages.

Durkin identifies seven basic factors that affect ability in comprehension. These are oral language, intelligence, features of the material read, motivation, interest, familiarity with the content being read, and the relevance of the correspondence between the dialect of the reader and that of the author.[1]

Harris and Smith identified five factors they believe are the primary determinants of reading comprehension. These factors include background experience, language abilities, thinking abilities, affection (including such areas as interests, motivation, attitudes, beliefs, and feelings), and reading purposes.[2]

Spache and Spache arrange the factors affecting reading comprehension into three broad categories dealing with the material being read, the characteristics of the reader, and the influences dependent upon the manner of reading. Under these three major categories are various sub-areas such as vocabulary development, word analysis skills, intelligence, beliefs, attitudes and prejudices of the reader, interest, purposes for reading, and rate of reading.[3]

In addition to these three sources, some of the factors outlined in chapter 9 that influence prereading also apply to the area of comprehension—intelligence and environment. The environmental factors can be further sub-divided into social/cultural awareness, background of experiences, oral language, and interests in reading.

Obviously, there is considerable overlap among the various sources cited; however, there are also subtle differences in almost every instance. Because of the numerous factors interacting with the comprehension process, it is difficult to reach a definite agreement on one complete list. As a result, a single source may include one or two factors more or less than another; this is to be expected. Each of the major factors is briefly discussed in the following pages in an effort to examine its impact upon the comprehension process and to assist teachers in providing better instruction in the comprehension skills.

Intelligence is a critical factor in every area; however, it is especially vital to comprehension. Recalling simple details from a story, while considered by some to be a lower-level comprehension skill, requires a rather complex thinking process with inferential and analytical understanding often necessitating even more intelligence in comprehension, a student must use deductive/inductive reasoning capabilities as well; therefore, intelligence plays a key role in the comprehension process.

Other key factors, categorized as environmental, include sociocultural awareness, background of experience, oral language, and interests in reading. Sociocultural factors are extremely important to comprehension. Often students from lower socioeconomic backgrounds have had very little opportunity to familiarize themselves with printed material. Generally, verbal rather than written stimuli are used for communication, making it difficult for these students to comprehend printed materials with any depth of understanding. Another unfortunate aspect is that comprehending the printed page may have little or no status in some neighborhoods where little reading is done. An integral part of the sociocultural factor is related to dialectical differences. Many linguists have voiced concern that students using nonstandard American-English orthography, or divergent speakers, experience so much difficulty in reading materials written in standard American-English that comprehension of the printed material is virtually impossible. However, Gemake has suggested that the dialect pattern of nonstandard black English does not interfere in the reading comprehension process of the third grade black student. It does however, interfere with oral reading. Gemake further suggests that comprehension of complex sentence patterns is more difficult for students speaking nonstandard black English.[4]

It is important for students to have varied experiences upon entering school, since comprehending the reading material is often contingent upon having some experiences related to the information encountered. An example of this is noted when an inner-city student is asked to read a story about a vacation at the beach, an experience of which the student has no knowledge. This lack of experience will probably increase the difficulty level of the material and decrease the student's chances for success. Stevens found that background knowledge is a significant factor in comprehension of information read by all ability groups of ninth graders.[5] Therefore, various experiences are desirable as aids to comprehension.

Oral language is important simply because it is easier to understand written words which are part of the student's oral and listening vocabulary. This is, of course, the premise upon which the language-experience approach is built. In a review of research, Christie found that students have difficulty comprehending written materials which contain syntactic structures not found in their oral language. This is significant in instructing those who speak English as a second language, those whose dialect differs substantially from standard English, as well as language delayed children who have been mainstreamed into the regular classroom.[6] The language experience approach as well as an intensive language development program are necessary to develop oral language to the point that it is not a major obstacle to reading comprehension.

Another essential factor is the interest level of the material. Assuming that the readability level of the material is appropriate, comprehension is better when a student is interested in the subject. Some materials are difficult for students to comprehend because of specific features, such as vocabulary, the presentation of too many complex ideas, and the rate at which they occur.[7] Thus, related to the interest of the material, the written message itself must be considered as a critical

factor affecting comprehension. Sentence structure, text structure, as well as the organization of ideas can enhance or deter a student's comprehension of information.

When students are given an assignment or are enjoying recreational reading, it is necessary to aid comprehension by setting a purpose for their reading. Accordingly, another factor affecting comprehension relates to the teacher or reader setting a purpose or having a reason for reading material. When students are aware of why they are reading, they derive more information and enjoyment from the selection.[8] Although this has been a common assumption about reading instruction, current research in schema theory reiterates the need to have students recall what they know about a topic before they begin to read about it. The idea of establishing readiness for reading is further supported by many studies investigating the use of advance organizers and structured overviews for use in content reading.[9] Research has established the value in aiding students to relate their present knowledge to what they are expected to learn from new materials.

Another factor affecting comprehension is the reading rate. All students should be taught to adjust their reading rate to the type of material read. Difficult material will require slower reading for better comprehension, while easier material will allow the students to increase their rate without impairing their comprehension.[10]

Many factors affecting comprehension also influence other areas of reading; therefore, the primary purpose of this discussion is to focus the teacher's attention on the various aspects involved when teaching comprehension. Often students do not read well because of these factors, thus experiencing the frustration and hostility frequently witnessed by the teacher.

## Relating Taxonomies and Comprehension

Comprehension is a thinking process, a process which Carey suggests as difficult to define, is not easily quantified, is ultimately not precisely observable, and which begets other processes.[11] For many years comprehension has been viewed as a process involving the development and application of a variety of subskills. These subskills were arranged in some systematic sequence according to various taxonomies of learning. The hierarchies progress from the lower levels of thinking to the higher levels. Teachers and materials are criticized because in the elementary grades students are not given the opportunity to develop their cognitive abilities as highly as possible. This is due to the questioning strategies used by some teachers. Often elementary students are asked low-level, literal questions which require only basic knowledge and result in one- or two-word answers. These literal-level questions force students to read strictly for main ideas, specific details, and other such information. Rarely are students asked to synthesize and evaluate the information read. As a result, they do not develop their thinking abilities to the highest possible degree.

Taba found that teachers tend to pour out information to students and, as a result of the low level of questioning, encourage them to recite this material back almost word for word. She felt that thinking was incorrectly perceived "as a global

**Table 11.1**

Relating Taxonomies to Levels of Comprehension

| Levels of Comprehension | Taxonomies | | |
|---|---|---|---|
| | *Bloom* | *Sanders* | *Barrett* |
| Literal | Knowledge<br>Comprehension | Memory<br>Translation | Recognition<br>Recall |
| Interpretive<br>(Inferential) | Application<br>Analysis<br>Synthesis | Interpretation<br>Application<br>Analysis<br>Synthesis | Inference |
| Critical | Evaluation | Evaluation | Evaluation<br>Appreciation |

process which seemingly encompassed anything that goes on in the head, from daydreaming to constructing a concept of relativity."[12]

A later study by Guszak further substantiated the theory that levels of questioning used in elementary grades were primarily of the literal type. He found that recognition and recall or memory questions formed 78.8 percent of all questions in the second grade, 64.7 percent in the fourth grade, and 57.8 percent in the sixth grade. Questions at the higher levels, such as translation and evaluation, were used only 20 percent of the time and in many cases required only a yes or no response.[13] As a result of these and other studies, many elementary teachers are becoming more aware of the need to enhance their students' development in cognition by improving their questioning strategies.

In an effort to help teachers improve learning, several important taxonomies, indicating how the learner progresses from the lowest levels of thinking to the highest, have developed. The primary purpose of these taxonomies is to enable the teacher to examine the learning process and to assist in the development of more appropriate questioning strategies for students.

Three of the more widely used taxonomies and their correlation to the three levels of comprehension skills suggested by the authors are presented in table 11.1. The taxonomies depicted were developed by Bloom, Sanders, and Barrett.[14]

However, current research is questioning whether these taxonomies do indeed reflect actual level of questioning difficulty for students. Moreover, questions are being asked about the teaching of subskills as a means of improving comprehension. The discussions as to the levels of thinking as well as the teaching of subskills have divided reading researchers into three groups who debate whether the reading process is best described through a top-down, bottom-up, or interactive model.

Those who believe that reading is a top-down process suggest that the student brings more information to the page than the page brings to him. This prior knowledge is used to make good guesses about the nature of the text. The student

reads to confirm or modify the hypothesis as well as to appreciate the style and ideas of the author. In the top-down model, the student starts with a hypothesis and attempts to verify it by reading. Theorists who support this model maintain that students even use this hypothesis testing procedure in recognizing words: they sample a few features of the word and confirm its identity. In this model, the higher levels in the taxonomies are used by the students in unlocking new information which is often considered as lower levels of thinking.[15]

Another hypothesis of thinking is called the bottom-up model. Researchers who adhere to this position believe that the page brings more information to the student than the student brings to the page. This position is also referred to as text driven, because the student begins with little information about the text, but as the print is sequentially processed, the message is understood. The bottom-up model was the first used to depict information as a series of discrete stages which agree to a great extent with the levels in the learning taxonomies.[16]

Because many researchers have not agreed with either of these models as being descriptive of the reading process, particularly the comprehension phase, a third hypothesis has emerged, the interactive model. This theory is based on the work of Rumelhart; it involves the reader and text working in concert to reveal a meaning. Strange contends that his interactive model begins as the student first attends to print. Then prior knowledge is used to make decisions about the print; these are decoding and comprehension decisions. These, plus other sources such as past experiences, help the student derive a unique meaning. This idea of an interactive model using past experiences (concepts) combined with new information from the text, leads to further research in reading comprehension under the label of schema theory which attempts to describe how old information is combined with new ideas to enhance comprehension.[17]

Schema theory is not a totally new idea nor is it a new name for an old idea, it is an old idea which has been expanded. Schema theory, as discussed by Durkin, supports the notion "of building up understandings, concepts, and vocabulary; and to review whatever experiences and concepts are relevant before children read a selection."[18] However, schema theory research offers more to aid in developing comprehension. According to this schema theory, to understand information the reader uses what is in his head and adds to his store of information as new related information is read. Furthermore, according to schema theory research, the ability to infer and the nature of the inference depend on the reader's knowledge; even explicit text is interpreted in different ways when the student constructs meaning from the text as well as from his previous knowledge. Schema theory supports our common sense about reading: "the more we know before we read, the more we learn when we read."[19]

The concepts of taxonomies, levels of questions, and specific subskills in comprehension acquire a different meaning as these new research areas become better understood. Sheridan argues that schema theory provides evidence that comprehension is a holistic process. Comprehension skills instruction is necessary, but in relation to the schemata, rather than as isolated skills.[20] The way

students organize information in their minds is an aid as they organize new information. Different researchers have investigated the organization of text materials, using a procedure known as discourse analysis. By identifying the text structure of materials, students can be taught to identify various organizational patterns of text in order to better understand new information. Meyer identified five basic patterns: response, comparison, antecedent/consequent, description, and collections.[21] Although these organizational patterns have been identified from an analysis of students' writing, the concept of identifying the organizational patterns in text is not new. As early as 1917, Thorndike reported that one reason for failure in reading is the student's inability to organize and to understand organizational relationships in written materials.[22] In 1964, Nila Banton Smith and James McCallister maintained that different patterns of writing exist in various content areas and serve as aids to understanding.[23] However, here too schema theory research has provided additional insight into the use of organizational patterns to aid comprehension. Cheek and Cheek analyzed content textbooks and identified four organizational patterns commonly used in content writing. These patterns are enumeration, relationship, problem-solving, and persuasion.[24] Further research has indicated that by teaching those organizational patterns to middle school students, comprehension is significantly improved.[25]

Schema theorists suggest that if students were taught to recognize the organization of materials and if materials were written so as to follow the logical patterns which students understand, then comprehension would be a natural process of understanding. Rosenshine goes further to suggest that there is no clear evidence for distinct reading skills or for a skills hierarchy.[26] Readance and Harris have more cautiously considered those skills which seem essential to comprehension. They studied nine comprehension subskills—identifying main ideas, identifying outcomes, drawing conclusions, determining sequence, identifying pronoun referents, deriving meaning from context, using punctuation clues, understanding syntax and affixes. One skill, affixes, was determined to be a false prerequisite for comprehension. Identifying outcomes, using punctuation clues, and understanding syntax were found to be possibly necessary, but insufficient in themselves to assure comprehension. The five remaining skills were deemed to be associated with competency.[27]

Although much of the current research in comprehension has questioned the teaching of comprehension skills as well as their arrangement in some learning hierarchy, the fact is that very little research has been conducted in a classroom setting, nor has it examined the effect of the findings over a long period of time or on different types of students. Consequently, although many of these new ideas seem to have great potential, classroom teachers must continue to use what they know and are expected to teach in the best possible way. They cannot ignore the need to view comprehension as an integral part of language as well as student experiences; but neither can they escape from the real world of state and local assessments of isolated comprehension skills. Thus, while this section has provided some insight into the current interests in comprehension, the following sections will address what teachers must teach in their classes.

## Comprehension Skills

The comprehension skills are divided into three basic areas: literal, interpretive (inferential), and critical. The specific skills within the areas are listed later in this chapter and are summarized in appendix A. This section provides a discussion on each of the basic areas and furnishes some insight into the importance of the area according to research findings.

## Literal Skills

Developing literal comprehension skills is an integral part of the total reading process. Some believe that students must deal with these basic, low-level comprehension skills, developing proficiency in their use in order to progress to more difficult interpretive and critical skills.

Such subskills as finding the main idea, recalling details, contrasts and comparisons, interpretation of abbreviations, symbols and acronyms, and several others, are classified as literal skills.[28]

Of particular importance to this area is the development of vocabulary. Students with adequate vocabularies find that understanding the meaning of material is generally less difficult for them than for students with inadequate vocabularies. Vineyard and Massey found this to be true even when intelligence was held constant; they supported a continuation of teaching strategies for improving comprehension through the improvement of vocabulary.[29]

Other subskills of particular importance to literal comprehension are identifying the main idea and reading for details. Dechant states that the ability to identify the main idea is essential to the understanding of what is written. Dawson and Bamman suggest looking for a definite sequence of details when learning to follow directions.[30] Without mastery of these skills, comprehension would be very difficult.

Organization of skills into some meaningful order is valuable in assisting students to grasp many of the skills included not only in the literal area, but in the interpretive and critical areas as well. This is particularly helpful in the skill of recalling information.[31] Also, organizing words in meaningful units such as phrases, clauses, and sentences further assists in the comprehension process.[32]

From the research related to the area of literal comprehension, it is logical to conclude that many variables interact at this level to promote or deter comprehension.

## Interpretive (Inferential) Skills

Interpretive skills are believed by some to require a higher level of cognition and perception than literal skills. Drawing inferences and interpreting the language and mood of the writer become vitally important in comprehending the inner meaning of the material read. Interpretation involves examining more than the superficial aspects of a selection; it involves drawing conclusions, making generalizations, predicting outcomes, and synthesizing ideas, as well as using other inferential skills.

In order to facilitate comprehension at a higher cognitive level, it is essential that the reader delve further into the meaning of the material. A closer examination of language patterns and syntax indicates that these contribute to successful comprehension. This closer examination of language patterns will enhance

the perception of the deep structure of a sentence.[33] Deese reinforced this concept by describing the syntax of a language as the bridge between the sound system and the semantic or meaning system in the language.[34]

The use of context clues in grasping the meaning of selections is essential. Earlier on, reading teachers felt that the student's use of these clues was beneficial to comprehension. Burmeister felt that word meaning was aided by the use of context clues, while Allen states that a student's experiential background plays a major role in gaining information from material through the use of context. Emans found that context clues could aid students in identifying words they had forgotten, checking the accuracy of words identified through the use of other clues, anticipating words (thus increasing the rate of recognition), and identifying totally unfamiliar words.[35]

Another valuable ally in promoting interpretive comprehension is to understand the proper use of signal words. These conjunctions can enable students to determine the meaning of sentences and passages.[36]

Other useful skills that assist students in acquiring meaning from materials are figurative language and punctuation. Figurative language can be most helpful to elementary students, enriching their vocabulary and improving their ability to gain meaning from materials they encounter.[37] Often punctuation replaces the intonation pattern in speech, necessitating the mastery of this skill as quickly as possible.[38] A task possibly not as difficult as some other interpretive skills, but certainly a challenge for the elementary school student, is the proper use of punctuation as an aid in comprehension.

As with literal skills, many factors interact to influence interpretation of printed materials; however, it is essential that every student have the opportunity to develop these skills in order to go beyond superficial understanding to a deeper understanding of the meaning of that material.

## Critical Reading Skills

Just as interpretive skills sometimes are more difficult for students to master than literal skills, critical reading skills are believed to require an even higher level of cognition than either literal or interpretive skills. Critical reading skills require that evaluative judgments be made about the material read and that the reader's reasoning abilities be used at their highest level.

The importance of the development of critical reading skills is further emphasized by the numerous efforts to reach a comprehensive, yet specific, definition of this area. Durkin views critical reading as both reading and reacting to printed material. Ives defines critical readers as those who, in addition to identifying facts and ideas accurately as they read, engage in interpretive and evaluative thinking. Burns and Roe state that critical reading is the evaluation of written material.[39] There seems to be little doubt that critical reading is the application of specific criteria, such as validity, accuracy, and truthfulness, in evaluating material.[40]

Teaching students to read critically is essential because of the various types of printed material that they will deal with in school and throughout their adult life. They will have to perceive bias, identify relevant and irrelevant information, differentiate between fact and opinion, understand fallacies in reasoning, and deal with many other situations which require critical evaluations of printed material. As a result, teachers should condition their students to read critically by expanding their knowledge, showing them how to question and use sound judgment in applying logic to all situations, then instruct them to reach a decision based on the analysis of all the data.[41]

Unfortunately, critical reading is not emphasized as much in the lower elementary grades as it could be,[42] even though research has shown that students at this level can read critically when given the opportunity and the appropriate instruction.[43] When teachers include critical reading skills in their instructional programs, it is important to use good questioning techniques, encourage discussions, analyze propaganda, and use sound reasoning in order to provide for a broader range of expression and ideas in the classroom. These techniques have been quite successful in improving critical reading skills.[44]

Perhaps the skill most widely used in teaching critical reading is that of analyzing propaganda. Since the Institute of Propaganda Analysis released its list of techniques for influencing opinion in 1937, teachers have taught these techniques extensively. Those techniques identified by the Institute are: (1) name calling, (2) glittering generalities, (3) transfer, (4) plain folks, (5) testimonials, (6) bandwagon, and (7) card stacking. Although instruction using these techniques has been most effective,[45] the perception of propaganda does not ensure that students will always be able to resist its more insidious aspects.[46]

As the research clearly indicates, developing the ability to read critically is very necessary to comprehension. Unless this ability is developed to its fullest, students may be unable to distinguish between important and unimportant information, may be unable to detect bias, or may fall prey to a fast-talking salesman, or to others who do not have their best interests at heart. Thus, it is essential to help students develop the ability to read critically, so that they can make good evaluative judgments.

**Prescriptive Teaching of Comprehension Skills**

The final portion of this chapter is involved with the concept of using prescriptive techniques to provide instruction in the various comprehension skill areas. A portion of this last section recommends several methods of evaluating students' strengths and weaknesses in the skill areas. In an effort to enhance its usefulness, this information is presented in a chart format. The remaining part of this chapter then deals with specific comprehension skills and some techniques for implementing prescriptions for teaching the comprehension skills.

As in chapters 9 and 10, several diagnostic procedures for evaluating each skill are presented. As previously mentioned, the authors are aware that some valuable diagnostic procedures and instruments may not be included. In using table 11.2, please note that several of the instruments listed do not separate comprehension into various skill area subtests; therefore, it is necessary that the teacher evaluate these tests more carefully, using an item analysis technique, to arrive at more definitive information. The instruments or procedures which fall into this category are listed under each skill area to which they apply, with no subtest specified. The informal procedures that are included, as well as the *Reading Miscue Inventory,* depend upon the teacher's questioning techniques for diagnosing the three categories of comprehension; thus, they are listed under all three skill areas.

The procedures presented in table 11.2 are intended to indicate ways of evaluating the strengths and weaknesses of each student in the various comprehension skill areas. When this evaluation has been completed, adequate prescriptive techniques can be implemented so that each student receives appropriate instruction. In using various instruments to diagnose comprehension, great caution should be taken to avoid making decisions about the students' strengths and weaknesses in comprehension, especially on the basis of too limited information. Niles and Harris[47] recommend that teachers consider the following as reading diagnosis is conducted in comprehension.

*Method of measurement:* Are the questions oral or written? Is a recall or multiple choice format used? What is the level of the question? Is the question a quality question?

*Instructional environment:* Does the environment provide a quality setting for reading? Is reading done orally or silently? What is the teacher's attitude toward reading?

*Text:* What is the content and style of presentation?

*Reader:* What does the reader bring to the situation in terms of interests, experiences, and intelligence?

Each of these factors will affect the results of diagnosis in comprehension. For example, Wilson found that average readers in the sixth and seventh grades performed significantly better but there was no difference between the two groups on responses to factual questions.[48] Thus, test scores, especially in comprehension, should be analyzed to determine the validity of the information.

**Table 11.2**
Diagnostic Techniques for Evaluating Comprehension Skill Areas

| Skill Areas | Procedures |
|---|---|
| **Literal and Interpretive** (Inferential) | Cloze test |
| | Criterion-referenced tests |
| | *Diagnostic Reading Scales* (Instructional Level; Independent Level) |
| | *Durrell Analysis of Reading Difficulty* (Oral Reading; Silent Reading) |
| | *Gates-MacGinitie Reading Test* (Comprehension) |
| | *Gilmore Oral Reading Test* (Comprehension) |
| | *Gray Oral Reading Test* (Comprehension—literal only) |
| | Group Reading Inventory |
| | Informal Reading Inventory |
| | *Iowa Silent Reading Test* (Reading Comprehension) |
| | Observation checklist |
| | *Reading Miscue Inventory* |
| | *Stanford Diagnostic Reading Test (Red Level—* Comprehension; *Green Level—*Literal and Inferential Comprehension; *Brown Level—*Literal and Inferential Comprehension; *Blue Level—*Literal and Inferential Comprehension) |
| | *Woodcock Reading Mastery Tests* (Word Comprehension Test; Passage Comprehension Test) |
| **Critical** | Criterion-referenced tests |
| | Group Reading Inventory |
| | Informal Reading Inventory |
| | Observation checklist |
| | *Reading Miscue Inventory* |

In providing prescriptive instruction in comprehension, teachers must be sure that they are instructing and modeling the behavior which is desired. Durkin has characterized the state of instruction in reading comprehension as basically no instruction.[49]

While there is no one way of teaching comprehension there are some basic guidelines which should be followed.

1. *The teacher should introduce the skill by telling and showing examples of the skill as used in the reading situation.*
2. *The teacher should show the students how to use the skill in their reading.*
3. *Opportunities should be provided for the students, working together, to demonstrate their understanding of the skill.*
4. *Once the students demonstrate an understanding as they work with the teacher and peers, their individual knowledge can be evaluated through individual activities.*

Elliott and Carroll recommend several strategies for increasing learning from reading. They suggest that teachers should provide developmentally appropriate instruction to create mental images, that they verbally elaborate on ideas, and that new information be related to prior knowledge.[50]

For instructors who continue to be troubled by the teaching of isolated comprehension skills and who view the current research in comprehension as a glimmer of hope of being able to approach comprehension instruction as a language process, Strange offers seven uses of the schema theory which will aid in prescriptive teaching, yet not require major changes in what we do.

1. *Prereading instruction:* Continue to motivate and provide purposes for reading. Add to your prereading instruction the notion of schema theory by helping students organize their related past experiences and make predictions about what will be learned from the new information.
2. *Vocabulary instruction:* Provide more instruction in vocabulary helping students learn specific labels for their schemata.
3. *Analyze question/answer relationships:* Consider the lower and higher levels of questioning as outlined in the taxonomies but also consider the text material to determine if, indeed, the question responses require literal, inferential, or critical thinking skills. Pearson and Johnson's refinement of the taxonomies may aid teachers in the analysis of question/answer relationships.

   Textually explicit: Both the question and answer are derived from the text and the relationship between them is explicitly cued by the text.

   Textually implicit: Both the question and answer are derived from the text but no explicit cue is provided to tie the question to the answer.

   Scriptually implicit: The question is derived from the text with the answer not given directly in the text but enough information provided to develop a plausible response.[51]
4. *Recall important details:* Noting details or recalling factual information is only valuable in helping students add to or change their existing schemata. Thus, minimal time should be spent on recalling details, and more time spent on helping students infer new ideas.
5. *Compare stories:* Help students learn to compare stories by looking at the plots, characters, settings, events, etc. Story grammar research indicates that stories should not be dealt with as isolated units but should be interrelated to note similarities and differences.
6. *Model/stimulate:* Modeling is an important instructional element in teaching comprehension. Teachers can stimulate students to think of the stories they read by talking about the story, comparing it to another, or predicting what will happen. This modeling of the comprehension process helps students realize that understanding information goes beyond the answering of isolated questions.

7. *Understand miscomprehension:* There are many reasons for incorrect or different answers to comprehension questions. Answers are not merely right or wrong; some answers which differ from those given in the teacher's manual may actually appear more correct when the students schemata is considered. Possible explanations which may help the teacher better understand miscomprehension include

No existing schema when students lack background in an area;

Naive schema when the students have only limited experiences to related to the topic;

No new information when a story adds nothing to the students existing knowledge, thus causing them to ignore the details because they are predictable and well understood;

Poor story which does not assist the students in integrating or relating the new ideas to their schemata;

Many schemata are appropriate in some stories which allows for different interpretations;

Schema instrusion allows a response to a question to come from the student's mind with no plausible line of reasoning;

Textual intrusion is used to respond incorrectly to a question when students give a response based on information from the text but the response is unrelated to the question.

The idea of miscomprehension provides another way of looking at answers to comprehension questions, just as miscues have added a dimension to the analysis of word recognition errors.[52] Both consider the student, his background of experience, and the impact of the error on the reading process.

These ideas regarding comprehension instruction should be considered when classroom teachers are planning their prescriptive teaching. Instruction by means of modeling is essential; isolated comprehension skills teaching must be related to practical situations in order for students to view reading as a helpful process which may be used to gain new information or for enjoyment.

In the final section of this chapter, the various comprehension skills and ideas for implementing prescriptions for each skill are presented in table 11.3.

**Table 11.3**
Comprehension Skills

| Skill | Prescriptive Techniques |
|---|---|
| **Literal Skills** | |
| *Understand concrete words, phrases, clauses, and sentence patterns* | Give students pictures of objects or situations and words or sentences that correspond. Ask them to match the picture to the word or sentence it represents. |
| | List several words from a book, magazine, or newspaper for which students may not know the meaning. Begin a word chain that contains the word and a sentence on one side of the strip of paper and the dictionary definition on the other side. Each student may have a paper chain or a group may develop one to hang in the classroom. |
| *Identify stated main idea* | Ask students to read a paragraph and circle in red the sentence that tells what the paragraph is about. |
| | Let each student in a group read one sentence from a paragraph containing a stated main idea. The student who reads the main idea sentence and identifies it as the main idea is crowned "Mr. or Ms. M. I." for most important sentence or main idea. |
| *Recall details* | Give students a paragraph to read. Ask them to circle the details that answer who, what, when, where, and how in green ink. |
| | Use a newspaper article and ask students to underline details that tell more about the title of the article. |
| *Remember stated sequence of events* | Give students a short story to read that contains a sequence of events. Ask them to retell the events in the proper sequence. If an event is skipped, the group must begin the sequence again. |
| | Ask students to read a story that has a sequence of events. Cut the story into sentence strips, giving each student one or more strips. Let them reconstruct the story in sequence. This is especially fun with a language-experience story and big sentence strips that can be taped to the floor. |
| *Select stated cause-effect relationships* | Give students a story with a stated cause-effect relationship. Ask them why the effect occurred or what caused something to happen. For example, "Why was the store owner angry?" or "What caused the bike tire to go flat?" |
| | After reading a story containing cause-effect relationships, ask students to identify each cause-effect situation. Help them relate these to real life situations. |

| Skill | Prescriptive Techniques |
|---|---|
| *Contrast and compare information* | Use two or more ideas in a story and ask students to tell how each is like or unlike the other. For example, compare a bear and a dog in the story. Give students two sentences in which ideas or objects are being compared. Ask them to underline the things that are being compared. |
| *Identify character traits and actions* | After reading a selection containing characters, ask students to act out designated characters, noting specific habits, behaviors, or actions. Ask students to read a story about a famous person. Then list the traits of the person that they think helped make him or her famous. |
| *Interpret abbreviations, symbols, and acronyms* | Ask students to list abbreviations or acronyms from a selection. Then write the meaning of each. Make a list of abbreviations, symbols, and acronyms that students find as they read. Develop a class dictionary or card file. |
| *Follow written directions* | Give students sets of written directions. As they follow the directions, a picture of some object will be formed. Ask students to read directions for playing a game, tell the directions to another student, and follow the directions in playing the game. |
| *Classify information* | Give students lists of items and ask them to classify or group them according to some appropriate title or heading. Ask students to take sentences from various stories and group them according to some topic. They may use some as topic sentences and others as supporting sentences. |

**Interpretive Skills**

| Skill | Prescriptive Techniques |
|---|---|
| *Predict outcomes* | Tell students to read a story to a designated point. They should stop and predict what will happen next or how the story will end. This may be done orally, as a written paper, or through illustrations. Give students a comic strip with the last frame missing. Ask them to predict how the comic ends. |
| *Interpret character traits* | After reading a story that contains different characters, ask students to describe how they think a character would act in a given situation. Use puppets and let students write a script for them based on the characters they have read about in another story. |

**Table 11.3**
Comprehension Skills (continued)

| Skill | Prescriptive Techniques |
|---|---|
| *Draw conclusions* | Give students several sentences that could be the beginning of a story. Ask them to develop a conclusion for the story from the given information.<br>After reading a story, ask students questions that require them to reach some conclusions from the information. |
| *Make generalizations* | Let students read a story and ask them to respond to questions that require them to make generalizations, such as these: Do the people in the story like each other? Which ones? Why do you think so? Could this story have happened in our city? Why?<br>After reading a story, ask students to decide when the story took place and to say why they think it happened at that certain time. They may also make generalizations about the story setting and characters. |
| *Perceive relationships* | Give students a selection that shows a relationship between two ideas. Ask them to identify the relationship, such as the way a little girl acted at a party and the way her mother acted.<br>Using several selections, ask students to identify the relationships of some similiar ideas, such as the time at which the various ideas occurred, or the different ways the characters responded to problems. |
| *Understand implied causes and effects* | Give students a story that contains the cause of a situation and ask students to decide the possible effects. For example, the law says that dogs cannot be loose in the city, but Mr. Jones refuses to put his dogs in a pen. What may happen? Why will these things happen?<br>Give students a list of effects of situations and ask them to identify the possible causes. For example: the ship spilled oil; the house burned down; the boy got a new bike. Tell why these things may have A happened. |
| *Identify implied main ideas* | Ask students to read a selection in which the main idea is not stated. Have them relate the main idea.<br>After reading a story, have students decide on a good title for the story. |
| *Interpret figurative language* | Develop a class file of figurative expressions found while reading. Use these expressions to create a booklet that depicts the expression in a literal manner and in its intended way.<br>Have students read a selection containing figurative language. Each expression should be underlined, and groups of students asked to discuss them to interpret the meaning. |

| Skill | Prescriptive Techniques |
|---|---|
| *Interpret meaning of capitalization and punctuation in a selection* | Give students some sentences without capitalization or punctuation and ask them to read the sentences. As a group, add the correct capital letters and marks. See how much easier the sentences are to read.<br>Give students two sentences that are alike except for punctuation. Discuss the differences in meaning. For example: ''Vicki,'' said her mother, ''is nice.'' Vicki said her mother is nice. |
| *Understand mood and emotional reactions* | After reading a story, ask students to identify the emotions expressed through the actions of the characters and the words used by the author.<br>Ask students to read a poem containing emotion. Let some students act out the various lines, while others guess which line is being dramatized. |
| *Interpret pronouns and antecedents* | Give students several sentences containing pronouns and antecedents. Ask them to identify the appropriate antecedents for each pronoun.<br>Select a passage containing pronouns and antecedents. Delete the pronouns and have students try to interpret the ideas and add the correct pronouns. |
| *Understand author's purpose and point of view* | Have students read letters from the editorial page of the newspaper and decide the writer's point of view.<br>After reading a story, ask students to decide why the author wrote the story and how he or she felt about the topic. |
| *Construe meaning by signal words* | Give students a selection containing signal words, e.g. *first, last, in summary, therefore.* Ask them to underline each signal word and tell what the word is signaling in this selection.<br>Play a game giving clues about signal words. Ask students to identify the appropriate signal word from a given selection. For example, which word in the last paragraph tells you the story is almost finished? |
| *Understand meaning of abstract words* | Ask students to circle all words in a paragraph that cannot be defined through concrete objects or actions. Then discuss the meanings of these abstract words.<br>Use a list of abstract words such as democracy, freedom, love, and identify concepts that help define these words. See how many ideas students can list to assist a person from outer space in understanding the words. |
| *Summarize information* | Give students a story and ask them to summarize it to send as a telegram to a friend. Tell them that it costs 5¢ for each word used, so the message must be short but complete. |

*How Is Comprehension Developed through Prescriptive Teaching?*

**Table 11.3**

Comprehension Skills (continued)

| Skill | Prescriptive Techniques |
|---|---|
| | Ask students to take a newspaper article and underline the key parts. They should summarize the article in several sentences to share with the class. |
| *Recognize implied sequence* | Use information from various sources and ask students to organize the ideas into a logical sequence.<br>Give students a story that uses a flash-back technique and ask them to identify the actual sequence of events. |
| *Use context clues to determine meaning* | Use sentences with the students containing comparisons, antonyms, or synonyms that can aid in determining the meanings of other words in the sentence. Ask them to underline the context clue word and circle the word it defines.<br>Select a list of multiple-meaning words and use them in sentences. Ask students to read the sentences and tell how the meanings are different. |
| *Synthesize data* | Use the summary statements from various sources and ask students to synthesize all of them to formulate their own statement.<br>Give students some information regarding a topic and ask them to synthesize it to form their own story. |

**Critical Reading Skills**

| Skill | Prescriptive Techniques |
|---|---|
| *Identify relevant and irrelevant information* | Give students a passage that contains some information that does not belong. Ask them to mark through the irrelevant information.<br>Ask students to organize some information from materials that you give them. In order to complete the task, they must discard some material that does not belong and use only the relevant information. |
| *Interpret propaganda techniques* | Show students samples of literature from various groups who promote their beliefs through propaganda. Identify specific parts of the material and discuss the ideas or possible reasons for the statements.<br>Give students some statements that are fact and others that are propaganda. Discuss how they differ. |
| *Perceive bias* | Give students selections to read that contain bias regarding local or national events. Ask them to identify the bias and to debate the issue with another student of a different opinion.<br>Use the editorial page of the newspaper or magazine and ask students to locate articles or letters that reflect a bias. |

| Skill | Prescriptive Techniques |
|---|---|
| *Identify adequacy of materials* | Ask students to review several materials and determine which is adequate to answer a list of questions that have been provided.<br>Assign topics to the students. Give each four books and ask them to select two that provide the most information on the topic. |
| *Understand reliability of author* | Look at the information provided on the author and the topic of the material. Ask students to evaluate the qualifications of the author in terms of the topic.<br>Give students a list of book titles and a list of authors with information on each. Ask them to match the title with the most appropriate author. |
| *Differentiate facts and opinions* | Give students a list of facts and opinions. Ask them to circle each opinion statement and tell why it is an opinion.<br>Ask students to read several short selections on a topic and determine which is factual and which is opinion. |
| *Separate real and unreal information* | Give students a list of ideas. Ask them to identify the ideas which are real and to tell why they are real.<br>Read passages to the students and ask them to stand up or clap when the information is unreal or cannot happen. |
| *Understand fallacies in reasoning* | Give students paragraphs that contain fallacies in reasoning, such as name calling, the bandwagon technique, stereotypes, etc. Ask them to underline the sentences that show these fallacies and to explain them.<br>Use the advertisements in a newspaper to identify the fallacies in reasoning that attempt to lure people into buying merchandise. |

The preceding tables present informal and formal diagnostic procedures, along with prescriptive techniques for each comprehension skill area, in an effort to facilitate the teachers' use of this information. Its purpose is to enable the teachers to use the activities and to develop additional activities which will enhance the effectiveness of the diagnostic-prescriptive reading programs in their classrooms.

## Summary

Comprehending printed material is the purpose and goal of reading. For a student to be a successful reader, he or she must comprehend. However, comprehension occurs at various levels. For example, some students may comprehend well at the literal level, but experience great difficulty in interpreting information or evaluating material. Thus, it is essential that students be taught to read on all three comprehension levels: literal, interpretive, and critical.

Why some students comprehend well at all levels of reading and others do not has always puzzled teachers. Some of the reasons include the various factors which affect reading comprehension; among those mentioned were experiences, language capabilities, intelligence, motivation, interests, attitudes, dialect, and purposes for reading. One or more of these may prevent many students from realizing their potential.

Another important factor in teaching students to comprehend materials is related to cognitive development. Many teachers do not assist students in reaching their highest level of cognition because of the types of questioning they use. It is essential to question students at interpretive and critical levels, not just at the literal level. Taxonomies have been developed in an effort to assist teachers in achieving this goal. Three taxonomies developed by Bloom, Sanders, and Barrett were presented.

Current research in comprehension questions the teaching of specific subskills and encourages comprehension development using the student's knowledge structure or schema. Although new ideas are provided in this research, much of the information only amplifies many of the present classroom practices.

To assist classroom teachers in applying these new research findings as well as coping with current requirements for instruction in the many comprehension subskills, the final section of this chapter provided diagnostic information as well as prescriptive techniques for implementing instruction in comprehension. These were summarized in chart form in an effort to be of greater value to the teacher.

## Applying What You Read

You have been transferred to a new school to teach the second grade. Your students have had very limited experiences and have poor oral language skills. How important are these impediments to the development of comprehension? How can these factors be partially nullified or reversed?

Using the taxonomies presented in this chapter as a model, develop your own taxonomy for teaching the comprehension skills. Discuss the role which taxonomies have in the reading comprehension process.

Design a program for diagnosing comprehension skills. Apply this diagnostic program to your classroom by selecting those procedures best suited to your students' needs.

After obtaining accurate diagnostic information about your students' strengths and weaknesses in comprehension skills, design appropriate prescriptive techniques for each student. Implement these prescriptions as early as possible.

1. Dolores Durkin, *Teaching Them to Read,* 3rd ed., pp. 393–95.

2. Larry A. Harris and Carl B. Smith, *Reading Instruction: Diagnostic Teaching in the Classroom,* 2nd ed., pp. 48–51.

3. George D. Spache and Evelyn B. Spache, *Reading in the Elementary School,* 4th ed., pp. 447–51.

4. Josephine Gemake, "Interference of Certain Dialect Elements with Reading Comprehension for Third Graders." *Reading Improvement.*

5. Kathleen C. Stevens. "The Effect of Background Knowledge on the Reading Comprehension of Ninth Graders." *Journal of Reading Behavior.*

6. James F. Christie, "Syntax: A Key to Reading Comprehension," *Reading Improvement.*

7. Durkin, *Teaching Them to Read,* pp. 394–95.

8. Harris and Smith, *Reading Instruction,* pp. 87–89.

9. Dolores Durkin, "What Is the Value of the New Interest in Reading Comprehension?" *Language Arts.*

10. Spache and Spache, *Reading in the Elementary School,* pp. 450–51.

11. Robert F. Carey, "Toward a More Cognitive Definition of Reading Comprehension," *Reading Horizons* 20 (Summer 1980):293.

12. Hilda Taba, "The Teaching of Thinking," *Elementary English.*

13. Frank J. Guszak, "Teacher Questioning and Reading," *The Reading Teacher.*

14. Benjamin Bloom, et al., *Taxonomy of Educational Objectives—Handbook I: The Cognitive Domain,* pp. 168–72; Norris M. Sanders, *Classroom Questions—What Kinds?* p. 3; Thomas C. Barrett and R. Smith, *Teaching Reading in the Middle Grades.*

15. Michael Strange, "Instructional Implications of a Conceptual Theory of Reading Comprehension," *The Reading Teacher;* Keith E. Stanovich, "Toward an Interactive-Compensatory Model of Individual Differences in the Development of Reading Fluency," *Reading Research Quarterly;* H. Levin and E. L. Kaplan, "Grammatical Structure and Reading," In H. Levin and J. Williams (Eds.), *Basic Studies in Reading;* Kenneth S. Goodman, "Reading: A Psycholinguistic Guessing Game," In Harry Singer and Robert Ruddell (eds.) *Theoretical Models and Processes of Reading* (2nd ed.).

16. Michael Strange, "Instructional Implications . . . Reading Comprehension," p. 392; K. Stanovich, "Toward an Interactive . . . Reading Fluency," p. 33–34; D. LaBerge and S. Jay Samuels, "Toward a Theory of Automatic Information Processing in Reading," *Cognitive Psychology.*

17. Michael Strange, "Instructional Implications . . . Reading Comprehension," p. 393; David Rumelhart, *Toward an Interactive Model of Reading;* Richard Rystrom, "Reflections of Meaning" *Journal of Reading Behavior;* Richard Anderson, Rand Spiro, and Mark Anderson, *Schemata as Scaffolding for the Representation of Information in Connected Discourse.*

18. Durkin, "What Is the . . . Reading Comprehension?" p. 24.

19. Durkin, "What Is the . . . Reading Comprehension?" p. 27.

20. E. Marcia Sheridan, "A Review of Research on Schema Theory and Its Implications for Reading Instruction in Secondary Reading."

21. Bonnie J. F. Meyer, "Structure of Prose: Implications for Teachers of Reading."

22. Edward Thorndike, "Reading and Reasoning: A Study of Mistakes in Paragraph Reading," *Journal of Educational Psychology.*

23. Nila Banton Smith, "Patterns of Writing in Different Subject Areas," *Journal of Reading;* James M. McCallister, "Using Paragraph Clues as Aids to Understanding," *Journal of Reading.*

24. Earl H. Cheek and Martha Collins Cheek, "Organizational Patterns: Untapped Sources for Better Reading," *Reading World.*

25. Martha D. Collins-Cheek, "Organizational Patterns: An Aid to Comprehension," American Reading Forum Proceedings.

26. Barak V. Rosenshine, "Skill Hierarchies in Reading Comprehenson," In Rand J. Spiro, Bertram C. Bruce, William F. Brewer (eds.) *Theoretical Issues in Reading Comprehension.*

27. John E. Readence and Mary McDonnel Harris, "False Prerequisites in the Teaching of Comprehension," *Reading Improvement.*

28. Miles V. Zintz, *The Reading Process,* pp. 231–32; Frank B. May, *Reading as Communication,* pp. 127–44, 160–73; John N. Mangieri, Lois A. Bader, and James E. Walker, *Elementary Reading,* pp. 66–74.

29. Edwin E. Vineyard and Harold W. Massey, "The Interrelationship of Certain Linguistic Skills and Their Relationship with Scholastic Achievement When Intelligence is Ruled Constant," *Journal of Educational Psychology.*

30. Emerald V. Dechant and Henry P. Smith, *Psychology in Teaching Reading,* 2nd ed., p. 254; Mildred A. Dawson and Henry A. Bamman, *Fundamentals of Basic Reading Instruction,* p. 182.

31. Jerome S. Bruner, "The Act of Discovery," *On Knowing,* pp. 81–96.

32. Robert Oakan, Morton Wierner, and Ward Cormer, "Identification, Organization, and Reading Comprehension for Good and Poor Readers," *Journal of Educational Psychology.*

33. Herbert D. Simons, "Linguistic Skills and Reading Comprehension," in *The Quest for Competency in Reading,* p. 165; F. A. Briggs, "Grammatical Sense as a Factor in Reading Comprehension," in *The Psychology of Reading Behavior,* pp. 145–49; Mary Anne Hall and Christopher J. Ramig, *Linguistic Foundations for Reading,* pp. 61–79.

34. James Deese, *Psycholinguistics,* p. 1.

35. Lou E. Burmeister, *From Print to Meaning,* pp. 112–13; Roach Van Allen, *Language Experiences in Communication,* pp. 370–71; Robert Emans, "Use of Context Clues," in *Teaching Word Recognition Skills,* pp. 181–87.

36. Barbara D. Stoodt, "The Relationship Between Understanding Grammatical Conjunctions and Reading Comprehension," *Elementary English.*

37. Harris and Smith, *Reading Instruction,* p. 225.

38. Edna L. Furness, "Pupils, Pedagogues, and Punctuation," *Elementary English.*

39. Durkin, *Teaching Them to Read,* p. 431; Josephine Piekarz Ives, "The Improvement of Critical Reading Skills," in *Problem Areas in Reading—Some Observations and Recommendations,* p. 5; Burns and Roe, *Teaching Reading,* p. 218.

40. Helen M. Robinson, "Developing Critical Readers," in *Dimensions of Critical Reading;* William Eller and Judith G. Wolf, "Developing Critical Reading Abilities," *Journal of Reading.*

41. David H. Russell, *Children's Thinking,* chapter 5.

42. Mary Austin and Coleman Morrison, *The First R: The Harvard Report on Reading in Elementary Schools,* chapter 12.

43. Constance McCullough, "Responses of Elementary School Children to Common Types of Reading Comprehension Questions," *Journal of Educational Research.*

44. Charlotte Agrast, "Teach Them to Read Between the Lines," *Grade Teacher;* Alan R. Harrison, "Critical Reading for Elementary Pupils," *The Reading Teacher.*

45. Agrast, "Teach Them to Read"; Evelyn Wolfe, "Advertising and the Elementary Language Arts," *Elementary English.*

46. Robert R. Nardelli, "Some Aspects of Creative Reading," *Journal of Educational Research.*

47. Jerome A. Niles and Larry A. Harris, "The Context of Comprehension," *Reading Horizons* 22.

48. Molly M. Wilson, "The Effect of Question Types in Varying Placements on the Reading Comprehension of Upper Elementary Students," *Reading Psychology.*

49. Dolores Durkin, "What Classroom Observations Reveal About Reading Comprehension Instruction." *Reading Research Quarterly;* Dolores Durkin, "Reading Comprehension Instruction in Five Basal Reader Series," *Reading Research Quarterly.*

50. Stephen N. Elliot and James L. Carroll. "Strategies to Help Children Remember What They Read," *Reading Improvement.*

51. P. David Pearson and Dale Johnson *Teaching Reading Comprehension.*

52. Michael Strange, "Instructional Implications . . . Reading Comprehension," pp. 394–97.

**Other Suggested Readings**

Adams, Anne H., and Harrison, Cathy B. "Using Television to Teach Specific Reading Skills." *The Reading Teacher* 29 (October 1975):45–51.

Degler, Lois Sauer. "Using the Newspaper to Develop Reading Comprehension Skills." *Journal of Reading* 21 (January 1978):339–42.

Duffelmeyer, Frederick A. "Promoting Reading Comprehension." *Reading Improvement* 17 (Winter 1980):269–71.

Fowler, Elain D., and Lamberg, Walter J. "Effect of Pre-Questions on Oral Reading by Elementary Students." *Reading Improvement* 16 (Spring 1979):71–74.

Gall, M. D.; Ward, B. A.; Berliner, D.C.; Cahen, L. S.; Winne, P. H.; Elashoff, J. D.; and Stanton, G. C. "Effects of Questioning Techniques and Recitation on Student Learning." *American Educational Research Journal* 15 (1978):175–99.

Goodman, Yetta, and Watson, Dorothy J. "A Reading Program to Live With: Focus on Comprehension." *Language Arts* 45 (November-December 1977):868–79.

Guthrie, John, ed. *Cognition, Curriculum and Comprehension.* Newark, Delaware: International Reading Association, 1977.

Hansen, J. "The Effects of Inference Training and Practice on Young Children's Reading Comprehension." *Reading Research Quarterly* 30 (1981):52–64.

Hodges, C. A. "Toward a Broader Definition of Comprehension Instruction." *Reading Research Quarterly* 15 (1980):299–306.

Isakson, Richard L.; Miller, John W.; and O'Harra, Nancy J. "Finding the Main Idea: Can Your Students Do It?" *Reading World* 19 (October 1979):28–35.

Kauchak, Don; Eggen, Paul; and Knollman, Patricia. "Mathemagenic Behaviors: Implications for the Classroom Teacher." *Reading Improvement* 15 (Spring 1978): 60–64.

Lesiak, Judi. "The Origin of Words: A Unit of Study." *Language Arts* 55 (March 1978):317–19.

McKenna, Michael. "Portmanteau Words in Reading Instruction." *Language Arts* 55 (March 1978):315–17.

Reder, Lynne M. "The Role of Elaboration in the Comprehension and Retention of Prose: A Critical Review." *Review of Educational Research* 50 (Spring 1980): 5–53.

Reed, Kathleen. "Improving Comprehension in Content Areas Through Questioning Strategies." *The New England Reading Association Journal* 14 (1979):29–36.

Riley, James D., and Pachtman, Andrew B. "Reading Mathematical Word Problems: Telling Them What to Do Is Not Telling Them How to Do It." *Journal of Reading* 21 (March 1978):531–34.

Schallert, Diane Lemmonier. "The Role of Illustrations in Reading Comprehension." In Rand J. Spiro, Bertram C. Bruce, William F. Brewer (eds.) *Theoretical Issues in Reading Comprehension.* Hillsdale, New Jersey: Lawrence Erlbaum Associates, 1980. pp. 503–24.

Schulwitz, Bonnie Smith, ed. *Teachers, Tangibles, Techniques: Comprehension of Content in Reading.* Newark, Delaware: International Reading Association, 1975.

Singer, Harry. "Active Comprehension: From Answering to Asking Questions." *The Reading Teacher* 31 (May 1978):901–908.

Sloat, K. C. M. "Characteristics of Effective Instruction." *Educational Perspectives* 20 (1981):10–12.

Taschow, Horst G. "How to Teach Critical Reading." *Insights into Why and How to Read.* Edited by Robert T. Williams. Newark, Delaware: International Reading Association, 1976.

Tatham, Susan Masland. "Comprehension Taxonomies: Their Uses and Abuses." *The Reading Teacher* 32 (November 1978):190–94.

Tharp, Roland G. "The Effective Instruction of Comprehension: Results and Description of the Kamehameha Early Education Program." *Reading Research Quarterly* 17 (1982):503–27.

# 12

Just as prereading skills provide a foundation for reading, word recognition skills assist word analysis, and comprehension skills improve thinking abilities, so study skills foster independence in reading. Study skills are intended to help students use reading skills in their daily activities and content areas. For example, skills such as how to organize information, use reference skills, read maps or tables, and use parts of a book are essential to becoming an independent reader. Thus, learning the proper use of study skills becomes another important task in the reading process.

This chapter contains a list of the various study skills, together with research relevant to each area that the teachers at Seabreeze School used in planning prescriptive instruction in the content areas. To provide prescriptive information regarding the development of the study skills, ideas for teaching are included along with specific procedures for diagnosing the study skills. Specific questions which the Seabreeze teachers discussed are:

Why are study skills important?

What are the study skills?

What information does research provide about the development of study skills?

Which diagnostic procedures are most effective in this area?

What are some prescriptive teaching ideas that can be used to develop study skills?

# How are study skills developed through prescriptive teaching?

The significant terms to remember as this chapter is read are listed below.

| | |
|---|---|
| Organizational skills | Specialized vocabulary |
| Reference skills | SQ3R |
| Specialized study skills | Study skills |
| | Typographical aids |

**Vocabulary to Know**

**The Importance of Study Skills**

The development of study skills is extremely important because of the high correlation between knowing how to use the skills and success in reading content materials. One of the first procedures which students must learn when reading content materials is which skills to use to understand the material. Although there is some emphasis on the development of study skills in basal readers, these skills are not fully developed until students become more involved in reading science, literature, social studies, and other content materials.

Study skills are generally not used so much in pleasure reading as they are in learning situations involving content reading assignments. Quite often, completing these assignments is a task that few students enjoy. Smith summarizes quite well the special situation which exemplifies the use of study skills. He states that this is an assignment made by another person, materials are chosen by someone else, and testing will be conducted by this other person.[1] The other person, of course, is the teacher; however, practically speaking, the one who will benefit from the assignments is the student. The result of these assignments should be the development of specific study skills which are ingrained in the student's memory for use as needed.

Much of the responsibility for learning to use study skills effectively rests with the student; however, it is incumbent upon the teacher to provide the necessary instruction if the learning of these skills is to occur. Unfortunately, instruction in this area often does not occur as frequently or with as much emphasis as is required. If students are to learn the effective use of study skills, they must receive carefully planned instruction in a variety of situations in the different content areas, and be provided appropriate assignments to sharpen these skills.

Although material in which these skills must be used becomes more complex as the level increases, the basic application of the study skills remains unchanged. Thus, application in each of the content areas is the key to efficient use of the study skills.

There are various techniques for teaching the study skills. Perhaps the most effective way to instruct students is to demonstrate the skills, although many teachers use inductive approaches such as inquiry, discovery, and problem solving.[2] An integral part of the instructional process, as previously mentioned, is the application of this skill knowledge to materials. Perhaps the use of content materials for this purpose is most efficient.

Study skills are important because they represent a structure of knowledge that must be transferred from one set of materials to another. The structure is adapted to the content dealt with, and allows for the consistent application of these skills to various types of content materials. As a result, students learn to apply these skills with some degree of consistency, thus becoming more independent readers.

In an effort to better understand the complex nature of the process involved in studying and learning, teachers may wish to consider several ideas about this complex act. Four major factors which are determining influences on studying have been identified. They include

1. the nature of the criterion task or goal for which the student is preparing;
2. the nature of the material the student is studying;
3. the cognitive and affective characteristics of the student; and
4. the strategies the student uses to learn the material.[3]

The interaction of these factors in many different ways certainly compounds the difficult task of teaching students how to study.

It is necessary that the student not only be given a purpose for reading by the teacher initially, but also that he or she develop the skill of learning to establish this individual's personal reason or goal for studying. Students can best acquire this skill through the use of study strategies such as SQ3R, which is discussed in Chapter 3.

The second factor affecting studying concerns the materials used by students. Effective content instruction requires the use of textbooks as well as supplementary materials. Because of the special relationship between the use of study skills and the acquisition of knowledge in the various content areas, it is essential that materials be carefully selected and that students understand how the information in the material is organized. Difficulties frequently arise in studying content materials because students are unable to determine which comprehension skills to apply when reading the material. This difficulty results primarily from a lack of understanding of the organization of the material used by the authors. Understanding text structure or organizational patterns is a key to learning the material. For a more thorough discussion of organizational patterns, see Chapter 11.

Because students are different in their learning styles, it is frequently difficult for teacher to identify their various cognitive and affective characteristics. Dunn and Dunn have explored this particular area and have identified four categories consisting of eighteen elements which influence how a student learns. They include

1. The Environmental Elements of Learning Style
    a) Sound: To what extent does background noise enhance or distract the learner?
    b) Light: Is study done best in a low or high lighting environment?
    c) Temperature: Is attention better focused in a warm or cool room?
    d) Design: Is a casual or structured environment preferred for study?
2. The Emotional Elements of Learning Style
    a) Motivation: To what extent do the students perceive a need to learn what they must study?
    b) Persistence: How long can the student work at a task before losing interest or giving up?

**Figure 12.1**
Elements of Learning
Style

Diagnosing Learning Style

| Stimuli | Elements | | | | | |
|---|---|---|---|---|---|---|
| Environmental | Sound | | Light | Temperature | | Design |
| Emotional | Motivation | | Persistence | Responsibility | | Structure |
| Sociological | Peers | Self | Pair | Team | Adult | Varied |
| Physical | Perceptual | | Intake | Time | | Mobility |

Designed by Dr. Rita S. Dunn, Dr. Kenneth J. Dunn

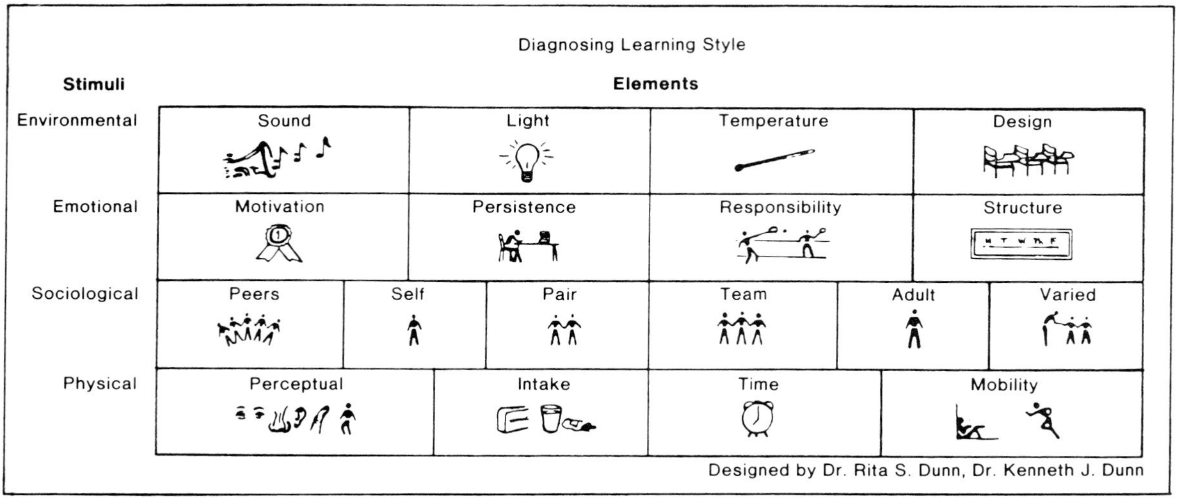

    c) Responsibility: How much direct supervision does the student need in order to complete a task?

    d) Structure: To what extent does the teacher have to organize, manage, and direct the students' learning experience?

3. The Sociological Elements of Learning Style

Does the student learn best in an individual or group situation?

4. The Physical Elements of the Learning Styles

    a) Perceptual: Does the student learn best visually, auditorially, tactually, or through kinesthetic learning?

    b) Intake: Is learning enhanced if the students drink or nibble, or do they learn better when slightly hungry?

    c) Time: At what time during the day does the student prefer to study?

    d) Mobility: How much movement does the student need when studying?[4]

Teachers may wish to consider these elements as a starting point for planning the most appropriate learning environment for students, since the development of study skills is directly related to the cognitive and affective characteristics of the learner.

When study skills are discussed, it is not unusual for the primary topic to indicate whether one strategy is more effective than another in helping the student learn the material. Although notetaking, outlining, summarizing, using book parts, and map reading are useful in the study process, research has failed to substantiate the superiority of one technique over another. What it indicates, however, is that the appropriate study strategy with the right material will enable

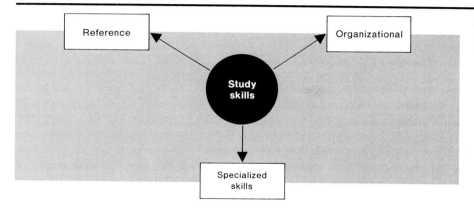

**Figure 12.2**
Categories of Study
Skills

the student to understand the information better, and that if students are taught the use of study strategies, then they must be taught to use the strategy appropriately.[5] Furthermore, research confirms that introducing students who already study effectively to a new strategy, may be harmful rather than helpful.[6] Thus, teachers must know the strengths and weaknesses of their students, so that appropriate instruction in the study skills can be provided.

## Study Skills

The study skills are divided into three basic categories: reference skills, organizational skills, and specialized study skills (see figure 12.2). Each of these skill areas is discussed in more detail in separate sections of this chapter. They also appear in a list later in the chapter, and in appendix A. In addition to a discussion of each skill category, some research is provided to give insight into the importance of the various areas and findings that must be considered in developing the skills.

## Reference Skills

Reference skills are primarily concerned with locating information in various sources. Skills in this category involve learning to use the dictionary and its subskills, using encyclopedias, using specialized reference materials, such as the atlas and the almanac, and using the library card catalog.

Obviously, students need to understand the proper use of all the reference skills in order to gain information necessary for the further understanding of content materials. As students become more involved in the content areas in upper elementary school, the middle school, and the junior high school, these skills become more and more important. Students are frequently given assignments requiring them to locate information which can only be found in reference materials. The use of these skills becomes an indispensable tool for acquiring knowledge.

Unfortunately, many students from the upper elementary through the high school levels lack proficiency in using reference skills; although a summary of British research studies indicates that a majority of students with access to an atlas at home were able to use it to some extent[7]—how many students have an

atlas in their home? When these deficiencies occur, little is gained from criticizing prior instruction in the lower grades; it becomes the responsibility of teachers at these upper levels to improve the students' skills.

Even with appropriate instruction, many students will still experience difficulty in using reference materials effectively because of the readability level of much of the material. When students read on lower instructional levels than their grade placement, reference materials written on an even higher level represent a serious obstacle to acquiring information. Thus, teachers must assist students in using reference materials written at levels that most closely meet their students' reading levels.

Bond and Wagner suggest that skill in locating information in reference materials is dependent upon certain abilities: (1) appraisal of the problem, (2) knowledge of appropriate sources, (3) locating a desired source, (4) using the index and table of contents, and (5) skimming.[8]

Because learning to use reference materials is so vital to the learning process and is one of the primary objectives of the upper elementary grades,[9] Nelson recommends closer cooperation between the librarian and the teacher. She also recommends that games, films, and periodicals, such as *Sports Illustrated* and *Hot Rod,* should be used more in teaching reference skills.[10]

A suggestion for improving the students' skill in using the dictionary, in an effort to relieve some of the boredom, is the use of word games featuring limericks and synonyms.[11]

Learning to use reference skills is essential. Instruction in the various content areas places certain demands on students, requiring some degree of expertise in using reference skills. Without these skills, success will be hampered.

## Organizational Skills

For some students an even more difficult task than learning to use reference skills is developing organizational skills. These require the ability to synthesize and evaluate the material read so that it can be organized into a workable format. A high level of cognition is required. The skills included in this area deal with developing outlines, underlining important points or key ideas, and taking notes during reading.

The need to outline compels students to locate the main idea in a passage and whatever details are essential to its development. The primary purpose of the outline technique is to help students locate the relevant information in a passage or series of materials. It is often suggested as a technique in studying for exams or preparing material for a research paper. Harris recommends teaching the use of outlines prior to teaching note-taking skills,[12] while Hansell found that appropriate training improves the ability to outline.[13]

The skill of underlining is another valuable tool for organizing data and highlighting relevant information. It is also useful in studying for exams and gathering information for research papers. An interesting aspect of underlining is that research has clearly indicated its superiority to outlining in gathering information.[14] It is also clear that underlining key words in a passage increases the likelihood that the information will be remembered.[15]

Note-taking is the third important skill involved in organizing material. It is helpful when attending classes or perhaps listening to a speaker, because the student learns to write down only the important points. The primary task involved in taking notes is to distinguish relevant from irrelevant information. For taking notes, Hafner suggests the following procedures:

1. List the main points with necessary clarifying statements.
2. List illustrations (graphic and verbal) and experiments useful for clarifying points.
3. List key terms and their definitions.
4. List terms or concepts that need further clarification.[16]

According to various research studies, notetaking appears to be a useful skill for students to develop as a technique for acquiring important information in both text material and in listening situations.[17]

The importance of these organizational skills cannot be overemphasized. They play a major role in successful reading. Research clearly indicates that training in these skills improves success in content reading, and that many students in the content areas are deficient in these skills.[18]

## Specialized Study Skills

The specialized study skills are essential in obtaining as much information as possible from a book or other materials. In this particular skill area, all parts of a book or materials are analyzed to determine what information can be obtained from them and how best to understand the information presented. Some skills included in this area are previewing; scanning and skimming materials; reading maps, tables, graphs, and diagrams; adjusting rate according to material and purpose; and using appropriate study techniques, such as SQ3R.

Previewing, scanning, and skimming content materials are valuable tools for learning about the organizational structure of materials, determining whether or not the information is useful, locating details, and determining the main ideas. Research indicates that previewing is especially valuable as an initial step in reading, and that instruction in how to read and interpret subheadings when previewing is essential.[19]

Another very important skill, especially in social studies, science, and math, is concerned with reading maps, tables, graphs, and diagrams. Unfortunately, research does not indicate clearly the order in which these subskills should be presented; however, no one disputes their usefulness.[20]

Adjusting rate according to the material and purpose is a third valuable skill that students must learn. Rate should be adjusted according to the difficulty level of the material and the purpose for which it is being read. For example, students should realize that they do not read a comic book in the same manner or at the same rate as they read their social studies book. Hafner and Jolly suggest that an appropriate rate is the maximum comfortable speed at which one can read and still understand the passage.[21]

A fourth valuable skill in reading content material is using appropriate study techniques, such as SQ3R (chapter 3). These techniques are being used more widely by teachers, and research indicates that they are being used successfully, especially SQ3R,[22] which was developed by Robinson.[23]

Learning the proper use of study skills is essential to the reading process. These skills are particularly vital to comprehension of content materials. Without the ability to organize materials, use the dictionary, outline, understand specialized vocabulary, use parts of a book, read maps and charts, and the many other skills, learning to read content-related material is a very difficult task.

## Prescriptive Teaching of Study Skills

The last section of this chapter explores two concepts. The first relates to diagnostic procedures for the teachers' use. The second concerns the application of prescriptive techniques to the various study skill areas. Each of these concepts is explored individually in a table format.

Since the importance of diagnosis is evident, the first concept presented concerns the application of appropriate diagnostic procedures to the various skill areas (see table 12.1). Each primary skill is represented, allowing the teacher to use the table efficiently. Unfortunately, the lack of formal diagnostic procedures related to study skills to some extent impedes diagnosis; however, using informal diagnostic procedures does yield much specific information, which is of great value to the teacher.

Since so few diagnostic procedures are available as compared to the other skill areas, all of the study skills are listed together with the appropriate corresponding diagnostic procedures. In some instances, the diagnostic tools specify a particular study skill area that is measured. Those instances are clearly noted in the table.

The diagnostic procedures presented in table 12.1 give information that can be used in diagnosing students' strengths and weaknesses in the study skills. When this diagnostic information has been used by the teacher, the next step is the implementation of a prescriptive program.

**Table 12.1**

Diagnostic Procedures for Evaluating Study Skill Areas

| Skill Areas | Procedures |
|---|---|
| **Reference, Organizational, and Specialized Study Skills** | *California Achievement Test* (Reference Skills) |
| | *Comprehensive Test of Basic Skills* |
| | Criterion-referenced tests |
| | Group Reading Inventory |
| | *Iowa Silent Reading Test* (Directed Reading Subtest measuring Dictionary, Library, Locational, Skimming, Scanning, and Encyclopedia skills) |
| | Observation checklist |

Prescriptive techniques for use in the classroom are presented in the final portion of this chapter. Each of the major study skill areas is divided according to specific skills, with activities presented to assist teachers in their instructional programs. These ideas are presented in table 12.2.

**Table 12.2**
Study Skills

| Skill | Prescriptive Technique |
|---|---|
| **Reference Skills** | |
| *Use dictionary* | Divide the group into teams. Call out a word and see which group can locate the word first. They must give the guide words in order to score a point. |
| | Give students a pronunciation key from the dictionary and a list of words spelled using the symbols from the pronunciation key. Take turns pronouncing the words using the appropriate accent. |
| *Use encyclopedia* | Put various topics on slips of paper and let students select one. Ask them to find the appropriate encyclopedia to locate information on the topic. Then identify five important facts about the topic. |
| | Play a game with the students taking turns being the librarian. The other students select prepared questions or make up questions to ask the librarian. When the librarian locates the answer in the encyclopedia, another student becomes the librarian. |
| *Use specialized reference materials* | Give students cards that tell about a trip they have won. Use an atlas to determine the roads they should take to get to their destination. |
| | Use questions that students prepare and that can be answered with an almanac. Let a student ask a question and see who can locate the information first. The winner gets to ask the next question. |
| *Use library card catalog* | Give assignments that can be answered from the card catalog. Let students work in teams to locate the information requested. |
| | Ask students to prepare questions that other students may answer using the card catalog. Different classes may exchange their questions and have contests. |
| **Organizational Skills** | |
| *Develop outlines* | Prepare a large model of an outline, omitting the words. Tape it to the floor or the wall. Give students the information that could complete the outline. Let them fill in the blanks. |
| | Give students sentence strips containing information that could be put together to form an outline. Ask them to develop the outline. Two groups may compete to see who can finish first. They may then write a story from the outline. |

**Table 12.2**

Study Skills (continued)

| Skill | Prescriptive Technique |
|-------|------------------------|
| *Underline important points or key ideas* | Give each team a short selection and a red pen. Get them to discuss and agree upon the important points that should be remembered and underlined. |
| | Use several copies of a selection and ask students to underline the key ideas. Then compare what each student marked. For any points that differ, ask the student to explain why they were underlined. |
| *Take notes during reading* | Ask students to take notes as they read by listing important points. Then ask them to use their notes to report what they read to another student. Let them check one another to be sure all important points were covered. |
| | Let students read different sections of a chapter and take notes. Then combine the notes to see if the most important information is included as they use the notes to answer questions. |

**Specialized Study Skills**

| Skill | Prescriptive Technique |
|-------|------------------------|
| *Use title page* | Give students several title pages and a list of questions that can be answered using the title page. Keep score as to who can answer the most questions. |
| | Ask each student to develop one question that can be answered from the title page. Let them ask the question of the class. When all the questions are answered, ask students to work in pairs and design their own title page. |
| *Use table of contents and lists of charts* | Play a game in which students give clues to locate information in the table of contents. For example, "I'm looking for the page number for the story, 'The Gray Fox.'" |
| | Give students a book without the table of contents and ask them to make one to go with the book. |
| *Locate introduction, preface, and foreword* | Have a treasure hunt in the classroom to locate books containing an introduction, preface, or foreword. Award one point for each one with an introduction, two points for each preface, three points for each foreword, and four bonus points for a book with all three components. |
| | Go through a book containing two or three of these components and develop questions from the information provided. To answer the questions, students must read the information in the book. |
| *Use appendix* | Give students materials that refer them to the appendices in the material. Ask them to follow the reference and locate specific information in the designated appendix. |

**Table 12.2**
Study Skills (continued)

| Skill | Prescriptive Technique |
|---|---|
| | Play "I Am Looking For" by telling the students things that you are looking for. All the information should be located in one of the appendices in a book that they have. |
| *Identify bibliography and lists of suggested readings* | After reading material in a book containing a list of suggested readings, refer the students to this list and ask them to select the two readings that seem most interesting to them and tell why they seem interesting.<br>Ask students to look at the bibliography in a book and find one or more of the materials listed in the bibliography. Then look at the material and determine what the author used from this source in writing the material. |
| *Use glossary and index* | Give students a crossword puzzle using words from the glossary in the book. In order to complete the puzzle, the student must use the glossary.<br>Ask students questions that can be answered from a book. However, to answer the questions they must locate the information in the index of the book. |
| *Use study questions* | Direct students to use the study questions to help establish their purposes for reading a material. They may try to answer the questions prior to reading the material and then answer them after they read.<br>Let students read a material and develop study questions that would aid other students as they read the material. |
| *Read maps, tables, graphs, and diagrams* | Draw a map to be followed as students go on a treasure hunt around the classroom or school. As they reach certain points, other maps are given until they find the one that directs them to the hidden treasure.<br>Get one group in the class to make a graph or table about the class, the weather, or something of interest to the students. Then let this group explain to the others in the class how the information can be read. |
| *Use footnotes, typographical aids, and marginal notes* | Give students a material containing footnotes and ask them to answer a question from the information in a footnote. For example, "What is the first page of the information that the author used in this reference?"<br>Ask students to make an outline of a chapter using only the words in bold and italic type. Then ask them to read the chapter to see if these were actually the most important ideas. |

| Skill | Prescriptive Technique |
|---|---|
| *Preview, skim, or scan materials* | Give students a short selection and two questions that can be answered from the selection. Allow them a very short time to skim the material to locate the answer.<br><br>Ask students to preview a chapter before they read it and list at least two questions that they want to answer as they read the material. |
| *Adjust rate according to material and purpose* | Give students two selections to read, one technical and one light narrative. Ask them to choose a selection and tell how quickly they will read it by placing a SLOW or FAST sign on their desk.<br><br>Prior to each reading activity, ask students why they are reading the material and at what rate the material should be read according to their purpose. Let them keep a log for several days to note the material, the purpose for reading it, and the rate. |
| *Understand general and specialized vocabulary* | Develop a vocabulary bank that contains all new words learned in each class. Each card in the bank should contain the word, the definition, and a sentence. If the word is general or relates to every content area, a red line should be placed across the card; if it relates to math, a blue line, and so on for each subject area. Words relating to several areas would have the various definitions and colors on the card.<br><br>Identify all vocabulary words in each lesson that may cause problems in reading the material. Discuss these words and their meanings as used in the context of the material. Use the newspaper and search for the words to see if they can be used to mean other things. |
| *Use appropriate study techniques, such as SQ3R* | Make a large sign to hang as a mobile in the classroom to remind the students to use the appropriate study technique as they read. Periodically review the study technique with the students to encourage them to use the procedure correctly.<br><br>As students are introduced to the different study procedures appropriate to particular content areas, tell them they will have their own codes or formulas that other classes in the school will not know. These formulas, such as SQ3R, will help them read the content material more easily. Then continuously use the "code" language with them to encourage its use. |

Each of the preceding tables represents an effort to provide diagnostic-prescriptive information in a format that is usable and that will enhance teachers' effectiveness in developing study skills.

**Summary**

Study skills provide the essential structure for the acquisition of knowledge from the printed page. The development of these skills is crucial to becoming an independent reader with the ability to comprehend specific information, especially from the various content materials.

The three primary categories of study skills are reference, organizational, and specialized study skills. Various techniques for teaching these skills include demonstration, inquiry, discovery, and problem solving.

Reference skills involve such skills as using the dictionary, encyclopedias, and library card catalog, while organizational skills include outlining, underlining, and note-taking. The third category, specialized study skills, stresses learning skills, such as how to use parts of a book, previewing, skimming, scanning, and SQ3R.

Diagnostic-prescriptive procedures and techniques were presented in tables to provide specific information to teachers for use in their classrooms.

**Applying What You Read**

You are the language arts teacher for the sixth grade. The students have difficulty in using materials in the library. Which skills would you need to develop, and how would you go about it?

Study skills are used most often in the content areas. How can the content teacher develop these skills? Select one content area and some specific study skills to use as an example.

Design a study skills program that would involve all the content teachers in your school. Decide how diagnostic data will be obtained, and which content areas will be used to develop and review the specific skills.

**Notes**

1. Carl B. Smith, *Teaching in Secondary School Content Subjects,* p. 252.
2. Larry A. Harris and Carl B. Smith, *Reading Instruction: Diagnostic Teaching in the Classroom,* p. 334.
3. Bonnie B. Armbruster and Thomas H. Anderson, "Research Synthesis on Study Skills," *Educational Leadership,* p. 154.
4. Rita Dunn and Kenneth Dunn, *Teaching Students Through Their Individual Learning Styles,* 1978, pp. 5–17. Reprinted with permission of Reston Publishing Co., a Prentice-Hall Co., 11480 Sunset Hills Road, Reston, VA 22090.
5. Bonnie B. Armbruster and Thomas H. Anderson, "Research Synthesis on Study Skills," p. 155.
6. B. Y. L. Wong and W. Jones, "Increasing Metacomprehension in Learning Disabled and Normally-Achieving Students Through Self-Questioning Training."
7. Herbert A. Sandford, "Directed and Free Search of the School Atlas Map," *The Cartographic Journal.*
8. Guy L. Bond and Eva B. Wagner, *Teaching The Child To Read,* 4th ed., Chapters 10–11.
9. Ryland W. Crary, *Humanizing The School: Curriculum Development and Theory,* p. 195.

10. Raedeane M. Nelson, "Getting Children into Reference Books," *Elementary English,* 884–87.
11. Mary Louise Labe, "Improve the Dictionary's Image," *Elementary English.*
12. Albert J. Harris and Edward R. Sipay, *How To Increase Reading Ability,* 6th ed., p. 491.
13. T. Stevenson Hansell, "Stepping Up to Outlining," *Journal of Reading.*
14. James Crewe and Dayton Hullgren, "What Does Research Really Say About Study Skills?" in *The Psychology of Reading Behavior,* pp. 75–78.
15. James Hartley, Sally Bartlett, and Alan Branthwaite, "Underlining Can Make a Difference-Sometimes," *Journal of Educational Research.*
16. Lawrence E. Hafner, *Developmental Reading in Middle and Secondary Schools: Foundations, Strategies, and Skills for Teaching,* p. 176.
17. James W. Dyer, James Riley, and Frank Yekovich, "An Analysis of Three Study Skills: Notetaking, Summarizing, and Rereading," *Journal of Educational Research;* Vincent P. Orlando, "Notetaking vs. Notehaving: A Comparison While Studying From Text," In Michal L. Kamil and Alden J. Moe (eds.) "Reading Research: Studies and Applications," *Twenty-eighth Yearbook of the National Reading Conference,* pp. 177–81; Carol A. Carrier and Amy Titus, "Effects of Notetaking Pretraining and Test Mode Expectations on Learning from Lectures," *American Educational Research Journal.*
18. George D. Spache and Evelyn B. Spache, *Reading in the Elementary School,* 4th ed., p. 291.
19. Spache and Spache, *Reading in the Elementary School,* p. 278; J. K. Hirstendahl, "The Effect of Subheads on Reader Comprehension," *Journalism Quarterly.*
20. Spache and Spache, *Reading in the Elementary School,* p. 282.
21. Lawrence E. Hafner and Hayden B. Jolly, *Patterns of Teaching Reading in the Elementary School,* p. 176.
22. Abby Adams, Douglas Carnine, and Russell Gersten, "Instructional Strategies for Studying Content Area Texts in the Intermediate Grades," *Reading Research Quarterly.*
23. Francis P. Robinson, *Effective Study,* 4th ed.

**Other Suggested Readings**

Ankney, Paul, and McClurg, Pat. "Testing Manzo's Guided Reading Procedure." *The Reading Teacher* 34 (March 1981):681–85.
Cushenberry, Donald C. "Effective Procedures for Teaching Reference Study Skills." *Reading Horizons* 19 (Spring 1979):245–47.
Earle, Richard A. *Teaching Reading and Mathematics.* Newark, Delaware: International Reading Association, 1976.
Fay, Leo. "How Can We Develop Reading Study Skills for the Different Curriculum Areas?" *Individualized Reading Instruction: A Reader.* Edited by Larry A. Harris and Carl B. Smith. New York: Holt, Rinehart and Winston, 1972.
Fry, Edward. "Graphical Literacy." *Journal of Reading* 24 (February 1981):383–90.
Levin, Joel R.; Berry, Jill Kessley; Miller, Gloria E.; and Bartell, Nina P. "More on How (and How Not) to Remember the States and Their Capitals." *The Elementary School Journal* 82 (March 1982):379–88.
Laughlin, Rosemary M. "Fun in the Word Factory: Exercises with the Dictionary." *Language Arts* 55 (March 1978):310–21.

Lundstrum, John P., and Taylor, Bob L. *Teaching Reading in the Social Studies.* Urbana, Illinois: ERIC Clearinghouse on Reading and Communication Skills, 1978.

Mattleman, Marciene S., and Blake, Howard E. "Study Skills: Prescriptions for Survival." *Language Arts* 54 (November–December 1977):925–27.

Norton, Donna E. "A Web of Interest." *Language Arts* 54 (November–December 1977):928–32.

Riley, James D., and Dyer, James. "The Effects of Notetaking While Reading or Listening." *Reading World* 19 (October 1979):51–56.

Thelen, Judith. *Improving Reading in Science.* Newark, Delaware: International Reading Association, 1983.

Thompson, Mark E. "Flexibility: A Key Element for Reading and Study Skills Specialists." *Reading Horizons* 21 (Summer 1981):252–57.

# 13

Up to this point, some teachers at Seabreeze perceived prescriptive reading instruction as involving strictly the teaching of individual skills. This is definitely not true in a good diagnostic-prescriptive reading program. The major component which distinguishes a skill-development program from a diagnostic-prescriptive program is that of personal reading. Until students have the opportunity to use reading skills in a reading situation and choose to read, the program has not fulfilled all of its objectives.

Personal reading development is not included in all classes at Seabreeze School. This was vividly pointed out as one of the students eagerly told a class visitor that she was working on compound words in reading. When asked what she used these skills for, the student replied, "I don't know, but I get a check mark when I finish the game!" Without personal reading skills, the word recognition, comprehension, and study skills remain fragmented parts that do not contribute to the development of a mature reader.

To provide ideas regarding the incorporation of personal reading skills into the diagnostic-prescriptive program, this chapter is designed to answer the following questions:

What is personal reading?

Why is personal reading important in a diagnostic-prescriptive reading program?

How is personal reading developed?

How does personal reading relate to the other reading skills?

How can students be motivated to read?

What are some techniques for developing personal reading habits?

# Why are personal reading skills included in prescriptive teaching?

While reading this chapter, note the following terms.

Affective domain
Bibliotherapy
Creative reading

Personal reading
Recreational reading
Sustained silent reading

**Vocabulary to Know**

**Personal Reading**

Recreational reading, reading for enjoyment, and application of reading skills are terms sometimes used when referring to personal reading. Regardless of what this crucial area is called, the idea is the same. In personal reading, students apply all their reading skill knowledge to decode words and interpret the printed symbol in order to increase their enjoyment and knowledge.

Students who have mastered the prereading, word recognition, comprehension, and study skills, yet do not use these skills to enrich their lives, need prescriptive instruction in personal reading, just as do students who have difficulty in understanding cause-effect relationships. Unless students perceive the learning of reading skills as an aid in reading materials and developing a lifetime habit of reading, then their skill knowledge is little more than isolated learning and is of little benefit. Therefore, teachers and students should continuously remind themselves that skill knowledge in reading is a *means* of assisting the student to learn the necessary fundamentals in order to develop personal reading habits. Students learn to read by reading.

In a diagnostic-prescriptive reading program, teachers and students sometimes become so involved with skill development that the application of the skills in personal reading becomes secondary. Teachers and administrators must make personal reading the major goal of the school reading program and demonstrate to students that reading is more than skill development. This point cannot be overemphasized, as the authors noted in working with approximately sixty second and third graders. When asked to draw a picture of what reading meant to them, two drew a picture of the teacher reading to a class, five drew themselves

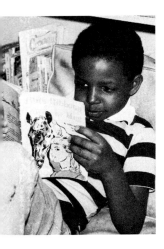

reading books on their own, and the remainder showed skill development activities ranging from the basal reader groups to doing worksheets! Thus, the prescriptive reading program must include reading experiences which are meaningful and which help students want to read.

The following five areas of personal reading must be included for all students in the prescriptive program (see figure 13.1):

*Enjoy and respond to stories and poems read by others.*

This is a personal reading skill that is begun at a very young age, prior to school entrance, as parents read to their children. This should be a pleasant experience and initiate enjoyment of the rhythm of language as well as the information from the story. Teachers should continue to read to students in order to broaden their background of experience and to motivate them to read on their own.

*Read materials for enjoyment.*

This includes reading books, comic books, or any material which gives the student pleasure. These materials are usually written at the student's independent reading level.

*Read materials to gain information.*

Students should appreciate using the reading skills to gain information. This may include using reference materials, reading books and magazines, brochures, or any other printed material.

*Learn more about self through reading.*

As students read they learn about other people, their joys and sorrows as well as how they cope in life situations. This knowledge of others not only teaches the students about life, it also helps them learn more about themselves as they face daily life situations. Books which relate to situations a student can identify with often help in dealing with problems or experiences the student is facing.

*Share enjoyment of reading with others.*

The student who has fully developed personal reading habits not only reads, but also shares with others the ideas gained from the materials.

Personal reading involves the reading skills in the affective domain, while skills in the other areas emphasize the cognitive aspect of reading. In order for students to succeed with the cognitive skills, the affective domain must be considered. This includes not only learning to enjoy reading, but also the development of a positive self-image. Pryor suggests that "changing a poor reader's self-concept by bolstering his feeling about himself is perhaps the first step toward improving the academic problem."[1] Additional ideas regarding the interrelationship of self-concept and reading are presented by Quandt.[2] This affective component of reading aids in the development of interests, attitudes, and personal values, as well as in reading for information and enjoyment. These areas are addressed more specifically in the following pages. It is sufficient to say at this time that teachers must use informal measures along with their own knowledge of children to diagnose a student's status in the development of personal reading skills and to provide the proper direction for growth in the affective areas.

**Figure 13.1**
Goals of Personal
Reading Skill
Development in a
Diagnostic-Prescriptive
Reading Program

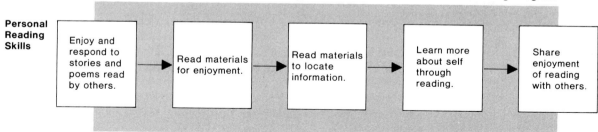

**Personal Reading Skills**

Enjoy and respond to stories and poems read by others. → Read materials for enjoyment. → Read materials to locate information. → Learn more about self through reading. → Share enjoyment of reading with others.

Motivating students to read is probably a greater challenge to teachers than teaching the cognitive skills in reading. Motivation to learn involves two basic components: interests and attitudes. There is no simple way to motivate students, but much can be done to interest them in reading.

Attitudes can be improved by providing appropriate instruction in an exciting manner, rewarding the student with words of praise, using appropriate techniques, and providing materials which are interesting and written at the appropriate level.

Much research has been conducted regarding students' reading interests.[3] From this vast amount of information teachers have attempted to select materials based on the age level of the students. Weintraub concluded that no single category of books will give children of the same age what they want to read. Thus, he suggests that each teacher identify the unique reading interests of the students in the classroom and select books with this knowledge in mind. This procedure was discussed in chapter 4, and a sample interest inventory appears in appendix E.

Moray presented a summary of the research in the area of reading interests. She concludes that:

Sex is a more important factor than intelligence, race, grade, or economic level in determining reading preferences at each age and grade level.

At the age of 9 or 10, girls will read books that interest boys, but boys will not read books that interest girls.

Teachers must be aware of individual student interests, rather than relying on broad generalizations.

Materials other than textbooks must be included in the reading program, as basals do not contain the variety of stories necessary to meet the identified interests of students.

Although reading interests vary from student to student, in a review of research relating to student's reading interests, Huus found several patterns which may be helpful in motivating students to read. She noted that primary level students like animals, home and family, make-believe, and cowboys as topics, but they also express interest in history and science informational materials. Through the middle years of elementary school, although sex differences in interests appear, both boys and girls like mystery, animals, adventure, comics, and humor. Huus also observed that interests in reading appear to have changed little over the years, and that the factors which affect reading interest are sex, age, literary quality, and the reading program.[4]

If teachers expect students to develop personal reading skills, they must provide interesting materials. This includes not only library books, but also magazines, newspapers, and comic books. The latter will sometimes interest students in reading; they seem to be more fun to read because they differ from the traditional school reading materials.[5] Developing an interest in some material and allowing the student to complete the material successfully is a motivating experience that will begin to change negative attitudes towards reading.

Alexander and Filler identify several variables which seem to be associated with attitudes toward reading: These are: achievement, self-concept, parents and the home environment, the teacher and classroom environment, instructional practices and special programs, sex, test intelligence, socioeconomic status, and interests.[6] As teachers attempt to improve students' attitudes toward reading, these ideas should be kept in mind:

> In order to have a positive feeling toward themselves and what they are doing, students must be successful and be commended for their efforts. Reading is no exception. Materials should be appropriate for the students' reading levels.
>
> Teachers need to be aware of the students' attitudes toward reading. This can be learned from observation and possibly through the use of a more formal attitude inventory. Some questions relating to attitude toward reading are included in the interest inventory instrument in appendix E.
>
> A student's attitude toward reading material affects comprehension of the material. For example, the student who does not like social studies but enjoys science will probably read science material with greater understanding than social studies material.
>
> Initial attitudes towards reading are formed by parents and the home environment. This factor must be accepted and an effort made to help parents realize the effect of their attitude on the student's progress in reading.
>
> Parental cooperation is extremely important in overcoming negative attitudes toward reading.
>
> Schools can communicate either positive or negative feelings about reading. Teachers who are enthusiastic about reading, classrooms which invite students to read, and a program which stresses reading as an exciting part of the school, greatly assist in the development of positive attitudes toward reading.

Flexible grouping and varied instruction are more conducive to improving attitudes toward reading than rigid ability groups.[7]

Teachers must be cautious about making generalizations regarding students' attitudes toward reading. Girls do not necessarily have better attitudes toward reading than boys,[8] just as brighter students do not always have a better attitude than less intelligent students.[9] Moreover, teachers should not assume that students from lower socioeconomic backgrounds are more likely to have negative attitudes toward reading.[10]

Roettger found that high attitude/low performance students viewed reading as important to life survival while low attitude/high performance students perceived reading as a means of personal improvement and academic success. Both groups felt, however, that too little time and concern was given to personal reading in their classrooms.[11]

In order to teach the cognitive reading skills, teachers must motivate students to read. This means increasing interests and improving attitudes toward reading. The following section presents more ideas that can be used in the prescriptive teaching of personal reading skills.

## Techniques for Developing Personal Reading Skills

Motivate students to read, persuade students to be excited about reading, improve their attitudes toward reading—how many times do teachers hear these requests! In the area of personal reading, it is difficult to identify specific skills and to assess specific strengths or weaknesses; likewise it is difficult to suggest definite ways to develop the skills. This is because (1) the behaviors are not easily identifiable and (2) students respond differently. Teachers find, as they review activity books such as those listed in appendix D, that most suggestions are directed toward the development of cognitive skills, but few ideas are presented for the personal reading skills.

To assist teachers in developing these personal reading skills, this section presents ideas that can be used in improving the classroom atmosphere through the use of activities, bibliotherapy, and creative reading. Teachers must remember to share ideas with parents in order to derive maximum benefit from the school activities.

## Classroom Atmosphere

It is the first day of school, as students go into their classroom they notice it is clean and colorful. The bulletin boards invite them into the room and give clues that learning will be fun this year. Book jackets and words indicating that reading is important are displayed throughout the room. In a back corner is a rug with bright cushions scattered around. Several shelves of books, magazines, comic books, and even a newspaper arouse the curiosity of the students. How soon can they go to the corner and stretch out on the floor to read a magazine?

The atmosphere in this room is conducive to the development of personal reading skills. However, the teacher must plan for the students to obtain maximum benefit from these resources. Each student must have time to look at books every day, to expand interests in reading, and to use the reading skills which are being taught. These things do not just happen; the teacher must, through careful planning, structure the opportunities and instruction, yet make it appear to be unstructured learning.

To provide students with opportunities to read and to see others read, many teachers are using USSR (Uninterrupted Sustained Silent Reading), SSR (Substantial or Sustained Silent Reading), or SQRT (Sustained Quiet Reading Time) in their classrooms. This procedure may be used with a total classroom or a total school so as to involve everyone in reading. In attaining this objective the key to the success is that *everyone* be involved. If the idea is used in a total school, all of the students, teachers, administrators, and staff must observe the time and read some material silently for a designated ten to fifteen minutes per day or at least twice a week. This brief time for silent reading is not a break for the teacher to plan or grade papers, or for the principal to check to see who is following directions. It is a time for reading or looking at a book. This procedure can serve as a motivational tool for many students if it is introduced in a positive manner and if everyone reads. The principal may want to read with various classes so that students can see another adult reading model. After the designated time for reading, the students proceed with their other work unless someone wants to share what was read. This is not a requirement and is done only if initiated by the student and for only a brief period of time.

A classroom teacher may wish to initiate this idea for fifteen minutes one day a week to begin motivating students to read on their own. The time can be increased as students become more familiar with the procedure, and it may be expanded to include the entire school. This uninterrupted silent reading time is provided to allow students time to experience the joys of silent reading and to begin to develop good reading habits.

A modification of SSR may be used with beginning readers. "Booktime" should be held at the same time each day, beginning with one to five minutes per group and progressing to ten to fifteen minutes. The teacher works with five to seven students at a time and places books into a reading center area which have been introduced by the teacher as stories are read to the class. Just as in SSR, the teacher reads while the students read, but she may also answer questions and pronounce words as the students request. During "Booktime" the students may read in pairs and talk quietly about the books.[12]

Another inviting way to motivate students to read in their extra time is through the use of a reading area or center in the classroom. This classroom library should contain a variety of books displayed in an interesting manner. The center may have some paperbacks in a book rack along with the books borrowed from the school library. The teacher may add a rug and some large pillows to make the area more exciting. The authors have seen many motivating reading centers in classrooms at all levels. Some teachers add old bathtubs or sofas to encourage students to relax as they read. Another idea is to add a tree house in one corner of the room. This may consist of a large tree limb planted in a container with paper leaves on which new words are written. More elaborate tree houses may be made by painting a large tree on the wall and ceiling, then building a small platform where students can sit while they read.

Some teachers may build a "reading shack" in their reading area. This is made of a wooden, house-shaped frame covered with chicken wire. Cushions on the floor enable the students to sit comfortably as they read in a more isolated environment.

In addition to a motivating reading area, teachers can enhance the classroom atmosphere by using colorful bulletin boards that encourage students to read. These displays are changed frequently and may be done by students as a way of sharing what they read. Other ideas for motivating students to read are presented by Fennimore, Roeder and Lee, and Johns and Lunt.[13]

The physical classroom atmosphere has a marked effect on student interest in reading. Desk arrangement, grouping procedures, reading centers, and displays can work to encourage or to deter reading progress. However, teachers should remember that the classroom atmosphere also includes teacher-student relationships, teacher attitude toward reading, and the overall attitude of the teacher concerning the school and the students. An attractive room will not overcome a negative teacher attitude. Thus, the classroom teacher must be positive about learning and show a feeling of concern about meeting the individual reading needs of each student. When both students and teachers feel good about where they are, the atmosphere is more conducive to learning.

## Bibliotherapy

Bibliotherapy is defined as "getting the right book to the right child at the right time."[14] This procedure is used to help students acquire insight into areas of interest or problems that they may be facing. It is a way of providing therapy through books. For example, the student whose parents are getting a divorce may get some help in dealing with the problem by reading *It's Not the End of the World,* by Judy Blume (Bantam Press, 1972), or *The Boys and Girls Book About Divorce,* by Richard A. Gardner, M.D. (Bantam Press, 1970), or *Chloris and the Creeps,* by Kin Platt (Dell, 1973). Huck suggests that the three processes in bibliotherapy correspond to the three phases of psychotherapy: identification, catharsis, and insight. In the identification phase, the student associates self with another person. Catharsis is the release of the emotion in some manner. Insight is the emotional awareness to deal with the problem.[15]

The classroom teacher can use bibliotherapy to interest students in reading by guiding them to materials that relate to their particular needs. This may motivate them to read more on their own in order to identify with others in similar situations. Thus, bibliotherapy is another way to assist students in developing personal reading skills. A bibliography of books that may be used in bibliotherapy is provided in appendix K.

## Creative Reading

As the cognitive reading skills are developed, students are encouraged to react to the printed word by expressing their own ideas about what they have read. This expression of feeling may be done through dramatics, writing, art, music, or thought. Creative reading is based on an expansion of the cognitive comprehension skills into the affective areas of individual reaction and expression.

Many students expand their personal reading skills because of the enjoyment of expressing their interpretation about what the author has said. Language arts activities, including creative thinking, are often used to enhance the development of creative reading skills. Turner and Alexander have suggested:

> A classroom environment in which reading is perceived by the teacher as a creative activity will be more likely to develop in children a view that reading is a fascinating and wonderful adventure. This concept of reading will not easily be lost in later years. But if it is not instilled early in school experiences, it will be even more difficult to gain in upper grades.[16]

Turner and Alexander suggest four areas that need to be considered in developing creative reading:

The types of reading materials that provide the best stimulus for creative thinking.

Ways of structuring oral questions and discussions to help students think creatively about reading.

Reading tasks that open rather than close doors to productive creative thoughts.

Environments that encourage creative behavior.

Teachers must provide opportunities for students to read creatively as another means of developing personal reading skills. Although creative reading is sometimes viewed as the highest-level cognitive skill, it is to be developed even with beginning readers so as to encourage their expression and reaction to the printed word. Activities such as role playing, dramatics, puppetry, composition, pantomime, and dance may be used to enhance the development of creative reading skills and to motivate students to apply the reading skills.

Personal reading is the culmination of the development of reading skills. Teachers must use many techniques to interest students in reading as a personal habit rather than just an assigned task. Materials such as paperback books seem to improve students' attitudes toward reading.[17] Bissett as well as Burger, Cohen, and Bisgaler found that by making books available and encouraging students to read them, the amount of personal reading triples.[18] Bamberger has pointed out that in areas throughout the world where personal reading habits have remained highly developed, the school library is the hub of the curriculum.[19] Thus, teachers should realize the importance of using many strategies to encourage personal reading. Strickler summarizes personal reading ideas as follows:

Use the students' interests in planning instruction.

Assure the students' success in the mastery of reading skills and strategies.

Help students discover their own purposes for reading.

Read often to the students.

Carefully select books for the literature program, using children's literature to supplement the curriculum.

Be an enthusiastic model of reading habits.

Fill bookshelves in the classroom.

Provide time for independent reading.

Encourage students to read and share what they have read.

Develop a literature program to help students realize the potential literature has for widening their world.[20]

## Summary

Personal reading is an integral part of diagnostic-prescriptive instruction. Too much stress on skill development without adequate opportunities for application of these skills makes learning a boring process for students. This is especially desirable, since one of the primary goals of reading instruction is to enable students to read for pleasure as well as to gain information.

Fostering personal reading in the classroom enables the teacher to develop the affective domain, in addition to the skills-oriented cognitive domain. This is important in developing a student's self-concept and awareness. It also plays a major role in motivating students by using high-interest books and other materials.

Developing personal reading skills is not an easy task. In order to facilitate this task, it is necessary to motivate students, to excite them about reading, and to build upon their interests. Some techniques for achieving this goal are: enhancing the classroom atmosphere, using bibliotherapy, and encouraging creative reading.

The successful development of personal reading in the classroom will provide much needed pleasure for students and will certainly increase the effectiveness of the diagnostic-prescriptive reading program. A bibliography of high interest children's books is found in appendix L.

## Applying What You Read

You have a group of students who seem to be developing their word recognition and comprehension skills adequately; however, they are somewhat unenthusiastic about learning to read. Outline a program to develop their personal reading habits.

The atmosphere within a classroom frequently affects learning in either a positive or negative manner. Give some specific examples of how your classroom could be changed to promote a more positive atmosphere toward reading.

Using bibliotherapy in your classroom can exert a positive influence on the students. In order to implement this, go to the library, check out some books, and categorize them according to areas of need, so that they are available when needed.

Creative reading allows students to express their own ideas and to interpret what they read. Identify five activities you could do in your classroom to enhance creative reading.

1. Frances Pryor, "Poor Reading—Lack of Self-esteem?" *The Reading Teacher.*
2. Ivan Quandt, *Self-Concept and Reading.*
3. Helen M. Robinson and Samuel Weintraub, "Research Related to Children's Interests and to Developmental Values of Reading," *Library Trends;* Stephen Meisal and Gerald G. Glass, "Voluntary Reading Interests and the Interest Content of Basal Readers," *The Reading Teacher;* Samuel Weintraub, "Children's Reading Interests," *The Reading Teacher;* Beta Upsilon Chapter, Pi Lambda Theta, "Children's Interests Classified by Age Level," *The Reading Teacher;* Geraldine Moray, "What Does Research Say About the Reading Interests of Children in the Intermediate Grades?" *The Reading Teacher.*
4. Huus, Helen, "A New Look at Children's Interests." In Jon E. Shapiro (ed.) *Using Literature and Poetry Affectively*, pp. 37–45.
5. Constance V. Alongi, "Response to Kay Haugaard: Comic Books Revisited," *The Reading Teacher.*
6. J. Estell Alexander and Ronald Claude Filler, *Attitudes and Reading,* p. 3.
7. Ann Kirtland Healy, "Effects of Changing Children's Attitudes Toward Reading," *Elementary English.*
8. Terry Denny and Samuel Weintraub, "First Graders' Responses to Three Questions About Reading," *Elementary School Journal.*
9. Harlan S. Hansen, "The Impact of the Home Literacy Environment on Reading Attitude," *Elementary English.*
10. M. J. Heimberger, "Sartain Reading Attitudes Inventory."
11. Doris Roettger, "Elementary Students' Attitudes Toward Reading," *The Reading Teacher.*
12. Laraine K. Hong, "Modifying SSR for Beginning Readers," *The Reading Teacher.*
13. Flora Fennimore, "Projective Book Reports," *Language Arts;* Harold H. Roeder and Nancy Lee, "Twenty-five Teacher Tested Ways to Encourage Voluntary Reading," *The Reading Teacher;* Jerry L. Johns and Linda Lunt, "Motivating Reading: Professional Ideas," *The Reading Teacher.*
14. Sara W. Lundsteen, *Children Learn to Communicate,* p. 216.
15. Charlotte S. Huck and Doris Young Kuhn, *Children's Literature in the Elementary School,* 2nd ed., p. 264.
16. Thomas N. Turner and J. Estill Alexander, "Fostering Early Creative Reading," *Language Arts.*
17. Lawrence F. Lowrey and William Grafft, "Paperback and Reading Attitudes," *The Reading Teacher.*
18. Donald J. Bissett, "The Amount and Effect of Recreational Reading in Selected Fifth Grade Classrooms"; Victor Burger, T. A. Cohen, and P. Bisgaler, *Bringing Children and Books Together.*
19. Richard Bamberger, *Promoting the Reading Habit.*
20. Darryl J. Strickler, "Planning the Affective Component," in Richard A. Earle, ed., *Classroom Practice in Reading,* p. 6.

**Other Suggested Readings**

Ashley, L. F. "Bibliotherapy, etc." *Language Arts* 55 (April 1978):478–81.

Cacha, Frances B. "Book Therapy for Abused Children." *Language Arts* 55 (February 1978):199–202.

Colvin, Marilyn A., and Stetson, Elton. "A Recreational Reading Program for Disabled Readers: It Works!" *Reading Horizons* 20 (Summer 1980):247–51.

Cullinan, Bernice E., and Carmichael, Carolyn W., editors. *Literature and Young Children*. Urbana, Illinois: National Council of Teachers of English, 1977.

Estes, Thomas H., and Johnstone, Julie P. "Twelve Easy Ways to Make Readers Hate Reading (and One Difficult Way to Make Them Love It)." *Language Arts* 54 (November–December 1977):891–97.

Fredericks, Anthony D. "Developing Positive Reading Attitudes." *The Reading Teacher* 36 (October 1982):38–40.

Gray, Mary Jane. "Does the Teacher's Attitude Toward Reading Affect the Attitude Toward Reading Held By The Studetns?" *Reading Horizons* 21 (Summer 1981): 239–43.

Harker, W. John. "Children's Literature and Back to the Basics." *Reading Horizons* 20 (Spring 1980):159–64.

Hunt, Lyman C. "The Effect of Self-Selection, Interest, and Motivation Upon Independent, Instructional and Frustration Levels." *The Reading Teacher* 24 (November 1970):146–51.

Huus, Helen, ed. *Evaluating Books for Children and Young People*. Newark, Delaware: International Reading Association, 1968.

Martin, Charles B.; Cramond, Bonnie; and Safter, Tammy. "Developing Creativity Through the Reading Program." *The Reading Teacher* 35 (February 1982):568–72.

Monson, Dianne, and Peltola, Bette J. *Research in Children's Literature*. Newark, Delaware: International Reading Association, 1976.

Mork, Theodore A. "Sustained Silent Reading in the Classroom." *The Reading Teacher* 25 (February 1972):438–41.

Shapiro, Jon B., ed. *Using Literature and Poetry Affectively*. Newark, Delaware: International Reading Association, 1979.

Shepherd, Terry, and Slees, Lynn B. "What Is Bibliotherapy?" *Language Arts* 53 (May 1976):569–71.

Spiegel, Dixie Lee. *Reading for Pleasure*. Newark, Delaware: International Reading Association, 1981.

Spiess, Jo Ann. "Literature and Hidden Handicaps." *Language Arts* 53 (April 1976):435–37.

Stevens, Kathleen C. "The Effect of Interest on the Reading Comprehension of Gifted Readers." *Reading Horizons* 21 (Fall, 1980):12–15.

Stewig, John Warren, and Sebesta, San L., ed. *Using Literature in the Elementary Classroom*. Urbana, Illinois: National Council of Teachers of English, 1978.

Tanyzer, Harold, and Karl, Jean, editors. *Reading, Children's Books, and Our Pluralistic Society*. Newark, Delaware: International Reading Association, 1972.

Tibbetts, Sylvia-Lee. "Sex Differences in Children's Reading Preferences." *The Reading Teacher* 28 (December 1974):279–81.

Yatvin, Joanne. "Recreational Reading for the Whole School." *The Reading Teacher* 31 (November 1977):185–88.

# 14

As the Seabreeze School faculty gathered to review their diagnostic-prescriptive reading program, several of the classroom teachers indicated concern about how the students who were mainstreamed into the regular classrooms as mandated by P.L. 94–142 would fit into the program. Another group was concerned about meeting the needs of several new students who spoke little or no English. During discussions of these two groups of students with special needs, questions about students with other language variations were asked repeatedly—questions about students who are considered to have language deficiencies due to a limited background of experiences and about students who have speech problems.

Because of their concerns about students with special needs in the diagnostic-prescriptive reading program, the teachers decided to investigate several areas in greater detail in order to better meet the individual needs of the learner. As these teachers read and reported back to the faculty, it became evident that students with special needs have always been a concern for the classroom teacher. However, because many of them were taught primarily in a special setting away from the regular classroom, or received special teaching assistance, the classroom teacher did not have a major responsibility in meeting such specialized needs. With the passage of P.L. 94–142, the influx of students with a primary language other than English, and the recognized special language needs of other students, the classroom teacher has become the manager of instruction for a very diverse population. Many teachers do not feel qualified to fill this role. Thus, this chapter presents some ideas on how to provide prescriptive reading instruction to students with special needs. The following questions will be addressed:

Who are the students with special needs?

What effect has the concept of mainstreaming had on diagnostic-prescriptive reading instruction?

How can students who are mainstreamed become involved in diagnostic-prescriptive reading instruction?

How do language variations affect diagnostic-prescriptive reading instruction?

How are students with language variations involved in the diagnostic-prescriptive reading program?

# How does the teacher in a diagnostic-prescriptive program deal with special needs in the classroom?

As you read this chapter, note the following terms.

Bilingual
Culturally disadvantaged
Educable mentally retarded
Educationally different
Emotionally disturbed
Gifted
Hearing-impaired
Language variations

Learning disabled
Mainstreaming
Multicultural
Physically impaired
Psychologically impaired
Speech disorders
Visually impaired

**Students with Special Needs**

Many students in our schools have special needs which must be accommodated. These needs range from physical impairments to language variations. It is imperative for the classroom teacher to be aware of ways to deal with these problems so that students with special needs are integrated into the class diagnostic-prescriptive reading program. In order to discuss these special problems, it is necessary to identify specific categories of needs that the classroom teacher may encounter.

For clarity, the authors have divided these areas of special needs into four broad categories, with subcategories under each. These broad categories include: students who have (1) physical impairments, (2) psychological impairments, (3) educational differences, and (4) language variations (see figure 14.1). Each of these areas is defined, with general suggestions for prescriptive teaching strategies provided for the categories.

Before beginning the discussion of these various categories of students with special needs, it would be useful to examine more closely the definition of mainstreaming and its implications for these students, as mandated by P. L. 94–142.

**Figure 14.1**
Types of Special Needs

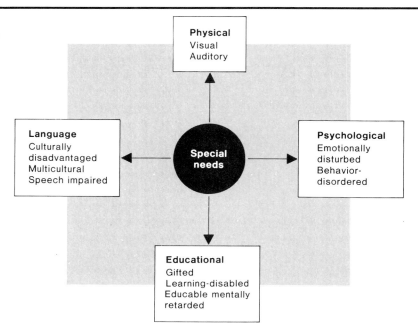

Birch[1] defines mainstreaming as an amalgamation of regular and special education into one system to provide a spectrum of services for all children according to their learning needs. Wang[2] interprets mainstreaming as the integration of regular and exceptional children in a school setting where all children share the same resources and opportunities for learning on a full-time basis. In fact, it represents an effort to provide the most equitable educational opportunity for all students, including those with special needs. It is further intended to create an environment for students with special needs to associate with other students of their age. The implications for the classroom teacher are clear. Opportunities for all students to improve their reading capabilities must be provided; this implies the wider use of diagnostic-prescriptive instruction. Keep these definitions and implications in mind as the various categories of special needs are discussed in the following pages.

**Table 14.1**
Public Law 94–142.

---

**General Provisions of Public Law 94–142**
PART X—EDUCATION AND TRAINING OF THE HANDICAPPED
EDUCATION OF THE HANDICAPPED ACT

Part A—General Provisions
Short Title; Statement of Findings & Purpose
Definitions

Sec. 601.

(a) This title may be cited as the "Education of the Handicapped Act".

"(b)-The Congress finds that—

"(1) there are more than eight million handicapped children in the United States today;

"(2) the special educational needs of such children are not being fully met;

"(3) more than half of the handicapped children in the United States do not receive appropriate educational services which would enable them to have full equality of opportunity;

"(4) one million of the handicapped children in the United States are excluded entirely from the public school system and will not go through the educational process with their peers;

"(5) there are many handicapped children throughout the United States participating in regular school programs whose handicaps prevent them from having a successful educational experience because their handicaps are undetected;

"(6) because of the lack of adequate services within the public school systems, families are often forced to find services outside the public school system, often at great distance from their residence and at their own expense;

"(7) developments in the training of teachers and in diagnostic and instructional procedures and methods have advanced to the point that, given appropriate funding, State and local educational agencies can and will provide effective special education and related services to meet the needs of handicapped children;

"(8) State and local educational agencies have a responsibility to provide education for all handicapped children, but present financial resources are inadequate to meet the special educational needs of handicapped children; and

"(9) it is in the national interest that the Federal Government assist State and local efforts to provide programs to meet the educational needs of handicapped children in order to assure equal protection of the law.

"(c) It is the purpose of this Act to assure that all handicapped children have available to them, within the time periods specified in section 612(2) (B), a free appropriate public education which emphasizes special education and related services designed to meet their unique needs, to assure that the rights of handicapped children and their parents or guardians are protected, to assist States and localities to provide for the education of all handicapped children, and to assess and assure the effectiveness of efforts to educate handicapped children".

---

On November 19, 1975, Congress passed Public Law 94–142. The law mandates significant changes regarding the education of children with special needs. The most significant change is the requirement that handicapped children be educated with their nonhandicapped peers as much as possible.

Hedley suggests several principles to consider in implementing mainstreaming. These are

1. Work in a consistently congenial and scheduled manner with the child study team.
2. Include parents in the planning and implementation of the individual study program.
3. Stress diagnostic-prescriptive approaches and a more complete knowledge of the dimensions of language assessment.
4. Stress non-biased, non-discriminatory assessment in terms of specific disability while assessing reading ability.
5. Commitment to a highly individualized program for the special learner and for the class, is necessary.
6. Emphasis on small group instruction, peer-tutoring, parent-tutoring, and the use of the support staff, especially in the classroom is helpful.
7. Openness to task analysis and break-down of instructional tasks for the learner, as well as reduced or changed pace of presentation based on educational need of the student.
8. Openness to using techniques and materials modeled by the special educator and the corrective reading teacher.
9. Stress on greater knowledge of the linguistic and reading processes in terms of cognitive strategies for the special student.
10. Knowledge of what impairs receptive and expressive language.
11. Arrangement of planning periods where the child study team discusses and coordinates instruction for the class as a whole as well as for the exceptional student.
12. Increased awareness of social problems and group dynamics when dealing with exceptional students.
13. Self awareness of attitudes and abilities for working with special students.
14. Emphasis on reduced class size in order to give more individual attention and to do more planning.[3]

**Physical Impairments**

Students with physical impairments include those with disorders of the nervous or musculoskeletal system, the visually disabled, and the hearing impaired. Because this book is limited to addressing the reading needs of students, the authors include under this category only those physical impairments that affect reading performance, namely the visual and hearing disorders. Students with such impairments experience difficulties in performing tasks because of a loss of acuity in either the visual or auditory mode. As a result of these losses, they must receive special assistance from the teacher in performing certain learning tasks. Students

with severe losses in vision or hearing are generally referred to more specialized school settings, which are better equipped to cope with their special needs than the regular classroom. Thus, the regular classroom teacher will probably not have totally blind or deaf students in the classroom.

*Visual Impairments*

In discussing visually impaired students, teachers may wish to use the three different types of impairments identified by Barraga. The *blind* students have only light perception, or have no vision and learn through Braille or media that do not require vision. Students with *low vision* "have limitations in distance vision but are able to see objects and materials when they are within a few inches or a maximum of two feet away." Barraga's third type of visual impairment is known as *limited vision* and includes students whose vision can be corrected.[4]

Research in the area of the partially sighted, or students with low vision, suggests that these students do perform in the normal range on standardized tests due to their ability to communicate with others via oral means. Bateman found that the partially sighted students in her study were normally distributed, with an average IQ of 100 on the Binet or Wechsler scales. She also found that on the *Illinois Test of Psycholinguistic Ability* the students were normal in the auditory-vocal channel subtests but performed significantly lower on the visual reception, visual association, motor expression, and visual sequential memory subtests.[5] Studies such as that of Demott indicate that there are no differences between sighted and visually impaired students in their understanding of ideas and concepts. He concluded that the visually impaired student, like the sighted, learns words and their meaning through use in the language rather than via direct experience.[6]

Teachers should recognize that research findings indicate that blind students are equal to the sighted in reading comprehension when provided more time to read the tests. Bateman found that partially sighted students in grades two to four

Were similar to the reading achievement level of sighted students;
Scored highest on a silent reading test and lowest on a timed oral reading test, and
Made more reversal errors than the sighted group but either did not differ or made fewer errors in other areas than the sighted.[7]

With this research information, teachers should recognize that educational objectives for the visually impaired are the same as for the sighted student, only the methods and materials must be changed. Lowenfeld suggests three basic ideas for the teacher to consider in teaching the visually impaired.

*Concreteness:* Students must be provided with objects that can be manipulated and touched in order to learn about their size, shape, weight, etc.
*Unifying experiences:* Systematic stimulation is necessary in order for the visually impaired to learn how parts relate to the total picture. For example, in order to learn how one part of the neighborhood connects to

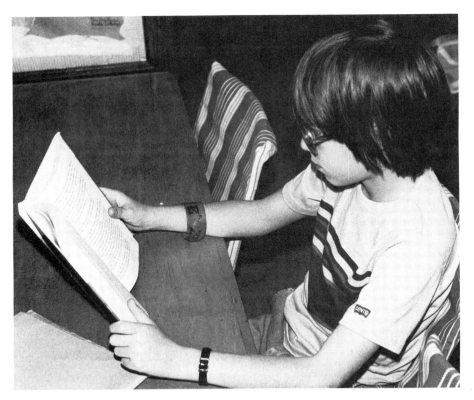

another the student must be taken to the places and provided explanations. Without adequate vision it is difficult for a person to unify parts into a meaning whole.

*Learning by doing:* The visually impaired student must be stimulated by sight, touch, or hearing to become involved with an activity. Thus, visually impaired students must be invited and shown how to become involved in a learning task because they cannot see the learning activity to automatically involve themselves.[8]

Classroom teachers can greatly assist the visually impaired student by providing instruction in listening skills. Because so much of their education comes through listening to information, this area must be strengthened through direct instruction. Additionally classroom teachers should be aware of special materials and equipment that assist in providing prescriptive instruction in reading.

For the visually impaired student, lighting is one of the most important considerations. Glare and direct sunlight limit vision, while evenly distributed light and appropriate artificial illumination assist the visually impaired reader. These students may also need adjustable desks to assure the right angle of light, gray-green chalkboards that reflect more light, typewriters, dictaphones, record players, magnifying lenses, large-type books, three-dimensional maps, and other specially designed teaching-learning aids.[9]

Classroom teachers should realize that visually impaired students fit into the diagnostic-prescriptive reading program just as other students with specific reading needs. The only difference is that specialized materials and techniques are needed to further assist them. These are provided, along with teaching assistance, by a special teacher who can help the regular teacher and the student to have positive teaching-learning experiences.

As with the visually impaired, hearing-impaired students can be grouped in two basic categories. According to Moores, the following definitions can be used to describe the hearing impaired: *Hearing Impairments*

A 'deaf person' is one whose hearing is disabled to an extent (usually 70 dB ISO or greater) that precludes the understanding of speech through the ear alone, with or without the use of a hearing aid.

A 'hard-of-hearing' person is one whose hearing is disabled to an extent (usually 35 to 69 dB ISO) that makes difficult, but does not preclude, the understanding of speech through the ear alone, with or without a hearing aid.[10]

The regular classroom teacher is not trained to provide appropriate instruction to the totally deaf student; however, the hard-of-hearing student can function in the classroom with assistance from the classroom teacher, who consults with a special teacher. It is important to note that students with a mild to moderate hearing loss are less likely to exhibit significant academic problems than students with more severe deficits, especially over longer periods of time.[11]

The hearing-impaired student suffers handicaps in many developmental areas, with language and related areas, such as reading, being most severely affected. Gentile has found that hearing-impaired students at age eight scored at about grade two in reading and math computation, and at age seventeen the children scored at about grade four in reading and grade six in math computation. These findings are substantiated by similar results in a study by Trybus and Karchmer.[12] Plaster indicates that the factors that appear to relate more directly to academic performance of hearing-impaired students are oral communication, personality, and linguistic competence.[13]

Although hearing-impaired students seem to do poorly in language-related areas, their intelligence range is like the range for normal children on nonverbal intelligence measures.[14]

In teaching the hearing-impaired student, Kirk and Gallagher note the use of special educational procedures, such as the use of hearing aids, auditory training, speech or lipreading, oral speech remediation, speech development, and language development.[15] Many of these procedures are used by a special teacher and may be adapted for use in the regular classroom. One example is the use of lipreading. Hard-of-hearing students often rely on this procedure to supplement the faint voices they hear. Students learn to see or hear a few clues in a sentence

and fill in the gaps from the context. In using lipreading, teachers must be aware that some sounds are more difficult to "read" or hear than others. For example:

> Vowels are more difficult to discriminate by lipreading, but are easier to discriminate through hearing because they are in lower-frequency ranges.
> Consonants such as *s* are in a higher-frequency range and are sometimes more difficult to hear.
> Sounds such as *k, h,* and *g* cannot be discriminated visually.

Thus, the teacher must realize that the hard-of-hearing student who uses lipreading may miss some information because of the formation or frequency of the sounds.

Larson and Miller provide a list of suggestions for the classroom teacher to consider in teaching the hearing-impaired student in the classroom:

1. Give the child favorable seating in the classroom and allow him or her to move to the source of speech within the room; let the child turn around or have speakers turn toward the child, to allow visual contact with anyone who is speaking.
2. Encourage the student to look at the speaker's lips, mouth, and face. Speech-reading should help clarify many of the sounds the child cannot hear.
3. Speak naturally—neither mumbling nor overarticulating. Speak neither too fast nor too slow, too loud or too soft.
4. Keep hands away from the mouth when speaking, and make sure that books, papers, glasses, pencils, and other objects do not obstruct the visual contact.
5. Take note of the light within the room so that the overhead light or window light is not at the speaker's back. Speechreading is difficult when light shines in the speechreader's eyes. Try to prevent shadows from falling on the speaker's mouth.
6. Stand in one place while dictating spelling words or arithmetic problems to the group, allowing the hard-of-hearing child to see better, as well as to give a sense of security that the teacher will be there when he or she looks up.
7. Speak in complete sentences. Single words are more difficult to speechread than are complete thoughts. Approximately 50 percent of the words in the English language look alike on the lips. Such groups of words are termed *homophenous.* (Examples: *man, pan, ban, band, mat, pat, bat, mad, pad, bad.*) Phrases and sentences placing the word in context help promote visual differentiation among homophenous words.
8. Give the student assignments in advance, or give the topic which will be discussed. A list of new vocabulary to be used in an assignment also assists the student. Familiarity may help the child understand the word in context and help promote visual differentiation among homophenous words.
9. Occasionally, have the hearing-impaired child repeat the assignment to some other child so you are sure the assignment has been understood.
10. Remember at all times that this is a normal child with a hearing handicap; never single out a hearing-impaired child in front of the group or in any other manner encourage an attitude of being "different."

11. Understand that the child with a hearing loss may tire faster than a child with normal hearing. The demands placed upon a child in speechreading and listening are greater than for hearing people.
12. Take into consideration that many children hear better on some days than they do on others. Also, children may suffer from tinnitus (hearing noises within the head), which may make them nervous and irritable.
13. Restate a sentence, using other words that have the same meaning, when the hearing-impaired individual does not understand what has been said. The reworded sentence might be more visible. (Example: Change, "Close your book," to "Shut the book," or "Please put your book away now." Look in a mirror and observe the difference.)
14. Encourage the hearing-impaired child to participate in all school and community activities. This child is just as much a part of the environment as any other child.
15. Help the child to accept mistakes humorously. The deaf and the hard-of-hearing resent being the target of laughter just as much as anyone else. Laugh with them, not at them.
16. Encourage an understanding of and interest in the handicap of a hearing-impaired child by the entire group.[16]

In the diagnostic-prescriptive reading program, hearing-impaired students must develop the same basic skills as normal students. These students may learn them more slowly and in different ways because of their difficulty with language, but they can, with the guidance of patient teachers, become adequate readers.

## Psychological Impairments

Teaching emotionally disturbed or behavior-disordered students is a cause of great concern to educators. Many of these students are quite capable of performing school tasks; however, they are often unable to do so because of psychological problems manifested in deviate or disruptive behavior in the classroom. These students may show great enthusiasm for completing an assigned task, only to suddenly explode into disruptive behavior, creating many problems for the classroom teacher. They may also be totally withdrawn from classroom activities.

Bower has identified some specific behavior patterns of emotionally disturbed students. While the presence of these problems does not always mean that the student has a psychological impairment, their incidence over a long period of time deserves attention. They are:

Absence of knowledge and skill acquisition in academic and social behaviors not attributed to intellectual capability, hearing and visual status, or physical health anomalies.

Absence of positive, satisfying interpersonal relationships with adults and peers.

Frequent instances of inappropriate behavior episodes which are surprising or unexpected for the conditions in which they occur.

Observable periods of diminished verbal and other motor activity (e.g., moods of depression or unhappiness).

Frequent complaints of a physical nature, such as stomach aches, soreness in the arm, and general fatigue.[17]

When classroom teachers identify students with these characteristics and refer them for further evaluation, or when they have a student who has already been formally identified as having emotional problems, they must have strategies for dealing with these students in the classroom. Such students follow the same basic procedures in the diagnostic-prescriptive reading program; however, the teacher must adjust teaching strategies to meet the personal needs of a student with a sometimes unpredictable reaction.

Kirk and Gallagher suggest some specific procedures which may be used with the emotionally disturbed student. These include psychodynamic strategies, the psychoeducational strategy, the behavior modification strategy, the developmental strategy, the learning disability strategy, and the ecological strategy.[18] Of these strategies the most useful in the classroom setting seem to be the behavior modification strategy and the learning disability strategy. The behavior modification strategy applies the principles of respondent and operant conditioning, in which the student is rewarded for the desired behavior.

The learning disability strategy is proposed by those who believe that emotional disturbances and learning disabilities are interrelated. This approach attempts to modify behavior by developing a more positive self-concept through successful experiences in school work.

As classroom teachers work with the emotionally disturbed student in the diagnostic-prescriptive reading program, consideration may be given to the basic guidelines outlined below:

> Be sure that instruction is based on the student's needs and interests, and that learning experiences are successful for the student.
> Offer options for learning a specified skill and allow the student to choose.
> Work with other resource persons in the community, such as social workers and psychiatrists, to meet the student's social and academic needs.
> Establish a positive relationship with the student. Teachers must sometimes have a high degree of tolerance for hate and aggressive reactions.
> Provide guidance to help students realize the seriousness of their actions and to take steps toward self-control.
> Learn to "read" the student; try to determine why certain actions or reactions occur. Then try to be empathetic and help the student work out dilemmas.

## Educational Differences

Three rather large groups of students comprise an area of special needs arising from educational differences. These can be classified as mentally retarded students, ranging from mildly to profoundly retarded; learning-disabled students; and gifted students. Each of these areas is discussed separately in the following pages.

As mainstreaming procedures are implemented in the school system, a major trend is to provide Educable Mentally Retarded (EMR) students with opportunities to associate with other students of their age. In some systems this includes placing the EMR student in the regular classroom during some designated class, or possibly on a permanent basis. The classroom teacher may also be involved in teaching EMR students whose parents will not allow them to be tested or placed in special classes.

*Educable Mentally Retarded*

For many years, IQ scores were used exclusively to determine who was mentally retarded, with ranges anywhere from 55 to 80 indicating EMR classification. Recently, the debate over the accuracy of IQ scores, especially in regard to blacks and Hispanics from culturally deficient or different backgrounds, has resulted in the consideration of other criteria along with IQ scores.

Several characteristics of the EMR student, which will assist the classroom teacher in providing appropriate reading instruction, are highlighted by Kirk:

> Such areas as auditory and visual memory, language use, conceptual and perceptual abilities, and imaginative and creative abilities may develop slowly.
>
> Academically, the EMR student experiences great difficulty with reading, writing, and spelling activities on entering school. These skills are often not acquired until the student is eight or even eleven years old.

Progress in school is at one-half to three-quarters the rate of the average student, which is comparable to the student's mental development.

EMR students often exhibit short attention spans and are easily frustrated; however, this situation improves when instruction is geared to meet the student's needs.

EMR students often create more behavior problems in school than other students; however, much of this can be alleviated through the use of appropriate instructional techniques.[19] Despite this reputation for disruptive behavior, evidence indicates that there is no significant difference between EMR students' behavior in the classroom and that of educationally handicapped students.[20]

As teachers plan for providing diagnostic-prescriptive instruction to the EMR student, they must recognize that these students need the same basic reading skills presented at a slower rate. Kolstoe has some additional recommendations for presenting learning tasks to the EMR student:

1. The tasks should be uncomplicated. The new tasks should contain the fewest possible elements, and most of the elements should be familiar, so [the student] has few unknowns to learn.

2. The task should be brief. This assures that [the student] will attend to the most important aspect of the task and not get lost in a sequence of interrelated events.

3. The task should be sequentially presented so the learner proceeds in a sequence of small steps, each one built upon previously learned tasks.

4. Each learning task should be the kind in which success is possible. One of the major problems to be overcome is that of failure-proneness. This major deterrent to learning can be effectively reduced through success experiences.
5. Overlearning must be built into lessons. Drills in game form seem to lessen the disinterest inherent in unimaginative drill.
6. Learning tasks should be applied to objects, problems, and situations in the learner's life environment. Unless the tasks are relevant, the learner has great difficulty in seeing their possible importance.[21]

More specifically, EMR students may benefit from using self-paced modules,[22] from computer-assisted instruction in learning sight words,[23] and by learning how to compare unknown words to words that they already have in their sight vocabulary.[24]

Knowledge of these procedures should assist the classroom teacher in providing appropriate prescriptive instruction for the EMR student.

In the context of this chapter, learning-disabled refers to the area classified as Specific Learning Disabilities. More and more students are being placed in this category for the purpose of receiving special instruction in the regular classroom as well as in special resource programs.

*Learning-Disabled*

Several definitions of specific learning disabilities have been offered; however, the most widely accepted definition was proposed by the National Advisory Committee on Handicapped Children in 1968. It states that

> Children with special (specific) learning disabilities exhibit a disorder in one or more of the basic psychological processes involved in understanding or in using spoken or written language. These may be manifested in disorders of listening, thinking, talking, reading, writing, spelling, or arithmetic. They include conditions which have been referred to as perceptual handicaps, brain injury, minimal brain dysfunction, dyslexia, developmental aphasia, etc. They do not include learning problems which are due primarily to visual, hearing, or motor handicaps, to mental retardation, emotional disturbance, or to environmental disadvantage.[25]

Although this is the more widely accepted definition of learning disabilities, the U.S. National Joint Committee on Learning Disabilities is urging that this definition be revised to better facilitate the identification and treatment of the individual.[26]

Gilliland enumerates some characteristics of the learning-disabled student which should provide the classroom teacher with insight into how better to meet their learning needs. These characteristics are outlined below.

*Characteristics of Learning-Disabled Students*
Students are usually much better in mathematics than reading.
Word recognition skills are poorly developed in comparison to other reading skills.
Many students are hyperactive, experiencing difficulty in sitting still while working on a task.

Concentration on interesting tasks is interrupted because of sounds or movement around them.

There are difficulties in recognizing likenesses and differences in similar spoken or printed words.

Students have difficulty in drawing simple shapes.

Reversals of letters or changes of the order of sounds in a word are symptoms of specific learning disabilities.

There is some lack of coordination in writing or walking.

The student tends to repeat the same errors over and over.

Many students have great difficulty in following directions.

There is quite a lot of variance in performance in different areas. Mathematics may be very high and reading very low.

Students experience difficulty in organizing their work.

Many students are very slow in finishing their work.[27]

Since students with specific learning disabilities are difficult to diagnose and even more difficult to teach, it is imperative that classroom teachers use all their skills to identify these students as soon as possible. However, there are educators who believe that because faulty assumptions have been made, students identified as learning disabled have not really benefited as much as they could have profited from the increased emphasis on early identification and intervention. Such assumptions concern the ease of identifying an L.D. student by trained professionals, the ease of defining the area of learning disabilities, and that intervention naturally follows identification.[28] Thus, in implementing a prescriptive reading program, it is imperative to consider each student's needs and plan accordingly.

In discussing learning disabilities as related to reading, Johnson and Myklebust suggest two types of reading disorders—visual processing and auditory processing.[29] Disorders in visual processing are recognized through—

Visual discrimination difficulties and confusion of similar letters and words,

Slow rate or perception,

Letter and word reversals and inversions,

Difficulty in following and retaining visual sequences,

Associated visual memory problems,

Inferior drawings,

Difficulty in visual analysis and synthesis,

Marked inferiority of visual skills in relation to auditory skills on diagnostic tests.

In instructing students with this type of disorder, the teacher should use the auditory skills by teaching sounds and words through association.

Auditory processing disorders are characterized by—

Associated auditory discrimination and perceptual problems which hinder the use of phonetic analysis,

Difficulty in separating words into their component phonemes and syllables or in blending them into whole words,

Difficulty in spontaneous recall of the sounds associated with letters or words,
Disturbances in auditory sequencing,
A general preference for visual activities over auditory tasks.

Students with this type of disorder should be taught by using strategies which emphasize the visual recognition of whole words while the auditory skills are being developed.

In implementing instruction for L.D. students, it is essential that the amount of on-task reading time be augmented; increase the amount of direct, supervised instruction the student receives, and be more aware of those students who are falling behind their classmates.[30]

Although teachers may note that learning-disabled students seem to have greater difficulties in one modality than the other, there is no one method of reading instruction that can be suggested for learning-disabled students. Through the use of many techniques in the prescriptive process, the special needs of these students can be met.

Until recently, gifted students have been neglected. This occurred primarily because many educators believed that these students were quite capable of fulfilling their own needs. Further, concern for the gifted seemed to decrease as a result of the increased interest in providing better educational opportunities for minorities and low socioeconomic groups. However, in the 1970s there was a renewed concern for providing more appropriate educational experiences for the gifted student.

*Gifted*

Just as in the other areas of special needs, it is important to identify at an early age those students exhibiting superior talent in one or more areas, and to promote opportunities for developing their potential. To assist in identifying these students, it is necessary to define the term *gifted*. The most widely accepted definition of the gifted student was proposed by Marland in 1972. He stated that perhaps as many as 3 to 5 percent of the school-age population are gifted, and defined this group in the following way:

> Gifted and talented children are those identified by professionally qualified persons who, by virtue of outstanding abilities, are capable of high performance. These are children who require differentiated educational programs and services beyond those normally provided by the regular program in order to realize their contribution to self and society.[31]

Children capable of high performance include those with demonstrated achievement or potential ability in any of the following areas:

General intellectual ability
Specific academic aptitude
Creative or productive thinking
Leadership ability
Visual and performing arts
Psychomotor ability

This rather broad definition encompasses a larger population and recognizes those students exhibiting talent in areas other than intelligence, as determined by IQ scores; actually, this allows for some affective assessment of what constitutes giftedness.

Classroom teachers may wish to note the following characteristics of giftedness as suggested by Terman and Oden in order to facilitate more individualized learning experiences for such students.

Gifted students exhibit above-average health and physical characteristics.
Gifted students are two to four years beyond the average level in school work.
Mental health problems are rare in the gifted population.
Contrary to some belief, gifted students interact well with peers.
Wide ranges of interests are enjoyed by gifted students.
Gifted students tend to be very successful adults.[32]

In the past, the classroom teacher has been totally responsible for providing instruction to this group of students with educational differences. However, with the renewed interest in the gifted student, school systems are developing programs which should help in meeting these special needs. These programs may be in the form of ability grouping, acceleration to provide more advanced content, enrichment programs to supplement the regular school offerings, and special classes within a school, or perhaps even Saturday sessions.

In the prescriptive reading program, the gifted student follows the same scope and sequence of skills but move at a faster rate and have more instruction in the higher-level reading skills. Bynum has proposed that curricula activities provide opportunities for students to do some of the following:

Add breadth and depth to present knowledge.
Use many instructional media, especially those which free the student from limited content restrictions.
Develop efficient reading and study skills.
Raise the conceptual level on which they function, and think conceptually.
Use problem-solving techniques.
Develop and use critical thinking skills.
Develop and use creative abilities.
Do independent work.
Explore under guidance and independently many fields of interest.
Deal with high-level abstractions.
Converse with students of like abilities.
Participate in planning learning experiences.
Apply theory and principles to solving life problems.
Develop leadership abilities or become effective followers.
Develop a personal set of values.
Set and reach immediate and ultimate goals.
Develop self-discipline and a sense of social responsibility.[33]

Teachers should remember that the gifted need planned reading instruction to assist in expanding their vocabulary and in using the many ideas these students learn so quickly. They also need opportunities to interact with other students at all levels in order to become better adjusted citizens in the school and community.

In this section, the focus is on the special needs of three specific groups of students who have one common bond—language variations. The groups discussed are the culturally disadvantaged, multicultural, and students with speech impairments.

**Language Variations**

The term culturally disadvantaged is often used to describe a particular segment of the population of the United States that is thought of as underfed, undereducated, and underprivileged. This group is also often referred to as culturally deprived, culturally different, and educationally disadvantaged. An equally descriptive term, societally neglected, is defined by Swanson and Willis to include those children and youth whose experienced environmental, cultural, and economic societal conditions consistently prevent them from realizing their potential within the dominant educational, vocational, and social structures of present society.[34]

*Culturally Disadvantaged*

These students usually experience great difficulty with reading and communicating orally in the school setting. Part of the problem can be ascribed to environmental factors; however, most of the difficulty is with language acquisition. The language of the culturally disadvantaged student is typically nonstandard American English, usually dialectical in nature; this creates many problems when these students encounter teachers and the type of reading material used in most schools. Teachers are often not accustomed to divergent speaking patterns, and students are unaccustomed to the speaking patterns and value system of the teachers. Moreover, these students may receive most of their reading instruction from a basal reader written in standard American English, depicting a way of life that is unfamiliar to the culturally disadvantaged student. As a result of these and other factors, such students lag behind others who have a wider background of experiences and are better able to cope with the language of the materials and the teacher. This situation creates frustration for the disadvantaged student and begins a cycle that may perpetuate a lifetime of failure.

To better meet the needs of these students, the teacher must first recognize the characteristics of these students:

Most are from families below the poverty level.
Many suffer from malnutrition and diseases such as severe anemia, rickets, and vitamin and protein deficiencies.
Often these students suffer from retarded physical growth.[35]

The limiting factors for the culturally disadvantaged as they develop their reading skills are poor language development, low self-concept, improper nutrition, and lack of motivation. Each of these factors affects the development of any learning skill.

Language development is limited, as these students often come from homes where there is little verbal interaction and few, if any, reading materials. Verbal communication lacks content and is given primarily in brief commands. This language background does not provide the type of stimulation that the student needs for developing good expressive or receptive language skills. Thus, as discussed in chapter 9, the students' prereading skills are poorly developed.

Students from culturally disadvantaged homes may also have a poor self-concept because of a lack of identity in the home and of recognition in areas that are important to them. These feelings are more prevalent in students from lower socioeconomic levels where positive feelings are often not expressed in the home. When the child with a poor self-concept enters school and is confronted with frustrating language experiences, reading difficulties have begun.

An added impediment in teaching the disadvantaged student is nutritional deprivation or malnutrition. Malnutrition has an effect on both physical and mental development prior to school entrance and continues to retard learning by leaving the student with a physiological need. Until this basic need is fulfilled, maximum learning cannot occur.

All the above factors contribute to a lack of motivation to learn to read. The constant feelings of frustration and failure are reflected by an apathetic reaction to learning. Classroom teachers must attempt to deal with this problem by improving the students' language skills and self-concept while the school provides nutritious meals. Language skills may be improved through the use of oral language activities throughout the school day. More specific suggestions are discussed in chapter 9. Self-concept can be improved as the student is given learning activities at which he or she can succeed. These students also need much positive reinforcement. Harber and Beatty concluded that:

> To improve the self-image and academic achievement among black, lower socioeconomic status children, teachers need to be trained to expect more from them, to judge their capabilities independent of race and socio-economic status, and to understand and respect their dialect and cultural background.[36]

Dennard supports this position by indicating that "we have overintellectualized the differences between the dialect of Blacks versus the dialects of other groups. It's time we return to teaching the language and giving all students a chance to use every aspect of it."[37] Thus, classroom teachers must make every effort to help these students succeed by

*Carefully introducing vocabulary, as well as concepts.* Because of these students' limited background experiences, they need more preparation for learning in order to increase the likelihood of success.

*Being patient with their language usage.* Never ridicule a person's language. Language is essential for expressing emotions and ideas.

*Providing an atmosphere conducive to class discussions involving everyone.* Involving each student in the learning improves self-concept, and the students begin to feel that they are an integral part of the class.

*Being enthusiastic and receptive in dealing with the students.* Enthusiasm is contagious. If the teacher enjoys teaching, the students will enjoy learning.

In order to better understand the differences between standard English and black English, teachers may wish to examine tables 14.2 and 14.3. Awareness of differences may give teachers a better understanding of these language variations, as well as increasing their understanding of students with dialects.

In teaching the culturally disadvantaged, classroom teachers must provide carefully planned prescriptive instruction and attempt to deal also with an enormous societal problem. This is not an easy task.

The multicultural segment of the school population comprises students who do not use American English as their primary language. Included here are Hispanics (Mexican-American, Cuban, Puerto Rican), Vietnamese, Europeans, Asians, and any other group that does not speak American English or uses American English as a secondary language. Obviously, difficulties in communicating orally and learning to read are inherent in these situations.

*Multicultural*

**Table 14.2**

Phonological differences between standard English and black English.

| Feature | Example (SE — BE) |
|---|---|
| Simplification of consonant clusters | Test—tes, past—pas, went—win |
| th sounds | |
|     voiceless th in initial position | think—tink or think |
|     voiced th in initial position | the—de |
|     voiceless th in medial position | nothing—nofin' |
|     voiced th in medial position | brother—brovah |
|     th in final position | tooth—toof |
| r and l | |
|     in postvocalic position | sister—sistah, nickel—nickuh |
|     in final position | Saul—saw |
| Devoicing of final b, d, and g | cab—cap, bud—but, pig—pik |
| Nasalization | |
|     -ing suffix | doing—doin' |
|     i and e before a nasal | pen—pin |
| Stress—absence of the first syllable of a multisyllabic word when the first syllable is unstressed | about—'bout |
| Plural marker* | three birds—three bird or three birds<br>the books—de book or de books |
| Possessive marker* | the boy's hat—de boy hat |
| Third person singular marker* | He works here—He work here |
| Past tense—simplification of final consonant clusters* | passed—pass, loaned—loan |

*Some authorities include these under syntactical differences.

Reprinted with permission of Jean R. Harber and Jane N. Beatty, and the International Reading Association, from *Reading and the Black English Speaking Child,* Newark, Delaware: International Reading Association, 1978, p. 46.

**Table 14.3.**
Syntactic differences between standard English and black English.

| Feature | SE | BE |
|---|---|---|
| Linking verb | He is going. | He goin'. or He is goin'. |
| Pronomial apposition | That teacher yells at the kids. | Dat teachah, she yell at de kid (kids). |
| Agreement of subject and third person singular verb | She runs home. | She run home. |
| | She has a bike. | She have a bike. |
| Irregular verb forms | They rode their bikes. | Dey rided der bike (bikes). |
| Future form | I will go home. | I'm a go home. |
| "If" construction | I asked if he did it. | I aks did he do it. |
| Indefinite article | I want an apple. | I want a apple. |
| Negation | I don't have any. | I don't got none. |
| Pronoun form | We have to do it. | Us got to do it. |
| Copula (verb "to be") | He is here all the time. | He be here. |
| | No, he isn't. | No, he isn't. or No, he don't. |
| Prepositions | Put the cat out of the house. | Put de cat out de house. |
| | The dress is made of wool. | De dress is made outta wool. |

Reprinted with permission of Jean R. Harber and Jane N. Beatty, and the International Reading Association, from *Reading and the Black English Speaking Child*, Newark, Delaware: International Reading Association, 1978, p. 46–47.

Students who speak English as a second language may be referred to as bilingual. Those who speak only their native language are monolingual. Lacking English as a primary language, many students who are very capable of learning are unable to do so because of the language barrier. Justin, for example, indicates that almost one million Spanish-speaking students in the Southwest will be unable to go beyond the eighth grade because of the language factor. Cordasco also found similar problems among Puerto Rican students on the east coast.[38]

Another serious concern to the multicultural population is the erosion and, in some cases, complete loss of their cultural identity. Many in this group see the American school system as an instrument of destruction of their culture. Until recently, U.S. education perceived its role as a "melting pot," where the various cultural and language differences were replaced by American standards, mores, and language, thus projecting these students into the mainstream of the American way of life. Although most of these cultural groups want to participate in the American way of life, they also wish to maintain their cultural heritage.

Fortunately, some change of attitude on the part of educators is apparent in the advent of a trend toward providing better educational services to our multicultural population. There is a belief that these multicultural groups should not be stripped of their culture, which is experiencing something of a renaissance in multicultural activities, a return to their "roots," a feeling many Americans are experiencing.

In an effort to ensure the right of students to an appropriate education, the U.S. Department of Health, Education, and Welfare has issued guidelines to prevent any type of language discrimination.[39] Another organization, the NEA, has

set up a Task Force on Bilingual/Multicultural Education, which defines bilingual education as "A process which uses a pupil's primary language as the principal medium of instruction while teaching the language of the predominant culture in a well-organized program, encompassing a multicultural curriculum."[40]

As classroom teachers attempt to teach reading to monolingual or bilingual students, they should remember that prescriptive instruction must be adapted to individual needs. Furthermore, the same sequence in learning words is used for the multicultural student as for the English speaker. The students learn first through *listening,* add the word to the *speaking* vocabulary, then use it in *reading,* and finally learn to *write* the word. Employing this procedure, students can learn words more quickly. Perez found that extending practice in oral language skills through the elementary grades appears to increase the likelihood of reading success.[41]

Some other suggestions which the teacher of the multicultural student should remember are listed below.

Become familiar with the students' culture so that cultural habits are understood.

Teach the student some survival words in English, e.g., name, address, restroom, etc.

Teach sentence formation by speaking in simple sentences.

Use resources from within the community to help the student. Adults or other students who speak the language can be valuable in teaching English to the student.

Identify concepts, such as numbers, letters, time, colors, etc., that the student needs to learn. Provide systematic instruction.

Do not automatically place these students in the low reading group. They probably need to be placed in several groups in order to gain more experience with the language.

Team the student with another student who acts as a "big brother" in helping the foreign speaker become acquainted with the school.

Most important, use variety in teaching and do not drill the student in phonics. English has sounds which do not exist in other languages; thus, the teacher should not expect Spanish-speaking students to learn immediately the *j* sound, as in *jump,* because this sound does not exist in their native language.

**Speech Problems**

Language disorders have always handicapped students; and efforts to correct the problems have been going on in the American school system for many years. Educators recognized early the special needs of these students, and as a result, speech-language pathologists have been furnishing instructional assistance for quite some time. Since World War II, this area has experienced considerable expansion, and most school systems now have access to the services of a speech specialist.

Language disorders exist in many students and can be caused by organic (neurological) factors, as well as developmental lag, and psychological, cultural, or environmental conditions.[42] Language is considered to be defective when—

the speaker attracts unfavorable attention,
it disrupts communication, and
the speaker or listener is adversely affected.[43]

According to Bankston, speech disorders are classified into areas of articulation disorders, fluency disorders, and voice disorders.[44] These disorders can affect all segments of the population and are not restricted to one group; they are, in fact, the largest group of special needs in the elementary schools.

Language disorders affect reading more directly, because many classroom teachers use a great deal of oral reading, especially in the primary grades. Therefore, it is necessary to remember that placing students with language problems under the stress of reading aloud only increases their lack of confidence and, in some instances, leads to the humiliation of the students before their peers. This is unnecessary and should be strictly avoided.

Because most schools have speech therapists available to work with students or to consult with teachers, the classroom teacher must coordinate instruction with the therapist. This is part of providing prescriptive instruction in the classroom. The teacher is aware of the sounds which students are working on with the therapist, and provides reinforcement activities in the classroom. In coordinating instruction for students with language disorders, the classroom teacher may use expansion and modeling techniques. In the *expansion* technique the teacher uses the student's incomplete sentence and repeats it to the student in a complete sentence. The *modeling* technique requires the teacher restructure the concept expressed by the student and express it as a complete sentence. These classroom activities help students to overcome their problems and assist the speech therapist in meeting their special needs. Geoffrion advocates the use of a language experience approach as an effective instructional strategy to use with these students.[45] Teamwork is an essential component in the diagnostic-prescriptive process. In dealing with language disorders, the classroom teacher's primary role is early detection and referral, adjusting instruction to the student's needs, and coordination with the therapist.

## Summary

In the diagnostic-prescriptive reading program, the classroom teacher must be aware of the special needs of some students. The goal of this chapter was to help classroom teachers acquire some knowledge of these special needs and ideas on how to deal with them in the reading program.

Students with special needs were divided into four basic types, with various specific subcategories under each type. The basic types discussed were—

Students with physical impairments, which included visually impaired and hearing-disabled students;

Students with psychological impairments, including emotionally disturbed or behaviorally disordered students;

Students with educational differences, including the educable mentally retarded, specific learning-disabled, and gifted students;

Students with language variations. Included in this category are culturally disadvantaged, multicultural, and speech-impaired students.

In addition to defining and describing the characteristics of each group, ideas for developing prescriptive reading techniques were presented.

Because of the emphasis being placed on mainstreaming, as mandated by P. L. 94–142, the classroom teacher again assumes the primary responsibility for educating all students and must acquire the skills essential for dealing with those students and their special needs in the school reading program.

**Applying What You Read**

In your classroom, you have several students who fit into the special needs category as defined in this chapter. How can they be included in the diagnostic-prescriptive reading program?

Some parents have just been told that their visually impaired children will be mainstreamed into your classroom. How would you explain to them how the children will function in the regular classroom?

You have just been assigned two new students who speak only Vietnamese. What should you do to help them learn English?

**Notes**

1. J. W. Birch, *Mainstreaming: Educable Mentally Retarded Children in Regular Classes.*
2. Margaret C. Wang, "Mainstreaming Exceptional Children: Some Instructional Design and Implementation Considerations," *The Elementary School Journal.*
3. Carolyn N. Hedley, "Mainstreaming and the Classroom Teacher: A Practical Approach," *Reading Horizons.*
4. Natalie Barraga, *Visual Handicaps and Learning,* p. 14.
5. Barbara Bateman, *Reading and the Psycholinguistic Processes of Partially Seeing Children.*
6. Richard M. Demott, "Verbalism and Affective Meaning for Blind, Severely Visually Impaired and Normally Sighted Children," *The New Outlook for the Blind.*
7. Bateman, *Reading and the Psycholinguistic Process of Partially Seeing Children.*
8. Berthold Lowenfeld, ed. *The Visually Handicapped Child in School.*
9. Samuel A. Kirk and James J. Gallagher, *Educating Exceptional Children,* 3rd ed., p. 268.
10. Donald F. Moores, *Educating the Deaf: Psychology, Principles and Practices,* p. 5.
11. Julia M. Davis; Patricia G. Stelmachovicz; Neil T. Shepard; and Michael P. Gorga, "Characteristics of Hearing-Impaired Children in the Public Schools: Part II-Psychoeducational Data," *Journal of Speech and Hearing Disorders.*
12. A. Gentile, *Further Studies in Achievement Testing, Hearing Impaired Students;* Raymond J. Trybus and Michael A. Karchmer, "School Achievement Scores of Hearing Impaired Children: National Data on Achievement Status and Growth Patterns," *American Annals of the Deaf.*
13. Gail Pflaster, "A Factor Analysis of Variables Related to Academic Performance of Hearing-Impaired Children in Regular Classes," *The Volta Review.*
14. Richard G. Brill, "The Relationship of Wechsler IQ's to Academic Achievement Among Deaf Students," *Exceptional Children.*
15. Kirk and Gallagher, *Educating Exceptional Children,* pp. 213–23.
16. Alfred D. Larson and June B. Miller, "The Hearing Impaired," in *Exceptional Children and Youth: An Introduction,* ed. by Edward L. Meyen, pp. 463–65.
17. Eli M. Bower, *Early Identification of Emotionally Handicapped Children in School,* 2nd ed.
18. Kirk and Gallagher, *Educating Exceptional Children,* pp. 406–20.
19. Kirk and Gallagher, *Educating Exceptional Children,* pp. 140–52.
20. Steven R. Forness; Arthus B. Silverstein; and Donald Guthrie, "Relationship Between Classroom Behavior and Achievement of Mildly Mentally Retarded Children," *American Journal of Mental Deficiency.*

21. Oliver P. Kolstoe, *Teaching Educable Mentally Retarded Children,* 2nd ed., p. 27.
22. David C. Gardner and Margaret Kurtz, "Teaching Technical Vocabulary to Handicapped Students," *Reading Improvement.*
23. M. Lally, "Computer-assisted Teaching of Sight-Word Recognition for Mentally Retarded School Children," *American Journal of Mental Deficiency.*
24. Frances M. Guthrie and Patricia M. Cunningham, "Teaching Decoding Skills to Educable Mentally Handicapped Children," *The Reading Teacher.*
25. National Advisory Committee on Handicapped Children, *First Annual Report, Subcommittee on Education of the Committee on Labor and Public Welfare, U.S. Senate,* p. 14.
26. U.S. National Joint Committee on Learning Disabilities, "Revised Definition of LD," *The Reading Teacher.*
27. Hap Gilliland, *A Practical Guide to Remedial Reading,* pp. 282–83.
28. Carol Strickland Beers and James Wheelock Beers, "Early Identification of Learning Disabilities: Facts and Fallacies," *The Elementary School Journal.*
29. Donald J. Johnson and Helmer R. Myklebust, *Learning Disabilities: Educational Principles and Practices.*
30. Gaea Leinhardt; Naomi Zigmond; and William W. Cooley, "Reading Instruction and Its Effects," *American Educational Research Journal.*
31. Sidney P. Marland, *Education of the Gifted and Talented,* p. 10.
32. Lewis M. Terman and Melita H. Oden, *The Gifted Group at Midlife: Thirty-Five Years' Follow-Up of the Superior Child, Genetic Studies of Genius.*
33. Margaret Bynum, *Curriculum for Gifted Students.*
34. B. Marian Swanson and Diane J. Willis, *Understanding Exceptional Children and Youth,* p. 133.
35. Swanson and Willis, *Understanding Exceptional Children and Youth,* pp. 137–40.
36. Jean R. Harber and Jane N. Beatty, *Reading and the Black English Speaking Child,* p. 20.
37. Kha Dennard, "Commentary: A Black Educator Speaks About Black English," *The Reading Teacher.*
38. Neal Justin, "Culture Conflict and Mexican-American Achievement," *School and Society.* F. Cordasco, "Puerto Rican Pupils and American Education," in *Education and the Many Faces of the Disadvantaged: Cultural and Historical Perspectives,* ed. W. W. Brickman and S. Lehrer, pp. 126–31.
39. Swanson and Willis, *Understanding Exceptional Children and Youth,* p. 154.
40. National Education Association, "America's Other Children-Bilingual Multicultural Education: Hope for the Culturally Alienated," *NEA Reporter.*
41. Eustolia Perez, "Oral Language Competence Improves Reading Skills of Mexican American Third Graders," *The Reading Teacher.*
42. Kirk and Gallagher, *Educating Exceptional Children,* pp. 357–78.
43. Kirk and Gallagher, *Educating Exceptional Children,* p. 350.
44. Nicholas W. Bankston, "The Speech and Language Impaired," in *Exceptional Children and Youth,* ed. Edward L. Meyen, p. 390.
45. Leo D. Geoffrion, "Reading and the Nonvocal Child," *The Reading Teacher.*

**Other Suggested Readings**

Adams, Phyllis J., and Anderson, Peggy L. "A Comparison of Teachers' and Mexican-American Children's Perceptions of the Children's Competence." *The Reading Teacher* 36 (October 1982):8–13.

Baratz, Joan C., and Shuy, Roger W., ed. *Teaching Black Children to Read.* Washington, D.C.: Center for Applied Linguistics, 1969.

Barnitz, John G. "Orthographies, Bilingualism, and Learning to Read English as a Second Language," *The Reading Teacher* 35 (February 1982):560–67.

Bauer, Richard H. "Memory, Acquisition, and Category Clustering in Learning Disabled Chidlren," *Journal of Experimental Child Psychology* 27 (June 1979):365–83.

Brooks, C. R., and Riggs, S. T. "WISC-R, WISC, and Reading Achievement Relationships Among Hearing-Impaired Children Attending Public Schools." *The Volta Review* 82 (February/March 1980):96–102.

Caton, Hilda, and Rankin, Earl. "Variability in Age and Experience Among Blind Students Using Basal Reading Materials." *Visual Impairment and Blindness* 74 (April 1980):147–49.

Cermak, Laird S.; Goldberg, Judith; Cermak, Sharon; and Drake, Charles. "The Short-term Memory Ability of Children with Learning Disabilities." *Journal of Learning Disabilities* 13 (January 1980):20–24.

Cohen, S. Alan, and Rodriquez, Samuel. "Experimental Results that Question the Ramirez-Castaneda Model for Teaching Reading to First Grade Mexican Americans." *The Reading Teacher* 34 (October 1980):12–18.

Cohen, Sandra, and Plaskon, Stephen P. "Selecting a Reading Approach for the Mainstreamed Child." *Language Arts* 55 (November/December 1978):966–70.

Dean, Raymond S. "The Use of the Peabody Picture Vocabulary Test with Emotionally Disturbed Adolescents." *Journal of School Psychology* 18 (Summer 1980): 172–75.

Feitelson, Dina. *Cross-Cultural Perspectives on Reading Research.* Newark, Delaware: International Reading Association, 1978.

Feitelson, Dina, ed. *Mother Tongue or Second Language?* Newark, Delaware: International Reading Association, 1979.

Gamez, Gloria I. "Reading in a Second Language: 'Native Language Approach' vs. 'Direct Method'." *The Reading Teacher* 32 (March 1979):665–70.

"Gifted Education." *The Elementary School Journal* 82 (January 1982):179–307.

Gilliland, Hap. "The New View of Native Americans in Children's Books." *The Reading Teacher* 35 (May 1982):912–17.

Johnson, Roger T., and Johnson, David W. "Building Friendships Between Handicapped and Nonhandicapped Students: Effects of Cooperative and Individualistic Instruction." *American Educational Research Journal* 18 (Winter 1981):415–24.

Kirchner, Corinne; Peterson, Richard; and Suhr, Carol. "Trends in School Enrollment and Reading Methods Among Legally Blind School Children, 1963–1978." *Journal of Visual Impairment and Blindness* 73 (November 1979):373–79.

Meyer, Linda A. "The Relative Effects of Word-analysis and Word-supply Correction Procedures with Poor Readers During Word-attack Training." *Reading Research Quarterly* XVII (1982): 544–55.

Miller, Robert. "The Mexican Approach to Developing Bilingual Methods and Teaching Literacy to Bilingual Students." *The Reading Teacher* 35 (April 1982):800–05.

Onativia, Oscan V., and Donoso, Maria Alejandra Reyes. "Basic Issues in Establishing a Bilingual Method." *The Reading Teacher* 30 (April 1977):727–34.

Parr, Gerald D.; Baca, Fernie; and Dixon, Paul. "Individualized versus Group Instruction in Bilingual Education: A Two-Year Study." *The Elementary School Journal* 81 (March 1981):223–27.

Pflaum, Susanna W., and Pascarella, Ernest T. "Interactive Effects of Prior Reading Achievement and Training in Context on the Reading of Learning-Disabled Children." *Reading Research Quarterly* XVI (1980):138–58.

Rigg, Pat. "Dialect and/in/for Reading." *Language Arts* 55 (March 1978):285–90.

Rodrigues, Raymond J. "Toward Pluralism: Multicultural Learners." *Language Arts* 55 (September 1978):728–32.

Rupley, William H., and Blair, Timothy R. "Mainstreaming and Reading Instruction." *The Reading Teacher* 32 (March 1979):762–65.

Scofield, Sandra J. "The Language-delayed Child in the Mainstreamed Primary Classroom." *Language Arts* 55 (September 1978):719–23, 732.

Strom, Robert D., and Johnson, Aileen. "The Elementary School Experience of Children from Mexico." *The Elementary School Journal* 82 (September 1981):37–48.

Thonis, Eleanor Wall. *Literacy for America's Spanish-Speaking Children.* Newark, Delaware: International Reading Association, 1976.

Valverde, Leonard A., ed. *Bilingual Education for Latinos.* Washington, D.C.: Association for Supervision and Curriculum Development, 1978.

Wagener, Elaine H. "Language Arts for the Visually Impaired Child." *Language Arts* 53 (April 1976):432–34.

Wiig, Elizabeth, and Semel, Eleanor M. *Language Disabilities in Children and Adolescents.* Columbus, Ohio: Charles Merrill, 1976.

Wilsendanger, Katherine D., and Birlem, Ellen Davis. "Adapting Language Experience to Reading for Bilingual Pupils." *The Reading Teacher* 32 (March 1979):671–73.

# Fitting the Parts Together

T he teachers at Seabreeze School have examined the concept of diagnostic-prescriptive instruction through the various steps. Each of the components in the steps is essential to the overall effectiveness of the program. Now that the steps have been implemented, the teachers must evaluate the results to see how well they have blended them to form a total diagnostic-prescriptive program.

# 15

As teachers and administrators initially implement a diagnostic-prescriptive reading program, there is a tendency to follow a step-by-step procedure without seeing a total program emerge. Thus, this chapter is designed to review the essential components of a diagnostic-prescriptive reading program and to show how they fit together to make a total program. This review may serve as a standard for evaluating any diagnostic-prescriptive reading program.

# How do all these parts fit together in a diagnostic-prescriptive reading program?

**Vocabulary to Know: A Review**

As the concepts presented in this book are summarized in this chapter, note these terms as designating the major ideas.

Approaches
Continuum of skills
Coordination
Diagnosis
Diagnostic-prescriptive
    reading instruction
Directed reading lesson

Grouping
Parental involvement
Personal reading
Prescriptions
Record-keeping procedure
Scope and sequence

**Components of the Diagnostic-Prescriptive Reading Program**

In reviewing a total diagnostic-prescriptive reading program, it is necessary to examine the component parts of the program. Each of these constituents must be considered if the effectiveness of the total program is to be evaluated. A weakness in any one of them results in a program that may not provide maximum learning opportunities for the student. Therefore, faculties must continuously assess their programs and strive to improve. The essential components of the diagnostic-prescriptive reading program are outlined on the following pages and summarized in table 15.1.

**A scope and sequence or continuum of reading skills guides the teacher in reading skill development.** As discussed in previous chapters, a hierarchy of reading skills is an essential component since the diagnostic-prescriptive program is predicated on the theory of skill development for each student. It is essential to determine the students' strengths and weaknesses in the various skills, so that the teacher can develop an effective prescription for each student. Even though a basal reading series employs a planned scope and sequence of skills, instructors may be unaware of this structure and fail to use it except as outlined by the teacher's manual. Teachers who do not use basal materials must adapt, adopt, or develop a continuum of skills to guide their skills teaching in reading.

To provide for continuous reading skill development, a successful diagnostic-prescriptive reading program should have a good scope and sequence concept of reading skills as its foundation. This hierarchy will assist teachers in introducing skills in a systematic manner for each student in the class.

**Diagnosis determines the reading needs of each student.** Diagnosing the strengths and weaknesses of each student in the classroom is vital to the success of a diagnostic-prescriptive reading program. Determining instructional, independent, and frustrational reading levels, interests, and specific strengths and weaknesses in the skill areas enables the teacher to locate appropriate materials and to develop prescriptions which best meet the needs of the students. These data are obtained through the use of informal and formal testing procedures. Unquestionably, diagnosis is a cornerstone in this total process, and as such it is essential to successful prescriptive teaching.

**A variety of approaches, materials, and activities aids in providing prescriptive instruction.** As teachers learn about student needs in reading through the different diagnostic procedures, they soon realize that there is no one material, approach, or technique that is appropriate for all students. Various approaches, including language-experience and individualized reading, in conjunction with the other approaches described in chapter 8, must be considered in developing prescriptive strategies.

Teachers must also be concerned with how well materials meet student needs. Schools implementing a diagnostic-prescriptive reading program need a variety of materials that accommodate not only the skill needs, but also the interests and learning styles of the students. Using this assortment of approaches and materials, the teacher matches the instructional techniques with the diagnosed student needs. Thus, in a diagnostic-prescriptive reading program, the teacher is the manager of the instructional program.

**The guided or directed reading lesson format leads the teacher in providing reading instruction.** Teachers organize the reading lessons used for prescriptive instruction. The guided or directed reading lesson format helps the teacher to organize lessons through the use of a specified step-by-step procedure that incorporates the areas important to the development and application of reading skills.

This procedure is presented in chapter 8. The steps include

*Readiness:* Developing background for the material to be read together with the vocabulary needed for reading it, is the essential first step.
*Skill development:* The teacher introduces or reviews the skills which students must have in order to read the material.
*Review:* The concepts, vocabulary, and skills should be reviewed to help students relate these to the material to be read. In addition, the teacher and students should establish purposes for reading the material to guide their silent reading.

*Guided Reading:* With purposes for reading the material clearly established, the students should be asked to read the material silently. Following the silent reading, the material must be discussed. At this time the teacher may ask students to read portions aloud as they locate specific information or to identify character moods by verbalizing their statements with appropriate expression.

*Follow-up:* After the students have read the material and discussed it with others so as to summarize the ideas of the author, some follow-up activities may be done. They may include more skill development in areas of need, or activities to encourage students to extend the information given by the author. Activities such as reading other materials related to the topic or interpreting what has been read through art work or creative writing are some of the things that are done as follow-up. Personal reading habits can be greatly enhanced at this time.

Teachers may wish to deviate from this structured format in order to have more variety in their reading lessons. However, they should keep this procedure in mind for every lesson so that the necessary elements of a good reading lesson are always present.

**A systematic record-keeping procedure helps monitor the skill development of the students.** The concept of a diagnostic-prescriptive reading program is based on the idea that the teacher knows the reading needs of the students and provides appropriate instruction based on these needs. Thus, the teacher must have a systematic way of recording the strengths and weaknesses of the entire class as well as of individual students.

As discussed in the section on "Management Systems" in chapter 7, teachers sometimes get so involved in the record-keeping aspect of the program that they lose sight of teaching. This must not happen. Record-keeping procedures should serve to help in the instructional program; they should not interfere with teaching. Schools which have a diagnostic-prescriptive reading program usually have a record-keeping procedure that is used throughout the school. This provides more continuity, and enabling the school to have a record on each student as progress is made from level to level.

The record-keeping procedure is based on the hierarchy of reading skills. There are usually two forms, a class profile and an individual student profile. The class profile sheet is a listing of all students in the class with spaces to mark strengths and weaknesses under each skill. The teacher uses this sheet to group students for specific skill development. The student profile contains information on the individual student and follows the student throughout school.

Record-keeping procedures are crucial in the diagnostic-prescriptive reading program. It is unrealistic to expect teachers to remember the specific needs of every student without some systematic way of recording the information.

**Teachers and administrators must commit themselves to meeting the individual reading needs of each student in the school.** In the diagnostic-prescriptive reading program, the school staff believes that every student can learn to read and communicates this belief to the students. The staff provides various types of learning experiences to help students overcome skill weaknesses and to extend their reading performance to their potential level. In this type of reading program, the teachers realize that students read at many different levels and have varying skill needs. Thus, they use various approaches and materials.

The school atmosphere encourages students to read because the adult models in the school think reading is important; they demonstrate this by reading to the students, and talk about what they read. The teachers motivate the students to read and help them understand how the many skills are used in their reading.

In a school where the entire school staff is committed to reading improvement and individual reading needs are considered, students feel good about learning; therefore, they tend to learn more.

**Teachers work together to develop reading skills and good reading habits for each student in all classes.** As teachers diagnose specific reading needs and record this information for use in providing appropriate prescriptive instruction, it is essential that the information be shared with all teachers who work with the student. This means that diagnostic information determined by the classroom teacher, the special reading teacher, and the content teacher must be combined, so that each teacher can provide the most appropriate instruction for each student.

Coordination is an essential ingredient in the diagnostic-prescriptive program. As outlined in chapter 1, many people must work together in order to implement the program. This involves working together to share diagnostic information and to plan for prescriptive instruction. The classroom teacher and the special reading teacher, such as the Chapter I teacher, must coordinate the instructional program for the students that they share. This is essential because without such coordination, the two teachers may be working against one another by using different approaches and materials to develop the needed skills. Additionally, it is a waste of time to repeat diagnostic procedures when the information could be shared.

Content teachers are also a part of this coordinated effort. All teachers in a departmentalized situation have responsibilities regarding the development of the reading skills appropriate to their content area. This includes determining the strengths and weaknesses in the skills areas and incorporating skill development into their instructional program. The diagnostic data collected by the language arts teacher should be shared with all of the other content teachers. Conversely, the diagnostic information from the various content teachers is shared with the language arts teacher, who may keep the up-to-date diagnostic records on the students. This exchange of information will enhance the coordination and planning of units and skill activities that can be developed jointly.

Planning with the media specialist and guidance counselor can greatly assist in the development of personal reading habits. Their encouragement and leadership will guide students into areas of reading that they have not explored.

**Students spend time reading as a leisure-time activity and to gain knowledge.** One of the major weaknesses of many diagnostic-prescriptive reading programs is the overemphasis on isolated skill development and the virtual exclusion of the application or personal reading aspect of the program. In a good program, students are encouraged to read materials on their own during their extra time and during planned free reading times. Moreover, students are shown how to read materials to gain information.

To enhance reading as a leisure-time activity, many schools have incorporated Sustained Silent Reading activities as described in chapter 13. Through community efforts, other schools have initiated Reading Is Fundamental (RIF) programs sponsored by the Smithsonian Institute. There are many ways to encourage students to read. Teachers must continuously try to motivate students to develop their personal reading skills, because without this aspect of the diagnostic-prescriptive program, reading has no purpose.

**Table 15.1**
Diagnostic-Prescriptive Reading Instruction

| Continuum of Skills | Diagnosis | Prescriptions | Directed Reading Lesson | Record-keeping Procedure |
|---|---|---|---|---|
| Basis for diagnosis and prescriptions | Identify skill strengths and weaknesses | Based on diagnosis | Provides format for reading lessons | Based on continuum of skills |
| Guides record-keeping system | Use variety of instruments | Use variety of approaches and materials | May be adapted as necessary | Record strengths and weaknesses of students |

**The use of various grouping procedures helps to meet the needs of the students.** In some classrooms, students spend most of their time with the students in their group. If this is the "low" group, these students are immediately labeled and tend to associate primarily with others in their group. Their performance seldom improves because they are expected to be the "low" group. The same is true for the other groups when only achievement grouping is used for instruction. Thus, teachers must use a variety of grouping patterns to enhance learning as well as social development.

Interest groups and skill groups provide some shifts in the composition of groups. At some points instruction must be individualized, and occasionally the entire class may work together on a task. Various grouping procedures are used in a diagnostic-prescriptive program to meet student needs, and students move from group to group as instruction is provided to aid their reading development.

**Parents are involved in the program.** No diagnostic-prescriptive reading program is fully functional until parents are involved. Parents assist in reading development in many ways. They serve as reading models in the home environment. This has been identified continuously as a significant factor in reading development.

Parents can also assist in reinforcing skills introduced at school. Teachers involve parents in the development of necessary reading skills when this seems feasible for the student, and when the parent is willing to work with the teacher. Some parents may pressure students to such an extent that more harm than good results. Other parents may determine their own instructional procedures, which may confuse the student. These situations exist; and teachers must consider this in involving parents. However, this should not discourage the inclusion of parents in the reading program.

| Commitment | Coordination | Personal Reading | Grouping | Parental Involvement |
|---|---|---|---|---|
| Encourage students to read | Work together to diagnose | Develop leisure-time reading habits | Use variety of groups | Invite parents into school |
| Meet individual student needs | Plan together for instruction | Learn to read for information | Aids in organizing and managing the class | Tell them about program |
| | | Use SSR and RIF | Have flexible groups | Train them to assist |
| | | Motivate students to read | | |

Some parents may prefer to work in the school as volunteers to tutor students or perform clerical tasks for the teacher. They are welcome additions.

When including parents in the reading program, the school faculty needs to consider the development of a training course to help parents understand the program and develop activities that can be used to help their children. Some schools include information regarding child growth and development and ideas on getting along with children. These programs help parents to feel a part of the school, to meet other parents with similar concerns, and to learn how they can help their children. The total diagnostic-prescriptive program is not functioning properly until parents are welcomed as a part of the school team.

As these points are reviewed, it is very evident that the diagnostic-prescriptive reading program include everyone working together to help develop the reading skills necessary for students to become lifetime readers.

## Summary

The different components of the diagnostic-prescriptive reading program have been summarized in this chapter and in table 15.1. As schools implement a reading program, they must consider all these parts in order to develop a balanced program which meets the needs of all students. These constituents may serve as evaluative criteria as the program is reviewed and revised.

A diagnostic-prescriptive reading program requires faculty commitment and administrative leadership to develop a program that meets the needs of the students. This is not an easy assignment; the rewards of seeing students who enjoy learning because they can read, and the feelings of satisfaction which teachers reflect as they guide these learning experiences, make teaching and learning joyous experiences for all.

**Applying What You Read**

As a reading teacher in a middle school, you are asked to help evaluate a diagnostic-prescriptive reading program. What would you look for?

Ten components of a diagnostic-prescriptive reading program have been identified. Which component do you feel is the most important, and why? How would you rank the others?

**Other Suggested Readings**

Gates, Arthur S. "Teaching Reading Tomorrow." *The Reading Teacher* 23 (December 1969):231–38.

Heathers, Glen. "A Working Definition of Individualized Instruction." *Educational Leadership* 34 (February 1977):342–45.

Hunter, Madeline. "A Tri-Dimensional Approach to Individualization." *Educational Leadership* 34 (February 1977):351–55.

Rupley, William H. "Effective Reading Programs." *The Reading Teacher* 29 (1976):116–20.

Schubert, Delwyn, and Torgerson, Theodore. *Improving the Reading Program.* Dubuque, Iowa: William C. Brown Company Publishers, 1981.

Strange, Michael C. "Considerations for Evaluating Reading Instruction." *Educational Leadership* 36 (December 1978):178–81.

Webb, L. Leon, and Howard, Theresa E. "Individualized Learning: An Achievable Goal for All!" *Educational Leadership* 34 (February 1977):356–60.

# Appendixes

## Appendix A

**Reading Skills List**

*Prereading Skills*

A. Oral Language Skills
1. Recognize word boundaries.
2. Use adequate vocabulary.
3. Understand basic concepts such as colors, shapes, size, direction.
4. Tell about a picture or object.
5. Express ideas in complete sentences.
6. Relate story in sequence.
7. Participate in discussions.

B. Visual-Motor Skills
1. Coordinate eye-hand movements.
2. Execute directionality in coordinated eye-hand movements.
3. Draw specified designs such as circles and lines.
4. Reproduce designated designs, numerals, letters, or words.
5. Reproduce own name in manuscript.

C. Visual Discrimination/Visual Memory Skills
1. Match shapes, objects, and pictures.
2. Recognize likenesses and differences in objects and designs.
3. Recognize likenesses and differences in numerals, letters, and words.
4. Match uppercase and lowercase letters.
5. Identify from memory, objects, pictures, or designs briefly presented.
6. Classify objects or pictures.

7. Recognize own name in manuscript.
8. Recognize designated designs, numerals, letters, or words.
9. Match colors.
10. Follow picture, design, letter or word in sequence.
11. Identify uppercase and lowercase letter symbols.

D. Visual Comprehension Skills
1. Identify details in pictures.
2. Identify missing parts in picture/symbol.
3. Identify sequence of pictures/story from pictures.
4. Identify common characteristics of objects.

E. Auditory Discrimination/Auditory Memory Skills
1. Discriminate among various environmental sounds.
2. Discriminate among different sounds of letters and words.
3. Identify simple everyday sounds.
4. Recognize rhyming words.
5. Follow simple one- and two-step directions.
6. Identify sounds in words.
7. Reproduce simple sounds, letters, and words.
8. Identify beginning sounds in words.
9. Identify ending sounds in words.
10. Identify medial sounds in words.
11. Use rhyming words to complete sentences.
12. Identify syllables in words.

F. Auditory (Listening) Comprehension Skills
   1. Follow directions.
   2. Associate object or picture with oral description.
   3. Identify main idea.
   4. Identify main character.
   5. Identify details in sentence and story.
   6. Identify sequence of events.
   7. Identify relationships such as cause-effect and comparisons.
   8. Interpret descriptive language.
   9. Recognize emotions of characters and story.
   10. Draw conclusions.
   11. Anticipate outcomes.

## Word Recognition Skills

A. Sight Vocabulary
   1. Identify familiar words, i.e., nouns, verbs, etc.
   2. Identify basic sight words in context.

B. Phoneme-Grapheme Correspondences (Phonics)
   1. Reproduce from memory uppercase and lowercase letter symbols.
   2. Associate concept of consonants with appropriate letters.
   3. Associate concept of vowels with appropriate letters.
   4. Associate sounds and symbols for initial, medial, and final consonant sounds.
   5. Recognize sounds and symbols of variant consonant patterns.
   6. Associate sounds and symbols for initial, medial, and final long and short vowel patterns.
   7. Recognize sounds and symbols of variant vowel patterns.
   8. Blend sounds to form words.
   9. Substitute initial, medial, and final sounds to form new words.

C. Structural Analysis
   1. Recognize compound words.
   2. Recognize contractions and original word forms.
   3. Analyze affixes (suffixes and prefixes) in words.
   4. Recognize inflectional endings.
   5. Divide unknown words into syllables.
      a. Dividing between two consonants
      b. Dividing between single consonants
      c. Dividing with *le* endings
      d. Dividing words with prefixes and suffixes
      e. Dividing words with common endings
   6. Accent appropriate syllables in words.
      a. Accenting first syllable
      b. Accenting compound words
      c. Accenting base word with prefix or suffix
      d. Using primary and secondary accents

D. Contextual Analysis
   1. Use picture clues to determine unknown words.
   2. Use context clues to determine unknown words.
      a. Sentence sense (missing word) clue
      b. Synonym, antonym, and homonym clue
      c. Familiar expression clue
      d. Comparison and contrast clue
      e. Words and multiple-meaning clue
      f. Summary Clue

## Comprehension Skills

A. Literal Skills
   1. Understand concrete words, phrases, clauses, and sentence patterns.
   2. Identify stated main ideas.
   3. Recall details (who, what, when, where, how).
   4. Remember stated sequence of events.
   5. Select stated cause-effect relationships.
   6. Contrast and compare information.
   7. Identify character traits and actions.
   8. Interpret abbreviations, symbols, and acronyms.
   9. Follow written directions.
   10. Classify information.

B. Interpretive (Inferential) Skills
   1. Predict outcomes.
   2. Interpret character traits.
   3. Draw conclusions.
   4. Make generalizations.
   5. Perceive relationships.
   6. Understand implied causes and effects.
   7. Identify implied main ideas.
   8. Interpret figurative language.
   9. Interpret meaning of capitalization and punctuation in a selection.
   10. Understand mood and emotional reactions.
   11. Interpret pronouns and antecedents.

12. Understand author's purpose and point of view.
13. Construe meaning by signal words.
14. Understand meaning of abstract words.
15. Summarize information.
16. Recognize implied sequence.
17. Use context clues to determine meaning.
    a. Synonym, antonym, and homonym clue
    b. Familiar expression clue
    c. Comparison and contrast clue
    d. Words and multiple meaning clue
    e. Summary clue
18. Synthesize data.

C. Critical Reading Skills
1. Identify relevant and irrelevant information.
2. Interpret propaganda techniques.
3. Perceive bias.
4. Identify adequacy of materials.
5. Understand reliability of author.
6. Differentiate facts and opinions.
7. Separate real and unreal information.
8. Understand fallacies in reasoning.

*Study Skills*

A. Reference Skills
1. Use dictionary.
    a. Alphabetical order and guide words
    b. Pronunciation symbols
    c. Accent marks
    d. Syllabication

2. Use encyclopedias.
3. Use specialized reference materials such as the atlas and almanac.
4. Use library card catalog.

B. Organizational Skills
1. Develop outlines.
2. Underline important points or key ideas.
3. Take notes during reading.

C. Specialized Study Skills
1. Use title page.
2. Use table of contents and lists of charts.
3. Locate introduction, preface, and foreword.
4. Use appendix.
5. Identify bibliography and lists of suggested readings.
6. Use glossary and index.
7. Use study questions.
8. Read maps, tables, graphs, and diagrams.
9. Use footnotes, typographical aids, and marginal notes.
10. Preview, skim, or scan materials.
11. Adjust rate according to material and purpose.
12. Understand general and specialized vocabulary.
13. Use appropriate study techniques such as SQ3R.

# Appendix B

## Informal Reading Inventories

Austin, M. C.; Bush, C. L.; and Huebner, M. H. *Reading Evaluation.* New York: Ronald Press, 1961.

Bader, Lois A. *Bader Reading and Language Inventory.* New York: Macmillan Publishing Company, Inc., 1983.

Botel, Morton. *Botel Reading Inventory.* Chicago, Illinois: Follett, 1978.

Brown, Don A. *Reading Diagnosis and Remediation.* Englewood Cliffs, New Jersey: Prentice-Hall, Inc., 1982, pp. 318–55.

Burns, Paul C., and Roe, Betty D. *Informal Reading Assessment.* Chicago: Rand McNally, 1980.

Ekwall, Eldon E. *Ekwall Reading Inventory.* Rockleigh, New Jersey: Allyn and Bacon, 1979.

Jacobs, Donald, and Searfoss, Lyndon. *Diagnostic Reading Inventory.* Dubuque, Iowa: Kendall/Hunt Publishing Company, 1978.

Johns, Jerry L. *Basic Reading Inventory,* 2nd ed. Dubuque, Iowa: Kendall-Hunt, 1981.

McCracken, Robert A. *Standard Reading Inventory.* Klamath Falls, Oregon: Klamath Printing Company, 1966.

Rakes, Thomas A.; Choate, Joyce S.; and Waller, Gayle Lane. *Individual Evaluation Procedures in Reading.* Englewood Cliffs, New Jersey: Prentice-Hall, Inc., 1983.

Rubin, Dorothy. *Diagnosis and Correction in Reading Instruction*. New York: Holt, Rinehart and Winston, 1982.

Silvaroli, N. J. *Classroom Reading Inventory,* 4th ed. Dubuque, Iowa: William C. Brown, 1982.

Smith, Nila Banton. *Graded Selections for Informal Reading Diagnosis—Grades 1–3*. New York: New York University Press, 1959; *Grades 4–6,* 1962.

Sucher, Floyd, and Allred, Ruel A. *Sucher-Allred Reading Placement Inventory*. Oklahoma City, Oklahoma: Economy Company, 1981.

Woods, Mary Lynn, and Moe, Alden J. *Analytical Reading Inventory,* 2nd ed. Columbus, Ohio: Charles E. Merrill, 1981.

**Listening Comprehension Inventories**

Durrell, Donald D., and Catterson, Jane. *Durrell Analysis of Reading Difficulty*. New York: The Psychological Corporation, 1981.

Durrell, Donald D.; Hayes, Mary T.; and Brassard, Mary B. *Durrell Listening-Reading Series*. New York: The Psychological Corporation, 1970.

———. *Sequential Tests of Educational Progress.* 3rd ed. Menlo Park, California: Addison-Wesley Testing Service, 1977.

Spache, George D. *Diagnostic Reading Scales*. 3rd ed. Monterey, California: CTB McGraw-Hill Inc., 1981.

## Appendix C

### Sources for Observation Checklists

Barbe, Walter B. *Educator's Guide to Personalized Reading Instruction*. Englewood Cliffs, New Jersey: Prentice-Hall, 1976.

Durrell, Donald D. *Durrell Analysis of Reading Difficulty*. New York: The Psychological Corporation, 1981.

Miller, Wilma A. *Reading Diagnosis Kit*. New York: The Center for Applied Research in Education, Inc., 1978.

Otto, Wayne, et al. *Focused Reading Instruction*. Reading, Mass.: Addison-Wesley, 1974.

Spache, George D., and Spache, Evelyn B. *Reading in the Elementary School*. 4th ed. Boston: Allyn and Bacon, 1977.

### Sources for Interest Inventories

Brown, Don A. *Reading Diagnosis and Remediation*. Englewood Cliffs, New Jersey: Prentice-Hall, Inc., 1982, pp. 373–75.

Fry, Edward. *Elementary Reading Instruction*. New York: McGraw-Hill Book Company, 1977.

Gillet, Jean Wallace, and Temple, Charles. *Understanding Reading Problems: Assessment and Instruction*. Boston: Little, Brown and Company, 1982, pp. 325–28.

Harris, Larry A., and Smith, Carl B. *Reading Instruction*. New York: Holt, Rinehart and Winston, 1980.

Potter, Thomas C., and Rae, Gwenneth. *Informal Reading Diagnosis*. Englewood Cliffs, New Jersey: Prentice-Hall, Inc., 1973.

Rakes, Thomas A.; Choate, Joyce S.; and Waller, Gayle Lane. *Individual Evaluation Procedures in Reading*. Englewood Cliffs, New Jersey: Prentice-Hall, Inc., 1983.

Rubin, Dorothy. *Diagnosis and Correction in Reading Instruction*. New York: Holt, Rinehart and Winston, 1982, pp. 172–74.

Silvaroli, Nicholas J.; Kear, Dennis J.; and McKenna, Michael C. *A Classroom Guide to Reading Assessment and Instruction*. Dubuque, Iowa: Kendall/Hunt Publishing Company, 1982. pp. 95–104.

Strang, Ruth. *Diagnostic Teaching of Reading,* 2nd ed. New York: McGraw-Hill Book Company, 1969.

# Appendix D

**Bibliography of Activity Books for Reading and Language Arts**

Aeemer, Gail, and Fowler, Christopher. *Frosty Main Ideas*. Akron, Ohio: Carson-Dellosa Publishing, 1981.

Anderson, Sandra; Archibald, Georgia; and McRee, Nancy J. *Activities for Auditory Learning Skills*. St. Louis, Missouri: Milliken Publishing Company, 1977.

Anderson, Sandra; Archibald, Georgia; and McRee, Nancy J. *Visual Learning Skills*. St. Louis, Missouri: Milliken Publishing Company, 1977.

Artman, John, *Slanguage*. Carthage, Illinois: Good Apple Inc., 1980.

————. *Newspaper Primary Reading Program-Level I*. Atlanta, Georgia: Atlanta Newspapers, 1978.

————. *Newspaper Primary Reading Program-Level II*. Atlanta, Georgia: Atlanta Newspapers, 1979.

Barkman, Vickie Rochelle. *Learning From Soup to Nuts*. Danville, New York: The Instructor Publications, Inc., 1978.

Barrett, Sally. *The Sound of the Week*. Carthage, Illinois: Good Apple, Inc., 1980.

Bauman, Toni, and Zinkgraf, June. *Fall Fantasies*. Carthage, Illinois: Good Apple, Inc., 1980.

Bauman, Toni, and Zinkgraf, June. *Spring Surprises*. Carthage, Illinois: Good Apple, Inc., 1980.

Bentson, Linda. *Claimed Story*. Grand Forks, North Dakota: Grand Forks Herald, 1979.

Berryman, Charles. *Improving Reading Skills*. Atlanta, Georgia: Atlanta Journal and Constitution, 1973.

Bohlen, Sue; Digby, Joyce; and Larson, Betty. *Just Hanging Around*. Minneapolis, Minnesota: T. S. Denison and Compnay, Inc., 1979.

Borba, Craig, and Borba, Michele. *The Good Apple Guide to Learning Centers*. Carthage, Illinois: Good Apple, Inc., 1978.

Borba, Michelle, and Ungaro, Dan. *The Complete Letter Book*. Carthage, Illinois: Good Apple, Inc., 1980.

————. *Imagineering the Reading Process*. Carthage, Illinois: Good Apple, Inc., 1980.

Breznau, Claudia Blamer. *The Real Happily Ever After Book*. Nashville, Tennessee: Incentive Publications, Inc., 1980.

Brosnahan, JoAnne Patricia, and Milne, Barbara Walters. *A Calendar of Home/School Activities*. Santa Monica, California: Goodyear Publishing Company, Inc., 1978.

Carlson, Ruth Kearney. *Poetry for Today's Child*. Dansville, New York: The Instructor Publications, Inc., 1972.

Carsetti, Janet K. *Motivational Activities for Reluctant Readers*. Columbia, Maryland: Read Inc., 1979.

Carson, Patti, and Dellosa, Janet. *All Aboard for Readiness Skills*. Akron, Ohio: Carson-Dellosa Publishing, 1982.

————. *Cartloads of Creative Story Starters*. Akron, Ohio: Carson-Dellosa Publishing, 1982.

————. *Swinging Into Vowels*. Akron, Ohio: Carson-Dellosa Publishing, 1978.

Cheyney, Arnold B., *Press*. Stevensville, Michigan: Educational Service, Inc., 1978.

————. *Video*. Stevensville, Michigan: Educational Service, Inc., 1980.

————. *Newspaper Reading Activities*. Cincinnati, Ohio: Cincinnati Enquirer and Cincinnati Post, 1981.

Colvin, Mary Paris (ed.). *Instructor's Big Idea Book*. Dansville, New York: The Instructor Publications, 1978.

Coudron, Jill M. *Alphabet Puppets*. Belmont, California. Fearon Teacher Aids, 1979.

————. *Everybody Loves the Comics*. Louisville, Kentucky: Courier Journal-Louisville Times, 1979.

Criscuola, Nicholas. *Look It Up!* Belmont, California: Fearon Pitman Publishers, Inc., 1980.

————. *137 Activities for Reading Enrichment*. Dansville, New York: The Instructor Publications, Inc., 1975.

Daily, Sandra S. *The Newspaper as a Focus for Compositions*. Houston, Texas: Houston Post, 1981.

D'Ambrosia, Roberta; Strock, Virginia; and Zographos, Marget, *Spell Well*. Belmont, California: Fearon Teacher Aids, 1980.

Davidson, Tom and others. *The Learning Center Book: An Integrated Approach.* Pacific Palisades, California: Goodyear Publishing Company, Inc., 1976.

Dellosa, Janet, and Carson, Patti. *Prize Winning Learning Activities.* Akron, Ohio: Carson-Dellosa Publishing, 1980.

——— . *Racing Into Reading Skills.* Akron, Ohio: Carson-Dellosa Publishing, 1978.

——— . *Rolling Into Primary Comprehension.* Akron, Ohio: Carson-Dellosa Publishing, 1978.

——— . *Throw Your Whole Self Into Comprehension.* Akron, Ohio: Carson-Dellosa Publishing, 1977.

——— . *Well "Seasoned" Story Starters.* Akron, Ohio: Carson-Dellosa Publishing, 1979.

Dey, Denny, and Grimm, Gary. *Storytelling.* Carthage, Illinois: Good Apple, Inc., 1979.

Dietrich, Wilson G. *Create With Paper Bags.* Minneapolis, Minnesota: T. S. Denison and Company, Inc., 1972.

Ellis, Mary Jackson. *Finger Play Approach to Dramatization.* Minneapolis, Minnesota: T. S. Denison and Company, Inc., 1960.

Farnette, Cherrie. *Newspaper Know-How.* Nashville, Tennessee: Incentive Publications, 1981.

Farnette, Cherrie; Forte, Imogene; and Loss, Barbara. *Kids' Stuff Reading and Writing Readiness.* Nashville, Tennessee: Incentive Publications, Inc., 1975.

Forgan, Harry W. The Reading Corner: *Ideas, Games and Activities for Individualizing Reading.* Pacific Palisades, California: Goodyear Publishing Company, Inc., 1977.

Forte, Imogene. *Skillstuff, Vol. 1. Reading.* Nashville, Tennessee: Incentive Publications, Inc., 1979.

Forte, Imogene and others. *Cornering Creative Writing.* Nashville, Tennessee: Incentive Publications, 1974.

Forte, Imogene; Frank, Marjorie; and MacKenzie, Joy. *Kid's Stuff-Reading and Language Experiences Intermediate—Jr. High.* Nashville, Tennessee: Incentive Publications, 1973.

Forte, Imogene; MacKenzie, Joy; and Collier, Mary Jo. *Kid's Stuff-Kindergarten and Nursery School.* Nashville, Tennessee: Incentive Publications, Inc., 1981.

Forte, Imogene, and MacKenzie, Joy. *Skillstuff. Volume II. Writing.* Nashville, Tennessee: Incentive Publications, Inc., 1980.

——— . *Skillstuff-Volume III. Reasoning.* Nashville, Tennessee: Incentive Publications, Inc., 1976.

——— . *The Yellow Pages for Students and Teachers.* Nashville, Tennessee: Incentive Publications, Inc., 1980.

Forte, Imogene, and Pangle, Mary Ann. *Comprehension Magic.* Nashville, Tennessee: Incentive Publications, Inc., 1977.

——— . *Mini-Center Stuff.* Nashville, Tennessee: Incentive Publications, Inc., 1976.

——— . *More Center Stuff for Nooks. Crannies and Corners.* Nashville, Tennessee: Incentive Publications, 1976.

——— . *P's and O's For The Sounds We Use.* Nashville, Tennessee: Incentive Publications, Inc., 1978.

——— . *Spelling Magic.* Nashville, Tennessee: Incentive Publications, Inc., 1976.

Forte, Imogene; Pangle, Mary Ann; and Tupa, Robbie. *Pumpkins, Pinwheels, and Peppermint Packages.* Nashville, Tennessee: Incentive Publications, Inc., 1974.

Frank, Marjorie. *If You're Trying to Teach Kids How to Write, You've Gotta Have This Book.* Nashville, Tennessee: Incentive Publications, Inc., 1979.

——— . *Creative Newspaper Innovations.* Colorado Springs, Colorado: The Gazette Telegraph, 1979.

Glover, Susanne, and Grewe, Georgeann. *Bone Up on Book Reports.* Carthage, Illinois: Good Apple, Inc., 1981.

——— . *The Newspaper as a Means of Horizontal Enrichment.* Grand Forks, North Dakota: Grand Forks Herald, 1977.

Grimm, Gary, and Mitchell, Don. *The Good Apple Creative Writing Book.* Carthage, Illinois: Good Apple, Inc., 1978.

——— . *The Good Apple Spelling Book.* Carthage, Illinois: Good Apple, Inc., 1976.

Gutzler, Dorothy, and Linn, Helen. *110 Reading Comprehension Activities.* Dansville, New York: The Instructor Publications, Inc., 1976.

Harris, Dorothy M. *Hayes Phonics Guide and Handbook.* Wilkinsburg, Pennsylvania, 1975.

Hendricks, William. *Scribe*. Stevensville, Michigan: Educational Services, Inc., 1976.

Hiebert, Jim. *Super Cereal Box Activities*. Belmont, California: Fearon Teacher Aids, 1981.

Hoover, Rosalie, and Murphy, Barbara. *Learning About Our 5 Senses*. Carthage, Illinois: Good Apple, Inc., 1981.

Hoover, Sharon. *Reading Ideas*. Dansville, New York: The Instructor Publications, Inc., 1981.

Indrisano, Roselmina. *Resource Activity Book Reading: The Fourth Dimension*. Dallas, Texas: Ginn and Company, 1976.

————. *Easy Do-Its*. Dansville, New York: The Instructor Publications, Inc., 1981.

Jordan, Anna. *Using the Newspaper to Reinforce Communication Skills*. Tampa, Florida: The Tampa Tribune/The Tampa Times, 1979.

Jay, Flora, and Richardson, Lynn J. *Humorous Antonym Hunt, Homograph Hunt, Homaphone Hunt and Vocabulary through Cartoons*. Johnson City, Tennessee, 1980.

Kahle, Gratia Underhill. *Favorite Finger Plays and Action Rhymes*. Minneapolis, Minnesota: T. S. Denison and Company, Inc., 1978.

Kaplan, Sandra Nina and others. *The Big Book of People and Word Games and Activities*. Pacific Palisades, California: Goodyear Publishing Company, Inc., 1976.

Kay, Drina. *All the Desk's A Stage*. Nashville, Tennessee. Incentive Publications, 1982.

Kay, Evelyn. *Games that Teach for Children Three Through Six*. Minneapolis, Minnesota: T. S. Denison and Company, Inc., 1981.

Keith, Joy L. *Comprehension Joy*. Naperville, Illinois: Joy L. Keith, 1974.

Kindig, Dean. *Ready!Set!Read!* Dansville, New York: The Instructor Publications, Inc., 1978.

Krakker, Valeria. *Teaching with Games in the Classroom*. Minneapolis, Minnesota: T. S. Denison and Company, Inc., 1966.

Krisvoy, Juel. *The Good Apple Puppet Book*. Carthage, Illinois: Good Apple, Inc., 1981.

Lass-Kayser, Mary Jo. *Teacher's Treasury of Classroom Reading Activities*. West Nyack, New York: Parker Publishing Company, Inc., 1979.

Linder, Jay. *Newspaper Learning Package*. Wenatchee, Washington: The Wenatchee World, 1971.

Lipson, Greta Barclay, and Romatowski, Jane A. *Calliope*. Carthage, Illinois: Good Apple, Inc., 1981.

Lipson, Greta Barclay, and Greenberg, Bernice N. *Extra! Extra! Read All About It*. Carthage, Illinois: Good Apple, Inc., 1981.

Lipson, Greta, and Morrison, Baxter. *Fact, Fantasy, and Folklore*. Carthage, Illinois: Good Apple, Inc., 1977.

Love, Marla. *20 Reading Comprehension Games*. Belmont, California: Fearon Pitman Publishers, Inc., 1977.

Lucas, Virginia H. *Chalkboard Techniques and Activities for Teaching Writing*. Columbus, Ohio: Zaner-Bloser, Inc., 1976.

Mallett, Jerry J. *Classroom Reading Games Activities Kit*. New York: The Center for Applied Research in Education, Inc., 1975.

Michener, Dorothy Muschlitz. *First Place: Skills and Activities for Early Learning*. Nashville, Tennessee: Incentive Publications, Inc., 1982.

Minn, Loretta Brandt. *Teach Speech*. Carthage, Illinois: Good Apple, Inc., 1982.

Mitchell, Glenda. *Food, Fun and Fundamental Skills*. Carthage, Illinois: Good Apple Inc., 1980.

Moldenhauer, Janice. *Developing Dictionary Skills*. Carthage, Illinois: Good Apple, Inc., 1979.

Montgomery, Maxine. *Dramatizations for Young Children Using Three-Dimensional Masks*. Minneapolis, Minnesota: T. S. Denison and Company, Inc., 1979.

Moore, Nancy M. *Everything Under the Sun for Teaching*. Paoli, Pennsylvania: Instructo/McGraw-Hill, 1980.

Obriecht, Carole Hillman. *The Learning Center*. Illinois: Ideal Publications, 1976.

Pike, Harper. *Here's Extra Help*. Carthage, Illinois: Good Apple, Inc., 1980.

Platts, Mary E. *Phonics*. Stevensville, Michigan: Educational Service, Inc., 1980.

Raskin, Bruce, ed. *Mud Puddles, Rainbows and Asparagus Tips. Learning's Best Language Arts Ideas*. Palo Alto, California: Education Today Company, Inc., 1979.

Roderman, W. *Using the Want Ads*. Hayward, California: Janus Book Publishers, 1977.

Sawitz, Mike, and Ourth, John. *Physical Fun for Everyone*. Carthage, Illinois: Good Apple, Inc., 1980.

Schasre, June Marie. *Study Work Assignments for Primary Grades*. Minneapolis, Minnesota: T. S. Denison & Co., Inc., 1974.

Schrader, Diana. *A Guide for Using Television In Your Classroom*. Carthage, Illinois: Good Apple, Inc., 1980.

Schurr, Sandra. *Library Lingo*. Nashville, Tennessee: Incentive Publications, 1981.

Schurr, Sandra. *Poetry Pack Rat*. Nashville, Tennessee: Incentive Publications, 1979.

Sealey, Leonard; Sealey, Nancy; and Millmore, Marcia. *Children's Writing*. Newark, Delaware: International Reading Association, 1979.

Smith, Charlene W. *The Listening Activity Book*. Belmont, California: Fearon Publishers, Inc., 1975.

Short, J. Rodney, and Dickerson, Bev. *The Newspaper*. Belmont, California: Pitman Learning, Inc., 1980.

Spache, Evelyn B. *Reading Activities for Child Involvement*. 2nd ed. Boston: Allyn and Bacon, Inc., 1976.

Stanish, Bob. *Hippogriff Feathers-Encounters with Creative Thinking*. Carthage, Illinois: Good Apple, Inc., 1981.

——— . *Sunflowering-Thinking, Feeling Doing Activities for Creative Expression*. Carthage, Illinois: Good apple, Inc., 1977.

Sylvester, Diane, and Schwartz, Linda. *Macmillan Instant Activities Program*. Macmillan Educational company: 1981.

Taetzsch, Sandra Zeitlin, and Taetzsch, Lyn. *Preschool Games and Activities*. Belmont, California: Fearon Teacher Aids, 1974.

Thompson, Richard A.; McGregor, Carlyne Ussery; and Thompson, Janet R. *Teacher's Galaxy of Reading Improvement Activities—With Model Lesson Plans*. West Nyack, New York: Parker Publishing Company, Inc., 1979.

Verner, Zenobia. *Collections: A Newsbook of Vocabulary Activities*. Houston, Texas: Clayton Publishing Company, 1979.

——— . *Newsbook of Capitalization*. Houston, Texas: Clayton Publishing Company, 1979.

——— . *Newsbook of Reading Comprehension Activities*. Houston, Texas: Clayton Publishing Company, 1978.

Walling, Elaine (ed.) *Path to Reading A Resource Guide for Prereading Experiences*. New York: Random House, Inc., 1977.

Wayman, Joe. *The Other Side of Reading*. Carthage, Illinois: Good Apple, Inc., 1980.

Wayman, Joe, and Plum, Lorraine. *Secrets and Surprises*. Carthage, Illinois: Good Apple, Inc., 1977.

Waynant, Louise F. *Learning Centers II*. Paoli, Pennsylvania: Instructo/McGraw-Hill, 1977.

Waynant, Louise F., and Wilson, Robert M. *Learning Centers . . . A Guide for Effective Use*. Paoli, Pennsylvania: The Instructo Corporation, 1974.

Wedemeyer, Avaril, and Cejka, Joyce. *Intermediate Language Arts Classroom Ideas and Activities*. Colorado: Love Publishing Company, 1978.

——— . *Primary Language Arts*. Colorado: Love Publishing Company, 1978.

Williams, DeAtna M. *More Paper-Bag Puppets*. Belmont, California: Fearon Teacher Aids, 1968.

——— . *Paper-Bag Puppets*. Belmont, California: Fearon-Pitman Publishers, Inc., 1966.

Wilson, Robert M., and Barnes, Marcia M. *Using Newspapers To Teach Reading Skills*. Maryland: ANPA Foundation, 1975.

Zinkgraf, June, and Bauman, Toni. *Winter Wonders*. Carthage, Illinois: Good Apple, Inc., 1978.

Compiled by Lucille K. Johnson, East Baton Rouge Parish Schools, Louisiana.

## Appendix E

**Interest and Attitude Inventory**

Name _____ Date _____

Grade in School _____ Age _____ Teacher_____

I. Home Relationships

   1. Do you have any brothers or sisters? _____

      Do you play together? _____

      What kinds of activities do you like to do with them? _____

      _____

   2. What do you enjoy doing with your mother? _____

      _____

      With your father? _____

   3. Do you help with the chores at home? _____

      What do you do to help? _____

   4. When you have an hour or two at home that you can spend just as you

      please, what do you like best to do? _____

      _____

II. Personal Life

   1. What would you like to be when you grow up? _____

      _____

   2. What frightens or upsets you the most at home? _____

      At school? _____

   3. What do you like most about yourself? _____

      _____

      What do you dislike most about yourself?_____

   4. Do you have a place to go and be alone? _____

      Where? _____

   5. I am happy when _____

      My greatest worry is _____

      The best thing that ever happened to me was _____

      _____

Printed with permission of Patti Russell, Martha Collins-Cheek, and Earl Cheek.

I am really afraid when _____

When I was younger _____

III. Reading

  1. What is the name of your favorite book? _____

     _____

     Why do you like it? _____

  2. Do you have any books of your own to read at home? _____ What are

     the names of some of them? _____

     _____

  3. Do your parents read stories to you? _____

     Do you sometimes read to your parents? _____

  4. How much do you like to read? Very much _____

     Not very much _____ Not at all _____

  5. Do you ever read magazines? _____ Comics? _____

     Newspapers? _____

  6. How important do you think it is to learn to read? Very important _____

     A little _____ Not at all _____

  7. I love to read when _____

     Reading _____

IV. School

  1. Do you like school? _____

     What is your favorite subject? _____

     Why? _____

     What is your least favorite subject? _____

     Why? _____

  2. What did you enjoy most about school during the past year? _____

  3. Do you ever get into trouble at school? If so, what kind? _____

  4. When do you do your homework? _____

     Where do you do it? _____

  5. Do you have a set time to go to bed on school days? _____

     What time do you go to bed? _____

  6. School would be better if only _____

     _____

V. Peer Relationships

1. Do you have a best friend? _____

   Why is he/she your best friend? _____

   _____

2. What do you enjoy doing most with your friends? _____

   _____

3. What would you like to do best? Play with a friend _____

   Be by yourself _____

4. I wish that my friends _____

VI. Interests

1. What are your favorite games to play outdoors? _____

   Indoors? _____

2. Do you like sports? _____ Which sports do you like best?_____

3. Do you have an after-school activity, such as team practice, boosters, or any

   lessons? _____

4. Do you have any hobbies or collections? _____

   What are they? _____

   Do you like to make or fix things? _____

   What do you like to make or fix? _____

5. Do you have any pets at home? _____ What kind? _____

   If you do not have any pets, what kind of pet would you choose if you could

   have one? _____

6. If you could have three wishes and they might all come true, what would you

   wish for? _____

   _____

7. What do you usually like to do after school? _____

   When it rains? _____On Saturdays? _____

   In the summer? _____

8. Who do you admire the most? _____

   If you could be somebody else, who would you want to be? _____

9. I wish more than anything else _____ .

VII. Television, Movies, and Radio

   1. What are some of your favorite TV programs? _____

      _____

      What programs do you watch on school days? _____

      _____

      Weekends? _____

   2. Do you like to go to the movies? _____

      Who do you usually go with? _____

      What were some of your favorite movies? _____

      _____

   3. Do you listen to the radio? Every day _____Once a week _____

      Never _____

VIII. Firsthand Experiences

   1. Have you ever been to the circus? _____ On an airplane? _____ To the zoo?
      _____On a boat? _____ On a farm? _____ To summer camp? _____ To a
      museum? _____ Swimming in a pool? _____ To the beach/mountains?
      _____ To the grocery? _____ On a picnic? _____ On a long vacation trip?
      _____ To a restaurant/cafe? _____

IX. Unaided Questions

   1. Now that I have asked you these questions, is there something else you
      would like to tell me about yourself?

# Appendix F

**A Scale of Reading Attitude Based on Behavior**

Name of student _____ Grade _____ Date _____

School _____ Observer _____

Directions: Check the most appropriate of the five blanks by each item below. Only one blank by each item should be checked.

| | Always Occurs | Often Occurs | Occasionally Occurs | Seldom Occurs | Never Occurs |
|---|---|---|---|---|---|
| 1. The student exhibits a strong desire to come to the reading circle or to have reading instruction take place. | _____ | _____ | _____ | _____ | _____ |
| 2. The student is enthusiastic and interested in participating once he or she comes to the reading circle or the reading class begins. | _____ | _____ | _____ | _____ | _____ |
| 3. The student asks permission or raises his or her hand to read orally. | _____ | _____ | _____ | _____ | _____ |
| 4. When called upon to read orally, the student eagerly does so. | _____ | _____ | _____ | _____ | _____ |
| 5. The student very willingly answers a question asked in the reading class. | _____ | _____ | _____ | _____ | _____ |
| 6. Contributions in the way of voluntary discussions are made by the student in the reading class. | _____ | _____ | _____ | _____ | _____ |
| 7. The student expresses a desire to be read to by you or someone else, and listens attentively while this is taking place. | _____ | _____ | _____ | _____ | _____ |
| 8. The student makes an effort to read printed materials on bulletin boards, charts, or other displays having writing on them. | _____ | _____ | _____ | _____ | _____ |

C. Glennon Rowell, "An Attitude Scale for Reading." *The Reading Teacher* 25 (February 1972):444. Reproduced with permission of Glennon Rowell and the International Reading Association.

| | Always Occurs | Often Occurs | Occasionally Occurs | Seldom Occurs | Never Occurs |
|---|---|---|---|---|---|
| 9. The student elects to read a book when the class has permission to choose a "free-time" activity. | ____ | ____ | ____ | ____ | ____ |
| 10. The student expresses genuine interest in going to the school's library. | ____ | ____ | ____ | ____ | ____ |
| 11. The student discusses with you (the teacher) or members of the class those items he or she has read from the newspaper, magazines, or similar materials. | ____ | ____ | ____ | ____ | ____ |
| 12. The student voluntarily and enthusiastically discusses with others the book he or she has read or is reading. | ____ | ____ | ____ | ____ | ____ |
| 13. The student listens attentively while other students share their reading experiences with the group. | ____ | ____ | ____ | ____ | ____ |
| 14. The student expresses eagerness to read printed materials in the content areas. | ____ | ____ | ____ | ____ | ____ |
| 15. The student contributes to group discussions that are based on reading assignments made in the content areas. | ____ | ____ | ____ | ____ | ____ |

## Appendix G

**Observation Checklist for Reading**

Name _____ Grade _____ Age _____

Teacher_____ Date _____

A. General Skills

_____ 1. Reads in spare time

_____ 2. Cooperates in school

_____ 3. Plays well with peers

_____ 4. Shares with others

_____ 5. Expresses interest in group and individual activities

_____ 6. Works well independently

_____ 7. Seeks help when needed

_____ 8. Respects peers

_____ 9. Respects authority

_____10. Gets along well with girls; _____ with boys

_____11. Has varied interests

_____12. Assumes leadership role when appropriate

_____13. Has good rapport with teacher

_____14. Accepts responsibility

_____15. Organizes time efficiently

_____16. Works well in a committee situation

_____17. Other _____

B. Oral Reading Skills

_____ 1. Pronounces words accurately

_____ 2. Enunciates words in a natural speaking voice

_____ 3. Uses pleasing voice skills (rate, pitch, expression)

_____ 4. Uses correct phrasing

_____ 5. Reads fluently

_____ 6. Holds book correctly

_____ 7. Reads without pointing to words

_____ 8. Does not lose place while reading

_____ 9. Reads without thrusting head

_____10. Recognizes and uses appropriate punctuation

_____11. Reads without repeating words or phrases

_____12. Reads without making omissions or additions of words

_____13. Other _____

C. Silent Reading Skills

_____ 1. Holds book correctly

_____ 2. Reads without moving head

_____ 3. Reads without pointing to words

_____ 4. Does not vocalize

_____ 5. Uses no lip movement

_____ 6. Reads at a steady rate

_____ 7. Other _____

D. Listening Skills

_____ 1. Listens to follow directions

_____ 2. Listens for different purposes

_____ 3. Listens to remember sequence of ideas

_____ 4. Listens to answer questions

_____ 5. Listens to understand main ideas

_____ 6. Listens to predict outcomes

_____ 7. Listens to summarize

_____ 8. Listens when someone reads or speaks

_____ 9. Other _____

E. Prereading Skills

_Oral Language Skills_

_____ 1. Participates freely and easily in discussions

_____ 2. Speaks in complete sentences

_____ 3. Expresses experiences

_____ 4. Uses an adequate vocabulary

_____ 5. Develops sequence of ideas in conversation

_____ 6. Uses descriptive words and phrases

_____ 7. Describes simple objects

_____ 8. Relates words and pictures

_____ 9. Other _____

*Visual Perception Skills*

_____ 1. Notes similarities in objects and words

_____ 2. Classifies objects into appropriate categories

_____ 3. Identifies from memory what is seen briefly

_____ 4. Recalls items in sequence

_____ 5. Recognizes likenesses and differences in objects and words

_____ 6. Matches picture parts

_____ 7. Matches numbers

_____ 8. Recognizes capital and lower case letters

_____ 9. Matches words

_____10. Recognizes geometric shapes

_____11. Recognizes colors

_____12. Recognizes own name

_____13. Reproduces numerals, letters, and words

_____14. Other _____

*Auditory Perception Skills*

_____ 1. Identifies and differentiates between common sounds

_____ 2. Differentiates sounds of loudness, pitch, and sequence

_____ 3. Identifies rhyming words

_____ 4. Hears differences in environmental, letter, and word sounds

_____ 5. Imitates sound sequences

_____ 6. Repeats words and sentences in sequence

_____ 7. Hears beginning, medial, and final sounds

_____ 8. Other _____

*Visual-Motor Skills*

_____ 1. Develops left-to-right eye movement

_____ 2. Coordinates hand-eye movement

_____ 3. Other _____

F. Word Recognition Skills

*Sight Vocabulary*

_____ 1. Recognizes words in isolation

_____ 2. Recognizes words in context

*Phonetic Analysis*

_____ 1. Identifies initial consonant sounds in words

_____ 2. Identifies medial consonant sounds in words

_____ 3. Identifies final consonant sounds in words

_____ 4. Substitutes initial consonant sounds to form new words

_____ 5. Substitutes medial consonant sounds to form new words

_____ 6. Substitutes final consonant sounds to form new words

_____ 7. Identifies vowel sounds in initial position

_____ 8. Identifies vowel sounds in medial position

_____ 9. Identifies vowel sounds in final position

_____ 10. Substitutes vowel sounds in initial position to form new words

_____ 11. Substitutes vowel sounds in medial position to form new words

_____ 12. Substitutes vowel sounds in final position to form new words

*Structural Analysis*

_____ 1. Recognizes compound words

_____ 2. Recognizes contractions

_____ 3. Recognizes base (root) words

_____ 4. Recognizes suffixes

_____ 5. Recognizes prefixes

_____ 6. Identifies common word endings

_____ 7. Divides words into syllables

_____ 8. Accents appropriate syllables when sounding out words

_____ 9. Recognizes possessive forms of nouns

_____ 10. Knows common rules for forming the plural of nouns

_____ 11. Other _____

*Contextual Analysis Skills*

_____ 1. Uses context to read unfamiliar words

_____ 2. Other _____

G. Comprehension Skills

*Literal Skills*

_____ 1. Reads for detail (who, what, when, where, why)

_____ 2. Reads for the main idea

_____ 3. Reads for a purpose

_____ 4. Reads to follow directions

_____ 5. Reads to follow sequence of events

_____ 6. Understands cause and effect in stories

_____ 7. Identifies meanings of words, phrases, and sentences

_____ 8. Identifies character traits

_____ 9. Understands the sense of the sentence

_____10. Other _____

*Interpretive Skills*

_____ 1. Reads to interpret illustrations

_____ 2. Reads to draw conclusions

_____ 3. Reads to make generalizations

_____ 4. Reads to get implied meaning

_____ 5. Reads to understand author's purpose

_____ 6. Interprets and appreciates figurative language

_____ 7. Understands writing style and literary quality of material

_____ 8. Makes inferences

_____ 9. Predicts outcomes

_____10. Recognizes mood of the story

_____11. Identifies character feelings and actions

_____12. Uses punctuation to interpret author's message

_____13. Other _____

*Critical Skills*

_____ 1. Differentiates between real and unreal

_____ 2. Determines propaganda in material

_____ 3. Identifies relevant and irrelevant information

_____ 4. Notes qualifications of the author

_____ 5. Reads to evaluate and judge

_____ 6. Distinguishes between fact and opinion

_____ 7. Discerns the attitudes of the writer

_____ 8. Other _____

H. Study Skills

    _____ 1. Alphabetizes words by _____ 1, _____ 2, _____ 3, _____4, _____ 5 letters.

    _____ 2. Finds words using guidewords in dictionary

    _____ 3. Locates main entry for a word containing an inflectional ending or suffix

    _____ 4. Uses the key in a dictionary to pronounce words

    _____ 5. Outlines a paragraph

    _____ 6. Outlines a chapter

    _____ 7. Develops an outline using several sources

    _____ 8. Summarizes a paragraph

    _____ 9. Summarizes a chapter

    _____10. Synthesizes information from several sources

    _____11. Skims or scans material when appropriate

    _____12. Locates information using an encyclopedia

    _____13. Locates information using the card catalog

    _____14. Locates information using the table of contents

    _____15. Locates information using an index

    _____16. Locates information using an appendix

    _____17. Locates information using a glossary

    _____18. Locates information using an atlas

    _____19. Interprets diagrams

    _____20. Interprets charts and tables

    _____21. Interprets maps

    _____22. Adjusts rate of reading according to material and purpose for reading

    _____23. Other

I. Other Observations

_____

_____

_____

# Appendix H

## Cheek Master Word List with Readability Level of Words

**A**

1 a
3 ability
2 able
3 aboard
1 about
1 above
4 accept
4 accident
3 according
4 account
1 across
3 act
4 action
4 actual
3 actually
2 add
3 address
4 admit
3 adventure
4 advice
4 afford
2 afraid
1 after
3 afternoon
1 again
2 against
2 age
2 ago
3 agree
2 ahead
4 aid
3 aim
2 air
3 alike
3 alive
1 all
3 allow
1 almost
2 alone
1 along
4 alphabet

3 already
1 also
2 although
1 always
1 am
3 among
3 amount
1 an
3 ancient
1 and
4 anger
2 angry
1 animal
1 another
2 answer
1 any
4 anybody
2 anyone
2 anything
4 anyway
4 anywhere
3 apart
2 apartment
3 appear
4 appearance
2 apple
4 approach
3 April
1 are
4 area
3 aren't
4 arithmetic
2 arm
3 army
1 around
4 arrange
3 arrive
3 arrow
3 art
3 article
1 as
4 aside

1 ask
1 asked
3 asleep
1 at
3 attack
3 attention
4 audience
4 August
4 author
3 automobile
4 autumn
3 average
4 avoid
3 awake
4 aware
1 away

**B**

1 baby
1 back
4 background
2 bad
3 balance
1 ball
1 balloon
3 band
2 bank
3 bar
4 bare
2 bark
1 barn
3 base
3 baseball
2 basket
3 bat
3 battle
1 be
3 beach
1 bear
3 beat
2 beautiful
3 beauty
2 became

1 because
3 become
1 bed
3 bedroom
2 been
1 before
1 began
2 begin
2 beginning
3 begun
1 behind
1 being
2 believe
2 bell
2 belong
3 below
3 belt
3 beneath
3 bend
3 bent
2 beside
1 best
4 bet
1 better
1 between
3 beyond
3 bicycle
1 big
1 bird
3 birth
1 birthday
2 bit
3 bite
1 black
3 blanket
2 blew
4 blind
2 block
2 blood
2 blow
1 blue
2 board

1 boat
2 body
2 bone
1 book
2 born
2 both
2 bottle
2 bottom
2 bought
4 bound
3 bow
3 bowl
1 box
1 boy
4 brain
2 branch
4 brass
2 brave
3 bread
2 break
2 breakfast
3 breath
4 breathe
4 breeze
3 brick
2 bridge
2 bright
1 bring
3 broke
2 broken
2 brother
2 brought
1 brown
3 brush
3 buffalo
2 build
2 building
3 built
2 burn
4 burst
2 business
1 bust

| | | | |
|---|---|---|---|
| 2 busy | 4 character | 3 company | 3 dangerous | 2 doing |
| 1 but | 3 charge | 2 complete | 1 dark | 2 doll |
| 2 butter | 3 check | 4 condition | 3 darkness | 3 dollar |
| 2 button | 4 cheese | 3 consider | 4 date | 1 done |
| 2 buy | 3 chest | 4 constant | 3 daughter | 3 donkey |
| 1 by | 3 chicken | 4 contain | 4 dawn | 1 don't |
| C | 3 chief | 3 content | 1 day | 1 door |
| 3 cabin | 2 child | 3 contest | 2 dead | 4 doubt |
| 2 cage | 1 children | 3 continue | 3 deal | 1 down |
| 1 cake | 4 chocolate | 3 control | 2 dear | 4 dozen |
| 1 call | 4 choice | 4 conversation | 4 death | 3 Dr. |
| 1 called | 2 choose | 3 cook | 3 decide | 3 draw |
| 3 calm | 4 chose | 3 cool | 4 deck | 4 drawing |
| 1 came | 3 chosen | 3 copper | 2 deep | 3 drawn |
| 3 camera | 3 church | 4 copy | 2 deer | 3 dream |
| 3 camp | 3 circle | 2 corn | 4 degree | 2 dress |
| 1 can | 2 circus | 2 corner | 4 department | 3 drew |
| 2 candle | 1 city | 4 correct | 4 depend | 2 drink |
| 3 candy | 4 claim | 3 cost | 4 describe | 2 drive |
| 2 cannot | 2 class | 4 cotton | 3 desert | 4 driven |
| 4 canoe | 3 clay | 1 could | 4 design | 3 driver |
| 1 can't | 2 clean | 2 couldn't | 4 desire | 3 drop |
| 3 cap | 2 clear | 4 council | 3 desk | 3 drove |
| 3 captain | 2 clever | 2 count | 4 destroy | 2 dry |
| 1 car | 2 climb | 1 country | 3 develop | 1 duck |
| 2 card | 2 clock | 4 couple | 4 dictionary | 3 dug |
| 4 cardboard | 2 close | 3 courage | 1 did | 4 dull |
| 2 care | 3 cloth | 2 course | 1 didn't | 1 during |
| 2 careful | 2 clothes | 4 court | 3 die | 3 dust |
| 2 carry | 3 cloud | 3 cousin | 2 difference | 4 duty |
| 3 case | 3 club | 2 cover | 1 different | E |
| 4 cast | 3 coach | 1 cow | 2 difficult | 1 each |
| 4 castle | 3 coast | 3 crack | 2 dinner | 3 eager |
| 1 cat | 1 coat | 2 cream | 3 direct | 2 ear |
| 1 catch | 4 code | 4 creature | 2 direction | 1 early |
| 3 cattle | 3 coffee | 4 crew | 3 dirt | 3 earn |
| 2 caught | 1 cold | 4 crop | 3 dirty | 2 earth |
| 3 cause | 4 collect | 2 cross | 3 discover | 3 easily |
| 3 cave | 4 collection | 3 crown | 4 discovery | 3 east |
| 2 cent | 4 colony | 1 cry | 4 disease | 2 easy |
| 3 center | 1 color | 3 cup | 2 dish | 1 eat |
| 3 century | 3 column | 3 curious | 3 distance | 2 edge |
| 3 certain | 1 come | 3 current | 4 distant | 4 effect |
| 3 certainly | 4 comfort | 4 curve | 3 divide | 4 effort |
| 4 chain | 3 comfortable | 1 cut | 1 do | 2 egg |
| 2 chair | 2 coming | 3 cutting | 3 doctor | 2 eight |
| 2 chance | 4 command | D | 1 does | 3 either |
| 2 change | 4 committee | 2 dance | 3 doesn't | 3 electric |
| | 2 common | 3 danger | 1 dog | 3 electricity |

| | | | | |
|---|---|---|---|---|
| 2 elephant | 4 fail | 2 flat | 4 furniture | 3 guard |
| 3 eleven | 2 fair | 2 flew | 4 further | 1 guess |
| 2 else | 2 fall | 2 flight | 4 future | 4 guest |
| 2 empty | 3 familiar | 3 float | G | 3 guide |
| 1 end | 1 family | 2 floor | 1 game | 2 gun |
| 3 enemy | 3 famous | 3 flour | 3 garage | H |
| 2 engine | 1 far | 3 flow | 2 garden | 4 habit |
| 4 engineer | 1 farm | 2 flower | 3 gas | 1 had |
| 3 enjoy | 2 farmer | 1 fly | 2 gate | 3 hadn't |
| 4 enormous | 3 farther | 4 fog | 3 gather | 2 hair |
| 1 enough | 1 fast | 2 follow | 1 gave | 2 half |
| 3 enter | 3 fat | 1 food | 4 general | 2 hall |
| 4 entire | 1 father | 3 fool | 3 gentle | 1 hand |
| 3 equal | 4 favor | 3 foolish | 1 get | 3 handle |
| 3 equipment | 3 favorite | 2 foot | 4 ghost | 4 handsome |
| 3 escape | 4 fear | 4 football | 1 giant | 3 hang |
| 3 especially | 3 fed | 1 for | 3 gift | 2 happen |
| 1 even | 2 feed | 2 force | 1 girl | 1 happy |
| 2 evening | 2 feel | 4 foreign | 1 give | 3 harbor |
| 3 event | 3 feeling | 2 forest | 2 given | 1 hard |
| 1 ever | 1 feet | 4 forever | 2 glad | 3 hardly |
| 1 every | 2 fell | 3 forget | 4 glance | 1 has |
| 3 everybody | 3 fellow | 3 forgot | 2 glass | 1 hat |
| 2 everyone | 2 felt | 3 forgotten | 1 go | 3 hate |
| 2 everything | 2 fence | 2 form | 4 god | 1 have |
| 4 everywhere | 1 few | 4 former | 2 goes | 4 haven't |
| 3 exactly | 2 field | 4 fort | 1 going | 2 having |
| 4 examine | 3 fierce | 3 forth | 2 gold | 3 hay |
| 2 example | 3 fifteen | 3 forty | 3 golden | 1 he |
| 4 excellent | 3 fifth | 2 forward | 1 gone | 1 head |
| 2 except | 3 fifty | 4 fought | 1 good | 3 health |
| 4 exchange | 3 fight | 1 found | 2 goodbye | 1 hear |
| 3 excitement | 2 figure | 1 four | 2 goose | 1 heard |
| 3 exercise | 2 fill | 2 fourth | 1 got | 2 heart |
| 4 expensive | 3 final | 2 fox | 4 government | 3 heat |
| 4 experience | 2 finally | 3 frame | 3 grain | 4 heaven |
| 3 experiment | 1 find | 3 free | 4 grand | 2 heavy |
| 3 expert | 2 fine | 4 freedom | 2 grandfather | 3 he'd |
| 3 explain | 3 finger | 3 fresh | 2 grandmother | 2 held |
| 4 explanation | 2 finish | 3 Friday | 1 grass | 1 hello |
| 4 explore | 1 fire | 1 friend | 2 gray | 1 help |
| 4 express | 4 firm | 2 friendly | 1 great | 4 helpful |
| 3 expression | 1 first | 2 frog | 1 green | 1 her |
| 3 extra | 1 fish | 1 from | 2 grew | 3 herd |
| 2 eye | 3 fit | 2 front | 1 ground | 1 here |
| F | 1 five | 4 frozen | 2 group | 4 hero |
| 1 face | 2 fix | 2 full | 2 grow | 2 herself |
| 2 fact | 3 flag | 1 fun | 2 grown | 3 hidden |
| 4 factory | 3 flame | 1 funny | | 2 hide |
| | | 3 fur | | |

| | | | |
|---|---|---|---|
| 1 high | 4 improvement | 2 kitchen | 2 lion | 3 mass |
| 4 highway | 1 in | 1 knew | 4 liquid | 3 master |
| 2 hill | 3 inch | 3 knife | 2 list | 3 match |
| 1 him | 3 increase | 1 know | 2 listen | 3 material |
| 1 himself | 3 indeed | 3 knowledge | 1 little | 2 matter |
| 1 his | 4 information | 2 known | 1 live | 1 may |
| 3 history | 3 insect | | 3 lively | 2 maybe |
| 2 hit | 2 inside | **L** | 1 living | 4 mayor |
| 1 hold | 4 instant | 4 lack | 3 load | 1 me |
| 2 hole | 2 instead | 2 ladder | 4 locate | 3 meal |
| 4 hollow | 4 instrument | 3 lady | 3 log | 4 mean |
| 1 home | 3 interest | 3 laid | 4 lonely | 3 measure |
| 4 honest | 3 interesting | 2 lake | 1 long | 3 meat |
| 3 honor | 1 into | 4 lamp | 1 look | 4 medical |
| 2 hope | 4 invention | 2 land | 1 looked | 4 medicine |
| 2 horn | 2 iron | 3 language | 3 loose | 2 meet |
| 1 horse | 1 is | 1 large | 3 lord | 3 member |
| 3 hospital | 2 island | 2 larger | 3 lose | 4 memory |
| 2 hot | 2 isn't | 1 last | 4 loss | 1 men |
| 3 hotel | 1 it | 2 late | 1 lost | 4 mention |
| 1 house | 1 its | 1 later | 2 lot | 3 message |
| 1 how | 1 it's | 1 laugh | 2 loud | 1 met |
| 3 however | 2 itself | 4 laughter | 2 love | 3 metal |
| 2 huge | 2 I've | 3 law | 3 lovely | 3 mice |
| 4 human | | 2 lay | 2 low | 2 middle |
| 2 hundred | **J** | 2 lead | 2 lower | 1 might |
| 3 hung | 4 jacket | 3 leader | 4 luck | 3 mile |
| 2 hungry | 4 January | 4 leaf | 4 lumber | 2 milk |
| 2 hunt | 3 jar | 3 learn | 2 lunch | 3 mill |
| 4 hunter | 3 jet | 2 least | 3 lying | 2 million |
| 1 hurry | 2 job | 4 leather | | 2 mind |
| 2 hurt | 3 join | 2 leave | **M** | 3 mine |
| 3 husband | 4 journey | 2 leaves | 2 machine | 3 mint |
| | 4 joy | 2 led | 3 mad | 2 minute |
| **I** | 3 judge | 1 left | 1 maid | 3 mirror |
| 1 I | 4 juice | 2 leg | 4 magazine | 1 miss |
| 1 ice | 3 July | 2 length | 2 magic | 3 mistake |
| 3 I'd | 1 jump | 3 less | 3 mail | 4 mixture |
| 2 idea | 3 June | 3 lesson | 2 main | 3 model |
| 1 if | 4 jungle | 1 let | 1 make | 3 modern |
| 3 ill | 1 just | 2 let's | 2 making | 2 moment |
| 1 I'll | | 1 letter | 4 mama | 1 money |
| 1 I'm | **K** | 4 level | 1 man | 2 monkey |
| 4 imagination | 1 keep | 2 library | 3 manner | 3 month |
| 3 imagine | 2 kept | 3 lie | 1 many | 4 mood |
| 3 immediately | 3 key | 1 life | 3 map | 2 moon |
| 1 important | 4 kid | 3 lift | 3 march | 1 more |
| 3 impossible | 2 kill | 1 light | 2 mark | 1 morning |
| 4 improve | 1 kind | 1 like | 3 market | 1 most |
| | 2 king | 1 line | 4 married | |

| 1 mother | 2 noise | 1 out | 2 piece | 2 present |
|----------|---------|-------|---------|-----------|
| 4 motion | 3 none | 2 outside | 1 pig | 4 president |
| 3 motor | 4 noon | 1 over | 2 pile | 3 press |
| 2 mountain | 2 nor | 2 owl | 3 pilot | 2 pretty |
| 2 mouse | 2 north | 1 own | 3 pine | 3 price |
| 2 mouth | 4 northern | 4 oxygen | 3 pink | 4 pride |
| 2 move | 3 nose | **P** | 3 pipe | 4 private |
| 1 Mr. | 1 not | | 3 pitch | 1 prize |
| 1 Mrs. | 2 note | 3 pack | 2 place | 3 probably |
| 1 much | 1 nothing | 3 package | 3 plain | 2 problem |
| 3 mud | 3 notice | 3 page | 2 plane | 4 professor |
| 2 music | 1 now | 3 paid | 3 planet | 4 program |
| 1 must | 1 number | 4 pain | 2 plant | 3 promise |
| 1 my | | 2 paint | 3 plate | 3 proper |
| 2 myself | **O** | 4 painted | 3 platform | 4 property |
| 4 mysterious | 4 object | 2 pair | 1 play | 4 protect |
| 4 mystery | 3 ocean | 3 palace | 4 player | 4 protection |
| **N** | 3 o'clock | 3 pale | 3 pleasant | 2 proud |
| 3 nail | 4 October | 2 pan | 2 please | 3 prove |
| 1 name | 4 odd | 4 papa | 4 pleasure | 3 provide |
| 3 narrow | 1 of | 2 paper | 3 plenty | 2 pull |
| 3 nation | 1 off | 4 paragraph | 1 pocket | 4 pure |
| 4 national | 3 offer | 3 park | 3 poem | 3 purple |
| 4 native | 2 office | 2 part | 4 poet | 4 purpose |
| 3 natural | 4 officer | 4 particular | 1 point | 2 push |
| 4 nature | 4 official | 1 party | 3 pole | 1 put |
| 4 navy | 2 often | 2 pass | 3 police | **Q** |
| 1 near | 1 oh | 2 past | 2 policeman | 3 quarter |
| 3 nearby | 2 oil | 4 pasture | 2 pong | 3 queen |
| 3 necessary | 1 old | 3 path | 1 pony | 2 question |
| 2 neck | 3 older | 3 patient | 3 pool | 2 quick |
| 1 need | 1 on | 4 pattern | 2 poor | 2 quickly |
| 3 needle | 1 once | 2 pay | 3 popular | 2 quiet |
| 2 neighbor | 1 one | 4 peace | 4 porch | 2 quite |
| 4 neighborhood | 1 only | 3 pen | 4 port | **R** |
| 3 neither | 3 onto | 3 pencil | 3 position | 1 rabbit |
| 4 nervous | 1 open | 1 penny | 3 possible | 2 race |
| 2 nest | 4 opinion | 1 people | 4 possibly | 2 radio |
| 1 never | 4 opposite | 3 perfect | 3 post | 4 railroad |
| 1 new | 1 or | 4 perform | 3 pot | 1 rain |
| 3 news | 3 orange | 3 perhaps | 3 potato | 3 raise |
| 3 newspaper | 4 orbit | 4 period | 3 pound | 1 ran |
| 1 next | 2 order | 2 person | 3 pour | 2 ranch |
| 2 nice | 3 ordinary | 1 pet | 3 power | 3 range |
| 1 night | 3 original | 4 phone | 4 practical | 3 rapidly |
| 3 nine | 1 other | 3 piano | 3 practice | 4 rare |
| 1 no | 3 ought | 2 pick | 4 prairie | 3 rather |
| 3 nobody | 1 our | 1 picture | 4 preparation | 4 raw |
| | 4 ourselves | 2 pie | 3 prepare | |

| | | | | | | | | |
|---|---|---|---|---|---|---|---|---|---|
| 2 | reach | 2 | round | 2 | sent | 2 | sight | 3 | somebody |
| 1 | read | 4 | route | 4 | sentence | 2 | sign | 3 | somehow |
| 4 | reader | 2 | row | 3 | separate | 3 | signal | 2 | someone |
| 1 | ready | 4 | royal | 4 | September | 4 | silence | 1 | something |
| 2 | real | 3 | rubber | 3 | serious | 3 | silent | 1 | sometimes |
| 3 | realize | 3 | rule | 3 | serve | 4 | silk | 3 | somewhat |
| 1 | really | 4 | ruler | 4 | service | 2 | silly | 3 | somewhere |
| 3 | rear | 1 | run | 1 | set | 2 | silver | 3 | son |
| 2 | reason | 2 | running | 3 | setting | 2 | simple | 2 | song |
| 3 | receive | 3 | rush | 4 | settle | 3 | simply | 1 | soon |
| 3 | recognize | | S | 2 | seven | 2 | since | 3 | sorry |
| 2 | record | | | 2 | several | 1 | sing | 3 | sort |
| 1 | red | 2 | sad | 3 | shade | 2 | single | 1 | sound |
| 3 | regular | 4 | saddle | 3 | shadow | 4 | sink | 2 | soup |
| 4 | relief | 2 | safe | 3 | shake | 3 | sir | 2 | south |
| 3 | remain | 3 | safety | 2 | shall | 2 | sister | 4 | southern |
| 4 | remarkable | 1 | said | 4 | shallow | 1 | sit | 3 | space |
| 2 | remember | 3 | sail | 2 | shape | 3 | sitting | 3 | speak |
| 4 | remove | 3 | sale | 3 | share | 4 | situation | 2 | special |
| 4 | repeat | 3 | salt | 3 | sharp | 2 | six | 3 | speech |
| 3 | reply | 2 | same | 1 | she | 2 | size | 3 | speed |
| 3 | report | 2 | sand | 3 | shed | 4 | skill | 4 | spell |
| 4 | represent | 1 | sang | 2 | sheep | 3 | skin | 3 | spend |
| 4 | research | 1 | sat | 3 | sheet | 3 | sky | 3 | spent |
| 3 | respect | 3 | Saturday | 3 | shelf | 1 | sleep | 3 | spider |
| 4 | responsible | 3 | save | 3 | shell | 3 | slept | 3 | spin |
| 2 | rest | 1 | saw | 4 | shelter | 3 | slide | 3 | spirit |
| 3 | result | 1 | say | 4 | she's | 4 | slight | 4 | spite |
| 2 | return | 3 | scale | 4 | shift | 3 | slip | 4 | split |
| 3 | rice | 3 | scene | 3 | shine | 4 | slope | 3 | spoke |
| 3 | rich | 1 | school | 2 | ship | 2 | slow | 4 | spoken |
| 1 | ride | 2 | science | 3 | shirt | 2 | slowly | 3 | spot |
| 2 | riding | 3 | scientific | 1 | shoe | 1 | small | 3 | spread |
| 4 | rifle | 3 | scientist | 2 | shoes | 2 | smell | 2 | spring |
| 1 | right | 3 | score | 2 | shook | 2 | smile | 2 | square |
| 2 | ring | 4 | screen | 3 | shoot | 3 | smoke | 3 | stage |
| 3 | rise | 2 | sea | 2 | shop | 3 | smooth | 4 | stairs |
| 2 | river | 3 | search | 3 | shore | 4 | snake | 2 | stand |
| 1 | road | 3 | season | 2 | short | 2 | snow | 3 | star |
| 2 | roar | 2 | seat | 3 | shot | 1 | so | 2 | start |
| 2 | rock | 1 | second | 1 | should | 4 | soap | 3 | state |
| 2 | rode | 3 | secret | 3 | shoulder | 4 | society | 4 | statement |
| 2 | roll | 2 | section | 2 | shout | 2 | soft | 2 | station |
| 2 | roof | 1 | see | 1 | show | 4 | soil | 1 | stay |
| 1 | room | 3 | seed | 2 | shown | 3 | sold | 3 | steady |
| 3 | root | 2 | seem | 2 | shut | 4 | soldier | 4 | steel |
| 2 | rope | 1 | seen | 3 | shy | 4 | solid | 3 | steep |
| 3 | rose | 2 | sell | 3 | sick | 3 | solve | 3 | stem |
| 4 | rough | 2 | send | 1 | side | 1 | some | 1 | step |
| | | 3 | sense | | | | | | |

2 stick
3 stiff
1 still
4 stomach
2 stone
2 stood
1 stop
1 stopped
1 store
2 stories
3 storm
1 story
2 straight
2 strange
4 stranger
3 straw
3 stream
1 street
4 strength
3 stretch
3 strike
2 string
3 strip
2 strong
3 struck
3 structure
3 struggle
3 stuck
3 student
3 study
3 style
2 subject
3 success
3 successful
1 such
4 sudden
2 suddenly
3 sugar
4 suggest
2 suit
4 sum
2 summer
1 sun
3 Sunday
2 supper
4 supplies
3 supply
4 support
3 suppose
1 sure
2 surface
1 surprise
3 swam
3 sweet
4 swept
2 swim
4 swing
3 switch
4 swung
4 syllable
4 symbol

T

2 table
2 tail
1 take
2 taken
1 talk
2 tall
4 tank
4 tape
4 task
3 taste
4 tea
3 teach
2 teacher
3 team
4 tear
3 teeth
2 telephone
4 telescope
3 television
1 tell
3 temperature
2 ten
2 tent
3 terrible
2 test
1 than
1 thank
1 that
2 that's
1 the
1 their
1 them
3 themselves
1 then
1 there
4 therefore
3 there's
1 these
1 they
3 they're
3 thick
3 thin
1 thing
1 think
2 third
3 thirty
1 this
1 those
2 though
1 thought
3 thousand
3 thread
1 three
2 threw
4 throat
1 through
3 throughout
2 throw
4 thrown
4 thumb
2 thus
4 tide
2 tie
3 tight
3 till
1 time
4 tin
2 tiny
3 tip
3 tired
1 to
1 today
1 together
1 told
3 tomorrow
3 tongue
3 tonight
1 too
1 took
3 tool
2 top
3 total
3 touch
3 tough
1 toward
3 tower
1 town
1 toy
2 tract
3 trade
3 traffic
3 trail
1 train
3 trap
3 travel
1 tree
3 tribe
2 trick
2 tried
2 trip
4 tropical
2 trouble
1 truck
2 true
2 trunk
4 trust
3 truth
1 try
3 tube
3 tune
2 turn
3 twelve
3 twenty
3 twice
1 two
1 type

U

3 uncle
1 under
2 understand
3 understood
2 unhappy
4 uniform
4 unit
4 unknown
3 unless
4 unlike
1 until
3 unusual
1 up
2 upon
3 upper
1 us
1 use
3 useful
3 usual
2 usually

V

3 vacation
3 valley
4 valuable
2 various
1 very
4 victory
3 view
3 village
2 visit
2 voice

W

1 wagon
2 wait
1 walk
2 walked
2 wall
1 want
3 war
2 warm
1 was
2 wash
2 wasn't
3 waste
2 watch
1 water
2 wave
1 way
1 we
3 weak
2 wear
3 weather
2 week
3 weigh
3 weight
3 welcome
1 well
2 we'll
1 went
1 were
3 we're
4 weren't
3 west

| | | | | |
|---|---|---|---|---|
| 4 western | 1 who | 2 wise | 3 wore | 1 years |
| 1 wet | 2 whole | 1 wish | 1 world | 1 yellow |
| 4 we've | 4 whom | 1 with | 3 worn | 1 yes |
| 3 whale | 2 whose | 1 within | 3 worry | 4 yesterday |
| 1 what | 1 why | 1 without | 3 worse | 2 yet |
| 3 whatever | 2 wide | 2 wolf | 3 worth | 1 you |
| 4 what's | 2 wife | 2 woman | 1 would | 2 you'll |
| 3 wheat | 2 wild | 2 women | 2 wouldn't | 1 young |
| 2 wheel | 1 will | 3 won | 3 wound | 1 your |
| 1 when | 3 willing | 2 wonder | 2 write | 2 you're |
| 4 whenever | 2 win | 2 wonderful | 2 writing | 2 yourself |
| 1 where | 2 wind | 2 won't | 2 written | 4 youth |
| 2 whether | 1 window | 2 wood | 2 wrong | 3 you've |
| 1 which | 2 wing | 4 wooden | 2 wrote | **Z** |
| 1 while | 2 winter | 4 wool | **Y** | 1 zoo |
| 2 whistle | 4 wisdom | 1 word | 2 yard | |
| 1 white | 3 wire | | 1 year | |

## Appendix I

### Interpretive Report: Student 2

Kristie is eight years old and the younger of two children. She is preparing to enter the fourth grade at Seabreeze School. Kristie enjoys school and is considered by her teachers to be very cooperative. She enjoys playing outdoors and especially likes to swim. Kristie enjoys math and indicates that she likes to read.

Several instruments were used to diagnose Kristie's reading problem. These included the *Wepman Auditory Discrimination Test, Slosson Intelligence Test, Sucher-Allred Reading Placement Inventory, Durrell Analysis of Reading Difficulty,* and the *Stanford Diagnostic Reading Test* (Green Level— Form A).

### Wepman Auditory Discrimination Test

Thirty-four of forty items correct; unsatisfactory for age.
Errors: Discriminating initial consonants—*v*ow and *th*ou; *f*ie and *th*igh. Discriminating medial vowels—b*u*m and b*o*mb; p*e*n and p*i*n. Discriminating final consonants—clo*th*e and clo*v*e; shea*f* and shea*th*.

### Slosson Intelligence Test

Average range.

### Sucher-Allred Reading Placement Inventory

#### Word Recognition Test

Primer: fourteen of fifteen words correct.
First Reader List: thirteen of fifteen words correct.
$2^1$ Reader List: fourteen of twenty words correct.
$2^2$ Reader List: six of twenty words correct.

On most words, Kristie put incorrect endings on the words such as pon*y* for pon*d*, go*es* for go*ne*, mu*st* for mu*ch*, and though*t* for throu*gh*.

#### Oral Reading Test

Independent Level: Primer.
Primer Paragraph: No word recognition or comprehension errors.
Instructional Level: First Reader.
First Reader Paragraph: Four word recognition errors (two mispronunciations— *lonesome* for *loud* and *after* for *afraid;* one nonpronunciation—*return;* one substitution—*chicks* for *chickens*). No comprehension errors.
Frustration Level: $2^1$ Reader.
$2^1$ Reader Paragraph: Ten word recognition errors (seven mispronunciations—*had* for *heard, lovely* for *loud, good* for *goose, lumpy* for *loud, floor* for *flapping, wishing*

for *wings*, *tumbling* for *landed;* one nonpronunciation—*surprise;* two substitutions—*Tom* for *Tim* and *bumpy* for *bump;* one insertion—*in*). Three of five comprehension questions correct—errors at the literal level.

Difficulties noted by the teacher consisted of such things as inability to use context clues or word analysis skills when an unknown word was encountered. Another observation made was that Kristie's speed was consistent and words were substituted quickly when the word to be read was unknown.

### Durrell Analysis of Reading Difficulty

*Subtest 1—Oral Reading*

Selection 1: No word recognition or comprehension errors. (High second-grade placement)

Selection 2: Four word recognition errors (two insertions— *did* and *a;* one mispronunciation—*went* for *wanted;* one omission—*go* following insertion of *a*). Five of six comprehension questions correct (missed literal questions involving recall of a number mentioned in the story). (Mid to high second-grade placement)

Selection 3: One word recognition error (one substitution—*after* for *afraid*). Six of seven comprehension questions correct (missed literal question dealing with recall of a number in the story). (High second-grade placement)

Selection 4: Eight word recognition errors (three nonpronunciations—*large, bottom, short;* two substitutions—*men* for *man* and *swim* for *swam;* three mispronunciations—*far* for *fast, martin* for *motorboat, shrore* for *shore*). Three of seven comprehension questions correct (difficulty with literal questions).

The median grade placement for the oral reading subtest was high second grade. Difficulties noted concerned her inadequate word analysis ability, failure to use context clues, and frequent disregard for punctuation.

*Subtest 2—Silent Reading*

Selection 1: Time—15 seconds. Recalled all five important events in story. Score—mid to high second-grade placement.

Selection 2: Time—24 seconds. Recalled four facts unaided and four more when aided. Score—high second-grade placement.

Selection 3: Time—29 seconds. Recalled nine facts unaided and four more when aided. Score—low to mid third-grade placement.

Selection 4: Time—47 seconds. Recalled fifteen facts unaided and two more when aided. Score—low third-grade placement.

Selection 5: Time—52 seconds. Recalled six facts unaided and two more when aided. Score—low to mid third-grade placement.

The median grade placement for silent reading is low third-grade with fair comprehension. Difficulties observed included poorly organized recall and poor recall of specific details, especially involving numbers. Kristie also had difficulty in recall of number-related facts on the *Sucher-Allred* oral reading selections.

*Subtest 3—Listening Comprehension*

Grade 2 Selection: Answered all questions correctly.

Grade 3 Selection: Answered seven of eight questions correctly.

Grade 4 Selection: Answered two of seven questions correctly.

Her listening comprehension score was judged to be at a third-grade level. During the administration of the subtest, Kristie appeared to concentrate well on the task.

*Subtest 4—Word Recognition and Analysis*

List 1, Grades 2–6: Flashed—nine of twenty-five correct. Analysis—no more correct. Grade placement of 2.5.

When attempting to analyze a word, Kristie looked at the initial consonant sound and substituted a word with the same initial sound, such as: *queen* for *quickly, question* for *quarter, ground* for *guard, crow* for *crawl, singing* for *single, strip* for *stamp,* and *trick* for *turkey.* She experienced difficulty in using all word analysis skills. Failure to look past the initial consonant sound in a word was a frequent error. She

would decode the first letter and then quickly say a word with the same letter in the initial position. She also failed to attend to blends in all cases and ignored vowel sounds and ending sounds. These problems were also observed on the *Sucher-Allred* and the oral reading section of the *Durrell*.

*Subtest 5—Visual Memory of Words, Primary*
> Nineteen of twenty items correct. 3.5 grade placement (highest level measured by this subtest).

*Subtest 6—Sounds, Primary*
> Twenty-eight of twenty-nine items correct. 3.5 grade placement (highest level measured by this subtest).

*Subtest 7—Visual Memory of Words, Spelling and Handwriting, Intermediate*
> Visual Memory: Recorded five of twelve words correctly. Grade placement of 4.

Kristie was able to remember correctly the first three to four letters of the words she missed.

> Phonic Spelling: None correct.

It was observed that Kristie was able to write the first three or four letters of the words correctly where blends were not involved. Ending sounds were omitted in several words.

> Spelling: List 1—eight of twenty words correct. Grade placement of 2.

Kristie omitted sounds and syllables in the words she missed. Incorrect vowel sounds were found as she substituted *piper* for *papers*, *trim* for *train*, *mark* for *market*, *pilt* for *planted*, *ment* for *minute*, and *print* for *promise*.

> Handwriting: Copied forty-five letters in one minute. Grade placement of 4.

### Stanford Diagnostic Reading Test (Green Level— Form A)
> Auditory Vocabulary: Stanine 3—Grade equivalent 3.0.
> Auditory Discrimination: Stanine 3—Grade equivalent 1.9.
> Phonetic Analysis: Stanine 2—Grade equivalent 1.5.
> Structural Analysis: Stanine 3—Grade equivalent 2.6.

Comprehension
> Literal: Stanine 3—Grade equivalent 2.1.
> Inferential: Stanine 2—Grade equivalent 1.4.
> Total: Stanine 3—Grade equivalent 2.9.

The subtests can be further analyzed to provide more specific diagnostic information.

*Subtest 1—Auditory Vocabulary*—measures the student's skill in selecting a word, read by the teacher, to complete a sentence, also read by the teacher. Questions are in the areas of math and science, social studies and art, and reading and literature. Kristie responded correctly to eighteen of forty items. Her errors were: seven reading and literature; nine in math and science, and six in social studies and art.

*Subtest 2—Auditory Discrimination*—assesses the skill of hearing similarities and differences among sounds in words. Kristie correctly identified thirteen of eighteen consonant sounds. The consonants missed involved one single consonant (*g*) and four consonant digraphs (*sh* twice, *ch*, and *th*). She was able to identify eleven of eighteen vowel sounds correctly. Her errors involved the short vowels *a*, *e*, and *i*, the long vowels *a* and *e* and the vowel sound *ou*.

*Subtest 3—Phonetic Analysis*—involves looking at a key word with one or two letters underlined and deciding which of three given words has the same sound as the underlined letters. Kristie correctly answered six of eighteen consonant sounds. Her errors were: three single consonants (soft *g*, soft *j*, and soft *c*); five consonant clusters (*gr*, *st*, *pr*, *ld*, and *sk*), and five consonant digraphs (*sh*, *ch*, *th*, *ng*, and *sh—tion*). She answered three of eighteen vowel sounds correctly. Her errors included: four short vowels ( *a*, *i*, *o*, and *u*); six long vowels (*a* twice, *i*, *u*, *e*, and *o*), and five other vowel sounds (*âr*, *ou*, *ôr*, *ô*, and *ər*).

Difficulties with consonant clusters, digraphs, and all vowel sounds on this section correlate highly with errors made previously on the auditory discrimination subtest. This is obviously an area of weakness for Kristie.

*Subtest 4—Structural Analysis*—Parts A and B deal with word division and blending as well as the ability to decode words through the analysis of word parts.

Kristie correctly responded to nineteen of thirty items on Part A. Her errors included: six affix errors (*in*vent, *com*plete, *re*port, *ex*claim, *pre*tend, and *ac*tion), and five syllable errors (*future, almost, pirate,*

*accent,* and *station*). On Part B, Kristie had a blending score of seventeen of thirty. Her errors were three compound words (*sidewalk, bathtub,* and *seaport*); five affixes (*go*ing, *play*ful, *ex*cuse, *ad*vance, and *short*est), and five syllable errors (*spider, hundred, moment, certain,* and *unit*).

Kristie shows more strength in the area of structural analysis than phonetic analysis. However, she still needs work in decoding word parts, especially affixes and syllables.

*Subtest 5—Comprehension*—Parts A and B assess comprehension using a cloze format and paragraphs followed by questions. On Part A, Kristie correctly responded to eighteen of twenty-four items, with three inferential errors and three literal errors. On Part B, she answered thirteen of thirty-six items correctly. Her errors included eight literal-level comprehension questions and fifteen inferential-level comprehension questions. Specifically, fourteen errors involved identifying details from the selection, two errors were in the area of anticipating outcomes; three errors dealt with drawing inferences; three errors required recognizing emotions of the characters, and one error required the identification of a cause and effect relationship. This clearly indicates that Kristie needs to attend to detail more carefully as she reads in order to improve her comprehension.

Kristie's failure to attend to details properly was also noted on the *Durrell* oral and silent reading subtests and on the *Sucher-Allred* oral reading paragraphs.

**Summarizing the Diagnostic Information**

On the *Wepman Auditory Discrimination Test* and the *Stanford Diagnostic Reading Test,* Auditory Discrimination Subtest, Kristie's scores indicated weaknesses in the areas of the initial and final consonant sounds *v, th,* and *f, th;* consonant digraphs *sh, ch,* and *th* in the initial position; the short and long vowel sounds of *a, e, i,* and *u;* and the other vowel sound of *ou.*

Her poor sight vocabulary was evident on the *Sucher-Allred* (Word Recognition Lists and Oral Reading Test), and the *Durrell* (Subtest of Oral and Silent Reading). On both of these instruments most of the words missed were basic sight words that she should have been able to recognize.

Word analysis skills were weak, as indicated by Kristie's performance on the *Durrell* (Word Analysis Subtest) where she used only initial consonants in analyzing words. Poor phonetic analysis was evident on the *Stanford Diagnostic Reading Test* (Phonetic Analysis Subtest), where she again had difficulty with short and long vowels, other vowel sounds, and consonant digraphs (*sh, ch, th, ng,* and *sh—tion*). Kristie had difficulty with the vowel sounds of *âr, ôr,* and *ǝr* and the consonant sounds of soft *g,* soft *j,* and soft *c.* On the *Sucher-Allred* she also experienced errors dealing with the same long and short vowels, consonant clusters, and other vowel sounds.

Structural analysis skills involving recognition of affixes, compound words, syllables, and the ability to blend words were poor on the *Stanford Diagnostic Reading Test* (Subtest on Structural Analysis), where Kristie made excessive errors on the items dealing with affixes and syllables. She also experienced difficulty with syllabication on the *Durrell* (Spelling Subtest), where she omitted syllables in attempting to spell many words.

On the *Durrell* (Oral and Silent Reading Subtests and Listening Comprehension Subtest), the *Sucher-Allred* (Oral Reading Test) and the *Stanford Diagnostic Reading Test* (Comprehension Subtest), Kristie exhibited deficiencies in both literal and inferential areas. Her specific comprehension problems involved the inability to identify details from selections read orally, silently, or from selections read to her. She had particular difficulty recalling details involving numbers read in selections (e.g. three boys, five dogs, six apples). Kristie also had poorly organized recall on the *Durrell* (Silent Reading Subtest), when she was asked by the teacher to tell everything she remembered about the story. Kristie was able to answer main idea questions correctly following both oral and silent reading on the *Durrell* (Oral and Silent Reading Subtests) and on the *Sucher-Allred* (Oral Reading Test).

She failed to use context clues to help her decode unknown words on the *Durrell* (Oral Reading Subtest) and on the *Sucher-Allred* (Oral Reading Test).

# Interpretive Report: Student 3

## Background Information

Detra, a fourth grader from Southside Elementary, was referred to the Reading Clinic by her guardian, Mrs. Byrd. In talking with Mrs. Byrd it was reported that Detra was a good reader, but comprehension was poor.

Case history information seemed to indicate a normal physical and developmental history. No problems were noted in the areas of speech, hearing, and vision. Mrs. Byrd reported that Detra never complained about her vision, but that she was never tested. Mrs. Byrd did not have any specific information in Detra's developmental history. She mentioned that Detra has only been with her for one year.

In talking with Detra, she appeared to be a very cooperative, quiet little girl. She stated that she liked to read very much and thought learning to read was very important. She sometimes reads to Mrs. Byrd. Her favorite book is *The Longest Birthday*. Detra enjoys playing baseball, bike riding, and swimming.

## Test Administered

*Slosson Intelligence Test*
*Slosson Oral Reading Test*
*Sucher-Allred Reading Placement Inventory*
*Stanford Diagnostic Reading Test* (Green Level)
*Durrell Analysis of Reading Difficulty*
*Wepman Auditory Discrimination Test*
Keystone
Audiometer

## Test Interpretation

*Slosson Intelligence Test*—Average Range

The *Slosson Intelligence Test* is a short screening intelligence test administered on an individual basis. The various items test areas of Visual Motor Skills, Auditory Memory, Auditory Association, Information, Math, Judgment Reasoning, and Vocabulary. Test results yielded a score in the average range of intelligence.

Areas of possible weaknesses appeared on math, judgment reasoning, and vocabulary items. Six errors were made from ten questions presented on math, five errors from a possible ten questions on judgment reasoning, and four errors out of a possible seven

questions were noted on vocabulary items. All five errors in judgment reasoning called for responses on how two objects were alike and different. Detra appeared to understand the concepts of same and different, but was unable to reason a correct response.

*Slosson Oral Reading Test*—Grade Equivalent 5.3

The *Slosson Oral Reading Test* consists of ten graded word lists varying in difficulty. Scores are based on the number of correct pronunciation. Detra correctly pronounced one hundred-six words. Grade equivalent for this test was 5.3. This appeared to be a strong area for Detra. She seemed to use phonetic and structural analysis in decoding new words. She was often heard sounding out words in their syllable units. Syllable blending, however did appear a little slow this appeared to account for the addition of syllables in some of the word errors. This was evident in the word errors *distanent* for *distant, comeon* for *common, dayinty* for *dainty, graysheus* for *gracious, dungēon* for *dungeon.*

*Sucher-Allred Reading Placement Inventory*

Word Recognition—Grade Equivalent 3.2
Independent Reading Level—
        Grade Equivalent 2.2
Instructional Reading Level—
        Grade Equivalent 3.2
Frustrational Reading Level—
        Grade Equivalent 4
Comprehension Errors—Main Idea, 1 error
                            Facts, 1 error
                            Inference, 1 error
                            Critical Thinking, 1
                            error

The *Sucher-Allred Reading Placement Inventory* consists of two parts: the Word-Recognition Test, and the Oral Reading Test. The range of the lists include primer throgh ninth grade reading level. The Oral Reading Test consists of twelve selections followed by comprehension questions.

On the Work Recognition Test of the *Sucher-Allred* errors were made on List D (2.2 Reader), List E (3.1 Reader) and List F (3.2 Reader). Two errors consisted of the omission of the /r/ in the words *tearsus* for *treasures,* and *weeking* for *wrecking.* Three errors consisted of the insertion of added syllables

evident in the words *breathering* for *breathing, partaly* for *partly,* and *woodchuckers* for *wookchuck's.* Slow syllable blending may have been a causal factor.

On the Oral Reading Test, the client's Independent Level appeared to be on grade equivalent 2.2. Three of the four word recognition errors on this selection appeared on basic sight vocabulary items. This was evident in the words *the* for *a, and* for *he, and had* for *and.* Detra missed one factual comprehension question.

The Instructional Level for the *Sucher-Allred* appeared to be on grade equivalent 3.2. Twelve word recognition errors consisting of four mispronunciations, one insertion, six substitutions, and repetition occurred on this passage. Five of the word recognition errors appeared on basic sight vocabulary items. Noted errors included *and* for *said, for* for *from, when* for *then, the* for *a,* and *the* for *its.* There appears to be a weakness in the recognition of basic sight vocabulary. A *b* for *d* reversal evident in the word *by* for *dry,* and the omission of the /r/ in the word *stuggled* for *struggled* were also noted in this passage. One critical thinking question and one-half of an inference question consisted of the comprehension errors.

Frustration Level for this test appeared to be on grade equivalent 4. Seventeen word recognition errors were made. All four of the substitution errors seemed to be contributed to poor recognition of basic sight vocabulary. This was evident in the words *the* for *that, to* for *at, there* for *here,* and *of* for *in.* There seems to be a weakness in this area. The articles *a* and *the* appeared account for the four insertion errors found in this selection. No other pattern of word recognition errors was noted. One main idea question, and one-half of an inference question constituted the errors made in comprehension.

*Stanford Diagnostic Reading Test* (Green Level)
 Auditory Vocabulary
  —Stanine 4 Grade Equivalent 3.2
 Auditory Discrimination
  —Stanine 5 Grade Equivalent 2.8
 Phonetic Analysis
  —Stanine 4 Grade Equivalent 2.5
 Structural Analysis
  —Stanine 5 Grade Equivalent 3.8
 Literal Comprehension
  —Stanine 5 Grade Equivalent 3.2

 Inferential Comprehension
  —Stanine 5 Grade Equivalent 3.2
 Comprehension Total
  —Stanine 5 Grade Equivalent 3.6

The *Stanford Diagnostic Reading Test* (Green Level) is a group diagnostic inventory which was given on an individual basis. The Green Level ranges approximately from grade equivalent 2.6 to 5.5. Stanine scores as well as grade equivalent scores will be presented in this summary. Stanine scores of 1, 2, and 3 can be interpreted as below-average performance; 4, 5, and 6 indicates average performance; and 7, 8, and 9 as above average performance.

Subtest 1, Auditory Vocabulary, consists of selected vocabulary items in the areas of reading and literature, math and science, social studies and the arts. The child is asked to identify the word that best fits the meaning of the sentence dictated. No reading is required.

Detra correctly identified twenty-one of the forty items presented. This yielded a grade equivalent of 3.2 and a stanine score of 4. The client appears to be in the low average range with an approximately equal number of errors occurring in the areas of reading and literature, math and science, social studies and the arts. A possible weakness is noted in auditory vocabulary.

Subtest 2, Auditory Discrimination, consists of items asking the child to make consonant and vowel discriminations. Items 1 through 12 test discrimination ability utilizing consonant sounds in the initial and final positions in words. The client is asked if the words dictated begin or end with the same sound. Detra correctly discriminated eleven out of the twelve word pairs presented. Items 13 through 36 test discrimination ability utilizing consonant and vowel sounds in the initial, medial, and final positions in words. Nineteen out of the twenty-four items presented were correctly discriminated. Detra appeared to have trouble with long vowel sounds on this part of the subtest. All five errors consisted of the incorrect discrimination of the similarities of long vowel sounds occurring in the initial medial and final positions of words. Specific problems were noted on /y$\overline{oo}$/ in the initial position, /$\overline{a}$/, /$\overline{o}$/ in the final positions, and /$\overline{oo}$/, /$\overline{i}$/ in the medial positions evident

in the words *union-useless, away-display, although-window, shoot-food,* and *night-slide.* Results of this totaled a raw score of 30 yielding a grade equivalent of 2.8, placing Detra in stanine 5. The grade equivalent score on this subtest indicates a possible weakness.

On subtest 3, Phonetic Analysis, the child is given an underlined grapheme. The child is to identify that same sound in another word. This task is done independently within a twenty minute time period. Sixteen of the thirty-six items were correctly identified. This resulted in a grade equivalent of 2.5 and a stanine score of 4. There appears to be a possible weakness in this area. Errors on this subtest were almost equally distributed in the analysis of consonant sounds (4/6 consisting of errors in /w/, /j/, /s/, /z/), consonant clusters (4/6 consisting of errors in /gr/, /st/, /ld/, /sk/), consonant digraphs (3/6 consisting of errors in /sh/, /ng/), short vowel sounds (4/6 consisting of errors in /e/, /o/, /u/, /oo/,) long vowel sounds (4/6 consisting of errors in /ī/, /ā/, /ē/, /ō/), and other vowel sounds (1/6 consisting of the error /ər/.) No pattern of errors was noted.

Subtest 4, Structural Analysis, is divided into two parts A and B. Part A consists of thirty items testing the child's ability to identify the first syllable in two syllable words. Detra correctly identified twenty-seven of the thirty items presented. No pattern of errors was noted.

On Part B of the subtest the child is given syllables, affixes, and root words. She is then asked to blend these elements together to make words. Detra successfully completed twenty of the thirty items presented. Errors were made on two of six items involving the rules for dividing and blending compound words evident in the incorrect selection of the word parts *havesome* for *someone,* and *toport* for *seaport;* three out of twelve items involving affixes, evident in the incorrect selection of *comvance* for *advance, shortless* for *shortest,* and *adin* for *inquire;* and five out of twelve items involving syllabification rules evident in the incorrect selection of *artion* for *question, otble* for *able, tarket* for *market, corcer* for *certain* and *tronit* for *unit.*

Detra received a total score of 47 on this subtest. Results indicated a grade equivalent of 3.8, and a stanine score of 5. This placed Detra in the average range for the task on structural analysis. It should be noted however, that Detra did significantly better on

items involving syllabification of whole words (Part A of the subtest). Detra appeared to have more problems on the more difficult task of blending parts of words into whole words.

The Reading Comprehension subtest of Stanford consists of two parts, A and B. Part A consists of twenty items presented in a modified cloze format. The task includes both literal and inferential comprehension questions. Detra successfully completed twenty-one of the twenty-four items presented on Part A of the subtest. Errors were noted on two literal and one inferential comprehension question.

Part B of the Reading Comprehension subtest consists of short paragraphs in the areas of reading and literature, math and science, social studies and the arts. Selections are read independently with literal and inferential comprehension questions following. On this portion of the subtest, Detra correctly answered twenty-five of the thirty-six items presented. Errors were noted on three literal and eight inferential comprehension questions. In combining the results from Part's A and B, a total of five literal and nine inferential comprehension errors were noed on this subtest. This yielded a stanine score of 5, and a grade equivalent of 3.2 in both the literal comprehension and inferential comprehension areas. A total comprehension stanine sscore of 5, and a grade equivalent of 3.6 was noted on this task. Detra appears to be in the average range in total reading comprehension on this particular subtest. Grade equivalent scores, however, do indicate a possible weakness in this area. Inferential questions appear to be more of a problem for Detra.

*Durrell Analysis of Reading Difficulty*

Oral Reading —Grade Equivalent Low 3
Silent Reading —Grade Equivalent Low 3
Listening Comprehension—Grade Equivalent 3
Word Recognition and Word Analysis:
    List 1 and 2 Flash —Grade Equivalent High 5
    List 1 and 2 Analysis —Grade Equivalent Middle 5
Naming Letters—No Errors
Visual Memory of Words (Primary)
                  —Grade Equivalent 3.5
Hearing Sounds in Words (Primary)
                  —Grade Equivalent 3.5
Phonic Spelling of Words—Below Test Norms
Spelling Test—Grade Equivalent 4
Handwriting—Grade Equivalent 3

The *Durrell Analysis of Reading Difficulty* consists of a variety of subtests that can be used to evaluate a readers ability.

The Oral Reading subtest contains short timed passages with comprehension questions. Detra obtained a median grade equivalent of Low 3 on this test. Comprehension appeared to be fair. Two fact questions were missed on selection 4, and three fact questions were missed on selection 5. Two significant word recognition errors appeared in the words *he* for *it,* and *an* for *the.* No other pattern of errors was noted.

Silent reading tests are also timed. The client is asked to recall memory items contained in the passages. Detra's median grade equivalent for this subtest was Low 3. Detra's speed for silent reading selections appeared to approximate the times received on the oral reading passages. Comprehension, however, did appear better on the Silent Reading subtest. In observing test behavior occasional lip movements, whispering, and finger pointing were noted.

Listening Comprehension scores yielded a grade equivalent of 3. In this subtest selections are read to the child with comprehension questions following. The grade equivalent score indicates a possible weakness in this area. It should be noted however that the grade 4 reading selection, "Peter Cooper's Engine" appeared to be a difficult selection.

On the Word Recognition and Word Analysis subtest the child is first flashed words for recognition. If items are missed on the flash, he is shown the word again for analysis. Scores from List 1 and 2 indicated a flash score of grade equivalent High 5, and an analysis score of grade equivalent Middle 5. Word recognition and word analysis appear to be a strong area for Detra. She appeared to use phonetic and structural analysis in decoding new words. Three errors on flashed words were characterized by the omission of the /er/ and /ry/ evident in the words *carpet* for *carpenter, advisment* for *advertisement,* and *battle* for *battery.* No other pattern of errors was noted.

Detra appeared to have a good knowledge of capital and small letter names. No errors were noted on the subtest Naming Letters.

On the Visual Memory of Words (Primary) subtest, Detra was asked to circle the letter on word flashed on the tachistoscope. A grade equivalent of 3.5 was obtained on this test. Errors consisted of *block* for *black, mentioned* for *mountains,* and *poultice* for *practice.* No significant pattern of errors was noted.

Hearing Sounds in Words (Primary) asks the child to identify words which begin, end, and some which begin and end like the words dictated. Twenty-eight of the twenty-nine items presented were correctly identified. This yielded a grade equivalent score of 3.5. This appeared to be a strong area for Detra. The one error consisted of a /d/ for /b/ in the final position evident in the word *crowd* for *crab.*

On the Phonetic Spelling of Words subtest the examiner dictates fifteen words to the client. The child must listen to the words presented and spell them as they sound. Results of this subtest were below the level of the norms presented. Fourteen errors were made. Only one word approximated the correct spelling of the dictated word. A pattern of errors was seen in the omission of the *r* in words containing /er/, and the omission of the final *e* in words needing a long vowel sound. This was evident in the words *intevit* for *intervent, introvet* for *introvert, iceotem* for *isotherm, carpulit* for *carpolite, ligulat* for *ligulate, expukat* for *explicate,* and *Aastolad* for *astrolabe.*

On the Spelling Test subtest of the *Durrell,* words were dictated from List 1, grade equivalent 2 and 3. Detra correctly spelled sixteen of the twenty words presented. Grade equivalent 4 was obtained on this task. This appeared to be a strong area for Detra. The *ai* in the words *hiar* for *hair* and *strat* for *straight* appeared to give Detra some trouble.

Detra scored a grade equivalent of 3 on the handwriting subtest. In observing test behavior, poor hand and pencil position were noted. Poor letter formation and slant also appeared to be a problem.

*Wepman Auditory Discrimination Test 5/30*

The *Wepman Auditory DIscrimination Test* (Form 1) consists of one syllable word pairs. As words are dictated the child is asked to respond if the words are the same or different. The child's back is turned toward the tester. No visual clues are given.

Test results indicated 5 y-errors. Two of the errors *clothe-clove* and *sheaf-sheath* appear to be due to regional dialect. Detra's auditory discrimination on this particular test appears adequate.

*Keystone Vision Screening Test*

Far Point Tests indicate a possible weakness
Near Point Tests indicate a possible weakness

Audiometer—Appears Adequate

Audiological screening was done at 20 dB. Results appear to indicate adequate hearing.

## Summary

In summarizing test results a profile of strengths and weaknesses can be identified. Detra appears to have good word recognition skills. She seemed to decode new words using skills in phonetic and structural analysis. This was evident in the grade equivalent score of 5.3 noted on the *Slosson Oral Reading Test*, and the grade equivalents of High 5 and Middle 5 noted on the Word Recognition and Word Analysis subtest of the *Durrell Analysis*. Hearing sounds in words also appeared to be a strong area for Detra. She successfully completed twenty-eight of the twenty-nine items presented. A grade equivalent of 3.5 was considered to be at the upper limits of this subtest on *Durrell*. A grade equivalent of 4 was obtained on the Spelling Test subtest of the *Durrell*. This appeared to be one of Detra's stronger areas.

As stated previously, Detra appeared to have good word recognition skills. A few problem areas seemed to appear, however, on the *Sucher-Allred* Word Recognition and Oral Reading subtests, and on the *Durrell* Word Recognition and Analysis subtest. Detra appeared to omit the /r/, /ər/, and /ry/ in selected words. On the Phonetic Spelling of Words subtest of the *Durrell*, Detra omitted the letter *r* in three of the words containing *er* spellings.

Detra also appeared to demonstrate slow syllable blending. This was evident in the errors made on the *Slosson Oral Reading Test*, and the *Sucher-Allred Word Recognition* subtest. Blending problems also appeared to emerge on the Structural Analysis subtest of the *Stanford*.

There appears to be a weakness in literal and inferential comprehension. Although both subtests in this area yielded average stanines on the Stanford, the 3.2 grade equivalents appear to indicate some problems. Errors consisted of nine out of thirty inferential questions, and five out of thirty literal comprehension questions. On the *Durrell* the opposite pattern occurred. On the Oral Reading subtest six of the seven comprehension errors were made on items calling for the literal interpretation of facts.

Detra appears to have a weak auditory vocabulary. This was evident on the items missed on the *Slosson Intelligence Test*, the 3.2 grade equivalent yielded on the Auditory Vocabulary subtest of the *Stanford*, and the grade equivalent 3 Listening Comprehension subtest score on the *Durrell*.

Judgment reasoning items on the *Slosson Intelligence Test* appeared to present a problem for Detra. An area of weakness appeared on items calling for a response on how two objects were alike and different. Detra appeared to understand the concepts of same and different, but was unable to reason a correct response.

Poor auditory discrimination was noted on the long vowels /oo/, /ā/, /ō/, /ī/ on the Auditory Discrimination subtest of the *Stanford*. The Phonetic Analysis subtest of the *Stanford* also indicated areas of possible weakness. The consonants /w/, /j/, /s/, /z/, the clusters /gr/, /st/, /ld/, /sk/, the digraphs /sh/, /ng/, the short vowels /e/, /o/, /u/, /oo/, the long vowels /ī/, /ā/, /ē/, /ō/, and the other vowel /ər/ appeared to be weak areas in phonetic analysis.

Poor recognition of basic sight vocabulary appeared to be a weakness on the oral reading selections of the *Sucher-Allred* and *Durrell Analysis*. Errors occurred on the words *a, and, at, from, he, here, in, its, said, that, then*, on the *Sucher-Allred*, and the words *the*, and *it* on the *Durrell*.

Poor visual acuity could have been a contributing factor. Both near point and far point test on the *Keystone Vision Screening Test* indicated a possible weakness.

Although a grade equivalent of 4 was obtained on th Spelling Test of the *Durrell*, Detra appeared to have problems with the phonetic spelling of words. Areas of weakness were noted on the omission of the *r* in the words containing the spelling *er*, and the omission of the silent *e* in words containing long vowel sounds. This was evident on the Phonetic Spelling of Words subtest of the *Durrell*. The /ā/ represented by the *ai* spelling gave Detra some problems on the Spelling Test subtest of the *Durrell*.

Poor handwriting skills characterized by poor hand and pencil position, and poor letter formation and slant appeared as a possible weakness on the *Durrell* Handwriting subtest.

## Appendix J

### Guidelines for Evaluating a Reading Management System

*Are the objectives included in the management system comprehensive for the reading program and do they relate to the scope and sequence in your school system?* Because the assessments and record-keeping procedures are based on the objectives, it is essential that the objectives be very specific, comprehensive, and reflect the needs of the students. Compare the skills included in the management system with the comprehensive list of reading skills found in appendix A and with your district's skills continuum.

*Do the assessments measure the given objectives?* It is essential that the assessments measure the specific objectives, otherwise, the instruments are invalid and of little value to the teacher. This should be checked carefully, as a problem with some criterion-referenced test items in their lack of correlation with the specific objectives.

*Are all assessments in the form of paper-pencil test* items? Teachers and administrators must realize that reading skills can be measured in various ways, one of which is the paper-pencil test. However, by identifying the specific reading skill, teachers can use activities in their learning centers, games, workbook pages, and observation techniques to determine the student's knowledge of the skill. The key is to know the skill and to identify alternative procedures for evaluation prior to beginning the use of the management system. For example, the teachers at Seabreeze School, working in teams, identified the exact procedures they would use to assess each reading skill in their scope and sequence listing. Thus, they did not use only written exercises to assess student knowledge of the skills; they used observation of reading activities in the basal groups and skill groups, student performance on designated games, and student responses in group discussions following the reading of a selection. These teachers determined numerous ways to assess reading skills and maintain objectivity in the process. Additionally, they were measuring reading performance through reading rather than always by asking the students to write.

*Are the objectives and assessments outlined for developing reading skills in a spiral curriculum, or are they given at only one level as mastery skills?*

Some management systems repeat objectives at several levels so that the student is exposed to the skill over a period of time and assessed on the skill at different levels. Other systems put the objective and assessments in at only one level—the level at which mastery is to occur. The authors favor the systems which encourage development of the skill over a period of time, because the learner is provided with instruction and review to better ensure the mastery of the skill. Although word recognition skills may be considered mastered when the student applies them in reading, comprehension and study skills must be reviewed and extended at each level. Thus, a management system which seeks to attain one level of mastery for all reading skills is not designed according to the learning process.

Some systems are inconsistent in the areas of management, learning tasks, skills hierarchy as well as instructional methods. In addition, the four elements in teaching a skill—cues, reinforcement, participation, and feedback are not used.

*Is the record-keeping procedure simple or extremely time consuming for the teacher?* Teachers will find that any record-keeping procedure is to some extent time consuming. However, this is an essential part of a good diagnostic-prescriptive reading program and essential for the teacher. Many times teachers feel that they can remember what each student knows and does not know—but this is impossible? How would you feel about a doctor who did not keep records on patients, but preferred to remember their illnesses and prescriptions? It is essential to keep records; however, the teacher must be sure that the records do not consume more time than teaching! Many school systems are addressing this problem through the use of microcomputers in the classrooms. Tests are given using the microcomputer, or at least results are recorded in lieu of a constant shuffling of papers to identify student needs.

*Are the objectives and assessments appropriate to the reading level of each student?* As objectives are assigned to the appropriate level in the continuum of skills, the teacher must be sure that the corresponding assessments are written at the appropriate readability levels. An objective placed at the third-grade level

with a corresponding assessment written at the fifth-grade level provides the teacher with little diagnostic data; does the student not know the skill or is he or she just unable to read the assessment?

*Are several assessments provided for each objective, and are these assessments equivalent for a given objective?* Two or more assessments are needed for each objective. This allows for pre- and post-assessment. The teacher should use one assessment prior to instruction to determine if the students knows the skill and a second to evaluate the achievement of the skill. If the teacher finds that the student has not learned the skill, still another assessment will be necessary at a later date. Thus, it is helpful if more than two assessments are provided, to permit the teacher to retest peiodically and make sure that the student is using the skill properly.

In addition, in selecting a management system be sure that the assessment items are equivalent in difficulty. If one is more difficult or easier than others that measure the same skill, the information gained will not be accurate.

*Are consultant services or training materials available in the school keyed to the objectives?* Teachers do not have time to locate materials to use in providing prescriptive instruction. Therefore, a complete management system refers to the materials that assist in developing specific objectives. Be sure that the materials that are keyed or referenced are current and available to the teacher using the system. A team of teachers should check these materials to be sure that they actually develop the appropriate reading skill. All too often teachers find that the material is either keyed incorrectly by a page or book number error or that the material was keyed by someone who mismatched reading skills! A quick spot check can save hours of frustration later.

## Appendix K

### Books to Use In Bibliotherapy

*Adoption*

Bates, Betty. *Bugs In Your Ears.* Holiday House, 1977.

Blue, Rose. *Seven Years From Home.* Raintree, 1976.

Budbill, David. *Bones on Black Spruce Mountain.* Dial Press, 1978.

Glass, Frankcina. *Marvin and Tige.* St. Martin's Press, 1977.

Pursell, Margaret S. *A Look At Adoption.* Lerner, 1978.

Rivera, Geraldo. *A Special Kind of Courage: Profiles of Young Americans.* Simon & Schuster, 1976.

Silman, Roberta. *Somebody Else's Child.* Frederick Warne, 1976.

Swetnam, Evelyn. *Yes, My Darling Daughter.* Harvey House, 1978.

Wasson, Valentina. *The Chosen Baby,* 3rd ed. rev. J. B. Lippincott, 1977.

*Child Abuse*

Anderson, Mary Q. *Step On A Crack.* Atheneum, 1978.

Bauer, Marion D. *Foster Child.* Seabury Press, 1977.

Hunt, Irene. *The Lottery Rose.* Charles Scribner's, 1976.

Mazer, Harry. *The War On Villa Street: A Novel.* Dalacorte Press, 1978.

Roberts, Willo D. *Don't Hurt Laurie!* Atheneum, 1978.

Ruby, Lois. *Arriving At A Place You've Never Left.* Dial Press, 1977.

*Death*

Alter, Judy. *After Pa Was Shot.* William Morrow, 1978.

Anders, Rebecca. *A Look At Death.* Learner, 1978.

Brown, Margaret Wise. *The Dead Bird.* Addison-Wesley, 1958.

Burch, Robert. *Simon and the Game of Chance.* New York: The Viking Press, 1970.

Carrick, Carol. *The Accident.* The Seabury Press, 1976.

Cleaver, Vera and Bill. *Grover.* J. B. Lippincott, 1970.

Colman, Hila Crayder. *Sometimes I Don't Love My Mother.* William Morrow, 1977.

De Paola, Tomie. *Nana Upstairs and Nana Downstairs.* G. P. Putnam's Sons, 1973.

Farley, Carol. *The Garden is Doing Fine.* Atheneum, 1975.

Greene, Constance Clarke. *Beat the Turtle Drum.* The Viking Press, 1976.

Harris, Audry. *Why Did He Die?* Lerner Publishing, 1965.

Smith, Doris. *A Taste of Blackberries.* New York: Crowell, 1973.

Warburg, Sandol Stoddard. *The Growing Time.* Houghton Mifflin, 1969.

White, E. B. *Charlotte's Web.* Harper & Row, 1952.

Zolotow, Charlotte. *My Grandson Lew.* Harper & Row, 1974.

### Divorce

Adams, Florence. *Mushy Eggs.* Putnam, 1973.

Berger, Terry. *How Does It Feel When Your Parents Get Divorced?* Julian Messner, 1977.

Blume, Judy. *It's Not the End of the World.* Bantam Press, 1972.

Caines, Jeannette F. *Daddy.* Harper & Row, 1977.

Christopher, Matthew F. *The Fox Steals Home.* Little, Brown, 1978.

Dexter, Pat Egan. *Arrow in the Wind.* Thomas Nelson, 1978.

Fox, Paula. *Blowfish Live in the Sea.* Bradbury Press, 1972.

Gardner, Richard A. *The Boys and Girls Book About Divorce.* Bantam Press, 1970.

Hazen, Barbara Shook. *Two Homes to Live In: A Child's-Eye View of Divorce.* Human Science Press, 1978.

Hunter, Evan. *Me and Mr. Stenner.* J. B. Lippincott, 1976.

Leshan, Eda J. *What's Going to Happen to Me? When Parents Separate or Divorce.* Four Winds Press, 1978.

Lexau, Joan M. *Me Day.* Dial, 1971.

Mann, Peggy. *My Father Lives in a Downtown Hotel.* Doubleday, 1973.

Newfield, Marcia. *A Book for Jodan.* Atheneum, 1975.

Platt, Kim. *Chloris and the Creeps.* Dell, 1973.

### Fear

Berkey, Barry, and Berkey, Velma. *Robbers, Bones and Mean Dogs.* Addison-Wesley, 1978.

Bloch, Marie H. *Displaced Person.* Lothrop, Lee & Shepard, 1978.

Cleary, Beverly B. *Ramona The Brave.* Morrow, 1975.

Clifton, Lucille. *Amifika.* E. P. Dutton, 1977.

Cohen, Miriam. *The New Teacher.* Macmillan, 1972.

Cohen, Miriam. *Will I Have A Friend?* Macmillan, 1967.

Clyne, Patricia E. *Tunnels of Terror.* Atlantic Monthly Press, 1977.

Griese, Arnold A. *The Way of Our People.* Dodd, Mead, 1975.

Leigh, Bill. *The Far Side of Fear.* Thomas Y. Crowell, 1975.

Lexau, Joan M. *Benjie.* Dial, 1964.

McCloskey, Robert. *One Morning in Maine.* Viking, 1952.

Miles, Miska, pseud. *Aaron's Door.* Viking Press, 1977.

### Handicaps

Albert, Louise. *But I'm Ready to Go.* Brady Press, 1976.

Baldwin, Anne Morris. *A Little Time.* The Viking Press, 1978.

Brown, Fern G. *You're Somebody Special on a Horse.* Albert Whitman, 1977.

Fanshawe, Elizabeth. *Rachel.* Bradbury Press, 1975.

Hark, Mildred. *Mary Lou and Johnny.* Watts, 1963.

Hirsch, Karen. *My Sister.* Carolrhoda Books, 1977.

Kingman, Lee. *Head Over Wheels.* Houghton Mifflin, 1978.

Litchfield, Ada B. *A Button in Her Ear.* Albert Whitman, 1976.

Litchfield, Ada B. *A Cane in Her Hand.* Albert Whitman, 1977.

Little, Jean. *Mine for Keeps.* Little, Brown, 1962.

Nicholson, William G. *Pete Gray: One Armed Major Leaguer.* Prentice-Hall, 1976.

Peusner, Stella. *Keep Stompin' Till the Music Stops.* The Seabury Press, 1977.

Pursell, Margaret S. *A Look at Physical Handicaps.* Lerner, 1976.

White, Paul. *Janet at School.* Thomas Y. Crowell, 1978.

Wolf, Bernard. *Don't Feel Sorry for Paul.* J. B. Lippincott, 1974.

### Hospitalization

Braithwaite, Althea. *Going Into Hospital.* Dinosaur Publications, 1974.

Bruna, Dick. *Miffy in the Hospital.* Methuen, 1975.

Collier, James L. *Danny Goes to the Hospital.* W. W. Norton, 1970.

Kay, Eleanor. *Let's Find Out About the Hospital.* Watts, 1971.

Rey, Margaret, and Rey, H. A. *Curious George Goes to the Hospital.* Houghton Mifflin, 1966.

Stein, Sara Bonnett. *A Hospital Story.* Walker & Company, 1974.

Sobol, Harriet L. *Jeff's Hospital Book.* Henry Z. Walck, 1975.

Weber, Alfons. *Elizabeth Gets Well.* Crowell, 1970.

Wolde, Gunilla. *Betsy and the Doctor.* Random House, 1978.

Ziegler, Sandra. *At the Hospital: A Surprise for Krissy.* The Child's World, 1976.

*Love*

Bornstein, Ruth. *Little Gorilla.* The Seabury Press, 1976.

Branscum, Robbie. *The Saving of P. S.* Doubleday, 1977.

Brown, Margaret Wise. *The Runaway Bunny.* Harper & Row, 1972.

Brown, Myra Berry. *The First Night Away From Home.* Watts, 1960.

Graham, John. *I Love You, Mouse.* Harcourt Brace Jovanovich, 1976.

McGee, Myra. *Lester and Mother.* Harper & Row, 1978.

Minarik, Else Holmeland. *Little Bear Series.* Harper & Row.

Sonneborn, Ruth. *Friday Night is Papa Night.* Viking, 1970.

Sonneborn, Ruth. *I Love Gram.* Viking, 1971.

Zolotow, Charlotte. *A Father Like That.* Harper & Row, 1971.

Zolotow, Charlotte. *Do You Know What I'll Do?* Harper & Row, 1958.

Zolotow, Charlotte. *William's Doll.* Harper & Row, 1972.

Viscardi, Henry. *The Phoenix Child: A Story of Love.* Paul S. Eriksson, 1975.

*Self-Awareness*

Ardizzone, Edward. *The Wrong Side of the Bed.* Doubleday, 1970.

Bradbury, Bianca. *"I'm Vinny, I'm Me."* Houghton Mifflin, 1977.

Brown, Marc Tolon. *Arthur's Nose.* Little, Brown, 1976.

Conaway, Judith. *Will I Ever Be Good Enough?* Raintree, 1977.

Danziger, Paula. *The Pistachio Prescription: A Novel.* Delacorte Press, 1978.

Dunn, Judy. *Having Fun.* Creative Educational Society, 1971.

French, Simon. *Cannily, Cannily.* Angus and Robertson, 1981.

Gripe, Maria Kristina. *The Green Coat.* Delacorte, 1977.

Hamilton, Gail, pseud. *Titania's Lodestone.* Atheneum, 1975.

Hooks, William H. *Doug Meets the Nutcracker.* Frederick Warne, 1977.

Hutchins, Pat. *Titch.* Macmillan, 1971.

Krasilovsky, Phyllis. *The Very Tall Little Girl.* Doubleday, 1969.

Lee, H. Alton. *Seven Feet Four and Growing.* The Westminster Press, 1978.

Noonan, Julia. *The Best Thing to Be.* Doubleday, 1971.

Preston, Edna. *The Temper Tantrum Book.* Viking, 1969.

*Sibling Rivalry*

Alexander, Martha G. *I'll Be the Horse If You'll Play With Me.* Dial, 1975.

Alexander, Martha. *Nobody Ever Asked Me If I Wanted a Baby Sister.* Dial, 1971.

Byars, Betsy C. *Go Hush the Baby.* Viking Press, 1971.

Cohen, Barbara Nash. *Benny.* Lothrop, Lee & Shepard, 1977.

Keats, Ezra Jack. *Peter's Chair.* Harper, 1967.

Lexau, Joan M. *Emily and the Klunky Baby and the Next Door Dog.* Dial, 1972.

Pearson, Susan. *Monnie Hates Lydia.* The Dial, 1975.

Steptoe, John. *Stevie.* Harper & Row, 1969.

Stolz, Mary S. *Ferris Wheel.* Harper & Row, 1977.

Viorst, Judith. *I'll Fix Anthony.* Harper & Row, 1969.

Voge, Ilse-Margret. *My Twin Sister Erika.* Harper & Row, 1976.

Zolotow, Charlotte. *If It Weren't For You.* Harper & Row, 1966.

Zolotow, Charlotte. *Someday.* Harper & Row, 1965.

Compiled by Adele Rutland.

## Appendix L

**A Selected Bibliography of Children's Books**

*Interest Level: Primer—2nd Grade*

Aardema, Verna. *Why Mosquitoes Buzz in People's Ears.* New York: Dial, 1975. (Folk Tale-Picture Book)

Adoff, Arnold. *All the Colors of the Race.* New York: Lothrop, Lee and Shepard, 1982. (Poetry)

Allen, Laura Jean. *Ottie and the Star.* New York: Harper & Row, 1979. (Animal)

Anderson, Karen Born. *What's the Matter, Sylvie, Can't You Ride?* New York: Dial, 1981. (Feelings—Picture Book)

Brandenberg, Fran. *Six New Students.* New York: Greenwillow, 1978. (Animals)

Brown, Palmer. *Hickory.* New York: Harper & Row, 1978. (Friendship)

Burningham, John. *Avocado Baby.* New York: Thomas Y. Crowell, 1982. (Tall Tale-Picture Book)

Caldecott, Randolph. *The Hey Diddle Diddle Picture Book.* London: Frederick Warne and Company, n.d. (Nursery Rhymes)

Carle, Eric. *The Honeybee and the Robber.* New York: Philomel Books, 1981. (Bees—Picture Book)

Cendrars, Blaise. *Shadow.* New York: Scribner's Sons, 1982. (Africa—Picture Book)

Cutler, Ivor. *The Animal House.* New York: Morrow, 1978. (Animal)

Delange, Ida. *ABC Christmas.* Champaign, Illinois: Garrard Publishing Company, 1978. (ABC's)

DeRegniers, Beatrice Schenk. *May I Bring A Friend?* New York: Atheneum, 1964. (Friends)

Gage, Wilson. *Mrs. Gaddy and the Ghost.* New York: Greenwillow, 1979. (Humor)

Garelick, May. *Where Does the Butterfly Go When It Rains?* New York: Scholastic Book Service, 1961. (Animals)

Goble, Paul. *The Girl Who Loved Wild Horses.* Scarsdale, N.Y.: Bradbury, 1978. (Animals—Picture Book)

Greene, Carol. *Hinny Winny Bunco.* New York: Harper & Row, 1982. (Fantasy—Picture Book)

Hall, Donald. *Ox-Cart Man.* New York: Viking Press, 1979. (Seasons—Picture Book)

Hoban, Tana. *Count and See.* New York: Macmillan, 1972. (Numbers)

Keats, Ezra Jack. *Apt. 3.* New York: Macmillan, 1971. (City Life)

Knotts, Howard. *Great-Frandfather, The Baby and Me.* New York: Antheneum, 1978. (Family)

Krauss, Ruth. *A Hole Is To Dig.* New York: Harper & Row, 1952. (Picture Book)

Langstaff, John. *Frog Went A-Courting'.* New York: Harcourt, Brace and World, 1955. (Animals)

Lenski, Lois. *The Little Airplane.* Henry Z. Walck, Inc., 1938. (Picture Book)

Leodhas, Sorche Nie. *Always Room For One More.* New York: Holt, Rinehart, and Winston, 1965. (Picture Book)

Lionn: Leo. *Geraldine the Music Mouse.* Pantheon, 1979. (Animal—Picture Book)

Lobel, Arnold. *Mouse Soup.* New York: Harper & Row, 1977. (Animals)

Nixon, Joan Lowery. *The Alligator Under the Bed.* New York: G. P. Putnam's Sons, 1974. (Animals)

Nolan, Madeena Spray. *My Daddy Don't Go to Work.* Minneapolis, Minnesota, 1978. (Family Problems)

Parker, Nancy W. *The Crocodile Under Louis Finneberg's Bed.* New York: Dodd, 1978. (Fantasy)

Peet, Bill. *Cowardly Clyde.* Boston: Houghton Mifflin, 1979. (Animal)

Perkins, Al. *The Nose Book.* A Bright and Early Book. New York: Random House, 1970. (Picture Book)

Plume, Ilse. *The Bremen-town Musicians.* Garden City, N.Y.: Doubleday, 1980. (Folk Tale—Animals)

Provensen, Alice, and Provensen, Martin. *The Year at Maple Hill Farm.* New York: Atheneum, 1979. (Seasons—Picture Book)

Raskin, Elen. *Spectacles.* New York: Atheneum, 1968. (Picture Book)

Rey, Margret. *Curious George Flies a Kite.* Boston: Houghton Mifflin, 1958. (Picture Book)

Rojankovsky, Feodor. *Animals on the Farm.* New York: Alfred A. Knopf, 1967. (Animals)

Suess, Dr. *The Foot Book.* New York: Random, 1968. (Picture Book)

Udry, Janice May. *A Tree is Nice.* (New York): Harper & Row, 1956. (Nature)

Ungerer, Tomi. *One, Two, Where's My Shoe?* New York: Harper & Row, 1964. (Picture Book)

Victor, Joan Berg. *SHH! Listen Again; Sounds of the Seasons.* Cleveland: The World Publishing Company, 1969. (The Seasons)

Waterton, Pettranella. *Pettranella.* Vancouver, B.C.: Douglas & McIntyre, 1981. (Historical Fiction)

Williams, Garth. *The Chicken Book.* New York: Delacorte Press, 1946. (Animals)

*Interest Level: 3rd—4th Grades*

Andersen, Hans Christian. *The Wild Swans:* Translated by M. R. James. New York: Charles Scribner's Sons, 1963. (Fairytale)

Anderson, Clarence W. *Blaze and the Gypsies.* New York: Macmillan, 1937. (Animals)

Anglund, Joan Walsh. *A Child's Book of Old Nursery Rhymes.* New York: Atheneum, 1973. (Nursery Rhymes)

Anglund, Joan Walsh. *A Friend is Someone Who Likes You.* New York: Harcourt, Brace & World, 1958. (Friendship)

Anglund, Joan Walsh. *Cowboy and His Friend.* New York: Harcourt, Brace & World, 1958. (Friendship)

Bolognese, Don. *A New Day.* New York: Delacorte Press, 1970. (Picture Book—Spanish-American)

Buck, Pearl S. *The Christmas Ghost.* New York: The John Day Company, 1960. (Christmas)

Burchard, Marshall. *Sports Hero: Rod Carew.* New York: Putnam, 1978. (Biography—Sports)

Burchard, Sue. *Sports Hero: Tony Dorsett.* New York: Harcourt Brace Jovanovich, 1979. (Biography—Sports)

Carlson, Natalie S. *Jaky or Dodo.* New York: Scribner's Sons, 1978. (Animal)

Carrick, Donald. *Harald and the Giant Knight.* Boston: Houghton Mifflin, 1982. (Knighthood—Boys)

Carrick, Malcolm. *I Can Squash Elephants! A Masai Tale About Monsters.* New York: Viking Press, 1978. (Fairytale)

Cleary, Beverly. *Henry Huggins.* New York: William Morrow & Company, 1950. (Fiction—Boys)

Cleary, Beverly. *Ramona and Her Father.* New York: Morrow, 1977. (Fiction—Girls)

Crane, Stephen. *The Red Badge of Courage and Other Stories.* Great Illustrated Classics Series. New York: Dodd, Mead & Company, 1957. (Story Collection)

Davis, Burke. *My Lincoln's Whiskers.* New York: Coward, 1979. (Historical fiction—Civil War)

Devaney, John. *The Picture Story of Terry Bradshaw.* New York: Julian Messner, 1977. (Biography—Picture Book)

Dietmeier, Mel. *Potato.* Reading, Massachusetts: Addison-Wesley Publishing Company, 1972. (Picture Book—Cats)

Dubelaar, Thea. *Maria.* Translated by Anthea Bell. New York: William Morrow, 1982. (Fiction—Family)

Clyne, Patricia Edwards. *Strange and Supernatural Animals.* New York: Dodd, 1979. (Mystery)

Collins, Jim. *Unidentified Flying Objects.* Milwaukee, WI: Raintree, 1977. (Science Fiction)

Cone, Molly. *Call Me Moose.* Boston: Houghton Mifflin, 1978. (Fiction—Girls)

Cormier, Robert. *The Chocolate War.* New York: Pantheon, 1974. (Friends)

Cormier, Robert. *I Am the Cheese.* New York: Pantheon, 1977. (Family)

Cox, William R. *Battery Mates.* New York: Dodd, 1978. (Sports—Boys)

Dahl, Ronald. *Charlie and the Chocolate Factory.* New York: Alfed A. Knopf, 1964. (Friends)

D'Aulaire, Ingri and Parin, Edgar. *Abraham Lincoln.* Garden City, New York: Doubleday and Company, 1939. (Biography)

D'Aulaire, Ingri and Parin, Edgar. *Columbus.* Garden City, New York: Doubleday and Company, 1955. (Biography)

Dixon, Franklin W. *The Mystery of Cabin Island.* New York: Grosset and Dunlap, 1966. (Mystery)

Dunlop, Eileen. *Fox Farm.* New York: Holt, 1979. (Fiction—Boys)

Edmonds, I. G. *The Magic Dog.* New York: E. P. Dutton, 1982. (Animals)

Elfman, Blossom. *The Girls of Huntington House.* Boston: Houghton Mifflin Company, 1972. (Unwed Mothers)

Farris, John. *When Michael Calls.* New York: Trident Press, 1967. (Mystery)

Farley, Walter. *The Black Stallion.* New York: Random House, 1941. (Horses)

Flack, Marjorie and Kurt Wiese. *The Story About Ping.* New York: Viking, 1933. (Animals)

Forbes, Esther. *Johnny Tremain.* New York: Houghton Mifflin Company, 1943. (Civil War)

Gag, Wanda. *Million of Cats*. New York: Coward, McCann, and Geoghegan, 1928. (Picture Book—Cats)

Galsone, Paul. *Henny Penny*. New York: Seabury Press, 1968. (Picture Book)

Galsone, Paul. *The Monkey and the Crocodile*. New York: Seabury Press, 1969. (Picture Book—Tale)

Hancock, Sibyl. *Theodore Roosevelt*. New York: Putnam, 1978. (Biography)

Hoff, Sydney. *Herschel the Hero*. New York: G. P. Putnam's Sons, 1969. (Picture Book)

Keats, Ezra Jack. *Hi, Cat!* New York: Macmillan, 1970. (Picture Book)

Langton, Jane. *The Fledgling*. New York: Harper & Row, 1980. (Fantasy—Adventure)

Lenski, Lois. *Strawberry Girl*. Philadelphia: J. B. Lippincott, 1946. (Fiction—Girls)

Lionni, Leo. *Frederick*. New York: Pantheon, 1967. (Picture Book)

McDermott, Gerald. *Arrow to the Sun*. New York: Viking Press, 1974. (Indian Tale—Picture Book)

Musgrove, Margaret. *Ashanti to Zulu: African Traditions*. New York: Dial, 1976. (Geography—Picture Book)

Myers, Elizabeth P. *Langston Hughes, Poet of His People*. Champaign, Illinois: Garrard Publishing Company, 1970. (Biography)

Osborne, Valerie. *One Big Yo to Go*. New York: Oxford University Press, 1980. (Poetry)

Robison, Nancy. *Tracy Austin*. New York: Harvey House, 1978. (Biography—Sports)

Sawyer, Ruth. *Journey Cake Ho!* New York: Viking, 1953. (Folktale)

Scribner, Charles Jr. *The Devil's Bridge*. New York: Scribner's Sons, 1978. (Folk—tale)

Spier, Peter. *Bored—Nothing to Do!* Garden City, New York: Doubleday, 1978. (Humor)

Sterling, Dorothy. *Freedom Train: The Story of Harriet Tubman*. New York: Scholastic Book Services, 1954. (Historical Fiction)

Stewart, Robert. *The Daddy Book*. New York: American Heritage Press, 1972. (Picture Book)

Van Allsburg. *Jumanj*. Boston: Houghton Mifflin, 1981. (Fantasy—Picture Book)

Viorst, Judith. *Alexander and the Terrible, Horrible, No Good, Very Bad Day*. New York: Atheneum, 1973. (Picture Book)

Wilde, Oscar. *The Happy Prince*. New York: Oxford University Press, 1981. (Social Consciousness)

Willard, Nancy. *A Visit to William Blake's Inn*. New York: Harcourt Brace Jovanovich, 1981. (Poetry)

Williams, Barbara. *Mitzi and the Terrible Tyrannosaurus Rex*. New York: E. P. Dutton, 1982. (Family Problems)

Zens, Patricia Martin: *The Gingerbread Man*. Racine, Wisconsin: A Whitman Book, 1963. (Fairytale—Picture Book)

*Interest Level: 5th—6th Grades*

Aiken, Joan. *The Faithless Lollybird*. Garden City, New York: Doubleday, 1978. (Fantasy)

Annixter, Jane, and Annixter, Paul. *The Year of the She-Grizzly*. New York: Coward, 1978. (Animals)

Arthur, Robert. *Alfred Hitchcock and the Three Investigators in the Mystery of the Silver Spider*. New York: Random House, 1967. (Mystery)

Atwater, Richard and Florence. *Mr. Popper's Penguins*. Boston: Little, Brown & Company, 1938. (Fiction—Animals)

Beatty, Patricia. *The Staffordshire Terror*. New York: Morrow, 1979. (Animals)

Bond, Michael and Banbery, Fred. *Paddington Bear*. New York: Random House, 1972. (Picture Book—Animals)

Brink, Carol Ryrie. *Caddie Woodlawn*. New York: Macmillan Company, 1935. (Frontier)

Bradford, Richard. *Red Sky at Morning*. Philadelphia: J. B. Lippincott Company, 1968. (Fiction—Family)

Burton, Virginia Lee. *The Little House*. Boston: Houghton Mifflin Company, 1942. (Picture Book)

Childress, Alice. *A Hero Ain't Nothin' But a Sandwich*. New York: Coward, McCann and Geoghegan, 1973. (Fiction—Boys)

Fuchshuber, Annegert. *The Wishing Hat*. New York: William Morrow and Company, 1977. (German Tale)

Galdone, Paul. *Puss in Boots*. New York: Seabury Press, 1976. (Fairytale)

Gipson, Fred. *Old Yeller*. New York: Harper & Row, 1956. (Animals)

Grenn, Hannah. *I Never Promised You a Rose Garden*. New York: Holt, Rinehart, and Winston, 1964. (Mental Illness)

Griese, Arnold A. *The Wind Is Not a River*. New York: Crowell, 1978. (Historical Fiction)

Godden, Rumer. *The Rocking Horse Secret*. New York: Viking Press, 1978. (Mystery—Girls)

Gormely, Beatrice. *Fifth Grade Magic.* New York: E. P. Dutton, 1982. (Fantasy—Girls)

Hader, Berton and Elmer. *The Big Snow.* New York: Macmillan Company, 1948.

Haley, Gail E. *A Story, A Story: An African Tale.* New York: Atheneum, 1970. (Tale)

Hamilton, Virginia. *M. C. Higgins, the Great.* New York: Macmillan, 1974. (Fictoin—Boys)

Hinton, S. E. *The Outsiders.* New York: Dell Publishing, 1967. (City Life—Gangs)

Hoban, Russell. *Best Friends for Frances.* New York: Harper & Row Publishers, 1969. (Picture Book)

Kerr, M. E. *Dinky Hocker Shoots Smack.* New York: Harper & Row Publishers, 1969. (Parent Problems)

Knight, Eric. *Lassie Come-Home.* New York: Holt, Rinehart & Winston, 1940. (Dogs)

Krumgold, Joseph. *Onion John.* New York: Thomas Y. Crowell Company, 1959. (Friends)

Lamorisse, Albert. *The Red Balloon.* Garden City, New York: Doubleday, 1956. (Friends)

Lindgren, Astrid. *Pippi Longstocking.* Translated by Florence Lamboro, New York: Viking Press, 1950. (Adventure—Girls)

Lord, Beman. *The Perfect Pitch.* New York: Henry Z. Walck, 1965. (Baseball)

Murphy, Barbara Beasley and Baker, Norman. *Navigator. The Heyerdahl and the Reed Boat "Ra".* Philadelphia: J. B. Lippincott Company, 1974. (Adventure—Sailing)

Neigoff, Mike. *Goal to Go.* Chicago: Albert Whitney & Company, 1970. (Football)

Nevill, Emily. *It's Like This, Cat.* New York: Harper & Row, 1963. (Animals)

Norton, Browning. *Wreck of the Blue Plane.* New York: Coward McCann, 1978. (Mystery—Boys)

O'Dell, Scott. *The Black Pearl.* Boston: Houghton Mifflin Company, 1967. (Family)

Paterson, Katherine. *The Bridge to Terabithia.* New York: Thomas Y. Crowell, 1977. (Fiction)

Pearce, Catherine Ownes. *The Helen Keller Story.* New York: Thomas Y. Crowell Company, 1959. (Biography)

Phillips, Betty Low. *Chris Evert, First Lady of Tennis.* New York: Julian Messner, 1977. (Biography)

Raskin, Ellen. *The Westing Game.* New York: E. P. Dutton, 1978. (Mystery)

Rawls, Wilson. *Where the Red Fern Grows.* Garden City, New York: Doubleday, 1961. (Dogs)

Reiss, Johanna. *The Upstairs Room.* New York: Thomas Y. Crowell Company, 1972. (World War II)

Shreve, Susan. *The Bad Dreams of a Good Girl.* New York: Alfred A. Knopf, 1982. (Fiction—Girls)

Spyri, Johanna. *Heidi.* Cleveland, Ohio: The World Publishing Company, 1946. (Friends)

Sutcliff, Rosemary. *The Road to Camlann: The Death of King Arthur.* New York: E. P. Dutton, 1982. (Historical Fiction)

Vance, Eleanor. *The Tall Book of Fairy Tales.* New York: Harper & Row, 1947. (Tales)

Wilder, Laura Ingalls. *Little House on the Prairie.* New York: Harper & Row, 1935. (Frontier)

Woody, Regina. *TV Dancer.* Garden City, New York: Doubleday & Company, 1967. (Careers)

Yates, Elizabeth. *Amos Fortune, Free Man.* New York: E. P. Dutton Company, 1950. (Biography)

Zindel, Paul. *My Darling. My Hamburger.* New York: Harper & Row, 1969. (Fiction—Girls)

*Interest Level: 7th—8th Grades*

Aldrich, Bess S. *A Lantern in Her Hand.* New York: Grosset & Dunlap, 1956. (Historical Fiction)

Arbuthnot, May Hill. *Time for Fairy Tales: Old and New.* Revised Edition. Glenview, Illinois: Scott, Foresman and Company, 1961. (Fairytales)

Beatty, Patricia. *Wait For Me, Watch For Me, Eula.* New York: Morrow, 1978. (Historical Fiction)

Bennett, Cathereen L. *Will Rogers: the Cowboy Who Walked With Kings.* Minneapolis, Minnesota: Lerner Publications Company, 1971. (Biography)

Blos, Joan. *A Gathering of Days: A New England Girl's Journal.* New York: Charles Scribner's Sons, 1979. (Historical Fiction)

Bonham, Frank. *Durango Street.* New York: E. P. Dutton and Company, 1965. (City Life)

Bonham, Frank. *The Mystery of the Red Tide.* New York: Scholastic Book Services, 1966. (Mystery)

Bova, Benjamin William. *City of Darkness: A Novel.* New York: Scribner's Sons, 1976. (Gangs)

Bowman, James Cloyd. *Pecos Bill.* Chicago: Abbret Whitman and Company, 1964. (Wild West Tales)

Bradbury, Ray. *The Golden Apples of the Sun.* Garden City, New York: Doubleday and Company, 1952. (Science Fiction)

Byars, Betsy. *The Summer of the Swans.* New York: Viking Press, 1970. (Family)

Chapin, Kim. *Fast as White Lightning: The Story of Stock Car Racing.* New York: Dial, 1981. (Cars)

Clemens, Samuel Langhorne. *The Prince and the Pauper.* Cleveland: The World Publishing Company, 1948. (Tale)

Daly, Maureen. *Seventeenth Summer.* New York: Dodd, Mead and Company, 1942. (Fiction—Girls)

Danziger, Paula. *The Cat Ate My Gymsuit.* New York: Delacorte Press, 1974. (Fiction—Girls)

DuMaurier, Daphne. *Rebecca.* New York: Doubleday and Company, 1938. (Fiction—Girls)

Dygard, Thomas J. *Winning Kicker.* New York: William Morrow, 1978. (Sports—Girls)

Edmonds. Walter D. *The Matchlock Gun.* New York: Dodd, Mead and Company, 1941. (Historical American Fiction)

Fernner, Phyllis P. *Behind the Wheel: Stories of Cars on Road and Track.* New York: William Morrow and Company, 1964. (Cars)

Gutman, Bill. *Duke: The Musical Life of Duke Ellington.* New York: Random House, 1977. (Biography)

Hanson, June Andrea. *Summer of the Stallion.* New York: Macmillan, 1979. (Fiction—Girls)

Haskins, James. *Sugar Ray Leonard.* New York: Lothrop, Lee and Shepard, 1982. (Biography)

Head, Ann. *Mr. & Mrs. Bo Jo Jones.* New York: G. P. Putnam's Sons, 1967. (Young Marriage)

Higdon, Hal. *Johnny Rutherford.* New York: Putnam, 1980. (Biography—sports)

Hunter, Kristin. *The Soul Brothers and Sister Lou.* New York: Charles Scribner's Sons, 1968. (Friends)

Kaplan, Bess. *The Empty Chair.* New York: Harper & Row, 1978. (Growing-up—Girls)

Kherdian, David. *The Road from Home: The Story of an Armenian Girl.* New York: Morrow, 1979. (Biography)

Lawson, Robert. *Ben and Me.* Boston: Little, Brown and Company, 1939. (Fiction)

Lee, Robert C. *I Was a Teenage Hero.* New York: McGraw-Hill Book Company, 1969. (Fiction—Basketball)

Leigh, Frances. *The Lost Boy.* New York: E. P. Dutton and Company, 1976. (Fiction)

L'Engle, Madeleina. *A Ring of Endless Light.* New York: Farrar, Straus & Giroux, 1980. (Fiction—Family)

Lipsyte, Robert. *The Contender.* New York: Harper & Row, 1967. (Fiction—Boxing)

Lowry, Lois. *Anastasia at Your Service.* Boston: Houghton Mifflin, 1982. (Fiction—Girls)

Lucas, George. *Star Wars.* New York: Ballantine Books, 1977. (Science Fiction)

Magorian, Michelle. *Good Night, Mr. Tom.* New York: Harper & Row, 1981. (Historical Fiction)

Masterman-Smith, Virginia. *The Great Egyptian Heist.* Four Winds Press, 1982. (Mystery)

McKinley, Robin. *The Blue Sword.* New York: Greenwillow Books, 1982. (Fantasy)

Miklowity, Gloria D. *Nadia Comaneci.* New York: Grosset and Dunlap, 1977. (Biography)

Murphy, Barbara, and Wolkoff, Judie. *Ace Hits the Big Time.* New York: Delacorte, 1981. (Gangs)

Myers, Walter D. *It Ain't All For Nothin'.* New York: Viking Press, 1978. (Growing up—Boys)

Newman, Robert. *The Case of the Baker Street Irregular.* New York: Atheneum, 1978. (Mystery—Boys)

Paterson, Katherine. *Jacob Have I Loved.* New York: Thomas Y. Crowell, 1980. (Historical Fiction—Girls)

Paterson, Katherine. *The Great Gilly Hopkins.* New York: Thomas Y. Crowell, 1978. (Fiction—Girls)

Schlee, Ann. *The Vandal.* New York: Crown, 1981. (Science Fiction)

Smith, Betty. *A Tree Grows in Brooklyn.* New York: Harper & Row Publishers, 1943. (Fiction—Girls)

Taylor, Mildred D. *Roll of Thunder. Hear My Cry.* New York: Dial Press, 1976. (Black History)

Travers, P. L. *Mary Poppins.* New York: Harcourt, Brace and World, 1962. (Friends)

Voight, Cynthia. *Dicey's Song.* New York: Atheneum, 1982. (Realist Fiction)

Wilder, Laura Ingalls. *Farmer Boy.* New York: Harper & Row, 1933. (Historical Fiction) RL

Wojciechowska, Maja. *Tuned Out.* New York: Harper & Row, 1968. (Teenage Problems)

Yep, Laurence. *The Dragon of the Lost Sea.* New York: Harper & Row, 1982. (Fantasy—Courage)

Compiled by Adele Rutland.

# Glossary

*Accent.* The part of a word which receives stress when it is spoken.

*Achievement Groups.* A system in which students are divided into several groups based upon their demonstrated ability and aptitude.

*Acronyms.* Abbreviations that consist of the first letter (or letters) of each word in a phrase, i.e., Nabisco from National Biscuit Company.

*Affective Domain.* That part of the taxonomic hierarchy that involves the feelings, emotions, and attitudes of a student.

*Affix.* A prefix or suffix added to a word to change its meaning.

*Analysis.* The evaluation of data to form a basis for decision making.

*Analytic Method.* A decoding method in which phonics is taught by presenting sounds in the context of words and helping students to generalize the sounds to different words.

*Analytic Phonics.* A method that begins with teaching an entire word and then teaching the sounds within a word.

*Approaches.* Different techniques used to provide reading instruction.

*Assessment.* The procedures and methods used to evaluate the progress that a student makes in skill development.

*Assessments.* Parts of a management system which are pre- and post-tests of knowledge of individual skills.

*Attitude Scales.* The rating forms used to assess a student's feelings toward reading.

*Auditory Comprehension.* The use of auditory discrimination and memory to interpret spoken symbols; frequently called listening comprehension.

*Auditory Discrimination.* The ability to differentiate between a variety of sounds.

*Auditory Memory.* The ability to recall the differentiation between a variety of sounds.

*Augumented Alphabet Approach.* A teaching method that incorporates materials which use some special coding procedure to change the traditional alphabet in order to develop one-to-one sound-symbol correspondences.

*Basal Reader.* A textbook used in the elementary grades, with the primary purpose of introducing students to reading skills in a sequential order.

*Bibliotherapy.* Encouraging a student to read a particular book that will help him/her gain insight into areas of interest to problems that he/she may be facing.

*Bilingual.* Students who speak two or more languages, with English often being the second language.

*Cause-And-Effect Relationships.* A comprehension skill which requires the reader to determine what event was precipitated by another event in the story.

*Classroom Teacher.* A teacher who has responsibility for a group of students.

*Cloze Procedure.* An informal diagnostic technique consisting of a 250-300 word passage from which every fifth word is deleted. Its primary purposes are to determine the students' instructional and independent reading levels, as well as ability to use context when reading.

*Cognitive Development.* The growth of the intellect in a normally developing child.

*Comparisons.* The ability to determine which ideas are alike and in what way they are alike.

*Compound Words.* Words that are composed of two or more shorter words which have independent meanings.

*Comprehension.* The understanding of the printed word.

*Comprehension Skills.* The skills through which the reader understands, organizes thought processes, and uses critical thinking while reading. These skills are combined into three basic areas: literal, interpretative, and critical.

*Concepts.* Abstract ideas generalized from several pieces of related specific information. They are theories, ideas, views or goals.

*Consonants.* The letters *b, c, d, f, g, h, j, k, l, m, n, p, q. r, s, t, v, w, x, y,* and *z.*

*Context Clue.* Other words which aid in obtaining the meaning or recognizing an unknown word.

*Contextual Analysis.* The use of the meaning of a phrase, sentence or passage, in conjunction with other word recognition skills to decode an unknown word or to derive meaning from a word or passage.

*Contextual Processing Approach.* Teaching reading by emphasizing the development of comprehension skills.

*Continuous Diagnosis.* The ongoing process of continuously updating previous diagnostic data.

*Continuum of Skills.* A hierarchical guide which a teacher uses to teach reading skills.

*Contractions.* A combination of two words from which one or more letters have been replaced by an apostrophe.

*Contrasts.* The ability to determine which ideas are different and in what ways they differ from each other.

*Coordination.* The cooperation of classroom teachers, reading specialists, and content teachers to ensure the success of the total school reading program.

*Correlation.* The degree of relationships between two variables expressed by the coefficient of correlation which extends along a scale from 1.00 (a perfect positive relationship) through .00 (no relationship) to -1.00 (a perfect negative relationship).

*Creative Reading.* A type of reading in which the reader reacts to the printed word by expressing his/her own ideas about what has been read.

*Criterion Referenced Tests.* A test based on objectives which contain the specific conditions, outcomes, and criteria that are expected for satisfactory completion of the task.

*Critical Reading.* The process of analyzing and evaluating what is read.

*Critical Skills.* Comprehension skills which require the reader to make an evaluation or judgment of the material read.

*Cross-Age Tutoring.* An instructional format in which an older student works with a younger student in an effort to improve the reading skills of the younger student.

*Culturally Disadvantaged.* The segment of the population which has limited cultural experiences to prepare them to fit into the mainstream of society.

*Data.* A body of information which has been gathered from a variety of sources.

*Decoding Approach.* Teaching reading by teaching the recognition of words; using some word identification strategy. This approach emphasized decoding to the exclusion of comprehension and other areas of reading.

*Diagnosis.* The act of determining the nature of a problem through careful examination and study.

*Diagnostic-Prescriptive Instruction.* A process in reading whereby the individual strengths and weaknesses of each student are identified through various diagnostic procedures, and appropriate instruction is provided based upon that diagnosis.

*Directed Learning Activity.* An organizational format for incorporating reading instruction and management techniques into a content classroom.

*Directed Reading Activity.* An instructional plan based on these five basic steps: readiness, skill development, review, guided reading, and follow-up.

*Directed Reading Lesson.* A format which helps the teacher to organize lessons through the use of a specified step-by-step procedure that incorporates the areas essential to the development and application of reading skills.

*Discourse Analysis.* The analysis of syntax in text materials in order to enhance reader comprehension.

*Eclectic Approach.* A method of teaching reading which stresses a variety of approaches selected based on individual students needs, learning styles, and interests.

*Educable Mentally Retarded.* Students within an I.Q. range of 55 to 80 who have slow auditory and visual memory, conceptual and perceptual ability, and imaginative and creative ability.

*Educationally Different.* This category includes mentally retarded students, learning disabled students, and gifted students.

*Emotionally Disturbed.* Students who are socially maladjusted, manifest inappropriate behavior, suffer periods of diminished verbal and motor activity, or have frequent complaints of a physical nature including general fatigue which interferes with their success in learning situations.

*Facilities.* The materials, physical features and physical arrangement of the classroom.

*Figurative Language.* Language that is rich in comparisons, similes, and metaphors.

*Formal Diagnostic Procedures.* The standardized techniques used by teachers and reading specialists to learn more about students' strengths and weaknesses in reading.

*Frustration Level.* The level at which a student has extreme difficulty in pronouncing words and comprehending the material.

*Gifted.* Students who exhibit superior talent in one or more areas.

*Grade Level.* The actual grade in which a student is enrolled.

*Grade Equivalent.* A score derived from the raw score on a standardized test, usually expressed in terms of a grade level divided into tenths.

*Grade Placement.* The level at which a student is placed for instruction.

*Graded Word Lists.* Word lists arranged according to the grade level at which each word is usually encountered by the student.

*Graded Basal Series.* A group of readers published by a specific publisher and intended for sequential use during the primary elementary years.

*Group Achievement Tests.* Tests administered to a large number of students simultaneously, which measure the depth of a student's knowledge of various broad areas of the curriculum.

*Group Administered Formal Tests.* These are diagnostic procedures which include diagnostic reading tests, achievement tests, and intelligence tests designed to be administered to a large number of students simultaneously and which have been standardized with populations of students.

*Group Diagnostic Tests.* Diagnostic instruments that are administered to many students simultaneously, and provide the teacher with in-depth information.

*Group Intelligence Tests.* Tests given to a large number of students simultaneously, to measure their aptitudes in such areas as verbal concepts, mathematical capabilities, and following directions.

*Group Survey Tests.* Diagnostic instruments which are administered to many students simultaneously providing scores for vocabulary, comprehension, and sometimes the rate of reading for each student.

*Grouping.* Any of a variety of methods by which a classroom of students is subdivided for appropriate reading instruction.

*Group Reading Inventory.* A procedure used by content teachers to diagnose the specific reading skills necessary to learn the concepts in a content area lesson.

*Grouping Procedures.* The methods and criteria used to combine students for instruction. These include achievement grouping, skills grouping, interest grouping, and cross-age or peer grouping.

*Hearing Impaired.* Students who have auditory processing impediments which make it difficult for them to function in the classroom.

*Hierarchy of Skills.* An ordering of reading skills from low to high levels of difficulty in order to facilitate the presentation and learning of the skills.

*Hesitations.* Pauses of more than five seconds between words during the administration of an informal reading inventory.

*Heterogeneous.* A word taken from the Greek term meaning different. Used in reading instruction to describe a randomly formed group.

*Homogeneous.* A word taken from the Greek term meaning same. Usually used in reading instruction to define a group formed on the basis of similarities of knowledge.

*Independent Level.* The level at which students read for recreational purposes. The material is easy enough to read quickly with maximum comprehension.

*Individualization.* Students are given assignments based on their own instructional level, and are engaged in tasks which meet their specific needs.

*Individual Diagnostic Reading Tests.* Instruments that provide the most thorough diagnosis of a student's reading problems by incorporating various subtests which aid the teacher in identifying specific reading strengths and weaknesses.

*Individual Auditory Discrimination Tests.* Instruments administered to a single student to determine his/her ability to distinguish likenesses and differences in sounds.

*Individual Auditory Screening Tests.* The use of an audiometer to measure the auditory acuity of a single student.

*Individual Intelligence Tests.* Tests given to a single student in order to predict the level of proficiency which may be expected from his performance of a specific activity.

*Individual Oral Reading Tests.* Instruments administered to a student by asking him to read aloud in order for the teacher to note such errors and difficulties as mispronunciations, omissions, repetitions, substitutions, unknown words, and sometimes hesitations.

*Individual Visual Screening Tests.* Instruments used to determine an individual student's visual acuity.

*Individual Instruction.* Instruction is provided, geared to the instructional level of each student, so that every student is working on an assignment to meet his or her specific needs.

*Individualized Reading Approach.* A teaching technique based on Olson's philosophy about child development, i.e., one which promotes the concepts of seeking, self-selection, and pacing.

*Individually-Administered Formal Tests.* Diagnostic instruments designed for use with a single student. These tests can be categorized as oral reading tests, diagnostic reading tests, auditory discrimination tests, auditory and visual screening tests, and intelligence tests.

*Inflectional Ending.* A word ending which, when added to a root word, denotes tense, number, degree, gender, or possession.

*Informal Diagnosis.* The use of nonstandardized techniques by teachers in order to determine their students' strengths and weaknesses in reading.

*Informal Reading Inventory.* A compilation of graded reading selections with comprehension questions to accompany each selection. This inventory is individually administered to determine the student's strengths and weaknesses in word recognition and comprehension.

*Initial Teaching Alphabet.* A forty-four-letter alphabet system that is used in an Augmented Alphabet Approach to teach beginning readers.

*Interactive Model.* A theory of the reading process, developed by Rumelhart, which postulates that the reader and the text work in concert to reveal the meaning of the passage.

*Interest Groups.* An organizational plan by which students with similar interests are allowed to work together in order to explore their mutual interests in greater depth.

*Interest Surveys.* Inventories used to measure a student's likes, dislikes, and areas of enjoyment, in order to provide reading materials which match these areas of individuality.

*Interpretation.* An in-depth evaluation of data by which the strengths and weaknesses of each student are examined, along with an exploration of the underlying causes for poor test results.

*Interpretive Comprehension.* The process of assimilating information in an effort to infer the author's meaning.

*Interpretive Skills.* A comprehension skill which involves comprehending the inner meanings of the material read.

*Insertions.* Words which do not appear on the printed page, added by the reader during the administration of an Informal Reading Inventory.

*Instructional Level.* The reading level at which a student can read the material, but has some difficulty with the recognition of words and comprehension, so that a teacher is required to assist him.

*Language Experience Approach.* A method in which instruction is built upon the use of reading materials created from the spoken language of the student, written initially by the teacher just as the student speaks.

*Language Variations.* Students who have a speech pattern which differs from standard American English usage. These variations may be related to pronunciation or syntax.

*Learning Centers.* Open areas in a classroom in which the students are motivated to participate because of the high interest level of the materials.

*Learning Disabled.* Students who exhibit a disorder in one or more of the basic neurological or psychological processes involved in understanding or in using spoken or written language.

*Linguistic Approach.* Teaching reading by using methods that consider the students' experiences and language patterns.

*Literal Comprehension.* The recall or recognition of explicitly stated ideas.

*Literal Skills.* Basic level comprehension skills such as recalling details, finding the main idea, or interpreting symbols and acronyms. This area of comprehension involves the recognition or recall of text information.

*Look-Say Method.* A technique for teaching reading that concentrates on memorization of "sight" words.

*Mainstreaming.* The act of integrating students with special needs into a normal classroom situation.

*Mean.* The average of a set of numbers derived by taking the sum of the set of measurements and dividing it by the number of measurements in the set.

*Median.* The central number in a set, above and below which an equal number of scores fall.

*Management.* The total process of selecting, organizing, and presenting classroom materials to the students.

*Management system.* A set of materials used to help the teacher organize and manage the reading program in the classroom.

*Miscomprehension.* Performance in which students frequently misunderstand questions and give different answers instead of wrong answers.

*Mispronunciations.* Words that are called incorrectly in the oral reading process or during an Informal Reading Inventory.

*Multicultural.* The segment of the population which has cultural values reflective of two or more cultures.

*Multi-Sensory Approach.* A teaching technique which involves the senses of touch and muscle movement, along with vision and hearing.

*Neurological Impress Method.* A multi-sensory approach which involves the teacher and student reading along together, while the teacher points to individual words.

*Normal Curve.* The bell curve, which has more scores at the mean or median and a decreasing number in equal proportions at the left and right of the center.

*Objective Based Tests.* Tests based on specific objectives, but for which no predetermined criteria for achievement are provided.

*Observation.* Teacher analysis of a student's knowledge, traits, behaviors, attitudes, and interaction, as part of the ongoing diagnostic program.

*Omissions.* Words that are left out by the reader during the administration of an informal reading inventory.

*Oral Language.* A pre-reading skill which emphasizes the development of speaking skills including vocabulary as well as syntactical ability.

*Organization.* The instructional design used to manage groups in a classroom situation effectively.

*Organization Patterns.* The manner in which textual material is written. In content writing these patterns appear as enumeration, relationship, problem solving, and persuasion.

*Organizational Skills.* A category of study skills which involves the ability to synthesize and evaluate material read so that it can be arranged into a workable format.

*Parental Involvement.* A facet of the total school reading program wherein parents act as reading models and are actively involved in their child's learning.

*Peer Tutoring.* An instructional format which involves students who are in the same grade level working together. These students do not have the same reading level or mastery of the same reading skills.

*Percentile.* The percentage score which rates a student relative to the percentage of others in a group who are below his score. Percentiles cannot be averaged, added together, subtracted, or treated arithmetically in any manner.

*Personal Reading.* The use of all reading skills by the student in order to develop reading into a leisure-time activity. Personal reading combines all the cognitive skills with a positive attitude towards reading.

*Phoneme-Grapheme Correspondences.* The association of specific sounds with specific symbols in beginning reading instruction.

*Phonics.* The association of specific phonemes (sounds) with the appropriate graphemes (symbols).

*Physically Impaired.* Students with disorders of the nervous system, musculo-skeletal system, visual impairments or hearing impairments.

*Picture Clue.* A clue to an unknown word that apears in the form of a picture in the text.

*Prefix.* A word component which is attached to the beginning of the root to change its meaning.

*Prereading Skills.* The basic skills necessary for developing a foundation that will enable a student to master higher-level reading skills and to learn to read. These skills include oral language development, visual perception, auditory perception listening comprehension, and visual-motor development.

*Prescription.* A specific direction which is recommended following a careful diagnosis.

*Prescriptive Instruction.* Reading instruction provided to meet the diagnosed reading needs of each student. It is based on the principles of teamwork, application of reading skills, positive self-concept, no one best way, varied aproaches, a hierarchy of skills, continuous diagnoses, and flexible instruction.

*Programmed Approach.* A system for developing reading proficiency through the systematic presentation of material and immediate feedback or responses.

*Psychologically Impaired.* Students who are emotionally disturbed or suffer from a behavior disorder.

*Range.* The distance between the largest and smallest numbers in a set.

*Raw Score.* An untreated test score usually obtained by counting the number of items correct. It is the basis for determining all the derived scores.

*Readability.* The determination of the approximate grade level at which various materials are written.

*Readiness.* 1) The preparation stage which is required to advance students to the beginning of formal reading instruction. Often known as pre-reading. 2) The preparation stage for teaching a lesson; a time in which new ideas are related to the previous experiences of the student.

*Reading Process.* The process used to identify printed symbols and associate meaning with those symbols in order to understand ideas conveyed by the writer.

*Reading Skills.* Skills which involve the learning of procedures or strategies necessary for decoding and understanding the meaning of printed symbols.

*Recreational Reading.* Reading done by a student for enjoyment and personal satisfaction.

*Record Keeping Procedure.* A system by which a teacher keeps track of the reading needs of the student in order to provide the appropriate ongoing instruction.

*Reference Skills.* Skills which are concerned with locating information in various sources.

*Relevant and Irrelevant Information.* A critical reading skill which requires the reader to determine whether the author's evidence or examples are germane to the subject matter at hand.

*Reliability.* A term which refers to the consistency with which the test agrees with itself or produces similar scores when readministered over a period of time by the same individual.

*Repetitions.* Words which are reread during the administration of an Informal Reading Inventory.

*Schema Theory.* A theory of comprehension which states that to understand information the reader uses what is in his mind, and adds to his store of information when new related information is read.

*Scope and Sequence.* The identification and orderly presentation of the reading skills to be taught at each level from kindergarten to the highest level.

*Sight Words.* The words which students see most frequently in reading and recognize instantly without using other decoding skills.

*Signal Words.* Connectors, such as conjunctions, which help the reader to understand the meaning of a passage, i.e., therefore, however, in addition, and, etc.

*Skills Approach.* Teaching reading through the development of individual skills in some systematic sequence.

*Skills Groups.* Using reading skills for the purpose of student placement in an individual situation.

*Specialized Study Skills.* A category of study skills which involves analyzing all parts of a book or material to determine what information can be obtained from it and how best to understand the information presented.

*Specialized Vocabulary.* Words that change in meaning from one content area to another.

*Speech Disorders.* Students who have problems in one of the following areas: articulation disorders, fluency disorders, or voice disorders.

*SQ3R.* A study strategy developed by Robinson that involves these five steps: survey, question, read, recite, and review.

*Standard Deviation.* A term used to describe the displacement of scores from the mean, a condition which varies with the range in a set of scores.

*Standard Score.* A raw score expressed in some form of standard deviation unit. They can be dealt with arithmetically and are easier to interpret than raw scores.

*Stanine.* A type of standard score which is based upon a nine point scale with a mean of 5 and a standard deviation of about 2.

*Structural Analysis.* The word recognition skill which stresses the analysis of word structure for purposes of pronunciation as well as comprehension.

*Study Skills.* The higher-level reading skills that require the application of many other reading skills.

*Substitutions.* Words which are given as replacements for the actual printed word during the administration of an Informal Reading Inventory.

*Suffix.* A word part which is attached to the end of the root to change its meaning.

*Summarizing.* Organizing interpreted data into a compact format which makes it easily accessible for classroom use.

*Sustained Silent Reading.* A classroom activity wherein everyone is required to read some material silently for a designated period of time.

*Syllabication.* The word recognition skill which consists of decoding words by dividing them into parts.

*Syllables.* Parts of a word which are combined to form the entire word. Each syllable has one vowel sound.

*Synthesis.* The ability to form a point of view after reading several sources of information.

*Synthetic Method.* A decoding method which involves learning individual letter sounds and combining these sounds into words.

*Synthetic Phonics.* A method that presents the isolated sounds in a word, then blends them to form the entire word.

*Taxonomy.* A hierarchy of the learning processes, classified from lowest to highest; categorizing.

*Teacher Effectiveness.* A concept which identifies the characteristics of teachers who are effective in helping students learn, as compared to those who are not as successful.

*Technical Vocabulary.* Words essential to the understanding of a specific content area. These words relate to only one content area and are crucial to the understanding of concepts in that area.

*Typographical Aids.* Material which is presented in boldface, italic or oversized type for purposes of emphasis.

*Use of Material.* The matching of available classroom teaching instruments to diagnosed student needs.

*VAKT.* Is an acronym for the Visual, Auditory, Kinesthetic, and Tactile approach. This technique was developed by Fernald as a multisensory approach to teaching reading. It has four basic stages: Tracing, Writing without tracing, Recognition in print, and Word Analysis.

*Validity.* The extent to which a test measures what it is designed to measure.

*Variant Patterns.* Vowel combinations in words which represent a unique sound or do not follow rules typically taught about decoding different sounds of unknown words.

*Visual Comprehension.* A prereading skill which comprises interpretive tasks necessary for understanding the visual stimuli presented in reading materials.

*Visual Discrimination.* The ability to differentiate between printed symbols.

*Visual Memory.* The ability to recall the differentation of printed symbols.

*Visual-Motor.* A prereading skill which includes such understandings as eye-hand coordination, directionality, and drawing specific designs using circles and lines.

*Visually Impaired.* Describes a student who is blind, has limited vision, or has low vision which prevents him from functioning normally in a classroom situation.

*Vocabulary Development.* Strategies taught to assist students in understanding new words found in reading.

*Vowels.* The letters *a, e, i, o, u* and sometimes *y* and *w*.

*Word Boundaries.* A prereading subskill which involves recognizing the spacing between words in oral language.

*Words in Color.* An augmented alphabet approach, using colors to distinguish the various sound-symbol correspondences.

*Word Recognition.* The use of prior memory or a decoding process by the reader to assist in the identification of words and the association of meaning with the identified symbols.

*Word Recognition Inventories.* Graded lists of words pronounced by a student in order for a teacher to learn more about his/her word recognition skills.

*Word Recognition Skills.* The wide range of subskills which provide students with different techniques for identifying a word. These skills include context, phonetic analysis, structural analysis, and sight word recognition.

# Bibliography

Adams, Abby; Carnine, Douglas; and Geisten, Russell. "Instructional Strategies for Studying Content Area Texts in the Intermediate Grades." *Reading Research Quarterly* 18 (Fall 1982):27–55.

Agrast, Charlotte. "Teach Them to Read Between the Lines." *Grade Teacher* 85 (November 1967):72–74.

Allen, M. "Relationship Between Kuhlmann-Anderson Intelligence Tests and Academic Achievement in Grade IV." *Journal of Educational Psychology* 44 (1944):229–39.

Allen, Roach Van. *Language Experiences in Communication.* Boston: Houghton Mufflin Company, 1976.

Allen, Roach Van. "The Language-Experience Approach." *Perspectives on Elementary Reading.* Edited by Robert Karlin. New York: Harcourt Brace Jovanovich, Inc., 1973.

Allington, Richard L., and McGill-Franzen, Anne. "Word Identification Errors in Isolation and in Context: Apples vs. Oranges." *The Reading Teacher* 33 (April 1980):795–800.

Alonge, Constance V. "Response to Kay Haugaard: Comic Books Revisited." *The Reading Teacher* 27 (May 1974):801–803.

Ames, W. S. "The Development of a Classification Schema of Contextual Aids." *Reading Research Quarterly* II (1966):57–82.

Anderson, Richard; Spiro, Rand; and Anderson, Mark. *"Schemata as Scaffolding for the Representation of Information in Connected Discourse.* Center for the Study of Reading, Technical Report No. 24. University of Illinois, Urbana-Champaign:1977.

Armbruster, Bonnie B., and Anderson, Thomas H. "Research Synthesis of Study Skills." *Educational Leadership* 39 (November 1981):154.

Armstrong, Robert J., and Mooney, Robert F. "The Slosson Intelligence Test: Implications for Reading Specialists." *The Reading Teacher* 24 (January 1971):336–40.

Arnold, Richard D. "Class Size and Reading Development." *New Horizons in Reading.* Edited by John E. Merritt. Newark, Delaware: International Reading Association, 1976.

Aukerman, Robert C. *Approaches to Beginning Reading.* New York: John Wiley, 1971.

Aukerman, Robert. *Reading in the Secondary School Classroom* New York: McGraw-Hill Book Company, 1972.

Austin, Mary, and Morrison, Coleman. *The First R: The Harvard Report on Reading in Elementary Schools.* New York: The Macmillan Company, 1963.

Bailey, Mildred H. "The Utility of Phonic Generalizations in Grades One Through Six." *The Reading Teacher* 20 (February 1967):413–18.

Bamberger, Richard. *Promoting the Reading Habit.* Paris: UNESCO Press, 1975.

Bankston, Nicholas W. "The Speech and Language Impaired." *Exceptional Children and Youth.* Edited by Edward L. Meyen. Denver, Colorado: Love Publishing Company, 1978.

Barraga, Natalie. *Visual Handicaps and Learning.* Belmont, California: Wadsworth Publishing Company, 1976.

Barrett, Thomas C. "The Relationship Between the Measures of Pre-reading Visual Discrimination and First-Grade Achievement: A Review of the Literature." *Reading Research Quarterly* I (Fall 1965):51–76.

Barrett Thomas, and Smith, R. *Teaching Reading in the Middle Grades.* Reading, Massachusetts: Addison-Wesley, 1976.

Bateman, Barbara. *Reading and the Psycholinguistic Process of Partially Seeing Children.* Arlington, Virginia: Council for Exceptional Children, 1963.

Beers, Carol S., and Beers, James W. "Early Identification of Learning Disabilities: Facts and Fallacies." *The Elementary School Journal* 81 (November 1980):67–76.

Belloni, Loretta Frances, and Jongsma, Eugene A. "The Effects of Interest on Reading Comprehension of Low-Achieving Students." *Journal of Reading*, 22 (November 1978):106–109.

Berry, Mildred F., and Eisenson, Jon. *Speech Disorders: Principles and Practices of Therapy.* New York: Appleton-Century Crofts, 1956.

Beta Upsilon Chapter, Pi Lambda Theta. "Children's Interests Classified by Age Level." *The Reading Teacher* 27 (April 1974):694–700.

Betts, Emmett A. *Foundations of Reading Instruction.* New York: American Book Company, 1957.

Birch, J. W. *Mainstreaming Educable Mentally Retarded Children in Regular Classes.* Reston, Virginia: Council for Exceptional Children, 1974.

Bissett, Donald J. "The Amount and Effect of Recreational Reading in Selected Fifth Grade Classrooms." Ph.D. Dissertation, Syracuse University, 1969.

Bloom, Benjamin, et al. *Taxonomy of Educational Objectives—Handbook I: The Cognitive Domain.* New York: David McKay, 1956.

Bloomfield, Leonard, and Barnhart, Clarence L. *Let's Read: A Linguistic Approach.* Detroit: Wayne State University Press, 1961.

Bond, Guy L., and Dykstra, Robert. "The Cooperative Research Program in First Grade Reading Instruction." *Reading Research Quarterly* 2 (Summer 1967):5–141.

Bond, Guy, and Dykstra, Robert. *Final Report, Project No. X-001.* Washington, D.C.: Bureau of Research, Office of Education, U.S. Department of Health, Education, and Welfare, 1967.

Bond, Guy, and Tinker, Miles A., and Wasson, Barbara B. *Reading Difficulties: Their Diagnosis and Correction.* 4th ed. Englewood Cliffs, New Jersey: Prentice-Hall, Inc., 1979.

Bond, Guy, and Wagner, Eva B. *Teaching The Child To Read*, 4th ed. New York: Macmillan, 1966.

Bormuth, John. "The Cloze Readability Procedure." *Elementary English* 45 (April 1968):429–36.

Botel, Morton. *Botel Reading Inventory*, Chicago: Follett Publishing Company, 1978.

Bower, Eli M. *Early Identification of Emotionally Handicapped Children in School*, 2nd ed. Springfield, Illinois: Charles C. Thomas, 1969.

Boyd, R. D. "Growth of Phonic Skills in Reading." *Clinical Studies in Reading III.* Edited by Helen M. Robinson, Supplementary Educational Monographs, No. 97. Chicago: University of Chicago Press, 1969, pp. 68–87.

Braun, Carl. "Interest-loading and Modality Effects on Textual Response Acquisition." *Reading Research Quarterly IV* (Spring 1969):428–44.

Briggs, F. A. "Grammatical Sense as a Factor in Reading Comprehension." *The Psychology of Reading Behavior.* Edited by G. B. Schick. Milwaukee: National Reading Conference, 1969.

Brill, Richard G. "The Relationship of Wechsler IQ's to Academic Achievement Among Deaf Students." *Exceptional Children* 28 (February 1962):315–21.

Britton, J. *Language and Learning.* Miami, Florida: University of Miami Press, 1970.

Brooks, Harold F., and Bruce, Paul. "The Characteristics of Good and Poor Readers as Disclosed by the Wechsler Intelligence Scale for Children." *Journal of Educational Psychology* (December 1955):488–93.

Brown, Linda L., and Sherbenin, Rita J. "A Comparison of Teacher Perceptions of Student Reading Ability, Reading Performance, and Classroom Behavior." *The Reading Teacher* 34 (February 1981):557–60.

Bruner, Jerome. *On Knowing.* Cambridge, Massachusetts: Harvard University Press, 1962.

Burger, Victor; Cohen, T. A.; and Bisgaler, P. *Bringing Children and Books Together*. New York: Library Club of America, 1956.

Burmeister, Lou E. *From Print to Meaning*. Reading, Massachusetts: Addison-Wesley, 1975.

Burns, Paul C., and Roe, Betty D. *Teaching Reading in Today's Elementary Schools*. 2nd ed. Chicago: Rand McNally College Publishing Company, 1980.

Buros, Oscar K., ed. *Reading Tests and Reviews II*. Highland Park, New Jersey: The Gryphon Press, 1975.

Bynum, Margaret. *Curriculum for Gifted Students*. Atlanta: State Department of Education, 1976.

Canney, George, and Achreiner, Robert. "A Study of the Effectiveness of Selected Syllabication Rules and Phonogram Patterns for Word Attack," *Reading Research Quarterly* 12 (1976–77): 102–24.

Carey, Robert F. "Toward a More Cognitive Definition of Reading Comprehension." *Reading Horizons* 20 (Summer 1980):293.

Carrier, Carol A., and Titus, Amy. "Effects of Notetaking Pretraining and Test Mode Expectations on Learning from Lectures." *American Educational Research Journal* 18 (Winter 1981):385–97.

Carroll, John B.; Davies, Peter; and Richman, Barry. *Word Frequency Book*. New York: American Heritage Publishing Company, Inc., 1971.

Cassidy, Jack. "Cross-Age Tutoring and the Sacrosanct Reading Period." *Reading Horizons* 17 (Spring 1977):178–80.

Chall, Jeanne C. "Minimum Competency in Reading." *Kappan* 60 (January 1979):351–52.

Cheek, Earl H. *Cheek Master Word List*. Waco, Texas: Educational Achievement Corporation, 1974.

Cheek, Earl H. "The Development of a Hierarchy for Teaching Phoneme-Grapheme Correspondences in Beginning Reading." Ph.D. dissertation, Florida State University, 1972.

Cheek, Earl H., and Martha Collins Cheek. "Organizational Patterns: Untapped Sources for Better Reading." *Reading World* 22 (May 1983).

Chernick, Eleanor. "Effects of the Feingold Diet on Reading Achievement and Classroom Behavior." *The Reading Teacher* 34 (November 1980):171–74.

Child Study Committee on the International Kindergarten Union. *A Study of the Vocabulary of Children Before Entering First Grade*. Washington, D.C.: The International Kindergarten Union, 1928.

Chomsky, Carol. *The Acquisition of Syntax in Children from 5 to 10*. Cambridge, Massachusetts: MIT Press, 1969.

Chomsky, Noam. *Language and Mind*. New York: Harcourt Brace Jovanovich, Inc., 1968.

Christie, James F. "Syntax: A Key to Reading Comprehension." *Reading Improvement* 17 (Winter 1980):313–17.

Clark, Ann D., and Richards, Charlotte J. "Auditory Discrimination Among Economically Disadvantaged and Nondisadvantaged Preschool Children." *Exceptional Children* 33 (1966):259–62.

Clarke, Barbara K. "A Study of the Relationship Between Eighth Grade Students' Reading Ability and Their Social Studies and Science Textbooks." Unpublished doctoral dissertation, Florida State University, 1977.

Clymer, Theodore. "The Utility of Phonic Generalizations in the Primary Grades." *The Reading Teacher* 16 (January 1963):252–58.

Clymer, Theodore. "What is 'Reading'?: Some Current Concepts." *Innovation and Change in Reading Instruction*, 67th Yearbook of the National Society for the Study of Education. Edited by Helen M. Robinson. Chicago: University of Chicago Press, 1968.

Cohen, Peter A.; Kulik, James A.; and Kulik, Chen-Lin C. "Educational Outcomes of Tutoring: A Meta-Analysis of Findings." *American Educational Research Journal* 19 (Summer 1982):237–248.

Collins-Cheek, Martha D. "Organizational Patterns: An Aid to Comprehension." American Reading Forum Conference Proceedings, 1982.

Cordasco, F. "Puerto Rican Pupils and American Education." *Education and the Many Faces of the Disadvantaged: Cultural and Historical Perspectives*. Edited by W. W. Brickman and S. Lehrer, New York: Wiley, 1962.

Courtney, Brother Leonard. "Methods and Materials for Teaching Word Perception in Grades 10–14." *Sequential Development of Reading Abilities.* Edited by Helen M. Robinson. Supplementary Educational Monographs, No. 90. Chicago: University of Chicago Press, 1960, pp. 42–46.

Crary, Ryland W. *Humanizing The School: Curriculum Development and Theory.* New York: Alfred Knopf, 1969.

Crewe, James, and Hullgren, Dayton. "What Does 'Research' Really Say about Study Skills?" *The Psychology of Reading.* 18th Yearbook National Reading Conference, 1969.

Cunningham, Patricia M. "A Teachers Guide To Materials Shopping." *The Reading Teacher* 35 (November 1981):180–84.

Dale, Edgar, and Chall, Jeanne. "A Formula for Predicting Readability." *Educational Research Bulletin* (January 21, 1948):11–20, 28.

Dallmann, Martha; Rouch, Roger L.; Chang, Lynette; and DeBoer, John J. *The Teaching of Reading.* 4th ed. New York: Holt, Rinehart and Winston, Inc., 1974.

Davis, Julia M.; Stelmachonicz, Patricia G.; Shepard, Neil J.; and Gorga, Michael P. "Characteristics of Hearing-Impaired Children in the Public Schools: Part II - Psychoeducational Data." *Journal of Speech and Hearing Disorders* 46 (May 1981):130–137.

Dawson, Mildred A., and Bamman, Henry A. *Fundamentals of Basic Reading Instruction.* New York: David McKay Co., 1959.

Dechant, Emerald V., and Smith, Henry P. *Psychology in Teaching Reading*, 2nd ed. Englewood Cliffs, New Jersey: Prentice-Hall, Inc., 1977.

Deese, James. *Psycholinguistics.* Boston: Allyn and Bacon, Inc., 1970.

Demott, Richard J. "Verbalism and Affective Meaning for Blind, Severely Visually Impaired and Normally Sighted Children." *The New Outlook for the Blind* 66 (January 1972):1–25.

Dennard, Kha. "Commentary: A Black Educator Speaks About Black English" *The Reading Teacher* 35 (November 1981):133.

Denny, Terry, and Weintraub, Samuel. "First Graders' Responses to Three Questions About Reading." *Elementary School Journal* 66 (May 1966):441–48.

Deutsch, Cynthia P., and Feldman, Shirley C. "A Study of the Effectiveness of Training for Retarded Readers in the Auditory Skills Underlying Reading." Title VII, Project No. 1127 Grant, U.S. Department of Health, Education and Welfare, Office of Education. New York: Medical College, 1966.

Deutsch, Martin et al. *Communication of Information in the Elementary School Classroom.* New York: Institute for Developmental Studies, New York Medical College, 1964.

Dickerson, Dolores P. "A Study of Use of Games to Reinforce Sight Vocabulary." *The Reading Teacher* 36 (October 1982):46–49.

Dixon, Carol N. "Selection and Use of Instructional Materials." in Calfee, Robert C., and Drumm, Priscilla A. (Eds.) *Teaching Reading in Compensatory Classes.* Newark, Delaware: International Reading Association, 1979, 104–113, 187–91.

Dore-Boyce, Kathleen; Misner, Marilyn S.; and McGuire, Lorraine D. "Comparing Reading Expectancy Formulas." *The Reading Teacher* 29 (October 1975):8–14.

Doren, Margaret. *Doren Diagnostic Reading Test of Word Recognition Skills Manual*, 2nd ed. Circle Pines, Minnesota: American Guidance Service, Inc., 1973.

Dreyer, Hal. "Rx for Pupil Tutoring Programs." *The Reading Teacher* 26 (May 1973):180–83.

Duffy, Gerald. "Maintaining A Balance in Objective-Based Reading Instruction." *The Reading Teacher* 31 (February 1978):519–23.

Duffy, Gerald G. *Teacher Effectiveness Research: Implications for the Reading Profession.* January 1981, ED 204 344.

Dunn, Rita, and Dunn, Kenneth. *Teaching Students Through Their Individual Learning Styles: A Practical Approach.* Reston, Virginia: Reston Publishing Company, 1978.

Durkin, Dolores. *Teaching Them to Read*, 3rd ed. Boston: Allyn and Bacon, Inc., 1978.

Durkin, Dolores. "What Is the Value of the New Interest in Reading Comprehension?" *Language Arts* 58 (January 1981):27.

Durkin, Dolores. "Reading Comprehension Instruction in Five Basal Reader Series." *Reading Research Quarterly* 16 (1981):515–44.

Durkin, Dolores. "What Classroom Observations Reveal About Reading Comprehension Instruction." *Reading Research Quarterly* 15 (1978–79):481–533.

Durrell, Donald D. *Durrell Analysis of Reading Difficulty: Manual of Directions*. New York: The Psychological Corporation, 1980.

Durrell, Donald, and Murphy, Helen A. "The Auditory Discrimination Factor in Reading Readiness and Reading Disability." *Education* 73 (May 1963):556–60.

Durrell, Donald, and Sullivan, H. B. *Durrell-Sullivan Reading Capacity and Achievement Manual for Primary and Intermediate Tests*. New York: Harcourt, Brace and World, 1945.

Dyer, James W.; Riley, James; and Yekonich, Frank P. "An Analysis of Three Study Skills: Notetaking, Summarizing, and Rereading." *Journal of Educational Research* 73 (September/October 1979):3–7.

Dykstra, Robert. "Auditory Discrimination Abilities and Beginning Reading Achievement." *Reading Research Quarterly* 1 (Spring 1966):5–34.

Dykstra, Robert. "Summary of the Second Phase of the Cooperative Research Program in Primary Reading Instruction." *Reading Research Quarterly* IV (Fall 1968): 49–70.

Eberwein, Lowell D. "The Variability of Readability of Basal Reader Textbooks and How Much Teachers Know About It." *Reading World* 18 (March 1979): 259–72.

Education Commission of the States. *National Assessment of Educational Progress: A Project of the Education Commission of the States*. Washington, D.C.: National Center for Educational Statistics, 1977.

Educational Products Information Exchange. *Report of a National Study of the Quality of Instructional Materials Most Used by Teachers and Learners*. Technical Report 76, New York: E.P.I.E. Institute, 1977.

Eisenhardt, Catheryn T. "Individualization of Instruction." *Elementary English* 48 (March 1971):341–45.

Ekwall, Eldon E. *Diagnosis and Remediation of the Disabled Reader*. Boston: Allyn and Bacon, Inc., 1976.

Ekwall, Eldon E. "Informal Reading Inventories: The Instructional Level. *The Reading Teacher*, 29 (April 1976):662–665.

Ekwall, Eldon. "Should Repetitions Be Counted as Errors?" *The Reading Teacher*, 27 (January 1974):365–367.

Eller, William, and Wolf, Judith G. "Developing Critical Reading Abilities." *Journal of Reading* 10 (December 1966):192–98.

Elliot, Stephen N., and Carroll, James L. "Strategies to Help Children Remember What They Read." *Reading Improvement* 17 (Winter 1980):272–77.

Emans, Robert. "Linguistics and Phonics." *The Reading Teacher* 26 (February 1973):477–82.

Emans, Robert. "The Usefulness of Phonic Generalizations Above the Primary Grades." *The Reading Teacher* 20 (February 1967): 410–25.

Emans, Robert. "Use of Context Clues." *Teaching Word Recognition Skills*. Compiled by Mildred A. Dawson. Newark, Delaware: International Reading Association, 1971.

Emans, Robert. "Use of Context Clues," in *Reading and Realism*. Newark, Delaware: International Reading Association, 1969, pp. 76–82.

Emans, Robert, and Fisher, Gladys Mary. "Teaching the Use of Context Clues." *Elementary English* 44 (1967): 243–46.

Evertson, Carolyn M. and Anderson, Linda M. "Beginning School." *Educational Horizons* 57 (Summer 1979):164–68.

Farr, Roger, ed. *Iowa Silent Reading Test: Manual of Direction*. New York: Harcourt Brace Jovanovich, Inc., 1973.

Farr, Roger; Fay, Leo; and Negley, Harold. *Then and Now: Reading Achievement in Indiana (1944–45 and 1976)*. Bloomington, Indiana: School of Education, Indiana University, 1978.

Fay, Leo. "Reading Study Skills: Math and Science," in *Reading and Inquiry*. Edited by J. Allen Figurel. Newark, Delaware: International Reading Association, 1965.

Fennimore, Flora. "Projective Book Reports." *Language Arts* 54 (February 1977):176–79.

Fernald, Grace M. *Remedial Technique in Basic School Subjects*. New York: McGraw-Hill, 1943.

Fidell, Rachel, and Fiddell, Estelle A., eds. *Children's Catalog*, 13th ed. Bronx, New York: H. W. Wilson Company, 1976.

Flesch, Rudolf F. "A New Readability Yardstick." *Journal of Applied Psychology* 32 (June 1948):221–33.

Flesch, Rudolf F. *Why Johnny Can't Read and What You Can Do About It.* New York: Harper and Row, 1955.

Fogarty, Joan L., and Wang, Margaret C. "An Investigation of the Cross-Age Peer Tutoring Process: Some Implications for Instructional Design and Motivation." *The Elementary School Journal* 82 (May 1982):451.

Forness, Steven R.; Silverstein, Arthur B.; and Guthrie, Donald. "Relationship Between Classroom Behavior and Achievement of Mildly Mentally Retarded Children." *American Journal of Mental Deficiency* 84 (November 1979):260–265.

Frenzel, Norman J. "Children Need a Multipronged Attack in Word Recognition." *The Reading Teacher* 31 (March 1978):627–31.

Fries, Charles C. *Linguistics and Reading.* New York: Holt, Rinehart and Winston, Inc., 1963.

Fry, Edward B. *Elementary Reading Instruction.* New York: McGraw-Hill Book Company, 1977.

Fry, Edward B. "Fry's Readability Graph: Clarifications, Validity, and Extension to Level 17." *Journal of Reading* 21 (December 1977):242–52.

Furness, Edna L. "Pupils, Pedagogues, and Punctuation." *Elementary English* 37 (1960):184–89.

Gagné, Robert M. *The Conditions of Learning,* 2nd ed. New York: Holt, Rinehart, and Winston, 1970.

Gardner, David C., and Kurtz, Margaret. "Teaching Technical Vocabulary to Handicapped Students." *Reading Improvement* 16 (Fall 1979):252–57.

Gates, Arthur I. *A Reading Vocabulary for the Primary Grades.* New York: Teachers College, Columbia University, 1926.

Gates, Arthur I.; McKillop, Anne S.; and Horowitz, E. C *Gates-Mckillop-Horowitz Reading Diagnostic Tests (2nd Ed.).* New York: Teachers College Press, 1981.

Gemake, Josephine. "Interference of Certain Dialect Elements With Reading Comprehension for Third Graders." *Reading Improvement* 18 (Summer 1981):183–189.

Gentile, A. *Further Studies in Achievement Testing, Hearing Impaired Students.* Annual Survey of Hearing Impaired Children and Youth. Washington, D.C.: Gallaudet College. 1973.

Gibson, E. J. "The Ontogeny of Reading." *American Psyhologist* 25 (1970):136–43.

Geoffrion, Leo D. "Reading and The Non-Vocal Child." *The Reading Teacher* 35 (March 1982): 662–669.

Gilliland, Hap. *A Practical Guide to Remedial Reading.* Columbus, Ohio: Charles E. Merrill Publishing Company, 1978.

Gilmore, John V., and Gilmore, Eunice C. *Gilmore Oral Reading Test: Manual of Directions.* New York: Harcourt Brace Jovanovich, 1968.

Glass, Gerald G., and Burton, Elizabeth H. "How Do They Decode Verbalizations and Observed Behaviors of Successful Decoders." *The Reading Teacher* 26 (March 1973):645.

Gleitman, Lila R., and Rozin, Paul. "Teaching Reading by Use of Syllabary." *Reading Research Quarterly* VIII (1973):447–83.

Gollin, E. S. "Developmental Studies of Visual Recognition of Incomplete Objects." *Perceptual and Motor Skills* II (1960):289–98.

Goodman, Kenneth S. "A Linguistic Study of Cues and Miscues in Reading." *Elementary English* 42 (1965):639–43.

Goodman, Kenneth S. "Behind the Eye: What Happens in Reading." *Reading Process and Program.* Edited by Kenneth Goodman and Olive Niles. Urbana, Illinois: National Council of Teachers of English, 1970.

Goodman, Kenneth S. "Let's Dump the Up-tight Model in English." *Elementary School Journal* 69 (October 1969), pp. 1–13.

Goodman, Kenneth S. "Miscues: Windows on the Reading Process." *Miscue Analysis.* Edited by Kenneth Goodman. Urbana, Illinois: ERIC Clearinghouse on Reading and Communication Skills, 1973.

Goodman, Kenneth S. "Reading: A Psycholinguistic Guessing Game." *Theoretical Models and Processes of Reading.* Edited by Harry Singer and Robert B. Ruddell. Newark, Delaware: International Reading Association, 1970.

Goodman, Kenneth S. "The 13th Easy Way to Make Learning to Read Difficult: A Reaction to Gleitman and Rozin." *Reading Research Quarterly* VIII (1973):484–93.

Goodman, Kenneth S., with Buck, Catherine. "Dialect Barriers to Comprehension Revisited." *The Reading Teacher* 25 (October 1973):6–12.

Goodman, Yetta M. "Reading Diagnosis—Qualitative or Quantitative" *The Reading Teacher* 26 (October 1972):37.

Goodman, Yetta M., and Burke, Carolyn L. "Reading: Language and Psycholinguistic Bases." *Reading: Foundations and Instructional Strategies*. Edited by Pose Lamb and Richard Arnold. Belmont, California: Wadsworth Publishing Company, Inc., 1976.

Goodman, Yetta, and Burke, Carolyn L. *Reading Miscue Inventory*. New York: Macmillan Publishing Company, Inc., 1972.

Grant, Linda, and Rothenberg, James. *Charting Educational Futures: Interaction Patterns in First and Second Grade Reading Groups*. Washington, D.C.: National Institute of Education (April 1981), ED 200 902.

Gray, William S. *On Their Own in Reading*. Chicago: Scott, Foresman, 1948.

Gray, William S. "Reading and Physiology and Psychology of Reading." *Encyclopedia of Educational Research*. Edited by E. W. Harris. New York: Macmillan, 1960.

Guszak, Frank J. "Teacher Questioning and Reading." *The Reading Teacher* 21 (December 1967): 227–34.

Guthrie, Frances M., and Cunningham, Patricia M. "Teaching Decoding Skills to Educable Mentally Handicapped Children." *The Reading Teacher* 35 (February 1982):54–59.

Guthrie, John J. "Effective Teaching Practices." *The Reading Teacher* 35 (March 1982):766–68.

Hafner, Lawrence E., and Jolly, Hayden B. *Patterns of Teaching Reading in the Elementary School*. New York: Macmillan, 1972.

Hafner, Lawrence. *Developmental Reading in Middle and Secondary Schools: Foundations, Strategies, and Skills for Teaching*. New York: Macmillan Publishing Company, Inc., 1977.

Hall, Mary Anne, and Ramig, Christopher J. *Linguistic Foundations for Reading*. Columbus, Ohio: Charles E. Merrill Publishing Company, 1978.

Hall, Mary Anne. *Teaching Reading as a Language Experience*. Columbus, Ohio: Charles E. Merrill, 1976.

Hall, Mary Anne. *The Language Experience Approach for Teaching Reading*, 2nd ed. Newark, Delaware: International Reading Association, 1978.

Haller, Emil J., and Davis, Sharon A. "Does Socio-Economic Status Bias the Assignment of Elementary School Students to Reading Groups" *American Educational Research Journal* (Winter 1980):409–418.

Hammill, Donald; Goodman, Libby; and Wilderholt, J. Lee. "Visual-Motor Processes: Can We Train Them?" *The Reading Teacher* 27 (February 1974): 469–78.

Hanna, Paul R., and Moore, James I. "Spelling—From Spoken Word to Written Symbol." *Elementary School Journal* 53 (1953):329–37.

Hansell, Stevenson T. "Stepping Up to Outlining." *Journal of Reading* 22 (December 1978): 248–252.

Hansen, Harlan S. "The Impact of the Home Literacy Environment on Reading Attitude." *Elementary English* 46 (January 1969):17–24.

Harber, Jean R. "Auditory Closure and Reading." *Reading Horizons* 21 (Winter 1981):134–38.

Harber, Jean R., and Beatty, Jane N. *Reading and the Black English Speaking Child*. Newark, Delaware: International Reading Association, 1978.

Hargis, Charles H., and Gickling, Edward F. "The Function of Imagery in Word Recognition Development." *The Reading Teacher* 31 (May 1978):870–73.

Harris, Albert J. *How to Increase Reading Ability*, 4th ed. New York: David McKay Co., Inc., 1961.

Harris, Albert J. "Practical Applications of Reading Research." *The Reading Teacher* 29 (March 1976):559–65.

Harris, Albert J. "Review of Gilmore Oral Reading Test." *Reading Tests and Reviews*. Edited by Oscar K. Buros, Highland Park, New Jersey: The Gryphon Press, 1968.

Harris, Albert J. "Review of Gray Oral Reading Test." *Reading Tests and Reviews*. Edited by Oscar K. Buros. Highland Park, New Jersey: The Gryphon Press, 1968.

Harris, Albert J., and Jacobson, Milton D. *Basic Elementary Reading Vocabularies*. New York: The Macmillan Company, 1972.

Harris, Albert J.; Serwer, Blanche; and Gold, Laurence. "Comparing Approaches in First Grade Teaching with Disadvantaged Children Extended into Second Grade." *The Reading Teacher* 20 (May 1967):698–703.

Harris, Albert J., and Sipay, Edward R. *How to Increase Reading Ability*, 6th ed. New York: David McKay Company, Inc., 1975.

Harris, Larry A. "Interest and the Initial Acquisition of Words." *The Reading Teacher* 22 (January 1969):312–14, 362.

Harris, Larry A., and Smith, Carl B. *Reading Instruction: Diagnostic Teaching in the Classroom*, 2nd ed. New York: Holt, Rinehart, and Winston, 1976.

Harris, Larry A., and Smith, Carl B. *Reading Instruction: Diagnostic Teaching in the Classroom*, 3rd ed. New York: Holt, Rinehart, and Winston, 1980.

Harris, Richard L. "Research Evidence Regarding the Impact of Class Size on Pupil Academic Achievement." Phoenix, Arizona: Maricopa County Schools, 1977.

Harrison, Alan R. "Critical Reading for Elementary Pupils," *The Reading Teacher* 21 (1967):244–52.

Hartley, James; Bartlett, Sally; and Branthwaite, Alan. "Underlining Can Make a Difference-Sometimes." *Journal of Educational Research* 74 (March/April 1980):218–24.

Hays, Warren S. "Criteria for the Instructional Level of Reading." 1975, Microfiche ED 117 665.

Healey, Ann Kirtland. "Effects of Changing Children's Attitudes Toward Reading." Elementary English 40 (November 1963): 255–57, 279.

Hedley, Carolyn N. "Mainstreaming and the Classroom Teacher: A Practical Approach." *Reading Horizons* 21 (Spring 1981):189–95.

Heimberger, M. J. "Sartain Reading Attitudes Inventory." April 1970. ERIC, ED 045 291.

Hiatt, Diana Buell. "Time Allocation In The Classroom: Is Instruction Being Shortchanged?" *Phi Delta Kappan* 61 (December 1979):289–90.

Hillerich, Robert L. "The Truth About Vowels." *Insights Into Why and How to Read*. Edited by Robert Williams. Newark, Delaware: International Reading Association, 1976.

Hillerich, Robert L. "Vowel Generalizations and First Grade Reading Achievement." *Elementary School Journal* 67 (1967):246–50.

Hillerich, Robert L. "Word Lists: Getting It All Together." *The Reading Teacher* 27 (January 1974):353–60.

Hirstendahl, J. K. "The Effect of Subheads on Reader Comprehension." *Journalism Quarterly* 45 (1968):123–25.

Hittleman, Daniel R. "Seeking a Psycholinguistic Definition of Readability." *The Reading Teacher* 26 (May 1973):783–89.

Holland, Howard K., and Galfo, Armand J. *An Analysis of Research Concerning Class Size*. Richmond, Virginia: State Department of Education, 1964.

Hollingsworth, Paul M. "Can Training in Listening Improve Reading?" *The Reading Teacher* 18 (1964):121–23, 127.

Holmes, Jack A., and Singer, Harry. *The Substrata-Factor Theory: The Substrata-Factor Difference Underlying Reading in Known Groups*. Final report, Contracts 538 and 538A. Washington, D.C.: Office of Education, U.S. Department of Health, Education and Welfare, 1961.

Hong, Laraine K. "Modifying SSR for Beginning Readers." *The Reading Teacher* 34 (May 1981): 888–91.

Huck, Charlotte S. and Kuhn, Doris Young. *Children's Literature in the Elementary School*, 2nd ed. New York: Holt, Rinehart and Winston, 1968.

Hurey, Edmund B. *The Psychology and Pedagogy of Reading*. New York: The Macmillan Company, 1908.

Huus, Helen. "A New Look at Children's Interests." in Shapiro, Joe E. (ed.) *Using Literature and Poetry Affectively*. Newark, Delaware: International Reading Association, 1979, 37–45.

Ives, Josephine Pilkarz. "The Improvement of Critical Reading Skills." *Problem Areas in Reading—Some Observations and Recommendations*. Edited by Coleman Morrison. Providence, Rhode Island: Oxford Press, Inc., 1966.

Jarrett, James L. "I'm for Basics, But Let Me Define Them." *Kappan* 59 (December 1977):235–39.

Jastak, J.; Bijou, S.; and Jastak, S. *Wide Range Achievement Test*. New York: The Psychological Corporation, 1976.

Jobe, Fred W. *Screening Vision in Schools*. Newark, Delaware: International Reading Association, 1976.

Johns, Jerry L., and Lunt, Linda. "Motivating Reading: Professional Ideas." *The Reading Teacher* 28 (April 1975):617–19.

Johns, Jerry L.; Edmond, Rose M., and Manrogenes, Nancy A. "The Dolch Basic Sight Vocabulary: A Replication and Validation Study." *The Elementary School Journal* 78 (September 1977):31–37.

Johnson, Dale D. "Reading: Current Approaches, Part One." *Reading Foundations and Instructional Strategies*. Edited by Pose Lamb and Richard Arnold. Belmont, California: Wadsworth Publishing Company, Inc., 1976.

Johnson, Dale D. "Skills Management Systems: Some Issues." *Language Arts* 54 (1977):511–16.

Johnson, Dale D. "The Dolch List Re-Examined." *The Reading Teacher* 24 (February 1971):449–57.

Johnson, Dale D., and Pearson, P. David. "Skills Management Systems: A Critique." *The Reading Teacher* 28 (May 1975):757–64.

Johnson, Dale D.; Smith, Richard J.; and Jensen, Kenneth L. "Primary Children's Recognition of High Frequency Words." *The Elementary School Journal* 73 (December 1972):162–67.

Johnson, Donald J., and Myklebust, Helmer R. *Learning Disabilities*: *Educational Principles and Practices*. New York: Gruen and Stratton, 1967.

Johnson, Marjorie Seddon, and Kress, Roy A. *Informal Reading Inventories*. Newark, Delaware International Reading Association, 1965.

Jongsma, Eugene R. "The Cloze Procedure: A Survey of the Research." ED050893 Bloomington, Indiana: Indiana University, August, 1971.

Jongsma, Kathleen S., and Jongsma, Eugene A. (Reviewers). "Test Review: Commercial Informal Reading Inventories." *The Reading Teacher,* 34 (March 1981):697–705.

Jordan, William C. "Prime-o-tee: The New Reading Method." *Academic Therapy Quarterly* (Summer 1967):248–50.

Jorm, Anthony F. "Effect of Word Imagery on Reading Performance as a Function of Reading Ability." *Journal of Educational Psychology* 69 (February 1977):46–54.

Juel, Connie. "Comparison of Word Identification Strategies With Varying Context, Word Type, and Reader Skill." *Reading Research Quarterly* 15 (1980):358–76.

Justin, Neal. "Culture Conflict and Mexican-American Achievement." *School and Society* 98 (1970):27–28.

Karlsen, Bjorn; Madden, Richard; and Gardner, Eric F. *Stanford Diagnostic Reading Test*: *Manual for Administering and Interpreting*. New York: Harcourt Brace Jovanovich, Inc., 1976.

Kaufman, Maurice. *Perceptual and Language Readiness Programs*: *Critical Reviews*. Newark, Delaware: International Reading Association, 1973.

Kennan, Donna. "A Study of the Relationship Between Tenth Grade Students' Reading Ability and Their Comprehension of Certain Assigned Textbooks." Unpublished doctoral dissertation, Florida State University, 1976.

King, Ethel M., and Siegmar, Muehl. "Different Sensory Cues as Aids in Beginning Reading." *The Reading Teacher* 19 (December 1965):163–68.

Kirk, Samuel A., and Gallagher, James J. *Educating Exceptional Children*, 3rd ed. Boston: Houghton Mifflin Company, 1979.

Klein, Marvin L. "The Reading Program and Classroom Management: Panacea or Perversion?" *Elementary English* 52 (March 1975):351–55.

Kolker, Brenda, and Terwilliger, Paul N. "Sight Vocabulary Learning of First and Second Graders." *Reading World* 20 (May 1981): 251–58.

Kolstoe, Oliver P. *Teaching Educable Mentally Retarded Children*, 2nd ed. New York: Holt, Rinehart and Winston, 1976.

Kucera, Henry, and Francis, W. Nelson. *Computational Analysis for Present-Day American English*. Providence, Rhode Island: Brown University Press, 1967.

Labe, Mary Louise. "Improve the Dictionary's Image." *Elementary English* 48 (March 1971): 363–65.

LaBerge, D., and Samuels, S. Jay. "Toward a Theory of Automatic Information Processing in Reading." *Cognitive Psychology* 6 (1974): 293–323.

Lahey, Benjamin, and Drabman, Ronald. "Facilitation of the Acquisition and Retention of Sight-Word Vocabulary Through Token Reinforcement." *Journal of Applied Behavior Analysis* 7 (Summer 1974):307–12.

Lally, M. "Computer-Assisted Teaching of Sight-Word Recognition for Mentally Retarded School Children." *American Journal of Mental Deficiency* 85 (January 1981):383–88.

Lange, Bob. "Readability Formulas Second Looks, Second Thoughts." *The Reading Teacher* 35 (April 1982):858–61.

Larson, Alfred D., and Miller, June B. "The Hearing Impaired." *Exceptional Children and Youth: An Introduction.* Edited by Edward L. Meyen. Denver, Colorado: Love Publishing Company, 1978.

Leinhardt, Gaia; Zigmond, Naomi; and Cooley, William W. "Reading Instruction and Its Effects." *American Educational Research Journal* 18 (Fall 1981):356–58.

Lenen, H., and Kaplan, E. L. "Grammatical Structure and Reading." in Lenin, H. and Williams, J. (eds.) *Basic Studies In Reading*, New York: Basic Books, 1970.

Levin, Harry, and Watson, J. "The Learning of Variable Grapheme-to-Phoneme Correspondences: Variations in the Initial Consonant Position." *A Basic Research Program on Reading.* U.S. Office of Education Cooperative Research Project No. 639. Ithaca, New York: Cornell University, 1963.

Liebert, Robert E., and Sherk, John K. "Three Frostig Visual Perception Sub-tests and Specific Reading Tasks for Kindergarten, First, and Second Grade Children." *The Reading Teacher* 24 (November 1970):130–37.

Livingston, Howard F. "Measuring and Teaching Meaning with an Informal Reading Inventory." *Elementary English* 51 (September 1974): 878–79, 895.

Loban, Walter. *The Language of Elementary School Children.* Urbana, Illinois: National Council of Teachers of English, 1963.

Lowenfeld, Berthold, ed. *The Visually Handicapped Child in School.* New York: John Day Co., 1973.

Lowrey, Lawrence F., and Grafft, William. "Paperback and Reading Attitudes." *The Reading Teacher* 21 (April 1968):618–23.

Lundsteen, Sara W. *Children Learn to Communicate.* Englewood Cliffs, New Jersey: Prentice-Hall, Inc., 1976.

McBroom, Maude; Sparrow, Julia; and Eckstein, Catherine. *Scale for Determining a Child's Reader Level,* Iowa City: Bureau of Publications, Extension Division, State University of Iowa, 1944.

McCallister, James M. "Using Paragraph Clues as Aids to Understanding. *Journal of Reading* 8 (October 1965):11–16.

McCullough, Constance. "Responses of Elementary School Children to Common Types of Reading Comprehension Questions." *Journal of Educational Research* 51 (September 1957): 65–70.

McFeely, Donald C. "Syllabication Usefulness in a Basal and Social Studies Vocabulary." *The Reading Teacher* 27 (May 1974): 809–14.

MacGinitie, Walter H. et al. *Gates-MacGinitie Reading Tests Teacher's Manuals.* Boston: Houghton Mifflin, 1978.

McLaughlin, Harry G. "SMOG Grading—A New Readability Formula." *Journal of Reading* 12 (May 1969):639–46.

McKiernan, Jack, and Anakian, Margo. "Directional Awareness Training: Remediation of Receptive Letter Reversals." *Academic Therapy* 16 (November 1980):193–97.

McNeil, J. D., and Keislar, E. R. "Value of the Oral Response in Beginning Reading: An Experimental Study Using Programmed Instruction." *British Journal of Educational Psychology* 33 (1963): 162–68.

Mangieri, John N., and Kahn, Michael S. "Is the Dolch List of 220 Basic Sight Words Irrelevant?: *The Reading Teacher* 30 (March 1977):649–51.

Mangieri, John N.; Bader, Lois A.; and Walker, James E. *Elementary Reading.* New York: McGraw-Hill Book Company, 1982.

Many, Wesley A. "Is There Any Difference: Reading vs. Listening?" *The Reading Teacher* 19 (1965): 110–13.

Marshbanks, Gabrielle, and Levin, Harry. "Cues by Which Children Recognize Words." *Journal of Educational Psychology* 56 (1965):57–71.

Marland, Sidney P. *Education of the Gifted and Talented.* Washington, D.C: U.S. Office of Education, 1972.

Martin, Jeanne, and Evertson, Carolyn M. *Teachers' Interactions with Reading Groups of Differing Ability Levels.* Washington, D.C: National Institute of Education, (March 1980), ED 203 303.

Marzano, Robert J.; Case, Norma; DeBoog, Anne; and Prochoruk, Kathy. "Are Syllabication and Reading Ability Related?" *Journal of Reading* 19 (April 1976):545–47.

Mavrogenes, Nancy A.; Hanson, Earl F., and Winkley, Carol K. "A Guide to Tests of Factors that Inhibit Learning to Read." *The Reading Teacher* 29 (January 1976):343–58.

Maxwell, Martha. "Readability: Have We Gone Too Far?" *Journal of Reading* 21 (March 1978): 525–30.

May, Frank B. *Reading as Communication.* Columbus, Ohio: Charles E. Merrill Publishing Company, 1982.

Meisal, Stephen, and Glass, Gerald G. "Voluntary Reading Interests and the Interest Content of Basal Readers." *The Reading Teacher* 23 (April 1970):655–59.

Milaragno, Ralph J. *Tutoring With Students.* Englewood Cliffs, New Jersey: Educational Technology Publications, 1976.

Meyer, Bonnie J. F. "Structure of Prose: Implications for Teachers of Reading." Research Report No. 3. Tempe, Arizona: Arizona State University, Department of Educational Psychology, 2.

Moacdieh, Chris. "Grouping for Reading in the Primary Grades: Evidence on the Revisionist Argument." Paper presented at the Annual Meeting of the American Educational Research Association, Los Angeles, California: April 13–17, 1981.

Moe, Alden J. "Reading: Current Approaches, Part Two." *Reading Foundations and Instructional Strategies.* Edited by Pose Lamb and Richard Arnold. Belmont, California: Wadsworth Publishing Company, Inc., 1976.

Monroe, Marion. *Children Who Cannot Read.* Chicago: University of Chicago Press, 1932.

Moores, Donald F. *Educating the Deaf: Psychology, Principles and Practices.* Boston: Houghton Mifflin Company, 1978.

Moray, Geraldine. "What Does Research Say About the Reading Interests of Children in the Intermediate Grades?" *The Reading Teacher* 31 (April 1978):763–68.

Musgrave, G. R. *Individualized Instruction.* Boston: Allyn and Bacon, Inc., 1975.

Nardelli, Robert R. "Some Aspects of Creative Reading." *Journal of Educational Research* 50 (March 1957):495–508.

National Advisory Committee on Handicapped Children. *First Annual Report, Subcommittee on Education of the Committee on Labor and Public Welfare, U.S. Senate.* Washington, D.C.: U.S. Government Printing Office, 1968.

National Education Association. "America's Other Children-Bilingual Multicultural Education: Hope for the Culturally Alienated." *NEA Reporter* 15 (1976):13.

Neill, Shirley Boes, "A Summary of Issues in the Minimum Competency Movement." *Kappan* 60 (February 1979):452–53.

Nelson, Joan. "Readability: Some Cautions to the Content Area Teacher." *Journal of Reading* 21 (April 1978):620–25.

Nelson, Raedeane M. "Getting Children into Reference Books." *Elementary English* 50 (September 1973):884–87.

Newman, Susan B. "Creative Reading and the Skills Management System." *Reading Improvement* 181 (Summer 1981):190–92.

New England Educational Assessment Project. *Reading* Instruction in New England's Public Schools. ERIC/CRIER ED 032 996, 1969.

Niles, Jerome A., and Harris, Larry A. "The Context of Comprehension." *Reading Horizons* 22 (Fall 1981):33–42.

Oakan, Robert; Wierner, Morton; and Cormer, Ward. "Identification, Organization, and Reading Comprehension for Good and Poor Readers." *Journal of Educational Psychology* 62 (1971): 71–78.

Oakland, Thomas D. "Auditory Discrimination and Socioeconomic Status as Correlates of Reading Ability." *Journal of Learning Disabilities* 2 (June 1969):325–29.

Ollila, Lloyd. "Reading: Preparing the Child." *Reading: Foundations and Instructional Strategies.* Edited by Pose Lamb and Richard Arnold. Belmont, California: Wadsworth Publishing Company, 1976.

Olson, Arthur V., and Johnson, Clifford L. "Structure and Predictive Validity of the Frostig Developmental Test of Visual Perception in Grades One and Three." *Journal of Special Education* 4 (Winter-Spring 1970):49–52.

Olson, Willard C. *Child Development.* Boston, C. C. Heath and Company, 1949.

Orlando, Vincent P. "Notetaking vs. Notehaving: A Comparison While Studying From Text." in Kamil, Michael L. and Moe, Alden J. (eds). "Reading Research: Studies and Applications." *Twenty-Eighth Yearbook of the National Reading Conference* (1979):177–81.

Otto, Wayne. "Evaluating Instruments for Assessing Needs and Growth in Reading." *Assessment Problems in Reading.* Edited by Walter H. MacGinitie. Newark, Delaware: International Reading Association, 1973.

Otto, Wayne, and Chester, R. "Sight Words for Beginning Readers." *Journal of Educational Research* 65 (1971):425–43.

Paradis, Edward. "The Appropriateness of Visual Discrimination Exercise in Reading Readiness Materials." *Journal of Educational Research* 67 (February 1974):276–78.

Parker, Francis W. *Talks on Pedagogies.* Chicago: Kellog, 1894.

Pearson, P. David, and Fielding, Linda. "Research Update: Listening Comprehension." *Language Arts* 59 (September 1982):617–18.

Pearson, P. David, and Johnson, Dale. *Teaching Reading Comprehension.* New York: Holt, Rinehart, and Winston, 1978.

Perez, Eustolia. "Oral Language Competence Improves Reading Skills of Mexican American Third Graders." *The Reading Teacher* 35 (October 1981):24–29.

Pertz, Doris, and Putnam, Lillian R. "An Examination of the Relationship Between Nutrition and Learning." *The Reading Teacher* 35 (March, 1982):702–07.

Pflaster, Gail. "A Factor Analysis of Variables Related to Academic Performance of Hearing-Impaired Children in Regular Classes." *The Volta Review* 82 (February/March 1980):71–84.

Pieronek, Florence T. "Do Basal Readers Reflect the Interests of Intermediate Students?" *The Reading Teacher* 33 (January 1980):408–12.

Pikulski, John. "The Validity of Three Brief Measures of Intelligence for Disabled Readers." *Journal of Educational Research* 67 (October 1973):67–68, 80.

Pikulski, John. "A Critical Review: Informal Reading Inventories." *The Reading Teacher* 28 (November 1974): 141–51.

Pikulski, John J., and Kiroch, Irwin S. "Organization for Instruction." in Calfee, Robert C., and Drum, Priscilla A. (Eds.) *Teaching Reading In Compensatory Classes.* Newark, Delaware: International Reading Association, 1979. pp. 72–86, 187–91.

Pick, Anne D. "Some Basic Perceptual Processes in Reading," *The Young Child.* Edited by Willard W. Hartup. Washington, D.C.: National Association for the Education of Young Children, 1972.

Plattor, Emma E., and Woestehoff, Ellsworth S. "Specific Reading Disabilities of Disadvantaged Children." *Reading Difficulties: Diagnosis, Correction and Remediation.* Edited by William Durr. Newark, Delaware: International Reading Association, 1970.

Pollack, Cecelia; Nahem, Joseph; and Krippner, Stanley. "Developing Auditory Perception Skills in Kindergarten Children." *Academic Therapy* 14 (September 1978):73–80.

Powell, William R. "Measuring Reading Performance." November 1978. ERIC, ED 155 589.

Pryor, Frances. "Poor Reading—Lack of Self-Esteem?" *The Reading Teacher* 28 (January 1975):359.

Quandt, Ivan. *Self-Concept and Reading.* Newark, Delaware: International Reading Association, 1972.

Rankin, Earl F., and Overholzer, Betsy, M. "Reaction of Intermediate Grade Children to Contextual Clues." *Journal of Reading Behavior* 1 (Summer 1969):50–73.

Ransom, Grayce A. *Preparing to Teach Reading.* Boston: Little, Brown and Company, 1978.

Raybin, Ron. "Minimum Essentials and Accountability." *Kappan* 60 (January 1979): 374–75.

Readence, John E., and Harris, Mary McDonnell. "False Prerequisites in the Teaching of Comprehension." *Reading Improvement* 17 (Spring 1980):18–21.

Reeves, Harriet Ramsey. "Individual Conferences— Diagnostic Tools." *The Reading Teacher* 24 (February 1971):411–15.

Robeck, Mildred C., and Wilson, John A. R. *Psychology of Reading: Foundations of Instruction.* New York: John Wiley and Sons, Inc., 1974.

Robinson, Francis P. *Effective Study*, 4th ed. New York: Harper and Row, 1970.

Robinson, Helen M. "Developing Critical Readers." *Dimensions of Critical Reading.* Edited by Russell G. Stauffer. Newark, Delaware: University of Delaware, Proceedings of the Annual Education and Reading Conference, 1964.

Robinson, Helen, ed. *Manual: Gray Oral Reading Test.* Indianapolis: Bobbs-Merrill Company, Inc., 1967.

Robinson, Helen. "Perceptual Training: Does It Result in Reading Improvement?" *Some Persistent Questions on Beginning Reading.* Edited by Robert C. Aukerman. Newark, Delaware: International Reading Association, 1972.

Robinson, Helen, and Weintraub, Samuel. "Research Related to Children's Interests and to Developmental Values of Reading." *Library Trends* 22 (October 1973):81–108.

Robinson, Violet B.; Strickland, Dorothy S.; and Cullinan, Bernice. "The Child: Ready or Not?" *The Kindergarten Child and Reading.* Edited by Lloyd Ollila. Newark, Delaware: International Reading Association, 1977.

Roeder, Harold H., and Lee, Nancy. "Twenty-five Teacher Tested Ways to Encourage Voluntary Reading." *The Reading Teacher* 27 (October 1973):48–50.

Roettger, Doris. "Elementary Students' Attitudes Toward Reading." *The Reading Teacher* 33 (January 1980): 451–53.

Rosenblatt, L. M. "Towards a Transactional Theory of Reading." *Journal of Reading Behavior* 1 (1969): 31–49.

Rosenshine, Barak V. "Skill Hierarchies in Reading Comprehension." in Spiro, Rand J., Bruce, Bertram C., and Brewer, William F. (eds.) *Theoretical Issues in Reading Comprehension.* Hillsdale, New Jersey: Lawrence Erlbaum Associates 1980, 535–554.

Ross, Ramon. "A Look at Listeners." *Elementary School Journal* 64 (April 1964):369–72.

Rothrock, Dayton. "The Rise and Decline of Individualized Instruction." *Educational Leadership* 39 (April 1982):528–30.

Ruck, L. V. "Some Questions About the Teaching of Syllabication Rules." *The Reading Teacher* 27 (March 1974):583–88.

Ruddell, Robert B. *Reading-Language Instruction: Innovative Practices.* Englewood Cliffs, New Jersey: Prentice-Hall, 1974.

Rumelhart, David. *Toward an Interactive Model of Reading.* Center for Human Information Services, Technical Report No. 56. University of California, San Diego: 1976.

Rupley, William H., and Blair, Timothy R. "Teacher Effectiveness Research in Reading Instruction: Early Efforts to Present Focus." *Reading Psychology* 2 (November 1980):49–56.

Russell, David H. *Children's Thinking.* Boston, Massachusetts: Ginn and Company, 1956.

Ryystrom, Richard. "Reflections of Meaning." *Journal of Reading Behavior* 9 (Summer 1977): 193–200.

Sanders, Norris M. *Classroom Questions—What Kinds?* New York: Harper and Row, 1966.

Sandford, Herbert A. "Directed and Free Search of the School Atlas Map." *The Cartographic Journal* 71 (December 1980):83–92.

Saunders, David R. "A Factor Analysis of the Picture Completion Items of the WAIS." *Journal of Clinical Psychology* 16 (April 1960):146–47.

Schell, Leo M. "The Validity of the Potential Level Via Listening Comprehension: A Cautionary Note." *Reading Psychology* 3 (1982):271–76.

Schell, Leo M., and Jennings, Robert E. "Test Review: Durrell Analysis of Reading Difficulty (3rd Edition)." *The Reading Teacher* 35 (November 1981):204–10.

Schell, Leo M. "Teaching Structural Analysis." *The Reading Teacher* 21 (November 1967):133–37.

Searls, Evelyn F. *How to Use WISC Scores in Reading Diagnosis.* Newark, Delaware: International Reading Association, 1975.

Sewell, Trevor E. "Intelligence and Learning Tasks as Predictors of Scholastic Achievement in Black and White First-Grade Children." *Journal of Psychology* 17 (Winter 1979): 325–32.

Shannon, Patrick. "Some Subjective Reasons for Teachers' Reliance on Commercial Reading Materials." *The Reading Teacher* 35 (May 1982):884–89.

Sheridan, E. Marcia. "A Review of Research on Schema Theory and Its Implications for Reading Instruction in Secondary Reading." ED 167 947, Indiana University, South Bend: 1978.

Simons, Herbert D. "Linguistic Skills and Reading Comprehension." *The Quest for Competency in Reading.* Edited by Howard A. Klein. Newark, Delaware International Reading Association, 1972.

Singer, Harry. "Teaching Word Recognition Skills." *Teaching Word Recognition Skills.* Edited by Mildred A. Dawson. Newark, Delaware: International Reading Association, 1971.

Singer, Harry. "Theoretical Models of Reading." *Journal of Communications* 19 (1969):134–56.

Singer, Harry, and Ruddell, Robert, eds. *Theoretical Models and Processes of Reading*, 2nd ed. Newark, Delaware: International Reading Association, 1976.

Singer, Harry; Samuels, S. Jay; and Spiroff, Jean. "The Effect of Pictures and Contextual Condition on Learning Responses to Printed Words." *Reading Research Quarterly* 9 (1973–74): 555–67.

Sipay, Edward R. *Sipay Word Analysis Tests.* Cambridge, Massachusetts: Educators Publishing Service, Inc., 1974.

Skinner, B. F. *Verbal Behavior.* New York: Appleton-Century-Crofts, 1957.

Slater, Mallie. "Individualized Language Arts in the Middle Grades." *The Reading Teacher* 27 (December 1973):253–56.

Slosson, Richard L. *Slosson Oral Reading Test.* East Aurora, New York: Slosson Educational Publications, Inc., 1963.

Smith, Carl B. *Teaching in Secondary School Content Subjects.* New York: Holt, Rinehart and Winston, 1978.

Smith, E. Brooks; Goodman, Kenneth; and Meredith, Robert. *Language and Thinking in the Elementary School.* New York: Holt, Rinehart and Winston, Inc., 1970.

Smith, Frank. *Psycholinguistics and Reading.* New York: Holt, Rinehart and Winston, Inc., 1973.

Smith, Frank. *Understanding Reading: A Psycholinguistic Analysis of Reading and Learning to Read* 3rd ed. New York: Holt, Rinehart, and Winston, 1982.

Smith, Henry P., and Dechant, Emerald V. *Psychology in Teaching Reading.* Englewood Cliffs, New Jersey: Prentice-Hall, Inc., 1961.

Smith, Nila Banton. *American Reading Instruction*, 3rd ed. Newark, Delaware: International Reading Association, 1974.

Smith, Nila Banton. "Patterns of Writing in Different Subject Areas." *Journal of Reading* 8 (October 1965):31–37.

Snyder, Geraldine V. "Learner Verification of Reading Games." *The Reading Teacher* 34 (March 1981): 686–91.

Spache, George D. *Diagnosing and Correcting Reading Disabilities*, 2nd ed. Boston: Allyn and Bacon, Inc., 1981.

Spache, George D. *Diagnostic Reading Scales.* Revised. Monterey, California: CTB/McGraw-Hill, 1972.

Spache, George D. *Diagnostic Reading Scales. Technical Bulletin.* Monterey, California: CTB/McGraw-Hill, 1973.

Spache, George D. *Good Reading for Poor Readers.* Champaign, Illinois: Garrard, 1974.

Spache, George. *Investigating the Issues of Reading Disabilities.* Boston: Allyn and Bacon, Inc., 1976.

Spache, George. *Toward Better Reading.* Champaign, Illinois: Garrard Press, 1963.

Spache, George, and Spache, Evelyn B. *Reading in the Elementary School*, 4th ed. Boston: Allyn and Bacon, Inc., 1977.

Stanchfield, Jo M. "Development of Prereading Skills in an Experimental Kindergarten Program." *Some Persistent Questions on Beginning Reading.*

Edited by Robert C. Aukerman. Newark, Delaware: International Reading Association, 1972.

Stanovich, Keith E. "Toward an Inter-active Compensatory Model of Individual Differences in the Development of Reading Fluency." *Reading Research Quarterly* 16 (1980):34–35, 42–45.

Stauffer, Russell G. *The Language-Experience Approach to the Teaching of Reading.* New York: Harper and Row, 1970.

Stern, Paula R., and Shanelson, Richard. "The Relationship Between Teachers' Grouping Decisions and Instructional Behavior: An Ethnographic Study of Reading Instruction." Paper presented at the Annual Meeting of the American Educational Research Association, Los Angeles, California, April 13–17, 1981.

Stevens, Kathleen C. "The Effect of Background Knowledge on the Reading Comprehension of Ninth Graders." *Journal of Reading Behavior* 12 (Summer 1980):451–54.

Sticht, Tom G.; Beck, L. J.; Hanke, R. N.; Kleiman, G. M.; and James, J. H. *Auding and Reading: A Developmental Model.* Alexandria, Virginia: Human Resource Research Organization, 1974.

Stoodt, Barbara D. "The Relationship Between Understanding Grammatical Conjunctions and Reading Comprehension." *Elementary English* 49 (1972):502–504.

Strang, Ruth. *Diagnostic Teaching of Reading.* New York: McGraw-Hill, 1969.

Strange, Michael. "Instructional Implications of a Conceptual Theory of Reading Comprehension." *The Reading Teacher* 33 (January 1980): 392.

Strickland, Dorothy. "Black is Beautiful vs. White is Right." *Elementary English* 49 (February 1972): 220–24.

Strickler, Darryl J. "Planning the Affective Component." *Classroom Practice in Reading.* Edited by Richard A. Earle. Newark, Delaware: International Reading Association, 1977.

Swalm, James E. "Is Listening Really More Effective for Learning in the Early Grades?" *Elementary English* 51 (1974):110–13.

Swanson, B. Marian, and Willis, Diane J. *Understanding Exceptional Children and Youth.* Chicago: Rand McNally College Publishing Company, 1979.

Taba, Hilda. "The Teaching of Thinking." *Elementary English* 42 (May 1976):534.

Taylor, Stanford E.; Frackenpohl, Helen; and White, Catherine. *A Revised Core Vocabulary: A Basic Vocabulary for Grades 1–8, An Advanced Vocabulary for Grades 9–13.* Huntington, New York: Educational Development Laboratories, 1969.

Taylor, Wilson L. "Cloze Procedure: A New Tool for Measuring Readability." *Journalism Quarterly* 30 (Fall 1953):415–33.

Terman, Lewis M., and Oden, Melita H. *The Gifted Group on Midlife: Thirty-Five Years' Follow-up of the Superior Child. Genetic Studies of Genius,* Vol. 5. Stanford California: Stanford University Press, 1959.

"The Minimum Competency Testing Movement." *Kappan* 59 (May 1978): entire issue.

Thorndike, Edward. "Reading and Reasoning: A Study of Mistakes in Paragraph Reading." *Journal of Educational Psychology* 8 (1917): 323–32.

Thorndike, Robert L. *Reading Comprehension in Fifteen Countries.* New York: John Wiley and Sons, 1973.

Thorndike, Robert. *The Concepts of Over and Under-achievement.* New York: Teachers College Press, Columbia University, 1963.

Tibbetts, Sylvia-Lee. "How Much Should We Expect Readability Formulas to Do?" *Elementary English* 50 (January 1973):75–76.

Tinko, H. G. "Letter Position in Trigram Discrimination by Beginning Readers." *Perceptual and Motor Skills* 35 (1972):153–54.

Torgenson, T. L., and Adams, G. S. *Measurement and Evaluation for the Elementary School Teacher.* New York: Holt, Rinehart, and Winston, 1954.

Trybus, Raymond J., and Karchmer, Michael A. "School Achievement Scores of Hearing Impaired Children National Data on Achievement Status and Growth Patterns." *American Annals of the Deaf* 122 (April 1977):62–69.

Turner, Thomas N., and Alexander, J. Estill. "Fostering Early Creative Reading." *Language Arts* 52 (September 1975):786.

U.S. National Joint Committee on Learning Disabilities. Revised Definition of LD. *The Reading Teacher* 35 (November 1981):134–35.

Valmont, William J. "Creating Questions for Informal Reading Inventories." *The Reading Teacher* 25 (March 1972):509–12.

Veatch, Jeanette. *Individualizing Your Reading Program*. New York: G. P. Putnam's Sons, 1959.

Vignocchi, Nillo. "What Research Says About the Effect of Class Size on Academic Achievement." *Illinois School Research and Development* 17 (Spring 1981):51–54.

Vineyard, Edwin E., and Massey, Harold W. "The Interrelationship of Certain Linguistic Skills and Their Relationship with Scholastic Achievement When Intelligence is Ruled Constant." *Journal of Educational Psychology* 48 (1957):279–86.


Walker, Susan M.; Noland, Ronald G., and Greenshields, C. "The Effect of High and Low Interest Control on Instructional Levels in Informal Reading Inventories." *Reading Improvement*, 16 (Winter 1979):297–300.

Wallen, Carl J. "Independent Activities: A Necessity, Not a Frill." *The Reading Teacher* 27 (December 1973):257–62.

Wang, Margaret C. "Mainstreaming Exceptional Children: Some Instructional Design and Implementation Considerations." *The Elementary School Journal* 81 (March 1981):195–221.

Walter, R. H., and Kosowski, Irene. "Symbolic Learning and Reading Retardation." *Journal of Consulting Psychology* 27 (1963):75–82.

Wardhaugh, Ronald. "Syl-lab-i-ca-tion." *Elementary English* 43 (November 1966):785–88.

Waugh, R. F., and Howell, K. W. "Teaching Modern Syllabication." *The Reading Teacher* 29 (October 1975):20–25.

Weintraub, Samuel. "Children's Reading Interests." *The Reading Teacher* 22 (April 1969):655–59.

Wepman, Joseph M. "Auditory Discrimination, Speech and Reading." *Elementary School Journal* 60 (1960):325–33.

Wheeler, H. E. and Howell, Emma A. "A First Grade Vocabulary Study." *Elementary School Journal* 31 (September 1930):52–60.

Whipple, Clifford L., and Kodman, Frank. "A Study of Discrimination and Perceptual Learning with Retarded Readers." *Journal of Educational Psychology* 60 (1969):1–5.

Williams, Joanna P. "Learning to Read: A Review of Theories and Models." *Reading Research Quarterly* 8 (1973):121–46.

Williams, Joanna P. "Successive vs. Concurrent Presentations of Multiple Grapheme-Phoneme Correspondences." *Journal of Educational Psychology* 59 (1968):309–14.

Wilson, Molly M. "The Effect of Question Types in Varying Placements on the Reading Comprehension of Upper Elementary Students." *Reading Psychology* 1 (Spring 1980):93–102.

Wilson, Robert M. *Diagnostic and Remedial Reading for Classroom and Clinic*, 4th ed. Columbus, Ohio: Charles E. Merrill Publishing Company, 1981.

Winkley, Carol. "Which Accent Generalizations are Worth Teaching?" *The Reading Teacher* 20 (December 1966):219–24, 253.

Wohlwill, J. F. "From Perception to Inference: A Dimension of Cognitive Development." *Thought in the Young Child*. Edited by W. Kessen and C. Kuklman. Chicago: University of Chicago Press, 1970.

Wolfe, Evelyn. "Advertising and the Elementary Language Arts." *Elementary English* 42 (January 1965):42–44.

Wong B. Y. L., and Jones, W. "Increasing Metacomprehension in Learning Disabled and Normally Achieving Students Through Self-Questioning Training." Burnaby, B. C. Canada: Simon Frasei University, 1981: Mimeographed.

Wood, Martha, and Brown, Mavis. "Beginning Readers' Recognition of Taught Words in Various Contextual Settings." in Kamil, Michael L. and Moe, Alden J. (eds.) *Reading Research: Studies and Applications*. Twenty-eighth Yearbook of the National Reading Conference 1979, 55–61.

Woodstock, Richard W. *Woodstock Reading Mastery Tests: Manual*. Circle Pines, Minnesota: American Guidance Service, Inc., 1973.


Zintz, Miles V. *The Reading Process* Dubuque, Iowa: Wm. C. Brown Company Publishers, 1980.

# author index

Horn, Alice, 169
Horowitz, Elizabeth C., 133, 146
Howell, Emma A., 90, 104
Howell, K. W., 286 n.24, 300
Huck, Charlotte S., 358, 361
Huey, Edmund B., 123, 146
Hullgren, Dayton, 338 n.14, 347
Huus, Helen, 354, 361

# i

Ingram, Barbara, 208
Ives, Josephine Piekarz, 314, 328

# j

Jacobson, Milton D., 90, 104
James, J. H., 260 n.27, 274
Jarrett, James, 28 n.4, 36
Jastak, J. F., 90 n.21, 104
Jastak, S. R., 90 n.21, 104
Jennings, Robert E., 133, 146
Jensen, Kenneth L., 281, 299
Jobe, Fred R., 139 n.31, 146
Johns, Jerry L., 281, 299
Johnson, Clifford I., 257, 273
Johnson, Dale, 90, 104, 182, 211, 229,
    247, 281, 299, 318, 329
Johnson, Donald J., 378, 389
Johnson, Marjorie Seddon, 72, 103
Jolly, Hayden B., 340, 347
Jones, Nancy R., 208
Jones, W., 337 n.6, 346
Jongsma, Eugene A., 65 n.2, 68, 96
    n.25, 103, 104
Jongsma, Kathleen S., 68, 103
Jordan, William C., 230 n.6, 247
Jorm, Anthony F., 280, 299
Juel, Connie, 288, 301
Justin, Neal, 384, 389

# k

Kahn, Michael S., 281, 299
Kaplin, E. L., 310 n.15, 327
Karchmer, Michael A., 371, 388
Karlsen, Bjorn, 116, 146
Kaufman, Maurice, 200
Keislar, E. R., 280, 299
King, Ethel M., 280, 299
Kirk, Samuel A., 370 n.9, 271, 274,
    276, 286 n.42, 386 n.43, 389
Kiroch, Irwin S., 188 n.10, 211

Kleiman, G. M., 260 n.27, 274
Klein, Marvin L., 182, 211
Kodman, Frank Jr., 259, 273
Kolker, Brenda, 280, 299
Kolstoe, Oliver P., 376–377, 389
Kosowski, Irene, 259, 274
Kress, Roy A., 72, 103
Krippner, Stanley, 259 n.23, 274
Kucera, Henry, 90, 92, 104
Kuhn, Doris Young, 358, 361
Kulik, Chen-Lin C., 190 n.16, 211
Kulik, James A., 190 n.16, 211
Kurtz, Margaret, 377 n.22, 389

# l

Labe, Mary Louise, 338 n.11, 347
LaBerge, D., 310 n.16
Lahey, Benjamin, 281, 299
Lally, M., 377 n.23, 389
Lange, Bob, 202, 212
Larson, Alfred D., 372–373, 388
LeButt, Marlene, 208
Lee, Nancy, 358, 361
Leibert, Robert E., 257, 273
Leinhardt, Gaea, 379 n.30, 389
Levin, Harry, 256, 273, 285, 300, 310
    n.15, 327
Lewis, Phyllis G., 98
Livingston, Howard F., 72, 104
Loban, Walter, 254, 272
Lowenfeld, Berthold, 369–370, 388
Lowrey, Lawrence F., 359 n.17, 361
Lundsteen, Sara W., 358 n.14, 361
Lunt, Linda, 358, 361

# m

McBroom, Maude, 75 n.8, 104
McCullough, Constance, 315 n.43,
    329
McFeely, Donald C., 287, 301
McGill-Franzen, Anne, 280, 299
MacGinitie, Walter H., 110, 111, 113
    n.2, 145
McGuire, Lorraine D., 169 n.5, 170
McKiernan, Jack, 256, 273
McKillop, Anne S., 133, 146
McLaughlin, Harry G., 202, 212
McNeil, J. D., 280, 299
Madden, Richard, 116, 146
Mangieri, John N., 281, 299, 312
    n.28, 328

Many, Wesley A., 261, 274
Marland, Sidney P., 379, 389
Marshall, Kim, 208
Marshbanks, Gabrielle, 256, 273
Martin, Jeanne, 188 n.12, 211
Marzano, Robert J., 286, 300
Massey, Harold W., 312, 328
Mavrogenes, Nancy A., 109, 145, 281,
    299
Maxwell, Martha, 202, 212
May, Frank B., 312 n.28, 328
Melaragno, Ralph J., 190 n.16, 211
Meredith, Robert, 237, 248
Meyer, Bonnie F., 311, 327
Miller, June B., 372–373, 388
Misner, Marilyn S., 169, 170
Moacdieh, Chris, 188 n.10, 211
Moe, Alden J., 229, 247
Monroe, Marion, 169, 170
Mooney, Robert F., 144, 147
Moore, James T., 284, 300
Moores, Donald F., 371, 388
Moray, Geraldine, 353, 361
Morrison, Coleman, 315 n.42, 328
Muehl, Siegmar, 280, 299
Murphy, Helen A., 137, 146
Musgrave, G. R., 186, 211
Myklebust, Helmer R., 378, 389

# n

Nahem, Joseph, 259 n.23, 274
Nardelli, Robert R., 315 n.46, 329
Negley, Harold, 13, 20
Neill, Shirley, 26 n.1, 35
Nelson, Joan, 202, 212
Nelson, Raedeane M., 338, 347
Neuman, Susan, 181 n.4, 211
Niles, Jerome A., 316, 329
Noland, Ronald G., 70 n.5, 10

# o

Oakan, Robert, 312 n.32, 328
Oakland, Thomas D., 137, 146
Oden, Melita H., 380, 389
Ollila, Lloyd, 256, 257, 259, 273, 274
Olson, Arthur V., 257, 273
Olson, Willard C., 232, 247
Orlando, Vincent P., 339 n.17, 347
Otto, Wayne, 90, 104
Overholzer, Betsy M., 288, 301

# subject index

Heterogeneous group, 187
Hierarchy of skills, 6, 31–32, 218
  scope and sequence, 218
High imagery words, 280, 286
High Intensity, 95
High interest material, 64–65
Hoffman Audiovisual Instructional
  System, 237
Holistic process of comprehension, 310
Homogeneous group, 187
Homonyms, 49
Horn Reading Expectancy Formula,
  168, 169
*How to Use WISC Scores in Reading
  Diagnosis,* 143
Hyperopia, 139

# i

Idea
  sequence of, 48
  understanding main, 49
Illinois Test of Psycholinguistic
  Ability, 360
Independent reading level, 75,
  183–184
Individual diagnostic reading tests,
  127–142
Individual formal diagnostic
  procedures, 108
Individualization, 183–186
Individualized Criterion Referenced
  Testing, 95
Individualized instruction, 40, 186
Individualized reading approach,
  232–234
Inductive approach, 334
Inferential skills, 312–314, 321–324
Informal diagnostic procedures
  attitude inventories, 60–64
  cloze procedure, 96–98
  criterion referenced tests, 93–96
  informal reading inventories, 67–85
  interest inventories, 64–66
  observation, 86–88
  tips on, 101–102
  word recognition inventories, 89–93
Informal Reading Inventory, 67–85,
  102, 110, 263, 290, 291, 317
  administration, 75–77
  analysis of miscues, 81–85
  construction of, 68–74
  interpretation, 77–81

response sheets, 72–74
sample marked passage, 84
scoring, 76
Initial Teaching Alphabet, 238
Insertions, 77, 83
Institute of Propaganda Analysis, 315
Instruction, reading
  diagnostic-prescriptive, 6–7
  individualized, 40
  traditional, 8
Instructional games, 101
Instructional reading level, 75
Integration, 5
Intelligence, 253, 278, 306
Intelligence tests, individual, 143, 144
Interactive model, 310
Interclass grouping format, 191–193
Interest
  groups, 189–190
  level, material, 307–308
  reading, 353–354
  student, 64–65
  surveys, 66–67, 102
International Kindergarten Union, 90
Interpretation of data, 159, 162
Interpretive level of comprehension,
  309
Interpretive skills, 30, 48, 59, 312–314
  diagnostic techniques, 317
  prescriptive techniques, 321–324
Interviews, 63
Intraclass grouping
  achievement, 187–188
  interest, 189–190
  peer, 190–191
  skills, 188–189
Introspective inventory, 61
Inventory
  attitude, 61–65
  Botel Reading, 122, 128–129, 290,
    291
  group reading, 99–100, 103, 222,
    224, 317, 341
  informal reading, 67–85
  interest, 66–67
  Interest and Attitude, 411–414
  introspective, 61
  Reading Miscue, 81–82, 290, 291,
    316, 317
  retrospective, 61
  screening, 58–59
  Sucher-Allred Reading Placement,
    161, 163, 166
  word recognition, 89–93, 102, 290

Iowa Silent Reading Test, 111,
  113–114, 317, 343
I.Q., 143–144
IRI. *See* Informal Reading Inventory
Irrelevant information, 314
ISRT. *See* Iowa Silent Reading Test
*It's Not the End of the World,* 358

# j

Judgments, evaluative, 314

# k

Keystone Telebinocular, 139, 140
Keystone Visual Survey Tests, 139,
  140
Kinesthetic approach, 229
Kucera-Francis Corpus, 90–92

# l

Language
  communication, 255
  development, 382
  patterns, 312
  variations, 365, 381–387
Language experience approach, 205,
  231–232
Laubach Method, 240
Leading questions, 62
Learning centers, 100–101, 206, 208
Learning disabilities, 377–379
Learning skills, content areas, 48, 49
Learning styles, 279, 335–336
*Learning to Read: The Great Debate,*
  283
Left-to-right progression, 256
Librarian's role in reading program,
  14, 219, 338
Limited vision student, 369
Linear technique, 238
Linguistic approach, 237–238, 284
Linguists, research by, 285
Lipreading, 371–372
Listening comprehension, 85, 260, 262
Listing format, 157
Literal level of comprehension, 309
Literal skills, 30, 47, 59, 312
  diagnostic techniques, 317
  prescriptive techniques, 320–321
Literary styles, 41
Literature, learning skills, 48–49